HOMELAND SECURITY

RESPONDING TO THE THREAT

Taken from:

Homeland Security for Policing
by Willard M. Oliver

Terrorism in the Twenty-First Century, Fourth Edition
by Cindy C. Combs

Understanding Terrorism: Groups, Strategies, and Responses, Second Edition
by James M. Poland

When Terrorism Strikes Home: Defending the United States
by James A. Fagin

Understanding Terrorism: Threats in an Uncertain World
edited by Akorlie A. Nyatepe-Coo and Dorothy Zeisler-Vralsted

PEARSON CUSTOM PUBLISHING
75 Arlington Street, Suite 300, Boston, MA 02116
A Pearson Education Company

This textbook, *Homeland Security: Responding to the Threat*, combines content from five leading publications into one custom textbook specifically chosen for this course. The publisher has attempted to renumber internal references to maintain uniformity for this custom title.

Many thanks to Dr. Jeffrey Rush, Criminal Justice Program Director, Virginia College, Birmingham, Alabama and to Dr. Robert Hanser, of the University of Louisiana at Monroe for their editorial review and selection of this content.

The following is a summary of the book chapters.

Contents

PART 1

The Need for Homeland Security

CHAPTER 1

The Era of Homeland Security

Our nation has been put on notice: We are not immune from attack. We will take defensive measures against terrorism to protect Americans. Today, dozens of federal departments and agencies, as well as state and local governments, have responsibilities affecting homeland security.

President George W. Bush, September 20, 2001
(See Appendix B for full speech)

INTRODUCTION

On September 11, 2001, policing entered the era of homeland security. Prior to the attack on America by Osama bin Laden and his terrorist group, Al Qaeda, on that fateful day, policing in America recognized that various crime problems had international implications, but there was little acknowledgment of how these crimes would impact state and local police directly. Issues such as international and transnational crimes, particularly organized and white-collar crime, and both drug and human trafficking, were issues of concern, but generally concerns for either the federal government and their criminal justice assets or for the international community. The realization that global concerns, such as terrorism, were indeed a state and local concern changed on September 11, 2001. That day policing in America moved out of the community policing era and into the era of homeland security.

To understand how this came about, it is important to first review the threat that Osama bin Laden and his terrorist organization, Al Qaeda, posed to America prior to September 11th. In addition, reviewing the actual events of the attack helps place the significance of that day in better context. Perhaps more importantly, reviewing how the local police responded to the attacks provides us some insight into what the era of Homeland Security means for policing. Therefore, this chapter will review the threat, the attack, and the response to better understand the significance of the threat, see how that attack moved American policing into the era of Homeland Security, and provide the context for understanding the role state and local police will play in this new era.

3

BOX 1-1

TERRORISM TIME LINE (ABBREVIATED) PRIOR TO FIRST WORLD TRADE CENTER (1993)

Kidnappings of U.S. Citizens in Colombia, January 31, 1993:
Revolutionary Armed Forces of Colombia (FARC) terrorists kidnapped three U.S. missionaries.

Kidnapping of U.S. Businessmen in the Philippines, January 17–21, 1992:
A senior official of the corporation Philippine Geothermal was kidnapped in Manila by the Red Scorpion Group, and two U.S. businessmen were seized independently by the National Liberation Army and by Revolutionary Armed Forces of Colombia (FARC).

Sniper Attack on the U.S. Embassy in Bonn, February 13, 1991:
Three Red Army Faction members fired automatic rifles from across the Rhine River at the U.S. Embassy Chancery. No one was hurt.

Attempted Iraqi Attacks on U.S. Posts, January 18–19, 1991:
Iraqi agents planted bombs at the U.S. ambassador to Indonesia's residence and at the USIS library in Manila.

U.S. Soldiers Assassinated in the Philippines, May 13, 1990:
The New People's Army (NPA) killed two U.S. Air Force personnel near Clark Air Force Base in the Philippines.

U.S. Embassy Bombed in Peru, January 15, 1990:
The Tupac Amaru Revolutionary Movement bombed the U.S. Embassy in Lima, Peru.

Assassination of U.S. Army Officer, April 21, 1989:
The New People's Army (NPA) assassinated Colonel James Rowe in Manila. The NPA also assassinated two U.S. government defense contractors in September.

Pan Am 103 Bombing, December 21, 1988:
Pan American Airlines Flight 103 was blown up over Lockerbie, Scotland, by a bomb believed to have been placed on the aircraft by Libyan terrorists in Frankfurt, West Germany. All 259 people on board were killed.

Attack on U.S. Diplomat in Greece, June 28, 1988:
The defense attaché of the U.S. Embassy in Greece was killed when a car bomb was detonated outside his home in Athens.

Naples USO Attack, April 14, 1988:
The Organization of Jihad Brigades exploded a car bomb outside a USO club in Naples, Italy, killing one U.S. sailor.

Kidnapping of William Higgins, February 17, 1988:
U.S. Marine Corps Lieutenant Colonel W. Higgins was kidnapped and murdered by the Iranian-backed Hizballah group while serving with the United Nations Truce Supervisory Organization (UNTSO) in southern Lebanon.

Servicemen's Bar Attack, December 26, 1987:
    Catalan separatists bombed a Barcelona bar frequented by U.S. servicemen, resulting in the death of one U.S. citizen.

Bus Attack, April 24, 1987:
    Sixteen U.S. servicemen riding in a Greek Air Force bus near Athens were injured in an apparent bombing attack, carried out by the revolutionary organization known as November 17.

Berlin Discothèque Bombing, April 5, 1986:
    Two U.S. soldiers were killed and 79 American servicemen were injured in a Libyan bomb attack on a nightclub in West Berlin, West Germany. In retaliation U.S. military jets bombed targets in and around Tripoli and Benghazi.

Aircraft Bombing in Greece, March 30, 1986:
    A Palestinian splinter group detonated a bomb as TWA Flight 840 approached Athens airport, killing four U.S. citizens.

Airport Attacks in Rome and Vienna, December 27, 1985:
    Four gunmen belonging to the Abu Nidal Organization attacked the El Al and Trans World Airlines ticket counters at Rome's Leonardo da Vinci Airport with grenades and automatic rifles. Thirteen persons were killed and 75 were wounded before Italian police and Israeli security guards killed three of the gunmen and captured the fourth. Three more Abu Nidal gunmen attacked the El Al ticket counter at Vienna's Schwechat Airport, killing three persons and wounding 30. Austrian police killed one of the gunmen and captured the others.

Egyptian Airliner Hijacking, November 23, 1985:
    An EgyptAir airplane bound from Athens to Malta and carrying several U.S. citizens was hijacked by the Abu Nidal Group.

Achille Lauro Hijacking, October 7, 1985:
    Four Palestinian Liberation Front terrorists seized the Italian cruise liner in the eastern Mediterranean Sea, taking more than 700 hostages. One U.S. passenger was murdered before the Egyptian government offered the terrorists safe haven in return for the hostages' freedom.

Attack on a Restaurant in El Salvador, June 19, 1985:
    Members of the FMLN (Farabundo Marti National Liberation Front) fired on a restaurant in the Zona Rosa district of San Salvador, killing four Marine security guards assigned to the U.S. Embassy and nine Salvadoran civilians.

TWA Hijacking, June 14, 1985:
    A Trans-World Airlines flight was hijacked en route to Rome from Athens by two Lebanese Hizballah terrorists and forced to fly to Beirut. The eight crew members and 145 passengers were held for seventeen days, during which one American hostage, a U.S. Navy sailor, was murdered. After being flown twice to Algiers, the aircraft was returned to Beirut after Israel released 435 Lebanese and Palestinian prisoners.

(continued)

Kidnapping of U.S. Officials in Mexico, February 7, 1985:
Under the orders of narcotrafficker Rafael Caro Quintero, Drug Enforcement Administration agent Enrique Camarena Salazar and his pilot were kidnapped, tortured, and executed.

Restaurant Bombing in Spain, April 12, 1984:
Eighteen U.S. servicemen were killed and 83 people were injured in a bomb attack on a restaurant near a U.S. Air Force base in Torrejon, Spain.

Kidnapping of Embassy Official, March 16, 1984:
The Islamic Jihad kidnapped and later murdered Political Officer William Buckley in Beirut, Lebanon. Other U.S. citizens not connected to the U.S. government were seized over a succeeding two-year period.

Naval Officer Assassinated in Greece, November 15, 1983:
A U.S. Navy officer was shot by the November 17 terrorist group in Athens, Greece, while his car was stopped at a traffic light.

Bombing of Marine Barracks, Beirut, October 23, 1983:
Simultaneous suicide truck-bomb attacks were made on American and French compounds in Beirut, Lebanon. A 12,000-pound bomb destroyed the U.S. compound, killing 242 Americans, while 58 French troops were killed when a 400-pound device destroyed a French base. Islamic Jihad claimed responsibility.

Naval Officer Assassinated in El Salvador, May 25, 1983:
A U.S. Navy officer was assassinated by the Farabundo Marti National Liberation Front.

Bombing of U.S. Embassy in Beirut, April 18, 1983:
Sixty-three people, including the CIA's Middle East director, were killed and 120 were injured in a 400-pound suicide truck-bomb attack on the U.S. Embassy in Beirut, Lebanon. The Islamic Jihad claimed responsibility.

Colombian Hostage-taking, April 8, 1983:
A U.S. citizen was seized by the Revolutionary Armed Forces of Colombia (FARC) and held for ransom.

Murder of Missionaries, December 4, 1981:
Three American nuns and one lay missionary were found murdered outside San Salvador, El Salvador. They were killed by members of the National Guard, and the killers are currently in prison.

Assassination of Egyptian President, October 6, 1981:
Soldiers who were secretly members of the Takfir Wal-Hajira sect attacked and killed Egyptian President Anwar Sadat during a troop review.

U.S. Installation Bombing, August 31, 1981:
The Red Army exploded a bomb at the U.S. Air Force Base at Ramstein, West Germany.

Grand Mosque Seizure, November 20, 1979:
200 Islamic terrorists seized the Grand Mosque in Mecca, Saudi Arabia, taking hundreds of pilgrims hostage. Saudi and French security forces retook the shrine after an intense battle in which some 250 people were killed and 600 wounded.

Iran Hostage Crisis, November 4, 1979:
> After President Carter agreed to admit the Shah of Iran into the United States, Iranian radicals seized the U.S. Embassy in Tehran and took 66 American diplomats hostage. Thirteen hostages were soon released, but the remaining 53 were held until their release on January 20, 1981.

Ambassador to Afghanistan Assassinated, February 14, 1979:
> Four Afghans kidnapped U.S. Ambassador Adolph Dubs in Kabul and demanded the release of various "religious figures." Dubs was killed, along with four alleged terrorists, when Afghan police stormed the hotel room where he was being held.

Assassination of Former Chilean Diplomat, September 21, 1976:
> Exiled Chilean Foreign Minister Orlando Letelier was killed by a car bomb in Washington.

Domestic Terrorism, January 27–29, 1975:
> Puerto Rican nationalists bombed a Wall Street bar, killing four and injuring 60; two days later, the Weather Underground claims responsibility for an explosion in a bathroom at the U.S. Department of State in Washington.

Ambassador to Cyprus Assassinated, August 19, 1974:
> U.S. Ambassador to Cyprus Rodger P. Davies and his Greek Cypriot secretary were shot and killed by snipers during a demonstration outside the U.S. Embassy in Nicosia.

Attack and Hijacking at the Rome Airport, December 17, 1973:
> Five terrorists pulled weapons from their luggage in the terminal lounge at the Rome airport, killing two persons. They then attacked a Pan American 707 bound for Beirut and Tehran, destroying it with incendiary grenades and killing 29 persons, including 4 senior Moroccan officials and 14 American employees of ARAMCO. They then herded 5 Italian hostages into a Lufthansa airliner and killed an Italian customs agent as he tried to escape, after which they forced the pilot to fly to Beirut. After Lebanese authorities refused to let the plane land, it landed in Athens, where the terrorists demanded the release of 2 Arab terrorists. In order to make Greek authorities comply with their demands, the terrorists killed a hostage and threw his body onto the tarmac. The plane then flew to Damascus, where it stopped for two hours to obtain fuel and food. It then flew to Kuwait, where the terrorists released their hostages in return for passage to an unknown destination. The Palestine Liberation Organization disavowed the attack, and no group claimed responsibility for it.

Consul General in Mexico Kidnapped, May 4, 1973:
> U.S. Consul General in Guadalajara, Terrence Leonhardy, was kidnapped by members of the People's Revolutionary Armed Forces.

Ambassador to Sudan Assassinated, March 2, 1973:
> U.S. Ambassador to Sudan, Cleo A. Noel, and other diplomats were assassinated at the Saudi Arabian Embassy in Khartoum by members of the Black September organization.

Munich Olympic Massacre, September 5, 1972:
> Eight Palestinian "Black September" terrorists seized eleven Israeli athletes in the Olympic Village in Munich, West Germany. In a bungled rescue attempt by West German authorities, nine of the hostages and five terrorists were killed.

(continued)

"Bloody Friday," July 21, 1972:
> An Irish Republican Army (IRA) bomb attack killed eleven people and injured 130 in Belfast, Northern Ireland. Ten days later, three IRA car bomb attacks in the village of Claudy left six dead.

U.S. Agency for International Development Adviser Kidnapped, July 31, 1970:
> In Montevideo, Uruguay, the Tupamaros terrorist group kidnapped AID Police adviser Dan Mitrione; his body was found on August 10.

Ambassador to Brazil Kidnapped, September 3, 1969:
> U.S. Ambassador to Brazil Charles Burke Elbrick was kidnapped by the Marxist revolutionary group MR-8.

Ambassador to Japan Attacked, July 30, 1969:
> U.S. Ambassador to Japan, A. H. Meyer, was attacked by a knife-wielding Japanese citizen.

Ambassador to Guatemala Assassinated, August 28, 1968:
> U.S. Ambassador to Guatemala, John Gordon Mein, was murdered by a rebel faction when gunmen forced his official car off the road in Guatemala City and raked the vehicle with gunfire.

First U.S. Aircraft Hijacked, May 1, 1961:
> Puerto Rican born Antuilo Ramierez Ortiz forced at gunpoint a National Airlines plane to fly to Havana, Cuba, where he was given asylum.

Source: U.S. Army—Timeline of Terrorism, Available online at http://www.army.mil/terrorism

THE THREAT—AL QAEDA

Thomas Friedman, a columnist for the *New York Times*, argued in an op-ed piece that America in the 1990s experienced the growth of three bubbles, all of which burst at the beginning of the twenty-first century.[1] The three bubbles included the stock market, corporate governance, and terrorism. The first bubble burst when the various dot-com organizations became greatly inflated in the 1990s, and the stock market simply adjusted their values downward in 2000. The second bubble burst at about the same time, when a number of ethical lapses were allowed to go unchecked throughout the 1990s until the illegal activities of corporate firms Enron and Arthur Andersen were revealed. The third bubble burst on September 11, 2001, and resulted from the terrorism bubble that was allowed to grow during the 1990s.

The terrorism bubble, Friedman asserted, "started with the suicide bombings against U.S. troops in Saudi Arabia, was followed by attacks on the U.S. Embassies in East Africa and on the USS *Cole*, then ballooned with the rise of Palestinian suicide terrorism in Israel and finally peaked with Al Qaeda's attack on 9/11."[2] Friedman traced most of what led up to the third bubble as being the result of Osama bin Laden and the terrorist organization Al Qaeda's ability to grow in power unchecked during the 1990s. He explained that like the other two bubbles, "the terrorism bubble was the product of a kind of temporary insanity, in which basic norms were ignored and excessive behavior was justified by new theories."[3] The threat of Al Qaeda was ultimately what led to the bubble bursting and ushering in the post–September 11th world, or as Friedman calls it, the "post-bubble world."[4] Understanding the origin of this threat, namely Osama bin Laden and his terrorist network Al Qaeda, and how this threat developed is important to understanding what led us into the era of Homeland Security.

The Bubble Forms

Al Qaeda was founded by Osama bin Laden in Afghanistan in 1988.[5] Osama bin Laden was born in July 1957, the seventeenth of twenty sons of a Saudi construction magnate of Yemeni origin. Many Saudis were conservative Sunni Muslims, and bin Laden adopted militant Islamist views while studying at King Abdul Aziz University in Jeddah, Saudi Arabia. There he studied Islam under Muhammad Qutb, brother of Sayyid Qutb, the key idealogue of a major Sunni Islamist movement, the Muslim Brotherhood.[6] Another of bin Laden's instructors was a major figure in the Jordanian branch of the Muslim Brotherhood, Dr. Abdullah Azzam. Azzam has been identified by some experts as the intellectual architect of the *jihad* against the 1979–1989 Soviet occupation of Afghanistan and ultimately of Al Qaeda itself;[7] he cast the Soviet invasion as an attempted conquest by a non-Muslim power of sacred Muslim territory and people.

Bin Laden went to Afghanistan shortly after the December 1979 Soviet invasion and joined Azzam there. He reportedly used some of his personal funds[8] to establish himself as a donor to the Afghan *mujahedin* and a recruiter of Arab and other Islamic volunteers for the war. In 1984 Azzam and bin Laden structured this assistance by establishing a network of recruiting and fund-raising offices in the Arab world, Europe, and the United States. That network was called the *Maktab al-Khidamat* (Services Office), also known as *Al Khifah;* many experts consider the *Maktab* network to be the organizational forerunner of Al Qaeda. Another major figure who utilized the *Maktab* network to recruit for the anti-Soviet *jihad* was Umar Abd al-Rahman (also known as "the blind shaykh"), the spiritual leader of radical Egyptian Islamist group Al Jihad. Bin Laden also fought in the anti-Soviet war, participating in a 1986 battle in Jalalabad and, more notably, a 1987 frontal assault by foreign volunteers against Soviet armor. Bin Laden has said he was exposed to a Soviet chemical attack and slightly injured in that battle.[9]

During this period, most U.S. officials perceived the volunteers as positive contributors to the effort to expel Soviet forces from Afghanistan, and U.S. officials made no apparent effort to stop the recruitment of non-Afghan volunteers for the war. U.S. officials have repeatedly denied that the United States directly supported the volunteers, although the United States did covertly finance (about $3 billion during 1981–1991) and arm (via Pakistan) the Afghan *mujahedin* factions, particularly the Islamic fundamentalist Afghan factions, fighting Soviet forces. At this time, neither bin Laden, Azzam, nor Abd al-Rahman was known to have openly advocated, undertaken, or planned any direct attacks against the United States, although they were critical of U.S. support for Israel in the Middle East.

In 1988, toward the end of the Soviet occupation, bin Laden and Azzam began contemplating how, and to what end, to utilize the Islamist volunteer network they had organized. U.S. intelligence estimates of the size of that network was about 10,000 to 20,000, although not all of these necessarily supported or joined Al Qaeda terrorist activities.[10] Azzam reportedly wanted this "Al Qaeda" (Arabic for "the base") organization to become an Islamic "rapid reaction force," available to intervene wherever Muslims were perceived to be threatened. Bin Laden differed with Azzam, hoping instead to dispatch the Al Qaeda activists to their home countries to try to topple secular, pro-Western Arab leaders, such as President Hosni Mubarak of Egypt and Saudi Arabia's royal family. Some attribute their differences to the growing influence on bin Laden by the Egyptians in his inner circle, such as Abd al-Rahman, who wanted to use Al Qaeda's resources to install an Islamic state in Egypt. Another close Egyptian confidant was Dr. Ayman al-Zawahiri, operational leader of Al Jihad in Egypt. Like Abd al-Rahman, Zawahiri had been imprisoned but ultimately acquitted for the October 1981 assassination of Egyptian President Anwar Sadat, and he permanently left Egypt for Afghanistan in 1985. There, he used his medical training to tend to wounded fighters in the anti-Soviet war. In November 1989, Azzam was assassinated, and some allege that bin Laden might have been responsible for the killing to resolve this power struggle. Following Azzam's death, bin Laden gained control of the *Maktab*'s funds and organizational mechanisms. Abd al-Rahman later came to the United States and was convicted in October 1995 for terrorist plots related to the February 1993 bombing of the World Trade Center. Zawahiri stayed with bin Laden to serve as bin Laden's main strategist; he is believed to still be serving in that role today.

The Bubble Grows

The August 2, 1990, Iraqi invasion of Kuwait apparently turned bin Laden from a de facto U.S. ally against the Soviet Union into one of its most active adversaries.[11] Bin Laden had returned home to Saudi Arabia in 1989 after the completion of the Soviet withdrawal from Afghanistan that February. While back home, he lobbied Saudi officials not to host the 500,000 U.S. combat troops that defended Saudi Arabia from the Iraqi invasion and ultimately expelled Iraq from Kuwait in Operation Desert Storm (January 17–February 28, 1991). He argued instead for the raising of a "mujahedin" army to oust Iraq from Kuwait, but his idea was rebuffed as impractical, causing a falling out with Saudi leaders. He relocated to Sudan in 1991, buying property there that he used to host and train Al Qaeda militants—this time, for use against the United States and its interests, as well as for *jihad* operations in the Balkans, Chechnya, Kashmir, and the Phillipines. He remained there until the Sudanese government, under U.S. and Egyptian pressure, expelled him in May 1996; he then returned to Afghanistan and helped the Taliban gain and maintain control of Afghanistan. The Taliban would capture the capital, Kabul, in September of 1996.

Bin Laden and Zawahiri apparently believed that the only way to bring Islamic regimes to power was to oust from the region the perceived backer of secular regional regimes, the United States. During the 1990s, bin Laden and Zawahiri transformed Al Qaeda into a global threat to U.S. national security by engaging in a number of attacks against the United States and its interests. In 1992, Al Qaeda claimed responsibility for bombing a hotel in Yemen where 100 U.S. military personnel were awaiting deployment to Somalia for Operation Restore Hope. No one was killed. However, Al Qaeda was responsible for the tragedy that subsequently followed during this operation in Somalia. Al Qaeda claimed responsibility for arming Somali factions, who battled U.S. forces there

BOX 1-2

Philippines Hostage Incident, May 27, 2001:

Muslim Abu Sayyaf guerrillas seized 13 tourists and 3 staff members at a resort on Palawan Island and took their captives to Basilan Island. The captives included three U.S. citizens: Guellermo Sobero and missionaries Martin and Gracia Burnham. Philippine troops fought a series of battles with the guerrillas between June 1 and June 3, during which nine hostages escaped and two were found dead. The guerrillas took additional hostages when they seized the hospital in the town of Lamitan. On June 12, Abu Sayyaf spokesman Abu Sabaya claimed that Sobero had been killed and beheaded; his body was found in October. The Burnhams remained in captivity until June 2002.

Manila Bombing, December 30, 2000:

A bomb exploded in a plaza across the street from the U.S. Embassy in Manila, injuring nine persons. The Moro Islamic Liberation Front was likely responsible.

Helicopter Hijacking, October 12, 2000:

In Sucumbios Province, Ecuador, a group of armed kidnappers led by former members of defunct Colombian terrorist organization the Popular Liberation Army (EPL) took hostage 10 employees of Spanish energy consortium REPSOL. Those kidnapped included five U.S. citizens, one Argentine, one Chilean, one New Zealander, and two French pilots, who escaped four days later. On January 30, 2001, the kidnappers murdered American hostage Ronald Sander. The remaining hostages were released on February 23 following the payment of $13 million in ransom by the oil companies.

Attack on USS *Cole*, October 12, 2000:

In Aden, Yemen, a small dinghy carrying explosives rammed the destroyer USS *Cole*, killing seventeen sailors and injuring 39 others. Supporters of Osama bin Laden were suspected.

Church Bombing in Tajikistan, October 1, 2000:

Unidentified militants detonated two bombs in a Christian church in Dushanbe, killing seven persons and injuring 70 others. The church was founded by a Korean-born U.S. citizen, and most of those killed and wounded were Korean. No one claimed responsibility.

Kidnappings in Kyrgyzstan, August 12, 2000:

In the Kara-Su Valley, the Islamic Movement of Uzbekistan took four U.S. citizens hostage. The Americans escaped on August 12.

ELN Kidnapping, June 27, 2000:

In Bogota, Colombia, ELN militants kidnapped a five-year-old U.S. citizen and his Colombian mother, demanding an undisclosed ransom.

RUF Attacks on U.N. Mission Personnel, May 1, 2000:

On May 1 in Makeni, Sierra Leone, Revolutionary United Front (RUF) militants kidnapped at least 20 members of the United Nations Assistance Mission in Sierra Leone (UNAMSIL) and surrounded and opened fire on a UNAMSIL facility, according to press reports. The

(continued)

militants killed five UN soldiers in the attack. RUF militants kidnapped 300 UNAMSIL peacekeepers throughout the country, according to press reports. On May 15 in Foya, Liberia, the kidnappers released 139 hostages. On May 28 on the Liberia and Sierra Leone border, armed militants released unharmed the last of the UN peacekeepers.

PLA Kidnapping, December 23, 1999:

Colombian People's Liberation Army (PLA) forces kidnapped a U.S. citizen in an unsuccessful ransoming effort.

Burmese Embassy Seizure, October 1, 1999:

Burmese dissidents seized the Burmese Embassy in Bangkok, Thailand, taking 89 persons hostage, including one U.S. citizen.

AFRC Kidnappings, August 4, 1999:

An Armed Forces Revolutionary Council (AFRC) faction kidnapped 33 UN representatives near Occra Hills, Sierra Leone. The hostages included one U.S. citizen, five British soldiers, one Canadian citizen, one representative from Ghana, one military officer from Russia, one officer from Kyrgystan, one officer from Zambia, one officer from Malaysia, a local bishop, two UN officials, two local journalists, and 16 Sierra Leonean nationals.

Shell Platform Bombing, June 27, 1999:

In Port Harcourt, Nigeria, armed youths stormed a Shell oil platform, kidnapping one U.S. citizen, one Nigerian national, and one Australian citizen and causing undetermined damage. A group calling itself "Enough is Enough in the Niger River" claimed responsibility. Further seizures of oil facilities followed.

ELN Hostage-taking, May 30, 1999:

In Cali, Colombia, armed ELN militants attacked a church in the neighborhood of Ciudad Jardin, kidnapping 160 persons, including six U.S. citizens and one French national. The rebels released approximately 80 persons, including three U.S. citizens, later that day.

ELN Hostage-taking, March 23, 1999:

Armed guerrillas kidnapped a U.S. citizen in Boyaca, Colombia. The National Liberation Army (ELN) claimed responsibility and demanded $400,000 ransom. On 20 July, ELN rebels released the hostage unharmed following a ransom payment of $48,000.

Hutu Abductions, March 1, 1999:

150 armed Hutu rebels attacked three tourist camps in Uganda, killed four Ugandans, and abducted three U.S. citizens, six Britons, three New Zealanders, two Danish citizens, one Australian, and one Canadian national. Two of the U.S. citizens and six of the other hostages were subsequently killed by their abductors.

FARC Kidnappings, February 25, 1999:

FARC kidnapped three U.S. citizens working for the Hawaii-based Pacific Cultural Conservancy International. On March 4, the bodies of the three victims were found in Venezuela.

Ugandan Rebel Attack, February 14, 1999:

A pipe bomb exploded inside a bar, killing five persons and injuring 35 others. One Ethiopian and four Ugandan nationals died in the blast, and one U.S. citizen working for

USAID, two Swiss nationals, one Pakistani, one Ethiopian, and 27 Ugandans were injured. Ugandan authorities blamed the attack on the Allied Democratic Forces (ADF).

Angolan Aircraft Downing, January 2, 1999:
A UN plane carrying one U.S. citizen, four Angolans, two Philippine nationals, and one Namibian was shot down, according to a UN official. No deaths or injuries were reported. Angolan authorities blamed the attack on National Union for the Total Independence of Angola (UNITA) rebels. UNITA officials denied shooting down the plane.

Armed Kidnapping in Colombia, November 15, 1998:
Armed assailants followed a U.S. businessman and his family home in Cundinamarca Department and kidnapped his 11-year-old son after stealing money, jewelry, one automobile, and two cell phones. The kidnappers demanded $1 million in ransom. On January 21, 1999, the kidnappers released the boy.

Colombian Pipeline Bombing, October 18, 1998:
A National Liberation Army (ELN) planted bomb exploded on the Ocensa pipeline in Antioquia Department, killing approximately 71 persons and injuring at least 100 others. The pipeline is jointly owned by the Colombia State Oil Company Ecopetrol and a consortium including U.S., French, British, and Canadian companies.

U.S. Embassy Bombings in East Africa, August 7, 1998:
A bomb exploded at the rear entrance of the U.S. Embassy in Nairobi, Kenya, killing 12 U.S. citizens, 32 Foreign Service Nationals (FSNs), and 247 Kenyan citizens. Approximately 5,000 Kenyans, 6 U.S. citizens, and 13 FSNs were injured. The U.S. Embassy building sustained extensive structural damage. Almost simultaneously, a bomb detonated outside the U.S. Embassy in Dar es Salaam, Tanzania, killing 7 FSNs and 3 Tanzanian citizens, and injuring 1 U.S. citizen and 76 Tanzanians. The explosion caused major structural damage to the U.S. Embassy facility. The U.S. Government held Osama bin Laden responsible.

Somali Hostage-takings, April 15, 1998:
Somali militiamen abducted nine Red Cross and Red Crescent workers at an airstrip north of Mogadishu. The hostages included a U.S. citizen, a German, a Belgian, a French, a Norwegian, two Swiss, and one Somali. The gunmen were members of a subclan loyal to Ali Mahdi Mohammed, who controlled the northern section of the capital.

FARC Abduction, March 21–23, 1998:
FARC rebels kidnapped a U.S. citizen in Sabaneta, Colombia. FARC members also killed 3 persons, wounded 14, and kidnapped at least 27 others at a roadblock near Bogota. Four U.S. citizens and one Italian were among those kidnapped, as well as the acting president of the National Electoral Council (CNE) and his wife.

Murder of U.S. Businessmen in Pakistan, November 12, 1997:
Two unidentified gunmen shot to death four U.S. auditors from Union Texas Petroleum Corporation and their Pakistani driver after they drove away from the Sheraton Hotel in Karachi. The Islami Inqilabi Council, or Islamic Revolutionary Council, claimed responsibility in a call to the U.S. Consulate in Karachi. In a letter to Pakistani newspapers, the Aimal Khufia Action Committee also claimed responsibility.

(continued)

Yemeni Kidnappings, October 30, 1997:
> Al-Sha'if tribesmen kidnapped a U.S. businessman near Sanaa. The tribesmen sought the release of two fellow tribesmen who were arrested on smuggling charges and several public works projects they claim the government promised them. They released the hostage on November 27.

Israeli Shopping Mall Bombing, September 4, 1997:
> Three suicide bombers of HAMAS detonated bombs in the Ben Yehuda shopping mall in Jerusalem, killing eight persons, including the bombers, and wounding nearly 200 others. A dual U.S./Israeli citizen was among the dead, and 7 U.S. citizens were wounded.

Hotel Nacional Bombing, July 12, 1997:
> A bomb exploded at the Hotel Nacional in Havana, injuring three persons and causing minor damage. A previously unknown group calling itself the Military Liberation Union claimed responsibility.

FARC Kidnapping, March 7, 1997:
> FARC guerrillas kidnapped a U.S. mining employee and his Colombian colleague, who were searching for gold in Colombia. On November 16, the rebels released the two hostages after receiving a $50,000 ransom.

ELN Kidnapping, February 24, 1997:
> National Liberation Army (ELN) guerrillas kidnapped a U.S. citizen employed by a Las Vegas gold corporation, who was scouting a gold mining operation in Colombia. The ELN demanded a ransom of $2.5 million.

Empire State Building Sniper Attack, February 23, 1997:
> A Palestinian gunman opened fire on tourists at an observation deck atop the Empire State Building in New York City, killing a Danish national and wounding visitors from the United States, Argentina, Switzerland, and France before turning the gun on himself. A handwritten note carried by the gunman claimed this was a punishment attack against the "enemies of Palestine."

Venezuelan Abduction, February 14, 1997:
> Six armed Colombian guerrillas kidnapped a U.S. oil engineer and his Venezuelan pilot in Apure, Venezuela. The kidnappers released the Venezuelan pilot on February 22. According to authorities, the FARC is responsible for the kidnapping.

Egyptian Letter Bombs, January 2–13, 1997:
> A series of letter bombs with Alexandria, Egypt, postmarks were discovered at Al-Hayat newspaper bureaus in Washington, New York City, London, and Riyadh, Saudi Arabia. Three similar devices, also postmarked in Egypt, were found at a prison facility in Leavenworth, Kansas. Bomb disposal experts defused all the devices, but one detonated at the Al-Hayat office in London, injuring two security guards and causing minor damage.

Tupac Amaru Seizure of Diplomats, December 17, 1996:
> Twenty-three members of the Tupac Amaru Revolutionary Movement (MRTA) took several hundred people hostage at a party given at the Japanese Ambassador's residence in Lima, Peru. Among the hostages were several U.S. officials, foreign ambassadors, and other diplomats, Peruvian Government officials, and Japanese businessmen. The group demanded

the release of all MRTA members in prison and safe passage for them and the hostage takers. The terrorists released most of the hostages in December but held 81 Peruvians and Japanese citizens for several months.

Abduction of U.S. Citizen by FARC, December 11, 1996:
Five armed men claiming to be members of the Revolutionary Armed Forces of Colombia (FARC) kidnapped and later killed a U.S. geologist at a methane gas exploration site in La Guajira Department.

Paris Subway Explosion, December 3, 1996:
A bomb exploded aboard a Paris subway train as it arrived at the Port Royal station, killing two French nationals, a Moroccan, and a Canadian and injuring 86 persons. Among those injured were one U.S. citizen and a Canadian. No one claimed responsibility for the attack, but Algerian extremists are suspected.

Red Cross Worker Kidnappings, November 1, 1996:
In Sudan a breakaway group from the Sudanese People's Liberation Army (SPLA) kidnapped three International Committee of the Red Cross (ICRC) workers, including a U.S. citizen, an Australian, and a Kenyan. On December 9 the rebels released the hostages in exchange for ICRC supplies and a health survey for their camp.

PUK Kidnapping, September 13, 1996:
In Iraq, Patriotic Union of Kurdistan (PUK) militants kidnapped four French workers for Pharmaciens Sans Frontieres, a Canadian United Nations High Commissioner for Refugees (UNHCR) official, and two Iraqis.

Sudanese Rebel Kidnapping, August 17, 1996:
Sudan People's Liberation Army (SPLA) rebels kidnapped six missionaries in Mapourdit, including a U.S. citizen, an Italian, three Australians, and a Sudanese. The SPLA released the hostages 11 days later.

Khobar Towers Bombing, June 25, 1996:
A fuel truck carrying a bomb exploded outside the U.S. military's Khobar Towers housing facility in Dhahran, killing 19 U.S. military personnel and wounding 515 persons, including 240 U.S. personnel. Several groups claimed responsibility for the attack.

Zekharya Attack, June 9, 1996:
Unidentified gunmen opened fire on a car near Zekharya, killing a dual U.S./Israeli citizen and an Israeli. The Popular Front for the Liberation of Palestine (PFLP) was suspected.

AID Worker Abduction, May 31, 1996:
A gang of former Contra guerrillas kidnapped a U.S. employee of the Agency for International Development (AID) who was assisting with election preparations in rural northern Nicaragua. She was released unharmed the next day after members of the international commission overseeing the preparations intervened.

West Bank Attack, May 13, 1996:
Arab gunmen opened fire on a bus and a group of Yeshiva students near the Bet El settlement, killing a dual U.S./Israeli citizen and wounding three Israelis. No one claimed responsibility for the attack, but HAMAS was suspected.

(continued)

Dizengoff Center Bombing, March 4, 1996:
> HAMAS and the Palestine Islamic Jihad (PIJ) both claimed responsibility for a bombing outside Tel Aviv's largest shopping mall that killed 20 persons and injured 75 others, including 2 U.S. citizens.

HAMAS Bus Attack, February 26, 1996:
> In Jerusalem, a suicide bomber blew up a bus, killing 26 persons, including three U.S. citizens, and injuring some 80 persons, including three other U.S. citizens.

ELN Kidnapping, February 16, 1996:
> Six alleged National Liberation Army (ELN) guerrillas kidnapped a U.S. citizen in Colombia. After nine months, the hostage was released.

Athens Embassy Attack, February 15, 1996:
> Unidentified assailants fired a rocket at the U.S. Embassy compound in Athens, causing minor damage to three diplomatic vehicles and some surrounding buildings. Circumstances of the attack suggested it was an operation carried out by the 17 November group.

IRA Bombing, February 9, 1996:
> An Irish Republican Army (IRA) bomb detonated in London, killing 2 persons and wounding more than 100 others, including 2 U.S. citizens.

Tamil Tigers Attack, January 31, 1996:
> Members of the Liberation Tigers of Tamil Eelam (LTTE) rammed an explosives-laden truck into the Central Bank in the heart of downtown Colombo, Sri Lanka, killing 90 civilians and injuring more than 1,400 others, including 2 U.S. citizens.

Kidnapping in Colombia, January 19, 1996:
> Revolutionary Armed Forces of Colombia (FARC) guerrillas kidnapped a U.S. citizen and demanded a $1 million ransom. The hostage was released on May 22.

Saudi Military Installation Attack, November 13, 1995:
> The Islamic Movement of Change planted a bomb in a Riyadh military compound that killed one U.S. citizen, several foreign national employees of the U.S. government, and over 40 others.

Attack on U.S. Embassy in Moscow, September 13, 1995:
> A rocket-propelled grenade was fired through the window of the U.S. Embassy in Moscow, ostensibly in retaliation for U.S. strikes on Serb positions in Bosnia.

Jerusalem Bus Attack, August 21, 1995:
> HAMAS claimed responsibility for the detonation of a bomb that killed 6 and injured over 100 persons, including several U.S. citizens.

Kashmiri Hostage-taking, July 4, 1995:
> In India six foreigners, including two U.S. citizens, were taken hostage by Al-Faran, a Kashmiri separatist group. One non–U.S. hostage was later found beheaded.

Bombing of the Federal Building in Oklahoma City, April 19, 1995:
> Right-wing extremists Timothy McVeigh and Terry Nichols destroyed the Federal Building in Oklahoma City with a massive truck bomb that killed 166 and injured hundreds more in what was up to then the largest terrorist attack on American soil.

Attack on U.S. Diplomats in Pakistan, March 8, 1995:
　　Two unidentified gunmen killed two U.S. diplomats and wounded a third in Karachi, Pakistan.

FARC Hostage-taking, September 23, 1994:
　　FARC rebels kidnapped U.S. citizen Thomas Hargrove in Colombia.

Hebron Massacre, February 25, 1994:
　　Jewish right-wing extremist and U.S. citizen Baruch Goldstein machine-gunned Moslem worshippers at a mosque in the West Bank town of Hebron, killing 29 and wounding about 150.

Attempted Assassination of President Bush by Iraqi Agents, April 14, 1993:
　　The Iraqi intelligence service attempted to assassinate former U.S. President George Bush during a visit to Kuwait. In retaliation, the U.S. launched a cruise missile attack two months later on the Iraqi capital Baghdad.

World Trade Center Bombing, February 26, 1993:
　　The World Trade Center in New York City was badly damaged when a car bomb planted by Islamic terrorists exploded in an underground garage. The bomb left 6 people dead and 1,000 injured. The men carrying out the attack were followers of Umar Abd al-Rahman, an Egyptian cleric who preached in the New York City area.

Source: U.S. Army—Timeline of Terrorism, Available on-line at http://www.army.mil/terrorism

in October 1993 and who killed 18 U.S. special operation forces in Mogadishu in October 1993, as depicted in the book and movie by the same title, *Black Hawk Down*.

Earlier that same year, Al Qaeda was involved in a more direct attack on the United States and its first on American soil. A growing body of information about central figures in the February 1993 bombing of the World Trade Center in New York City, particularly the reputed key bomb maker Ramzi Ahmad Yusef, suggests possible Al Qaeda involvement. As noted earlier, Abd Al-Rahman was convicted for plots related to this attack.

The next attack by Al Qaeda came in June of 1995, in Ethiopia, when operatives of Al Qaeda allegedly aided the Egyptian militant Islamic Group in a nearly successful assassination attempt against the visiting Egyptian President Hosni Mubarak. That fall, Al Qaeda would strike America in Saudi Arabia. The four Saudi nationals who confessed to a November 1995 bombing of a U.S. military advisory facility in Riyadh, Saudi Arabia, claimed on Saudi television to have been inspired by bin Laden. Five Americans were killed in that attack. In addition, it is commonly believed that another attack on Americans in Saudi Arabia that occurred the next year was also by Al Qaeda. Specifically, the 9/11 Commission report indicates that Al Qaeda might have had a hand in the June 1996 bombing of the Khobar Towers complex near Dhahran, Saudi Arabia, although FBI officials have attributed the attack primarily to Shiite Saudi dissidents working with Iranian agents. Nineteen U.S. airmen were killed.

The next attack that Al Qaeda is alleged to have been responsible for was the August 1998 bombings of U.S. embassies in Kenya and Tanzania, which killed about 300. On August 20, 1998, two weeks after the attacks, the United States launched a cruise missile strike against bin Laden's training camps in Afghanistan, reportedly missing him by a few hours. In July 1999 President Clinton imposed a ban on U.S. trade with Taliban-controlled Afghanistan and froze Taliban assets in the United States. Then, in December 1999, U.S. and Jordanian authorities separately thwarted related Al Qaeda plots against religious sites in Jordan and apparently against the Los Angeles International Airport. This prompted the issuance of UN Security Council Resolution 1333, on December 19, 2000, which banned any arms shipments or provision of military advice to the Taliban. The Clinton administration also pursued a number of covert operations against bin Laden during this same time frame of 1999–2000. Later, after President Bush entered the White House in January of 2001, nine months before the attacks of September 11th, his administration considered some new options, which included arming anti-Taliban opposition groups.[12]

The last significant attack by Al Qaeda before September 11th occurred in October 2000, when Al Qaeda activists attacked the USS *Cole* in a ship-borne suicide bombing while the *Cole* was docked at the harbor in Aden, Yemen. The ship was damaged, and 17 sailors were killed. The next attack and the bursting of the terrorism bubble came with the September 11, 2001, attacks. By this time, Al Qaeda had become a coalition of factions of radical Islamic groups operating throughout the Muslim world, mostly groups opposing their governments. Cells and associates have been located in over 70 countries, according to U.S. officials. Among the groups in the Al Qaeda coalition, virtually all of which are still active today, are the Islamic Group and Al Jihad (Egypt), the Armed Islamic Group and the Salafist Group for Call and Combat (Algeria), the Islamic Movement of Uzbekistan (IMU), the Jemaah Islamiyah (Indonesia), the Libyan Islamic Fighting Group (Libyan opposition), and Harakat ul-Majahedin (Pakistan, Kashmiri).

THE ATTACK: SEPTEMBER 11, 2001

Tuesday September 11 dawned temperate and nearly cloudless in the eastern United States.[13] Millions of men and women readied themselves for work. Some made their way to the Twin Towers, the signature structures of the World Trade Center complex in New York City. Others went to Arlington, Virginia, to the Pentagon. Across the Potomac River, the U.S. Congress was back in session. At the other end of Pennsylvania Avenue, people began to line up for a White House tour. In Sarasota, Florida, President George W. Bush went for an early morning run.

For those heading to an airport, weather conditions could not have been better for a safe and pleasant journey. Among the travelers were Mohamed Atta and Abdul Aziz al Omari, who arrived at the airport in Portland, Maine.

Boston: American 11 and United 175

Atta and Omari boarded a 6:00 a.m. flight from Portland to Boston's Logan International Airport.

When he checked in for his flight to Boston, Atta was selected by a computerized prescreening system known as CAPPS (Computer Assisted Passenger Prescreening System), created to identify passengers who should be subject to special security measures. Under security rules in place at the time, the only consequence of Atta's selection by

The Collapse of the World Trade Center Building, September 11, 2001. (*Source: AP Wide World Photos.*)

CAPPS was that his checked bags were held off the plane until it was confirmed that he had boarded the aircraft. This did not hinder Atta's plans.

Atta and Omari arrived in Boston at 6:45 a.m. Seven minutes later, Atta apparently took a call from Marwan al Shehhi, a longtime colleague, who was at another terminal at Logan Airport. They spoke for three minutes. It would be their final conversation.

Between 6:45 and 7:40, Atta and Omari, along with Satam al Suqami, Wail al Sherhi, and Waleed al Shehri, checked in and boarded American Airlines Flight 11, bound for Los Angeles. The flight was scheduled to depart at 7:45 a.m.

In another Logan terminal, Shehhi, joined by Fayez Banihammad, Mohand al Shehri, Ahmed al Ghamdi, and Hamza al Ghamdi, checked in for United Airlines Flight 175, also bound for Los Angeles. A couple of Shehhi's colleagues were obviously unused to travel; according to the United ticket agent, they had trouble understanding the standard security questions, and she had to go over them slowly until they gave the routine, reassuring answers. Their flight was scheduled to depart at 8:00 a.m.

The security checkpoints through which passengers, including Atta and his colleagues, gained access to the American 11 gate were operated by Globe Security under a contract with American Airlines. In a different terminal, the single checkpoint through which passengers for United 175 passed was controlled by United Airlines, which had contracted with Huntleigh USA to perform the screening.

In passing through these checkpoints, each of the hijackers would have been screened by a walk-through metal detector calibrated to detect items with at least the mental content of a .22 caliber handgun. Anyone who might have set off that detector would have been screened with a hand wand—a procedure requiring the screener to identify the metal item or items that caused the alarm. In addition, an X-ray machine would have screened the hijackers' carry-on belongings. The screening was in place to identify and confiscate weapons and other items prohibited from being carried onto a commercial flight. None of the checkpoint supervisors recalled the hijackers or reported anything suspicious regarding their screening.

As Atta had been selected by CAPPS in Portland, three members of his hijacking team—Suqami, Wail al Shehri, and Waleed al Shehri—were selected in Boston. Their selection affected only the handling of their checked bags, not their screening at the checkpoint. All five men cleared the checkpoint and made their way to the gate for American 11. Atta, Omari, and Suqami took their seats in business class. The Shehri brothers had adjacent seats in row 2, in the first-class cabin. They boarded American 11 between 7:31 and 7:40. The aircraft pushed back from the gate at 7:40.

Shehi and his team, none of whom had been selected by CAPPS, boarded United 175 between 7:23 and 7:28. Their aircraft pushed back from the gate just before 8:00.

Washington Dulles: America 77

Hundreds of miles southwest of Boston, at Dulles International Airport in the Virginia suburbs of Washington, D.C., five more men were preparing to take their early morning flight. At 7:15, a pair of them, Khalid al Mihdhar and Majed Moqed, checked in at the American Airlines ticket counter for Flight 77, bound for Los Angeles. Within the next 20 minutes, they would be followed by Hani Hanjour and two brothers, Nawaf al Hazmi and Salem al Hazmi.

Hani Hanjour, Khalid al Mihdhar, and Majed Moqed were flagged by CAPPS. The Hazmi brothers were also selected for extra scrutiny by the airline's customer service representative at the check-in counter. He did so because one of the brothers did not have photo identification nor could he understand English, and because the agent found both of the passengers to be suspicious. The only consequence of their selection was that their checked bags were held off the plane until it was confirmed that they had boarded the aircraft.

All five hijackers passed through the main terminal's west security screening checkpoint; United Airlines, which was the responsible air carrier, had contracted out the work to Argenbright Security. The checkpoint featured closed-circuit television that recorded all passengers, including the hijackers, as they were screened. At 7:18, Mihdhar and Moqed entered the security checkpoint.

Mihdhar and Moqed placed their carry-on bags on the belt of the X-ray machine and proceeded through the first metal detector. Both set off the alarm, and they were directed to a second metal detector. Mihdhar did not trigger the alarm and was permitted through the checkpoint. After Moqed set it off, a screener wanded him. He passed this inspection.

About 20 minutes later, at 7:35, another passenger for Flight 77, Hani Hanjour, placed two carry-on bags on the X-ray belt in the main terminal's west checkpoint and proceeded, without alarm, through the metal detector. A short time later, Nawaf and Salem al Hazmi entered the same checkpoint. Salem al Hazmi cleared the metal detector and was permitted through; Nawaf al Hazmi set off the alarms for both the first and second metal detectors and was then hand-wanded before being passed. In addition, his over-the-shoulder carry-on bag was swiped by an explosive trace detector and then passed. The video footage indicated that he was carrying an unidentified item in his back pocket, clipped to its rim.

When the local civil aviation security office of the Federal Aviation Administration (FAA) later investigated these security screening operations, the screeners recalled nothing out of the ordinary. They could not recall that any of the passengers they screened were CAPPS selectees. The 9/11 Commission asked a screening expert to review the videotape of the hand-wanding, and he found the quality of the screener's work to have been "marginal at best." The screener should have "resolved" what set off the alarm; and in the case of both Moqed and Hazmi, it was clear that he did not.

At 7:50, Majed Moqed and Khalid al Mihdhar boarded the flight and were seated in 12A and 12B coach. Hani Hanjour, assigned to seat 1B (first class), soon followed. The Hazmi brothers, sitting in 5E and 5F, joined Hanjour in the first-class cabin.

Newark: United 93

Between 7:03 and 7:39, Saeed al Ghamdi, Ahmed al Nami, Ahmad al Haznawi, and Ziad Jarrah checked in at the United Airlines ticket counter for Flight 93, going to Los Angeles. Two checked bags; two did not. Haznawi was selected by CAPPS. His checked bag was screened for explosives and then loaded on the plane.

The four men passed through the security checkpoint, owned by United Airlines and operated under contract by Argenbright Security. Like the checkpoints in Boston, it lacked closed-circuit television surveillance, so there is no documentary evidence to indicate when the hijackers passed through the checkpoint, what alarms may have been triggered, or what security procedures were administered. The FAA interviewed the screeners later; none recalled anything unusual or suspicious.

The four men boarded the plane between 7:39 and 7:48. All four had seats in the first-class cabin; their plane had no business-class section. Jarrah was in seat 1B, closest to the cockpit; Nami was in 3C, Ghamdi in 3D, and Haznawi in 6B.

The 19 men were aboard four transcontinental flights. They were planning to hijack these planes and turn them into large guided missiles, loaded with up to 11,400 gallons of jet fuel. By 8:00 a.m. on the morning of Tuesday, September 11, 2001, they had defeated all the security layers that America's civil aviation security system then had in place to prevent a hijacking.

The Hijacking of American 11

American Airlines Flight 11 provided nonstop service from Boston to Los Angeles. On September 11, Captain John Ogonowski and First Officer Thomas McGuinness piloted the Boeing 767. It carried its full capacity of nine flight attendants. Eighty-one passengers boarded the flight with them (including the five terrorists).

The plane took off at 7:59. Just before 8:14, it had climbed to 26,000 feet, not quite its initial assigned cruising altitude of 29,000 feet. All communications and flight profile data were normal. About this time the Fasten Seatbelt sign would usually have been turned off, and the flight attendants would have begun preparing for cabin service.

At that same time, American 11 had its last routine communication with the ground when it acknowledged navigational instructions from the FAA's air traffic control (ATC) center in Boston. Sixteen seconds after that transmission, ATC instructed the aircraft's pilots to climb to 35,000 feet. That message and all subsequent attempts to contact the flight were not acknowledged. From this and other evidence, the 9/11 Commission believes the hijacking began at 8:14 or shortly thereafter.

Reports from two flight attendants in the coach cabin, Betty Ong and Madeline "Amy" Sweeney, tell us most of what we know about how the hijacking happened. As it began, some of the hijackers—most likely Wail al Shehri and Waleed al Shehri, who were seated in row 2 in first class—stabbed the two unarmed flight attendants who would have been preparing for cabin services.

The 9/11 Commission does not know exactly how the hijackers gained access to the cockpit; FAA rules required that the doors remained closed and locked during flight. Ong speculated that they had "jammed their way" in. Perhaps the terrorists stabbed the flight attendants to get a cockpit key, to force one of them to open the cockpit door, or to lure the captain or first officer out of the cockpit. Or the flight attendants may just have been in their way.

At the same time or shortly thereafter, Atta—the only terrorist on board trained to fly a jet—would have moved to the cockpit from his business-class seat, possibly accompanied by Omari. As this was happening, passenger Daniel Lewin, who was seated in the row just behind Atta and Omari, was stabbed by one of the hijackers—probably Satam al Suqami, who was seated directly behind Lewin. Lewin had served four years as an officer in the Israeli military. He may have made an attempt to stop the hijackers in front of him, not realizing that another was sitting behind him.

The hijackers quickly gained control and sprayed Mace, pepper spray, or some other irritant in the first-class cabin to force the passengers and flight attendants toward the rear of the plane. They claimed they had a bomb.

About five minutes after the hijacking began, Betty Ong contacted the American Airlines Southeastern Reservations Office in Cary, North Carolina, via an AT&T airphone to report an emergency aboard the flight. This was the first of several occasions on 9/11 when flight attendants took action outside the scope of their training, which emphasized that in a hijacking they were to communicate with the cockpit crew. The emergency call lasted approximately 25 minutes, as Ong calmly and professionally relayed information about events taking place aboard the airplane to authorities on the ground.

At 8:19, Ong reported: "The cockpit is not answering, somebody's stabbed in business class—and I think there's Mace—that we can't breathe—I don't know, I think we're getting hijacked." She then told of the stabbings of the two flight attendants.

At 8:21, one of the American employees receiving Ong's call in North Carolina, Nydia Gonzalez, alerted the American Airlines operations center in Fort Worth, Texas, reaching Craig Marquis, the manager on duty. Marquis soon realized this was an emergency and instructed the airline's dispatcher responsible for the flight to contact the cockpit. At 8:23, the dispatcher tried unsuccessfully to contact the aircraft. Six minutes later, the air traffic control specialist in American's operation center contacted the FAA's Boston Air Traffic Control Center about the flight. The center was already aware of the problem.

Boston Center knew of a problem on the flight in part because just before 8:25 the hijackers had attempted to communicate with the passengers. The microphone was keyed, and immediately one of the hijackers said, "Nobody move. Everything will be okay. If you try to make any moves, you'll endanger yourself and the airplane. Just stay quiet." Air traffic controllers heard the transmission; Ong did not. The hijackers probably did not know how to operate the cockpit radio communication system correctly and thus inadvertently broadcast their message over the air traffic control channel instead of the cabin public-address channel. Also at 8:25, and again at 8:29, Amy Sweeney got through to the American Flight Services Office in Boston but was cut off after she reported someone was hurt aboard the flight. Three minutes later, Sweeney was reconnected to the office and began relaying updates to the manager, Michael Woodward.

At 8:26, Ong reported that the plane was "flying erratically." A minute later, Flight 11 turned south. American also began getting identifications of the hijackers, as Ong and then Sweeney passed on some of the seat numbers of those who had gained unauthorized access to the cockpit.

Sweeney calmly reported on her line that the plane had been hijacked; a man in first class had his throat slashed; two flight attendants had been stabbed—one was seriously hurt and was on oxygen whereas the other's wounds seemed minor; a doctor had been requested; the flight attendants were unable to contact the cockpit; and there was a bomb in the cockpit. Sweeney told Woodward that she and Ong were trying to relay as much information as they could to people on the ground.

At 8:38, Ong told Gonzalez that the plane was flying erratically again. Around this time Sweeney told Woodward that the hijackers were Middle Easterners, naming three of their seat numbers. One spoke very little English, and one spoke excellent English. The hijackers had gained entry to the cockpit, and she did not know how. The aircraft was in a rapid descent.

At 8:41, Sweeney told Woodward that passengers in coach were under the impression that there was a routine medical emergency in first class. Other flight attendants were busy at duties such as getting medical supplies while Ong and Sweeney were reporting the events.

At 8:41, in America's operations center, a colleague told Marquis that the air traffic controllers declared Flight 11 a hijacking and "think he's [American 11] headed toward Kennedy [airport in New York City]. They're moving everybody out of the way. They seem to have him on a primary radar. They seem to think that he is descending."

At 8:44, Gonzalez reported losing phone contact with Ong. About this same time Sweeney reported to Woodward, "Something is wrong. We are in a rapid descent . . . we are all over the place." Woodward asked Sweeney to look out the window to see if she could determine where they were. Sweeney responded: "We are flying low. We are flying very, very low. We are flying way too low." Seconds later she said, "Oh my God we are way too low." The phone call ended.

At 8:46:40, American 11 crashed into the North Tower of the World Trade Center in New York City. All on board, along with an unknown number of people in the tower, were killed instantly.

The Hijacking of United 175

United Airlines Flight 175 was scheduled to depart for Los Angeles at 8:00. Captain Victor Saracini and First Officer Michael Horrocks piloted the Boeing 767, which had seven flight attendants. Fifty-six passengers boarded the flight.

United 175 pushed back from its gate at 7:58 and departed Logan Airport at 8:14. By 8:33, it had reached its assigned cruising altitude of 31,000 feet. The flight attendants would have begun their cabin service.

The flight had taken off just as American 11 was being hijacked, and at 8:42 the United 175 flight crew completed their report on a "suspicious transmission" overheard from another plane (which turned out to have been Flight 11) just after takeoff. This was United 175's last communication with the ground.

The hijackers attacked sometime between 8:42 and 8:46. They used knives (as reported by two passengers and a flight attendant), Mace (reported by one passenger), and the threat of a bomb (reported by the same passenger). They stabbed members of the flight crew (reported by a flight attendant and one passenger). Both pilots had been killed (reported by one flight attendant). The eyewitness accounts came from calls made from the rear of the plane, from passengers originally seated further forward in the cabin, a sign that passengers and perhaps crew had been moved to the back of the aircraft. Given similarities to American 11 in hijacker seating and in eyewitness reports of tactics and weapons, as well as the contact between the presumed team leaders, Atta and Shehhi, the 9/11 Commission believes the tactics were similar on both flights.

The first operational evidence that something was abnormal on United 175 came at 8:47, when the aircraft changed beacon codes twice within a minute. At 8:51, the flight deviated from its assigned altitude, and a minute later New York air traffic controllers began repeatedly and unsuccessfully trying to contact it.

At 8:52, in Easton, Connecticut, a man named Lee Hanson received a phone call from his son Peter, a passenger on United 175. His son told him: "I think they've taken over the cockpit—An attendant has been stabbed—and someone else up front may have been killed. The plane is making strange moves. Call United Airlines—Tell them it's Flight 175, Boston to LA." Lee Hanson then called the Easton Police Department and relayed what he had heard.

Also at 8:52, a male flight attendant called a United office in San Francisco, reaching Marc Policastro. The flight attendant reported that the flight had been hijacked, both pilots had been killed, a flight attendant had been stabbed, and the hijackers were probably flying the plane. The call lasted about two minutes, after which Policastro and a colleague tried unsucessfully to contact the flight.

At 8:58, the flight took a heading toward New York City.

At 8:59, Flight 175 passenger David Sweeney tried to call his wife, Julie. He left a message on their home answering machine that the plane had been hijacked. He then called his mother, Louise Sweeney, told her the flight had been hijacked, and added that the passengers were thinking about storming the cockpit to take control of the plane away from the hijackers.

At 9:00, Lee Hanson received a second call from his son Peter:

> It's getting bad, Dad—A stewardess was stabbed—They seem to have knives and Mace—They said they have a bomb—It's getting very bad on the plane—Passengers are throwing up and getting sick—The plane is making jerky movements—I don't think the pilot is flying the plane—I think we are going down—I think they intend to go to Chicago or someplace and fly into a building—Don't worry, Dad—If it happens, it'll be very fast—My God, my God.

The call ended abruptly. Lee Hanson had heard a woman scream just before it cut off. He turned on a television, and in her home so did Louise Sweeney. Both then saw the second aircraft hit the World Trade Center.

At 9:03:11, United Airlines Flight 175 struck the South Tower of the World Trade Center. All on board, along with an unknown number of people in the tower, were killed instantly.

The Hijacking of American 77

American Airlines Flight 77 was scheduled to depart from Washington Dulles for Los Angeles at 8:10. The aircraft was a Boeing 757 piloted by Captain Charles F. Burlingame and First Officer David Charlebois. There were four flight attendants. On September 11, the flight carried 58 passengers.

American 77 pushed back from its gate at 8:09 and took off at 8:20. At 8:46, the flight reached its assigned cruising altitude of 35,000 feet. Cabin service would have begun. At 8:51, American 77 transmitted its last routine radio communication. The hijacking began between 8:51 and 8:54. As on American 11 and United 175, the hijackers used knives (reported by one passenger) and moved all the passengers (and possibly crew) to the rear of the aircraft (reported by one flight attendant and one passenger). Unlike the earlier flights, the Flight 77 hijackers were reported by a passenger to have box cutters. Finally, a passenger reported that an announcement had been made by the "pilot" that the plane had been hijacked. Neither of the firsthand accounts mentioned any stabbings or the threat or use of either a bomb or Mace, though both witnesses began the flight in the first-class cabin.

At 8:54, the aircraft deviated from its assigned course, turning south. Two minutes later the transponder was turned off, and even primary radar contact with the aircraft was lost. The Indianapolis Air Traffic Control Center repeatedly tried and failed to contact the aircraft. American Airlines dispatchers also tried, without success.

At 9:00, American Airlines Executive Vice President Gerald Arpey learned that communications had been lost with American 77. This was now the second American aircraft in trouble. He ordered all American Airlines flights in the Northeast that had not taken off to remain on the ground. Shortly before 9:10, suspecting that American 77 had been hijacked, American headquarters concluded that the second aircraft to hit the World Trade Center might have been Flight 77. After learning that United Airlines was missing a plane, American Airlines headquarters extended the ground stop nationwide.

At 9:12, Renee May called her mother, Nancy May, in Las Vegas. She said her flight was being hijacked by six individuals who had moved them to the rear of the plane. She asked her mother to alert American Airlines. Nancy May and her husband promptly did so.

At some point between 9:16 and 9:26, Barbara Olson called her husband, Ted Olson, the Solicitor General of the United States. She reported that the flight had been hijacked, and the hijackers had knives and box cutters. She further indicated that the hijackers were not aware of her phone call, and that they had put all the passengers in the back of the plane. About a minute into the conversation, the call was cut off. Solicitor General Olson tried unsuccessfully to reach Attorney General John Ashcroft.

Shortly after the first call, Barbara Olson reached her husband again. She reported that the pilot had announced that the flight had been hijacked, and she asked her husband what she should tell the captain to do. Ted Olson asked for her location and she replied that the aircraft was then flying over houses. Another passenger told her they were traveling northeast. The Solicitor General then informed his wife of the two previous hijackings and crashes. She did not display signs of panic and did not indicate any awareness of an impending crash. At that point, the second call was cut off.

At 9:29, the autopilot on American 77 was disengaged; the aircraft was at 7,000 feet and approximately 38 miles west of the Pentagon. At 9:32, controllers at the Dulles Terminal Radar Approach Control "observed a primary radar target tracking eastbound at a high rate of speed." This was later determined to have been Flight 77.

At 9:34, Ronald Reagan Washington National Airport advised the Secret Service of an unknown aircraft heading in the direction of the White House. American 77 was then 5 miles west-southwest of the Pentagon and began a 330-degree turn. At the end of the turn, it was descending through 2,200 feet, pointed toward the Pentagon and downtown Washington. The hijacker pilot then advanced the throttles to maximum power and dove toward the Pentagon.

At 9:37:46, American Airlines Flight 77 crashed into the Pentagon, traveling at approximately 530 miles per hour. All on board, as well as many civilian and military personnel in the building, were killed.

The Battle for United 93

At 8:42, United Airlines Flight 93 took off from Newark (New Jersey) Liberty International Airport bound for San Francisco. The aircraft was piloted by Captain Jason Dahl and First Officer Leroy Homer, and there were five flight attendants. Thirty-seven passengers,

BOX 1-3

REMARKS BY THE PRESIDENT AFTER TWO PLANES CRASH INTO WORLD TRADE CENTER EMMA BOOKER ELEMENTARY SCHOOL SARASOTA, FLORIDA SEPTEMBER 11, 2001, 9:30 A.M.

THE PRESIDENT: Ladies and gentlemen, this is a difficult moment for America. I, unfortunately, will be going back to Washington after my remarks. Secretary Rod Paige and the Lt. Governor will take the podium and discuss education. I do want to thank the folks here at Booker Elementary School for their hospitality.

Today we've had a national tragedy. Two airplanes have crashed into the World Trade Center in an apparent terrorist attack on our country. I have spoken to the Vice President, to the Governor of New York, to the Director of the FBI, and have ordered that the full resources of the federal government go to help the victims and their families, and to conduct a full-scale investigation to hunt down and to find those folks who committed this act.

Terrorism against our nation will not stand.

And now if you would join me in a moment of silence. May God bless the victims, their families, and America. Thank you very much.

including the hijackers, boarded the plane. Scheduled to depart the gate at 8:00, the Boeing 757's takeoff was delayed because of the airport's typically heavy morning traffic.

The hijackers had planned to take flights scheduled to depart at 7:45 (American 11), 8:00 (United 175 and United 93), and 8:10 (American 77). Three of the flights had actually taken off within 10 to 15 minutes of their planned departure times. United 93 would ordinarily have taken off about 15 minutes after pulling away from the gate. When it left the ground at 8:42, the flight was running more than 25 minutes late.

As United 93 left Newark, the flight's crew members were unaware of the hijackings of American 11. Around 9:00, the FAA, American, and United were facing the staggering realization of apparent multiple hijackings. At 9:03, they would see another aircraft strike the World Trade Center. Crisis managers at the FAA and the airlines did not yet act to warn other aircraft. At the same time, Boston Center realized that a message transmitted just before 8:25 by the hijacker pilot of American 11 included the phrase, "We have some planes."

No one at the FAA or the airlines that day had ever dealt with multiple hijackings. Such a plot had not been carried out anywhere in the world in more than 30 years, and never in the United States. As news of the hijackings filtered through the FAA and the airlines, it does not seem to have occurred to their leadership that they needed to alert other aircraft in the air that they too might be at risk.

United 175 was hijacked between 8:42 and 8:46, and awareness of that hijacking began to spread after 8:51. American 77 was hijacked between 8:51 and 8:54. By 9:00, the FAA and airline officials began to comprehend that attackers were going after multiple aircraft. American Airlines' nationwide ground stop between 9:05 and 9:10 was followed by a United Airlines ground stop. FAA controllers at Boston Center, which had tracked the first two hijackings, requested at 9:07 that Herndon Command Center "get messages to airborne aircraft to increase security for the cockpit." There is no evidence that Herndon took such action. Boston Center immediately began speculating about other aircraft that might be in danger, leading them to worry about a transcontinental flight—Delta 1989—that in fact was not hijacked. At 9:19, the FAA's New England regional office called Herndon and asked that Cleveland Center advise Delta 1989 to use extra cockpit security.

Several FAA air traffic control officials told the 9/11 Commission that it was the air carrier's responsibility to notify their planes of security problems. One senior FAA air traffic control manager said that it was simply not the FAA's place to order the airlines what to tell their pilots. The Commission believes that such statements did not reflect an adequate appreciation of the FAA's responsibility for the safety and security of civil aviation.

The airlines bore responsibility, too. They were facing an escalating number of conflicting and, for the most part, erroneous reports about other flights, as well as a continuing lack of vital information from the FAA about the hijacked flights. The 9/11 Commission found no evidence, however, that American Airlines sent any cockpit warnings to its aircraft that day. United's first decisive action to notify its airborne aircraft to take defensive action did not come until 9:19, when a United flight dispatcher, Ed Ballinger, took the initiative to begin transmitting warnings to his 16 transcontinental flights: "Beware any cockpit intrusions—Two a/c (aircraft) hit World Trade Center." One of the flights that received the warning was United 93. Because Ballinger was still responsible for his other flights as well as Flight 175, his warning message was not transmitted to Flight 93 until 9:23.

By all accounts, the first 46 minutes of Flight 93's cross-country trip proceeded routinely. Radio communications from the plane were normal. Heading, speed, and altitude ran according to plan. At 9:24, Ballinger's warning to United 93 was received in the cockpit. Within two minutes, at 9:26, the pilot, Jason Dahl, responded with a note of puzzlement: "Ed, confirm latest mssg plz—Jason."

The hijackers attacked at 9:28. While traveling 35,000 feet above eastern Ohio, United 93 suddenly dropped 700 feet. Eleven seconds into the descent, the FAA's air traffic control center in Cleveland received the first of two radio transmissions from the aircraft. During the first broadcast, the captain or first officer could be heard declaring "Mayday" amid the sounds of a physical struggle in the cockpit. The second radio transmission, 35 seconds later, indicated that the fight was continuing. The captain or first officer could be heard shouting: "Hey get out of here—get out of here—get out of here."

On the morning of 9/11, there were only 37 passengers on United 93—33 in addition to the 4 hijackers. This was below the norm for Tuesday mornings during the summer of 2001. But there is no evidence that the hijackers manipulated passenger levels or purchased additional seats to facilitate their operation.

The terrorists who hijacked three other commercial flights on 9/11 operated in five-man teams. They initiated their cockpit takeover within 30 minutes of takeoff. On Flight 93, however, the takeover took place 46 minutes after takeoff, and there were only four hijackers. The operative likely intended to round out the team for this flight, Mohamed al Kahtani, had been refused entry by a suspicious immigration inspector at Florida's Orlando International Airport in August.

Because several passengers on United 93 described three hijackers on the plane, not four, some have wondered whether one of the hijackers had been able to use the cockpit jump seat from the outset of the flight. FAA rules allow use of this seat by documented and approved individuals, usually air carrier or FAA personnel. The 9/11 Commission found no evidence indicating that one of the hijackers, or anyone else, sat there on this flight. All the hijackers had assigned seats in first class, and they seem to have used them. It is more likely that Jarrah, the crucial pilot-trained member of their team, remained seated and inconspicuous until after the cockpit was seized; and once inside, he would not have been visible to the passengers.

At 9:32, a hijacker, probably Jarrah, made or attempted to make the following announcement to the passengers of Flight 93: "Ladies and Gentlemen: Here the captain, please sit down keep remaining sitting. We have a bomb on board. So, sit." The flight data recorder (also recovered) indicates that Jarrah then instructed the plane's autopilot to turn the aircraft around and head east.

The cockpit voice recorder data indicate that a woman, most likely a flight attendant, was being held captive in the cockpit. She struggled with one of the hijackers who killed or otherwise silenced her.

Shortly thereafter, the passengers and flight crew began a series of calls from GTE airphones and cellular phones. These calls between family, friends, and colleagues took place until the end of the flight and provided those on the ground with firsthand accounts. They enabled the passengers to gain critical information, including the news that two aircraft had slammed into the World Trade Center.

At 9:39, the FAA's Cleveland Air Route Traffic Control Center overheard a second announcement indicating that there was a bomb on board, that the plane was returning to the airport, and that passengers should remain seated. Although it apparently was not heard by the passengers, this announcement, like those on Flight 11 and Flight 77, was intended to deceive them. Jarrah, like Atta earlier, may have inadvertently broadcast the message because he did not know how to operate the radio and the intercom. To the 9/11 Commission's knowledge, none of them had ever flown an actual airliner before.

At least two callers from the flight reported that the hijackers knew that passengers were making calls but did not seem to care. It is quite possible Jarrah knew of the success of the assault on the World Trade Center. He could have learned of this from messages being sent by United Airlines to the cockpits of its transcontinental flights, including Flight 93, warning of cockpit intrusion and telling of the New York attacks. But even without them, he would have certainly understood that the attacks on the World Trade Center would already have unfolded, given Flight 93's tardy departure from Newark. If Jarrah did know that the passengers were making calls, it might not have occurred to him that they were certain to learn what had happened in New York, thereby defeating his attempts at deception.

At least 10 passengers and 2 crew members shared vital information with family, friends, colleagues, or others on the ground. All understood the plane had been hijacked. They said the hijackers wielded knives and claimed to have a bomb. The hijackers were wearing red bandanas, and they forced the passengers to the back of the aircraft.

Callers reported that a passenger had been stabbed and that two people were lying on the floor of the cabin, injured or dead—possibly the captain and first officer. One caller reported that a flight attendant had been killed.

One of the callers from United 93 also reported that he thought the hijackers might possess a gun. But none of the other callers reported the presence of a firearm. One recipient of a call from the aircraft recounted specifically asking her caller whether the hijackers had guns. The passenger replied that he did not see one. No evidence of firearms or of their identifiable remains were found at the aircraft's crash site, and the cockpit voice recorder gives no indication of a gun being fired or mentioned at any time. The 9/11 Commission believes that if the hijackers had possessed a gun, they would have used it in the flight's last minutes as the passengers fought back.

Passengers on three flights reported the hijackers' claim of having a bomb. The FBI told the 9/11 Commission they found no trace of explosives at the crash sites. One of the passengers who mentioned a bomb expressed his belief that it was not real. Lacking any evidence that the hijackers attempted to smuggle such illegal items past the security screening checkpoints, the 9/11 Commission believes the bombs were probably fake.

During at least five of the passengers' phone calls, information was shared about the attacks that had occurred earlier that morning at the World Trade Center. Five calls described the intent of passengers and surviving crew members to revolt against the hijackers. According to one call, they voted on whether to rush the terrorists in an attempt to retake the plane. They decided and acted.

At 9:57, the passenger assault began. Several passengers had terminated phone calls with loved ones to join the revolt. One of the callers ended her message as follows: "Everyone's running up to first class, I've got to go. Bye."

The cockpit voice recorder captured the sounds of the passenger assault muffled by the intervening cockpit door. Some family members who listened to the recording report that they could hear the voice of a loved one among the din. The 9/11 Commission could not identify whose voices can be heard. But the assault was sustained.

In response, Jarrah immediately began to roll the airplane to the left and right, attempting to knock the passengers off balance. At 9:58:57, Jarrah told another hijacker in the cockpit to block the door. Jarrah continued to roll the airplane sharply left and right, but the assault continued. At 9:59:52, Jarrah changed tactics and pitched the nose of the airplane up and down to disrupt the assault. The recorder captured the sounds of loud thumps, crashes, shouts, and breaking glasses and plates. At 10:00:03, Jarrah stabilized the airplane.

Five seconds later, Jarrah asked, "Is that it? Shall we finish it off?" A hijacker responded, "No. Not yet. When they all come, we finish it off." The sounds of fighting continued outside the cockpit. Again, Jarrah pitched the nose of the aircraft up and down. At 10:00:26, a passenger in the background said, "In the cockpit. If we don't we'll die!" Sixteen seconds later, a passenger yelled, "Roll it." Jarrah stopped the violent maneuvers at about 10:01:00 and said, "Allah is the greatest! Allah is the greatest!" He then asked another hijacker in the cockpit, "Is that it? I mean, shall we put it down?" to which the other replied, "Yes, put it in it, and pull it down."

The passengers continued their assault and at 10:02:03, a hijacker said, "Pull it down! Pull it down!" The hijackers remained at the controls but must have judged that the passengers were only seconds from overcoming them. The airplane headed down; the control wheel was turned hard to the right. The airplane rolled onto its back, and one of the hijackers began shouting, "Allah is the greatest! Allah is the greatest!" With the sounds of the

BOX 1-4

REMARKS BY THE PRESIDENT UPON ARRIVAL AT BARKSDALE AIR FORCE BASE, LOUISIANA

THE PRESIDENT: I want to reassure the American people that the full resources of the federal government are working to assist local authorities to save lives and to help the victims of these attacks. Make no mistake: The United States will hunt down and punish those responsible for these cowardly acts.

I've been in regular contact with the Vice President, the Secretary of Defense, the national security team and my Cabinet. We have taken all appropriate security precautions to protect the American people. Our military at home and around the world is on high alert status, and we have taken the necessary security precautions to continue the functions of your government.

We have been in touch with the leaders of Congress and with world leaders to assure them that we will do whatever is necessary to protect America and Americans.

I ask the American people to join me in saying a thanks for all the folks who have been fighting hard to rescue our fellow citizens and to join me in saying a prayer for the victims and their families.

The resolve of our great nation is being tested. But make no mistake: We will show the world that we will pass this test. God bless.

passenger counterattack continuing, the aircraft plowed into an empty field in Shanksville, Pennsylvania, at 580 miles per hour, about 20 minutes' flying time from Washington, D.C.

Jarrah's objective was to crash his airliner into symbols of the American Republic, the Capitol or the White House. He was defeated by the alerted unarmed passengers of United 93.

THE RESPONSE: SEPTEMBER 11, 2001

New York, NY

The World Trade Center (WTC) complex was built for the Port Authority of New York and New Jersey.[14] Construction began in 1966, and tenants began to occupy its space in 1970. The Twin Towers came to occupy a unique and symbolic place in the culture of New York City and America.

The WTC actually consisted of seven buildings, including one hotel, spread across 16 acres of land. The buildings were connected by an underground mall (the concourse). The Twin Towers (1 WTC, or the North Tower, and 2 WTC, or the South Tower) were the signature structures, containing 10.4 million square feet of office space. Both towers had 110 stories, were about 1,350 feet high, and were square; each wall measured 208 feet in length. On any given workday, up to 50,000 office workers occupied the towers, and 40,000 people passed through the complex.

In New York City, the city government had ready at their disposal a number of plans for critical incidents that may have potentially occurred in the city, with the Office of Emergency Management and Interagency Preparedness (OEM) established to coordinate the workings of such agencies as the New York Police Department (NYPD), the Port Authority Police Department (PAPD), and the Fire Department of New York (FDNY). In 1996 Mayor Rudolph Giuliani created the Mayor's Office of Emergency Management, which had three basic functions. First, OEM's Watch Command was to monitor the city's key communications channels—including radio frequencies of FDNY dispatch and the NYPD—and other data. A second purpose of the OEM was to improve New York City's response to major incidents, including terrorist attacks, by planning and conducting exercises and drills that would involve multiple city agencies, particularly the NYPD and the FDNY. Third, the OEM would play a crucial role in managing the city's overall response to an incident. After OEM's Emergency Operations Center was activated, designated liaisons from relevant agencies, as well as the mayor and his or her senior staff, would respond there. In addition, an OEM field responder would be sent to the scene to ensure that the response was coordinated.

The OEM's headquarters was located at 7 WTC. Some questioned locating it both so close to a previous terrorist target (the 1993 bombing) and on the 23rd floor of a building (difficult to access should elevators become inoperable). There was no backup site. The site was activated shortly after the first plane hit the North Tower. However, after the South Tower was hit, an evacuation order was issued. Prior to its evacuation, no outside agency liaisons had reached OEM.

The NYPD on September 11 stood at 40,000 police officers and was led by Police Commissioner Bernard Kerik, whose duties were not primarily operational but who retained operational authority. Much of the NYPD's operational activities were run by the chief of department. In the event of a major emergency, a leading role would be played by the Special Operations Division. This division included the Aviation Unit, which provided helicopters for surveys and rescues, and the Emergency Services Unit (ESU), which carried out specialized rescue missions. The NYPD had specific and detailed standard operating procedures for the dispatch of officers to an incident's depending on the incident's magnitude.

The Port Authority of New York and New Jersey Police Department consisted of 1,331 officers, many of whom were trained in fire suppression methods as well as in law enforcement. The PAPD was led by a superintendent. There was a separate PAPD command for each of the Port Authority's nine facilities, including the World Trade Center.

As of September 11, the Port Authority lacked any standard operating procedures to govern how officers from multiple commands would respond to and then be staged and utilized at a major incident at the WTC. In particular, there were no standard operating procedures covering how different commands should communicate via radio during such an incident.

At 8:46:40, the hijacked American Airlines Flight 11 flew into the upper portion of the North Tower, cutting through floors 93 to 99. Within minutes, New York City's 911 system was flooded with eyewitness accounts of the events. Most callers correctly identified the target of the attack. Some identified the plane as a commercial airliner.

Numerous NYPD officers saw the plane strike the North Tower and immediately reported it to NYPD communications dispatchers.

At 8:58, while en route, the NYPD Chief of Department raised the NYPD's mobilization to level 4, thereby sending to the WTC approximately 22 lieutenants, 100 sergeants, and 800 police officers from all over the city. The Chief of Department arrived at Church and Vesey at 9:00.

At 9:01, the NYPD patrol mobilization point was moved to West and Vesey to handle the greater number of patrol officers dispatched in the higher-level mobilization. These officers would be stationed around the perimeter of the complex to direct the evacuation of civilians. Many were diverted on the way to the scene by intervening emergencies related to the attack.

At 8:50, the Aviation Unit of the NYPD dispatched two helicopters to the WTC to report on conditions and assess the feasibility of a rooftop landing or of special rescue operations. En route, the two helicopters communicated with air traffic controllers at the area's three major airports and informed them of the commercial airplane crash at the World Trade Center. The air traffic controllers had been unaware of the incident.

At 8:56, an NYPD ESU team asked to be picked up at the Wall Street heliport to initiate rooftop rescues. At 8:58, however, after assessing the North Tower roof, a helicopter pilot advised the ESU team that they could not land on the roof because "it is engulfed in flames and heavy smoke conditions."

Two on-duty NYPD officers were on the 20th floor of the North Tower at this time. They climbed to the 29th floor, urging civilians to evacuate, but did not locate a group of civilians trapped on the 22nd floor.

Just before 9:00, an ESU team began to walk from Church and Vesey to the North Tower lobby, with the goal of climbing toward and setting up a triage center on the upper floors for the severely injured. A second ESU team would follow them to assist in removing those individuals.

Numerous officers responded to help injured civilians and to urge those who could walk to vacate the area immediately. Putting themselves in danger of falling debris, several officers entered the plaza and successfully rescued at least one injured, nonambulatory civilian, and attempted to rescue others.

Also by about 9:00, transit officers began shutting down subway stations in the vicinity of the World Trade Center and evacuating civilians from those stations.

Around the city, the NYPD cleared major thoroughfares for emergency vehicles to access the WTC. The NYPD and PAPD coordinated the closing of bridges and tunnels into Manhattan.

The Port Authority's on-site commanding police officer was standing in the concourse when a fireball erupted out of elevator shafts and exploded onto the mall concourse, causing him to dive for cover. The on-duty sergeant initially instructed the officers in the WTC Command to meet at the police desk in 5 WTC. Soon thereafter, he instructed officers arriving from outside commands to meet him at the fire safety desk in the North Tower lobby. A few of these officers from outside commands were given WTC Command radios.

One Port Authority police officer at the WTC immediately began climbing stairwell C in the North Tower. Other officers began performing rescue and evacuation operations on the ground floors and in the PATH (Port Authority Trans-Hudson) station below the WTC complex.

Within minutes of impact, Port Authority police officers from the PATH, bridges, tunnels, and airport commands began responding to the WTC. The PAPD lacked written standard operating procedures for personnel responding from outside commands to the WTC during a major incident. In addition, officers from some PAPD commands lacked interoperable radio frequencies. As a result, there was no comprehensive coordination of PAPD's overall response.

At 9:00, the PAPD commanding officer of the WTC ordered an evacuation of all civilians in the World Trade Center complex because of the magnitude of the calamity in the North Tower. Also, at 9:00, the PAPD Superintendent and Chief of Department arrived separately and made their way to the North Tower.

In the 17-minute period between 8:46 and 9:03 a.m. on September 11, New York City and the Port Authority of New York and New Jersey had mobilized the largest rescue operation in the city's history. Well over a thousand first responders had been deployed, an evacuation had begun, and the critical decision that the fire could not be fought had been made. Then the second plane hit.

At 9:03:11, the hijacked United Airlines Flight 175 hit WTC (the South Tower) from the south, crashing through the 77th to 85th floors. What had been the largest and most complicated rescue operation in city history instantly doubled in magnitude.

Immediately after the second plane hit, the Chief of Department of the NYPD ordered a second Level 4 mobilization, bringing the total number of NYPD officers responding to close to 2,000.

The NYPD Chief of Department called for Operation Omega, which required the protection of sensitive locations around the city. NYPD headquarters were secured, and all other government buildings were evacuated.

The ESU command post at Church and Vesey streets coordinated all NYPD ESU rescue teams. After the South Tower was hit, the ESU officer running this command post decided to send one ESU team (each with approximately six police officers) up each of the Twin Towers' stairwells. While he continued to monitor the citywide SOD channel, which NYPD helicopters were using, he also monitored the point-to-point tactical channel that the ESU teams climbing in the towers would use.

Initial responders from outside PAPD commands proceeded to the police desk in 5 WTC or to the fire safety desk in the North Tower lobby. Some officers were then assigned to assist in stairwell evacuations; others were assigned to expedite evacuation in the plaza, concourse, and PATH station. As information was received of civilians trapped above ground-level floors of the North Tower, other PAPD officers were instructed to climb to those floors for rescue efforts. Still others began climbing toward the impact zone.

At 9:11, the PAPD superintendent and an inspector began walking up stairwell B of the North Tower to assess damage near and in the impact zone. The PAPD chief and several other PAPD officers began ascending a stairwell to reach the Windows on the World restaurant on the 106th floor, from which calls had been made to the PAPD desk reporting at least 100 people trapped.

The first NYPD ESU team entered the West Street–level lobby of the North Tower and prepared to begin climbing at about 9:15 a.m. They attempted to check in with the FDNY chiefs present, but were rebuffed. OEM personnel did not intervene. The ESU team began to climb the stairs. Shortly thereafter, a second NYPD ESU team entered the South Tower. The OEM field responder present ensured that they check in with the FDNY chief in charge of the lobby, as it was agreed that the ESU team would ascend and support FDNY personnel.

Many PAPD officers from different commands responded on their own initiative. By 9:03, the PAPD central police desk requested that responding officers meet at West and Vesey and await further instructions. In the absence of a predetermined command structure to deal with an incident of this magnitude, a number of PAPD inspectors, captains, and lieutenants stepped forward at around 9:30 to formulate an on-site response plan. They were hampered by not knowing how many officers were responding to the site and where those officers were operating. Many of the officers who responded to this command post lacked suitable protective equipment to enter the complex.

At 9:37, a civilian on the 106th floor of the South Tower reported to a 911 operator that a lower floor—the "90-something floor"—was collapsing. This information was conveyed inaccurately by the 911 operator to an NYPD dispatcher. The dispatcher further confused the substance of the 911 call by telling NYPD officers at the WTC complex that "the 106th floor is crumbling" at 9:52, 15 minutes after the 911 call was placed. The NYPD dispatcher conveyed this message on the radio frequency used in precincts in the vicinity of the WTC and subsequently on the Special Operations Division channel, but not on City Wide channel 1.

A third ESU team subsequently entered the North Tower at its elevated mezzanine lobby level and made no effort to check in with the FDNY command post. A fourth ESU team entered the South Tower. By 9:59, a fifth ESU team was next to 6 WTC and preparing to enter the North Tower.

By approximately 9:50, the officer running the ESU command post on Church and Vesey streets had a final radio communication with one of the ESU teams in the South Tower. The team then stated that it was ascending via stairs, was somewhere in the 20s, and was making slow progress because of the numerous descending civilians crowding the stairwell.

Three plainclothes NYPD officers without radios or protective gear had begun ascending either stairwell A or C of the North Tower. They began checking every other floor above the 12th for civilians. Only occasionally did they find any, and in those few cases they ordered the civilians to evacuate immediately. While checking floors, they used office phones to call their superiors. In one phone call an NYPD chief instructed them to leave the North Tower, but they refused to do so. As they climbed higher, they encountered increasing smoke and heat. Shortly before 10:00 they arrived on the 54th floor.

By 9:58, one PAPD officer had reached the 44th floor sky lobby of the North Tower. Also in the North Tower, one team of PAPD officers was in the mid-20s and another was in the lower 20s. Numerous PAPD officers were also climbing in the South Tower, including the PAPD ESU team. Many PAPD officers were on the ground floor of the complex—some assisting in evacuation, others manning the PAPD desk in 5 WTC or assisting at lobby command posts.

Throughout this period (9:03 to 9:59), a group of NYPD and Port Authority police officers, as well as two Secret Service agents, continued to assist civilians leaving the North Tower. They were positioned around the mezzanine lobby level of the North Tower, directing civilians leaving stairwells A and C to evacuate down an escalator to the concourse. The officers instructed those civilians who seemed composed to evacuate the complex calmly but rapidly. Other civilians exiting the stairs, who were either injured or exhausted, collapsed at the foot of these stairs; officers then assisted them out of the building.

When civilians reached the concourse, another NYPD officer stationed at the bottom of the escalator directed them to exit through the concourse to the north and east and then out of the WTC complex. This exit route ensured that civilians would not be endangered by falling debris and people on West Street, on the plaza between the towers, and on Liberty Street.

Some officers positioned themselves at the top of a flight of stairs by 5 WTC that led down into the concourse, going into the concourse when necessary to evacuate injured or disoriented civilians. Numerous other NYPD officers were stationed throughout the concourse, assisting burned, injured and disoriented civilians, as well as directing all civilians to exit to the north and east. NYPD officers were also in the South Tower lobby to assist in civilian evacuation. NYPD officers stationed on Vesey Street between West Street and Church Street urged civilians not to remain in the area and instead to keep walking north.

At 9:58:59, the South Tower collapsed in 10 seconds, killing all civilians and emergency personnel inside, as well as a number of individuals—both first responders and civilians—in the concourse, in the Marriott, and on neighboring streets. The building collapsed into itself, causing a ferocious windstorm and creating a massive debris cloud. The Marriott Hotel suffered signficant damage as a result of the collapse of the South Tower.

A member of the NYPD Aviation Unit radioed that the South Tower had collapsed immediately after it happened and further advised that all people in the WTC complex and nearby areas should be evacuated. At 10:04, NYPD aviation reported that the top 15 stories of the North Tower "were glowing red" and that they might collapse. At 10:08, a helicopter pilot warned that he did not believe the North Tower would last much longer.

Immediately after the South Tower collapsed, many NYPD radio frequencies became overwhelmed with transmissions relating to injured, trapped, or missing officers. As a result, NYPD radio communications became strained on most channels. Nevertheless, they remained effective enough for the two closest NYPD mobilization points to be moved further from the WTC at 10:06.

Just like most firefighters, the ESU rescue teams in the North Tower had no idea that the South Tower had collapsed. However, by 10:00 the ESU officer running the command post at Church and Vesey ordered the evacuation of all ESU units from the WTC complex. This officer, who had observed the South Tower collapse, reported it to ESU units in the North Tower in his evacuation instructions.

This instruction was clearly heard by the two ESU units already in the North Tower and the other ESU unit preparing to enter the tower. The ESU team on the 31st floor found the full collapse of the South Tower so unfathomable that they radioed back to the ESU officer at the command post and asked him to repeat his communication. He reiterated his urgent message.

The ESU team on the 31st floor conferred with the FDNY personnel there to ensure that they, too, knew that they had to evacuate, then proceeded down stairwell B. During the descent, they reported seeing many firefighters who were resting and did not seem to be in the process of evacuating. They further reported advising these firefighters to evacuate, but said that at times they were not acknowledged. In the opinion of one of the ESU officers, some of these firefighters essentially refused to take orders from cops. At least one firefighter who was in the North Tower has supported this assessment, stating that he was not going to take an evacuation instruction from a cop that morning. However, another firefighter reports that ESU officers ran past him without advising him to evacuate.

The ESU team on the 11th floor began descending stairwell C after receiving the evacuation order. Once near the mezzanine level—where stairwell C ended—this team spread out in chain formation, stretching from several floors down to the mezzanine itself. They used their flashlights to provide a path of beacons through the darkness and debris for civilians climbing down the stairs. Eventually, when no one else appeared to be descending, the ESU team exited the North Tower and ran one at a time to 6 WTC, dodging those who still were jumping from the upper floors of the North Tower by acting as spotters for each other. They remained in the area, conducting additional searches for civilians; all but two of them died.

After surviving the South Tower's collapse, the ESU team that had been preparing to enter the North Tower spread into chain formation and created a path for civilians (who had exited from the North Tower mezzanine) to evacuate the WTC complex by descending the stairs on the north side of 5 and 6 WTC, which led down to Vesey Street. They remained at this post until the North Tower collapsed, yet all survived.

The three plainclothes NYPD officers who had made it up to the 54th floor of the North Tower felt the building shake violently at 9:59 as the South Tower collapsed (although they did not know the cause). Immediately thereafter, they were joined by three firefighters from an FDNY engine company. One of the firefighters apparently heard an evacuation order on his radio, but responded in a return radio communication, "We're not fucking coming out!" However, the firefighters urged the police officers to descend because they lacked the protective gear and equipment needed to handle the increasing smoke and heat. The police officers reluctantly began descending, checking that the lower floors were clear of civilians. They proceeded down stairwell B, poking their heads into every floor and briefly looking for civilians.

Other NYPD officers helping evacuees on the mezzanine level of the North Tower were enveloped in the debris cloud that resulted from the South Tower's collapse. They struggled to regroup in the darkness and to evacuate both themselves and civilians they encountered. At least one of them died in the collapse of the North Tower. At least one NYPD officer from this area managed to evacuate out of 5 WTC, where he teamed up with a Port Authority police officer and acted as a spotter in advising the civilians who were still exiting when they could safely run from 1 WTC to 5 WTC and avoid being struck by people and debris falling from the upper floors.

At the time of the collapse of the South Tower, there were numerous NYPD officers in the concourse, some of whom are believed to have died there. Those who survived struggled to evacuate themselves in darkness, assisting civilians as they exited the concourse in all directions.

The North Tower collapsed at 10:28:25 a.m., killing all civilians alive on upper floors, an undetermined number below, and scores of first responders. The FDNY Chief of Department, the Port Authority Police Department Superintendent, and many of their senior staff were killed. Incredibly, 12 firefighters, 1 PAPD officer and 3 civilians who were descending stairwell B of the North Tower survived its collapse.

On September 11, the nation suffered the largest loss of life—2,973—on its soil as a result of hostile attack in its history. The FDNY suffered 343 fatalities—the largest loss of life of any emergency response agency in history. The PAPD suffered 37 fatalities—the largest loss of life of any police force in history. The NYPD suffered 23 fatalities—the second-largest loss of life of any police force in history, exceeded only by the number of PAPD officers lost the same day.

Mayor Guiliani, along with the Police and Fire commissioners and the OEM director, moved quickly north and established an emergency operations command post at the Police Academy. Over the coming hours, weeks, and months, thousands of civilians and city, state, and federal employees devoted themselves around the clock to putting New York City back on its feet.

Arlington, VA

At 9:37 a.m., the west wall of the Pentagon was hit by hijacked American Airlines Flight 77, a Boeing 757. The crash caused immediate and catastrophic damage. All 64 people aboard the airliner were killed, as were 125 people inside the Pentagon. One hundred six people were seriously injured and would be transported to area hopitals.[15]

At approximately 9:37 a.m., Arlington County Police Department (ACPD) Corporal Barry Foust and Officer Richard Cox, on patrol in south Arlington, saw a large American Airlines aircraft in steep descent on a collision course with the Pentagon.[16] They immediately radioed the Arlington County Emergency Communication Center (ECC). ACPD Headquarters issued a simultaneous page to all members of the ACPD with instructions to report for duty. Two-way pagers are standard issue only for the Emergency Response Team, hostage negotiators, members of the Special Weapons and Tactics (SWAT) team, and several command officials. Media reports of the attack alerted those who did not receive the pager message.

BOX 1-5

REMARKS OF ATTORNEY GENERAL JOHN ASHCROFT; SEPTEMBER 11, 2001

Today America has experienced one of the greatest tragedies ever witnessed on American soil.

These heinous acts of violence are an assault on the security of our nation and every American citizen.

We will not tolerate such acts and we will expend every effort and devote all necessary resources to bring the people responsible for these crimes to justice.

Now is the time for us to come together as a nation and offer our support and prayers for victims and their families, for the rescue workers and law enforcement, and for every one of us who has been changed forever by this horrible tragedy.

The following is a summary of the known facts surrounding today's incidents:

American Airlines flight 11 departed Boston for Los Angeles, was hijacked by suspects armed with knives. This plane crashed into the World Trade Center.

United Airlines flight 175 departed Boston for Los Angeles, was hijacked and crashed into the World Trade Center.

American Airlines flight 77 departed Washington Dulles for Los Angeles, was hijacked and crashed into the Pentagon.

United Airlines flight 93 departed Newark for San Francisco, was hijacked and crashed in Shanksville, Pennsylvania.

Crime scenes have been established by federal authorities in New York, Washington, D.C., Pittsburgh, Boston, and Newark.

The full resources of the Department of Justice, including the Federal Bureau of Investigation, the Immigration and Naturalization Service, the U.S. Attorneys offices, the U.S. Marshals Service, the Bureau of Prisons, the Drug Enforcement Administration and the Office of Justice programs, have been deployed to investigate these crimes and to assist victim survivors and victim families.

Thousands of FBI agents in all of the field offices across the country and in the international legats assisted by personnel from the other Department of Justice agencies are cooperating in this investigation.

The FBI has established a website where people can report any information about these crimes. That address is www.ifccfbi.gov.

The FBI is also in the process of establishing a toll free 800 number for the same purpose.

It takes courage to come forward in situations like this and I urge anyone with information that may be helpful to the authorities to use these resources.

The Office of Victims of Crime has established a toll free 800 for family and friends of victims. They can call 800-331-0075 to leave contact information for a future time when more information is available, to find out information about a victim or to find out information about the rights of victims and the services available to victim survivors and victim families.

The determination of these terrorists will not deter the determination of the American people. We are survivors and freedom is a survivor.

A free American people will not be intimidated or defeated. We will find the people responsible for these cowardly acts and justice will be done.

Local, regional, state, and federal agencies immediately responded to the Pentagon attack. In addition to county fire, police, and sheriff's departments, the response was assisted by the Metropolitan Washington Airports Authority, Ronald Reagan Washington National Airport Fire Department, Fort Myer Fire Department, the Virginia State Police, the Virginia Department of Emergency Management, the FBI, FEMA, a National Medical Response Team, the Bureau of Alcohol, Tobacco, and Firearms, and numerous military personnel within the Military District of Washington.[17]

The ACPD response to the incident was also immediate, with the on-duty shift engaged in minutes and most ACPD officers arriving on the scene within the first three hours.[18] Several ACPD senior officers were out of the county when the incident occurred. Chief Flynn was attending a conference in Atlantic City, New Jersey, where he was the featured speaker on the subject of racial profiling. Deputy Chief Holl was at a Virginia Police Corps meeting in Richmond, Virginia. Both Chief Flynn and Deputy Chief Holl immediately began driving back to Arlington. Deputy Chief John Haas was in Miami, Florida, participating in a police chief's assessment program and was unable to arrange immediate transportation back to Arlington. This delay turned out to be fortuitous. When Deputy Chief Haas reported for duty on Monday, September 17, he brought fresh leadership to a command section that had been continuously engaged for nearly a week.

Lieutenant Robert Medarios was the first ACPD command-level official to arrive on the scene; he assumed command of the ACPD response. Lieutenant Medarios quickly reached an agreement with a Defense Protective Service (DPS) official that the ACPD would assume responsibility for the outer perimeter. This was an important decision because the DPS exercises exclusive federal legislative jurisdiction at the Pentagon and its surrounding grounds. In these instances, the federal government acquires all the authority usually reserved by the state.

Lieutenant Medarios, Lieutenant Brian Berke, and Sergeant Jim Daly quickly assessed the road network conditions and identified 27 intersections that required immediate police posting. Sergeant Daly began organizing the staging area at Fire Station 5 and the adjacent park. The parking lot and adjacent field were cordoned off and guards posted around the perimeter. By 11:00 a.m., more than 100 law enforcement personnel had reported to the staging area representing the ACPD, Arlington County Sheriff's Office, Fairfax County Police Department, Alexandria Police Department, Arlington County Park Rangers, and the Immigration and Naturalization Service (INS). Officers were assigned to a particular post for 2 or 3 hours, given an hour of relief, then assigned to a different post to minimize boredom.

Many ACPD officers attempting to reach the Pentagon, including detectives who were responding from headquarters, found themselves fully engaged in rerouting traffic and clearing a path for fire, rescue, and medical units. Although they had difficulty reaching their intended destination, these officers knew precisely what needed to be done and acted on their own initiative, radioing to ACPD Headquarters their respective locations and activities. Detectives from the ACPD Vice Control Section assumed general patrol of the county away from the incident site to augment remaining officers in the event of a major criminal incident.

At 9:55, the incident commander ordered an evacuation of the Pentagon impact area because a partial collapse was imminent; it occurred at 9:57, and no first responders were injured.[19]

At about 10:15 a.m., Arlington County Fire Department Chief James Schwarz ordered a site-clearing evacuation because of the report of a second hijacked aircraft heading toward the Washington Metropolitan Area.[20] This was the first of three evacuations caused by reports of incoming aircraft, and the evacuation order was well communicated and well coordinated.[21] After this first evacuation, the ACPD incident command post (ICP) moved to an area beneath the I-395 overpass at Hayes Street and set up near the Arlington County Fire Department (ACFD) ICP to facilitate communications and coordination.[22]

At ACPD Headquarters, Captain Rich Alt, Captain Mary Gavin, Lieutenant Karen Hechenroder, and Administrative Assistant Barbara Scott began organizing the departmentwide response. Officers were being deployed throughout the county, and information had to be gathered regarding their locations and times of arrival so replacements could be scheduled and relief coordinated. The roll call room is a natural meeting place in the police department for gathering and distributing information. It became the home of the ACPD Incident Command System (ICS) staffing command for the duration of operations. The ACPD previously adopted the ICS as the appropriate response structure for large-scale incidents. Moreover, less than two weeks prior to the terrorist attack on the Pentagon, all ACPD command officers participated in routine recurring ICS training.

Shortly after Lieutenant Medarios assumed initial command at the incident site on September 11, Captain Rebecca Hackney arrived and took over as Incident Commander. Captain Hackney sketched the initial ACPD ICS assignments on a notepad. Acting Chief James Younger arrived, reviewed Captain Hackney's ICS assignments, then directed Captain Daniel Murray to be ACPD liaison to the ACFD ICP and Captain David Herbstreit to liaison with the FBI. By telephone, he spoke with Deputy Chief Holl, who was returning from Richmond, and requested that he respond directly to the incident site. Deputy Chief Holl arrived at about noon and took over as the ACPD incident commander. Deputy Chief Younger reported to the Arlington County Emergency Operation Center, as requested by the County Manager.

The ACPD loaned its mobile command post to the ACFD to serve as the initial ICP. The ACFD did not have a similar capability. Deputy Chief Holl worked out of the Watch Commander's Ford Expedition. The ACPD formulated a plan to screen pedestrian and vehicular traffic and assign ACPD representatives to the ACPD ICP, the FBI Command Post, Emergency Medical Services Control, the Arlington County EOC, and the Emergency Communication Center. Captain Murray reported to the ACFD ICP and told Chief Edward Plaugher he would remain with the ACFD throughout the fire and rescue operations.

Recognizing that minute-to-minute activities would be all consuming, early in the afternoon of September 11, Deputy Chief Holl assigned Lieutenant Steve Broadhurst to forecast the issues that would confront the department during the next 6 to 12 hours. Captain Roy Austin was assigned responsibility for department routine operations away from the incident site.

The Arlington County Sheriff's Office (ACSO) also immediately responded to the attack. Sheriff Beth Arthur and Chief Deputy Sheriff Mike Raffo were watching the World Trade Center attacks on television when they were notified that an airliner crashed into the Pentagon. They immediately headed to the Arlington County Emergency Operations Center (EOC). ACSO recall procedures were implemented, and an ICP was set up on the first floor of the courthouse building. The ICP was subsequently relocated to a large conference room in the Arlington County Detention Facility.

Some deputies not already on assignment rushed to the Pentagon, arriving in time to help rescue a few of the victims. Other deputies began directing traffic, as roadways became jammed.

One of the first actions taken by the ACSO was closing the courts and evacuating the judges and staff. This action was in consultation with the Arlington County judges, who approved the closure. This decision freed up approximately 20 deputies who were then able to assist with the response to the attack on the Pentagon.

Several factors facilitated the response to this incident and distinguished it from the far more difficult task in New York. There was a single incident, and it was not 1,000 feet above ground. The incident site was relatively easy to secure and contain, and there were no other buildings in the immediate area. There was no collateral damage beyond the Pentagon.[23] In the end, the emergency response at the Pentagon represented a mix of local, state, and federal jurisdictions and was generally effective.[24] It overcame the inherent complications of a response across jurisdictions because the ICS, a formalized management structure for emergency response, was in place in the National Capital Region on 9/11.

BOX 1-6

STATEMENT BY THE PRESIDENT IN HIS ADDRESS TO THE NATION SEPTEMBER 11, 2001, 8:30 P.M.

THE PRESIDENT: Good evening. Today, our fellow citizens, our way of life, our very freedom came under attack in a series of deliberate and deadly terrorist acts. The victims were in airplanes, or in their offices; secretaries, businessmen and women, military and federal workers; moms and dads, friends and neighbors. Thousands of lives were suddenly ended by evil, despicable acts of terror.

The pictures of airplanes flying into buildings, fires burning, huge structures collapsing, have filled us with disbelief, terrible sadness, and a quiet, unyielding anger. These acts of mass murder were intended to frighten our nation into chaos and retreat. But they have failed; our country is strong.

A great people has been moved to defend a great nation. Terrorist attacks can shake the foundations of our biggest buildings, but they cannot touch the foundation of America. These acts shattered steel, but they cannot dent the steel of American resolve.

America was targeted for attack because we're the brightest beacon for freedom and opportunity in the world. And no one will keep that light from shining.

(continued)

Today, our nation saw evil, the very worst of human nature. And we responded with the best of America—with the daring of our rescue workers, with the caring for strangers and neighbors who came to give blood and help in any way they could.

Immediately following the first attack, I implemented our government's emergency response plans. Our military is powerful, and it's prepared. Our emergency teams are working in New York City and Washington, D.C. to help with local rescue efforts.

Our first priority is to get help to those who have been injured, and to take every precaution to protect our citizens at home and around the world from further attacks.

The functions of our government continue without interruption. Federal agencies in Washington which had to be evacuated today are reopening for essential personnel tonight, and will be open for business tomorrow. Our financial institutions remain strong, and the American economy will be open for business, as well.

The search is underway for those who are behind these evil acts. I've directed the full resources of our intelligence and law enforcement communities to find those responsible and to bring them to justice. We will make no distinction between the terrorists who committed these acts and those who harbor them.

I appreciate so very much the members of Congress who have joined me in strongly condemning these attacks. And on behalf of the American people, I thank the many world leaders who have called to offer their condolences and assistance.

America and our friends and allies join with all those who want peace and security in the world, and we stand together to win the war against terrorism. Tonight, I ask for your prayers for all those who grieve, for the children whose worlds have been shattered, for all whose sense of safety and security has been threatened. And I pray they will be comforted by a power greater than any of us, spoken through the ages in Psalm 23: "Even though I walk through the valley of the shadow of death, I fear no evil, for You are with me."

This is a day when all Americans from every walk of life unite in our resolve for justice and peace. America has stood down enemies before, and we will do so this time. None of us will ever forget this day. Yet, we go forward to defend freedom and all that is good and just in our world.

Thank you. Good night, and God bless America.

UNDERSTANDING THE THREAT

To understand the implications that the September 11th attacks had on policing, one must understand the threat behind the attack as well as the threat in a post–9-11 world. The threat that led to the September 11th attack, as previously detailed, came from Osama bin Laden and his terrorist network, Al Qaeda. This terrorist group was unique for the fact it was not a state-sponsored terrorist group, nor did it have a state to call its own. Although bin Laden had established his operations first in Sudan and later Afghanistan, political pressure removed him from the former, and military pressure removed him from the latter. Although it is believed that bin Laden has moved his operations into the mountains of Pakistan, Al Qaeda has continued to operate, increasing the number of its attacks by hitting "soft targets," such as nightclubs, synagogues, and train/subway stations.[25] In addition, most of the attacks since 9-11 have been on a much smaller scale. These attacks have included the Jemaah Islamiya (Indonesian affiliate) attack on a Bali nightclub, killing 180 (October 2002); the bombing of an Israeli-owned hotel and the related firing (and near miss) of shoulder-fired missiles at an Israeli passenger aircraft, both in Mombasa, Kenya (November 2002); suicide car bomb attacks against three housing compounds in Riyadh, Saudi Arabia, killing 20 people, including eight Americans (May 2003); a suicide bomb attack against five sites in Casablanca killing about 40 people (May 2003); and the bombing of a commuter train in Madrid, Spain, killing about 300 (March 2004).[26] Numerous smaller attacks have also been conducted against U.S. interests and personnel in Saudi Arabia, Turkey, East Asia, and other areas where Al Qaeda affiliates operate.

It has, however, been noted that no attacks have occurred on American soil since September 11th, which the Bush administration, as well as Thomas Friedman of the *New York Times*, have attributed to the work of the F.B.I., the C.I.A., and the Department of Homeland Security and for the fact that the fight has been brought to the Middle East in terms of both wars in Afghanistan and Iraq.[27] This, however, should not negate the emphasis of state and local police on homeland security, for Al Qaeda's history of attacks against U.S. interests has consistently retained a time lag between attacks. Al Qaeda has also been quite adept at adapting to the changing environment in which it finds itself, thus although our attention may be on airport security, this focus may very well leave other sectors vulnerable to attack. Therefore, it should be stated that although Al Qaeda has not carried out a direct attack on the United States since September 11th, it is true that their ability to survive and adapt continues to leave future attacks a reality.

Although Al Qaeda is assuredly the terrorist group of concern, it is important that police come to understand that they are not the only threat to homeland security. Other international terrorist organizations and extremist groups exist that perceive the United States as a target of interest.[28] In addition, other international crime problems cross countries, and thus transnational crimes such as drug trafficking, human trafficking, and the black market sales of both conventional weapons and weapons of mass destruction have become a threat to homeland security. Taken further, the United States also has its own domestic terrorism threats that are of concern, and past threats, such as organized crime and gangs, continue to pose a threat to homeland security. Just like these latter threats, good information and intelligence are the primary means by which police can make arrests; therefore, the key to dealing effectively with the threat of terrorism, both international and domestic, is having good information and intelligence and the ability to act on it. This is why understanding the threat America faces, not only from Al Qaeda, but other terrorist organizations, is critical to today's modern police.

Police, however, are better able to comprehend the threat of crime, rather than the threat of terrorism. Police operate in an environment of law-based violations and the enforcement of these laws. The fact that there are conceptual similarities between crime and terrorism provides for a better understanding of terrorism from a police perspective. First and foremost, it should be noted that terrorism is criminal in nature. According to McVey, "virtually all terrorist acts violate some criminal statutes of the host jurisdiction," making it "the easiest element for local law enforcement to appreciate."[29] In addition, it has been noted that both crime and terrorism are almost always the work of young males, similar to the majority of crimes, especially violent crimes.[30] And, at a more conceptual level, it has also been noted that both the terms *crime* and *terrorism* are often hard to define, are social constructs, and when committed, serve to undermine social trust.[31] From these viewpoints, terrorism is an issue with which police can play a role.

Crime and terrorism are different, however, in that the targets of terrorism are often symbolic, the terrorist's actions are almost always violent, terrorists are primarily seeking publicity, and their goals are largely political.[32] Unlike crime, there are few laws regulating terrorism, and the response to terrorism is not limited to the local level, but almost always rises to the highest levels of government.[33] In addition, unlike criminals who tend to commit crimes in a very similar manner (modus operandi), terrorists tend to adapt and innovate, thus making it more difficult to utilize traditional investigatory methods. Finally, although only some crime tends to operate within an organizational structure, terrorist groups almost always operate by some operational structure, even if the structural organization is not fully clear.

BOX 1-7

REMARKS BY THE PRESIDENT TO POLICE, FIREMEN AND RESCUE WORKERS MURRAY AND WEST STREETS, NEW YORK, NEW YORK SEPTEMBER 14, 2001

CROWD: U.S.A.! U.S.A.!

THE PRESIDENT: Thank you all. I want you all to know—

Q: Can't hear you.

THE PRESIDENT: I can't talk any louder. (Laughter.)

I want you all to know that America today—that America today is on bended knee in prayer for the people whose lives were lost here, for the workers who work here, for the families who mourn. This nation stands with the good people of New York City, and New Jersey and Connecticut, as we mourn the loss of thousands of our citizens.

Q: I can't hear you.

THE PRESIDENT: I can hear you. (Applause.) I can hear you. The rest of the world hears you. (Applause.) And the people who knocked these buildings down will hear all of us soon. (Applause.)

CROWD: U.S.A.! U.S.A.!

THE PRESIDENT: The nation sends its love and compassion to everybody who is here. Thank you for your hard work. Thank you for making the nation proud. And may God bless America. (Applause.)

CROWD: U.S.A.! U.S.A.!

Understanding the threat first entails understanding the ideological motivations behind terrorism. It then necessitates an understanding of the various groups and the threat they pose to America. Specifically, it entails not only a generic understanding of terrorism and terrorist groups, but also a continual update of potential threats and the potential targets, especially those in each police department's jurisdiction. But perhaps before any of this can occur, the police must first understand the impact that September 11th has had on policing and that because of that attack, the police now play a crucial role in the era of homeland security.

UNDERSTANDING THE ATTACK[34]

On September 11, 2001, when Al Qaeda terrorists hijacked four planes and attacked the World Trade Center buildings in New York City and the Pentagon in Arlington County, Virginia, little did anyone know that they would set in motion a new era of policing, namely the era of homeland security.[35] In the wake of 9-11 it has become evident that many state and local police agencies across the country have found themselves adapting to this new role in policing. Whether they have adopted the concepts of Homeland Security by force (e.g., New York City, Arlington County (VA), Washington, D.C.), by local circumstances (e.g., San Francisco, Chicago, Houston), by lure of grant dollars (e.g., City of Pine Bluff Police Department, Arkansas; Town of Kittery Police Department, Maine; Casper Police Department, WY), by state directive, or simply by local government and citizen demand, police agencies are beginning to wrestle with what homeland security means to their particular agencies. As one author has stated, the overriding question today for police management is, "What is the role of state and local law enforcement in a post–September 11 environment?"[36]

The new role in American policing in the post–September 11 environment is not only a response to the specific events on that fateful day, but they are also an amalgam of change brought about by various political, economic, and social factors in the United States. The political implications have been derived by the president winning a second term and his agenda focus on the "war on terrorism" and Homeland Security. In addition, Congress has played a major role in the passage of legislation that created the Department of Homeland Security and enacted the myriad laws encapsulated in the USA PATRIOT Act.

The economic factors that followed in kind are found in the spending by the national government, and to some degree by state governments, in the area of homeland security. Many government agencies have seen their budgets slashed while budgets for homeland security have risen. In fact, even police-related grant programs such as the Edward Bryne and COPS grants have seen their budgets drastically cut by the Bush administration, while funding for homeland security has continued to rise substantially.

No less important than the political and economic factors shaping the concepts of homeland security are the social factors. The social implications for the movement toward homeland security are derived from public concern regarding terrorism, which has moved from little to no concern in the pre–9-11 years to ranking as one of the three most important problems facing our country ever since.[37] Americans now agree that government should address the problems of terrorism and homeland/domestic security. This may be from a high level of concern that there will be another terrorist attack in the United States and that they or someone in their family could become a victim of terrorism. According to a recent Pew Research poll, since 9-11, 23 percent of respondents stated they were very worried, whereas an additional 44 percent have stated they are somewhat worried about another terrorist attack.[38] And, in a Gallup poll during the same time period, 9 percent of respondents have stated they were very worried, and an additional 29 percent have stated they are somewhat worried that they or a member of their family would fall victim to a terrorist act.[39] In fact, concern among Americans has risen so high that approximately half of Americans surveyed by the Pew Research Center stated that to "curb terrorism" they believe it will be necessary to "give up some of their civil liberties," and they favor the requirement that all citizens carry a national identification card.[40] It is perhaps not all too surprising, then, to find that over 81 percent of citizens favor government expanding under-cover activities to penetrate groups under suspicion, over 67 percent of citizens favor closer monitoring of banking and credit card transactions to trace funding sources, and over 54 percent favor law enforcement monitoring Internet discussions in chat rooms and other forums.[41] The movement toward the era of homeland security by police is not emerging in some police management vacuum, but rather it is coming about as part of a larger environmental change.

The movement to an era of homeland security in policing should also not be all too surprising. The previous paradigm[42] or epicycle[43] in policing that has lasted for well over 25 years has been the philosophy of community policing. It will later be noted that community policing moved through three generations of policy development, namely innovation (early 1980s), diffusion (late 1980s and early 1990s), and institutionalization, achieving this by the mid to late 1990s.[44] What typically follows the institutionalization of a policy is the process of disappearance, which generally takes the form of new innovations being integrated into the institutionalized model as a means of dealing with change. This eventually gives way to the new innovations and ideas beginning to stand more firmly on their own, thus giving rise to the new policy and diminishing the old.[45] We witnessed the adoption of "Homeland Security through Community Policing" in the wake of 9-11, but as the idea of a policing role in homeland security took shape, homeland security has been more recently thought of as its own distinct policy. As a result, Pelfrey's assertion in 1998 that "the current paradigm, community policing, will be refined . . . and may eventually be replaced by a different paradigm"[46] is possibly coming to fruition.

To understand the implications of the September 11th attack for state and local policing, it is necessary to explore this new era of policing by drawing on past conceptual frameworks of policing. To do so, we must look to the organizational strategies of policing used by Kelling and Moore to explain the three previous eras of policing, specifically the political, reform, and community eras.[47] As they once stated, "This concept can be used not only to describe the different styles of policing in the past and the present, but also to sharpen the understanding of police policy makers of the future."[48] Still further, we must draw on the previous work of Greene[49] and his comparison of various models of policing to compare and contrast the various social interactions and social components of American policing, by highlighting these same concepts under the homeland security form of policing.

BOX 1-8

THE FOUR ERAS OF POLICING BASED ON ORGANIZATIONAL STRATEGY

Elements	Political Era	Reform Era	Community Era	Homeland Security Era
Authorization	Politics and law	Law and professionalism	Community support (political), law, professionalism	National/international threats (politics), law (intergovernmental), professionalism
Function	Broad social services	Crime control	Broad, provision of service	Crime control, antiterrorism/counterterrorism, intelligence gathering
Organizational design	Decentralized	Centralized, classical	Decentralized, task forces, matrices	Centralized decision making, decentralized execution
Relationship to environment	Intimate	Professionally remote	Intimate	Professional
Demand	Decentralized, to patrol and politicians	Centralized	Decentralized	Centralized
Tactics and technology	Foot patrol	Preventive patrol and rapid response to calls for service	Foot patrol, problem solving, etc.	Risk assessment, police operations centers, information systems
Outcome	Citizen political satisfaction	Crime control	Quality of life and citizen satisfaction	Citizen safety, crime control, antiterrorism

Adapted by author from Kelling, G. L. & Moore, M. H. (1988). "The Evolving Strategy of Policing." *Perspectives on Policing, No. 4.* Washington, D.C.: National Institute of Justice.

The Four Eras of Policing

According to researchers Kelling and Moore, American policing has moved through three distinct eras: the political, the reform, and the community eras.[50] In explaining these three distinct eras, the authors used the conceptual framework of "corporate strategy," which was defined as "the pattern of major objectives, purposes, or goals and essential policies and plans for achieving these goals."[51] Based on this framework, Kelling and Moore looked at police organizational strategies in seven topical areas: authorization, function, organization, demand, environment, tactics, and outcomes to distinguish how policing has evolved throughout American history. Authorization, the first of these seven dimensions, referred to the underlying source of authority given to the police. This was essentially the mandate for police operations. Function detailed the values, mission, and goals of the organization, which focused on the police role in society. Organization consisted of the structure, human resources, and management processes of an agency. Demand entailed the source of the demand for police services, whereas environment dealt with the varied relationship of the organization with those elements external to the agency. Tactics described the methods and technologies the organization used to obtain their goals, and outcomes are the results of these activities. By detailing the changes in policing across these seven dimensions throughout the history of American policing, Kelling and Moore were able to describe these three distinct eras in policing (see Box 1-8).

The first era of policing, the political era, began around the 1840s with the creation of the first bona fide police agencies in America. Although people recognized the need for a police force at the time, they were not sure of its role in society. As the political machines of the day had full control over the machinations of government, policing became part and parcel to the politics of the day. The authorization for the police during the political era was largely derived from these same political machines. Because no one was certain as to their specific function and for the fact few social agencies existed at the time, police delivered a broad array of services from dealing with criminals, to keeping immigrant workers in line and running soup kitchens. Although the organization of these early police had military overtones, they were largely decentralized in their deployment with poor supervision and little in the way of management. As a result of this and the strong political ties, the police were very intimate and close to the people they policed. The demands on these early police came first and foremost from the ward politicians, who made their demands for political gain, while the local citizens made their demands directly to the local beat cop. There was little in the way of tactics or technology at the time, although call boxes would later be a factor, so local beat officers and foot patrol was the overriding method of police delivery. The outcome of policing during the political era was largely aimed at implementing the political machine's will and keeping the citizens satisfied by officers maintaining some semblance of order. The political era, however, was not successful in any right as it was ill-suited for controlling crime, delivering social services, or maintaining control, for it was largely corrupt and often very brutal.

The time period of the 1920s through the 1970s is marked as the "reform era" by Kelling and Moore.[52] The political corruption and rampant brutality among the police, exacerbated by their ties to the local political machines, reached a zenith at the turn of the century, as citizens began calling for the reform of the police. Progressive police chiefs such as August Vollmer and professional-minded leaders like J. Edgar Hoover helped create a model of policing that would take decades to implement, but the changes would help reign in control of the police. The authorization of the police became more entrenched in the law, especially the criminal law, and rooted in the concept of police professionalism. Its function, stripped of all the social services, became centered on crime control. In addition, to rein in corruption it adopted a very paramilitary template formed around the classical hierarchical organizational method. The demand for police services was more centralized by directing calls toward the police station itself, and police became more professionally detached from the citizens they policed. The overriding methods of police deployment came about as a result of technology, police vehicles, and radios and emphasized preventive patrol and rapid response to the centralized calls for service. The outcome of policing was solely focused on crime control. The reform era was somewhat successful in removing corruption and brutality from policing through its centralized control and its move toward professionalism. However, the distancing of the police from the citizens generated new problems and conflicts, especially during the array of social changes that occurred during the 1960s.

This realization, that for police to effectively perform their job they need the assistance of the citizenry, led to the third era of policing, the "community era."[53] The authorization for the police, although still rooted in the law and professionalism, focused more heavily on local community support. To deal more effectively with crime, fear of crime, and disorder, police began focusing on those factors that contribute to crime by providing a broad array of services beyond the crime control methods of the previous era. The police organized themselves through a more decentralized geographical neighborhood identity method of policing and responded to the demands of these citizens by working more closely with them on a routine basis. The tactics employed included a return to foot patrols (and bicycle, horse, etc.) to enhance contact with citizens, and it used various problem-solving and geographical information systems to identify trends and solve underlying problems rather than symptoms. As a result, the focus of the community era was on the outcome of citizen satisfaction with the police and the quality of life of the local communities and neighborhoods. Although the community era has been marginally successful in reducing the fear of crime and increasing the quality of life, there is little evidence that its ability to control crime has had equal success, if any at all.

In terms of the era of homeland security, by applying the framework used by Kelling and Moore to describe the political, reform, and community eras, it helps clarify the direction of this new era in policing. The authorization for this era has largely come from the national and international threat that is terrorism, driven by the events of September 11, 2001. In addition, citizen awareness of the issue of terrorism reached a critical juncture on that day, and as a result, citizens have given authorization to the government to target terrorism and protect the home front.[54] Thus the authorization for policing is derived from the national and international threats, but it has played out through government and citizens giving this new role in policing legitimacy. In addition, the era is still marked by an adherence to the law, but more so in that intergovernmental law (and relations) are becoming an overriding concern. Professionalism of the police also continues to play a role in authorizing the police to take on this role in that police were and, in the event of future attacks, will continue to be the first responders and an integral part of the recovery process.

The function of police under homeland security is marked by a more focused concentration of its resources into crime control, for it is through crime control, enforcement of the criminal law, and traffic law that many potential threats can be exposed and intelligence gathered. In addition, police have begun to take on the role of antiterrorism by focusing on various passive measures that can reduce the vulnerabilities of their communities to future terrorist attacks. Much of this is being done through local threat assessments, intelligence gathering, and intergovernmental information sharing. Another added function of the police is counterterrorism, which are those offensive measures taken to respond to terrorist acts through the process of preparedness training, creation of emergency (and routine) operations centers, large-scale crisis intervention, and special reaction team training. Moreover, the collection, processing, and analysis of intelligence are also becoming a necessary and crucial function of the police in this current era.

The organizational design of the police agency would seem to entail another pendulum swing bringing it back to the centralized design. This is only partially the case. Although the era of homeland security would entail a more centralized organizational control, especially in dealing with information coming from the enhanced intergovernmental relations and information sharing, it primarily entails a centralized decision-making process. The actual execution of the organization will, like the community era, entail a decentralized and flexible approach. It is internal information sharing that will feed the centralized decision making, but it is the officer on the street that will execute these decisions with the flexibility of street-level decision making.

Because the demand on the organization will be somewhat more centralized, the demand for the agency's services will be more centralized as well. Hence, under the role of the police in homeland security the relationship to their environment will be professional. Unlike the professionally remote relationship that marked the reform era, policing under homeland security will not isolate themselves from the community, which is a crucial source of information and intelligence, but will by the nature of demand, function, and organizational design be professionally oriented.

Tactics and technology are perhaps one of the most critical areas due to the nature of homeland security concepts and one in which police are most deficient and for which they will remain on a learning curve for some time to come. The concepts of conducting risk assessments, intelligence gathering and processing, and developing large-scale crisis response, although not completely foreign to policing, will necessitate more training and education. The employment of tactics related to antiterrorism and counterterrorism is partially a continuation of past police practices, but with a wider array of information to process. It is the adoption of new technologies that police will need and the protection of these technologies that police will be engaged in for some time to come.

The outcome of homeland security continues to bear elements of previous eras—crime control, citizen satisfaction, and quality of life. However, the primary emphasis of this new era will be citizen safety and antiterrorism methods aimed at the mitigation of future attacks. Although crime prevention will also still be a desired outcome, preventing future terrorist acts is the new challenge to law enforcement in America.

The Five Models of Policing

A more recent analysis of policing styles comes from a leading researcher in the policing field, Jack R. Greene.[55] Greene articulated that there were currently (at the time of his writing) four models of policing in America. These four models included traditional policing, community policing, problem-oriented policing, and zero-tolerance policing. To clarify the differences among these four models, Greene compared them across 12 dimensions related to the "police role and function, interaction with the community, formal and social organization, and service delivery."[56] These dimensions consisted of the following: (1) focus of policing, (2) forms of intervention, (3) range of police activity, (4) level of discretion at line level, (5) focus of police culture, (6) locus of decision making, (7) communication flow, (8) range of community involvement, (9) linkage with other agencies, (10) types of organization and command focus, (11) implications for organizational change and development, and (12) measurement of success (see Box 1-9).[57] Although Greene acknowledges this typology was largely a heuristic device it does provide "a useful way to contrast and compare potentially differing paradigms of policing."[58]

BOX 1-9

COMPARISONS OF SOCIAL INTERACTIONS AND STRUCTURAL COMPONENTS OF VARIOUS FORMS OF POLICING INCLUDING HOMELAND SECURITY

Social Interaction or Structural Dimension	Traditional Policing	Community Policing	Problem-Oriented Policing	Zero-Tolerance Policing	Homeland Security Policing
Focus of policing	Law enforcement	Community building through crime prevention	Law, order, and fear problems	Order problems	Security, antiterrorism, counter terrorism, law and order
Forms of intervention	Reactive, based on criminal law	Proactive, on criminal, and administrative law	Mixed, on criminal, and administra-tive law	Proactive, uses criminal, civil, and administra-tive law	Proactive, on criminal law and for mitigation and preparedness
Range of police activity	Narrow, crime focused	Broad crime, order, fear, and quality-of-life focused	Narrow to broad— problem focused	Narrow, location and behavior focused	Broad, security, terrorism, crime, fear
Levels of discretion at line level	High and unaccountable	High and accountable to the community and local commanders	High and primarily accountable to the police administra-tion	Low, but primarily accountable to the police administra-tion	High and primarily accountable to the police administration
Focus of police culture	Inward, rejecting community	Outward, building partnerships	Mixed depending on problem, but analysis focused	Inward focused on attacking the target problem	Mixed depending on threat, threat-analysis focused
Locus of decision making	Police directed, minimizes the involvement of others	Community– police coproduction —joint responsibility and assessment	Varied, police identify problems, but with community involvement and interaction	Police directed, some linkage to other agencies where necessary	Police directed with linkage to other agencies

(continued)

BOX 1-9 (continued)

Social Interaction or Structural Dimension	Traditional Policing	Community Policing	Problem-Oriented Policing	Zero-Tolerance Policing	Homeland Security Policing
Communication flow	Downward from police to community	Horizontal between police and community	Horizontal between police and community	Downward from police to community	Downward from police to community
Range of community involvement	Low and passive	High and active	Mixed depending on problem set	Low and passive	Mixed depending on threat
Linkage with other agencies	Poor and intermittent	Participative and integrative in the overarching process	Participative and integrative depending on the problem set	Moderate and intermittent	Participative and integrative in the overarching process
Type of organization and command focus	Centralized command and control	Decentralized with community linkage	Decentralized with local command accountability to central administration	Centralized or decentralized but internal focus	Centralized decision making, decentralized exectuion
Implications for organizational change/ development	Few, static organization fending off the environment	Many, dynamic organization focused on the environmental interactions	Varied, focused on problem resolution but with import for organization intelligence and structure	Few, limited interventions focused on target problems, using many traditional methods	Varied, focused on security and threat, but with import for intelligence and stucture

BOX 1-9

Social interaction or Structural Dimension	Traditional Policing	Community Policing	Problem-Oriented Policing	Zero-Tolerance Policing	Homeland Security Policing
Measurement of success	Arrest and crime rates, particularly serious Part I crimes	Varied, crime, calls for service, fear reduction, use of public places, community linkages and contacts, safer neighborhoods	Varied, problems solved, minimized, displaced	Arrests, field stops, activity, location-specific reductions in targeted activity	Arrests, field stops, intelligence gathering, mitigation, and preparedness

Adapted by author from Greene, J. R. (2000). "Community Policing in America: Changing the Nature, Structure, and Function of the Police." In *Criminal Justice 2000: Policies, Processes, and Decisions of the Criminal Justice System.* Vol. 3. Washington, D.C.: U.S. Department of Justice, Office of Justice Programs.

The traditional policing model is largely an early twentieth-century development, and like Kelling and Moore explained, it was primarily focused on crime control through law enforcement. By enforcing the criminal law after crimes occurred, it made the police largely a reactive organization with a very narrow focus. Gone were the social services provided in the nineteenth century, as other social service agencies came into creation and took over those various tasks. In addition, to overcome the past corruption and brutality, police were organized more along military lines with a strict chain of command, which did make them more accountable for their behaviors, but also distanced them from the citizens they policed. Police officers became a responsive agent of the police centralized bureaucracy, and they began taking their orders solely from the police hierarchy, thus making their interaction with community members and other social agencies extremely limited. Ultimately the measurement of success under traditional policing became focused on the number of arrests made and the ability to control the crime rate as exemplified by the Federal Bureau of Investigation's Uniform Crime Reports. The traditional policing model still exists today and for many agencies remains the primary model of policing.

The community policing model, largely derived from innovations in the 1980s, is primarily focused on building community partnerships and crime prevention. Although community policing still uses criminal law, it encompasses a wider scope of alternatives, including administrative and civil law, mediation and arbitration, as well as redirecting problems by working with other social service agencies. Police officers under community policing are more proactive, and they address not only problems of crime, but also of disorder, quality of life, and fear of crime. As police officers build these partnerships, they become coproducers of the solutions to various problems that plague specific neighborhoods and thus are more accountable to the citizens they serve. As a result, police are actively involved with the community, they communicate on a routine basis, and they work with other agencies in addressing crime and disorder. Organizationally, to achieve these ends, the police must be more decentralized. Finally, the outcomes of community policing are based on the needs of the specific neighborhoods policed.

Problem-oriented policing also became a key model of policing in the 1980s through the work of Herman Goldstein. Problem-oriented policing is also focused on crime, disorder, and fear of crime and utilizes a variety of means to address these problems. What sets problem-oriented policing apart is that police may engage in problem solving without the support or assistance of the community. Police identify specific problems in the neighborhoods they police, they research these problems, then develop solutions. After a period of implementation they assess the solution's effectiveness on the problem. Therefore, problem-oriented policing is problem centered, thus depending on the type of problem and the possible solutions selected, police may or may not have much discretion, contact with citizens, or engagement with other social agencies. The organization implementing problem-oriented policing in many ways has to allow decentralized local commands, but demands accountability to the central administration. The measurement of success under problem-oriented policing, then, is really based on the police officer's ability to solve problems, reduce the impact of the problem, or potentially to displace and disperse the problem from a concentrated area.

The final model of policing articulated by Greene is zero-tolerance policing. Largely a 1990s derived model of policing, its focus is on both crime and disorder problems through proactive means and calling on criminal, civil, and administrative law. It does this by targeting a specific crime (e.g., prostitution, open-air drug markets) or disorder (e.g., panhandlers, graffiti) that occurs in a specific time and place and then concentrating police resources on this specific problem. Police engaging in zero-tolerance policing tend to have a narrow range of focus, based on the behavior(s) they are trying to address. There tends to be a highly centralized control over this type of policing, which means communication is driven by the hierarchy with limited community or other social service agency involvement. The measurement of success for zero-tolerance policing, like traditional policing, emphasizes such things as the number of arrests, tickets, or field stops, with the desired outcome being a reduction in the undesirable behavior in a specific location.

Turning to the new model of policing, by applying Greene's 12 dimensions of policing to homeland security assists in clarifying the current and future direction of homeland security. The focus of policing under homeland security has incorporated the concepts of security and both antiterrorism and counterterrorism into its primary focus. Recognizing and assessing the level of threat, incorporating security measures to prevent future terrorist acts, and developing methods of mitigating threats and responding to both threats and actual incidents have become part of policing under homeland security. Despite these additions, more traditional methods of law enforcement and the focus on law and order still remain an important focus of homeland security policing, as this type of activity can serve the function of security through both arrests or simply intelligence gathering. This is why the forms of intervention under this model of policing will remain very proactive and will draw on the criminal law for enforcement. Although new laws oriented toward dealing with the problem of terrorism will be applied, especially in the area of investigations (e.g., USA PATRIOT Act), for the average line officer the basic means of intervention will remain criminal and traffic violations, as well as routine field stops.

Based on the focus and both new and old forms of intervention, the range of police activity is clearly going to be very broad under homeland security. New security measures will include threat assessments and risk analysis, antiterrorism practices for both mitigation and preparedness, as well as counterterrorism and recovery practices in the event of an actual attack. This will be combined with a concentration on crime, disorder, and fear of crime, especially when associated with terrorism. Because of the concentration of many of these activities at the line officer level, discretion for these officers will have to remain high, but due to the nature of intelligence gathering and information dissemination, these officers will be held accountable by the police administration.

The focus of the police culture, due to the nature of the threat, will be mixed. Although certain threats or information dissemination by such agencies as the U.S. Department of Homeland Security, or the state equivalent, may create a "police only" information dissemination, police will have to continue an outward focus in regard to their own low-level intelligence gathering. Police will need to rely on citizen support in providing information either through traditional means or through partnerships previously formed under the community policing model. This also means that the police will have a mixed range of community involvement as some aspects of the threat analysis may preclude citizen involvement, whereas others may rely heavily on their input and expertise.

Police and citizen participation may be mixed based on the threat, but police will have to link with other agencies, both governmental and nongovernmental to implement nearly any type of security measure. This will include other public safety agencies such as fire and code enforcement, it will include those in the medical and mental health community, and it will draw heavily on such agencies as public works, water treatment, and transportation. Police agencies will need to have far greater linkage with these types of agencies than ever before for security reasons, and this type of lateral linkage will be just as important as the vertical linkage with state and federal agencies.

Organizationally, police departments under homeland security will incorporate a strong centralized command structure, but it will need to maintain a largely decentralized method of execution. Because intelligence gathering and information sharing will be critical not only for the processing of information beyond the police agencies themselves, but also for quickly disseminating intelligence down to line officers, centralized control through active command operations centers that can link with these other agencies, both vertically and horizontally, will be critical. Because information has to be processed and disseminated in real time, the centralized operations command center with a decision-making staff element will become the means of organizational control. However, line officers will still need the flexibility of discretion for the implementation of centralized information and orders, as well as for the means of gathering and disseminating information through routine police procedures.

Ultimately, the measurement of success under the Homeland Security model will entail the traditional methods of arrest, field stops, and traffic enforcement, but it will include the ability to gather, process, and disseminate intelligence information. In addition, it will entail the agency's ability to mitigate security threats and be prepared for the possibility of an attack. Simply stated, preventing terrorism, mitigating the impact that a terrorist attack would have, and responding effectively to a terrorist attack are the key outcomes of policing for homeland security.

Recovery effort from the attack on the Pentagon, Arlington County, Virginia. (*Source: Photo Courtesy of the Federal Emergency Management Agency [FEMA].*)

UNDERSTANDING THE RESPONSE

Understanding the threat that America faced prior to September 11, 2001, the attack itself, and the local police response on that day provides us the context in which to understand that policing has moved into a new era, an era of homeland security. Recognizing that the threat from Al Qaeda and other terrorist organizations, as well as from other transnational crimes, remains provides the basis for which homeland security is now important to state and local police agencies. In addition, learning from the police response to the 9-11 attacks gives us some understanding of the issues that police face, not only in preparing to respond to future attacks, but to prevent future attacks as well.

As Melchor Guzman has so succinctly explained,

> The roles and strategies of the police are shaped by the need of the times. In this time of terror, police are required to be more vigilant and perhaps more suspicious. They are required to be more proactive both in detecting and investigating acts of terrorism. The community policing roles that they have embraced for the last decade should be examined in the light of its opposing tenets to the demands of providing police service in a time of terror. The police should lean toward a more legalistic style and begin to apply their innate talent for sensing danger. This is the philosophical shift that circumstances demand. This is probably the role that the American people demand from their law enforcement officers.[59]

BOX 1-10

Train Bombing, Madrid, Spain, March 11, 2004:
> Bombs were exploded simultaneously on commuter trains as they arrived at various train stations in Madrid. The bombings killed at least 192 people and wounded more than 1,400.

Restaurant Bombing in Baghdad, December 31, 2003:
> A car bomb explosion outside Baghdad's Nabil Restaurant killed 8 persons and wounded 35. The wounded included 3 *Los Angeles Times* reporters and 3 local employees.

Grenade Attacks in Bogota, November 15, 2003:
> Grenade attacks on two bars frequented by Americans in Bogota killed one person and wounded 72, including 4 Americans. Colombian authorities suspected FARC (the Revolutionary Armed Forces of Colombia). The U.S. Embassy suspected that the attacks had targeted Americans and warned against visiting commercial centers and places of entertainment.

Rocket Attack on the al-Rashid Hotel in Baghdad, October 26, 2003:
> Iraqis using an improvised rocket launcher bombarded the al-Rashid Hotel in Baghdad, killing one U.S. Army officer and wounding 17 persons. The wounded included 4 U.S. military personnel and 7 American civilians. Deputy Secretary of Defense Paul D. Wolfowitz, who was staying at the hotel, was not injured. After visiting the wounded, he said, "They're not going to scare us away; we're not giving up on this job."

Bomb Attack on U.S. Diplomats in the Gaza Strip, October 15, 2003:
> A remote-controlled bomb exploded under a car in a U.S. diplomatic convoy passing through the northern Gaza Strip. Three security guards, all employees of DynCorp, were killed. A fourth was wounded. The diplomats were on their way to interview Palestinian candidates for Fulbright scholarships to study in the United States. Palestinian President Arafat and Prime Minister Qurei condemned the attack, while the major Palestinian militant groups denied responsibility. The next day, Palestinian security forces arrested several suspects, some of whom belonged to the Popular Resistance Committees.

Car Bombings in Baghdad, October 12, 2003:
> Two suicide car bombs exploded outside the Baghdad Hotel, which housed U.S. officials. Six persons were killed and 32 wounded. Iraqi and U.S. security personnel apparently kept the cars from actually reaching the hotel.

Hotel Bombing in Indonesia, August 5, 2003:
> A car bomb exploded outside the Marriott Hotel in Jakarta, Indonesia, killing 10 persons and wounding 150. One of the dead was a Dutch citizen. The wounded included an American, a Canadian, an Australian, and two Chinese. Indonesian authorities suspected the Jemaah Islamiah, which had carried out the October 12, 2002, bombing in Bali.

Truck Bomb Attacks in Saudi Arabia, May 12, 2003:
> Suicide bombers attacked three residential compounds for foreign workers in Riyadh, Saudi Arabia. The 34 dead included 9 attackers, 7 other Saudis, 9 U.S. citizens, and one

(continued)

citizen each from the United Kingdom, Ireland, and the Philippines. Another American died on June 1. It was the first major attack on U.S. targets in Saudi Arabia since the end of the war in Iraq. Saudi authorities arrested 11 Al-Qaeda suspects on May 28.

Suicide Bombing in Haifa, March 5, 2003:
A suicide bombing aboard a bus in Haifa, Israel, killed 15 persons and wounded at least 40. One of the dead claimed U.S. as well as Israeli citizenship. The bomber's affiliation was not immediately known.

Assassination of an AID Official, October 28, 2002:
Gunmen in Amman assassinated Laurence Foley, Executive Officer of the U.S. Agency for International Development Mission in Jordan. The Honest People of Jordan claimed responsibility.

Ambush on the West Bank, September 18, 2002:
Gunmen ambushed a vehicle on a road near Yahad, killing an Israeli and wounding a Romanian worker. The al-Aqsa Martyrs' Brigades claimed responsibility.

Attack on a School in Pakistan, August 5, 2002:
Gunmen attacked a Christian school attended by children of missionaries from around the world. Six persons (two security guards, a cook, a carpenter, a receptionist, and a private citizen) were killed, and a Philippine citizen was wounded. A group called al-Intigami al-Pakistani claimed responsibility.

Bombing at the Hebrew University, July 31, 2002:
A bomb hidden in a bag in the Frank Sinatra International Student Center of Jerusalem's Hebrew University killed 9 persons and wounded 87. The dead included 5 U.S. citizens and 4 Israelis. The wounded included 4 U.S. citizens, 2 Japanese, and 3 South Koreans. The Islamic Resistance Movement (HAMAS) claimed responsibility.

Suicide Bombing in Jerusalem, June 19, 2002:
A suicide bombing at a bus stop in Jerusalem killed 6 persons and wounded 43, including 2 U.S. citizens. The al-Aqsa Martyrs' Brigades claimed responsibility.

Car Bombing in Pakistan, June 14, 2002:
A car bomb exploded near the U.S. Consulate and the Marriott Hotel in Karachi, Pakistan. Eleven persons were killed and 51 were wounded, including one U.S. and one Japanese citizen. Al Qaeda and al-Qanin were suspected.

Hostage Rescue Attempt in the Philippines, June 7, 2002:
Philippine Army troops attacked Abu Sayyaf terrorists on Mindanao Island in an attempt to rescue U.S. citizen Martin Burnham and his wife Gracia, who had been kidnapped more than a year earlier. Burnham was killed but his wife, though wounded, was freed. A Filipino hostage was killed, as were four of the guerrillas. Seven soldiers were wounded.

Suicide Bombing in the West Bank, March 31, 2002:
A suicide bombing near an ambulance station in Efrat wounded four persons, including a U.S. citizen. The al-Aqsa Martyrs' Brigades claimed responsibility.

Suicide Bombing in Israel, March 27, 2002:
A suicide bombing in a noted restaurant in Netanya, Israel, killed 22 persons and wounded 140. One of the dead was a U.S. citizen. The Islamic Resistance Movement (HAMAS) claimed responsibility.

Suicide Bombing in Jerusalem, March 21, 2002:
> A suicide bombing in Jerusalem killed 3 persons and wounded 86 more, including 2 U.S. citizens. The Palestinian Islamic Jihad claimed responsibility.

Car Bomb Explosion in Peru, March 20, 2002:
> A car bomb exploded at a shopping center near the U.S. Embassy in Lima, Peru. Nine persons were killed and 32 wounded. The dead included two police officers and a teenager. Peruvian authorities suspected either the Shining Path rebels or the Tupac Amaru Revolutionary Movement. The attack occurred 3 days before President George W. Bush visited Peru.

Grenade Attack on a Church in Pakistan, March 17, 2002:
> Militants threw grenades into the Protestant International Church in Islamabad, Pakistan, during a service attended by diplomatic and local personnel. Five persons, two of them U.S. citizens, were killed, and 46 were wounded. The dead Americans were State Department employee Barbara Green and her daughter, Kristen Wormsley. Thirteen U.S. citizens were among the wounded. The Lashkar-e-Tayyiba group was suspected.

Drive-by Shooting in Colombia, March 14, 2002:
> Gunmen on motorcycles shot and killed two U.S. citizens who had come to Cali, Colombia, to negotiate the release of their father, who was a captive of the FARC. No group claimed responsibility.

Suicide Bombing in Jerusalem, March 9, 2002:
> A suicide bombing in a Jerusalem restaurant killed 11 persons and wounded 52, one of whom was a U.S. citizen. The al-Aqsa Martyrs' Brigades claimed responsibility.

Suicide Bombing in the West Bank, March 7, 2002:
> A suicide bombing in a supermarket in the settlement of Ariel wounded 10 persons, 1 of whom was a U.S. citizen.

Suicide Bombing in Jerusalem, January 27, 2002:
> A suicide bomb attack in Jerusalem killed 1 person and wounded 100. The incident was the first suicide bombing made by a Palestinian woman.

Kidnapping of Daniel Pearl, January 23, 2002:
> Armed militants kidnapped *Wall Street Journal* reporter Daniel Pearl in Karachi, Pakistan. Pakistani authorities received a videotape on February 20 depicting Pearl's murder. His grave was found near Karachi on May 16. Pakistani authorities arrested four suspects. Ringleader Ahmad Omar Saeed Sheikh claimed to have organized Pearl's kidnapping to protest Pakistan's subservience to the United States and had belonged to Jaish-e-Muhammad, an Islamic separatist group in Kashmir. All four suspects were convicted on July 15. Saeed Sheikh was sentenced to death, the others to life imprisonment.

Drive-by Shooting at a U.S. Consulate, January 22, 2002:
> Armed militants on motorcycles fired on the U.S. Consulate in Calcutta, India, killing 5 Indian security personnel and wounding 13 others. The Harakat ul-Jihad-I-Islami and the Asif Raza Commandoes claimed responsibility. Indian police later killed two suspects, one of whom confessed to belonging to Lashkar-e-Tayyiba as he died.

(continued)

Ambush on the West Bank, January 15, 2002:

Palestinian militants fired on a vehicle in Beit Sahur, killing one passenger and wounding the other. The dead passenger claimed U.S. and Israeli citizenship. The al-Aqsa Martyrs' Battalion claimed responsibility.

Attack on the Indian Parliament, December 13, 2001:

Five gunmen attacked the Indian Parliament in New Delhi shortly after it had adjourned. Before security forces killed them, the attackers killed 6 security personnel and a gardener. Indian officials blamed Lashkar-e-Tayyiba and demanded that Pakistan crack down on it and on other Muslim separatist groups in Kashmir.

Suicide Bombing in Haifa, December 2, 2001:

A suicide bomb attack aboard a bus in Haifa, Israel, killed 15 persons and wounded 40. HAMAS claimed responsibility for both this attack and those on December 1 to avenge the death of a HAMAS member at the hands of Israeli forces a week earlier.

Anthrax Attacks, October–November 2001:

On October 7 the U.S. Centers for Disease Control and Prevention (CDC) reported that investigators had detected evidence that the deadly anthrax bacterium was present in the building where a Florida man who died of anthrax on October 5 had worked. Discovery of a second anthrax case triggered a major investigation by the Federal Bureau of Investigation (FBI). The two anthrax cases were the first to appear in the United States in 25 years. Anthrax subsequently appeared in mail received by television networks in New York and by the offices in Washington of Senate Majority Leader Tom Daschle and other members of Congress. Attorney General John Ashcroft said in a briefing on October 16, "When people send anthrax through the mail to hurt people and invoke terror, it's a terrorist act."

Source: U.S. Army—Timeline of Terrorism, Available online at http://www.army.mil/terrorism

September 11th spawned a number of changes related to law enforcement as the concepts of homeland security were put into place. These events include everything from the creation of the USA PATRIOT Act, a sweeping piece of legislation that was drafted and signed into law within six weeks, and the creation of the Department of Homeland Security, the largest reorganization of the federal bureaucracy since World War II. Although many of the changes have occurred at the national level, they place the role of state and local police in homeland security in context and is therefore the subject of the next chapter.

ENDNOTES

1. Friedman, T. L. (2003). "The Third Bubble." *New York Times,* Sunday, April 20, Section 4, p. 9; See also Friedman, T. L. (2003). *Longitudes and Attitudes.* New York: Anchor Books, pp. 316–317.
2. *ibid.*
3. *ibid.*
4. *ibid.*

5. This section is based largely on 9/11 Commission. (2004). *Final Report of the National Commission on Terrorist Attacks Upon the United States.* New York: W.W. Norton & Company; and Katzman, K. (2005). "Al Qaeda: Profile and Threat Assessment." *CRS Report for Congress,* February 10, pp. 1–3.

6. The Muslim Brotherhood was founded in 1928 in Egypt, and it has spawned numerous Islamist movements throughout the region since, some as branches of the Brotherhood, others with new names. For example, the Palestinian Islamist group Hamas traces its roots to the Palestinian branch of the Muslim Brotherhood.

7. Gunnaratna, R. (2002). *Inside Al Qaeda.* New York: Columbia University Press.

8. The September 11 Commission report says that U.S. officials obtained information in 2000 indicating that bin Laden received $1 million per year from his family from 1970 (two years after his father's death) until 1994, when his citizenship was revoked by the Saudi government. See 9/11 Commission (2004). *Final Report of the National Commission on Terrorist Attacks Upon the United States.* New York: W.W. Norton & Company, p. 170.

9. Gunnaratna, R. (2002). *Inside Al Qaeda.* New York: Columbia University Press, p. 21.

10. 9/11 Commission. (2004). *Final Report of the National Commission on Terrorist Attacks Upon the United States.* New York, NY: W.W. Norton & Company, p. 67.

11. This section is based largely on 9/11 Commission. (2004). *Final Report of the National Commission on Terrorist Attacks Upon the United States.* New York: W.W. Norton & Company; and Katzman, K. (2005). "Al Qaeda: Profile and Threat Assessment." *CRS Report for Congress,* February 10, pp. 3–4.

12. 9/11 Commission. (2004). *Final Report of the National Commission on Terrorist Attacks Upon the United States.* New York: W.W. Norton & Company, pp. 139, 203–214.

13. This section is derived from the 9/11 Commission Report. To date there has not been a more precise telling of the events of September 11, 2001, therefore, rather than composing yet another version, this section draws directly on the report's version of events. See 9/11 Commission. (2004). *Final Report of the National Commission on Terrorist Attacks Upon the United States.* New York: W.W. Norton & Company, pp. 1–14.

14. This section is derived from the 9/11 Commission Report. See 9/11 Commission. (2004). *Final Report of the National Commission on Terrorist Attacks Upon the United States.* New York: W.W. Norton & Company, chapter 9.

15. 9/11 Commission. (2004). *Final Report of the National Commission on Terrorist Attacks Upon the United States.* New York: W.W. Norton & Company, p. 314.

16. This section is derived largely from Arlington County. (2002). *Arlington County After-Action Report.* Arlington County, VA: Arlington County.

17. *ibid.*

18. Arlington County. (2002). *Arlington County After-Action Report.* Arlington County, VA: Arlington County.

19. 9/11 Commission. (2004). *Final Report of the National Commission on Terrorist Attacks Upon the United States.* New York: W.W. Norton & Company, p. 315.

20. Arlington County. (2002). *Arlington County After-Action Report.* Arlington County, VA: Arlington County.

21. 9/11 Commission. (2004). *Final Report of the National Commission on Terrorist Attacks Upon the United States.* New York: W.W. Norton & Company, p. 315.

22. Arlington County. (2002). *Arlington County After-Action Report.* Arlington County, VA: Arlington County.

23. 9/11 Commission. (2004). *Final Report of the National Commission on Terrorist Attacks Upon the United States.* New York: W.W. Norton & Company, p. 315.

24. 9/11 Commission. (2004). *Final Report of the National Commission on Terrorist Attacks Upon the United States.* New York: W.W. Norton & Company, p. 314.

25. Henry, T. (2005). "Al-Qaeda's Resurgence." *The Atlantic Monthly,* June: 54–55.

26. Katzman, K. (2005). "Al Qaeda: Profile and Threat Assessment." *CRS Report for Congress,* February 10, p. 6.

27. Katzman, K. (2005). "Al Qaeda: Profile and Threat Assessment." *CRS Report for Congress,* February 10; Friedman, T. (2005). "The Calm Before the Storm?" *The New York Times,* April 13, p. 19.

28. Hill, S. and Ward, R. H. (2004). *Extremist Groups: An International Compilation of Terrorist Organizations, Violent Political Groups, and Issue Oriented Militant Movements.* 2nd ed. Huntsville, TX: OICJ Publications.

29. McVey, P. M. (2003). "The Local Role in Fighting Terrorism." In *Homeland Security: Best Practices for Local Government,* edited by Roger L. Kemp, 125–130. Washington, D.C.: International City/County Management Association, p. 126.

30. LaFree, G. (2005). "Developing a Criminological Agenda for the Study of Terrorism and Homeland Security." Beto Lecture Series. Huntsville, TX. February 23, 2005.

31. *ibid.*

32. McVey, P. M. (2003). "The Local Role in Fighting Terrorism." In *Homeland Security: Best Practices for Local Government,* edited by Roger L. Kemp, 125–130. Washington, D.C.: International City/County Management Association.

33. LaFree, G. (2005). "Developing a Criminological Agenda for the Study of Terrorism and Homeland Security." Beto Lecture Series. Huntsville, TX. February 23, 2005.

34. This section is based on an earlier article by the author. Oliver, W. M. (2005). "The Era of Homeland Security: September 11, 2001 to . . ." *Crime & Justice International* 21, no. 85 (March/April): 9–17.

35. Oliver, W. M. (2004). "The Homeland Security Juggernaut: The End of the Community Policing Era?" *Crime & Justice International* 20, no. 79: 4–10.

36. Bodero, D. D. (2002). "Law Enforcement's New Challenge to Investigate, Interdict, and Prevent Terrorism." *The Police Chief* 69, no. 2: 41–48.

37. Maguire, K. and Pastore, A. L. (2005). *Sourcebook of Criminal Justice Statistics.* [Online]. Available at http://www.albany.edu/sourcebook/; downloaded January 17, 2005. Table 2.1.

38. Maguire, K. and Pastore, A. L. (2005). *Sourcebook of Criminal Justice Statistics.* [Online]. Available at http://www.albany.edu/sourcebook/; downloaded January 17, 2005. Table 2.0009.

39. Maguire, K. and Pastore, A. L. (2005). *Sourcebook of Criminal Justice Statistics.* [Online]. Available at http://www.albany.edu/sourcebook/; downloaded January 17, 2005. Table 2.30.

40. Maguire, K. and Pastore, A. L. (2005). *Sourcebook of Criminal Justice Statistics.* [Online]. Available at http://www.albany.edu/sourcebook/; downloaded January 17, 2005. Table 2.0010.

41. Maguire, K. and Pastore, A. L. (2005). *Sourcebook of Criminal Justice Statistics.* [Online]. Available at http://www.albany.edu/sourcebook/; downloaded January 17, 2005. Table 2.0011.

42. Greene, J. R. (2000). "Community Policing in America: Changing the Nature, Structure, and Function of the Police." In *Criminal Justice 2000: Policies, Processes, and Decisions of the Criminal Justice System*. Vol. 3. Washington, D.C.: U.S. Department of Justice; Oliver, W. M. and Bartgis, E. (1998). "Community Policing: A Conceptual Framework." *Policing: An International Journal of Police Strategies & Management* 21, no. 3: 490–509; Pelfrey, W. V., Jr. (1998). "Precipitating Factors of Paradigmatic Shift in Policing: The Origin of the Community Policing Era." In *Community Policing: Contemporary Readings*, edited by G. P. Alpert and A. Piquero, 79–94. Prospect Heights, IL: Waveland Publishers.

43. Gowri, A. (2003). "Community Policing Is an Epicycle." *Policing: An International Journal of Police Strategies and Management* 26, no. 4: 591–611.

44. Oliver, W. M. (2000). "The Third Generation of Community Policing: Moving Through Innovation, Diffusion, and Institutionalization." *Police Quarterly* 3, no. 4: 367–388.

45. Yin, R. (1979). *Changing in Urban Bureaucracies: How New Practices Become Routinized*. Lexington, MA: Lexington Books.

46. Pelfrey, W. V., Jr. (1998). "Precipitating Factors of Paradigmatic Shift in Policing: The Origin of the Community Policing Era." In *Community Policing: Contemporary Readings*. Edited by G. P. Alpert and A. Piquero, 79–94. Prospect Heights, IL: Waveland Publishers, p. 90.

47. Kelling, G. L. and Moore, M. H. (1988). "The Evolving Strategy of Policing." *Perspectives on Policing*, No. 4. Washington, D.C.: National Institute of Justice.

48. Kelling, G. L. and Moore, M. H. (1991). "From Political to Reform to Community: The Evolving Strategy of Police." In *Community Policing: Rhetoric or Reality?* Edited by J. R. Greene and S. D. Mastrofski, 3–25, New York: Praeger Publishers, p. 23.

49. Greene, J. R. (2000). "Community Policing in America: Changing the Nature, Structure, and Function of the Police." In *Criminal Justice 2000: Policies, Processes, and Decisions of the Criminal Justice System*. Vol. 3. Washington, D.C.: U.S. Department of Justice.

50. Kelling, G. L. and Moore, M. H. (1988). "The Evolving Strategy of Policing." *Perspectives on Policing*, No. 4. Washington, D.C.: National Institute of Justice; Kelling, G. L. and Moore, M. H. (1991). "From Political to Reform to Community: The Evolving Strategy of Police." In *Community Policing: Rhetoric or Reality?* Edited by J. R. Greene and S. D. Mastrofski, 3–25. New York: Praeger Publishers.

51. Chandler, 1962, as cited in Kelling, G. L. and Moore, M. H. (1991). "From Political to Reform to Community: The Evolving Strategy of Police." In *Community Policing: Rhetoric or Reality?* Edited by J. R. Greene and S. D. Mastrofski, 3–25. New York: Praeger Publishers, p. 3.

52. Kelling, G. L. and Moore, M. H. (1988). "The Evolving Strategy of Policing." *Perspectives on Policing*, No. 4. Washington, D.C.: National Institute of Justice; Kelling, G. L. and Moore, M. H. (1991). "From Political to Reform to Community: The Evolving Strategy of Police." In *Community Policing: Rhetoric or Reality?* Edited by J. R. Greene and S. D. Mastrofski, 3–25. New York: Praeger Publishers.

53. *ibid.*

54. Maguire, K. and Pastore, A. L. (2005). *Sourcebook of Criminal Justice Statistics*. [Online]. Available at http://www.albany.edu/sourcebook/; downloaded January 17, 2005. Table 2.0011.

55. Greene, J. R. (2000). "Community Policing in America: Changing the Nature, Structure, and Function of the Police." In *Criminal Justice 2000: Policies, Processes, and Decisions of the Criminal Justice System.* Vol. 3. Washington, D.C.: U.S. Department of Justice.

56. Greene, J. R. (2000). "Community Policing in America: Changing the Nature, Structure, and Function of the Police." In *Criminal Justice 2000: Policies, Processes, and Decisions of the Criminal Justice System.* Vol. 3. Washington, D.C.: U.S. Department of Justice, p. 309.

57. Greene, J. R. (2000). "Community Policing in America: Changing the Nature, Structure, and Function of the Police." In *Criminal Justice 2000: Policies, Processes, and Decisions of the Criminal Justice System.* Vol. 3. Washington, D.C.: U.S. Department of Justice.

58. Greene, J. R. (2000). "Community Policing in America: Changing the Nature, Structure, and Function of the Police." In *Criminal Justice 2000: Policies, Processes, and Decisions of the Criminal Justice System.* Vol. 3. Washington, D.C.: U.S. Department of Justice, p. 309.

59. Guzman, M. C. De. (2002). "The Changing Roles and Strategies of the Police in Time of Terror." *Academy of Criminal Justice Sciences Today,* Sept./Oct., pp. 8–13.

CHAPTER **2**

Homeland Security

*The enemies of freedom have no regard for the innocent, no concept of
the just and no desire for peace. They will stop at nothing to destroy our
way of life, and we, on the other hand, we stop at nothing to defend it.*

Secretary of Homeland Security Tom Ridge,
August 6, 2003

INTRODUCTION

The concepts of homeland security did not appear out of thin air in the wake of the terrorist attacks on September 11th, but rather were both an extension of the history of
homeland security, spanning nearly 80 years, and a result of policies that had been cir-
culating on Capitol Hill for nearly a decade. The first purpose of this chapter, then, is to
provide a historical perspective regarding the evolution of homeland security, from its
early conceptions in American history, through its more formal evolution during the two
World Wars, and finally to the more definitive restructuring throughout the latter half of
the twentieth century. Once insight is gained from the historical perspective of homeland
security, it helps to place the post–September 11th changes in perspective. Therefore,
the second purpose of this chapter is aimed at reviewing the legislative actions by Congress and the president and how the federal bureaucracy has realigned to fight terrorism
in the post–9/11 world. Specifically it will look at the largest overhaul of the federal bureaucracy since President Truman realigned the executive branch to transition America
from World War II to the Cold War. The overall intent of this chapter, and related to the
two main purposes, is to convey an understanding of how America has and is realigning
to fight this new war at the federal level, which serves to provide some key insights into
the role that state and local police will play in this era of homeland security.

HISTORY OF HOMELAND SECURITY

The Founding Fathers, under the U.S. Constitution, established a system that gave
the primary role of homeland security to state and local governments. The national

government essentially played a secondary role in the preservation of the homeland unless the state and local governments became so overwhelmed that they could no longer effectively deal with the situation. This particular relationship was embodied in Article 4, Section 4, of the U.S. Constitution, which declared that "the United States shall guarantee to every state in this Union a Republican form of government, and shall protect each of them against invasion; and on application of the legislature, or of the executive (when the legislature cannot be convened) against domestic violence."[1] The first clause gave the federal government the power and responsibility to protect all the states in the Union from an invasion by outside forces of any type. The second clause allowed for the federal government, primarily through the actions of the president, to intervene in cases of domestic disturbances on request of the state government.[2] This was mostly likely inserted by the founders as a result of Shays' Rebellion in Pennsylvania, which occurred just prior to the Constitutional Convention convening.[3]

Although presidential involvement in the issue of domestic disturbances would evolve over time, there was a profound realization that local disturbances were best left to the state and local governments. Federal intervention in local disturbances, the founders agreed, should be a last resort. Madison would highlight this fact, partially to alleviate the fears of the Anti-Federalists, in the Federalist Papers, Number 43, when he explained,

> Insurrection in a State will rarely induce a federal interposition, unless the number concerned in them bear some proportion to the friends of government. It will be much better that the violence in such cases should be repressed by the superintending power, than that the majority should be left to maintain their cause by a bloody and obstinate contest. The existence of a right to interpose will generally prevent the necessity of exerting it.[4]

However, this is not to say that Madison did not recognize the importance of maintaining civil order and that government, including the national government, had the right to intervene. As Madison explained in Federalist Number 37,

> Energy in government is essential to that security against external and internal danger and to that prompt and salutary execution of laws which enter into the very definition of good government. Stability in government is essential to national character and to the advantage annexed to it, as well as to that repose and confidence in the minds of the people, which are among the chief blessings of civil society.[5]

It was, however, Alexander Hamilton, who recognized that granting the state and local governments primary dominion over the issue of administering criminal and civil justice would give them a vested power over the national government. He wrote in Federalist Number 17,

> There is one transcendent advantage belonging to the province of the State governments, which alone suffices to place the matter in a clear and satisfactory light—I mean the ordinary administration of criminal and civil justice. This, of all others, is the most powerful, most universal, and most attractive source of popular obedience and attachment. It is this which, being the immediate and visible guardian of life and property, having its benefits and its terrors in constant activity before the public eye, regulating all those personal interests and familiar concerns to which the sensibility of individuals is more immediately awake, contributes more than any other circumstance to impressing upon the minds of the people affection, esteem, and reverence towards the government. This great cement of society,

which will diffuse itself almost wholly through the channels of the particular governments, independent of all other causes of influence, would insure them so decided an empire over their respective citizens as to render them at all times a complete counterpoise, and, not unfrequently, dangerous rivals to the power of the Union.[6]

Although perhaps overstating the case of power granted to state and local governments through their control of the criminal justice system, the important aspect of this lengthy quote is the fact that Hamilton recognized it was the state and local governments who had primary domain over the issue of law and order and continue to do so today.[7] The national government was a very limited, almost nonexistent, partner. The legal historian Lawrence Friedman has stated that the federal government, in regard to crime and order maintenance, had started "from a baseline of close to zero."[8]

It is evident that the founding fathers and the federal system they created left the primary task of maintaining law and order to the state and local governments. A combination of Article four, Section four, which guaranteed the states a "republican form of government" and the tenth amendment, which reserved the rights not granted by the Constitution to the states, vastly limited the power of the national government to intervene in matters of a criminal nature. Although it could most assuredly deal with crime in its territories and in the District of Columbia, as well as on the "high seas," it could not become directly involved in criminal matters, unless called on by the state legislature or state executive when the legislature could not convene. It is clear, then, that crime, criminal justice, and homeland security were, in the traditional sense, a state and local government matter and that presidents were greatly limited in their ability to address this issue.

Over time this would slowly change as critical events occurred throughout our history, the issue of federalism more fully developed, and people began looking to the national government to solve such problems. The federal government would begin to become more involved in issues of homeland security by various means of asserting federal authority. As Calder has explained, there are essentially three broad categories under which the federal government could intervene: "(1) incidents threatening the unity principle of the federal system of government; (2) incidents threatening the national security and involving foreign nations; and (3) incidents violating a federal law passed by Congress."[9] It was under these three categories that presidents would begin to expand the role of government in homeland security beyond that in which state and local governments continued to be primarily responsible.

It has been noted that one of the first cases of federal intervention in a disaster came in 1803, when three great fires swept through the town of Portsmouth, New Hampshire.[10] The town's ability to recover in the aftermath severely taxed both town and state, and the latter appealed to Congress for assistance. Congress introduced and passed legislation that would render financial assistance to the community. This was the first of what would become a common occurrence by which the national government would become involved in domestic disturbances.[11] Most of these early encounters consisted of natural disasters, such as the Johnstown (Pennsylvania) flood in 1889[12] or the San Francisco earthquake in 1906. In other cases, the national government responded to man-made disasters such as the great Chicago fire of 1871. And in still other cases the national government became involved in domestic disturbances through Article 4 Section 4 of the Constitution, commencing with the Whiskey Rebellion of 1794, and including such historical disturbances as the Dorr Rebellion of 1842, the Pullman Strike of 1894, the Detroit (Michigan) riots during World War II, and the race riots of the late 1960s.[13]

In terms of homeland security, however, little thought was given to the protection of the homefront until World War I. Prior to that time, America was largely isolated from the rest of the world and was protected by the two great oceans. America's entry into World War I would somewhat alter this notion, but not necessarily with any lasting effect. There was never truly any "concentrated, organized attempt to address the protection of the population because it was largely assumed that no one could launch any significant, direct attacks on the vast U.S. land mass."[14]

There was one minor effort to address the protection of the population when America entered World War I. Congress enacted the U.S. Army Appropriations Act, which included the establishment of the Council of National Defense (CND).[15] According to D.F. Houston, the Secretary of Agriculture at the time, "the council was charged with the duty of mobilizing military and naval resources, studying the location, utilization and coordination of railroads, waterways and highways, increase of domestic production for civil and military purposes, the furnishing of requisite information to manufacturers, and the creation of relations which would render possible the immediate concentration of national resources."[16] Related to this charge, the CND was also to create a War Industries Board that would encourage state governments to create state defense councils and in turn encourage local governments to create their own local defense councils.[17] These entities would be formed to provide for local security against external threats. Once the war ended in 1918, the program was largely discontinued and officially abolished in 1921. America returned to its isolationism.

During the Great Depression and the Dust Bowl years of the mid-1930s, America faced a number of emergencies that prompted Roosevelt to create the National Emergency Council within the confines of the White House. As America began to move more toward a war footing in the late 1930s, Roosevelt's concern shifted away from the natural emergencies and more toward the issue of national security. In 1939, "Roosevelt issued a statement on espionage requesting that all citizens, including state and local officials, turn over relevant information to the FBI."[18] The next year, Roosevelt would abolish the National Emergency Council and reconstitute it as the Office of Emergency Management, which would remain under the president in the White House. The next year, on May 20, 1941, just prior to America entering World War II, Roosevelt created the Office of Civil Defense (OCD) with New York City Mayor Fiorello La Guardia as its director. Roosevelt placed the OCD within the Office of Emergency Management.[19]

Like its predecessor from World War I, the OCD sought to have a nationwide network of Civil Defense councils that were established to protect the homeland from external threats to include the tasking as an early warning system, an entity to monitor the threat of espionage, and as a means of responding to attacks on the homefront. Eventually the OCD saw 44 states establish Civil Defense councils, and over 1,000 local defense councils were created. The OCD became primarily known for its local citizens, who were in charge of conducting air raid drills and preparing for another attack on American soil after the December 7, 1941, bombing of Pearl Harbor. By the end of World War II over ten million citizens had volunteered their time as part of the OCD.

After World War II, as America shifted from a hot war to a cold war, the status of the OCD was in question. Technically there was no need for the OCD, as it was largely based on the threat of another direct attack such as the one on Pearl Harbor. However, it did not take long to realize that the Cold War was just as serious as the hot war, as the threat of an attack by the Soviet Union became the direct attack that America feared. Toward this end, Truman created the National Security Resources Board (NSRB) in 1947, and it would assume all civil defense planning duties until 1950.[20] At the same time the Department of Defense also created an Office of Civil Defense Planning aimed at preparing civil defense plans from the military's perspective. This was renamed the Office of Civil Defense Liaison, as it would no longer be primarily responsible for civil defense plans, but would liaison with the NSRB.

The NSRB continued to function until 1953 as an office within the White House and under the authority of the Executive Branch.[21] However, because the issue of civil defense was becoming a primary concern of the American people, highlighted by the fact that the Soviet Union had tested an atomic bomb in 1949, Truman decided to do something more definitive. By signing Executive Order 10186[22] he created the Federal Civil Defense Administration (FCDA).[23] Because the newly named agency had no funding and because Congress wanted both a chance to engage in the politics of civil defense and have oversight authority regarding civil defense, it moved to pass legislation that would make the FCDA an independent agency of the federal government responsible for coordinating all civil defense planning. Congress passed a comprehensive bill known as the Civil Defense Act of 1950,[24] and one aspect of the bill was the creation of the FCDA, which came into existence on January 12, 1951. Both the NSRB and the Office of Civil Defense Planning under the Department of Defense were absorbed into this newly created independent agency. America now had a consolidated agency for coordinating all civil defense planning in the United States.

The only problem with the consolidated agency was determining what its primary function was. The Truman administration debated the proper role, and Congress debated the proper funding. Although there was an initiative to build bomb shelters, the funding was severely lacking. Although there was consideration for the creation of medical treatment capabilities for mass casualties, the funding was limited, thus limiting the stockpiles of medical supplies. In addition, mass evacuation plans were developed, but largely limited to federal considerations, such as Washington, D.C. In the end, states retained the basic responsibility for civil defense by developing local plans and coordinating among state and local officials. The FCDA did develop education materials and created school lesson plans teaching such things as "duck and cover" and the effects of radiation. Funding was also allocated for cities and towns to install warning sirens and in coordination with the FCC, the CONELRAD (CONtrol of ELectronic RADiation) system was created, which was the early protege of the Emergency Broadcast System (EBS).

Despite having one agency responsible for civil defense planning, the responsibilities were dispersed across existing agencies and newly created agencies. In 1950 Congress passed the Federal Disaster Relief Act, which was designed to provide relief to states in times of disaster.[25] To this end, the Office of Defense Mobilization (EOP) was created in the White House to coordinate this type of relief. Although initially this was to deal with wartime activities, it would pick up disaster relief responsibilities through another Executive Order (10427). In 1953, under reorganization plan #3, the FCDA would focus on war threats and the ODM would concentrate on peacetime threats. Although the administration was trying to make wartime civil defense and peacetime civil defense (natural and man-made disasters) distinct from each other, the reality was they were highly related. If a city in America was attacked by the Soviet Union, its evacuation plans would be no different than if a natural disaster occurred. Recognizing this duplication of effort, once again under a re-organization plan (this time #1 dated July 1, 1958), both the functions of the FCDA and ODM were consolidated under the Office of Defense and Civilian Mobilization (ODCM). The name aptly showed both concerns merging together.

The ODCM was placed under the control of the Executive Office of the President. Leading up to this consolidation, America experienced the impact of several hurricanes, and each one necessitated an individual response from Congress to provide for disaster relief. Recognizing the inefficiencies associated with responding to disasters in this manner, the newly created ODCM looked to establish a standard method of response. To ensure that there was adequate funding for this standard response, Congress amended the Federal Civil Defense Act to provide matching grants to help states and local governments share the cost of civil emergencies.

In 1961, with the election of John F. Kennedy as president, once again administrative priorities necessitated organizational changes. Kennedy, "sensing that the overwhelming majority of state and local governments were doing little if anything to develop a shelter-ing capability, decided to make civil defense preparedness once again a central issue."[26] The Kennedy administration's take on the issue of war and peace preparedness was that the functions should be split. Hence the Office of Civil and Defense Mobilization was split into two agencies, the Office of Emergency Planning (OEP), an office within the White House for civil emergencies, and the Office of Civil Defense, under the Department of Justice, for civil defense.

This was only the beginning of the fragmentation of various services related to civil defense. Beginning in the late 1960s and moving into the 1970s, state governors began to pressure Congress to once again consolidate civil defense and emergency prepared-ness. The main motivational factor was most likely the ability to allow for the dual use of funds, thus freeing up more support and financial assistance to state and local gov-ernments, regardless of the type of emergency. Although the dual use of funds became a reality, the two entities were not consolidated but fragmented even further. On the civil defense side of the equation, the Office of Civil Defense in 1964 retained its name, but the U.S. Army was given primary responsibility. In 1972, this was moved back to the Department of Defense's responsibility with another name change to the Defense Civil Preparedness Agency.

On the emergency preparedness side of the equation, the Office of Emergency Plan-ning (OEP) became the Office of Emergency Preparedness (still OEP) in 1968, which retained all of the previous preparedness functions, only losing the civil defense respon-sibilities. However, in the early 1970s, other agencies became responsible for various as-pects of preparedness. The OEP became the Office of Emergency Preparedness, but still being the OEP it was thus changed to the Federal Preparedness Agency (FPA) in 1975. The new OEP and later FPS was placed under the General Services Administration (GSA), thus downplaying its importance to the Nixon administration. In addition, the Of-fice of Telecommunication Policy, the Office of Science and Technology Policy, the De-partment of the Treasury, and the Federal Disaster Assistance Administration picked up various responsibilities, as did the Dam Safety Coordination office, the Earthquake Haz-ard Reduction office, the Consequence Management in Terrorism office, the Warning and Emergency Broadcast Agency, the Federal Insurance Administration, the National Fire Prevention and Control Administration, and the National Weather Service Community Preparedness Program. This fragmentation was also evident at the state level as well, as states attempted to align their respective agencies with the federal agencies dealing with particular aspects of civil defense and emergency preparedness. Clearly there was no single plan or any coordinated effort regarding civil defense or emergency preparedness throughout the 1970s, leaving the United States strategy toward civil defense and emergency management in total confusion.[27]

BOX 2-1

HISTORICAL ORGANIZATIONAL ANTECEDENTS OF THE DEPARTMENT OF HOMELAND SECURITY

National Defense Council	1917–1918
National Emergency Council	1933–1939
National Defense Council	1939–1941
Office for Emergency Management	1940–1950
Office of Civilian Defense	1941–1945
National Security Resources Board (National Security Act 1947)	1947–1949
Office of Civil Defense Planning (Department of Defense)	1948–1949
National Security Resources Board (White House)	1949–1953
Office of Civil Defense Liasison (Department of Defense)	1949–1950
Office of Defense Mobilization (Federal Civil Defense Act 1950)	1950–1953
Federal Civil Defense Administration	1950–1958
Office of Defense and Civilian Mobilization	1958
Office of Civil and Defense Mobilization	1958–1961
Office of Emergency Planning	1961–1968
Office of Civil Defense (Department of Defense)	1961–1964
Office of Civil Defense (U.S. Army)	1964–1972
Defense Civil Preparedness Agency (Department of Defense)	1972–1979
Office of Preparedness (General Services Administration)	1973–1975
Federal Preparedness Agency (General Services Administration)	1975–1979
Federal Emergency Management Agency (FEMA)	1979–2003
Department of Homeland Security (FEMA falls under DHS)	2003–present
U.S. Northern Command (Department of Defense)	2002–present

Sources: City of Fort Collins. (2005). *From Civil Defense to Emergency Management.* Retrieved July 12, 2005 from *http://www.ci.fort-collins.co.us/oem/civildefense.php*, Drabek, T. E. (1991). "The Evolution of Emergency Management." In *Emergency Management: Principles and Practices for Local Government.* Edited by Drabek, T. E. and Hoetmer, G. J., 3–29. Washington, D.C.: International City Management Association; Green, W. G. (2005). *Civil Defense and Emergency Management Organizational History.* Retrieved July 14, 2005 from *http://www.richmond.edu/~wgreen/Ecdflow.pdf*; The Tennessee Emergency Management Agency. (2005). "Tennessee Civil Defense History." Retrieved June 15, 2005 from *http://www.tnema.org/Archives/EMHistory/TNCDHistory10.htm*

In 1979, the Carter administration put an end to the confusion. The state governors had begun to call for a consolidation of federal emergency management in 1977, and they used the National Governors Association to make their demands known. In 1978, Carter submitted a reorganization plan to Congress, and debate ensued. Then, on March 28, 1979, the nuclear power plant at Three Mile Island began to malfunction, generating serious concern among the American people. Three days later, on March 31, 1979, President Carter signed Executive Order 12127, which established the Federal Emergency Management Agency (FEMA). An additional Executive Order (12148) mandated the consolidation of all the various agencies listed under this newly created agency.[28] Carter placed John Macy in charge of FEMA with the responsibility of unifying an agency that consisted of a number of varying agencies, under a number of different organizations, spread across Washington, D.C. Despite the consolidation being mandated by Executive Order, the reality was that FEMA remained a conglomerate of many different entities acting independent of one another.[29] In addition, "for many years the 'civil defense' and 'national security' planners were distinct from those that assisted state and local governments in preparing for and responding to disasters."[30] Macy argued that both emergency preparedness and civil defense activities shared many similarities and that responses to both would be roughly the same. As a result, Macy focused his efforts on the creation of the Integrated Emergency Management System (IEMS), which focused on the "direction, control and warning systems which are common to the full range of emergencies from small isolated events to the ultimate emergency—war."[31]

FEMA continued to face a number of problems in regard to its operations. A number of early crises and disasters included the contamination of Love Canal, the Cuban Refugee crisis, the Loma Prieta earthquake and Hurricanes Hugo in 1989 and Andrew in 1992. Each of these disasters only managed to highlight how woefully ill-prepared FEMA was in responding to disasters—its primary charge. Perhaps the most demoralizing emergency to FEMA was Hurricane Andrew; when FEMA could not adequately respond, President Bush placed the Secretary of Transportation in charge and mobilized the military to provide assistance. Several investigative reports by the General Accounting Office (GAO) revealed that FEMA was not able to coordinate or handle the management of catastrophic disasters and changes needed to be made.[32]

Upon taking office, President Clinton appointed James Lee Witt as the Director of FEMA, the first director to actually have a background in emergency management, having served as then-Governor Clinton's director of the Arkansas Office of Emergency Services.[33] Witt initiated sweeping reforms, attempting to address many of the criticisms laid out by the GAO in their investigations. He drew on the concepts of "reinventing government," concepts proposed by authors Osborne and Gaebler[34] and touted by then Vice-President Al Gore, such as customer service training and reorganizations, to break down and eliminate stovepipes by encouraging agencies within FEMA to begin communicating with one another. In addition, he encouraged the use of new technologies to better manage the vast amounts of information that occur during disasters. Moreover, Witt also began to improve the relationships and coordination, one of its primary functions, with state and local agencies. In the end, FEMA was also assisted by President Clinton elevating the FEMA director to cabinet-level status, thus giving Witt and his agency far more power inside the Beltway.[35]

FEMA was tested numerous times in the 1990s, including the first World Trade Center Bombing in 1993 and the Oklahoma City Bombing in 1995. Although they were successful, due to the nature of federalism in America, one defining question still remained: in the event of a disaster, who was the lead agency? Witt did not immediately claim the role for FEMA, having to recognize that first responders are local police and fire and that states have the right and responsibility under the Constitution to respond to such disasters.[36] However, as FEMA began to flex its muscle by way of newfound capabilities and resources, state directors began looking to FEMA to lead the way. FEMA's constraints, however, fell in the area of the amount of resources it was able to command. Other agencies with various related responsibilities often had greater resources, such as the Department of Justice and the Department of Defense. This created constraints regarding FEMA's ability to always assume the primary leadership role. Despite this political misgiving, whether FEMA wanted the role or not, it was fast becoming an administrative given.

In 2001, when President George W. Bush came into office, he appointed Joe M. Allbaugh as the new director of FEMA.[37] Within months FEMA's new director was faced with the greatest challenge in that organization's history, the terrorist attacks on September 11, 2001. The agency responded well under the circumstances and was able to provide both New York City and Arlington County, Virginia, with urban search and rescue support, give assistance in various lifesaving operations, meet individual and public assistance needs, implement human services and victims' assistance programs, and help with the removal of debris at ground zero.[38] Despite its success in responding to the terrorist attacks, there was still the realization that FEMA's resources and capabilities needed to be enhanced to protect the homeland, and within two years FEMA became one of the major components of the DHS.

In addition to the creation of the DHS, the Bush administration also expanded the U.S. military's focus on the world, by creating the U.S. Northern Command (NORTHCOM) in 2003.[39] NORTHCOM was devised to cover all North America, the only geographical area in the world that the Department of Defense did not cover at the time. Given the new command with a four-star general in charge, NORTHCOM became the primary command for homeland defense and was given authority, as specific in Article 1, Section 8, "to provide for calling forth the militia to execute the laws of the union, suppress insurrections, and repel invasions." Although the DHS assumed the emergency management and civil defense duties, any military considerations fell under U.S. Northern Command.

U.S.A. P.A.T.R.I.O.T. ACT 2001

In the immediate aftermath of the terrorist attacks on September 11, 2001, neither the DHS nor the U.S. Northern Command existed. Although consideration had been given prior to the attacks for a major bureaucratic reorganization, the plans were merely in the discussion stage within the executive and legislative branches. Other bills to address the issue of terrorist investigations, strengthen existing laws on terrorism, or create new laws were also under consideration at the time. When the hijacked planes struck the World Trade Center towers and the Pentagon, this moved any and all proposals from the consideration stage to placing them on the table for action. For example, one such bill, the

Combating Terrorism Act, had "proposed expanding the government's authority to trace telephone calls to include e-mails,"[40] thus expanding existing surveillance powers to include modern technological changes. According to O'Harrow, a reporter for the *Washington Post,* "it was hauled out and approved in minutes."[41]

Although from the time the bill was crafted to the time it was ultimately passed by Congress and signed into law was very short by Washington standards, the debate was nonetheless extremely intense. Much of the debate centered on the right balance between targeting the terrorists who had committed the attacks and balancing that with the civil liberties of all citizens to avoid government peering into the lives of everyday people.[42] The Bush administration, namely under the guidance of Attorney General John Ashcroft, pushed for expanded governmental powers. The chairman of the Judiciary Committee, Senator Patrick Leahy (D-VT), attempted to slow down the push toward expanding government powers of surveillance. American sentiments as represented through public opinion polls, however, "showed that most people were more than willing to trade off civil liberties and privacy protection for more security."[43] So, although the Democrats began drafting their own antiterrorism legislation (tentatively titled the Uniting and Strengthening America Act), many of the administration's policies were finding their way into the bill that was ultimately crafted. Although there were many similarities between the bills, the final bill went much further than the Democrats' bill. And although it was Dick Armey (R-TX) that began the discussion of placing a "sunset" provision in the bill, it was the Democrats that embraced the concept, thus making it more palatable for all concerned. As a result, the majority of the bill's new laws would have a four-year sunset, thus the provisions would expire at the end of 2005 unless renewed by Congress.

The bill, House Resolution 2975, originated in the House of Representatives and became widely known as the "Patriot Act." The official title, however, was the U.S.A. P.A.T.R.I.O.T. Act, which stands for "Uniting and Strengthening America By Providing Appropriate Tools Required to Intercept and Obstruct Terrorism." One month after the September 11th terrorist attacks, the Senate passed Senate Bill 1510, their version of the Patriot Act provisions. On that same day the House Judiciary Committee reported out an amended version of House Resolution 2975, and amendments were then offered by House members to this bill over the next several days.

On October 17, the U.S. Capitol and its lawmakers confronted a new terrorist threat—the anthrax attacks. This increased the urgency to get a final bill to the president's desk for his signature.[44] As a result, over the next several days, the House passed a clean bill (House Resolution 3162), which resolved the differences between their earlier bill and the Senate bill. The Senate agreed to the changes, and House Resolution 3162 and the U.S.A. PATRIOT Act[45] was sent to the president, who signed it on October 26, 2001, making it Public Law 107-56.

The U.S.A. PATRIOT Act has ten titles that provided for new powers for government to use against terrorists. In general, it gave federal officials greater authority to track and intercept communications, both for law enforcement and foreign intelligence-gathering purposes.[46] It vested the secretary of the treasury with regulatory powers to combat corruption of U.S. financial institutions for foreign money laundering purposes. It sought to further close our borders to foreign terrorists and to detain and remove those within our borders. It created new crimes, new penalties, and new procedural

BOX 2-2

REMARKS BY THE PRESIDENT AT SIGNING OF THE USA PATRIOT ACT

THE PRESIDENT: Good morning and welcome to the White House. Today, we take an essential step in defeating terrorism, while protecting the constitutional rights of all Americans. With my signature, this law will give intelligence and law enforcement officials important new tools to fight a present danger.

. . . The changes, effective today, will help counter a threat like no other our nation has ever faced. We've seen the enemy, and the murder of thousands of innocent, unsuspecting people. They recognize no barrier of morality. They have no conscience. The terrorists cannot be reasoned with. Witness the recent anthrax attacks through our Postal Service.

Our country is grateful for the courage the Postal Service has shown during these difficult times. We mourn the loss of the lives of Thomas Morris and Joseph Curseen; postal workers who died in the line of duty. And our prayers go to their loved ones.

I want to assure postal workers that our government is testing more than 200 postal facilities along the entire Eastern corridor that may have been impacted. And we will move quickly to treat and protect workers where positive exposures are found.

But one thing is for certain: These terrorists must be pursued, they must be defeated, and they must be brought to justice. And that is the purpose of this legislation. Since the 11th of September, the men and women of our intelligence and law enforcement agencies have been relentless in their response to new and sudden challenges.

We have seen the horrors terrorists can inflict. We may never know what horrors our country was spared by the diligent and determined work of our police forces, the FBI, ATF agents, federal marshals, Custom officers, Secret Service, intelligence professionals and local law enforcement officials, under the most trying conditions. They are serving this country with excellence, and often with bravery.

They deserve our full support and every means of help that we can provide. We're dealing with terrorists who operate by highly sophisticated methods and technologies, some of which were not even available when our existing laws were written. The bill before me takes account of the new realities and dangers posed by modern terrorists. It will help law enforcement to identify, to dismantle, to disrupt, and to punish terrorists before they strike.

For example, this legislation gives law enforcement officials better tools to put an end to financial counterfeiting, smuggling and money-laundering. Secondly, it gives intelligence operations and criminal operations the chance to operate not on separate tracks, but to share vital information so necessary to disrupt a terrorist attack before it occurs.

As of today, we're changing the laws governing information-sharing. And as importantly, we're changing the culture of our various agencies that fight terrorism. Countering and investigating terrorist activity is the number one priority for both law enforcement and intelligence agencies.

Surveillance of communications is another essential tool to pursue and stop terrorists. The existing law was written in the era of rotary telephones. This new law that I sign today will allow surveillance of all communications used by terrorists, including e-mails, the Internet, and cell phones.

As of today, we'll be able to better meet the technological challenges posed by this proliferation of communications technology. Investigations are often slowed by limit on the reach of federal search warrants. *(continued)*

Law enforcement agencies have to get a new warrant for each new district they investigate, even when they're after the same suspect. Under this new law, warrants are valid across all districts and across all states. And, finally, the new legislation greatly enhances the penalties that will fall on terrorists or anyone who helps them.

Current statutes deal more severely with drug-traffickers than with terrorists. That changes today. We are enacting new and harsh penalties for possession of biological weapons. We're making it easier to seize the assets of groups and individuals involved in terrorism. The government will have wider latitude in deporting known terrorists and their supporters. The statute of limitations on terrorist acts will be lengthened, as will prison sentences for terrorists.

This bill was carefully drafted and considered. Led by the members of Congress on this stage, and those seated in the audience, it was crafted with skill and care, determination and a spirit of bipartisanship for which the entire nation is grateful. This bill met with an overwhelming—overwhelming agreement in Congress, because it upholds and respects the civil liberties guaranteed by our Constitution.

This legislation is essential not only to pursuing and punishing terrorists, but also preventing more atrocities in the hands of the evil ones. This government will enforce this law with all the urgency of a nation at war. The elected branches of our government, and both political parties, are united in our resolve to fight and stop and punish those who would do harm to the American people.

It is now my honor to sign into law the USA Patriot Act of 2001.

efficiencies for use against domestic and international terrorists. Although it is not without safeguards, critics contended some of its provisions went too far.[47] And although it grants many of the enhancements sought by the Department of Justice, others are concerned that it did not go far enough.[48]

The titles and provisions of the USA PATRIOT Act that apply to law enforcement begin with Title I, which was designed to enhance domestic security. It created funding for various counterterrorist activities, authorized the Department of Justice to request assistance from the Department of Defense regarding enforcing laws related to weapons of mass destruction (specifically nuclear, chemical, and biological weapons), and it defined presidential authority in regard to terrorist attacks.

Title II was aimed at enhancing surveillance procedures for law enforcement to specifically target terrorists. Although many of these provisions have been used against organized crime and drug syndicates, the broader applications to terrorists, as well as some of the new powers, created much of the controversy over the Patriot Act. This title is broad in that it allowed for the seizure of voice mail messages under a warrant, it authorized intelligence agencies and federal law enforcement agencies to share noncriminal information, it permitted pen registers and trap and trace orders of electronic communication such as e-mail, and it encouraged cooperation between law enforcement and foreign intelligence investigators.

Title III was directed toward money laundering and expanding the powers of law enforcement to work with banking institutions to bring down those laundering money for terrorism purposes. In addition, it prohibited laundering the proceeds from such things as cybercrime, supporting a terrorist organization, and using American credit cards fraudulently overseas. Title IV contained a number of provisions designed to prevent alien terrorists from entering the United States, particularly from Canada, to enable authorities to detail and deport alien terrorists and those who support them, and to monitor the movement of foreigners in the United States. Title V was aimed at removing obstacles to investigating terrorism, including such provisions as allowing for DNA collection in terrorist offenses, and it increased the dollar amount for rewards that the Department of Justice may authorize for wanted terrorists. Title VI provided funding for the victims of terrorism, specifically public safety officers and their families. Title VII was focused on increasing information sharing for critical infrastructure protection allowing for the expansion of the Regional Information Sharing System (RISS) to be used to enhance cooperation between federal, state, and local law enforcement agencies to address multijurisdictional terrorist conspiracies and activities.

Title VIII of the Patriot Act focused on the creation of new crimes and new penalties. The Act created new federal crimes for terrorist attacks on mass transportation facilities, for biological weapons offenses, for harboring terrorists, for providing terrorists material support, for misconduct associated with money laundering as previously mentioned, for conducting the affairs of an enterprise that affects interstate or foreign commerce through the patterned commission of terrorist offenses, and for fraudulent charitable solicitation. Although strictly speaking these were new federal crimes, they generally supplemented existing laws by filling gaps and increasing penalties. More specifically, the Act did exclusively increase penalties for certain crimes that terrorists might commit. It established an alternative maximum penalty for acts of terrorism, raised the penalties for conspiracy to commit certain terrorist offenses, envisioned sentencing some terrorists to lifelong parole, and increased the penalties for counterfeiting, cybercrime, and charity fraud. Title IX was aimed at improving intelligence gathering through cooperation between the director of the Central Intelligence Agency and the attorney general. And, finally, Title X was a set of miscellaneous provisions that aimed to provide safeguards against civil rights abuses, to create the First Responders Assistance Act, which would give grants to state and local governments to assist them in preventing and responding to terrorist attacks, and authorized grants through such previous grants as the Office for State and Local Domestic Preparedness Support of the Office of Justice Programs and the Crime Identification Technology Act of 1998, greater appropriations for the purposes of antiterrorism.[49]

The vast majority of the USA PATRIOT Act is clearly aimed at providing provisions for the federal government to deal with the issue of terrorism, in particular federal law enforcement. However, some of the provisions have direct bearing on state and local law enforcement, and although it is federally driven, the Patriot Act cannot be ignored by local law enforcement, for they do play a role in the Act's enforcement. That particular role and which provisions apply and how they apply are still being determined. In addition, the sunset provisions could potentially impact the future application of the Patriot Act's provisions. As of this writing, however, Congress has made some minor changes to the bill, but for all intents and purposes it would appear that the majority of the provisions within the USA PATRIOT Act will be renewed with 14 of the sunset provisions becoming permanent, and two, one related to business records and the other to roving wiretaps, are being given a 10-year extension.[50]

BOX 2-3

THE PRESIDENT'S STATE OF THE UNION ADDRESS JANUARY 29, 2002

. . . The next priority of my budget is to do everything possible to protect our citizens and strengthen our nation against the ongoing threat of another attack. Time and distance from the events of September the 11th will not make us safer unless we act on its lessons. America is no longer protected by vast oceans. We are protected from attack only by vigorous action abroad, and increased vigilance at home.

My budget nearly doubles funding for a sustained strategy of homeland security, focused on four key areas: bioterrorism, emergency response, airport and border security, and improved intelligence. We will develop vaccines to fight anthrax and other deadly diseases. We'll increase funding to help states and communities train and equip our heroic police and firefighters. We will improve intelligence collection and sharing, expand patrols at our borders, strengthen the security of air travel, and use technology to track the arrivals and departures of visitors to the United States.

Homeland security will make America not only stronger, but, in many ways, better. Knowledge gained from bioterrorism research will improve public health. Stronger police and fire departments will mean safer neighborhoods. Stricter border enforcement will help combat illegal drugs. And as government works to better secure our homeland, America will continue to depend on the eyes and ears of alert citizens.

THE HOMELAND SECURITY ACT 2002

Although the U.S.A. P.A.T.R.I.O.T. Act gave the federal government new tools with which to track down terrorists, it did not rectify the organizational structure of the federal government for dealing with homeland security. At the time of the September 11th attacks, the federal government had over 100 agencies with some form of responsibility for homeland security. In addition, there was no entity or individual responsible for coordinating the work of these agencies to protect the homeland. Not to mention the fact that many of the agencies also worked with their state and local counterparts through joint efforts, various programs, and task forces. The Bush administration realized this problem immediately and attempted to rectify it by establishing the Office of Homeland Security within the White House through E.O. 13228, which was signed on October 8, 2001. Bush then selected Pennsylvania Governor Tom Ridge to serve as its director.

Shortly thereafter, realizing the political relationship that an Office of Homeland Security would cause, Senator Lieberman (D-CT) introduced a bill (S. 1534) with Senator Arlen Specter (R-PA) to establish a "Department of National Homeland Security." The bill would have made the head of the department a member of the cabinet and the National Security Council. The political issue centered around the fact that an "office" within the White House is part of the president's staff of advisors and does not have to appear before Congress when requested. A department head is part of the bureaucracy, which both the president and Congress control, and thus when Congress calls a department head to appear at a hearing, they must respond to this request. Senator Lieberman proposed the bill so as not to lose

Congressional control over the issue of homeland security. The bill did develop, albeit slowly, through Congress as it proceeded from one committee to the next. In the meantime, Lieberman's fears were realized when Tom Ridge, after becoming director, essentially refused to appear before Congress. Political pressure was brought on the president, giving impetus to the creation of a DHS.[51]

On June 6, 2002, President Bush proposed the creation of a DHS, a proposal that would move beyond the coordination efforts of the Office of Homeland Security to a strong administrative structure for managing consolidated programs concerned with border security and effective response to domestic terrorism incidents. On June 18th, the president transmitted to the House of Representatives proposed legislation to establish the new department. It was then introduced by request of the president as House Resolution 5005 and sponsored by Speaker of the House Dennis Hastert (R-IL) and the Minority Leader Richard Gephardt (D-MO).

The difficulties related to coordinating a massive overhaul of the federal bureaucracy are that Congress has the authority to reorganize the bureaucracy and allocate budgets for each of the agencies. As the discussion for reorganization centered on the creation of a new agency, the DHS, the debate was focused on what agencies, or what pieces of an agency, would fall under this new department-level organization. In addition, to move these particular agencies or subagencies out of their current agency, it would take the approval of the related committees in Congress to approve such a move. Hence, if a sub-agency was to be moved out of the Department of Agriculture, the Agriculture committee in the House would have to approve it before the entire House could make a motion. By the end of the summer the coordination of such a movement was underway.

President George W. Bush signing the Homeland Security Act. (*Source: AP Wide World Photos.*)

On June 19, 2002, the Agriculture, Armed Services, and Energy and Commerce committees approved plans for the reorganization of the federal bureaucracy. In addition, the Ways and Means Committee, the committee that approves budgetary allocations, also approved of the bill on June 19. Debate then began in the Judiciary, Science, and Transportation committees, as they had more agencies being affected by the proposed bill. All three of these committees, by voice vote, gave approval to moving forward with the proposals. As a result, the House of Representatives began open debate on House Resolution 5005, the Homeland Security Act of 2002, on June 25. The next day, debate in the House ended after 26 amendments to the bill were proposed, considered, and many adopted. Some of these amendments included establishing an office for state and local government coordination, retaining FEMA as an independent agency with responsibility for natural disaster preparedness, response, and recovery, and preserving the Customs Service as a distinct entity within the Department of Homeland Security. That same day, June 26, 2002, the House voted on the bill, and it passed with a 295 to 132 vote. The bill then moved to the Senate, where it went through a similar process of debate followed by reconciliation with the House bill, which came on November 19, 2002.[52]

A week later, in the East Room of the White House, President Bush made his remarks before signing the bill into law. He stated that "with my signature, this act of Congress will create a New DHS, ensuring that our efforts to defend this country are comprehensive and united." He further stated that the act, "takes the next critical steps in defending our country" and that "the continuing threat of terrorism, the threat of mass murder on our own soil will be met with a unified, effective response."[53]

The Homeland Security Act of 2002 consists of 17 titles. Title I of the act established the DHS and created the position for the Secretary of Homeland Security to be appointed by the president with the consent of the Senate and to be a part of the president's cabinet. Specifically, this first title sets out the responsibilities of the new department, which include preventing terrorist attacks within the United States, reducing the vulnerability of the United States to terrorism at home, and minimizing the damage and assisting in the recovery from any attacks that may occur. The DHS's primary responsibilities correspond to the five major functions established by the bill: information analysis and infrastructure protection (Title II); chemical, biological, radiological, nuclear, and related countermeasures (Title III); border and transportation security (Title IV); emergency preparedness and response (Title V); and coordination with other parts of the federal government, with state and local governments, and with the private sector (Title VII).[54]

Title II of the act is focused on information analysis and infrastructure and creates a corresponding undersecretary to the secretary for this purpose. The duties of this office include (1) receiving and analyzing law enforcement information, intelligence, and other information to understand the nature and scope of the terrorist threat to the American homeland and to detect and identify potential threats of terrorism within the United States; (2) comprehensively assessing the vulnerabilities of key resources and critical infrastructures; (3) integrating relevant information, intelligence analyses, and measures; (4) developing a comprehensive national plan for security key resources and critical infrastructures; (5) taking or seeking to effect necessary measures to protect those key resources and infrastructures; (6) administering the Homeland Security Advisory System, exercising primary responsibility for public threat advisories, and providing specific warning information to state and local governments, and the private sector, as well as advice about appropriate protective actions and countermeasures; and (7) reviewing, analyzing, and making recommendations for improvements in the policies and procedures governing the sharing of law enforcement, intelligence, and other information relating to homeland security within the federal government and between the federal government and state and local governments. In addition, this title transferred several agency systems related to information analysis to the DHS and granted the agency access to intelligence.[55]

Title III of the act focuses on chemical, biological, radiological, and nuclear countermeasures. As in Title II, this title creates an undersecretary position whose responsibilities include (1) securing the people, infrastructure, property, resources and systems in the United States from acts of terrorism involving chemical, biological, radiological, or nuclear weapons or other emerging threats; (2) conducting a national scientific research and development program to support the mission of the department, including developing national policy and coordinating the federal government's (nonmilitary) efforts to counter these types of terrorist threats, including relevant research and development; (3) establishing priorities and directing and supporting national research and development and procurement of technology and systems for detecting, preventing, protecting against, and responding to terrorist attacks using chemical, biological, radiological, nuclear, or related weapons and materials, and for preventing the importation of such weapons and materials into the United States; and (4) establishing guidelines for state and local efforts to develop and implement countermeasures in this area. This title also transferred a number of programs from various existing departments focused on these type of agents and to coordinate these programs with the public-health sector and Department of Health and Human Services.[56]

Title IV of the Homeland Security Act created an undersecretary for border and transportation security whose primary duties include (1) preventing the entry of terrorists and the instruments of terrorism into the United States; (2) securing the borders, territorial waters, ports, terminals, waterways, and air, land, and sea transportation systems of the United States; (3) administering the immigration and naturalization laws of the United States, including the establishment of rules governing the granting of visas and other forms of permission to enter the United States to individuals who are not citizens or lawful permanent residents; (4) administering the customs laws of the United States; and (5) ensuring the speedy, orderly, and efficient flow of lawful traffic and commerce in carrying out these responsibilities. Most significantly, this title transferred the United States Customs Service, the Immigration and Naturalization Service (INS), and the Coast Guard, along with several other agencies, under the DHS.[57]

Title V of the Act created the position of undersecretary for emergency preparedness and response. This undersecretary is responsible for (1) helping to ensure the preparedness of emergency response providers for terrorist attacks, major disasters, and other emergencies; (2) establishing standards, conducting exercises and training, evaluating performances, and providing funds in relation to the Nuclear Incident Response Team; (3) providing the federal government's response to terrorist attacks and major disasters; (4) aiding the recovery from terrorist attacks and major disasters; (5) working with other federal and nonfederal agencies to build a comprehensive national incident management system; (6) consolidating existing federal government emergency response plans into a single, coordinated national response plan; and (7) developing comprehensive programs for developing interoperative communications technology and ensuring that emergency response providers acquire such technology. The agencies transferred to the DHS under this title include the FEMA and several elements of both the Department of Justice and the Department of Health and Human Services. In addition, the title also gave DHS the ability to command certain elements of both the Department of Energy and the Environmental Protection Agency as they relate to nuclear threats and incidents.[58]

Title VI dealt with the treatment of charitable trusts for members of the armed forces and other government organizations. Title VII of the Homeland Security Act dealt with the management of the new agency and created the undersecretary for management whose responsibilities include (1) budget and fiscal matters; (2) procurement; (3) human resources and personnel; (4) information technology and communications systems; (5) facilities, property, equipment, and other material resources; (6) security for personnel, information technology and communications systems, and material resources; and (7) identification and tracking of performance measures. This undersecretary position did not absorb control of any outside agencies or their subagency parts.[59]

Title VIII of the act deals with coordination with nonfederal entities, the inspector general, the United States Secret Service, and general provisions. This title specifies the responsibilities of the secretary of homeland security relating to coordination with state and local officials and the private sector to ensure adequate planning, equipment, training, and exercise activities, coordinating and, as appropriate, consolidating, the federal government's communications and communications systems relating to homeland security with state and local governments, directing grant programs for state and local government emergency response providers, and distributing warnings and information to state and local governments and to the public. This title also created the office of Inspector General, transferred the U.S. Secret Service from the Treasury Department to DHS allowing it to maintain itself as a distinct entity, and it allowed for advisory committees to be created by the secretary of homeland security.[60]

Title IX created the National Homeland Security Council within the Executive Office of the president, much akin to the National Security Council that deals with foreign affairs. Title X focused on information security for the new department, whereas Title XI primarily involved the transfer of the Bureau of Alcohol, Tobacco, and Firearms from the Department of Treasury to the Department of Justice. Title XII dealt with airline liability arising out of insurance claims resulting from acts of terrorism, and Title XIII focused on federal workforce improvement. Title XIV allowed for the arming of airline pilots as a security measure against terrorism, and title XV of the act dealt with the transition of the various agencies as well as the appropriations originally allocated to the agencies and how this would be dealt with when the DHS was formed. And, finally, titles XVI and XVII dealt with legal changes that were necessary to have conformity in the law regarding all of the changes being made with the creation of the new department.[61]

The signature of the Homeland Security Act of 2002 by President Bush entered the act into law as Public Law 107-296. More significantly, it would stand as the largest change in the U.S. bureaucracy since President Harry S Truman's overhaul as America entered the Cold War. Bush announced that Tom Ridge, currently serving as the Director of the Office of Homeland Security, would serve as secretary, that Navy Secretary Gordon England would become the deputy secretary for homeland security, and DEA Administrator Asa Hutchinson would become the undersecretary for border and transportation security. On January 24, 2003, 60 days after the signing of the Homeland Security Act, the DHS came into existence.

OFFICE/DEPARTMENT OF HOMELAND SECURITY

On September 20, 2001, when President Bush addressed both Congress and the nation in the wake of the terrorist attacks on the United States, he announced that he was creating the Office of Homeland Security and that he was appointing Tom Ridge as its director. On October 8, President Bush did just that, swearing in Ridge as an assistant to the president for dealing with issues related to homeland security. The problems of having an executive office consisted not only of the political ramifications as previously detailed, but also centered on the fact that without its own budgetary allocations from Congress, the office would essentially be ineffective in trying to coordinate the numerous agencies responsible for securing the homeland. As a result, the Homeland Security Act of 2002 was passed that began the process of overhauling the federal bureaucracy to create the DHS. The department came into official existence on January 24, 2003, with Tom Ridge moving into the secretary's position, creating continuity in the transition from an office to a department. On March 1, 2003, nearly all the federal agencies were transferred into the DHS with the remaining agencies coming onboard June 1, 2003. Although some of the agencies remained intact and reported directly to the secretary for homeland security, most fell under the four new directorates: Border and Transportation Security, Information Analysis and Infrastructure Protection, Emergency Preparedness and Response, and Science and Technology. Secretary Ridge was given one year to develop a structural framework for organizing the 22 agencies absorbed and the over 179,000 employees. This was accomplished by August of 2004, but under the direction of the new secretary of homeland security, Michael Chertoff, it is undergoing revisions and is projected to reorganize again by the end of fiscal year 2005.

Vision, Mission, and Strategic Goals

In 2004, the DHS released its Strategic Plan that relayed its vision and mission statement and listed the key strategic goals to achieve this vision and implement its mission.[62]

Vision
Preserving our freedoms, protecting America . . . we secure our homeland.

Mission
We will lead the unified national effort to secure America. We will prevent and deter terrorist attacks and protect against and respond to threats and hazards to the nation. We will ensure safe and secure borders, welcome lawful immigrants and visitors, and promote the free flow of commerce.

Strategic Goals
Awareness—Identify and understand threats, assess vulnerabilities, determine potential impacts and disseminate timely information to our homeland security partners and the American public.

Prevention—Detect, deter and mitigate threats to our homeland.

Protection—Safeguard our people and their freedoms, critical infrastructure, property and the economy of our Nation from acts of terrorism, natural disasters, or other emergencies.

Response—Lead, manage and coordinate the national response to acts of terrorism, natural disasters, or other emergencies.

Recovery—Lead national, state, local and private sector efforts to restore services and re-build communities after acts of terrorism, natural disasters, or other emergencies.

Service—Serve the public effectively by facilitating lawful trade, travel and immigration.

Organizational Excellence—Value our most important resource, our people. Create a culture that promotes a common identity, innovation, mutual respect, accountability and teamwork to achieve efficiencies, effectiveness, and operational synergies.

Core Values

Integrity. "Service before self."   Each of us serves something far greater than ourselves. To our nation, we represent the President and the Congress. To the world, seeking to visit or do business with us, we are often the first Americans they meet. We will faithfully execute the duties and responsibilities entrusted to us, and we will maintain the highest ethical and professional standards.

Vigilance. "Guarding America."   We will relentlessly identify and deter threats that pose a danger to the safety of the American people. As a Department, we will be constantly on guard against threats, hazards, or dangers that threaten our values and our way of life.

Respect. "Honoring our Partners."   We will value highly the relationships we build with our customers, partners and stakeholders. We will honor concepts such as liberty and democracy, for which America stands.

Office of the Secretary

The secretary of homeland security is a cabinet-level official within the executive branch. The first secretary of homeland security was Tom Ridge, and the second and current secretary is Michael Chertoff. The staff functions in the office of the secretary oversee activities with other federal, state, local, and private entities as part of a collaborative effort to strengthen America's borders, provide for intelligence analysis and infrastructure protection, improve the use of science and technology to counter weapons of mass destruction, and create a comprehensive response and recovery division. Within the office of the secretary multiple offices contribute to the overall homeland security mission.[63]

The Privacy Office of the U.S. Department of Homeland Security

The DHS Privacy Office is the first statutorily required Privacy Office at any federal agency whose mission is to minimize the impact on individual's privacy, particularly the individual's personal information and dignity, while achieving the mission of the DHS. It operates under the direction of the chief privacy officer, who is appointed by

BOX 2-4

MEET THE SECRETARY OF HOMELAND SECURITY: MICHAEL CHERTOFF

On February 15, 2005, Judge Michael Chertoff was sworn in as the second secretary of the Department of Homeland Security. Chertoff formerly served as United States Circuit Judge for the Third Circuit Court of Appeals.

Secretary Chertoff was previously confirmed by the Senate to serve in the Bush administration as assistant attorney general for the criminal division at the Department of Justice. As assistant attorney general, he helped trace the 9/11 terrorist attacks to the Al-Qaida network, and worked to increase information sharing within the FBI and with state and local officials.

Before joining the Bush administration, Chertoff was a partner in the law firm of Latham & Watkins. From 1994 to 1996, he served as special counsel for the U.S. Senate Whitewater Committee.

(Source: Photo Courtesy of the Department of Homeland Security.)

(continued)

Prior to that, Chertoff spent more than a decade as a federal prosecutor, including service as U.S. Attorney for the District of New Jersey, First Assistant U.S. Attorney for the District of New Jersey, and Assistant U.S. Attorney for the Southern District of New York. As United States Attorney, Chertoff investigated and prosecuted several significant cases of political corruption, organized crime, and corporate fraud.

Chertoff graduated magna cum laude from Harvard College in 1975 and magna cum laude from Harvard Law School in 1978. From 1979–1980 he served as a clerk to Supreme Court Justice William Brennan, Jr.

Secretary Chertoff is married to Meryl Justin Chertoff and has two children.

Source: Department of Homeland Security website. (2005). Retrieved April 2005 from *http://www.dhs.gov/dhspublic/display?theme=11&content=4353.*

the secretary. Nuala O'Connor Kelly was appointed chief privacy officer of the DHS by Secretary Ridge on April 16, 2003.[64]

Office for Civil Rights and Civil Liberties

The mission of the Office for Civil Rights and Civil Liberties is to protect civil rights and civil liberties of American citizens and to support homeland security by providing the department with constructive legal and policy advice on the full range of civil rights and civil liberties issues the department will face. Specifically, the Office for Civil Rights and Civil Liberties provides legal and policy advice to departmental leadership on civil rights and civil liberties issues, investigates and resolves complaints filed by members of the public, provides leadership to the department's Equal Employment Opportunity Programs, and serves as an information and communication channel with the public. The office is led by Daniel Sutherland, Officer for Civil Rights and Civil Liberties, who provides legal and policy advice to the secretary and the senior officers of the department.[65]

Office of Counter Narcotics

The Office of Counter Narcotics is largely a liaison position with other agencies responsible for the coordination of drug control policy in the United States, particularly the White House Office of National Drug Control Policy (ONDCP). The purpose is to counter the narcotics trade, for many of the profits from illegal drugs are used to finance terrorism against the United States. The director of this office is a former Central Intelligence Agency employee, Roger Mackin, who is responsible for performing as the U.S. Interdiction Coordinator (USIC), a position within the ONDCP, with those of the newly established DHS Counter Narcotics Officer. The mission of this office is to ensure that all DHS counterdrug policies, initiatives, efforts, and resources are aligned with the President's National Drug Control Strategy. The director coordinates with department and agency heads, U.S. ambassadors and military commanders, interagency working groups, task forces, and coordinating centers having interdiction responsibilities. He will also review the assets committed by federal agencies for drug interdiction to ensure that they are sufficient and their use is properly integrated and optimized.

Office of General Counsel

The Office of General Counsel is a legal advisory office for the secretary of Homeland Security. In addition, the director of this office also advises other members of Homeland Security senior leadership on legal issues arising throughout the department, including those relating to immigration, customs enforcement, environmental compliance, international agreements, civil litigation, transportation security, labor and employment, incident management, public health, infrastructure protection, and intelligence sharing.

Office of Legislative Affairs

The Office of Legislative Affairs facilitates the development and advancement of the department's legislative agenda. The office focuses on providing members of Congress and Congressional staff information about departmental programs, policies, and initiatives on the impact of pending legislation on the department and through Congressional hearings, briefings, meetings, and other communications.

Office of National Capital Region Coordination

The Office of National Capital Region Coordination (NCRC) oversees and coordinates federal programs for and relationships with state, local, and regional authorities in the Washington, D.C., metropolitan area. The office's responsibilities include coordinating department activities relating to the NCR; coordinating to ensure adequate planning, information sharing, training, and execution of domestic preparedness activities in the NCR; and assessing and advocating for resources needed in the NCR.

Private Sector Office

The Office of the Private Sector provides the American business community with a direct line of communication to the DHS. The office works with businesses, trade associations, and other nongovernmental organizations to foster dialogue between the private sector and the department on the full range of issues and challenges faced by America's business sector. In addition to ensuring open communication between the department and the private sector, the office provides strategic guidance to the secretary on prospective policies and regulations and their impact and promotes public–private partnerships and best practices to improve the nation's homeland and economic security.

Office of Public Affairs

The Office of Public Affairs manages both internal and external communications for the DHS and all its 22 component agencies. More specifically, it serves as the public relations office coordinating all press releases, media press conferences, and public affair's requests.

Office of Security

The Office of Security protects and safeguards DHS personnel, property, facilities, and information. The Office of Security develops, implements, and oversees the department's security policies, programs, and standards; delivers security awareness training and education to department personnel; and provides security support to Homeland Security component agencies.

The Office of State and Local Government Coordination and Preparedness

The Office of State and Local Government Coordination and Preparedness is the federal government's lead agency responsible for preparing the nation against terrorism by assisting states, local and tribal jurisdictions, and regional authorities as they prevent, deter, and respond to terrorist acts. The office provides a broad array of assistance to America's first responders through funding, coordinated training, exercises, equipment acquisition, and technical assistance in support of implementing the national strategy for homeland security. The office is focused on implementing Homeland Security Presidential Directive-8, the establishment of a National Preparedness Goal that establishes mechanisms for improved delivery of federal preparedness assistance to state and local governments, and outlines actions to strengthen preparedness capabilities of federal, state, and local entities.

The Five Directorates

As previously detailed under the Homeland Security Act of 2002, five directorates were established to coordinate homeland security efforts regarding five key functioning areas: Border and Transportation Security (BTS), Emergency Preparedness and Response (EP&R), Information Analysis and Infrastructure Protection (IAIP), Science and Technology (S&T), and the Office of Management.

Border and Transportation Security (BTS)

Border and Transportation Security (BTS) is the largest of the five directorates and is focused on securing the nation's borders and transportation systems and enforcing the nation's immigration laws. The BTS absorbed the functions of six former federal agencies: the U.S. Customs Service, the INS enforcement division, the Animal and Plant Health Inspection Service, the Transportation Security Administration, the Office for Domestic Preparedness, and the Federal Protective Service.

Transportation Security Administration (TSA)   The Transportation Security Administration (TSA) was created in response to the terrorist attacks of September 11, 2001, as part of the Aviation and Transportation Security Act signed into law by President George W. Bush on November 19, 2001. TSA was originally in the Department of Transportation but was moved to the DHS in March 2003. TSA's mission is to protect the nation's transportation systems by ensuring the freedom of movement for people and commerce. In February 2002, TSA assumed responsibility for security at the nation's airports and by the end of the year had deployed a federal workforce to meet challenging Congressional deadlines for screening all passengers and baggage. TSA has also engaged in several programs aimed at enforcement including a canine program, training airline crews in self-defense, training pilots and flight deck crews in

BOX 2-5

DEPARTMENT OF HOMELAND SECURITY GOAL #1—AWARENESS

Objective 1.1—Gather and fuse all terrorism-related intelligence; analyze and coordinate access to information related to potential terrorist or other threats.

Objective 1.2—Identify and assess the vulnerability of critical infrastructure and key assets.

Objective 1.3—Develop timely, actionable, and valuable information based on intelligence analysis and vulnerability assessments.

Objective 1.4—Ensure quick and accurate dissemination of relevant intelligence information to homeland security partners, including the public.

Source: Department of Homeland Security. (2004). *Securing Our Homeland: U.S. Department of Homeland Security Strategic Plan.* Washington, D.C.: U.S. Department of Homeland Security.

firearms, and enhancing the screening of passengers and luggage through enhanced science technology.[66]

U.S. Customs and Border Protection (CBP)   U.S. Customs and Border Protection (CBP) is the unified border agency within the (DHS). The CBP combined the inspection workforce and broad border authorities of U.S. Customs, U.S. Immigration, Animal and Plant Health Inspection Service, and the entire U.S. Border Patrol. CBP includes more than 41,000 employees to manage, control, and protect the nation's borders, at and between the official ports of entry. CBP has two goals—antiterrorism and facilitating legitimate trade and travel into and out of the United States.

U.S. Immigration and Custom Enforcement (ICE)   The U.S. Immigration and Custom Enforcement (ICE) was created out of the functions, expertise, resources, and jurisdictions of several once-fragmented border and security agencies that were merged and reconstituted into ICE, the DHS's largest investigative bureau. The agencies that were either moved entirely or merged in part, based on law enforcement functions, included the investigative and intelligence resources of the U.S. Customs Service, the INS, the Federal Protective Service, and as of November 2003, the Federal Air Marshals Service. ICE is the investigative arm of the BTS, the operational directorate within the DHS tasked with securing the nation's borders and safeguarding its transportation infrastructure. The largest component within the DHS, BTS employs more than 100,000 men and women. ICE brings together more than 20,000 employees who focus on the enforcement of immigration and customs laws within the United States, the protection of specified federal buildings, and air and marine enforcement. By unifying previously fragmented investigative functions, ICE will deliver effective and comprehensive enforcement. ICE is led by an Assistant Secretary, who reports directly to the under secretary for BTS.

Federal Law Enforcement Training Center (FLETC)   The Federal Law Enforcement Training Center FLETC serves as an interagency law enforcement training organization for 81 federal agencies. The center also provides services to state, local, and international law enforcement agencies. The center is headquartered at Glynco, Georgia; however, the FLETC also operates two other residential training sites in Artesia, New Mexico, and Charleston, South Carolina. The FLETC also operates an in-service requalification training facility in Cheltenham, Maryland, for use by agencies with large concentrations of personnel in the Washington, D.C., area. The FLETC has oversight and program management responsibility for the International Law Enforcement Academy (ILEA) in Gaborone, Botswana, and supports training at other ILEAs in Hungary and Thailand. The center's parent agency, the Department of Homeland Security, supervises its administrative and financial activities. The FLETC director serves under the authority of the under secretary for border and transportation security.[67]

Emergency Preparedness and Response (EP&R)

The second directorate is the Emergency Preparedness and Response (EP&R), which is built on the foundation laid by the Federal Emergency Management Agency (FEMA), which ensures that our nation is prepared for incidents, whether natural disasters or terrorist assaults, and oversees the federal government's national response and recovery strategy. The undersecretary of Emergency Preparedness and Response also serves as the director of the Federal Emergency Management Agency, who reports directly to the Secretary of Homeland Security. Essentially the EP&R is FEMA.

Federal Emergency Management Administration (FEMA)   FEMA is part of the Department of Homeland Security's Emergency Preparedness and Response Directorate. FEMA has more than 2,600 full-time employees. They work at FEMA headquarters in Washington D.C., at regional and area offices across the country, the Mount Weather Emergency Operations Center, and the National Emergency Training Center in Emmitsburg, Maryland. FEMA also has nearly 4,000 standby disaster assistance employees who are available for deployment after disasters. Often FEMA works in partnership with other organizations that are part of the nation's emergency management system. These partners include state and local emergency management agencies, 27 federal agencies, and the American Red Cross.[68]

Information Analysis and Infrastructure Protection (IAIP)

The Information Analysis and Infrastructure Protection (IAIP) directorate performs the two functions implied within its name. To accomplish the first role, essentially aimed at reducing the vulnerability of the United States to terrorism and to detect, to prevent, and to respond to terrorist attacks, the Information Analysis and Infrastructure Protection was made a member of the Intelligence Community. IAIP's mission to disseminate information analyzed by the department to state and local government agencies and authorities and private-sector entities brings to the post–9/11 federal government a capability for the security and protection of the nation's domestic assets that did not previously exist.

The essential function of IAIP is mapping the vulnerabilities of the nation's critical infrastructure against a comprehensive analysis of intelligence and public source information. This function is unique to the federal government and fundamental to the nation's ability to better protect itself from terrorist attacks.

BOX 2-6

DEPARTMENT OF HOMELAND SECURITY GOAL #2—PREVENTION

Objective 2.1—Secure our borders against terrorists, means of terrorism, illegal drugs, and other illegal activity.

Objective 2.2—Enforce trade and immigration laws.

Objective 2.3—Provide operational end users with the technology and capabilities to detect and prevent terrorist attacks, means of terrorism, and other illegal activities.

Objective 2.4—Ensure national and international policy, law enforcement, and other actions to prepare for and prevent terrorism are coordinated.

Objective 2.5—Strengthen the security of the nation's transportation systems.

Objective 2.6—Ensure the security and integrity of the immigration system.

Source: Department of Homeland Security. (2004). *Securing Our Homeland: U.S. Department of Homeland Security Strategic Plan.* Washington, D.C.: U.S. Department of Homeland Security.

Office of Information Analysis (IA)   Within IAIP, the Office of Information Analysis (IA) performs the intelligence activities carried out within DHS. IA responsibilities are to (1) monitor, assess, and coordinate indications and warnings in support of the secretary of the DHS, who by Executive Order is responsible for implementing the Homeland Security Advisory System (HSAS); (2) access all information, assessments, analysis, and unevaluated intelligence relating to terrorist threats to the homeland; (3) maintain real-time intelligence connectivity to support situational awareness during implementation of protective measures and incident management; (4) assess the scope of terrorist threats to the homeland to understand such threats in light of actual and potential vulnerabilities of the homeland; (5) integrate threat information and analyses with vulnerability assessments from the DHS Office of Infrastructure Protection (IP) to identify priorities for protective and support measures by DHS, other agencies of the federal government, state and local government agencies and authorities, the private sector, and other entities; (6) respond to requirements from the assistant secretary for Infrastructure Protection for information analysis and intelligence requirements; (7) gather and integrate terrorist-related information from DHS component agencies, state and local government agencies and authorities, and private-sector terrorist-related reporting/information; process requests for information (RFI) from these component agencies, state and local government agencies and authorities and private-sector entities; and (8) disseminate threat information, intelligence and responses to RFI's to DHS component agencies, state and local government agencies and authorities, and private-sector entities.[69]

The Terrorist Threat Integration Center (TTIC)   The roles and functions of IAIP and the Terrorist Threat Integration Center (TTIC) are complementary and collaborative and enhance the national effort to detect, disrupt, and prevent terrorism. TTIC makes full use of all terrorist threat–related information and expertise available to the U.S. government and provides comprehensive all-source threat analysis to the president, to DHS, and to other federal agencies. IAIP provides intelligence analysts to the TTIC, who participates with analysts from other federal agencies in analyzing this all-source terrorist information. IAIP also provides TTIC with threat information gathered and integrated from DHS component agencies, state and local government agencies and authorities, and private-sector entities.

IAIP integrates all-source threat information and analysis received from TTIC and other agencies of the intelligence community with its own vulnerability assessments to provide tailored threat assessments, including priorities for protective and support measures to other agencies of the federal government, state and local government agencies and authorities, and private-sector entities. Finally, IAIP administers the HSAS to include exercising primary responsibility for public advisories.[70]

Homeland Security Operations Center (HSOC)   The Homeland Security Operations Center (HSOC) serves as the nation's nerve center for information sharing and domestic incident management—dramatically increasing the vertical coordination between federal, state, territorial, tribal, local, and private-sector partners. The HSOC collects and fuses information from a variety of sources every day to help deter, detect, and prevent terrorist acts. Operating 24 hours a day, 7 days a week, 365 days a year, the HSOC provides real-time situational awareness and monitoring of the homeland, coordinates incidents and response activities, and in conjunction with the DHS Office of Information Analysis, issues advisories and bulletins concerning threats to homeland security, as well as specific protective measures. Information on domestic incident management is shared with Emergency Operations Centers at all levels through the Homeland Security Information Network (HSIN).

The HSOC represents over 35 agencies ranging from state and local law enforcement to federal intelligence agencies. Information is shared and fused on a daily basis by the two halves of the HSOC that are referred to as the "Intelligence Side" and the "Law Enforcement Side." Each half is identical and functions in tandem with the other but requires a different level of clearance to access information. The "Intelligence Side" focuses on pieces of highly classified intelligence and how the information contributes to the current threat picture for any given area. The "Law Enforcement Side" is dedicated to tracking the different enforcement activities across the country that may have a terrorist nexus. The two pieces fused together create a real-time snapshot of the nation's threat environment at any moment.[71]

Office of Infrastructure Protection (IP)   The IAIP's other critical function, as performed by the Office of Infrastructure Protection (IP), is focused on securing the nation's 17 critical infrastructure and key resource sectors. Chemical facilities are one specific sector that is of significant focus for the department. Prior to the formation of DHS, responsibility for the nation's critical infrastructure was scattered over a patchwork of various federal agencies. With the creation of the department and Homeland Security Presidential Directive-7, DHS is the sector-specific agency responsible for coordinating the U.S. government's efforts to protect critical infrastructure across the chemical sector. The department develops and coordinates plans in close cooperation with its federal, state, local, tribal, and private-sector partners to aggressively reduce the nation's vulnerability to acts of terrorism in the chemical sector.[72]

Science and Technology (S&T)

The Directorate of Science and Technology (S&T) serves as the primary research and development arm of Homeland Security, using our nation's scientific and technological resources to provide federal, state, and local officials with the technology and capabilities to protect the homeland. The focus is on catastrophic terrorism—threats to the security of our homeland that could result in large-scale loss of life and major economic impact. S&T's work is designed to counter those threats, both by evolutionary improvements to current technological capabilities and development of revolutionary, new technological capabilities.

Office of National Laboratories   The Office of National Laboratories provides the nation with a unifying core of science, technology, and engineering laboratories, organizations, and institutions dedicated to securing the homeland. The mission of this office is to establish, develop, nurture, and sustain the people, places, programs, and capabilities of the Homeland Security Science and Technology Complex to: facilitate access and maximize capabilities of existing national assets; successfully execute research, development, testing, and evaluation programs; prevent technology surprise; and anticipate and deter future terrorist threats.[73]

Homeland Security Advanced Research Projects Agency (HSARPA)   The Homeland Security Advanced Research Projects Agency (HSARPA) is mainly responsible for issuing solicitations for research, for reviewing the research capabilities of both public and private entities that apply, and to manage the funding of the research. The HSARPA also conducts conferences and workshops related to their solicitations. Most of the solicitations to date have centered on biological and chemical agents as well as radiological and nuclear elements.[74]

BOX 2-7

DEPARTMENT OF HOMELAND SECURITY GOAL #3—PROTECTION

Objective 3.1—Protect the public from acts of terrorism and other illegal activities.

Objective 3.2—Reduce infrastructure vulnerability from acts of terrorism.

Objective 3.3—Protect against financial and electronic crimes, counterfeit currency, illegal bulk currency movement, and identity theft.

Objective 3.4—Secure the physical safety of the president, vice president, visiting world leaders, and other protectees.

Objective 3.5—Ensure the continuity of government operations and essential functions in the event of crisis or disaster.

Objective 3.6—Protect the marine environment and living marine resources.

Objective 3.7—Strengthen nationwide preparedness and mitigation against acts of terrorism, natural disasters, or other emergencies.

Source: Department of Homeland Security. (2004). *Securing Our Homeland: U.S. Department of Homeland Security Strategic Plan.* Washington, D.C.: U.S. Department of Homeland Security.

BOX 2-8

DEPARTMENT OF HOMELAND SECURITY GOAL #4—RESPONSE

Objective 4.1—Reduce the loss of life and property by strengthening nationwide response readiness.

Objective 4.2—Provide scalable and robust all-hazard response capability.

Objective 4.3—Provide search-and-rescue services to people and property in distress.

Source: Department of Homeland Security. (2004). *Securing Our Homeland: U.S. Department of Homeland Security Strategic Plan.* Washington, D.C.: U.S. Department of Homeland Security.

Office of Management

The under secretary for management is responsible for the budget, appropriations, expenditure of funds, accounting and finance, procurement, information technology systems, facilities, property, equipment, other material resources, and the identification and tracking of performance measurements relating to the responsibilities of Homeland Security. Key to the mission of the DHS is the success of its employees, and the Directorate for Management is responsible for ensuring that employees have clear responsibilities and means of communication with other personnel and management. An important resource for communications is the office of the Chief Information Officer, who is responsible for maintaining the information technology necessary to keep the more than 170,000 employees of DHS connected to and fully a part of the goals and mission of the department.[75]

Coast Guard

The Coast Guard became part of the DHS in March of 2003, but it was not absorbed under any of the five directorates. Rather, it was kept whole and intact with the Commandant of the Coast Guard reporting directly to the secretary of homeland security. In addition, prior to the move to DHS, the U.S. Coast Guard's powers and responsibilities increased after the passage of the Maritime Transportation Security Act of 2002.[76] According to the U.S. Coast Guard's *Maritime Strategy for Homeland Security,*[77] the Coast Guard now serves as the nation's "maritime first responder" and is a crucial and responsive element of the DHS. Its well-trained crews react to a wide variety of maritime disasters, such as plane crashes, groundings, bridge and waterway accidents, and other maritime calamities. The Coast Guard's specially trained National Strike Force teams around the nation provide a flexible and adaptive resource of the DHS, deploying swiftly to clean up oil spills and hazardous materials, provide assistance during natural disasters such as hurricanes and flooding, and work hand in hand with EPA, FEMA, state, local, and other key agencies to save lives and protect property.

The Coast Guard ensures that our maritime transportation system and its waterways are safe, as over 95 percent of U.S. trade comes by sea. Our waterways and maritime productivity depend on our nation's aids to navigation systems—buoys and markers, lighthouses,

BOX 2-9

DEPARTMENT OF HOMELAND SECURITY GOAL #5—RECOVERY

Objective 5.1—Strengthen nationwide recovery plans and capabilities.
Objective 5.2—Provide scalable and robust all-hazard recovery assistance.

Source: Department of Homeland Security. (2004). *Securing Our Homeland: U.S. Department of Homeland Security Strategic Plan.* Washington, D.C.: U.S. Department of Homeland Security.

and electronic navigation systems such as the Differential Global Positioning System (DGPS) along with Coast Guard Vessel Traffic Services in key ports—all combine to help keep our homeland waters safe, secure, and productive.

As the nation's lead agency for maritime law enforcement, Coast Guard vessels and aircraft constantly patrol both our offshore and coastal regions, "pushing our borders out" and extending our vigilance and awareness of potential approaching threats, enforcing U.S. immigration policies and customs laws, and stopping drug smugglers, all of which strengthen our nation's maritime homeland security. The Coast Guard interdicts thousands of illegal migrants each year, stops tons of drugs from reaching our streets and arrests hundreds of smugglers, and works tirelessly in interagency teams with its homeland security partners such as U.S. Customs, Immigration, Department of Defense, and state and local authorities to help identify threats far off our coasts and help secure our maritime borders and our homeland.

Specifically, the Coast Guard's mission includes (1) maritime safety: eliminate deaths, injuries and property damage associated with maritime transportation, fishing, and recreational boating. The Coast Guard's motto is Semper Paratus—(Always Ready), and the service is always ready to respond to calls for help at sea; (2) national defense: defend the nation as one of the five U.S. armed services. Enhance regional stability in support of the National Security Strategy, utilizing the Coast Guard's unique and relevant maritime capabilities; (3) maritime security: protect America's maritime borders from all intrusions by: (a) halting the flow of illegal drugs, aliens, and contraband into the United States through maritime routes; (b) preventing illegal fishing; and (c) suppressing violations of federal law in the maritime arena; (4) mobility: facilitate maritime commerce and eliminate interruptions and impediments to the efficient and economical movement of goods and people, while maximizing recreational access to and enjoyment of the water; and (5) protection of natural resources: eliminate environmental damage and the degradation of natural resources associated with maritime transportation, fishing, and recreational boating.[78]

U.S. Secret Service

The other agency that was transferred into the Department of Homeland Security intact, whose director reports directly to the secretary of homeland security, is the U.S. Secret

Service. Originally under the Department of the Treasury due to its responsibilities for investigating counterfeiting, the U.S. Secret Service was moved under the DHS. The U.S. Secret Service is mandated by statute and executive order to carry out two significant missions: protection and criminal investigations. The Secret Service protects the president and vice president, their families, heads of state, and other designated individuals; investigates threats against these protectees; protects the White House, Vice President's Residence, foreign missions, and other buildings within Washington, D.C.; and plans and implements security designs for designated National Special Security Events. The Secret Service also investigates violations of laws relating to counterfeiting of obligations and securities of the United States; financial crimes that include, but are not limited to, access device fraud, financial institution fraud, identity theft, computer fraud; and computer-based attacks on our nation's financial, banking, and telecommunications infrastructure.[79]

Office of Inspector General (OIG)

In addition to the U.S. Coast Guard and U.S. Secret Service, two other entities essentially stand alone in the DHS. The first is the Office of Inspector General (OIG). The inspector general is responsible for conducting and supervising audits, investigations, and inspections relating to the programs and operations of the department. The OIG is to examine, evaluate, and where necessary, critique these operations and activities, recommending ways for the department to carry out its responsibilities in the most effective, efficient, and economical manner possible. Specifically, the mission of the Inspector General's office is to serve as an independent and objective inspection, audit, and investigative body to promote effectiveness, efficiency, and economy in the DHS's programs and operations and to prevent and detect fraud, abuse, mismanagement, and waste in such programs and operations.[80]

BOX 2-10

DEPARTMENT OF HOMELAND SECURITY GOAL #6—SERVICE

Objective 6.1—Increase understanding of naturalization and its privileges and responsibilities.

Objective 6.2—Provide efficient and responsive immigration services that respect the dignity and value of individuals.

Objective 6.3—Support the U.S. humanitarian commitment with flexible and sound immigration and refugee programs.

Objective 6.4—Facilitate the efficient movement of legitimate cargo and people.

Source: Department of Homeland Security. (2004). *Securing Our Homeland: U.S. Department of Homeland Security Strategic Plan.* Washington, D.C.: U.S. Department of Homeland Security.

U.S. Citizenship & Immigration Services (USCIS)

The other entity that largely stands alone within the DHS is the Citizenship and Immigration Services (USCIS). The DHS has administered the nation's immigration laws since March 1, 2003, when the INS became part of DHS. Through the USCIS, DHS continues the tradition of processing immigrants into the country by administering services such as immigrant and nonimmigrant sponsorship, adjustment of status, work authorization and other permits, naturalization of qualified applicants for U.S. citizenship, and asylum or refugee processing. This function, along with immigration enforcement, was originally performed by the INS. These functions were split out with USCIS performing the administrative aspects of immigration law, whereas immigration enforcement became the responsibility of the Directorate of Border and Transportation Security. The USCIS states that the department tries to ensure that "America continues to welcome visitors and those who seek opportunity within our shores while excluding terrorists and their supporters."[81]

DHS, Six-Point Agenda—July 2005

In July of 2005, the DHS issued a six-point agenda for organizational change to ensure that the department's policies, operations, and structures are aligned in the best way to address the potential threats—both present and future—that face our nation. The six-point agenda is intended to guide the department in its current round of changes with the intent to (1) increase overall preparedness, particularly for catastrophic events; (2) create better transportation security systems to move people and cargo more securely and efficiently; (3) strengthen border security and interior enforcement and reform immigration processes; (4) enhance information sharing with our partners; (5) improve DHS financial management, human resource development, procurement, and information technology; and (6) realign the DHS organization to maximize mission performance.

Supporting the six-point agenda, the department has proposed to realign the DHS to increase its ability to prepare, prevent, and respond to terrorist attacks and other emergencies. These changes, according to Secretary Chertoff, will better integrate the department and give department employees better tools to accomplish their mission. These plans include the following.

Centralize and Improve Policy Development and Coordination

A new Directorate of Policy will be the primary departmentwide coordinator for policies, regulations, and other initiatives; ensure consistency of policy and regulatory development across the department; perform long-range strategic policy planning; assume the policy coordination functions previously performed by the BTS Directorate; and include the Office of International Affairs, Office of Private Sector Liaison, Homeland Security Advisory Council, Office of Immigration Statistics, and the Senior Asylum Officer.

Strengthen Intelligence Functions and Information Sharing

A new Office of Intelligence and Analysis will ensure that information is gathered from all relevant field operations and other parts of the intelligence community, analyzed with a

BOX 2-11

DEPARTMENT OF HOMELAND SECURITY GOAL #7—ORGANIZATIONAL EXCELLENCE

Objective 7.1—Protect confidentiality and date integrity to ensure privacy and security.

Objective 7.2—Integrate legacy services within the department improving efficiency and effectiveness.

Objective 7.3—Ensure effective recruitment, development, compensation, succession management, and leadership of a diverse workforce to provide optimal service at a responsible cost.

Objective 7.4—Improve the efficiency and effectiveness of the department, ensuring taxpayers get value for their tax dollars.

Objective 7.5—Lead and promote e-government modernization and interoperability initiatives.

Objective 7.6—Fully integrate the strategic planning, budgeting, and evaluation processes to maximize performance.

Objective 7.7—Provide excellent customer service to support the mission of the department.

Source: Department of Homeland Security. (2004). *Securing Our Homeland: U.S. Department of Homeland Security Strategic Plan.* Washington, D.C.: U.S. Department of Homeland Security.

mission-oriented focus, informative to senior decision makers, and disseminated to the appropriate federal, state, local, and private-sector partners. It will be led by a chief intelligence officer reporting directly to the secretary. The office is intended to be comprised of analysts within the former Information Analysis directorate and draw on expertise of other department components with intelligence collection and analysis operations.

Improve Coordination and Efficiency of Operations

A new director of Operations Coordination will conduct joint operations across all organizational elements, coordinate incident management activities, and use all resources within the department to translate intelligence and policy into immediate action. The Homeland Security Operations Center, which serves as the nation's nerve center for information sharing and domestic incident management on a 24/7/365 basis, will be a critical part of this new office.

Enhance Coordination and Deployment of Preparedness Assets

The Directorate for Preparedness will consolidate preparedness assets from across the department, facilitate grants and oversee nationwide preparedness efforts supporting first responder training, citizen awareness, public health, infrastructure, and cyber security and

DHS Organizational Chart

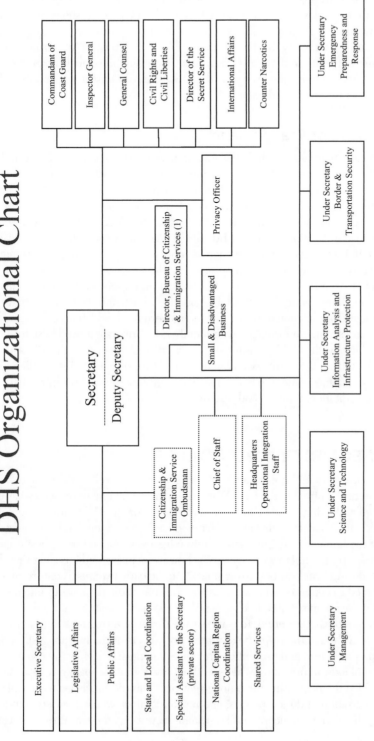

Secretary

Deputy Secretary

- Commandant of Coast Guard
- Inspector General
- General Counsel
- Civil Rights and Civil Liberties
- Director of the Secret Service
- International Affairs
- Counter Narcotics

- Director, Bureau of Citizenship & Immigration Services (1)
- Privacy Officer
- Small & Disadvantaged Business

- Citizenship & Immigration Service Ombudsman
- Chief of Staff
- Headquarters Operational Integration Staff

- Executive Secretary
- Legislative Affairs
- Public Affairs
- State and Local Coordination
- Special Assistant to the Secretary (private sector)
- National Capital Region Coordination
- Shared Services

- Under Secretary Management
- Under Secretary Science and Technology
- Under Secretary Information Analysis and Infrastructure Protection
- Under Secretary Border & Transportation Security
- Under Secretary Emergency Preparedness and Response

August 2004

Homeland Security

ensure proper steps are taken to protect high-risk targets, focus on cyber security and telecommunications, and will include a new Chief Medical Officer, responsible for carrying out the department's responsibilities to coordinate the response to biological attacks. Managed by an under secretary this Directorate will include infrastructure protection, assets of the Office of State and Local Government Coordination and Preparedness responsible for grants, training, and exercises, the U.S. Fire Administration, and the Office of National Capitol Region Coordination.[82]

Other Department Realignments

Other department realignments include the attempt to improve National Response and Recovery Efforts by focusing FEMA on its core functions. FEMA will report directly to the Secretary of Homeland Security. To strengthen and enhance our nation's ability to respond to and recover from man-made or natural disasters, FEMA will now focus on its historic and vital mission of response and recovery. It will integrate the Federal Air Marshal Service (FAMS) into Broader Aviation Security Efforts. The Federal Air Marshal Service will be moved from the ICE bureau to the TSA to increase operational coordination and strengthen efforts to meet this common goal of aviation security. The DHS will merge Legislative and Intergovernmental Affairs. This new Office of Legislative and Intergovernmental Affairs will merge certain functions among the Office of Legislative Affairs and the Office of State and Local Government Coordination to streamline intergovernmental relations efforts and better share homeland security information with members of Congress as well as state and local officials. And finally, the DHS plans to assign the Office of Security to the Management Directorate. The Office of Security will be moved to return oversight of that office to the Under Secretary for Management to better manage information systems, contractual activities, security accreditation, training, and resources.[83]

HOMELAND SECURITY AND POLICE

Just as the American federal bureaucracy was forced to realign itself in the wake of World War II with America's entry into the Cold War, the American federal bureaucracy has once again found itself realigning to fight a new war, a war on terrorism. The history of homeland security provides the perspective that although the federal government has been concerned about securing the homeland, the ultimate question has centered on how to best organize for such a complex problem. How we organize is how we manage, and it is clear that there has been much debate over how best to organize.[84] In the early twentieth century, much of the debate seemed to center on who was most responsible, the federal government or the state and local governments. Later, in the post–World War II era, it appeared that the debate centered around whether or not to combine the threat of terrorism with the threat of natural disasters. Although the response and recovery aspects of the two are vastly similar, the planning, preparedness, and prevention are not. Some presidents saw the two as highly related and combined the functions, whereas others saw them as separate responsibilities and, hence, divided the responsibilities among agencies. This ultimately led to the splintering and decentralization of duties, powers, and responsibilities, which resulted in little cohesion among the various concepts of homeland security. Although President Carter

Department of Homeland Security Organization Chart
(proposed end state)

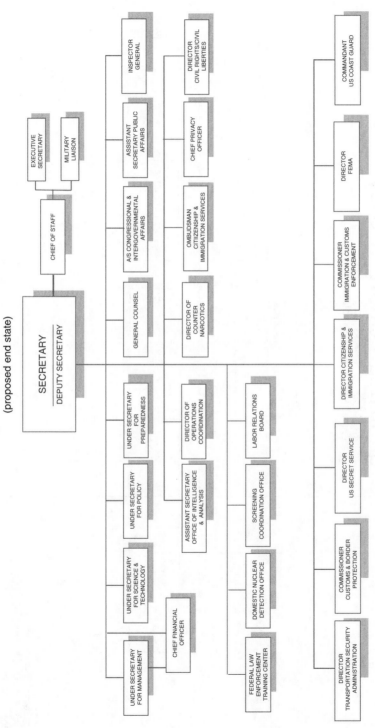

SECRETARY / DEPUTY SECRETARY

CHIEF OF STAFF

EXECUTIVE SECRETARY

MILITARY LIAISON

INSPECTOR GENERAL

ASSISTANT SECRETARY PUBLIC AFFAIRS

DIRECTOR CIVIL RIGHTS/CIVIL LIBERTIES

A/S CONGRESSIONAL & INTERGOVERNMENTAL AFFAIRS

CHIEF PRIVACY OFFICER

OMBUDSMAN CITIZENSHIP & IMMIGRATION SERVICES

GENERAL COUNSEL

DIRECTOR OF COUNTER NARCOTICS

UNDER SECRETARY FOR MANAGEMENT

UNDER SECRETARY FOR SCIENCE & TECHNOLOGY

UNDER SECRETARY FOR POLICY

UNDER SECRETARY FOR PREPAREDNESS

CHIEF FINANCIAL OFFICER

ASSISTANT SECRETARY OFFICE OF INTELLIGENCE & ANALYSIS

DIRECTOR OF OPERATIONS COORDINATION

FEDERAL LAW ENFORCEMENT TRAINING CENTER

DOMESTIC NUCLEAR DETECTION OFFICE

SCREENING COORDINATION OFFICE

LABOR RELATIONS BOARD

DIRECTOR TRANSPORTATION SECURITY ADMINISTRATION

COMMISSIONER CUSTOMS & BORDER PROTECTION

DIRECTOR US SECRET SERVICE

DIRECTOR CITIZENSHIP & IMMIGRATION SERVICES

COMMISSIONER IMMIGRATION & CUSTOMS ENFORCEMENT

DIRECTOR FEMA

COMMANDANT US COAST GUARD

07-27-05

Homeland Security

101

Department of Homeland Security
Organization Chart—Policy
(proposed end state)

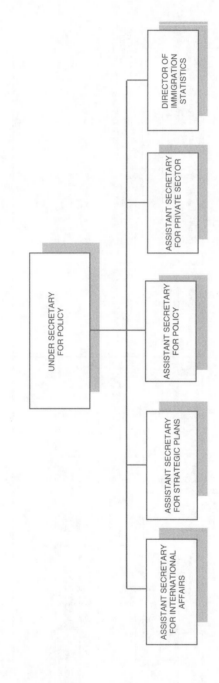

07-13-05

102

Department of Homeland Security
Organization Chart—Preparedness

(proposed end state)

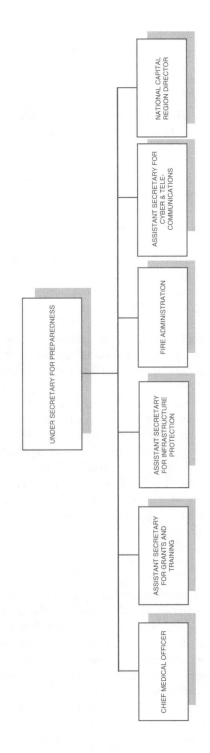

```
                    UNDER SECRETARY FOR PREPAREDNESS
    ┌──────────────┬──────────────┬──────────────┬──────────────┬──────────────┐
CHIEF MEDICAL   ASSISTANT      ASSISTANT      FIRE           ASSISTANT      NATIONAL
OFFICER         SECRETARY      SECRETARY      ADMINISTRATION  SECRETARY FOR  CAPITAL
                FOR GRANTS AND FOR INFRA-                     CYBER & TELE-  REGION DIRECTOR
                TRAINING       STRUCTURE                      COMMUNICATIONS
                               PROTECTION
```

07-13-05

Homeland
Security

brought the various agencies together under FEMA, this centralized agency would take over a decade before it became fully capable in its ability to respond to disasters. And despite FEMA's admirable response to the September 11th attacks, it was clear that America's needs for securing the homeland far exceeded FEMA's capabilities.

In the 1990s, with several terrorists attacks on America's assets and interests, policies for securing the homeland were advocated. However, according to John Kingdon, three streams must converge together for action to be taken.[85] These three streams are the problem stream, the political stream, and the policy stream. Regarding terrorism and homeland security, the problem stream did exist and was identified by researchers, analysts, and Congressional staffers who work on public policy issues. These same people also generated policy solutions to the terrorism problem, which circulated among those on Capitol Hill. However, what was lacking was the political stream that would create the impetus for acting on the policies to address the problems. September 11th, sadly, created the political stream that galvanized the public and demanded action. As the three streams merged, Congress and the president were able to secure the passage of several comprehensive bills, including the USA PATRIOT Act and the Homeland Security Act of 2002.

The impact of these broad pieces of legislation is still being worked out. The USA PATRIOT Act gave sweeping powers to law enforcement to pursue terrorists, would-be terrorists, and those that finance and support terrorism. The controversy over whether the laws went too far and invaded civil rights or simply did not go far enough aside, the majority of the act's provisions that were due to sunset on December 31, 2005, apparently will be renewed,[86] for as of March 2006, Congress had only left to workout differences between the Senate and House renewal bills. And despite the sweeping laws that were implemented by the act, law enforcement officials are still determining how best to use these new powers to fight terrorism. Equally, despite the passage of the Homeland Security Act of 2002 and the creation of the DHS, the federal bureaucratic structure continues to reorganize. And, more specifically, the DHS is still reorganizing to enhance its capabilities, as is evidenced by the six-point agenda released July 2005.[87] The DHS is still trying to determine how best to organize to secure the homeland. This then begs the question, if the federal bureaucracy is still busy trying to organize itself, where does that leave state and local police and their role in homeland security? That is the subject of the next three chapters.

CONCLUSION

Historically, state and local governments have played a role in protecting the homeland, albeit not a role that has been consistently defined. In the aftermath of September 11th, there has been a near consensus that state and local police will play a role in homeland security, but that role has also been ill defined. Legislative acts such as the USA PATRIOT Act and the Homeland Security Act all cite the role of state and local police and have established numerous liaison positions, operations centers, and various entities to work with the agencies, but like the Department of Homeland Security, it is a mosaic of plans and actions, rather than a unified concept. Therefore, it is the intent of the next three chapters to draw on this mosaic to try and clarify the role of the police in homeland security. Specifically, the next three chapters will attempt to identify the strategic, operational, and tactical roles of state and local police agencies in homeland security.

ENDNOTES

1. United States Constitution. Article 4, Section 4. According to James Madison's notes, there was actually much debate over this specific clause during the Constitutional Convention. Luther Martin, a delegate to the convention from Maryland, "opposed it as giving a dangerous and unnecessary power. The consent of the State ought to precede the introduction of any extraneous force whatever." In addition, "Mr. Gerry was against letting loose the myromidons of the United States on a State without its own consent. The States will be the best Judges in such cases. More blood would have been spilt in Massachusetts in the late insurrection, if the General authority had intermeddled." Gouverneur Morris of Pennsylvania is also reported to have remarked, "We are acting a very strange part. We first form a strong man to protect us, and at the same time wish to tie his hands behind him." Finally, George Mason remarked, "If the General Government should have no right to suppress rebellions against particular States, it will be a bad situation indeed."

2. The state legislature was preferred to make the decision of calling for federal assistance because it was feared that a future insurrection might occur by way of a despotic governor attempting to assume dictatorial powers over the people of that state.

3. Cronin, T. E., Cronin, T. Z., and Milakovich, M. E. (1981). *U.S. v. Crime in the Streets.* Bloomington: Indiana University Press, p. 2; Mahoney, B. 1976. *The Politics of the Safe Streets Act, 1965–1973: A Case Study in Evolving Federalism and the National Legislative Process.* Ph.D. Dissertation, Columbia University, p. 12. See also the discussion by Hamilton in Federalist Papers Number 74, in Rossiter, C. (1961). *The Federalist Papers.* New York: New American Library, pp. 447–449.

4. Rossiter, C. (1961). *The Federalist Papers.* New York: New American Library, p. 276.

5. Rossiter, C. (1961). *The Federalist Papers.* New York: New American Library, p. 226.

6. Rossiter, C. (1961). *The Federalist Papers.* New York: New American Library, p. 120.

7. Hamilton would also state, in speaking before the New York Ratifying Convention on June 28, 1788, ". . . but the laws of Congress are restricted to a certain sphere, and when they depart from this sphere, they are no longer supreme or binding. In the same manner the states have certain independent powers, in which their laws are supreme: for example, in making and executing laws concerning the punishment of certain crimes, such as murder, theft, etc., the states cannot be controlled." In addition he would also explain, "the state officers will ever be important, because they are necessary and useful. Their powers are such as are extremely interesting among the people; such as affect their property, their liberty, and life. What is more important than the administration of justice and the executive of the civil and criminal laws?"

8. Friedman, L. M. (1993). *Crime and Punishment in American History.* New York: Basic Books, p. 262.

9. Calder, J. D. (1978). *Presidents and Crime Control: Some Limitations on Executive Police Making.* Ph.D. Dissertation, Claremont University. Calder explains that these categories are purposely broad and that they were derived from reading several historical accounts, by noted historians and political scientists, of presidential intervention and justifications for such intervention.

10. The Tennessee Emergency Management Agency. (2005). "Tennessee Civil Defense History." Available online at http://www.tnema.org/Archives/EMHistory/TNCDHistory10.htm downloaded June 15, 2005.

11. *ibid.*

12. McCullough, D. (1987). *The Johnstown Flood*. New York: Simon & Schuster.

13. Oliver, W. M. (2003). *The Law & Order Presidency*. Upper Saddle River, NJ: Prentice Hall.

14. The Tennessee Emergency Management Agency. (2005). "Tennessee Civil Defense History." Available online at http://www.tnema.org/Archives/EMHistory/TNCD History10.htm; downloaded June 15, 2005.

15. National Archives and Records Administration. (2005). *Records of the Council of National Defense (CND)*. Available online at http://www.archives.gov/research_room/federal_records_guide/print_friendly.html?page=council_of_national_defense_rg062_content.html&title=NARA%20%7C%20Research%20Room%20%7C%2 0Guide%20to%20Records%20of%20the%20Council%20of%20National%20De fense%20%5BCND%5D; downloaded July 12, 2005.

16. Primary Documents: D F Houston on U.S. War Readiness, 1917. (2004). Available online at http://www.firstworldwar.com/source/uspreparation_houston.htm; downloaded on July 12, 2005. The original source is listed as Source Records of the Great War, Vol. V, ed. Charles F. Horne, National Alumni 1923.

17. The Tennessee Emergency Management Agency. (2005). "Tennessee Civil Defense History." Available online at http://www.tnema.org/Archives/EMHistory/TNCDHistory10.htm; downloaded June 15, 2005. See also the Encyclopedia of Civil Defense and Emergency Management. (2005). Available online at http://www.richmond.edu/ ~wgreen/ ECDnatdefcounI.html; downloaded July 12, 2005.

18. The Tennessee Emergency Management Agency. (2005). "Tennessee Civil Defense History." Available online at http://www.tnema.org/Archives/EMHistory/ TNCDHistory10.htm; downloaded June 15, 2005.

19. Drabek, T. E. (1991). "The Evolution of Emergency Management." In *Emergency Management: Principles and Practices for Local Government*. Edited by Drabek, T. E. and Hoetmer, G. J., 3–29, Washington, D.C.: International City Management Association.

20. Hunter, L. C. (1959). *Organization of the Federal Government for National Security*. Available online through the National Defense University Library at http:// www.ndu.edu/library/ic3/L60-039.pdf; downloaded July 14, 2005.

21. Neel, C. H. (1959). *Organization for National Security*. Available online through the National Defense University Library at http://www.ndu.edu/library/ic2/L51-010.pdf; downloaded July 14, 2005.

22. Executive Order 10186, Establishing the Federal Civil Defense Administration in the Office for Emergency Management of the Executive Office of the President. Signed: December 1, 1950 by President Harry S Truman. Reference Federal Register page and date: 15 FR 8557, December 5, 1950. Available online at http://www.archives.gov/ federal_register/executive_orders/1950.html

23. The American Experience. (1999). *Race for the Superbomb*. Interview with historian Laura McEnaney. Transcripts available online at http://www.pbs.org/wgbh/ amex/bomb/ filmmore/reference/interview/index.html; downloaded July 13, 2005.

24. 64 Stat. 1245

25. Sylves, R. and Cumming, W. R. (2004). "FEMA's Path to Homeland Security: 1979–2003." *Journal of Homeland Security and Emergency Management* 1, no. 2: 1–21.

26. The Tennessee Emergency Management Agency. (2005). "Tennessee Civil Defense History." Available online at http://www.tnema.org/Archives/EMHistory/TNCDHistory10.htm; downloaded June 15, 2005.

27. Drabek, T. E. (1991). "The Evolution of Emergency Management." In *Emergency Management: Principles and Practices for Local Government.* Edited by Drabek, T. E. and Hoetmer, G. J., 3–29, Washington, D.C.: International City Management Association.

28. Sylves, R. and Cumming, W. R. (2004). "FEMA's Path to Homeland Security: 1979–2003." *Journal of Homeland Security and Emergency Management* 1, no. 2: 1–21.

29. Federal Emergency Management Agency. (2003). *This is FEMA: A Look at the Federal Government's Primary Disaster Response and Recovery Resource.* Washington, D.C.: Department of Homeland Security.

30. The Tennessee Emergency Management Agency. (2005). "Tennessee Civil Defense History." Available online at http://www.tnema.org/Archives/ EMHistory/ TNCDHistory10.htm; downloaded June 15, 2005.

31. Federal Emergency Management Agency. (2005). *FEMA History.* Available online at http://www.fema.gov/about/history.shtm; downloaded July 14, 2005.

32. General Accounting Office. (1993). *Disaster Assistance: DOD's Support for Hurricanes Andrew and Iniki and Typhoon Omar.* Available online at www.gao.gov/cgi-bin/getrpt? NSIAD-93-180; downloaded July 14, 2005; General Accounting Office. (1993). *Disaster Management: Improving the Nation's Response to Catastrophic Disasters.* Available online at http://archive.gao.gov/t2pbat5/149631.pdf; downloaded July 14, 2005.

33. Drabek, T. E. (1991). "The Evolution of Emergency Management." In *Emergency Management: Principles and Practices for Local Government.* Edited by Drabek, T. E. and Hoetmer, G. J., 3–29. Washington, D.C.: International City Management Association.

34. Osborne, D. and Gaebler, T. (1992). *Reinventing Government.* New York: Addison Wesley Publishing Company.

35. Sylves, R. & Cumming, W. R. (2004). "FEMA's Path to Homeland Security: 1979–2003." *Journal of Homeland Security and Emergency Management* 1, no. 2: 1–21.

36. The Tennessee Emergency Management Agency. (2005). "Tennessee Civil Defense History." Available online at http://www.tnema.org/Archives/EMHistory/TNCDHistory 10.htm; downloaded June 15, 2005.

37. Federal Emergency Management Agency. (2005). *Federal Emergency Management Agency History.* Available online at http://www.fema.gov/about/history.shtm; downloaded July 15, 2005.

38. Allbaugh, J. M. (2001). Testimony by the Director, Federal Emergency Management Agency Before the Committee on Environment and Public Works, U.S. Senate October 16, 2001. Transcript available online at http://www.yale.edu/lawweb/avalon/sept_11/ fema_003.htm; downloaded July 14, 2005.

39. U.S. Northern Command. (2005). U.S. Northern Command Homepage. Available online at http://www.northcom.mil

40. O'Harrow, R., Jr. (2002). "Six Weeks in Autumn." *The Washington Post.* October 27, p. W06. Also available online at http://www.washingtonpost.com

41. *ibid.*

42. *ibid.*

43. *ibid.*

44. *ibid.*

45. The full text of the U.S.A. PATRIOT Act is available online through the Library of Congress at http://thomas.loc.gov/cgi-bin/bdquery/z?d107:h.r.03162.

46. See Doyle, C. (2002). "The USA PATRIOT Act: A Sketch." *CRS Report for Congress,* April 18 and the U.S.A. PATRIOT Act, available online through the Library of Congress at http://thomas.loc.gov/cgi-bin/bdquery/z?d107:h.r.03162.

47. Dempsey, J. X. (2005). "Patriot Act: Checks are Needed to Protect Rights." *National Public Radio Homepage.* Available online at http://www.npr.org/templates/story/ story.php? storyId=4763647; downloaded on July 29, 2005.

48. McDonald, H. (2005). "Patriot Act: Let Investigator's Do Their Job." *National Public Radio Homepage.* Available online at http://www.npr.org/templates/story/story.php?storyId= 4763326; downloaded July 29, 2005.

49. Doyle, C. (2002). "The USA PATRIOT Act: A Sketch." *CRS Report for Congress,* April 18. And the U.S.A. PATRIOT Act, available online through the Library of Congress at http://thomas.loc.gov/cgi-bin/bdquery/z?d107:h.r.03162:

50. See Doyle, C. (2005). "USA PATRIOT Act Sunset: A Sketch." *CRS Report for Congress,* June 29; Doyle, C. (2005). "USA PATRIOT Act Sunset: Provisions That Expire on December 31, 2005." *CRS Report for Congress,* June 29; National Public Radio. (2005). "Debating the Patriot Act." Available online at http://www.npr.org/templates/story/ story.php? storyId=4759727&sourceCode=gaw; downloaded July 29, 2005.

51. Relyea, H. C. (2002). "Homeland Security: Department Organization and Management." *CRS Report for Congress,* August 7.

52. *ibid.*

53. Bush, G. W. (2002). "President Bush Signs Homeland Security Act." White House Homepage. Available online at http://www.whitehouse.gov/news/releases/2002/11/ print/20021125-6.html#; downloaded August 9, 2005.

54. Department of Homeland Security. (2005). *Homeland Security Act of 2002.* Available online at http://www.dhs.gov/dhspublic/display?theme=46&content=410; White House. (2002). "Analysis for the Homeland Security Act of 2002." *White House Homepage.* Available online at http://www.whitehouse.gov/deptofhomeland/analysis/hsl-bill-analysis.pdf; downloaded August 9, 2005.

55. *ibid.*

56. *ibid.*

57. *ibid.*

58. *ibid.*

59. *ibid.*

60. *ibid.*

61. *ibid*

62. Department of Homeland Security. (2004). *Securing Our Homeland: U.S. Department of Homeland Security Strategic Plan.* Available online at http://www.dhs.gov/interweb/ assetlibrary/DHS_StratPlan_FINAL_spread.pdf; downloaded January 14, 2005.

63. Department of Homeland Security. (2005). *Department of Homeland Security Homepage.* Available online at http://www.dhs.gov/dhspublic/index.jsp; downloaded August 2, 2005.

64. *ibid.*

65. *ibid.*

66. Transportation Security Administration. (2005). *Transportation Security Administration Homepage.* Available online at http://www.tsa.gov/public/; downloaded August 12, 2005.

67. Federal Law Enforcement Training Center. (2005). *Federal Law Enforcement Training Center Homepage.* Available online at http://www.fletc.gov/; downloaded on August 10, 2005.

68. Federal Emergency Management Administration. (2005). *Federal Emergency Management Administration Homepage.* Available online at http://www.fema.gov/; downloaded August 4, 2005.
69. Department of Homeland Security. (2005). *Department of Homeland Security Homepage.* Available online at http://www.dhs.gov/dhspublic/index.jsp; downloaded August 2, 2005.
70. Terrorist Threat Integration Center. (2005). *Terrorist Threat Integration Center Homepage.* Available online at http://www.fas.org/irp/agency/ttic/; downloaded August 12, 2005.
71. Department of Homeland Security. (2005). *Department of Homeland Security Homepage.* Available online at http://www.dhs.gov/dhspublic/index.jsp; downloaded August 2, 2005.
72. *ibid.*
73. *ibid.*
74. *ibid.*
75. *ibid.*
76. The Maritime Transportation Security Act of 2002. *U.S. Coast Guard Homepage.* Available online at http://www.uscg.mil/hq/g-m/mp/pdf/MTSA.pdf; downloaded August 12, 2005.
77. U.S. Coast Guard. (2002). *Maritime Strategy for Homeland Security.* Available online at http://www.uscg.mil/news/reportsandbudget/Maritime_strategy/USCG_Maritme_Strategy.pdf; downloaded August 12, 2005.
78. U.S. Coast Guard. (2005). *U.S. Coast Guard Homepage.* Available online at http:// www .uscg.mil/USCG.shtm; downloaded August 12, 2005.
79. U.S. Secret Service. (2005). *U.S. Secret Service Homepage.* Available online at http://www.secretservice.gov/; downloaded August 12, 2005.
80. Department of Homeland Security. (2005). *Department of Homeland Security Homepage.* Available online at http://www.dhs.gov/dhspublic/index.jsp; downloaded August 2, 2005.
81. United States Citizenship and Immigration Services. (2005). *Department of Homeland Security Homepage.* Available online at http://www.dhs.gov/dhspublic/index.jsp; downloaded August 12, 2005.
82. Department of Homeland Security. (2005). *Department of Homeland Security Homepage.* Available online at http://www.dhs.gov/dhspublic/index.jsp; downloaded August 2, 2005.
83. *ibid.*
84. Gortner, H. F., Mahler, J., and Nicholson, J. B. (1997). *Organization Theory: A Public Perspective.* 2nd ed. Fort Worth, TX: Harcourt Brace College Publishers.
85. Kingdon, J. C. (1995). *Agendas, Alternatives, and Public Policies.* 2nd ed. New York: HarperCollins College Publishers.
86. Barret, T. (2005). "House Approves Renewal of Patriot Act." *CNN Homepage.* Available online at http://www.cnn.com/2005/POLITICS/07/21/patriot.act/; downloaded August 16, 2005; Lichtbu, E. (2005). "Congress Nears Deal to Renew Antiterror Law." *The New York Times,* November 17, p. 17.
87. Department of Homeland Security. (2005). Department of Homeland Security Homepage. Available online at http://www.dhs.gov/dhspublic/index.jsp; downloaded August 2, 2005.

3

Terrorism: Its Origin and History

John Weinzierl

The third chapter outlines the history of terrorism. Although living with the threat of terrorist attacks is a recent development in U.S. society, many parts of the world regard terrorism as part of the political landscape. Further, the use of violence to achieve political and/or religious goals dates back to the first century of the common era. In this chapter, Weinzierl provides historical context for understanding contemporary terrorism. One of the most compelling questions posed to the reader asks whether terrorism is effective. This essay reveals not only the longstanding use of violence as a political strategy, but the inadequacy of conventional means to stop terrorism. In this examination of the usefulness of violence as a political tool, the author provides an accessible and informative survey of the modern history of the Middle East.

On September 11, 2001, the United States experienced the brutal reality of terrorism. In the aftermath, many asked how could this happen. Is this a new kind of war and, if so, can we win? However, what many Americans do not realize is that these same questions have been asked for generations because terrorism is not new. It has a history that has been all too often ignored. Perhaps this is because terrorism has resurfaced in the late twentieth century after a period of relative calm. Before the challenges of terrorism can be understood, it is important to establish a historical context.

In addition to providing a historical perspective, the second objective of this chapter is to investigate the effectiveness of terrorism. History teaches us that terrorism is more effective today than ever before. As a result, an explanation of the methods, motivations, and objectives of contemporary terrorist groups—in particular, Hezbollah, Hamas, and al-Qaeda—is necessary. The future implications of terrorism are horrifying when one considers the ever-expanding availability of chemical, biological, and nuclear weapons. Can this new trend be stopped? The vast military and economic resources of the United States are intimidating and effective if brought to bear against a conventional military foe, however, international terrorist groups and networks do not fit this model.

DEFINITIONS

Arriving at a generally accepted definition of terrorism is not easy. Is it a term used by Western nations to condemn and define enemies of the state? Is terrorism just something you recognize and label when you see it, like bombings, assassinations, kidnappings, and skyjackings? Or, to quote the now common phrase, "Is one person's terrorist another person's freedom fighter?" Despite the difficulty in arriving at a precise definition, there are threads of commonality. Acts of terrorism are intended to evoke a response and generate fear from an audience much wider than the immediate victim. The psychological component of seeking to create fear as a primary goal, whether in an individual, a community, or a state, is essential to the concept of terrorism. It is difficult to measure this sense of terror, but what is clear is that there are advantages to be gained from it. Terrorism is also a potent way not only to communicate, but to send a message in an age dominated by the mass media (Weinberg & Davis, 1989, pp. 1–6).

Another important characteristic of terrorism is that it usually involves a well-planned, organized action, not a random, impulsive act of violence. Al-Qaeda has demonstrated this fact and set a new standard for terrorist effectiveness. Another element that needs to be understood is that terrorism is a feasible method of combat for groups and states that would not stand a chance in a conventional war against a particular opponent. In this respect terrorism provides a low-cost, low-risk, and potentially high-yield alternative. Lastly, a disturbing characteristic of terrorism, especially contemporary terrorism, is that it goes beyond the accepted rules in regard to humanitarian constraints. In other words, terrorist attacks cause the death of innocent people. This is above all true when considering the attacks of suicide bombers. Of course, this disregard of human life gives terrorism its shock power (Hoffman, 1998, p. 40).

Below are two definitions of terrorism. The first is official, while the second definition is scholarly. The second definition in particular tightly defines terrorism's major characteristics.

> Terrorism is the threat of violence and the use of fear to coerce, persuade, and gain public attention (National Advisory Committee, 1976, p. 3).

> Political terrorism is the use, or threat of use, of violence by an individual or a group, whether acting for or in opposition to established authority, when such action is designed to create extreme anxiety and/or fear-inducing effects in a target group larger than the immediate victims with the purpose of coercing that group into acceding to the political demands of the perpetrators (Wardlaw, 1982, p. 16).

Terrorism is not an ideology but a strategy that may be used by individuals, groups, or states for different purposes. It is a strategy that is often confused with guerrilla warfare. Although both rely upon unconventional military means with which to attack their opponents, there are differences between the two. Guerrilla war is rural in character, with guerrilla fighters establishing bases far from the reach of state power. Guerrilla war is typically a conflict between the insurgent guerrillas and the government. In the early phases of hostilities, guerrillas may turn to the strategy of terrorism to bring attention to their cause and show government vulnerability; however, as the chances for success improve, terrorism is likely to be used less. Ultimately, with popular support mounting, a "people's army" will rise up and defeat the government's regular forces and seize control of the state (Crozier, 1960, pp. 159–191).

The strategy of terrorism, on the other hand, avoids attacking government forces directly, preferring instead to commit acts of violence against unarmed civilians in hopes of achieving political change indirectly through fear and coercion. Terrorism, unlike guerrilla warfare, is typically an urban phenomenon, simply because cities offer targets that are more dramatic: public buildings, government apparatus, vulnerable populations, and full media coverage, all of which serve to generate publicity and magnify the crucial element of fear.

ORIGIN AND HISTORY

The earliest forms of terrorism, drawn from Jewish and Muslim histories, are religiously motivated and seek to influence not only the masses, but also God. Specifically, early terrorism focuses on the roles of the Sicarii, an extreme Jewish Zealot sect, in provoking a revolt against Rome (66–70 A.D.), and the Assassins, a radical Shiite Ismaili sect, which waged a campaign aimed at the purification of Islam for almost two centuries (1090–1275 A.D.) (Weinberg & Davis, 1989, p. 19).

Roman-Jewish historian Josephus Flavius tells of the Sicarii's unorthodox tactics, such as attacking enemies in broad daylight, preferably when crowds gathered on holidays in Jerusalem. Their weapon of choice was the dagger (*Sicarii* means dagger-wielders), which was hidden under the coat. It was thought that the crowd provided a sort of cover or anonymity for the assassin, who would simply blend in after the murder was committed (Laqueur, 2001, p. 7). Their actions created an environment of fear where no one was to be trusted and everyone was feared. The message of the Zealots–Sicarii was that all fellow Jews who accommodated with the Romans would be killed. Zealots mainly assassinated other Jewish moderates, but Greeks living in Judea and Roman rulers were targets as well. Their immediate goal was to eliminate Roman influence, but their ultimate goal was to initiate the coming of the Messiah by forcing an apocalyptic confrontation between Rome and the Jewish nation. The Zealots believed that by provoking such a crisis they could force God's direct intervention to save the people of Israel. Their God was a crucial part of the wider audience they were trying to influence.

The desired revolt began in 66: however, by 70 A.D. it was a catastrophe with thousands of Jews dead, the second Temple in ruins, and the Jewish state destroyed. The last of the Zealots fled and took refuge on top of Masada near the Dead Sea, where they committed mass suicide in 73 A.D. rather than surrender to the Romans besieging them. Like many religious extremists today, the Sicarii embraced their martyrdom as something joyful. Although the Zealots never witnessed the coming of the Messiah, the memory of their struggle and deep commitment persisted.

The medieval Assassins represent another religious sect that used terrorism in the eleventh and twelfth centuries. Some of the features of this movement remind one of contemporary terrorist movements. Their origins are found in the division among the followers of the Shiite tradition and in particular with the formation of a sect known as the Ismalis (centered in modern day Israel, Syria, and Iran). Followers of this group believed in the need for a purification of the Muslim community in order to hasten the arrival of the

Imam "the heir of the Prophet, the Chosen of God, and the sole rightful leader of mankind," who would establish a new and just society (Lewis, 1967, p. 27).

Outnumbered by the orthodox Sunni Muslim rulers, the Assassins sought to achieve their ends by unconventional means. Their leader, Hassan I Sabah, developed a strategy of using isolated mountain strongholds as bases to stage protracted campaigns of terror against Sunni religious and political leaders. According to the Assassins, these Sunni leaders had usurped leadership of Islam and corrupted its meaning (Weinberg & Davis, 1989, p. 21).

Acting as instruments of God, the Assassins would seek out and kill "enemy" leaders, despite the certainty of their own death. Using a short dagger, they would kill the enemy and, rather than flee, the Assassin would calmly await capture and execution. Most of the victims were Sunnis, but some Christians were taken as well, the most celebrated being Marquis Conrad of Montferrat, ruler of the kingdom of Jerusalem, who was killed by a group of Assassins disguised as monks. To counter the awe and respect these bold attacks generated among the common people, the Abbasids Arab dynasty spread rumors that the Assassins were not acting of their own accord but were really acting under the influence of hashish.

Overall, the impact of the Assassins was insignificant. They made few converts and never succeeded in reforming the Islamic faith. One of the greatest legacies of terror left behind by the Assassins was the origin of the suicide mission and the strategy of disguise or deception. For his martyrdom, the devout Assassin was promised admission to paradise—the same reward that motivates members of al-Qaeda, Hamas, Hezbollah, and other Islamic extremists today. The legends of the Assassins deeply impressed contemporaries and subsequent generations.

Throughout the Middle Ages and the subsequent religious wars of the fifteenth and sixteenth centuries in Europe, there was tremendous violence in which religious and political leaders were killed: however, there are no examples of terrorism equaling the sustained campaign of the Zealots or the Assassins. Perhaps one exception was the fanatical Anabaptist groups who represented the left wing of the sixteenth-century Reformation. Besides challenging infant baptism, they emphasized adherence to scripture and strict church discipline as ranking higher than the law of the state. The most spectacular example of Anabaptist success was the seizing of Münster (1533–1535) and the establishment of the "Kingdom of Saints." After gaining control of the city, the Anabaptists waged a campaign of terror against its "heretical" inhabitants in order to establish God's kingdom. "Christ will give the sword and revenge to them, the Anabaptists, to punish all sins, stamp out all governments, communize all property and slay those who do not permit themselves to be rebaptized" (Cohn, 1970, p. 255). This violence did much to discredit the movement and only redoubled the efforts of both Roman Catholics and Protestants to crush the movement.

So far, we have considered the earliest manifestations of terrorism associated with extreme religious beliefs. These terrorist activities, directed at both divine and human audiences, were intended to improve human existence both politically and religiously. But the purposes of these groups, though religiously inspired, were not exclusively religious in objective. Whether it was to seize political control or maintain it, overthrow the dominant wealthy class, or rid an area of Roman influence, secular objectives were inevitably part of the religious agenda. Much like the Islamic extremist groups today (Hezbollah, Hamas, al-Qaeda, and others), the religious terrorists of the ancient and medieval period attempted to modify the political order in the name of an ultimately religious purpose. There can be no doubt, however, that the members of these sects believed and saw their activities as serving God's will (Weinberg & Davis, 1989, p. 23).

MODERN TERRORISM

The late eighteenth century saw the nature of terrorism change with the coming of the French Revolution. The "Reign of Terror" did not initiate the Revolution but maintained and protected it from counterrevolution by spreading fear through violence. "The Terror" was a policy carried out by the French state and is an example of terrorism from above, or state terrorism. The state terrorism of the French Revolution pales in comparison to that practiced by Nazi Germany and Stalinist Russia, but nonetheless it established a precedent in the history of terrorism.

The French Revolution and the Terror were not legitimized in the name of God, but in the name of the *people*. With this concept, the motivational foundations for terrorism changed dramatically. In the century following the events in France, revolution against the established order was often justified by its proponents in the name of the people, the masses, or the proletariat. Like God for the religious fanatic terrorists, the people's will came to be viewed as transcendent—a substitute for God, in whose name everything was justifiable. With these developments came new definitions of citizen and state, and concepts such as nationalism and self-determination. All of this helped establish an intellectual climate that would give rise to the more radical political ideologies of Marx and Bakunin. In short, the French Revolution sparked an intellectual revolution that transformed terrorism from a religious to a predominantly secular phenomenon (Weinberg & Davis, 1989, pp. 24–25).

Modern non–state-sponsored terrorism, or terrorism from below, emerged during the last third of the nineteenth century because liberal, revolutionary changes failed to materialize. Frustration mounted as the revolutions of 1830 and 1848 failed to bring sweeping changes—Russia remained an autocracy controlled by the Czar, the French Republic was perverted into empire, and Germany remained unchanged. In addition, the masses seemed apathetic and the proletariat never rose up as Marx said they would. Some felt that terrorism could reignite the flame to unleash social or national revolution (Weinberg & Davis, 1989, p. 26).

Czarist Russia offers the first manifestations, both in theory and practice. The Russians Michael Bakunin and Sergey Nechayev published *Revolutionary Catechism* (1869), which provided an idealized guide that would be used by later generations as a model of a terrorist dedicated to his or her cause. According to Bakunin and Nechayev, the terrorist was a lost soul without an identity or ties to family and friends. The terrorist had broken with society and its laws and conventions and was consumed with only one passion: the revolution. All had to be sacrificed for the revolutionary cause. Reminiscent of Assassin tactics, the *Catechism* advised infiltration by way of disguise and dissimulation. The army, the bureaucracy, capitalists, and especially the church and royal palace were all targets. It was recommended to kill the most capable and intelligent enemies first, for such assassinations would inspire fear among society and government. The *Catechism* also defined anarchism by stressing the need for the total destruction of institutions, social structures, and civilization (Westwood, 1993, pp. 109–119).

Modern terrorism was first practiced by the Russian terrorist group Narodnaya Volya, or the People's Will. Its members were basically middle-class student–revolutionaries who had become disenchanted with the indifferent peasants, police repression, czarist tyranny, and absence of constitutional freedoms. In this light, terrorism in Russia was merely a manifestation of a general crisis in Russian society. The People's Will launched a terror campaign in 1878 against the Russian czarist regime culminating in the assassination of the Czar Alexander II in 1881. Instead of reviving the revolution, the only result of these efforts was a new more repressive czar. One can conclude that the terrorism of the People's Will, although a powerful statement of dissatisfaction, was ineffectual and indeed counterproductive. The assassination only shut the door to a political solution of the Russian crisis. The unrest did not spread and most of the members of the People's Will were quickly apprehended and executed. The demise of the People's Will effectively ended terrorism in Russia for two decades (Borcke, 1982, pp. 48–62).

The period between 1878 and 1914 saw a wave of terrorist activities carried out by anarchists (including the activities of the People's Will). They practiced the concept of "propaganda by deed," which believed that the most effective means of propaganda to draw people into the struggle was a violent deed. They felt that workers did not need to read—in other words, the propaganda of the idea had little effect—and violence is what awoke the consciousness, drew attention to, and generated publicity for a cause. Didactic violence would ultimately rally the masses behind the revolution. The deeds of the anarchists preoccupied public opinion, police chiefs, psychologists, and writers all over Europe for many years. Not only were bombs thrown into cafes, theaters, and parades, but there were many attempts on the lives of leading statesmen. U.S. presidents Garfield and McKinley were killed. There were attempts to assassinate Bismarck and Emperor William I of Germany. French President Carnot was killed in 1894; Antonio Canovas, the Spanish prime minister, in 1897; Elizabeth, Empress of Austria in 1898; and King Umberto of Italy in 1900 (Laqueur, 1999, p. 20). These examples, however, were isolated acts of violence and not part of a coordinated campaign of terror. Despite the deeds of violence, the social revolution never came, and in this respect the anarchists failed. Instead of mobilizing the masses, the violent deeds increased passivity, leaving people with the impression that these violent acts were the revolution, not a spark to ignite it (Joll, 1980, pp. 99–129).

Nationalism also became a powerful motive for terrorism in the late nineteenth and early twentieth century. Nationalists who practiced terrorism targeted the multinational empires of Britain, Austria–Hungary, and Ottoman Turkey. The objective was statehood for the respective nationalities under imperial control. Perhaps the most notorious example was the assassination of the Archduke Ferdinand in 1914. Young Gavrilo Princip, part of the Pan-Serbian secret society known as the Black Hand, hoped to further the cause of the southern Slavs by killing the Austrian heir. This act of terrorism precipitated a world war that directly led to the downfall of the Austrian Empire. Viewed in this light, the assassination of the archduke was extremely effective; however, it can be argued that war was inevitable because of the international rivalries (specifically Anglo-German antagonisms) of the time.

Between the world wars a new motive emerged as a major cause of terrorism in Europe. Until World War I, terrorism was mainly a left wing strategy, however, now groups seeking to preserve the status quo or prevent change turned to right wing or reactionary terrorism. The Ku Klux Klan provides an example of such terrorism; founded in 1865, it is still operational today. In Europe many people reacted to the Bolshevik Revolution in Russia (1917) with the fear that communism would take over the world. The objective became the repression of anyone who threatened the status quo: socialists, communists, liberals, and so on. The fascist movement, with its nationalistic, violent, and anticommunist ideology, arose and flourished in this climate. Eventually, the fascist and nazi movements established totalitarian regimes in Italy and Germany respectively. Along with Stalinist Russia, these totalitarian states used terrorism to repress and control the masses. Persecution of Jews, communists, and other "enemies of the state" was typical and ensured submissive compliance among the people (Hoffman, 1998, p. 24). During this period anarchists did not disappear entirely; however, many national terrorist groups derived ideological as well as material support from the fascists.

After World War II, the feared neo-Nazi or neo-Fascist specter never rose from the ashes, and terrorist activities shifted from Europe to North Africa, Middle East, and Asia where anticolonialism and nationalistic sentiments were gathering strength. Violent campaigns were launched by nationalist groups striving for independence. Terrorism had occurred in the Middle East before, but now with the weakening of colonial powers, terrorism only gained momentum. Successes, like the fall of Singapore, demonstrated that the once mighty empires of the West were vulnerable (Laqueur, 1999, p. 23).

In the British mandate of Palestine, Irgun and the Stern Gang (both of which were Zionist paramilitary organizations dedicated to the expulsion of the British forces and the Arab population from Palestine in efforts to establish a Jewish state) escalated their use of terrorism after the British White Paper of 1939, which severely restricted Jewish immigration to the Palestine region. The White Paper effectively closed one of the few remaining avenues of escape for European Jews fleeing the Holocaust (Ovendale, 1999, pp. 77–79).

The leader of Irgun, Menachem Begin, realized that a handful of men and few weapons could never hope to challenge the British Army on the battlefield. Instead, Irgun would launch a terrorist campaign and utilize the urban landscape of Palestine to blend in until the time was right to strike. Begin's objective was not to defeat Britain militarily, but to use terrorism to undermine Britain's prestige and confidence. If it cost the British too much prestige and too many young soldiers to control the mandate of Palestine, Begin was confident that the British public would insist upon withdrawal. Irgun bombed various British offices in Jerusalem, Tel Aviv, and Haifa frequently. The 1946 bombing of Jerusalem's King David Hotel, the site of the British Army headquarters, was the most spectacular operation of Irgun. Ninety-one people were killed in this tragedy that still holds the distinction of one of the world's single most deadly terrorist attacks (Hoffman, 1998, p. 51). Unwilling to enforce military rule, Britain turned Palestine over to the United Nations in 1947. Success vindicated Begin's strategy; the exclusive use of terrorism forced the British from Palestine. Interestingly, Menachem Begin later became prime minister of Israel, thus providing an excellent example of a terrorist leader achieving legitimate political success.

The Israelis were not alone in experiencing success. Mao Tse-tung in China, Ho Chi Minh in Vietnam, and Fidel Castro in Cuba had also emerged victorious in their struggle for national liberation or social revolution. Their strategy for success, unlike

Irgun's terrorist campaign, was a rural-based guerrilla war. Terrorism was used in these struggles, but it played a decidedly secondary role and was not a major factor in determining the outcome.

CONTEMPORARY TERRORISM

Terrorism is one of the greatest threats facing the world today, particularly when one considers the catastrophic potential of coupling a suicide bomber with a weapon of mass destruction (nuclear, biological, or chemical). Unlike war, terrorism is not a relatively constant factor in human history. Its violent outbreaks are unpredictable, sometimes with years, decades, or even centuries elapsing without much activity. It is evident that from the late 1960s to the present we have lived in an active period or a so-called "age of terrorism" (Weinberg & Davis, 1989, pp. 38–47). Many factors have contributed to this reality.

Technological innovation, in a sense, freed terrorism from any geographic or regional constraints. The 1960s saw the introduction of international commercial jet travel and the incredible proliferation of television. Terrorists could now strike at international targets of their choice and in a matter of hours have their message received by a mass audience—a situation undreamed of by the most dedicated Zealot, Assassin, or anarchist. Selecting the 1972 Munich Olympic Games and the 1978 World Cup Soccer tournament in Argentina as terrorist targets was no accident. In both cases, television audiences were estimated to number almost 800 million people (Weinberg & Davis, 1989). News coverage of these terrorist acts, especially when innocent victims were involved, created a major media event.

The ever-increasing use of jet aircraft to carry large numbers of people at great speeds and according to predetermined schedules created a situation vulnerable to skyjackings. Terrorists now had the opportunity to purchase their tickets and travel rapidly to other locations where new unsuspecting target populations could be exploited. Modern advances in communication (satellite/television) and transportation (commercial jet travel) effectively internationalized terrorism. These developments, particularly the emergence of modern communications (and its future development), go along way in explaining why we live in an "age of terrorism" (Weinberg & Davis, 1989).

Another dynamic force changing terrorism was the technological development in weaponry. Cold war competition created ballistic missiles and nuclear powered submarines, but it also yielded a completely new class of small weapons such as plastic explosives, armor-piercing bullets, hand-held rocket launchers, and the miniaturization of other existing weapons (Weinberg & Davis, 1989). Such improvements not only made daggers obsolete but made it easier for terrorists to conceal these weapons until they were ready for use or to detonate explosives from a safe distance. Among other things, the modern commercial jetliner has proven vulnerable to these new developments in explosives. It does not take an accomplished physicist to realize that only a small amount of explosives is needed to bring down an aircraft, while substantial quantities are required for a target on land (an estimated six tons for the 1983 attack on the U.S. Marine headquarters in Beirut). In short, these technological advances in weaponry increased the power of the terrorist to kill and become more difficult to detect.

International cold war competition between the Soviet Union and the United States was an important mechanism in the development of contemporary terrorism. In the 1980s, some regarded terrorism as a calculated means of the communist world to destabilize the West (Sterling, 1983). At the time this seemed plausible and the U.S. government was receptive to this conspiracy theory. By the middle of the decade, however, with a series of suicide bombings directed against many U.S. diplomatic and military targets in the Middle East, it became obvious that more than the Kremlin was funding terrorism. Attention began to shift to Iran, Iraq, Libya, and Syria as states sponsoring terrorism. With this development, one can see weaker states using terrorism as an alternate or "surrogate" form of warfare to inflict significant damage on the great power of the world without the risk of retribution (Hoffman, 1998, p. 27).

Another factor contributing to terrorism today is hostility toward the United States. During and after the cold war many peoples of the world began to perceive the United States as the imperialist power of the modern era. The growth of multinational corporations, the stationing of U.S. troops, and the coercive use of economic sanctions all strengthened this perception. In addition, tremendous differences between the levels of wealth and consumer consumption further accentuated the growing disparity between the developed world and the underdeveloped, or "third-world." Feeling economically exploited by U.S. capitalism, underdeveloped countries increasingly detested the intrusive foreign policy exercised by the United States (Hoffman, 1998, p. 80). Such impressions were destined to spawn feelings of intense antipathy, frustration, and indignation; these are the seeds of terrorism.

Today many frustrated people in third-world countries feel that the United States has so thoroughly monopolized and so formidably consolidated its global standing that there is no means of turning the tables besides terrorism. Terrorism is a ferocious strategy indeed, but many terrorists feel the situation is so irretrievable that any chance of change demands such tactics. No terrorist group—or country, for that matter—can hope to fight and win a conventional war against the United States; terrorism represents a feasible alternative (Baudrillard, 2001).

One of the most distinct features of contemporary terrorism is the resurgence of radical religious movements and terrorism of the extreme right. This should not come as a surprise, because religion was the original motivation for terrorism, as demonstrated by the examples of the Zealots and Assassins. Unfortunately, terrorism generated by religious motivation typically leads to greater bloodshed and destruction. This is especially true where violence is seen as a divine duty. In this situation, the religious terrorist is given unlimited means to legitimize and justify his or her actions. The terrorist feels no longer constrained by temporal morality and respect for fellow humans. The taking of innocent lives or his or her own life is not something to avoid; it is simply a means to a divinely directed end (Hoffman, 1998, p. 88).

TERRORISM IN THE MIDDLE EAST

Throughout history, religious fanaticism and terror are not exclusive to any one religion. Christian cults exist in the United States that spew hate propaganda of white supremacy and anti-Semitism and armed opposition to the federal government. It was precisely this type of attitude that was responsible for the bombing of the federal building in Oklahoma. Judaism also has its extremists. In 1984 Jewish extremists attempted to bomb the Dome on the Rock, one of the holiest sites in Islam; the plot was thwarted by Israeli security. In 1994, a Jewish fundamentalist massacred twenty-nine Muslims in a crowded mosque at Hebron. In 1995, a Jewish extremist assassinated Prime Minister Yitzhak Rabin two years after he signed the Oslo Peace Accords (Wilkinson, 2001, p. 59).

Although the current resurgence of religious terrorism is largely identified with the Muslim and Arab world, it would be ridiculous to associate mainstream Islamic religion with the terrorism of its most extreme elements. It is interesting to point out that, even though the anti-Western attitude of Islamic extremists is important, most violence practiced by extreme Muslims is directed against other Arabs or Muslims. Iraq, Afghanistan, and Algeria are examples of the *jihad* turning inward to destroy domestic evil before turning against the infidel abroad. Having stated this, one cannot overlook the fact that Muslim countries lead the world in terrorist activities. The frequency of Islamic/Arab-inspired terrorism is striking. In the last year alone the activities of Hezbollah, Hamas, and al-Qaeda have shaken Israel and the West to its core. It is interesting to note that of all armed conflict on the globe in 1999, Islam was involved in 80 percent. Of thirteen United Nations peace missions, nine concerned Muslim countries or interests (Laqueur, 1999, p. 129). It is for these reasons that discussion will now focus upon Islamic terrorism.

In the Middle East, discontent revolves around the survival of the Israeli state that was created by a U.N. resolution in 1948. Islamic and specifically Palestinian terrorism grew out of the resistance movement against Israel. There had been attacks against Israeli settlements since the state was created, mainly small raids across the border, but it was only after the Six Days' War of 1967 and the Israeli occupation of the West Bank, Gaza, and the Golan Heights that a major terrorist campaign began. It was after 1967, when a substantial number of Arabs came under Israeli rule, that well-organized terrorist groups with substantial budgets, sophisticated weapons, and their own intelligence services came into being. It can be concluded that the inability of the Arab states to effectively coordinate their military efforts and defeat Israel was a potent catalyst for terrorism in the Middle East (Laqueur, 1999, p. 134).

The Palestinian Liberation Organization (PLO) is an umbrella organization comprising Palestinian political and guerrilla groups. It remains the recognized governing institution of the Palestinian people. Yasser Arafat is not only Chairman of the PLO (since 1969), but founder of Fatah, the military branch and current dominant member of the PLO. The current goals of the PLO are to establish an independent, *secular* Palestinian state on part of historic Palestine liberated from Zionist occupation. The PLO accepts the existence of Israel.

The PLO has engaged in many notorious operations: Munich Olympics of 1972, blowing up jets at Dawson field in Jordan 1970, and other miscellaneous bombings and ambushes. These major operations brought reprisals from both Jordan and Israel; however, the PLO gained a considerable amount of international recognition. After Munich, because of international television broadcasting, the whole world was aware of the Palestinians and their cause. They could no longer be dismissed as insignificant. The PLO brought terrorism to the world and was an example to all future terrorist groups.

With this in mind, the 1980s witnessed the emergence of two of the more well-known extremist groups: Hezbollah in Lebanon and Hamas in Gaza and the occupied territories. Both of these groups are Muslim fundamentalist in origin and have caused far greater problems for Israel than Fatah or any other group. Their emergence was part of the wave of fundamentalism sweeping through the Muslim world, because of the recent success of the revolution in Iran. The Iranian revolution is held up as an example to Muslims worldwide that the West's intrusion into the Middle East can be resisted. The success of this revolution also gave strength to the reassertion of the fundamentalist teachings of the Qur'an (Laqueur, 1999).

Hezbollah, which means "party of God," was directly connected with the victory of Ayatollah Khomeini and his Shiite followers in Iran. The Iranian state helped to found and fund Hezbollah, hoping that this group would export the goals of Iran's successful Islamic revolution to Lebanon and create an exclusively Islamic state there. Another objective of Hezbollah is to drive Israel from the occupied territories. Hezbollah believes it is fighting a defensive struggle sanctioned by God and struggles against what it considers the arrogance and depravity of the West. The United States is perceived as the "great nemesis behind all problems of the region, due to its support for Israel and because it distances itself from all causes of liberty and freedom in the area" (Fadlallah, 1986, pp. 4–13).

Hezbollah was established by a contingent of 2,000 troops (Islamic Revolutionary Guards) sent to Lebanon in the summer of 1982 to expel an international force (Israeli, French, and United States) engaged in the war there. Eventually, Hezbollah gained substantial popular support and established a real political presence in Lebanon. This popular support was achieved by providing social services to its followers, such as schools and medical services. Providing such services has bolstered Hezbollah's image as the champion of the poor and oppressed; however, its sectarian, religious character has prevented it from becoming too powerful in Lebanon, although it has held tremendous sway over the Shiite minority there. It has engaged in a variety of business ventures, including supermarkets, bakeries, drugs, and farming to help finance its terrorist activities. While some of its income comes from wealthy Shiites in Lebanon, most comes from Iran (Laqueur, 1999, p. 137).

In 1983, Hezbollah conducted a lethal terrorist campaign against the Israeli, French, and U.S. military contingents in Lebanon. Its suicide bombings, which used vehicles packed with explosives, included attacks on the U.S. embassy in West Beirut (killing 61 persons), the U.S. Marine camp at Beirut Airport (killing 241), the French contingent's headquarters (killing 74), and the Israelis forces headquarters in Tyre (killing 30). Hezbollah was also responsible for numerous other activities such as hijackings and the keeping of hostages. The effectiveness of Hezbollah, especially during its early days, is impressive. The suicide bombings induced the United States and France to withdraw their forces from Lebanon. However, the ultimate objective of establishing an exclusive Islamic state remains elusive. Hezbollah has remained active during the 1990s, most prominently engaging in border warfare against Israel in south Lebanon. Using rockets and roadside bombs, Hezbollah has made life difficult for Israelis in the north and has continued fighting against Israeli forces in southern Lebanon. In May 2000, Israeli forces withdrew from Lebanon, vindicating the efforts of the Hezbollah guerrilla fighters.

The rise of Hamas was tied to the *intifada* that erupted in 1987. The *intifada* refers to the popular uprising of the Palestinians in the Gaza Strip and the West Bank against the Israeli occupation. This uprising broke out against the backdrop of twenty years of Israeli military occupation, during which the Palestinian population had met with frustrating political, economic, and social deprivation. While the early stages of the uprising involved youngsters throwing stones and taunting Israeli soldiers, it eventually spread and involved organized demonstrations, civil disobedience, and boycotting of Israeli goods and services. The magnitude and resilience of the *intifada* surprised Israel. Daily clashes attracted world media attention, which further fueled the fire of the grassroots movement. The international community began to sympathize with the Palestinian cause and voice concerns about alleged Israeli state terror perpetrated against Palestinians.

Hamas was the driving force behind the *intifada,* and in 1987, it formally declared its existence. Hamas is actually an acronym for the Arabic phrase "Islamic Resistance Movement." From the outset, the Sunni fundamentalist Hamas set a moral and political challenge to the national secular PLO. It insisted in remaining out of the PLO and soon became its primary opposition in the Palestinian political arena. One of the keys to Hamas's popularity is its large-scale welfare arm. Like Hezbollah, Hamas provides educational, medical, and other desperately needed welfare services in impoverished West Bank and Gaza towns, creating a marked contrast with the corrupt and ineffectual image of Arafat's administration (Sela, 1999, pp. 276–280).

Since the conclusion of the Israel–PLO Oslo Agreement in 1993, Hamas, through its armed struggle against Israel, has constituted a serious challenge to the peace process. The PLO's desire to establish a secular Palestinian state and its willingness to compromise and co-exist with Israel was unacceptable to Hamas, which called for nothing less than the complete destruction of the Jewish state. The ultimate goal is to create an Islamic state in all of pre-1948 Palestine (which includes all of Israel). The short-term objective is to drive the Israelis out of all the occupied territories. Hamas believes that the Palestinian struggle is part of the religious duty of *jihad* incumbent on all Muslims (Sela, 1999).

In the mid-1990s in response to the Oslo Agreement, Qassam units (Hamas military/terrorist units) carried out a number of suicide attacks against Israeli targets. Qassam operates entirely on a clandestine basis, and it is believed to have up to 500 young volunteers for suicide missions. Lack of resources, Israeli counterterrorism, and PLO authority, however, hampered their efforts. Not ready to fight the PLO as well as Israel, in the summer of 1997, Hamas made it known it would cooperate with Arafat. Although it will not abandon suicide attacks against Israel, it has agreed to refrain for defined periods. While it refuses the authority of the PLO domestically, it does accept Arafat's leadership in representing the Palestinians internationally. Both the PLO and Hamas want to avoid a Palestinian civil war, in which both sides feel Israel would be the winner (Laqueur, 1999, pp. 138–140).

While Hamas may be a lukewarm ally of the PLO in the day-to-day battle against Israel, it is resolutely opposed to restoring the peace process. Their latest *wave* of suicide attacks (2000–2002) is designed to sabotage the peace process and force Israel from the occupied territories. From October 2000 to June 2002, Hamas is thought to be responsible for no less then twenty-two suicide bombings in Israel targeting restaurants, malls, buses, and bus stations. Casualties from these bombings total over 1,000 people (175 dead and over 900 wounded). The Israeli military response has brought charges of state terrorism, particularly in the case of the Jenin refugee camp. The international pressure on Arafat to answer for and halt this latest round of suicide attacks has sent him on a collision course with Hamas. Arafat has little chance of controlling or eliminating Hamas. Opinion polls find 70 percent of Palestinians in support of the suicide bombings and opposed to a ceasefire. Many Palestinians feel that the suicide bombings are a means to an end and their only means of resistance. In fact, Arafat's own Fatah regards Hamas as comrades-in-arms against the Israelis, and there is little enthusiasm for the task of arresting Hamas leadership.

Another terrorist group involved in Middle Eastern politics is the organization or network known as al-Qaeda (Arabic for "the base"). This organization was created in 1990 by the Saudi multimillionaire Osama bin Laden to recruit Arab Muslims to fight against the Soviets in Afghanistan. In fact, the United States actually engaged in state sponsorship and helped train and fund al-Qaeda during the last phase of the cold war, hoping to defeat the Soviets indirectly. Al-Qaeda is a revolutionary group with the stated objective to unite all Muslims and establish a government under Sunni Muslim precepts. To achieve this goal it is thought that all Muslim governments, "corrupted by Western influence" (i.e., the Saudi government) must be overthrown by force. Eventually, Muslim state boundaries will be erased and replaced with a unified pan-Islamic state under the rule of the caliphs (Alexander & Swetnam, 2001, p. 2).

Al-Qaeda's activities are largely supported by the personal fortune of Osama bin Laden, (rumored to be worth upwards of $300 million), which he received from the bin Laden Group, his father's construction company. Bin Laden has augmented his fortune with various successful companies (construction, agriculture, investment, transportation) that he has established. Al-Qaeda also receives donations from all over the world to continue its *jihad.* Bin Laden, for all practical purposes, acts as the chief executive and chief financial officer of a loosely affiliated group of terrorist extremists who share resources and expertise and come together for an operation and then disperse. Al-Qaeda is just the most visible head of this international terrorist network (Cilluffo & Rankin, 2002, p.13).

In 1996, bin Laden issued a Declaration of Jihad against the United States and the Saudi government. He has endorsed a *fatwah* (religious ruling) stating that Muslims should kill Americans and their allies, military and civilian, anywhere in the world where they can be found. Al-Qaeda, and more generally all Islamic fundamentalist groups, detests U.S. global hegemony, the continued U.S. presence on the Arabian Peninsula following the Gulf War, and its seemingly unreserved support of Israel (Alexander & Swetnam, 2001, Appendices, pp.1–22).

In its efforts to spread *jihad* to all corners of the globe, al-Qaeda has been linked to many terrorist operations, such as the 1993 World Trade Center bombing in New York; the 1993 attack on U.S. troops in Somalia; the 1996 bombing of the Khobar Towers in Saudi Arabia; the 1998 U.S. embassy bombings in East Africa; the 2000 attack on the USS *Cole* in Aden, Yemen; and the 2001 assassination of Ahmad Shah Massoud, leader of the Northern Alliance in Afghanistan. In addition, al-Qaeda masterminded the September 11, 2001 attacks on the World Trade Center and the Pentagon, where nineteen suicide bombers hijacked four U.S. domestic flights and crashed three of them into their targets. The fourth flight crashed following an apparent struggle between hijackers and passengers. Almost 3,000 people perished in this most deadly terrorist attack in history.

How effective is al-Qaeda? It has not yet won its *jihad,* but it has won some skirmishes toward that ultimate objective. Al-Qaeda has done what no terrorist group has: It has successfully attacked and hurt the United States on American soil and demonstrated U.S. vulnerability. The propaganda from this deed automatically gives al-Qaeda a respect and visibility afforded to no other contemporary terrorist group. The United States, for all practical purposes, has won the war in Afghanistan and has crushed the Taliban, but although al-Qaeda has been wounded and forced from Afghanistan, it is impossible to ascertain its strike capabilities. Even if Osama bin Laden is captured or killed, al-Qaeda will survive and continue its activities. Al-Qaeda is an international terrorist network; it will take more than apprehending one of its chief lieutenants to stop it. It is important to understand that the United States has a difficult task because it must completely exterminate al-Qaeda to "win," while al-Qaeda merely has to survive to "win."

The al-Qaeda network has effectively exploited advances in technology unlike any other terrorist group. The ability to use the internet and satellite communications to recruit, propagandize, and coordinate strikes is impressive, but when you add to this the exceptional ability to organize globally, build clerical support, and attract recruits willing to martyr themselves, al-Qaeda becomes the most daunting terrorist organization to date. No single event better illustrates this fusion than the attacks of September 11.

Bin Laden is increasingly deified by many in the Islamic community. The headmaster of one the largest religious schools in Pakistan stated that Osama bin Laden is a "hero because he raises his voice against the outside powers that are trying to crush Muslims" (quoted in Bergen, 2001, p. 31). The young students at this school, needless to say, share this same view. In an interview before September 11, General Pervez Musharaf, the ruler of Pakistan, summarized bin Laden's appeal:

> The Western demonization of Osama bin Laden . . . made him a cult figure among Muslims who resent everything from the decline in moral values as conveyed by Hollywood movies and TV serials to America's lack of support for Palestinians being killed by Israeli occupation forces. . . . It is a very long list of complaints that has generated a strong persecution complex that the Osama bin Laden cult figure has come to embody. He is a hero figure on the pedestal of Muslim extremism (quoted in Bergen, 2001, p. 34).

What has caused U.S. officials great concern recently are the reports stating that al-Qaeda, Hezbollah, and Hamas are cooperating and may be in the process of establishing an alliance (Nasser, 2002). Such an alliance would be unprecedented and allow the organizations to collaborate on explosive and tactics training, money laundering, weapons smuggling, and sharing intelligence. If these organizations stood together, they could be more resilient in the "War on Terrorism" just begun by the United States. As an example, if al-Qaeda has been hobbled because its bases in Afghanistan are destroyed, members could assimilate into Hamas or Hezbollah and not only survive and continue to train and plan, but strengthen the global terrorist network. Hezbollah leadership categorically denies any link with al-Qaeda. Such a link would have to overcome different interpretations of Islam (al-Qaeda is Sunni, Hezbollah is Shiite)—not an easy task. However, Hamas has developed a working relationship with the PLO in order to focus better upon its enemy; perhaps Hezbollah and al-Qaeda will do the same (Nasser, 2002).

All of these organizations display a remarkable religious or ideological enthusiasm, resulting in fanatical acts such as suicide bombing. To Hezbollah, Hamas, and al-Qaeda, the suicide bomber is a martyr who believes his or her cause is both worthy and invincible. Because the secular cultures of the West place so much emphasis upon individual worth and freedom, it is perhaps more difficult to understand such a seemingly desperate strategy. In the United States in particular, where the media and, in some cases, government officials have given the impression that a clean, high-tech war can now be fought with almost no casualties, empathy is impossible.

Yet suicide missions have existed for as long as wars have been fought. The Assassins, discussed above, were a much-dreaded group that specialized in suicide missions. Most of the nineteenth-century anarchists were on suicide missions as well. Their bombs had to be thrown from short distances to be accurate, thus, the explosion would kill them, too. In fact, all attacks against public officials in countries that have capital punishment are suicide missions. The attacks have to be carried out at close range and the chances for the assassin to escape are poor (Laqueur, 1999, p. 140). Considering the above examples, it should not be a surprise that contemporary terrorist organizations use suicide missions, even though the media treated it as a new phenomenon in the early 1980s.

Islamic theological conflict surrounds the use of suicide bombers. The Qur'an does not permit suicide in principle; however, it can be interpreted as a religious duty to fight and die for Allah and Islam. In theory, the martyr is to submit to the will of Allah by his or her own free will and die an unavoidable and unsought death. In practice the candidates for martyrdom are heavily indoctrinated, selected by group leadership, and given a target. The typical suicide bomber is a male between the ages of 16 and 28. Most bombers come from poor families or refugee camps where living conditions are miserable. In most cases the main motivation is religious with patriotism and nationalism only secondary considerations. A very disturbing aspect of the September 11 attacks was that the suicide bombers involved did not follow the typical pattern. They all were generally middle-class, well educated, technically savvy young men who assimilated all too well into the communities in California and Florida. In fact, some of these men had been living unnoticed in the United States for several years and even learned how to fly passenger jets in the United States (Bergen, 2001, pp. 27–28). Suicide bombers in general present a difficult problem for authorities to defend against, because ordinarily authorities depend on the natural human fear of death as a deterrent, but the suicide bomber has already embraced death (Anderson & Sloan, 2002, p. 470).

It is important to understand that terrorists willing to martyr themselves, coupled with the development of weapons of mass destruction (WMD; biological, chemical, and nuclear), constitute one of the greatest threats to national security and humanity. The use of WMD has the potential to give terrorism unprecedented publicity, coercive power, and effectiveness. Incidences like the 1995 nerve gas attack on the Tokyo subway system, the 1995 bombing in Oklahoma City, and the devastating 2001 attack on the Pentagon and World Trade Center betray this reality and indicate the more lethal direction that terrorism is unfortunately headed. Such destructive power only a decade ago was monopolized by the nation–state; we are now on the brink of a new era where this type of destructive capability is increasingly in the hands of a few.

Another disturbing factor is the availability of material needed to make WMD. There is a great amount of fissionable material unaccounted for, mainly from the former Soviet Union, which has now entered the black market. Although much of this material is not suitable for constructing a nuclear weapon, it could be used to build a "dirty bomb"—in other words, coupling radioactive agents with conventional explosives. Although the device would fail to reach nuclear yield, it would nonetheless spread radioactive contamination with devastating economic and psychological consequences. The fallout would cause panic and people would have to stay inside to avoid it. Authorities would have to clean a tremendous amount of square miles. Buildings would have to be scrubbed, topsoil removed, and so on. The cost of such a cleanup would be unfathomable (Stern, 1999, p. 3).

Biological or chemical attack has the potential to be as devastating as a nuclear bomb. This type of attack is much more likely because the methods for making such weapons are simple and accessible. The formula for Sarin (nerve gas) is on the internet, and the materials and education needed to create other crude biological and chemical weapons are cheap and basic. At a different level, weaponized anthrax (which is difficult to create), if disbursed under optimal conditions in an urban setting, could kill several million people. Unlike a nuclear attack, however, some biological and chemical agents can be reversed if the population is aware of the attack and well-prepared medical personnel and vaccines or antidotes are on hand. The real danger of the biological threat lies in the highly infectious nature of its agents. If undetected, diseases such as smallpox or the plague can multiply exponentially and spread through a population. By the time the symptoms are recognized, it could be too late to contain an epidemic (Cilluffo & Rankin, 2002, p. 13).

Every modern society is vulnerable to terrorist attack. The United States is especially vulnerable because of its free and open nature. First Amendment protections allow the dissemination of printed materials that can help terrorists. The Bill of Rights that makes Americans free also makes terrorism more difficult to combat (Stern, 1999, p. 5). The above two statements are a reality. The question is, what is the balance between civil liberties and public safety? In June 2002, an ABC news poll reported that 79 percent of Americans feel it is more important to investigate terrorism, even if it means intruding on personal privacy. Just 18 percent said it was more important not to intrude on privacy, even if it limits counterterrorism efforts. The frequency of terrorist success in the United States will directly alter that cherished balance between civil liberties and public safety. If there are more attacks like September 11 and other landmark bridges or buildings crumble, or if there is a successful terrorist deployment of a weapon of mass destruction, measures will be called for that may well violate civil rights. These measures could include a more active FBI and CIA, curtailing the right of free speech, expanding the role of the military, and increasing surveillance and phone tapping.

In combating terrorism in the future, it is necessary to recognize that the terrorist threat is a permanent condition. The United States will always be vulnerable because of its openness, its huge urban centers, and its transportation systems. In this respect, complacency must be avoided and vigilance maintained. One of the most pressing needs of the United States is to improve intelligence capabilities. Accurate and timely information, coupled with proper analysis, is crucial in defending against terrorism and infiltrating terrorist groups. Terrorism is a dynamic and evolving force; so too must a nation's capabilities and responses improve and adapt. The area of human intelligence is critical. Technological gadgets are helpful to be sure, but to effectively combat terrorism the intelligence community needs up-to-date, accurate information from human agents and informants. There is also a wealth of information to be tapped in open literature and from the private sector. Journalists and entrepreneurs who work in "problem" areas of the world have a wealth of information to contribute (Hall & Fox, 2001/2002, p. 10).

Strengthened international cooperation is crucial as well. The coalition established to fight terrorism after September 11 still exists, but it has wavered at times. In this era of globalization and increasing interdependence, almost every terrorist campaign has an international dimension. It will take a long-term international commitment to effectively combat the terrorist threat that exists today. The United Nations' measures on human rights could be used to combat terrorism. The *Universal Declaration of Human Rights* (1948) specifically guarantees the right to life, liberty, and the security of the person. Several other U.N. covenants stress the right to enjoy "freedom from fear" (Wilkinson, 2001, p. 189). These provisions could be more rigorously enforced to help blunt terrorist success and establish a united international front (Hoffman, 1998, p. 211).

States that sponsor terrorism must be held accountable. If nations such as Iraq, Iran, Libya, Syria, and North Korea refuse to be brought into the international community and insist on funding terrorism, they are a large part of the problem and they must be stopped. How to do this is another matter; economic sanctions, diplomacy, and military action have been used in the past with varying results.

Shortly after September 11, the United States created the Office of Homeland Security to deal with the vulnerability of U.S. society. This unprecedented national response to the modern terrorist threat represents a new course for U.S. security. Congress appropriated a $40 billion Emergency Response Fund to wage war against al-Qaeda, help efforts to rebuild New York and Virginia, compensate victims, and strengthen home defenses. A total of $10 billion was dedicated to homeland security for such things as increased security for airports, nuclear facilities, dams, and bridges; employment of sky marshals on airlines; production of vaccines; installation of detection equipment in major mail sorting facilities; and many other measures. Another important objective for the Office of Homeland Security is to improve the use and coordination of intelligence across all levels of government (Bush, 2002, pp. 2–20). Only the future will demonstrate how effective these security efforts will be.

CONCLUDING REMARKS

As we have seen, terrorism can be defined in many ways because there are many types of terrorism. Terrorism has appeared in conjunction with a civil war or guerrilla warfare. It has been waged by religious and secular groups, by the left and the right, by nationalists and internationalist movements, and by state governments. Terrorism, unlike guerrilla movements, has rarely ever reached its final objective or changed the course of nations. Overall, the impact of terrorism on history has been minor. Then why use terrorism? Maybe some terrorists are poor students of history and continue to hope for an exceptional Irgun-like success. The likely answer is that the strategic limitations of terrorism are understood, but the tactical, short-term rewards (publicity, expression of belief, exhilaration, and revenge) make it worthwhile, at least to the terrorist (Laqueuer, 1999, pp. 46–48).

What the future holds for terrorism is unknown. Will the abysmal record of accomplishment continue? The answer is probably not. Over the last twenty-five years, terrorist attacks have become much more lethal. What began with hijackings soon escalated to sabotage bombing of jumbo jets, then to car and truck bombs capable of killing hundreds of people, and finally to commercial jet aircraft being used as weapons and flown into skyscrapers. What could be next? Everyone's fear, of course, is the use of WMD. If and when they are used, the potential for terrorism to reach its long-term, final objectives will increase dramatically.

To counteract this "age of terrorism," the international coalition must effectively mobilize its resources and ingenuity. The task is enormous and requires efforts on many fronts: law enforcement, military, intelligence, homeland security, health care. The international community can and must triumph over terrorism.

DISCUSSION QUESTIONS

1. What role has religion played in terrorist attacks over the last twenty years? Why is religion a key ingredient in the current wave of international terrorism?
2. What would you consider as an effective terrorist action? Why is terrorism more effective today than in the past?
3. What are the seeds of contemporary terrorism? The author recommends certain policies for governments trying to combat terrorism. Outline three of these policies. What are the potential problems with implementing these policies?

REFERENCES

ALEXANDER, Y, & SWETNAM, M. (2001). *Usama Bin Laden's al-Qaida: Profile of a terrorist network.* Ardsley, NY: Transnational Publishers.

ANDERSON, S., & SLOGAN, S. (2002). *Historical dictionary of terrorism* (2nd ed.). Lanham: The Scarecrow Press.

BAUDRILLARD, J. (2001, November 2). "L'esprit du terrorisme." *Le Monde* (Paris).

BERGEN, P. (2001). *Holy war, inc.* New York: The Free Press.

BORCKE, A. (1982). Violence and terror in Russian revolutionary terrorism: The Narodnaya Volya, 1879–83. In W. Mommsen & G. Hirschfeld (Eds.), *Social protest, violence and terror in nineteenth and twentieth century Europe* (pp. 48–62). New York: St. Martin's Press.

BUSH, G. (2002). Securing the homeland, strengthening the nation. *www.whitehouse.gov/homeland/homeland_security_book.html,* retrieved 7/1/2002.

CILLUFFO, F., & RANKIN, D. (Winter 2001/2002). Fighting terrorism. *NATO Review,* 12–15.

COHN, N. (1970). *The pursuit of the millennium.* New York: Oxford.

CROZIER, B. (1960). *The rebels.* Boston: Beacon Press.

ESPOSITO, JOHN. (1998). *Islam: The straight path.* Oxford: Oxford University Press.

FADLALLAH, M. H. (1986). Islam and violence in political reality. *Middle East Insight,* 4, 4–5.

HALL, R., & FOX, C. (Winter 2001/2002). Fighting terrorism. *NATO Review,* 8–11.

HOFFMAN, B. (1998). *Inside terrorism.* New York: Columbia University Press.

JOLL, J. (1980). *The anarchists.* Cambridge, MA: Harvard University Press.

LAQUEUR, W. (2001). *A history of terrorism.* New Brunswick: Transaction Publishers.

_____. (1999). *The new terrorism.* Oxford: Oxford University Press.

LEWIS, B. (1967). *The Assassins: A radical sect in Islam.* New York: Oxford University Press.

_____. (1997). *The Middle East.* New York: Simon and Schuster.

NASSER, C. (2002, July 1). Hizbullah denies Al-Qaeda link again; *Washington Post* claims groups 'coordinating.' *The Daily Star.* *www.hizbollah.org/english/press/p2002/p20020701.htm,* retrieved 7/4/2002.

National Advisory Committee on Criminal Justice Standards and Goals. (1976). *Report of the Task Force on Disorders and Terrorism.* Washington, DC: U.S. Government Printing Office.

OVENDALE, R. (1999). *The Arab-Israeli wars* (3rd ed). London: Longman.

PETERS, R. (1996). Jihad *in classic and modern times.* Princeton: Markus Wiener Publishers.

SELA, AVRAHAM. *Political Encyclopedia of the Middle East.* Continum: NY, 1999.

STERLING, C. (1983). *The terror network: The secret war of international terrorism.* New York: Holt, Rinehart & Winston.

STERN, J. (1999). *The ultimate terrorists.* Cambridge, MA: Harvard University Press.

WARDLAW, G. (1982). *Political terrorism: Theory, tactics, and counter-measures.* Cambridge, UK: Cambridge University Press.

WEINBERG, L., & DAVIS, P. (1989). *Introduction to political terrorism.* New York: McGraw Hill.

WESTWOOD, J. (1993). *Endurance and endeavor: Russian history 1812 to 1992* (4th ed.). Oxford: Oxford University Press.

WILKINSON, P. (2001). *Terrorism versus democracy.* London: Frank Cass.

CHAPTER 4

Criminals or Crusaders?

Key Concepts

crazies	soldiers of the revolution
criminals	al-Qaeda
crusaders	motivation
characteristics of a "successful" terrorist	group dynamics
	religion as a factor
fedayeen	trends in recruitment and membership
HAMAS	socialization toward violence
Irish Republican Army	Sicariis

Nothing is easier than to denounce the evil doer; nothing is more difficult than to understand him.

Fedor Dostoevsky

What kind of person becomes a terrorist? Perhaps an understanding of the dynamics of becoming a terrorist will increase our understanding of this phenomenon. Terrorist acts are committed for a wide variety of causes. It is also true that there are a wide variety of individuals and groups who commit terrorist acts. Although studying all such persons in detail is not feasible, a brief analysis of some of the important characteristics of modern terrorists might be informative.

The political world changed a great deal in the last two decades of the twentieth century. These political changes influenced the type of persons more likely to be recruited into terrorist groups. A study of the type of individuals known to be drawn to terrorism in the twentieth century will, perhaps, help us to predict the most probable type of twenty-first century terrorist. This could be an extremely useful tool for governments and institutions confronted with the need to plan to cope with terrorism.

PROFILE OF A TERRORIST

Why do people become terrorists? Are they crazy? Are they thrill seekers? Are they religious fanatics? Are they ideologues? Is there any way to tell who is likely to become a terrorist?

This final question provides a clue as to why political scientists and government officials are particularly interested in the psychological factors relating to terrorism. If one could identify the traits most closely related to a willingness to use terrorist tactics, then one would be in a better position to predict, and prevent, the emergence of terrorist groups.

Unfortunately, identifying such traits is not easy. Just as not all violence is terrorism, and not all revolutionaries are terrorists, not all persons who commit acts of terrorism are alike. Frederick Hacker suggests three categories of persons who commit terrorism: *crazies, criminals,* and *crusaders.* He notes that an individual carrying out a terrorist act is seldom "purely" one type or the other, but Hacker suggests that each type offers some insights into why an individual will resort to terrorism.[1]

Understanding the individual who commits terrorism is vital, not only for humanitarian reasons, but also to decide how best to deal with those individuals *while they are engaged in planning or carrying out terrorist acts.* From a law enforcement perspective, for example, it is important to appreciate the difference between a criminal and a crusading terrorist involved in a hostage-taking situation. Successful resolution of such a situation often hinges on understanding the mind of the individuals perpetrating the crime.

Let us consider the three categories of terrorists suggested by Hacker: crazies, criminals, and crusaders. For the purposes of this study, we need to establish loose descriptions of these three types. Hacker offers some useful ideas on what is subsumed under each label. **Crazies,** he suggests, are *emotionally disturbed individuals who are driven to commit terrorism "by reasons of their own that often do not make sense to anybody else."*

Criminals, on the other hand, *perform terrorist acts for more easily understood reasons: personal gain.* Such individuals transgress the laws of society knowingly and, one assumes, in full possession of their faculties. Both their motives and their goals are usually clear, if still deplorable, to most of mankind.

This is not the case with the **crusaders.** These individuals commit terrorism for reasons that are often unclear both to themselves and to those witnessing the acts. Their ultimate goals are frequently even less understandable. While such individuals are usually idealistically inspired, their idealism tends to be a rather mixed bag of half-understood philosophies. Crusaders, according to Hacker, *seek not personal gain, but prestige and power for a collective cause.* They commit terrorist acts in the belief "that they are serving a higher cause," in Hacker's assessment.

What difference does it make what kind of terrorist is behind the machine gun or bomb? To the law enforcement personnel charged with resolving the hostage situation, it can be crucial to know what type of person is controlling the situation. Criminals, for instance, can be offered sufficient personal gains or security provisions to induce them to release the hostages. Crusaders are far less likely to be talked out of carrying out their threats by inducements of personal gains, since to do so they would have to betray, in some sense, that higher cause for which they are committing the action.

For the same reason, it is useful for security agents to know what type of individual is likely to commit a terrorist act within their province. A criminal, for example, would be more likely to try to smuggle a gun aboard an airline than a bomb, since the criminal usually anticipates living to enjoy the reward of his or her illegal activities. Crusaders, however, are more willing to blow themselves up with their victims, since their service to that higher cause often carries with it a promise of a reward in the life to come.

The distinction between criminals and crusaders with respect to terrorism needs some clarification. Clearly, when anyone breaks the law, as in the commission of a terrorist act, he or she becomes a criminal, regardless of the reason for the transgression. The distinction between criminal and crusader, though, is useful in understanding the differences in the motives and goals moving the person to commit the act.

The majority of the individuals and groups carrying out terrorist acts in the world in the last decade of the twentieth and the beginning years of the twenty-first century have been crusaders. This does not mean there are not occasional instances in which individuals who, reacting to some real or perceived injury, decide to take a machine gun to the target of their anger and kidnap or destroy anyone in sight. Nor does it mean there are not individual criminals and criminal organizations that engage in terrorist activities.

Nonetheless, it is true that the majority of individuals who commit modern terrorism are, or perceive themselves to be, crusaders. According to Hacker, the typical crusading terrorist appears to be normal, no matter how crazy the cause or how criminal the means used for this cause may seem. He or she is neither an idiot nor a fool, neither a coward nor a weakling. Instead, the crusading terrorist is frequently a professional, well trained, well prepared, and well disciplined in the habit of blind obedience to a cause.

Table 4.1 indicates a few dramatic differences between the types of terrorist Hacker profiles. One is that crusaders are the least likely to negotiate a resolution to a crisis, both because such action can be viewed as a betrayal of a sublime cause and because there is little that the negotiator can offer, since neither personal gain nor safe

TABLE 4.1   Hacker's Typology of Terrorists

Type of Terrorist	Motive/Goal	Willing to Negotiate?	Expectation of Survival
Criminal	Personal gain/ profit	Usually, in return for profit and/or safe passage	Strong
Crusader	"Higher cause" (usually a blend of religious and political)	Seldom, since to do so could be seen as a betrayal of the cause	Minimal, since death offers reward in "afterlife"
Crazy	Clear only to perpetrator	Possible, but only if negotiator can understand motive and offer hope/alternatives	Strong, but not based on reality

passage out of the situation are particularly desired by true crusaders. Belief in the cause makes death not a penalty, but a path to reward and glory; therefore the threat of death and destruction can have little punitive value. What can a police or military negotiator offer to a crusader to induce the release of hostages or the defusing of a bomb?

Similar problems exist with crazies, depending upon how much in touch with reality such an individual is at the time of the incident. Negotiation is difficult, but not impossible, if the negotiator can ascertain the goal or motive of the perpetrator and offer some hope (even if it is not real) of success in achieving that goal by other, less destructive means. One of the critical elements is that crazies, according to Hacker's evaluation, have a limited grip on the reality that they themselves may die in the course of this action. Thus, the threat of death by a superior force carries diminished weight if the perpetrator cannot grasp the fact that he or she may die in this encounter. Just as very young children find the reality of death a difficult concept to grasp, Hacker suggests that crazies offer serious difficulties for negotiators because they often cannot grasp this reality.

Criminals, then, are the preferred perpetrators, since they will negotiate; their demands are generally logical (although often outrageous) and are based in terms that can be met or satisfied with rational alternatives. Criminals know they can be killed and have a strong desire to live to enjoy the rewards of the actions they are taking. Thus, negotiators have specific demands to be bartered, and their "clients" can be expected to recognize superior force and to respond accordingly in altering demands and resolving the incident.

These differences are critically important in at least two contexts: (1) resolving situations in which hostages are held by terrorists and (2) establishing security measures and training for vulnerable targets. The type of terrorist engaged in the incident significantly impacts the successful resolution of the situation. Hostage negotiators need to know whether they are dealing with a crusader or a criminal, know whether there is any potential for negotiation. If the individual(s) perpetrating the crime are crusaders, then an immediate hostage rescue attempt may be more appropriate than the initiation of a negotiation process.

In terms of security devices and training, the profiles become even more vital. The events of September 11, 2001, illustrate dramatically the consequences of training and equipping for the wrong type of perpetrators. Airline pilots in the United States had been trained to respond to attempts to take over flights as hostage situations. Thus the pilots of the doomed September 11 flights were engaged in trying to keep the situation calm and to "talk down" the plane, to initiate a hostage release without violence. But the individuals engaged in the takeover were crusaders, not criminals or crazies, who did not plan to live through the incidents. Only the passengers on the flight that crashed in Pennsylvania were able to offer substantial resistance—perhaps in part because they had not been trained to assume a peaceful solution could be negotiated with hostage takers.

This does not suggest that the pilots and crew were not vigilant and did not make every effort to save the lives of the passengers. But because the profile they had been trained to respond to did not match that with which they were confronted, they were unable to respond successfully to the demands of the situation. Thus, inaccurate profiling in pilot training was a serious contributing factor to the sequence of events on that day.

To political scientists, as well as to military, police, and other security and intelligence units assigned the task of coping with terrorism, an understanding of the type of person likely to commit acts of terrorism is invaluable. As our understanding of a phenomenon increases, our ability to predict its behavior with some accuracy also increases. Thus, as we try to understand who terrorists are and what they are like, we should increase our ability to anticipate their behavior patterns, thereby increasing our ability to respond effectively and to prevent more often the launching of successful terrorist attacks.

CAN WE GENERALIZE ABOUT A "TYPICAL" TERRORIST?

What, then, do we know about the type of individual who becomes a terrorist? Until fairly recently, with the in-depth coverage given to Osama bin Laden, we usually had very little personal data about successful perpetrators of terrorist attacks, because successful terrorists depend upon secrecy for protection. Through the capture of those less efficient in the art of terrorist operation, we have learned some useful information; our security and intelligence organizations continue to add substantially to that data pool.

Nevertheless, it remains true that to generalize about the "typical" terrorist can be very difficult with any degree of accuracy. The search for a "terrorist personality" is a legitimate exercise, but it is unlikely to produce any common denominator capable of uniting a wide variety of countries, periods of time, cultures and political alliances. In other words, the community of nations is unable, at this point, to agree on such a profile.

Some scholars, of course, have attempted to create a profile of a typical terrorist. Their successes are mixed, at best, but do offer some ideas that help us not only to understand what a typical terrorist may be like (if such a creature can be said to exist), but also to evaluate how terrorists as well as terrorism have changed in recent years.

Edgar O'Ballance offers one such critique of what he calls a "successful" terrorist (by which he appears to mean one who is neither captured nor dead). In his book, *The Language of Violence,* O'Ballance suggests several essential **characteristics of the "successful" terrorist:**

1. *Dedication.* To be successful, a terrorist cannot be a casual or part-time mercenary, willing to operate only when it suits his convenience or his pocket. He must become a **fedayeen,** a "man of sacrifice." Dedication also implies absolute obedience to the leader of the political movement.

2. *Personal Bravery.* As the terrorist must face the possibility of death, injury, imprisonment, or even torture if captured, O'Ballance regards this trait as important, to varying degrees, depending upon one's position within the terrorist group's hierarchy.

3. *Without the Human Emotions of Pity or Remorse.* Since most victims will include innocent men, women, and children, whom he or she must be prepared to kill in cold blood, the terrorist must have the killer instinct, able to kill without hesitation on receipt of a code or signal. As this expert notes, many can kill in the heat of anger or in battle, but few, fortunately, can do so in cold blood.

4. *Fairly High Standard of Intelligence.* As the would-be terrorist has to collect, collate, and assess information, devise and put into effect complex plans, and evade police, security forces, and other hostile forces, intelligence would appear to be a requisite.

5. *Fairly High Degree of Sophistication.* This is essential, according to O'Ballance, for the terrorist to blend into the first-class section on airliners, stay at first-class hotels, and mix inconspicuously with the international executive set.

6. *Be Reasonably Well Educated and Possess a Fair Share of General Knowledge.* By this, O'Ballance means that the terrorist should be able to speak English as well as one other major language. He asserts that a university degree is almost mandatory.

O'Ballance notes that "all terrorists do not measure up to these high standards, but the leaders, planners, couriers, liaison officers, and activists must."[2] This assertion is difficult to challenge effectively, because if the terrorist is successful, then the implication is that he or she has succeeded in evading law enforcement, security, and intelligence officers, and hence the information about the individual is necessarily either scant or unconfirmed.

We could conclude, with some justice, that most of O'Ballance's assertions, like most generalizations, are at least half-true, half-false, and largely untestable. But these generalizations, with their grains of truth, are still useful in analyzing terrorism and terrorist behavior. Let us instead examine each of his suggested attributes of a terrorist to discover whether they can be substantiated by insights into contemporary behavior.

Dedication certainly appears, on the surface, to be characteristic of modern terrorists. Palestinians involved in various groups, for example, have indicated a willingness to wait for as long as it takes them to realize their dream of a return to a nation of Palestine. They have been willing to wait as long as the Irgun waited, or longer, and many are reluctant to accept the current peace settlements, because that represents at this point less than full national independence for a nation of Palestine. Like the Irgun, they have unbounded faith in the justice of their cause and seem willing to die to achieve it.

The progress toward a comprehensive peace settlement in the Middle East in the last years of the twentieth century indicated that this tenacity may be a liability to the government established by Yasser Arafat in Gaza and parts of the West Bank, because this represents only a portion of the land that was Palestine and does not constitute full sovereignty from Israel for the Palestinians, particularly with the construction by the government of Israel of a formidable wall slicing through the West Bank and decimating parts of Palestinian territory. Anger by the Palestinian group **HAMAS,** *a radical Islamic movement supported throughout the Middle East by Iran,* indicates that a significant portion of the Palestinians remain committed to full restoration of Palestine to the Palestinian people. The suicide bombings in this area since 1994, which have claimed the lives of innocent men, women, and children, provoking harsh response by Israel in attacks that have claimed far more Palestinian lives, have given credence to this absolute resolve.

Nor is such dedication limited to Palestinians and Israelis. Observers in Northern Ireland have suggested that religious fanaticism is handed down from generation to generation in this region as well, carrying with it a willingness to fight and die for a cause. Schoolchildren in Northern Ireland have exhibited an intolerance and a bitterness that is too often translated into violence, and parents have even attacked groups of children walking to school. When children, parents, preachers, and priests join to commit murder in a "holy" cause, "dedication has produced countless bloody massacres and seemingly endless terrorism."

However, unlike the continuing violence in the Middle East, progress is being made toward a political settlement of the problem of Northern Ireland. Like the situation of Palestine, though, the solution will probably not satisfy all of the truly dedicated terrorists. The willingness of the **Irish Republican Army,** *radical Irish Catholics committed to the removal of British forces from Northern Ireland and to the unification of Ireland,* to negotiate a peace has angered radical elements in the Catholic community, and the movement of the British to negotiate with the IRA openly has raised equal anger in militant Protestant groups. If a resolution of the dispute of the British with the IRA *is* reached and a merging of Northern Ireland with the Republic of Ireland planned, there is reason to fear that a similarly dedicated group of terrorists will emerge, determined to force the United Kingdom into retaining sovereignty (thus keeping Protestant control).

Such dedication is not always directed at so specific a nationalist cause. The Japanese Red Army (JRA), for instance, founded in 1969, described themselves as **soldiers of the revolution,** *pledged to participate in all revolutions anywhere in the world through exemplary acts.* This group was responsible for the massacre of 26 tourists at Lod Airport in Tel Aviv, Israel. These dedicated revolutionaries undertook numerous terrorist attacks, many of which, like the Lod Airport massacre, were essentially suicide missions, because escape was scarcely possible.

The dedication of Osama bin Laden and his **al-Qaeda** network—*created by bin Laden in the late 1980s to bring together Arabs in Afghanistan against the Soviet Union and now engaged in attempting to establish an Islamic Caliphate throughout the world*—has also become apparent, as evidence has emerged that most of the attacks generated by this network involved years of preparation. Some of the individuals who carried out the September 11 attack came to the United States years in advance, slowly and carefully planning each stage of the operation. The dedication involved for those willing to leave home and live for years in the country to be attacked—learning about its airport security systems, taking lessons in the flight of its airliners, even traveling on the airlines to time and plan each step with accuracy—is difficult to assimilate but is clear from the evidence of their activities.

Personal bravery is also a characteristic often attributed to modern terrorists. There are, however, two views of the bravery that terrorists may possess. One might argue, with a great deal of justice, that it can scarcely be termed "brave" to use weapons mercilessly against unarmed and defenseless civilians. The men, women, and children at Lod Airport were wholly unable to defend themselves against the vicious attack of the JRA. Was it "brave" of the JRA to slaughter these innocent and unarmed people?

The opposing view, which does in fact attribute bravery to those perpetrating acts of terror, is that to be willing to carry out missions in which one's own death or imprisonment are inevitable argues no small degree of personal courage. A willingness to give one's life for a cause has commanded, throughout history, at least a reluctant admiration, even from one's enemies.

Bravery is, at best, a very subjective term. One may feel oneself to be very cowardly but be perceived by others to be quite fearless. The audience for one's deeds is often able to judge one's bravery only by the commission of the deed and is unaware of the inner doubts or demons that may have driven one to the act. Nor is the individual necessarily the best judge of his or her own personal bravery, since a person's capacity for self-deception makes it so that we often do not consciously admit (or refuse to be aware of) our true motives and fears.

The question as to whether or not terrorists who murder innocent persons, with the knowledge that their own survival is problematic, are brave may never be answered to anyone's satisfaction. Much depends on the way in which one describes the situation.

According to O'Ballance, a successful terrorist should be without the human emotions of pity or remorse. Given the necessity of being able to kill, in cold blood, unarmed and innocent persons, this would appear a reasonable assumption regarding the terrorist personality. Unlike criminals who may kill to prevent being captured or to secure some coveted prize, terrorists must, by the very nature of the act that they are often called upon to commit, kill persons against whom they have no specific grudge, whose life or death is not really material to their well-being or security.

Hacker states:

> Often, the terrorists do not know whom they will hurt, and they could not care less. Nothing seems important to them except they themselves and their cause. In planning and executing their deeds, the terrorists are totally oblivious to the fate of their victims. Only utter dehumanization permits the ruthless use of human beings as bargaining chips, bargaining instruments, or objects for indiscriminate aggression.[3]

This description creates a vivid portrait of a ruthless and, one would think, thoroughly unlikable killer. Yet those guilty of such acts have not always presented to the world such a vision of themselves.

Consider the following case: On July 22, 1946, an Irgun team, dressed as waiters, rolled seven milk churns full of dynamite and TNT into the empty Regency Grill of the King David Hotel in Jerusalem. At 12:37, the TNT in the milk cans exploded, creating pressure so great that it burst the hearts, lungs, and livers of the clerks working on the floors above.

Thurston Clarke gives a gruesome description of the fate of the people in the King David Hotel at that time:

> In that split second after 12:37, thirteen of those who had been alive at 12:36 disappeared without a trace. The clothes, bracelets, cufflinks, and wallets which might have identified them exploded into dust and smoke. Others were turned to charcoal, melted into chairs and desks or exploded into countless fragments. The face of a Jewish typist was ripped from her skull, blown out of a window, and smeared onto the pavement below. Miraculously it was recognizable, a two-foot-long distorted death mask topped with tufts of hair.
>
> Blocks of stones, tables and desks crushed heads and snapped necks. Coat racks became deadly arrows that flew across rooms, piercing chests. Filing cabinets pinned people to walls, suffocating them. Chandeliers and ceiling fans crashed to the floor, empaling and decapitating those underneath.[4]

Ninety-one people died in that bomb blast. Of these, 28 were British, 41 were Arabs, and 17 were Jews. Another 46 were injured.

Listen to the words of the person who commanded this attack:

> There is no longer any armistice between the Jewish people and the British administration of Eretz Israel which hands our brothers over to Hitler. Our people are at war with this regime—war to the end.[5]

Was this bombing the deed of a fanatic, a person who could murder in cold blood many innocent people in this "war to the end"? Certainly it would seem the case.

And yet the perpetrator of this atrocity, the man responsible for the terrible destruction of 91 lives, was Menachem Begin, who in the 1970s served as prime minister of Israel. The Irgun terrorist who plotted to destroy the hotel was the same man who, working with President Carter of the United States and President Anwar Sadat of Egypt, made significant efforts to move Israel on the road to peace with its Arab neighbors, signing the famous Camp David Accords, bringing a measure of peace between Israel and Egypt.

Are terrorists cold-blooded killers only at the time of the commission of their crime, or is that a trait endemic to their character? Do they, in fact, commit such acts because of a fatal flaw in their character that makes them unable to feel pity or remorse, or are they driven by circumstances and forces to commit acts that are personally abhorrent to them?

Just as there is no safe generalization with regard to the personal bravery of terrorists, so there seem pitfalls in making too broad a characterization of a terrorist as incapable of pity or remorse. Perhaps of all that O'Ballance had to say about this particular aspect of a terrorist's characteristics, it is accurate only to say that terrorists appear to have an image of the enemy that allows them to be willing to use lethal force.

Some may indeed kill without pity or remorse and may in fact be incapable of such emotions. But to say that terrorists as a whole are so constructed is a generalization for which there is insufficient data and conflicting indicators in known cases.

The characteristics that O'Ballance suggests of sophistication and education are less true of post-1970s terrorists than they were of terrorists prior to that time. Many nineteenth-century revolutionary terrorists were indeed intelligent, sophisticated, university educated, and even multilingual. Those responsible for the murder of Czar Alexander II of Russia in March 1881 were men and women who possessed a much higher level of education and sophistication than most other young people of their nation. They were led by Sophia Perovskaya, daughter of the wealthy governor-general of St. Petersburg, the empire's capital.

Similarly, the Tupamaros of Uruguay were primarily composed of the young, well-educated liberal intellectuals who sought, but never fully gained, the support of the less educated masses. The Baader-Meinhoff gang in West Germany, which terrorized that nation throughout the 1970s, was also composed of middle- and upper-class intellectuals. This gang's master strategist was Horst Mahler, a radical young lawyer, and it drew its membership and support system heavily from the student body of German universities.

The founder of one of Italy's first left-wing terrorist bands, the Proletarian Action Group (GAP), was Giangiacomo Feltrinelli, the heir to an immense Milanese fortune and head of one of Europe's most distinguished publishing houses. Like the Red Brigades, which would succeed this group as Italy's leading left-wing terrorist group, the GAP drew much of its initial membership from young, often wealthy, intellectuals.

Terrorists, in fact, tended to be recruited from college campuses until the 1980s. Many came from well-to-do families, so that sophistication and an ability to mix with the international set were well within their grasp. Intelligence, sophistication, education, and university training: not only the leaders but also many of the practitioners of both nineteenth-century anarchism and contemporary terrorism possessed these attributes.

But standards and modes of behavior among terrorists as we move forward in the twenty-first century are changing. The French anarchists would not have abducted children and threatened to kill them unless ransom was paid. The Narodnaya Volya would not have sent parts of their victims' bodies with little notes to their relatives as the right-wing Guatemalan National Revolutionary Unity did. Neither French nor Russian anarchists would have tormented, mutilated, raped, and castrated their victims, as too many terrorist groups have done in the latter part of the twentieth century. The Baader-Meinhoff would not have flown passenger airlines into the World Trade Center, killing thousands.

As Walter Lacquer pointed out:

> Not all terrorist movements have made a fetish of brutality; some have behaved more humanely than others. But what was once a rare exception has become a frequent occurrence in our time.[6]

According to Lacquer, the character of terrorism has undergone a profound change. Intellectuals, he contends, have made "the cult of violence respectable." In spite of the violence characterizing their movement, he asserts that no such cult existed among the Russian terrorists, a difficult claim to either prove or disprove.

Nevertheless, Lacquer is correct in his assertion that the terror of recent decades is different. That much has already been established in preceding chapters. It is also true that modern terrorists are significantly different and that the difference in the type of person becoming a terrorist today has a great deal to do with the difference in terrorism.

TERRORISM IS DIFFERENT TODAY

Motivation

Part of the difference lies in the **motivation** that drives individuals to embrace terrorism. Walter Lacquer summed up the situation very well in the 1980s:

> Whatever their motives may be, the "ardent love of other" which Emma Goldman observed is not among them. The driving force is hate not love, ethical considerations are a matter of indifference to them and their dreams of freedom, of national and social liberation are suspect. Nineteenth-century nationalist terrorists were fighting for freedom from foreign domination. More recently, appetites have grown, the Basques have designs on Galicia, the Palestinians not only want the West Bank but also intend to destroy the Jewish state, and the IRA would like to bomb the Protestants into a united Ireland. The aims of terrorism, in brief, have changed, and so have the terrorists.[7]

In the twenty-first century, a less-than-clear political purpose seems involved in much of the terrorism perpetrated. Moreover, the motives of individuals involved in a struggle against a cruel oppressor are surely significantly different from those of persons rebelling against a democratically elected government. Although idealism, a social conscience, or hatred of foreign oppression can serve to drive one to commit acts of terrorism, so can boredom, mental confusion, and what psychologists term "free-floating aggression."

Certainly religious fanaticism is today as strong a motivator for the commission of terrorism as it has been in previous centuries. The holy war waged by some Muslims on Christians and fellow Muslims is no less violent than that waged during the Middle Ages. The mixture of political and religious fanaticism has always been a volatile and often violent combination.

What difference does it make whether terrorism is committed by social idealists or persons suffering from free-floating aggression? We could speculate that a social conscience would be more likely to inhibit the perpetrator from the use of indiscriminate violence against the unprotected masses. Perhaps mental confusion contributes to an inability to recognize limits on the use of terror-violence.

Unfortunately, terrorists of the twenty-first century appear more willing to use weapons of mass destruction than have those of preceding decades, perhaps because more states have used these weapons in internal wars in recent years. Iraq's use of cyanide gas on the Kurds in Halabja in March 1988 dramatically illustrated the willingness of states to use such weapons. Thus, the news that al-Qaeda tested an air dispersal mechanism for cyanide, although a chilling thought, should hardly be surprising. If states, which set the norms that limit the use of such weapons, are using these weapons openly against their own citizens, then individuals engaged in terrorist acts can scarcely be expected to continue to refrain from the use of such weapons.

Group Dynamics

These are, at best, only suppositions as to why modern terrorists, although they may still be idealistic, are more brutal than their predecessors. Before considering demographic information that might help to substantiate and explain this difference, let us first consider the impact of the terrorist *group* upon the terrorist. If **group dynamics** *helps to shape terrorist thought and action,* then its impact must certainly be understood in order to comprehend the contemporary terrorist.

Modern terrorists are, for the most part, fanatics, whose sense of reality is distorted. They operate under the assumption that they, and they alone, know the truth and are therefore the sole arbiters of what is right and what is wrong. They believe themselves to be moralists, to whom ordinary law does not apply, because the law in existence is created by immoral persons for immoral purposes.

They are not, of course, consistent in their logic. For example, they demand that governments who capture terrorists treat them as prisoners of war, as they are involved in a war against either a specific government or society in general. But they vehemently deny the state's right to treat them as war criminals for their indiscriminate killing of civilians. In other words, they invoke the laws of war only in so far as it serves their purposes, but reject any aspect of such laws that limit their ability to kill at will.

Two other points should be made with respect to understanding the contemporary terrorist. The first point is relatively simple and involves what seems like a truism. *The less clear the political purpose that motivates terrorism, the greater its appeal is likely to be to unbalanced persons.* A rational individual will be more likely to require a clear purpose for the commission of an extraordinary act. Thus an act whose motivation is unclear is more likely to appeal to an irrational mind.

As already noted, contemporary terrorism has significantly less clear political purpose than that of earlier centuries. Thus, it seems fair to say that a larger proportion of contemporary terrorists may well be unbalanced persons, the crazies that Hacker described.

The second point relates to what psychologists term *group dynamics. If it is true that a terrorist's sense of reality is distorted, as discussed earlier in the context of terrorist images, then the greater the association the terrorist enjoys with his or her group of fellow terrorists, the greater that distortion will be.* The more, in other words, an individual perceives his or her identity in terms of the group of fellow terrorists, the less will be his or her ability to see the world as it really is. For the terrorist who is a member of a close-knit organization, reality is defined by the group. Remember, too, that this group rejects the reality of laws as they currently exist and morality as defined by anyone except the group itself.

Thus, conventional moral and legal constraints have little meaning to an individual deeply involved in a terrorist group. The group determines for itself what is moral and what is legal. An individual who has just joined the group may be able to perceive the difference between what the group declares to be morally or legally justified. The longer he or she remains with the group or the stronger the individual identifies with the norms of the group, the less able the individual becomes to see the difference between reality and "reality" as it is defined by the group.

The strength of the individual's acceptance of the group's definition of reality is particularly evident in situations in which terrorism has been a significant part of the culture for several generations. In Northern Ireland, for instance, young people have been "brought up to think of democracy as part of everyday humdrum existence, but of recourse to violence as something existing on a superior plane, not merely glorious but even sacred."[8]

Religion as a Factor in Group Dynamics

Consider the case of the individual who commits terrorism as a member of a fanatic religious group. Religions, as a rule, offer their own versions of reality, as well as a promise of reward for conformity to the norms of that reality. The reward is usually promised for a future time, when the present reality has passed away.

Thus, religious zealots committing an act of terrorism are assured by their religion and its leaders that their acts are acceptable to a higher morality than may currently exist. They are reinforced in their belief that what they are doing is right by the approval of their fellow zealots. Further, religious fanatics are assured of immortality and a suitable reward therein if they should die in the commission of the act of terrorism.

It would be difficult if not impossible to persuade such persons out of their beliefs by reasonable arguments. Little could be offered to such persons as an inducement for discontinuing the act of terrorism. What reward can compete with the promise of immortality, approval by one's peers, and religious sanctification?

Obviously, the dynamics of some groups are much more powerful than those of others whose reward system and expensive spiritual support system is less organized or persuasive. Certain types of terrorists are thus, much more difficult to deal with on a rational basis, due to this ability of a group to distort reality.

TRENDS IN TERRORIST RECRUITMENT AND MEMBERSHIP

So groups have an impact on modern terrorist behavior; some groups have more than others. Motivation has some effect on the type of individual involved in contemporary terrorism. Yet we have not established what a modern terrorist is really like, beyond a few generalizations. Is it, in fact, possible to be more specific about a typical terrorist personality?

It is unlikely that this search for a terrorist personality could be successful in creating a set of common denominators that could span several continents, time periods, cultures, and political configurations. All that most experts seem to agree on regarding terrorists today is that they are primarily young people. There are, it seems, very few old terrorists.

However, some demographic **trends in recruitment and membership** in modern terrorist affiliations offer clues as to who is currently becoming a terrorist. While this falls short of providing a profile of a modern terrorist, it does yield insights into not only who modern terrorists are, but also the impact of such a demographic configuration on contemporary terrorism.

Age

Terrorism is not only a pursuit of the young, it also became in the late 1970s and 1980s a pursuit of the *very* young. Although terrorists during the time of the Russian anarchists tended to be at least in their mid-20s, during these two decades in the late twentieth century, the average age steadily decreased. During the turbulent 1960s, many terrorists were recruited from college campuses throughout the Western world. This brought the average age down to around 20, give or take a year, because the leaders were several years older, often in their early thirties.

Research in 1977 indicated that the usual urban terrorist was between 22 and 25 years of age. Among the Tupamaros, the average age of arrested terrorists was around 24.1, while in Brazil and Argentina, the average was 23 and 24, respectively. These figures remained true for the ETA, the IRA, and groups in Iran and Turkey during that time.

As early as the spring of 1976, however, evidence of a change in the age level of terrorists began to emerge. Arrests of Spanish Euzkadita Azkutasuna (ETA) members revealed a number of youths in their teens. In Northern Ireland, some of the terrorists apprehended were as young as 12 to 14.[9]

Today, although the majority of active terrorists are in their twenties, there has been a tendency, particularly among the Arab and Iranian groups, to recruit children of 14 or 15 years of age. These children are used for dangerous, frequently suicidal, missions, partly because their youth makes them less likely to question their orders and partly because their extreme youth makes them less likely to attract the attention of the authorities.

One explanation of this phenomenon is that the anarchistic-revolutionary philosophy that had begun to infiltrate the province of the university students has begun to infiltrate the secondary school level, but this is a less persuasive explanation. Instead, researchers note the increasing level of media violence, access to weapons, development of satanic cults, and other sociological phenomenon are more likely to be found in young people today than in earlier decades.

Although these social patterns may explain part of this demographic trend, another explanation may lie in the number of children growing up in cultures in which violence is a way of life. In the Middle East and in Northern Ireland, for instance, children growing up in violent community struggles could easily become a part of terrorist activities spanning successive generations within the same family. Children were thus recruited, not by philosophy learned at university or secondary school, but by the dogma and lifestyles of their parents, facilitating a potentially more comprehensive assimilation into the terrorist group.

However, by the 1990s, this trend became less clear, as peace within at least one of these regions came closer to reality. Religious fanaticism is still a highly motivating factor compelling young teenagers into roles as suicide bombers; yet, studies of groups like HAMAS and Ansar al-Islam indicate most members are closer in age to the early 1970s terrorist profile. The individuals responsible for the bombing of the Pan Am flight over Lockerbie and those involved in either the 1993 bombing or the dramatically more successful 2001 attacks on the World Trade Center in New York City were certainly not 12 or 13 years of age!

Sex

During the earlier part of the twentieth century, the leaders of terrorist cadres included some women among their numbers, but the rank and file were usually predominantly male. In many such groups, women were assigned the less life-threatening roles of intelligence collection, courier, nurse or medical personnel, and maintenance of "safe houses" for terrorists on the run.

Terrorism of the late twentieth century, however, was an equal opportunity employer. The commander of the JRA for years, Fusako Shigenobu was a woman, and of the 14 most wanted West German terrorists in 1981, 10 were women. Moreover, studies have shown that female members of terrorist groups have proved to be tougher, more fanatical, more loyal, and possessors of a greater capacity for suffering. Women have also, in some terrorist groups, tended to remain members longer than men, on the average.

One example serves to demonstrate the difference in the roles played by women in terrorism today. It was a pregnant woman who was given the task of carrying a suitcase loaded with explosives aboard an airplane in the 1980s. Only a few decades ago, she would have been, at best, allowed to provide a safe haven for the man entrusted with that task. This is *not* to suggest that this is in any way "progress," but it does indicate a difference in the role women now play in terrorism.

Education

Until the mid-1970s, most of the individuals involved in terrorism were quite well educated. Almost two-thirds of the people identified as terrorists were persons with some university training, university graduates, or postgraduate students. Among the Tupamaros, for example, about 75 percent of their membership were very well educated, and of the Baader-Meinhof organization in West Germany, the figure reached almost 80 percent.

In the Palestinian groups, most members were university students or graduates, frequently those who, by virtue of their middle-class wealth, had been able to study at foreign universities. By 1969, several thousand Palestinians were studying abroad at universities, particularly in Europe, where they were exposed to anarchistic-Marxist ideas. This group became an important recruiting pool for the Popular Front for the

Liberation of Palestine (PFLP). Indeed, the chief of the PFLP for decades, George Habash, was a medical doctor who obtained his degree abroad.

But the level of education of the average terrorist is declining today, partly because of the trend in recruitment age of the last two decades of the twentieth century already noted. If young people are being recruited out of secondary school rather than out of college, then the number of individuals in terrorist groups with college educations will necessarily decline as well.

This trend brings with it another important decline: a diminishing of the understanding by the rank and file among terrorists of the political philosophies that have supposedly motivated the groups to adopt terrorist activities. As a rule, elementary school children are clearly unable to grasp the impetus of Marxist philosophy toward social revolution. Unlike the college students of the 1960s who studied and at least half-understood radical political philosophies, today's new terrorist recruits are fed watered-down versions of Marx and Lenin or religious philosophy by leaders whose own understanding of these philosophers is certainly suspect.

This downward trend in education and understanding of political philosophy is exhibited by terrorist leadership figures as well as by the cadres' rank-and-file memberships. The notorious terrorist, Abu Nidal, leader of the group bearing his name, only attended college in Cairo for two years. Contrary to his claim in subsequent years, he never obtained an engineering degree, or indeed any other degree.

Economic Status

During the 1960s, many young people joined terrorist organizations as a way of rejecting the comfortable, middle-class values of their parents. They were often children of parents who could afford to send them to private colleges, and they were rejecting the comparative wealth of their surroundings to fight for justice for those less fortunate.

Today's terrorists tend to be drawn more from the less fortunate than from the comfortable middle-class homes. Although some come from families who have had wealth but lost it through revolution or confiscation, most are from absolute destitution, individuals for whom terrorism represents the only way to lash out at society's injustices. In the terrorist group, these individuals find a collective wealth and ability to improve one's financial situation that is enormously appealing to the impoverished.

Again, Abu Nidal provides insight into the change in the economic circumstances of the type of person who becomes a terrorist today in many parts of the world. Nidal, born Sabri al-Banna, was the son of wealthy Palestinian parents who lost everything. From the lap of luxury, his family moved into the extreme poverty of refugee camps. The bitterness and frustration of this life of endless poverty and statelessness may well have produced the catalyst for the terrorist he was to become.

Osama bin Laden, however, clearly does not fit this trend in economic status. The son of a multimillionaire, inheriting substantial wealth, bin Laden was, in this respect, more like the terrorists of the 1970s, rejecting the life of wealth and perceiving himself as fighting on behalf of those victimized by the very economic system from which his family benefited. This is remarkably similar to the attitude of the founders of the Tupamaros in Uruguay.

Disturbing Patterns

Although the trends in recruitment of individuals into terrorist acts offer insights into the demographics of groups engaged in terrorism today, there are several more disturbing patterns also emerging. Many individuals who engage in terrorist acts share either a lack or a rejection of the desire for a peaceful society. Among many groups, too, is an emerging, and violent, antipathy toward Western cultures. When these two factors combine with religious fanaticism, the potential for escalating terrorism against Western targets by individuals and groups who share a common enemy and even a common religious motivation easily becomes a holy war of immense proportions.

Socialization toward Violence

As noted earlier, intellectuals have, during the past few decades, helped to make the cult of violence respectable. But for today's terrorists there has been a **socialization toward violence** in ways never experienced before in civilized society. Intellectual terrorists of the 1960s were, for the most part, first-generation terrorists. Today we see an increasing number of third- and even fourth-generation terrorists. Young people recruited in such circumstances have been *socialized to accept violence as a normal pattern of life*. Peace, as much of the rest of the world knows it, has no meaning for them, and the related values of a civilized society have equally little relevance in their lives.

In Northern Ireland and parts of the Middle East, until the peace efforts of the 1990s, this pattern of successive generations of terrorism has produced terrorists who have no understanding of the kind of limits on the use of violence regarded by much of the world as fundamental. Violence is not only a normal pattern of life, but also a means of survival. Its successful use offers a means of security and enhancement of one's own and one's family's, life.

This role of violence is made vividly clear by remarks made by the Reverend Benjamin Weir, a former U.S. hostage held by terrorists in Lebanon in the 1980s. He suggested that, for many Lebanese youths, the only employment open to them that offered both an income and some form of security for their families was with one of the warring militia factions. College was for decades either unavailable or unaffordable, and alternative employment in a nation whose economy was in shambles was unlikely. Life as a terrorist was, in some respects, the *only* alternative for many young people in that war-torn country.

Alienation toward Western Systems

Globalization has left at least 20 percent of the world's population completely stranded, alienated, and desperate, without hope of catching a ride on the accelerating economic train led by the West. Terrorism and violent religious funda-mentalism, however complex their causes, grow well in the soil of poverty and hunger. For people who struggle to feed their families and feel left behind by economic globalization, the call to radicalism is powerful. More than 800 million people globally are chronically undernourished, a condition with devastating con-sequences for their health and for the welfare of their communities. The poverty and hunger in the developing nations threaten social and political stability, while providing fertile ground for those who want to blame the Western governments for these conditions.

Clearly, many who responded to bin Laden's call for holy war against the United States were among those stranded and alienated by the Western-led pattern of globalization. Not only did the poverty and hunger breed resentment of those who appear to enjoy so much of the world's wealth, but the presence of the West, particu-larly the United States, in the Middle Eastern region provided a focus for the anger. When the U.S. presence could be described as desecrating the holy sites of Islam, then the fires of religious zeal could be added to the desperation of poverty and hunger, creating a lethal combination. Globalization was linked in the minds of many with the destitute living to which many were reduced and to threats to the culture by the presence of heretics within the region.

Religious Fanaticism

Like some of the earliest forms of terrorism, drawn from Muslim and Jewish histories, terrorists in the twenty-first century are increasingly motivated by religious zealotry, seeking not only to change a political system but also to purify a religious com-munity. Seeing themselves as called upon to engage in a holy war against infidels who threaten their faith, these modern zealots have begun to have an impact not enjoyed by their predecessors of earlier times. The **Sicariis,** *dagger-wielding Jewish zealots of an-cient Rome who sought to provoke an apocalyptic confrontation between Rome and the Jewish nation,* and the Assassins, noted in an earlier chapter, who tried to purify the Muslim community by assassination in order to hasten the arrival of the Imam, the heir of the Prophet, who would establish a new and just society, had either a negative or at best a relatively insignificant impact on the growth of their faith community.

Modern religious zealots emerging today have been able to seriously impact both political systems and the strength of faith communities in their movement toward holy wars. Extremists carrying out terrorism—by the state, by groups, or by individual suicide bombers—are making the emergence of a political state of Pales-tine and the survival of the state of Israel problematic. Religious leaders in several countries in the Middle East advocate instructing the very young to commit them-selves to religious fanaticism, which makes peace in that region unlikely. Religiously inspired terrorists carried out the attacks of September 11 and impede the rebuilding of both Afghanistan and Iraq by calls for a holy war to purify and protect a faith com-munity. Clearly, religious motivation for terrorism today has not only increased, but is also becoming more successful.

Mastermind of the attacks on the World Trade Center and the Pentagon, as well as the alleged architect of the bombings of the U.S. embassies in Kenya and Tanzania and the attack on the USS *Cole* in Yemen, Osama bin Laden is perhaps the world's best known terrorist. A brief review of his life to date offers interesting insights into the profile of this modern crusader terrorist.

Osama, which means "young lion," in Arabic, was born on March 10, 1957, in Riyadh, Saudi Arabia. His family moved to Medina when he was six months old, later dividing their time between Jeddah and the holy cities of Mecca and Medina. He was the seventeenth son of Mohammed, who had more than 50 sons and daughters by several wives. The construction company that Mohammed founded in 1931 helped to rebuild the al-Aqsa mosque in Jerusalem—the site to which the Prophet was transported in his Night Journey from Mecca—and to renovate the holy places in Mecca and Medina. Mohammed died in a plane crash in 1967, when Osama was 10 years old.

At 17, Osama married a Syrian relative (the first of his four wives) and began his studies at King Abdul-Aziz University in Jeddah soon after this, receiving his degrees in economics and public administration in 1981. At the university, bin Laden became acquainted with both the Muslim Brotherhood, an Islamic group, and the leading teachers in Islamic studies, Abdullah Assam and Muhammad Qutb. Both of these men would influence Osama's life significantly. Azzam would eventually create the first contemporary international jihadist network, and Qutb was the brother of Sayyid Qutb, author of *Signposts,* the key text of the jihadist movement.

Bin Laden absorbed Sayyid's writings with intensity; indeed, they shaped the way he saw the world and his role in it. Sayyid Qutb suggested that the way to establish the Islamic order desired by true Muslims is through an offensive jihad against the enemies of Islam, whether they be non-Islamic societies or Muslim societies that are not following the precepts of the Koran. As one scholar notes, "This is the ideological underpinning of bin Laden's followers, who target not only the West but also such rich Muslim regimes as Saudi Arabia, which they regard as apostates."[10]

In the middle of his studies of these writings, the Muslim world was undergoing a period of substantial change. In 1979, the shah of Iran was overthrown and a Muslim state under the leadership of Ayatollah Khomeini came to Tehran. Egypt and Israel signed a peace agreement in March of that year; in November, hundreds of armed Islamic militants seized the Grand Mosque in Mecca; and the Soviets invaded Afghanistan in late December.

Muslims from around the world were drawn to fight the Soviets in Afghanistan during the 1980s. Rob Schultheis, one of the few journalists who covered this largely ignored war, called it "the holiest of wars," as the Afghans rose up under the banner of Islam to drive the infidels out and to stop the carnage, which ultimately cost more than a million Afghan lives and displaced at least another five million.[11]

Bin Laden, then 22, headed to Pakistan to meet with the Afghan leaders who were calling for support from the Muslim world. He then returned home to Saudi

Arabia to lobby his family and friends for support of the mujahideen. During the next few years, he made several trips to Afghanistan, taking hundreds of tons of construction machinery from his family construction business, which he made available to the mujahideen to build roads, dig tunnels into the mountains for shelter, and build simple hospitals for the wounded.

Having lost his deeply religious father at a very early age, bin Laden was influenced throughout his life by older religious men, often radicals, but always men of strong faith. Each contributed to Osama's vision of the call for a holy war and of the focus of this struggle against the enemies of Islam. He told a Pakistani journalist that his father "was very keen that one of his sons should fight against the enemies of Islam," and he clearly saw himself as fulfilling his father's wishes.[12]

Bin Laden's contribution to the Afghan war was primarily in terms of the fundraising that he did for it and the intensity with which he advocated support for the mujahideen. Like most Afghans who fought in the war, the significance of their interaction lay in the lessons they learned from it, the network that emerged from contact with militants from dozens of countries, and the indoctrination in the most extreme ideas of jihad. All received at least some military training, a little battlefield experience, and went home to continue this jihad on another front.

The war in Afghanistan profoundly affected bin Laden, in what he viewed as a spiritual rather than a political or military context. In an interview with CNN, he stated:

> I have benefited so greatly from the jihad in Afghanistan that it would be impossible for me to gain such a benefit from any other chance . . . . What we benefited from most was [that] the glory and myth of the superpower was destroyed not only in my mind, but also in [the minds] of all Muslims.[13]

Bin Laden's subsequent willingness to call for a jihad against the remaining superpower, the United States, clearly grew from his experiences in the Afghan war. This, from his perspective, was his destiny. The events of September 11, 2001, although not necessarily planned by him, were certainly a fulfillment of his desire for such an attack on what he viewed as enemies of Islam.   ❑

CONCLUSIONS

These trends present an alarming portrait of modern terrorists. Some are younger, much younger than in previous centuries. As any parent (or older sibling) knows, younger children are harder to reach by logical argument. Their values are less clearly formed or understood. They are, as a whole, less rational, more emotional than their elders. They are also less likely to question the orders of their leaders, more likely to follow blindly where their trust is given.

Younger or older, they are less educated, so they are less likely to be following the dictates of their social conscience, or their political philosophy, and more likely to be simply following orders. It is very difficult to reason with someone who is "just following orders." Some of the world's greatest atrocities have been committed by those who were just following orders—who did not even have the excuse of being children.

Individuals committing terrorist acts today are less likely to have a comfortable home to fall back on or to cushion their failure. Instead, their families are increasingly likely to be extremely poor. For these new recruits, membership—and success—in a terrorist group is the only way out of abject poverty. For them, there can be no turning back.

They are used to violence; it is for them a daily occurrence. They neither understand nor recognize the need for limits on that violence. They have seen homes destroyed, families killed, in endless wars of attrition. The idea that civilization wishes to impose limits on the types or victims of violence is beyond their understanding, because they have seen almost every type of violence used against almost every conceivable victim.

Too often, their faith and the teachings of their religious leaders not only justify their actions but call upon them to do more. The agents of socialization—family, community, religion—are now offering increasing support for young people to carry out extreme acts of violence against enemies of their faith community.

These are the new terrorists, and they are a formidable force. Their youth and their patterns of socialization make them unique, even in the long history of terrorism. Whether it is possible for modern civilization to successfully counter this radicalization of the very young toward the violence of terrorism is questionable. What is beyond question is that unless we *can* reverse these trends, civilization will have to cope with an increasing spiral of terror-violence.

EVALUATION

The modern terrorist *is* different. The requisites suggested by O'Ballance are met less frequently, even by terrorist leaders, and the trends in terrorist recruitment suggest an increasing deviation from those norms suggested by that expert.

Taking Osama bin Laden as an example of a modern terrorist leader, try to resolve the following questions:

1. To what extent does bin Laden meet, or fail to meet, the criteria suggested by O'Ballance?
2. To what extent does bin Laden exemplify the trends discussed (toward youthful recruitment, education, etc.)?
3. If bin Laden is a "typical" modern terrorist, what does that suggest about terrorist acts today (more cruel, more indiscriminate)?
4. Are there other leaders who are more typical of modern terrorists?
5. Judging by the trends, from what areas or groups are terrorist recruits more likely to come?
6. Do the individuals who committed the September 11 attacks on the World Trade Center or the Oklahoma City bombing fit the typical pattern offered here?
7. What does this suggest for those who seek to diminish the incidence of terrorism in today's world?

SUGGESTED READINGS

Bergen, Peter L. *Holy War, Inc.: Inside the Secret World of Osama bin Laden.* New York: The Free Press, 2001.

Clarke, Thurston. *By Blood and Fire: The Attack on the King David Hotel.* New York: Putnam, 1981.

Hacker, Frederick J. *Crusaders, Criminals, Crazies: Terror and Terrorism in Our Time.* New York: Norton, 1976.

Hoffman, Bruce. "Defining Terrorism." In *Inside Terrorism.* New York: Columbia University Press, 1998.

Juergensmeyer, Mark. *Terror in the Mind of God: The Global Rise of Religious Violence.* Berkeley, CA: California University Press, 2000.

O'Ballance, Edgar O. *The Language of Violence: The Blood Politics of Terrorism.* San Rafael, CA: Presidio Press, 1979.

Pillar, Paul R., ed. "Dimensions of Terrorism and Counterterrorism." In *Terrorism and U.S. Foreign Policy.* Washington, DC: Brookings Institute Press, 2001.

NOTES

1. Frederick J. Hacker, *Crusaders, Criminals, Crazies: Terror and Terrorism in Our Time* (New York: Norton, 1976), 8–9.

2. Edgar O'Ballance, *The Language of Violence: The Blood Politics of Terrorism* (San Rafael, CA: Presidio Press, 1979), 300–301.

3. Hacker, *Crusaders,* 105.

4. Thurston Clarke, *By Blood and Fire: The Attack on the King David Hotel* (New York: Putnam, 1981), 45.

5. Quoted by Milton Meltzer, *The Terrorists* (New York: Harper & Row, 1983), 111.

6. Walter Lacquer, *The Age of Terrorism* (Boston: Little, Brown, 1987), 92.

7. Ibid., 93.

8. Connon Cruise O'Brien, "Reflecting on Terrorism," *New York Review of Books* (September 16, 1976): 44–48.

9. Charles Russell and Bowman Miller, "Profile of a Terrorist," *Terrorism: An International Journal* 1, no. 1 (1977): 20.

10. Peter L. Bergen, *Holy War, Inc.: Inside the Secret World of Osama bin Laden* (New York: The Free Press, 2001), 48.

11. Rob Schultheis, *Night Letters: Inside Wartime Afghanistan* (New York: Crown, 1992), 155.

12. Bergen, *Holy War,* 52.

13. Bin Laden interview with Peter Bergen and Peter Arnett, May 1997, CNN.

PART II

The Threat Against the Homeland

THE DYNAMICS OF HOSTAGE TAKING AND NEGOTIATION

CHAPTER OBJECTIVES

The study of this chapter will enable you to:

- Sketch the historical precedents of hostage taking
- Describe at least three categories of hostage takers
- Explain the Stockholm Syndrome
- Recognize the need for hostage guidelines
- Review hostage survival strategies
- Trace the historical experience of U.S. hostage-taking rescue attempts
- Describe the Good Guys hostage-taking incident.

INTRODUCTION

The last decade has witnessed a dramatic increase in hostage taking as a preferred tactic of political terrorists. The theatrical nature surrounding terrorist hostage situations has also provided the stimulus for the increase of criminal and psychotic hostage-taking episodes. The high visibility of instant media coverage of the hostage incident has also forced democratic governments and police administrators to develop extensive hostage antiterrorist training programs.

Police statistics reveal that nearly 2,000 people throughout the world have been taken hostage in the last decade; unofficially, several times that number may have been taken hostage. The onslaught of political, criminal, and psychotic hostage-taking incidents has challenged the criminal justice system to develop new countermeasures to control such crime. Recently hostage takers have demanded everything from the freeing of inmates during a prison riot, to the payment of a $100 million ransom for the release of a wealthy businessperson, to political asylum of Cuban skyjackers in the United States, and to demands that Russia end the war in Chechnya. No community or country is immune to the growing phenomenon of hostage taking.

Hostage-taking incidents can occur anytime, anywhere. A simple domestic dispute can quickly escalate into a hostage-taking situation, or a spectacular sporting event, like the Olympic games, can become the object of a hostage taking. The location of a hostage taking can be a government office, a library, or state prison. For the police, hostage taking has become commonplace. In fact, some criminal justice institutions can be described as "hostage prone"—particularly courthouses, jails, and prisons. Police officials responsible for the administration of such facilities must be prepared for the possibility of a hostage taking.

In this chapter, therefore, some of the basic factors related to government and police response to hostage takings are examined. Additionally, a **typology** of hostage takers will be presented; furthermore, the psychological manifestations of the **Stockholm Syndrome**, identification with the aggressor, response of the hostage victim, and techniques for surviving a hostage taking are explored. The purpose here is to alert the reader to the complex problems associated with a variety of hostage-taking scenarios. But first, a brief historical review of hostage taking is in order.

EARLY HISTORY OF HOSTAGE TAKING

Hostage taking has a long relationship with rebellion and warfare. For example, the Roman Empire suppressed revolts in Italy, Spain, and Gaul by requiring the vanquished tribes to give hostages as a guarantee of their future good behavior.[1] Similar tactics were used in Ireland by the Earl of Tyrone during the sixteenth century and again during the French Revolution. More recently, during World War II, Nazi Germany would take hostages in retaliation for acts of sabotage and assassination. In one such incident, during the Nazi occupation of Czechoslovakia in 1942, 10,000 Czech hostages were taken by the Nazis and randomly executed in reprisal for the attempted assassination of Reinhard Heydrich.[2] Likewise, today nuclear strategy based on the alleged balance of power is, as Schelling states, "simply a massive and modern version of an ancient institution: the exchange of hostages."[3]

However, a qualitative distinction in the selection of hostage victims appeared in the twelfth century. In Europe the hostage holding of a member of the nobility was considered to be an effective future bargaining tool. The best-known example was the abduction of Richard the Lionhearted by rival noblemen in Austria in 1193. In order to secure the release of Richard, a large ransom was paid to the Austrians. Similarly, Fredrich Barbarossa seized hundreds of noblemen and high-ranking military leaders in order to secure a favorable peace treaty with Milan in 1158. This pattern of holding powerful government officials or wealthy business tycoons as hostages has continued to the present, although today nonstate hostage takers have become more widespread. The taking of hostages to achieve political objectives by nonstate hostage takers has occurred with regularity in the United States, Northern Ireland, Spain, France, Italy, Germany, and Latin America.[4]

For example, the Zapatistas in Mexico in the spring of 1994 abducted several wealthy Mexican business tycoons and released them only after the payment of large ransoms. Equally, in Colombia, literally thousands of people were taken hostage and held for ransom in 1997. The U.S. State Department has labeled Colombia the kidnapping capital of the world. Colombian terrorist groups such as FARC (Revolutionary Armed Forces of Colombia) and the ELN (National Liberation Army) are responsible for most of the kidnappings and hostage takings.[5]

Thus, in the case of political terrorists, the strategy of taking high-ranking corporate officials hostage accomplishes four objectives for the terrorist organization:

1. The organization acquires large sums of ransom money needed to finance further terrorist activities.
2. The publicity generated by media attention brings the group national and international recognition.
3. The victim is often viewed as exploiting the poor people, which translates into much needed grassroots community support.
4. The free enterprise system is weakened by the intimidation of foreign investments.

TYPOLOGIES OF HOSTAGE TAKERS

There are a number of possible ways to categorize hostage takers, each of which may be used for decision-making purposes, developing negotiating styles, or for academic analysis. Stratton has identified three broad categories and delineates them as follows: (1) the mentally ill hostage taker, (2) the criminal hostage taker, and (3) the social, political, religious, or ethnic crusader hostage taker.[6] The mentally ill hostage taker most often seeks recognition from the intense media exposure that follows the hostage episode. The mentally ill hostage taker also has the ability to exercise considerable power over the police. This is especially true in the barricade/hostage situation where the hostage taker threatens suicide. This hostage-taking event can easily develop into a spectacle, emulating a Cecil B. deMille Hollywood production. For example, on April 3, 1986, a barricaded hostage taker in a crowded South Chicago tenement killed two hostages and was holding one captive and threatening suicide.[7] The building was surrounded by 150 police officers. The hostage taker demanded a pizza be delivered and vowed not to surrender until he had watched a movie on TV. He was permitted to watch his movie and eat his pizza uninterrupted by the police. In a related incident, a barricaded suspect holding two teenage hostages in a Newport, Kentucky, house held off police SWAT teams for over thirty hours, demanding heroin and $20,000 in ransom for the release of the hostages before being killed by a police sharpshooter.[8]

Virtually every police agency in the United States has its own version of the mentally disturbed hostage-taking scenario. The number of incidents is endless. Cooper suggests that the mentally disturbed hostage taker is a person with limited individual power who feels persecuted by the world or a segment of it and strikes back by attempting to physically control someone.[9] Mentally disturbed hostage takers are the most difficult to negotiate with since their actions are irrational and unpredictable.

Criminal hostage takers, on the other hand, are generally the most rational and predictable to negotiate with because they do not want to be arrested. Criminal hostage takers account for approximately 60 percent of all hostage-taking incidents in the United States. Criminals who are fleeing the scene of a felony, such as an armed robbery, often take hostages as a last resort when faced with the unexpected arrival of the police. The fleeing felon can most likely be negotiated out of a potentially dangerous situation by delineating the seriousness of the crime of kidnapping (hostage taking) or false imprisonment, as well as the charge of armed robbery. However, some criminals may try to convince the police they are political terrorists rather than criminals, thus complicating the negotiating process. This was the case when a man claiming to be a Palestinian guerrilla burst into a French courtroom and attempted to free two of France's most notorious criminals.[10] The two French criminals who were on trial for a series of armed robberies were provided with guns, and 35 hostages were taken, including the judge and jury. During the course of the courtroom siege, hostages were released sporadically; after two days, French police negotiators were able to convince the hostage takers that their escape was futile. The political cause proclaimed by the hostage takers was obscure, and few people understood their rhetoric. But what seemed to be yet another hostage tragedy ended with no injuries or deaths.

The social, political, religious, or ethnic crusader hostage taker is most often a member of a group falling within our definition of terrorism. The terrorist hostage taker generally has a strong commitment to a cause or a political ideology. Organizations that seek social change (e.g., Hizballah), political change (the Sikhs in India and the Palestinian Islamic Jihad of Israel), or independence for ethnic minorities (the ETA Basque separatist movement in Spain or the Tamils in Sri Lanka) are well known to the world because of their extranormal acts of terrorism and the publicity these acts generate through intense media involvement. Such groups are the most difficult to negotiate with because of their total commitment to a cause. The crusader terrorist is rational and often enters a hostage-taking situation with preconceived demands and identified limits as to how far the negotiator can be pushed in meeting the stated demands. Therefore, through extensive planning, individual determination, and the ability to manipulate the media, the negotiation process is quite complicated.

The three-way classification of hostage takers has also been analyzed by other criminal justice writers. Middendorff has identified three types of hostage takers: (1) politically motivated offenders, (2) those seeking to escape from something to somewhere, and (3) those seeking personal gain. Middendorff argues that the classification of hostage takers can only be based on motives.[11]

Like Middendorff and Stratton, the New York City hostage-negotiation training program identifies three categories of hostage takers: (1) professional criminals, (2) psychotics, and (3) terrorists. Trainers from that program claim that each type of hostage taker requires a different approach to handling the situation in the process of negotiation. In other words, different motives would require different response strategies by police **negotiators**. For example, a ransom demand can have quite a different meaning for the professional criminal and the terrorist. The professional criminal may use the ransom for personal gratification while the terrorist may use the ransom to purchase guns and explosives to further his terrorist activity.[12]

Richard Kobetz lists five types of hostage-taking situations: (1) prison takeovers and escape situations in which hostages are seized; (2) aircraft hijackings; (3) seizures of business executives, diplomats, athletes, and cultural personalities; (4) armed robberies in which innocent bystanders are seized to effect an escape; and (5) seizures of hostages by mentally disturbed individuals seeking personal recognition. Clearly, his typology involves a synthesis of hostage taker, hostage, and motive. Each category has its own unique features that demand an individual response by police negotiators.[13]

Cooper maintains that hostages are seized by those who perceive the hostage-taking event as a way of setting up a bargaining position that cannot be achieved by other means. He argues for a typology of seven hostage takers: (1) political extremists, (2) fleeing felons, (3) institutionalized persons, (4) estranged persons, (5) wronged persons, (6) religious fanatics, and (7) mentally disturbed persons. Cooper recognizes that his classification is subject to wide criticism since many categories may overlap. But from a police operational point of view, this classification can be used as a guide for action in organizing police/hostage training programs.[14]

Goldaber describes nine categories of hostage takers: (1) suicidal personality, (2) vengeance seeker, (3) disturbed individual, (4) cornered perpetrator, (5) aggrieved inmate, (6) felonious extortionist, (7) social protestor, (8) ideological zealot, and (9) terrorist extremist. The value of Goldaber's typology is that it reveals the complexity of responsive action by the police. For example, negotiating with a suicidal bank robber as opposed to a nonsuicidal bank robber, or a vengeance-seeking terrorist as opposed to a social protestor, requires an extraordinarily complex police response.[15]

The Los Angeles Sheriff's Office states that an understanding of the type of person holding hostages aids the negotiator in identifying the motivation of hostage takers. The Los Angeles Sheriff's Office, then, classifies hostage takers into four broad categories: (1) mentally disturbed persons, (2) common criminals,

TABLE 5.1   **Typology of Hostage Takers**

Criminal	Political Terrorist	Psychotic
Fleeing felon	Seeking media recognition for a cause	Mentally deranged
Prison inmate riots	Social protestor	Suicidal
Extortionist kidnapper	Religious zealot	Angry
Barricaded suspect	Seeking vengeance	Seeking personal recognition
	Air hijacking	Estranged from family
	State as hostage taker	Barricaded suspect

(3) prisoners, and (4) terrorists. The four categories were first introduced by the FBI in the mid 1970s. Since then the four category hostage-taker typology has become the standard for state and local law enforcement agencies in the United States.[16]

The creation of a hostage typology is a useful first step in coordinating police responses. This is the case even though no natural categories of hostage takers exist. The creation of any typology is bound to be arbitrary, reflecting the training and discipline of those who construct them. The most realistic arrangements are those that are able to reduce the subjectivity of the categories. Certainly, this is no easy task. Nonetheless, a typology clearly indicates that different responses (to different hostage types) require a wide variety of police strategies, negotiating skills, and tactical responses. Based on the previous review, we now seek to provide a reasonable typology of hostage takers. The typology is based on the hostage taker's motivation, with the creation of three broad categories and several subcategories. Conceivably, an individual hostage taker could be a psychotic, criminally inclined, political terrorist. (See Table 5.1.)

We will now review some of the general negotiating guidelines that apply most often to all hostage-taking situations.

TIME, TRUST, AND THE STOCKHOLM SYNDROME

The most important factor in any hostage negotiation situation is time. The first few minutes appear to be the most dangerous since the emotional level of both hostage takers and hostages is extremely unpredictable. The confusion, fear, and anxiety at the initial stage of the hostage-taking event predominate and can produce injury and death. However, as time passes and the agitated emotions of the hostage takers and the hostages subside, a period of calm begins. Generally, the longer the hostage-taking incident continues, the greater the probability the hostages will be released unharmed. This phenomenon can be explained in several ways. The passage of time allows the Stockholm Syndrome an opportunity to manifest itself. The Stockholm Syndrome was first observed on August 23, 1973, when a single gunman intent on robbery entered a bank in Stockholm, Sweden. The robbery attempt was interrupted by the police, whereupon the gunman took four bank employees hostage and retreated into an 11-foot by 42-foot carpeted bank vault. The hostage taking was to continue for 131 hours, affecting the lives of the hostages and giving rise to the psychological phenomenon eventually referred to as the Stockholm Syndrome.

The Stockholm Syndrome appears to be an unconscious emotional response to the traumatic experience of victimization. In the Stockholm bank robbery case, the armed bank robber was able to negotiate the release from prison of his former cellmate. This cellmate then joined the bank robber in the vault, thus further complicating negotiating procedures. Now there were four hostages and two hostage takers. During the course of the negotiations, it was discovered that the hostages feared the police more than they feared their captors. In a phone conversation with the prime minister of Sweden, one of the hostages expressed the feelings of the entire group when she stated, "The robbers are protecting us from the police." Eventually, after 131 hours, the bank siege ended; but for weeks after, the hostages complained to psychiatrists that they had chronic nightmares over the possibility that the hostage takers might escape and abduct them again. Yet strangely enough, the hostages felt no hatred toward their abductors. In fact, they felt emotionally indebted to the hostage takers for allowing them to remain alive and saving them from the police.[17]

The Stockholm Syndrome has been observed around the world in a variety of hostage situations. Participants in the hostage drama are cast together in a life-threatening environment where each must adapt in order to stay alive. The positive bond that develops between hostages and hostage takers serves to unite them against the outside influence of the police. Actually the Stockholm Syndrome has been known for quite some time to the psychiatric community, where it often is referred to as "identification with the aggressor." By any name, the syndrome works in favor of the police negotiator. The Stockholm Syndrome may manifest itself in three ways: (1) the positive feelings of the hostages toward the hostage takers; (2) the reciprocal, positive feelings of the hostage takers toward the hostages; and (3) the negative feelings of both the hostages and hostage takers toward the police and the government.[18] Strentz defends the position that hostages regress to an earlier period of development when they are in a state of extreme dependence and fear.[19] This situation is not unlike a parent/child relationship in which the child is emotionally attached to its parents. The positive feelings act as a defense mechanism to ensure the survival of the hostage. Simon and Blum maintain that hostages are in a cognitive bind. On the one hand, they are dependent on the hostage taker for their survival. On the other hand, they are dependent on the police for their rescue. Thus, the hostage is placed in a double jeopardy situation.[20]

Despite the involuntary manifestation of the Stockholm Syndrome, it is not a magical relationship that affects all hostage-taking incidents. The positive contact between hostage taker and hostages is largely determined by the absence of negative experiences during the hostage-taking incident. For example, if the hostages are beaten, raped, or physically abused, the Stockholm Syndrome is less likely to occur. In Iran, during the U.S. hostage crisis that lasted 444 days, few of the freed hostages had any favorable commentary about their captors. In order to prevent the positive feelings the hostage takers might feel toward the hostages, Iranian hostage takers would frequently change guards, and keep some hostages isolated and others blindfolded for long periods of time. In fact, one of the returning hostages stated that "students told him of being trained in the summer of 1979 at Palestine Liberation Organization camps on how to handle hostages."[21]

Aronson maintains that most people cannot harm another person unless the victim has been dehumanized.[22] When hostage takers and hostages are isolated together in a building, airplane, or a bank vault, a process of humanization apparently occurs. A hostage can then build empathy with the hostage taker while still maintaining his or her dignity and individuality, thus lessening the possibility of being physically abused or executed. The exception is the antisocial hostage taker, demonstrated by four Iranians in December 1984.[23] The four seized a Kuwaiti airliner and took refuge in Tehran. Two American hostages were summarily executed, and several other hostages reported being beaten, burned with cigarettes, and having their hair set on fire. Fortunately, this type of hostage incident is rare, and in most situations the Stockholm Syndrome will be present. As time passes and positive experiences begin to develop between hostage takers and hostages, then the hostage's chance of survival becomes much greater.

Certainly the relevance of the Stockholm Syndrome to the police negotiation process is clear. The syndrome's presence may save the life of hostages as well as hostage takers. Understanding the ultimate effects of the syndrome may also prevent the police from resorting too quickly to the use of deadly force. The experience of positive contact often prevents the hostage taker from injuring a hostage he has come to know and in some cases to love. The police negotiator can foster the Stockholm Syndrome by: (1) asking to check on the health of a hostage, (2) discussing the family responsibilities of the hostage with the hostage taker, and (3) requesting information on the treatment of the hostage. The police negotiator should not understate the importance of the human qualities of the victim or hostage.

Time is also important because it allows a "friendly" relationship between the hostage takers and the negotiator to develop. By stalling for time, the negotiator can use several strategies to build rapport and trust with the hostage takers. The improvement of trust between hostage takers and negotiator reduces the likelihood that victims or hostages will be harmed and increases the likelihood that the hostage takers will seriously consider the negotiator's suggestions. Miron and Goldstein outline several techniques for developing trust and rapport between negotiator and hostage takers, which include (1) self-disclosure, (2) empathy, (3) being a good listener, (4) being understanding and showing personal interest in the hostage taker's problems, (5) reflecting on the hostage taker's feelings, and (6) not rejecting outright all demands.[24] The primary role of the negotiator is to establish a favorable and supportive climate with the hostage takers. Even though **time and trust** are generally considered to be the most important factors in the hostage-taking episode, other management and psychological considerations are also very important.

LONDON SYNDROME

The London syndrome is yet another complex concept that occasionally occurs during a hostage-taking crisis. In 1980, hostage takers seized the Iranian embassy in London and took twenty-six people hostage. After six days of unproductive negotiations with the hostage takers, the British Special Air Services (SAS) planned to assault and rescue the hostages. While the SAS planned their assault and rescue, one of the hostages was shot and killed by the hostage takers, and his body was unceremoniously thrown out onto the street. The death of the hostage was the signal for the SAS to assault and attempt to rescue the remaining hostages. Thus began Operation Nimrod, one of the few major counterterrorist rescue operations to occur in front of television cameras. The rescue mission lasted eleven minutes. During the ensuing firefight, four of the five hostage takers were killed and one was captured. In the after-action report, the SAS noted that the hostage killed earlier after negotiations broke down was the only hostage killed or injured by the hostage takers.

Further investigation revealed that the hostage who was killed continually argued with the hostage takers and would at times physically challenge them. After several hours of haranguing the hostage takers, the hostage was shot and killed and his body removed from the hostage location. Hence, the term **London Syndrome** refers to a situation in which a hostage continuously argues or otherwise threatens the hostage takers and the hostage is killed by the hostage takers.[25] Several incidents since the London embassy rescue verify the syndrome. The admonition is as follows: "Don't argue with hostage takers because they will eventually eliminate the argumentative hostage." Obviously, the hostage takers have the power.

The best-known incident involving the London syndrome was the murder of Leon Klinghoffer.[26] Leon Klinghoffer was a passenger aboard the Italian cruise ship the *Achille Lauro*, which was seajacked by four Palestinian hostage takers on October 7, 1985. Once in control of the ship, the hostage takers demanded the release of fifty Palestinians being held in Israeli jails. When the negotiations began to falter, the hostage takers brutally murdered the 69-year-old, wheelchair-bound Leon Klinghoffer, dumping his body and wheelchair into the sea. Reportedly, Klinghoffer confronted the hostage takers and became extremely argumentative, even spitting on the hostage takers. Apparently agitated by the behavior of Klinghoffer, the hostage takers killed him, but killed no other hostages. Even so, there are specific recommended guidelines to resolve hostage-taking incidents.

GUIDELINES FOR HOSTAGE EVENTS

After the drama of the Munich Olympics in 1972, democratic nations recognized a need to deal with political hostage-taking incidents on more than an ad hoc basis. Eleven Israeli hostages, five Palestinian hostage takers, and one police officer were killed when negotiations collapsed and Munich police attempted to rescue the hostages.[27] The Palestinian hostage takers demanded the release of 200 "fedayeen" incarcerated in Israeli jails. The Israelis refused, but after a complicated negotiation process, the West Germans promised the Palestinian hostage takers safe passage to Egypt with their hostages. When Israeli hostages and their Palestinian captors arrived at the Furstenfeldbruck airport, German police sharpshooters were waiting for them. In the ensuing gun battle, the terrorists threw hand grenades into the helicopters holding the Israeli hostages, killing all on board. Police captured three terrorists after the gun battle. The West German police were widely criticized for their use of deadly force. The massacre at Munich caused police administrators worldwide to review carefully and analyze police response to hostage-taking situations. Police and democratic governments suddenly became conscious of their lack of understanding of terrorist hostage takers and the vulnerability of society's institutions. A series of well-trained, elite military units were organized, and the improvement of hostage negotiation skills was undertaken in response to the newest form of criminality: hostage taking.[28]

The circumstances surrounding every hostage-taking situation are somewhat different; however, there are recommended guidelines appropriate for most hostage situations. The selection and training of negotiators is of crucial importance since they provide the link between police authorities and hostage takers. Negotiators should be trained in hostage management strategy, terrorist ideologies, and the psychology of hostage takers. In the case of the **Munich Olympics**, no specifically trained negotiator was available. Several police and government officials representing West German, Israel, U.S., and Arab delegations attempted to negotiate the release of the Israeli hostages without success. One reason for this failure is that high-ranking officials acted as negotiators. Negotiators should be lower- or middle-ranking police officers who report to a decision maker. This buys time since the negotiator must always consult with his or her superiors before a decision is made. Other advantages are that unfavorable decisions will be accepted as coming from "higher-ups" and not the negotiator and, therefore, will not influence the trust that has developed, it is hoped, between negotiator and hostage taker. The negotiator can also direct his or her attention to the immediate task of

FIGURE 5.1 A masked hostage taker of the Black September Organization appears on the balcony in front of the location where Israeli athletes are being held hostage at the 1972 Olympic Games in Munich, Germany. (AP/Wide World Photos)

building rapport with the hostage takers and not be obstructed by management responsibilities.

Cooperation of the media is also essential not to reveal the tactical plans and resources of the police or military. In the Munich incident, no limit was placed on media reporting of West Germany's tactical response.

A chain of command must be established to ensure that communication among responding personnel is free of interference. Communications, firepower, assistance to negotiators, and related resources should be the responsibility of one ranking official.

All police and nonpolice personnel must be readily identifiable and distinguishable from hostages and hostage takers. In the event of an unexpected firefight, police personnel obviously must not be mistaken for hostage takers. In the Munich Olympics, a police officer was killed when he was mistaken for one of the Palestinian hostage takers.

The exact number and identity of hostage takers must be ascertained as quickly as possible. In the event of an assault, the police fire team must be able to distinguish the difference between hostages and hostage takers beyond mere clothing because hostage takers can easily switch clothing or other similar items to confuse or test the trustworthiness of the police. For example, in Munich the police misjudged the number of Palestinian hostage takers, assuming that there were only five holding the Israelis at the Olympic Village. Instead, there were eight. Five sharpshooters were stationed at strategic locations and instructed to "take out" the terrorists after they arrived at the airport with the hostages. Even under the best of conditions, it would have been difficult for the sharpshooters to kill all of the hostage takers before they retaliated against the hostage Israeli athletes. The problem was compounded when one of the police sharpshooters prematurely opened fire. Three hostage takers were disabled, but the others turned on the bound and helpless Israeli hostages with grenades, killing all. If possible, the negotiating team should make every effort actually to see all the hostages and hostage takers.[29]

The negotiator should avoid any shifts in location of hostages by the hostage takers. Most likely this demand is for an airplane, bus, or car for the purpose of escape. Once the hostage-taking location is moved, the negotiator loses the control of the situation that might possibly have been established at the original location. The movement of hostages creates a setting of unpredictability and compounds the task of the negotiator. This loss of control by the negotiator may prompt the mistimed use of deadly force to rescue the hostages, since new resources and new people for the hostage takers are now available. For example, as the hostages were being moved to the airport in Munich, the hostage takers were joined by three companions, seemingly to help control the hostages.

If hostage takers request others, such as relatives or friends, to be present at the scene, the negotiator should avoid this and stall the hostage taker. Like shifts in location, the presence of hostage takers' relatives or friends (religious or governmental) adds that element of unpredictability to the scenario. Friends or relatives may aid the hostage taker, become hostages, or act as an audience for the hostage taker who has suicidal tendencies. The way of handling such a request, rather than outright refusal, is to stall for time. However, there are exceptions, as with all guidelines. The Hanafi Muslim siege of Washington, DC, in 1977, for example, was resolved only after three outside negotiators representing the Islamic faith were requested; they successfully negotiated the release of the hostages,[30] although some experts believe that everything is negotiable.[31]

Certain items are universally accepted as nonnegotiable. Obviously, you would not want to negotiate for new weapons, explosives, or more ammunition, which would increase the level of power or violence potential of the hostage takers. Crelinsten and Szabo cite two additional nonnegotiable policies that are commonly adhered to by police negotiators throughout the world: (1) no exchange of hostages, and (2) no concessions without something in return.[32] Other nonnegotiable items are drugs, narcotics, and alcohol. A hostage situation becomes unpredictable and unduly dangerous when intoxicating substances are introduced. As with requests for others and shifts in location, the negotiator should stall for time.

The use of tricks and deceit by the negotiator during a hostage situation is yet another difficult management consideration. On the one hand, critics of the use of deception maintain that the negotiator must consider the long-term effects of dishonest negotiation because of widespread media reporting of the hostage incident. Then, hostage takers involved in the next incident may not trust any negotiators, thereby reducing the probability of a peaceful resolution of the incident. On the other hand, tricks and deceit are viewed as viable strategies if they work and hostage lives are saved. Evidence indicates, however, that tricks and deceit are likely to be more successful with psychotic and criminal hostage takers than with fanatical and devoted political terrorists. The dilemma is a realistic one and ultimately the use of deception should be based on the circumstances of each individual hostage situation. Generally, the negotiator should avoid promising to meet demands he cannot deliver, especially if the hostage incident generates intense media coverage that is observed by future hostage takers seeking to demonstrate the perfidy of a rival government or the treachery and brutality of the police. The reporting of a hostage-taking event in the United States might reach an audience of 40 million people. What's the chance that some borderline psychotic may be stimulated to take part in some future hostage-taking episode?

Finally, a style of negotiation or overall hostage strategy based on mutual concession is recommended. After reviewing hundreds of hostage-taking incidents, three styles of negotiation have been observed: (1) win/lose, or agitation, (2) harmony, and (3) mutual concession. The agitation style forces the hostage taker into a position where he has no other recourse but to harm the hostages. The negotiator who is more interested in harmony gives in easily, granting the demands of the hostage taker. The preferred style is, of course, one based on compromise, problem solving, and mutual concession.

In sum, the few guidelines highlighted in this section point out the complexity of hostage negotiations. A hostage incident is more than a few "crazy people" seeking recognition. In effect, hostage incidents are contests of power between police and governments on the one hand and a variety of hostage takers on the other hand, the latter representing criminals, political terrorists, and psychotics. The understanding of this power relationship should be an important element in formulating hostage-taking strategies by the police in order to cope with future hostage incidents. What has been the U.S. experience in responding to hostage-taking crises?

U.S. EXPERIENCE: HOSTAGE RESCUE

The most difficult decision during a hostage-taking episode concerns the appropriate time to use force and conduct a rescue attempt. The police and military record in using hostage rescue teams to free hostages is a mixed one. For every spectacular, successful hostage rescue operation, there are many more spectacular failures. A historical review of hostage-taking incidents illustrates the difficulty involved in hostage rescue attempts. The hostage rescue attempt must be perfectly timed and coordinated to catch the hostage takers by surprise and save as many hostage lives as possible. All of this raises the risk of a failed rescue attempt. No two hostage situations are exactly the same. In hostage-taking incidents the type of location may be similar (such as a house, public building, airplane), but the circumstances can vary greatly. What type of hostage takers are involved? What type of weapons do the hostage takers have? What impact will a successful or failed rescue attempt have on the community? What outside support do the hostage takers have? The United States has a long history of hostage rescue attempts, which include a few successes but a far greater number of failures. The following is a representative sample of U.S. government experiences in reacting to political hostage-taking episodes.

The earliest recorded hostage rescue attempt occurred in 1805 when President Thomas Jefferson attempted to rescue 307 Americans being held by Barbary pirates. The Barbary states of Tripoli, Tunis, Algiers, and Morocco had continually harassed American shipping in the Mediterranean Sea, where they seajacked passing American vessels, sold their cargoes, and held their crews for ransom. By 1805 President Jefferson had dispatched the U.S.S. *Philadelphia* to Tripoli to neutralize the Tripolitan Barbary pirates. While the U.S.S. *Philadelphia* was in pursuit of a Tripolitan pirate ship, it ran aground, and 307 U.S. sailors were taken hostage and held for a large ransom. President Jefferson refused to pay the ransom, stating that a ransom payment would only encourage the other Barbary states to take Americans hostage. After failed negotiations with the Tripolitan Barbary pirates, President Jefferson was convinced that the best course of action was to organize an expeditionary force to rescue the hostages. The U.S. expeditionary force or "hostage rescue team" landed on the shores of Tripoli, threatening to march on the capital city and destroy it if the hostages were not freed. The Barbary pirates countered with a threat of their own to kill the U.S. hostages if the expeditionary force did not pull back from the capital city of Tripoli. The stalemate lasted for several days. Finally, President Jefferson agreed to pay $60,000 in ransom for the U.S. hostages. Many people considered the rescue attempt a failure since President Jefferson eventually gave in to most of the demands of the Barbary pirates.[33]

Another 100 years passed before the United States was once again faced with a major hostage crisis overseas. In May 1904 Ion Perdecaris and his stepson were taken hostage in Morocco by a Berber chieftain. What eventually became known as the "Perdecaris incident" prompted President Theodore Roosevelt to dispatch immediately a unit of the U.S. Navy to rescue Perdecaris and his stepson. Turner reports that President Roosevelt's dramatic moves on behalf of two Americans electrified the country and ensured his reelection.[34] However, the U.S. Navy could do little in its efforts to secure the release of the two hostages. The hostage takers threatened to kill the hostages rather than surrender. Once again, a president of the United States was forced to make a deal with hostage takers. The hostage takers received almost everything they demanded, including a large ransom, and Perdecaris and his stepson were released unharmed.[35]

One of the most unusual and lesser known hostage-taking incidents involving negotiations occurred in January 1945. In Santo Tomas University, located in Manila, over 5,000 American and British civilians were being held as prisoners of war by the Japanese. The returning Gen. Douglas MacArthur wanted the prisoners released as soon as possible in order to boost the morale of invading American troops. MacArthur ordered Gen. William Chase to go to Manila and free the prisoners. As Chase and his column of tanks and infantry arrived at Santo Tomas University, the Japanese barricaded themselves in the courtyard and threatened to kill the American prisoners. Chase negotiated with the Japanese for three days. On the first day of negotiation, Chase was allowed to send in food and medical supplies for the American and British prisoners. By the second day the Japanese agreed to release all the children and the most seriously ill and wounded prisoners. Finally, Chase and the Japanese reached a mutual agreement. All the American prisoners were freed, and the Japanese soldiers were permitted to leave Santo Tomas University without their weapons and join elements of the Japanese army still fighting on the outskirts of Manila.[36]

Chase used many of the negotiating tactics considered standard procedure in hostage negotiations today. For example, Chase wisely used the element of time and dragged negotiations out for three days to calm the terrified Japanese hostage takers. He first negotiated for the release of sick and injured prisoners. He did not set deadlines for ending the crisis. He never gave up anything without getting something in return. He had a keen understanding of the personality of the Japanese commander. He would not negotiate for weapons and ammunition. He avoided dismissing any Japanese demand as trivial. He skillfully used the threat of force and violence. At one point in the negotiations, he warned the Japanese if one American was harmed the entire American brigade would attack the University (hostage stronghold). In sum, General Chase used his common sense and performed as a well-trained hostage negotiator.

The hostage incident that stirred the American public to demand immediate rescue was the seizing of the U.S.S. *Pueblo* by North Korea in early 1968. The *Pueblo* was a noncombatant, lightly armed, intelligence-gathering ship with eighty-three sailors on board. The North Koreans took the *Pueblo* to Wonsan, Korea, where the eighty-three sailors became hostages of the North Korean military. The North Koreans laid out their demands, which President Johnson refused to acknowledge. Instead, he called up 14,787 Air Force and Navy reservists, along with 372 aircraft, and positioned several aircraft carriers off the coast of North Korea, threatening to rescue the American seamen by force. North Korea stood firm, insisting that President Johnson acknowledge their demands. In the end, President Johnson agreed to the demands of the hostage-taking North Koreans, who insisted that the United States was spying on North Korea. Again, the threatened rescue mission failed, the hostage takers obtained almost everything they demanded, and the hostages were freed unharmed.[37]

On May 12, 1975, a Cambodian gunboat seized the **S.S. *Mayaguez***, an unarmed container ship off the coast of Cambodia. Thirty-nine American seamen were taken hostage. President Ford, seeking to avoid a *Pueblo*-type incident, immediately prepared to launch a military rescue of the thirty-nine hostages. He and his advisors prematurely concluded that it was futile to negotiate for the release of the hostages with "international pirates." Accordingly, that left only a military-style rescue option. U.S. aircraft and Marines were ordered to rescue the hostages with a land and sea assault, a costly rescue operation. Eighteen Marines were killed when they engaged the Cambodians, and twenty-three Marines lost their lives in a helicopter accident while preparing for the rescue operation. More U.S. troops were killed than the number of hostages taken by the Cambodians. At about the same time the tactical assault began, the Cambodian hostage takers released the thirty-nine American hostages unharmed. The rescue attempt lacked accurate and timely intelligence data. President Ford's decision to rescue the thirty-nine hostages was widely supported by the U.S. Congress, as well as presidential candidate Jimmy Carter.[38]

The most spectacular attempt to rescue U.S. hostages occurred during President Carter's term in office. On November 4, 1979, Iranian terrorists seized the American embassy in Tehran, and fifty-three Americans were taken hostage. Simon reports that preparation for an eventual military rescue operation was begun shortly after the embassy was overrun.[39] However, the implementation of a hostage rescue would be delayed until a coherent plan could be designed and rehearsed. By early April 1980 negotiations with the Iranian hostage takers were at a standstill, and President Carter announced that the United States was breaking off diplomatic relations with Iran. The stage was set for a rescue attempt. Unlike the previous rescue attempts, the newly formed counterterrorist team, **Delta Force**, was specially trained and prepared to rescue the American hostages in Iran. On April 11, 1980, President Carter ordered a military rescue mission for the American hostages, implemented by Delta Force on April 25, 1980.

Operation Eagle Claw, the code name for the hostage rescue operation in Iran, caught many people by surprise. Few people really expected the United States to attempt such a high-risk military rescue. Nonetheless, the rescue mission was plagued by unforeseen circumstances that doomed it from the start. In brief, the rescue plan was for eight helicopters to rendezvous with six C-130 tactical air transports about 150 miles southeast of Tehran. (The code name for the rendezvous point was **Desert One**.) The helicopters were to refuel and then, under the cover of darkness, fly to the outskirts of Tehran, rest until the following evening, and then, in buses and cars provided by Iranian intelligence agents, drive to the U.S. embassy and rescue the American hostages.[40]

However, en route to the Desert One location, two of the helicopters experienced engine problems and were forced to land in the Iranian desert, where the crew abandoned them. The remaining six helicopters became disoriented in a fierce, unpredicted desert sandstorm and lost their way. Thus, the six helicopters arrived at the rendezvous point almost one hour late. The six C-130s encountered no difficulties en route and arrived safely at Desert One. Unfortunately, a third helicopter was judged unsafe to continue the rescue mission, leaving five remaining helicopters, one below the minimum outlined in the original rescue plan. Not wanting to attempt the rescue mission with fewer than six helicopters, President Carter gave the order to abort the hostage rescue mission. As one of the remaining helicopters moved into position for refueling, it collided with a C-130. Both aircraft burst into flames, sending exploding shell casings in all directions and endangering the other aircraft.[41]

Eight members of the 140-man rescue team died in the collision, and their remains were left behind. Sick argues that the decision to leave the bodies of the rescue team behind was prompted by the urgency to flee the area before the Iranian military discovered the flames.[42] The remaining rescue team safely fled the Iranian desert. There is little doubt that the Iranian hostage rescue attempt was an utter disaster for the United States.

In fact, Paul Ryan, a high-ranking military official, maintains that the planning for such a rescue mission was inconceivable and was doomed to failure from

FIGURE 5.2 Iran releases American hostages who were held captive in Tehran for 444 days. The freed hostages arrive at Rhein-Main Air Base in then West Germany on January 21, 1981. (UPI/CORBIS BETTMAN)

the very start.[43] Even several American hostages believed the rescue mission had little chance of success.[44] Eventually, the Iranian military recovered the eight bodies of the rescue team and put them on display in front of the American embassy for the whole world to see. The failed rescue attempt was a great propaganda victory for Iran and a humiliating defeat for the U.S. Delta Force.

The Iranian hostage rescue mission is still widely debated, and it raised several questions regarding the problems associated with the hostage rescue operations. For example, the chances for failure were high since the hostage takers could easily kill all the hostages once the rescue effort began, even though the United States believed it caught the Iranians by surprise. It is conceivable that the Iranians could have learned of the rescue mission and could have been waiting to ambush the U.S. Delta Force once it entered the U.S. embassy. There is no doubt that the risks for a successful hostage rescue attempt in Iran were great. However, those who planned the Iranian rescue mission were confident that the highly trained rescue team, Delta Force, would succeed. The commandos of Delta Force were ready to distinguish themselves in the annals of hostage rescue operations, but unforeseen circumstances would postpone that effort. Probably the most bizarre hostage-taking incident and rescue attempt occurred at the Good Guys electronics store in Sacramento, California.

THE GOOD GUYS HOSTAGE INCIDENT[45]

On April 4, 1991, shortly after 1:00 P.M., four armed Asian males entered the **Good Guys** electronics store in Sacramento, California, in an apparent attempted robbery, and held forty-one men, women, and children hostage in a siege that was to last more than eight hours. Before the hostage-taking incident ended, three hostages were killed, and the hostage takers wounded eleven others. During the tactical assault by members of the Sacramento Sheriff's Selective Enforcement Detail (SED), three hostage takers were killed, and another suspect was seriously wounded. The hostage takers were described as part of a loosely knit Asian gang. According to the police the four hostage takers belonged to an Asian gang called the Oriental Boys, although the police maintained that the hostage-taking incident was not in any way gang related.

The Good Guys incident reflects a type of hostage-crisis negotiation seldom encountered, that is, negotiating with unfamiliar culture. Hammer observes that hostage-taking episodes involving significant cultural differences in beliefs, values, and communication style offer a difficult and uncertain negotiation situation.[46] The rules and principles commonly practiced by skilled negotiators may not be sufficient when cultural dynamics are present. The Good Guys hostage incident is a rare case of intercultural crisis negotiation.

The Good Guys hostage takers were four South Vietnamese males who arrived in Sacramento in 1980 with their parents. Three of the Good Guys hostage takers were brothers. The Nguyen brothers—Long Khoc, 17; Loi Khoc, 21; Pham Khoc, 19—lived with their parents and three other siblings in a cramped, two bedroom apartment complex in South Sacramento. The father of the three Nguyen brothers was a former soldier in the South Vietnamese army who first fled North Vietnam and then fled to Malaysia by fishing boat after the communist takeover of South Vietnam in 1975. Loi Nguyen was a high school dropout, while his brothers Long and Pham attended continuation high school for students with academic problems. Long Nguyen had previously been arrested for burglary and school vandalism. The three Nguyen brothers were fascinated with firearms and often talked of war and being in combat. The fourth member of the "gang" was Cuong Van Tran, 17, who came from an affluent family. Cuong Tran attended high school with Pham and Long Nguyen and, like Long, had a juvenile record of burglary and vandalism. On the day of the Good Guys hostage-taking episode, the Nguyen brothers asked their parents' permission to go fishing on the Sacramento River. However, they took a detour that eventually resulted in one of the most bizarre hostage-taking incidents ever recorded in California.

The Nguyen brothers and Cuong Tran attacked the Good Guys electronics store. Moving quickly through the electronics store with trained, brutal precision, they began rounding up hostages. One hostage stated that they moved through the store like trained commandos. They eventually secured 41 hostages within a defensive perimeter in the front of the store. The four hostage takers were armed with three 9-mm Parabellum 15-shot magazine pistols and a pump action 12-gauge shotgun. Loi Nguyen purchased their weapons at a West Sacramento gun store after waiting the required fifteen days for purchases of pistols. The fifteen-day waiting period is designed to give police authorities time to make a background check on gun buyers. The four hostage takers also had a quantity of .45 caliber ammunition in their possession.

The first police response came after dispatchers received a 911 call for a "robbery in progress, shots fired." At first police assumed they were dealing with ordinary holdup men, possibly attempting to escape from a botched stickup. When the first officers on the scene surrounded the building, it became apparent that this incident was no ordinary robbery-in-progress call. A tense standoff began between the police and the hostage takers who threatened to kill the hostages. Fearing for the safety of the hostages, the first officer on the scene attempted to negotiate with the hostage takers, who demanded his bulletproof vest in exchange for a hostage. The police officer gave up his bulletproof vest, and the hostage takers released a woman and two children. The bulletproof vest was retrieved by a hostage and taken into the store, where the hostage takers tested it by firing a single shot into it. The surviving hostage taker was wearing the bulletproof vest. Thereafter, the hostage takers gave the police more demands. By this time the Selective Enforcement Detail had arrived, and several trained police snipers surrounded the electronics store.

By midafternoon, the nature of the hostage-taking incident began to unfold. In a passionate diatribe, the hostage takers outlined their demands. First, they wanted forty 1,000-year-old ginseng plants or roots, and they wanted the police to cook ten of the ginseng plants to make tea and serve it to them. They also wanted four bulletproof vests, the kind of vests that cover a person from the toes to the neck. They also wanted $4 million in cash and transportation to Thailand, where they intended to shoot Viet Cong. They demanded a helicopter with a capacity for forty people to transport them to Sacramento Metropolitan Airport. They also demanded a .45 caliber pistol.

If these demands were not met, the hostage takers stated that they would start shooting the hostages at 6:00 P.M. They renewed their demands for bulletproof vests and transportation out of the country. They did not renew their demand for money or ginseng plants. In the meantime, the SED team had gained access to a rear storage room in the Good Guys store by entering through the ceiling in an adjoining store. Additionally, the SED team installed a camera lens in the wall of the Good Guys store, enabling them a partial view of the hostages gathered near the main entrance of the store. The hostage situation then entered the negotiation phase.

One of the hostage takers, known as Thailand, began to negotiate with the Sacramento sheriff's negotiator. The performance of the sheriff's negotiator was described by the media as professional and efficient during the siege. Thailand wanted to know when the mayor would arrive at the scene and told the police negotiator he knew they would not be able to get out of the store, but still the hostage takers refused to surrender. Thailand renewed his demand for the release of one hostage for one bulletproof vest. Thailand eventually became agitated with the stalling tactics of the police negotiators and turned the negotiation over to another hostage taker, known only as Number 1. Number 1 then replaced Thailand and also threatened to kill the hostages if the bulletproof vests were not placed in front of the store immediately. Number 1 stated, "We call the shots here," not the police. In fact, Number 1 did not believe the police negotiator had the power to meet any of the hostage takers' demands. At one point a hostage was put on the phone and reiterated the hostage takers' demands for the release of three hostages for three bulletproof vests, stating that the situation was critical and he was in danger of being killed.

By 7:30 P.M. tension began to mount, and the hostage takers tied the hands of several hostages behind their backs and tethered the hostages together. Hostages would later report a frightening ordeal of taunting, constant threats of death, and brutal beatings. The hostage takers flipped coins to see whom they were going to shoot first. The hostage takers told several hostages they would shoot them in the leg first, then the chest, and finally shoot them in the head. Even so, one hostage was sent out by the hostage takers to notify the police that the hostage takers were very serious, and if their demands were not met, hostages would die. When this hostage did not return to the hostage scene with the police response, the hostage takers became very angry. A negotiated settlement rapidly deteriorated.

A second hostage was shot in the leg and sent out to renew the hostage takers' threat that they were serious. The hostage takers demanded three bulletproof vests immediately or another hostage would be shot. The police negotiator stalled; another hostage was shot in the leg, and a third hostage was shot in the back after he collapsed to the floor. The police negotiator then decided to give the hostage takers one bulletproof vest. The bulletproof vest was placed in front of the main entrance to the store. The hostage takers sent a female hostage, who was tethered to a long length of rope with her hands tied to retrieve the bulletproof vest. The police, fearing more hostages would be shot, decided that the time had come to launch an attempted rescue mission. The rescue plan was to begin when the bulletproof vest was retrieved from the front of the store. The plan seemed simple enough. (See Figure 5.3.)

As the female hostage opened the door to pick up the bulletproof vest, an SED sharpshooter, his rifle mounted on a tripod, was given the go ahead to shoot a hostage taker standing near the front entrance as the door was opened. The action by the sharpshooter was the signal to other SED team members hidden in a rear storage room to "take out" the remaining hostage takers and rescue the hostages. However, as the door swung open, the police sniper's bullet shattered the glass door but missed the hostage taker. The hostage takers then turned on the hostages who were lying facedown on the floor in the front of the store and began to shoot several hostages in the back and head. At about the same time, the SED team emerged from the storage room and engaged the hostage takers in a brief but

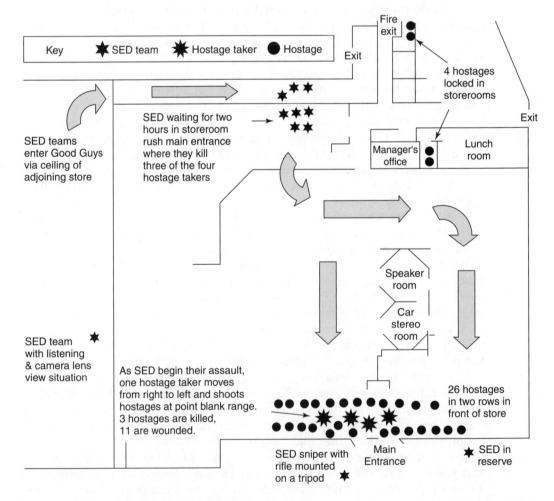

FIGURE 5.3 Good Guys hostage-taking floor plan.

deadly gun battle. Three hostage takers were killed, and one was seriously wounded. The surviving hostage taker, Loi Khoc Nguyen, was convicted on February 9, 1996, of fifty-one counts of murder and assault and was sentenced to life in prison without the possibility of parole.

The Good Guys hostage incident, and the manner in which it was resolved, has much to teach us. The Good Guys incident highlights the special problems of cooperation, personnel, and negotiations that occur when the hostage event involves multiple offenders and many hostages. It is a good example of the careful and coordinated use of highly skilled police personnel. The Good Guys incident underscores how crucial to the outcome are the negotiator's efforts to understand the hostage takers' motivations. Certainly the motivation behind the Good Guys incident was notoriety. The Nguyens and Tran were poor students who could not hold a steady job and blamed their problems on society. The irrationality of the Good Guys hostage takers' demands and the childlike display of anger illustrate the need to develop new strategies for dealing with this type of terrorist psychotic criminal hostage taker.

The Good Guys hostage-taking incident identifies several important topics relevant to hostage negotiations:

1. The need for patience and deliberation, balanced with appropriate levels of force
2. The expressive versus instrumental motivations of the hostage takers
3. The timing of rescue missions
4. Language differences between the negotiator and hostage takers (in the Good Guys incident the hostage takers spoke very poor English)
5. Hostage taking as a desperate cry for attention and affiliation

Reportedly, the Nguyen brothers and Cuong Tran were Hong Kong movie fanatics. All four youths watched the highly stylized films whose gun-toting detectives and gangsters fought it out amid Hong Kong streets and back alleys. The real motivation in the Good Guys hostage-taking incident may be these Hong Kong videos. Gangster films such as *A Better Tomorrow* and *Bullet in the Head* were popular among Vietnamese youth in the late 1980s. Police investigators speculate that such films' gang shooting scenes, in which gunmen coolly flipped coins to decide which of the hostages would be shot first, influenced the Good Guys hostage-taking incident.

In *Bullet in the Head*, three best friends, blood brothers from Hong Kong looking to make a name for themselves, travel to Vietnam during the war to smuggle drugs and instead begin to fight the Viet Cong. While in Vietnam, the blood brothers are searching for their souls. They cannot decide whether they are good guys or bad guys. Along the way the brothers are captured by the Viet Cong and tortured. Eventually, the brothers escape from the Viet Cong. Hence the rationale—the bad guys take hostages at the Good Guys electronic stores.

A few weeks after the Good Guys hostage-taking incident, the Sacramento Sheriff's Department received a threatening letter signed by the Brothers of the

Dragon: "On 4-4-91 you have killed our brothers in Sacramento for no reason. For this reason there must be revenge. The Brothers of the Dragon have decided in a meeting a lesson will be made." On the margins of the letter were the Vietnamese words that embody the gangster theme, words that many Vietnamese gang members have tattooed on their skin: Tinh, Tien, Tu, Toi, Thu—Love, Money, Prison, Sin, Revenge. However, the Brothers of the Dragon never carried out the threat.

Obviously, future negotiators will need to add an increased understanding of cultural awareness to their archives on negotiator behavior. Even so, groups motivated by political and religious beliefs have proven to be the most difficult, dangerous, and threatening for law enforcement to negotiate with. Negotiators must understand the group they confront.

OTHER RESCUE ATTEMPTS

Entebbe and Beyond

The raid on **Entebbe Airport** in Uganda by Israeli commandos has been considered the model for successful military hostage rescue attempts. Whenever the United States or other countries are confronted with a high-visibility hostage situation, the question often raised is whether they can duplicate the success of the Israelis. In a daring hostage rescue mission in 1976 that has yet to be duplicated, the Israelis flew more than 2,500 miles to Entebbe Airport in Uganda and freed over 100 Israeli hostages. During the raid 3 hostages were killed, along with 7 hostage takers, 40 Ugandan soldiers, and the Israeli operational leader of the rescue mission. Simon points out that the raid on Entebbe was unique and aided by several factors that are unlikely to be present in other hostage-taking episodes.[47]

First, the Israelis helped train the Ugandan military forces in the tactics of counterterrorism and hostage rescue. Thus, they were familiar with the Ugandan military defenses that surrounded Entebbe Airport. The Israelis also knew the physical layout of Entebbe Airport since an Israeli construction firm built much of it. Additionally, the rescue operation caught nearly everyone by surprise. The raid on Entebbe was the first long-range hostage rescue operation, and terrorist hostage takers were not yet familiar with counterterrorist military-style operations. The Israeli success at Entebbe stimulated the United States and other countries to develop their own counterterrorist and hostage rescue capabilities, with the result that several other countries have conducted successful hostage rescue missions. A few notable examples follow.

On Christmas Eve, 1994, four members of the **Armed Islamic Group (GIA)** of Algeria, posing as baggage handlers, boarded an Air France jetliner in Algiers and took 227 passengers and twelve crew members hostage. The hijackers were armed with AK-47s and at least two handguns. They demanded the release of their spiritual leader, who was being held in an Algerian jail, or hostages would be killed. Five hours after the hostage taking began, the hostage takers unexpectedly released nineteen women and children, although two hostages were brutally killed and their bodies thrown from the aircraft. On the second day of the hostage standoff, the hostage takers released more women and children and killed a third hostage. The hostage takers then issued a new demand. They wanted to leave Algiers and fly to Paris, the original destination of the hijacked plane. The Algerian government reluctantly allowed the plane to leave for Paris with a stop in Marseille for refueling. The elite French GIGN (Gendarmerie Nationale) counterterrorist hostage-rescue team was waiting.

As the hijacked plane sat on the runway in Marseille, negotiations were stalled, and the hostage takers would not surrender. The hijackers gave a new deadline for their demands and threatened to begin killing more hostages if their demands were not met. Not wanting to see another innocent hostage killed, GIGN assaulted the plane. The hostage rescue team yanked open the doors of the plane and threw "flash bangs" to confuse the hostage takers. Flash bangs produce a loud noise and a brief intense light designed to disorient hostage takers. Next the rescue team exchanged rapid bursts of gunfire with the hostage takers. In the end, the hostage-taking ordeal lasted for 54 hours; 25 people were injured, including 13 hostages, 9 members of the rescue team, the pilot, and 2 crew members. The 4 hostage takers were killed during the assault and rescue. The entire rescue operation took only seven minutes.[48]

The hijackers actually wanted to fly the plane into the Eiffel Tower and explode it over Paris. Freed hostages reported that the hostage takers had planted dynamite under the seats of the plane. The hijackers also demanded the plane's fuel tanks be filled with three times the amount of fuel to reach Paris. Because negotiators believed that the hijackers were creating a bomb, they decided to attempt a hostage-rescue effort. The rescue of the hostages was one of the most successful since the raid on Entebbe. It now seems clear that the terrorist GIA learned an important lesson. The plan was defeated partly because the hijackers could not fly the plane. Today we are confident that GIA has close ties with al Qaeda and Usama bin Laden.[49]

On December 17, 1996, Peru faced a hostage-taking crisis that would last for 126 days.[50] During a reception being held at the Japanese ambassador's residence in Lima, twenty terrorist hostage takers from MRTA or the **Tupac Amaru** suddenly appeared and took several hundred guests hostage. The Tupac Amaru is a symbol of rebellion in Peru. In 1572 the name belonged to an Incan chief who attempted to overthrow Spanish colonial rule in Peru. Thus, the name became a rallying cry for Peruvian peasants through the centuries and would not die. By the early 1980s the Tupac Amaru would become one of the most dangerous terrorist groups in Peru. In terrorist attacks across Peru, the group killed thousands of innocent civilians. However, after the election of a new Peruvian president, who vowed to eliminate terrorism in Peru, hundreds of members of Tupac Amaru were either killed or apprehended by Peruvian police. By late 1996 Peru's president boasted that he had "knocked out" terrorism in Peru. It seemed that way until the evening of December 17, 1996.[51]

During a reception, twenty terrorist hostage takers of the Tupac Amaru overran the Japanese ambassador's residence and took 600 of Peru's political, religious, and social elite hostage. Within minutes police arrived on the scene and engaged the hostage takers in a forty-minute gun battle, capturing six of the hostage takers. After about an hour, the hostage takers had secured the Japanese ambassador's residence and began to negotiate for the release of the hostages. In a goodwill gesture, the hostage takers released all the women and elderly hostages. By the fifth day the hostage takers released 225 additional hostages. After the ninth day the Tupac Amaru held 103 hostages. The Tupac Amaru demanded the release of 400 prisoners from Peruvian jails, including the wife of the leader of the hostage takers. In addition, an improvement in Peruvian prison conditions was demanded for all prisoners. The Peruvian government took a hard-line stance and refused to negotiate and make concessions for the release of the hostages. Instead, the Peruvian government formulated a complicated rescue plan.

The rescue plan was to build five tunnels under the hostage-taking location (Japanese ambassador's residence) that would allow a counterterrorist team to storm the site. Also, the Peruvians began to collect intelligence information on the daily routine of the hostage takers. The Peruvian president made his last negotiated offer that if hostages were freed the hostage takers would be granted political asylum in Cuba. The hostage takers refused. Tension and stress were building among negotiators, hostage takers, and hostages. A negotiated settlement seemed remote. Then on April 20, 1997, the 140 members of the Peruvian Counterterrorist Team gathered in the tunnels awaiting the signal for the attempted rescue. After two days the rescue team was in place, and on April 22, 1997, the rescue operation commenced. Explosives were placed at several locations that allowed the tactical team to breach the residence and engage the Tupac Amaru in a 23-minute gun battle. All fourteen hostage takers were killed. The hostage takers were completely taken by surprise. Two members of the counterterrorist team were killed, and one hostage died of a heart attack during the rescue. The daring rescue mission was an extraordinary success attributed to "state of the art" surveillance, superior intelligence information gathering, and careful, meticulous planning.[52]

On October 23, 2002, Russia was faced with an unusual hostage-taking event involving multiple hostages and multiple hostage takers. Fifty heavily armed Chechen hostage takers, including twenty women, seized over 800 hostages at a theater in central Moscow. The hostage takers identified themselves as members of the 29th Division of the Chechen Army. The Chechen hostage takers, dressed in camouflage clothing, wore suicide explosive belts around their bodies. They took up positions around the theater and planted mines and explosive charges at the entrances and exits of the theater. The women hostage takers moved into the crowded theater and sat among the terrified audience, threatening to detonate the suicide explosive belts wrapped around their bodies. During the next several hours, the hostage takers allowed water to be delivered to the hostages and released about eighty hostages, mostly women and children. Two hostages were killed when they attempted to escape.

The Chechen hostage takers demanded an end to the war in Chechnya between the Russian military and Chechen rebels. In addition the hostage takers wanted Russia to pull all its troops out of Chechnya within a week. If the Russians did not meet the Chechen demands, hostages would be killed, and the theater would be blown up. The hostage takers said they were ready to die along with the hostages if their demands were not met. Negotiations dragged on for three days. The hostage takers would not give up, and the Russian government would not give in.

Meanwhile, Russian troops and police surrounded the theater while the Russian special operations hostage-rescue team (Alpha) prepared to conduct a rescue of the hostages. On Saturday, October 26, the hostage takers presented a new demand that if Russian troops did not begin to pull out of Chechnya by 6:00 A.M. they would begin to execute the hostages. Fearing for the lives of the hostages, the Russians decided to attempt a risky rescue mission.

Under the cover of darkness, using night vision goggles, the hostage-rescue team moved into place around the theater. Once the rescue team was in place, the Russians released a deadly narcotic gas into the theater's ventilation system. The gas quickly immobilized the hostages and the hostage takers who were knocked unconscious. The rescue team blew a hole in the wall of the theater, entered, and killed forty-seven of the unconscious Chechen hostage takers and disarmed the explosive devices. Three hostage takers escaped but were apprehended two hours later. At first the rescue effort appeared to be successful. The gas was only to render the hostages and hostage takers unconscious for a short period of time. However, this was not the case.

The gas the Russians used was Fentanyl, an opiate-based narcotic a hundred times more powerful than morphine. Fentanyl not only causes extreme drowsiness but can also cause breathing to stop. Unfortunately Fentanyl killed 129 innocent hostages. Russian negotiators maintained that the use of the deadly gas was necessary in order to neutralize the hostage takers who were strapped with explosives and threatening to kill everyone. The Russians insisted that Fentanyl by itself could not have resulted in the deaths of so many hostages. Rather the deaths of the hostages resulted from their weakened condition: lack of movement, hunger, dehydration, severe stress, and a lack of oxygen after three days of being held captive. President Putin defended the rescue operation by stating we "managed to do the impossible" and saved most of the 800 hostages.[53]

Throughout the last few years, there have been several terrorist hostage-taking incidents carried out by Chechen rebels. For example, Chechen rebels have taken mostly Russian hostages at hospitals, and hijacked airplanes, ships, and busses all in an effort to force Russia to grant independence to Chechnya. In sum, in the breakaway Russian Republic of Chechnya, Russia says it is fighting terrorism while Chechen rebels say they are fighting for independence. The outcome seems to be an ongoing war that will continue for many years to come.

In summary, the rescue operations illustrate the importance of training, planning and the use of high-tech equipment. In addition, the effective use of diversions or distractions is apparent. The use of flash bangs and disabling gas illustrate the need for creative planning to gain a few seconds' advantage over the hostage takers. Split-second timing and close-quarters combat are skills often necessary for the safe release of the hostages. However, it must be restated that every hostage situation is different, and the tactical rescue attempt is never the same. A decisive turning point in the formation of highly trained hostage rescue units was the Munich Olympic hostage-taking episode.

SURVIVING A HOSTAGE SITUATION

Past experience has shown that people who are prepared suffer the least physical abuse and emotional trauma when taken hostage. Even though every hostage situation is somewhat different and every individual reacts differently, the following proposed guidelines may prove useful in surviving the growing threat of the sudden, unpredictable captivity of being held hostage. So, how does one prepare to be a hostage?

The most critical points of any type of hostage situation come at the moment of capture and release. The important thing is to remain calm and not to panic. During the capture phase of the incident, the hostage should avoid unnecessary or unexpected movements, crying out for help, or making loud noises. Obviously, the initial reactions of hostages are fear, disbelief, and shock. This fear must quickly be overcome so that the hostage can regain composure and recognize the reality of captivity. At the initial phase of captivity, should the hostage resist or surrender? Generally, this is a personal decision based on the circumstances and the amount of danger involved in trying to escape. Because of the uncertainty involved at the moment of capture, it is recommended that the hostage reassure the hostage taker of his or her intention to cooperate. The potential hostage must also be psychologically prepared to cope with blindfolds, gags, being bound, and drugs. Blindfolds and hoods are used to disorient and confuse the hostage. Gags prevent talking or shouting out and being bound hand and foot prevents escape. Being blindfolded, gagged, and bound, the hostage then becomes a mere object, less than a human being, making it easier for the hostage taker to assault the hostage.[54]

After the initial phase of captivity, the hostage must adjust. There are several recommendations: (1) exercise when possible and keep fit, (2) keep a sense of humor by remembering that others have survived similar or worse situations, (3) try to establish a routine; this gives the hostage the feeling of control over the environment, (4) try to keep a sense of time orientation by inwardly recording time, place, and routine of the hostage takers, (5) if singled out, try to relate to the

FIGURE 5.4   American journalist Terry Anderson was held hostage in Beirut, Lebanon, from March 1985 to December 1991. Anderson describes how he survived seven years as a hostage of Islamic extremists in his book *Den of Lions.* (AP/Wide World Photos)

hostage taker as a human being—for example, mention personal events, emphasizing children and family, (6) do not let hostage takers dehumanize you, (7) when physically beaten, do not be a hero; show pain; if you have any medical problems, notify the hostage takers immediately, (8) if interrogated by the hostage takers, tell the truth; avoid embellishments that will cause damage later in the situation, and (9) do not try to escape unless the probability of success is high.[55]

During the capture phase, the captors may also heighten fear by loading and unloading weapons in the presence of hostages, by staging mock executions, by dramatic displays of temper, by physical abuse, and by continually threatening to kill the hostages. But time is in the favor of the hostages. The longer the hostage situation continues, the greater the chance hostages will be released unharmed. Passage of time without rescue or release is quite depressing. To overcome this depression, the hostage can establish rapport with the hostage taker but should not fake interest in support for the hostage taker's cause. Terrorist hostage takers will use that support for propaganda purposes.

The most dangerous phase of any hostage-taking situation is during a negotiated release or a tactical rescue attempt. Seventy-five percent of all casualties occur during release and rescue operations. If a negotiated release is agreed upon, hostage takers may be nervous and fearful of a double cross, anxious to escape capture and punishment. Therefore, hostages must not act in any manner that would endanger their lives, such as an angry outburst toward the hostage takers. In the case of a tactical rescue attempt, hostages must avoid panic and remain as calm as possible. The tactical rescue is based largely on surprise and shock. During the rescue phase, hostages and hostage takers will experience momentary panic and fear. Confusion may also result from gunfire, explosions, and tactical team members shouting instructions to both hostages and hostage takers. The hostage must avoid the impulse to flee during the rescue operation. Rescue team members can easily mistake hostages for hostage takers. The safest response for hostages is to immediately drop to the ground and lie as flat as possible.[56]

The experience of being a hostage does not end with the resolution of the situation either by negotiated release or tactical rescue. Generally, the victimization hostages live through can be either uncomplicated or pathological. Following the hostage crisis, many hostages develop a variety of psychological problems, including nightmares, phobias, depression, and startle reactions. For example, five years after the Iranian hostage episode, at least one-half of the American hostages reported still having nightmares about their captivity in Iran.[57] A hostage may not suffer depression until after the situation has ended. The intense media coverage of hostage incidents makes celebrities of some hostages. This certainly was the case during the seventeen-day captivity of TWA 847 in June 1985. However, as the celebrity status begins to recede, depression may occur. Ochberg identifies additional psychological manifestations of postrelease hostages, including paranoid reactions, obsessions, idiosyncratic difficulties, and the Stockholm Syndrome.[58]

For some people (high-risk corporate executives, diplomats, and ranking military personnel) preparing for captivity is just as important as preparing tighter security measures to avoid being captured. Therefore, potential targets should realize what their own instinctive reactions will be during captivity, what hostage

TABLE 5.2 Hostage Event

Normal Response	Pathological Response
Outcry: fear, sadness, anger, rage	**Overwhelmed:** emotional reaction of panic and fear
Denial: "This cannot be happening to me"	**Extreme avoidance:** using drugs/alcohol to avoid pain
Intrusion: voluntary thoughts of the event	**Flooded states:** disturbing nightmares and thoughts of the event
Working through: facing reality of situation	**Psychosomatic responses:** developing new ailments
Completion: going on with life	**Character distortions:** long-term distortions of ability

takers might expect hostages to do, and what hostages can do to overcome the psychological and physical pressures of being held captive.

In sum, the psychological literature identifies five states of **hostage reaction** to captivity. The five states can be categorized into a normal response and a pathological response. The emotional impact of being held hostage has a devastating effect on some hostages—they may never outlive the experience of having been held hostage. (See Table 5.2.)

CONCLUSIONS

Hostage taking will continue to escalate because of the proven benefits of intense publicity and as a cost-effective method of extorting a ransom. Hostage taking does work. It works for criminals except in those countries where the police are efficient and trusted by the populace. In recent years, for example, Italy has reported the hostage taking of 334 people by criminal gangs and ransoms of $185 million paid for the release of the victims.[59] It works for terrorists except where states are repressive. Terrorist groups have taken hundreds of people hostage and millions of dollars have been paid in ransom by businesses and private citizens. But above all, the taking of hostages brings terrorists, psychotics, and criminals publicity and recognition. For example, little was known of Palestinians, Chechens, Peruvian rebels, Croatians, or Kashmiris until their criminal acts of hostage taking filled the media. One factor that could disrupt the trend of hostage taking is to establish stringent security measures. More effective security measures should deter and reduce attacks on corporations, embassies, airlines, and individuals by raising the potential risks, and the costs to hostage takers in terms of death or imprisonment. Another factor that could impinge on the escalation of hostage taking is the universal application of a no-ransom policy. If a policy of no ransom or no concessions were uniformly applied without major exceptions, then the probability of reducing hostage episodes might rise dramatically.

The possibility also exists that terrorists or psychotics could take mass hostages involving not just individual victims or corporations but the governments they represent. Nuclear threats by terrorists against major cities are not an unlikely scenario confined to paperback novels. Another reasonable conclusion is that as hostage taking increases, governments will be forced to devote sizable resources and money to the protection of key communication networks, nuclear plants, and energy systems. Recall that 9/11 began as a hostage-taking incident. Finally, the need to improve negotiation skills and tactical responses is imperative if we expect to effectively manage the hostage crisis. The next chapter examines the most common act of terrorism in the world today—indiscriminate bombing.

KEY TERMS

Delta Force	**hostage reaction**	**Stockholm Syndrome**
Desert One	**London Syndrome**	**time and trust**
Entebbe Airport	**Munich Olympics**	**typology**
GIA	**negotiator**	**Tupac Amaru**
Good Guys	**S.S. *Mayaguez***	

REVIEW QUESTIONS

1. Why was the Munich Olympics a turning point in hostage negotiation strategies and tactical response?
2. Describe the Stockholm Syndrome.
3. Why will hostage taking continue to be a major problem for police agencies?
4. How realistic is a repeat of the Good Guys hostage incident?
5. You are negotiating with a psychotic terrorist hostage taker who is prepared to surrender. As he approaches the door, he recognizes a police sniper stationed on a nearby rooftop. He runs back inside and begins to threaten the hostages, claiming you set him up to be killed. What would you say or do to get negotiations "back on track"?
6. When is the appropriate time to execute a hostage-rescue attempt? Be specific.
7. Identify the following:
   a. FARC
   b. USS *Pueblo*
   c. Operation Eagle Claw
   d. Entebbe Airport
   e. Armed Islamic Group (GIA)
   f. Tupac Amaru
   g. ETA
   h. Chechens
8. How do you determine when the Stockholm Syndrome is not developing?
9. Develop your own typology of hostage takers.
10. What differentiates criminal and political terrorist hostage-taking episodes?

11. List and describe at least six hostage-taking guidelines that are present in every hostage-taking incident.

WEB SITES

International Policy Institute for Counter-Terrorism
http://www.ict.org.il/
Security Resource Net's Counter Terrorism
http://nsi.org/terrorism.html
Human Rights Databank
http://www.hri.ca
Amnesty International
http://www.amnesty.org
Jewish Legal Intelligence
http://www.jurist.law.pitt.edu

ENDNOTES

[1] Robert B. Asprey, *War in the Shadows. The Guerrilla in History* (London: MacDonald and Jane's, 1975), p. 20.

[2] J. Bowyer Bell, *Assassin: The Theory and Practice of Political Violence* (New York: St. Martin's Press, 1979), p. 102.

[3] Thomas C. Schelling, *The Strategy of Conflict* (London: Oxford University Press, 1973), p. 239.

[4] Clive C. Aston, "Political Hostage Taking in Western Europe: A Statistical Analysis," in *Perspectives on Terrorism*, eds. Lawrence Z. Freedman and Yonah Alexander (Wilmington, DE: Scholarly Resources, 1983), p. 100.

[5] For example, see Ann Hagedorn Auerbach, *Ransom: The Untold Story of International Kidnapping* (New York: Henry Holt, 1998); Kirk Semple, "The Kidnapping Economy," *The New York Times Magazine*, June 3, 2001, p. 46.

[6] John G. Stratton, "The Terrorist Act of Hostage Taking: Considerations for Law Enforcement," *Journal of Police Science and Administration* 6 (1978), pp. 123–24.

[7] *Sacramento Bee*, April 4, 1986, sec. A, p. 10.

[8] *Sacramento Bee*, December 31, 1985, sec. A, p. 8.

[9] H. H. A. Cooper, *The Hostage Takers* (Boulder, CO: Paladin Press, 1981), pp. 53–61.

[10] *Time Magazine*, December 23, 1985, p. 35.

[11] Wolf Middendorff, *New Developments in the Taking of Hostages and Kidnapping: A Summary* (Washington, DC: National Criminal Justice Reference Service, 1975), pp. 1–9.

[12]Frank Bolz Jr., "The Hostage Situation: Law Enforcement Options," in *Terror-ism: Interdisciplinary Perspectives*, eds. Burr Eichelman, David A. Soskis, and William H. Reid (Washington, DC: American Psychiatric Association, 1983), pp. 99–116.

[13]Richard Kobetz, *Hostage Incidents: The New Police Priority* (Gaithersburg, MD: International Association of Chiefs of Police, undated mimeo).

[14]Cooper, *The Hostage Takers*, pp. 1–3.

[15]Irving Goldaber, "A Typology of Hostage Takers," *Police Chief* (June 1979), pp. 21–22.

[16]Los Angeles Sheriff's Office, *Special Enforcement Bureau (SEB): Hostage Guidelines*, July 1998.

[17]David A. Soskis and Clinton Van Zandt, "Hostage Negotiation: Law Enforcement's Most Effective Non-lethal Weapon," *FBI Management Quarterly* 6 (1986), pp. 1–8.

[18]Murray S. Miron and Arnold P. Goldstein, *Hostage* (New York: Pergamon, 1979), p. 9.

[19]Thomas Strentz, "Law Enforcement Policy and Ego Defenses of the Hostage," *F.B.I. Law Enforcement Bulletin* (April 1979), p. 4.

[20]Robert I. Simon and Robert A. Blum, "After the Terrorist Incident: Psychotherapeutic Treatment of Former Hostages," *American Journal of Psychotherapy*, 41 (April 1987), pp. 194–200.

[21]Robert D. McFadden, Joe B. Treaster, and Maurice Carroll, *No Hiding Place* (New York: Times Books, 1981), p. 120.

[22]Elliot Aronson, *Social Animal* (San Francisco, CA: W. H. Freeman, 1972), p. 168.

[23]*Sacramento Bee*, December 11, 1984, sec. A, p. 1.

[24]Miron and Goldstein, *Hostage*, pp. 101–102.

[25]Thomas Strentz, *FBI Hostage Negotiation Training Program*, San Diego, CA, March 17, 1986.

[26]For example, see Antonio Corsese, *Terrorism, Politics and Law: The* Achille Lauro *Affair* (Malden, MA: Blackwell Publishers, 1989).

[27]Manfred Schreiber, *After Action Report of Terrorist Activities 20th Olympic Games Munich, West Germany FRG*, September 1972, p. 14.

[28]Simon Reeve, *One Day in September: The Full Story of the 1972 Munich Olympics Massacre and the Israeli Revenge Operation "Wrath of God"* (New York: Arcade Publishing, 2000), pp. 20–48.

[29]Ibid., pp. 105–15.

[30]Miron and Goldstein, *Hostage*, pp. 53–62.

[31]For example, see Frank Bolz et al., *Counterterrorism Handbook: Tactics, Procedures, and Techniques* (New York: Elsevier, 1990).

[32]Ron A. Crelinsten and Denis Szabo, *Hostage Taking* (Lexington, MA: Lexington Books, 1979), p. 53.

[33]Jeffery D. Simon, *The Terrorist Trap: America's Experience with Terrorism* (Bloomington: Indiana University Press, 1994), pp. 29–33.

[34]Stansfield Turner, *Terrorism and Democracy* (Boston: Houghton Mifflin, 1991), pp. 8–9.

[35]For example, see Godfrey Fisher, *Barbary Legend: War, Trade and Piracy in North Africa* (Westport, CT: Greenwood, 1974).

[36]For example, see Frederic H. Stevens, *Santo Tomas Internment Camp* (New York: Stratford House, 1946); Emily Van Sickle, *The Iron Gates of Santo Tomas* (Chicago: Academy Chicago, 1992).

[37]For example, see Ed Brandt, *The Last Voyage of the USS* Pueblo (New York: Norton Press, 1969); Lloyd M. Bucher, *Bucher: My Story* (New York: Doubleday, 1970).

[38]For example, see Richard G. Head, *Crisis Resolution: Presidential Decision Making in the Mayaguez and Korean Confrontations* (Boulder, CO: Westview Press, 1978); Christopher Jon Lamb, *Belief Systems and Decision Making in the Mayaguez Crisis* (Gainesville: University of Florida Press, 1989).

[39]Simon, *The Terrorist Trap: America's Experience with Terrorism*, pp. 125–35.

[40]For example, see Charlie A. Beckwith and Donald Knox, *Delta Force* (New York: Dell Books, 1983); James H. Kyle, *The Guts to Try: The Untold Story of the Iranian Hostage Rescue Mission by the On-the-Scene Desert Commander* (New York: Orion Books, 1990).

[41]For example, see Gary Sick, *All Fall Down: America's Tragic Encounter with Iran* (New York: Random House, 1984); David P. Houghton, *U.S. Foreign Policy and the Iran Hostage Crisis* (New York: Cambridge University Press, 2001); Massoumeh Ebthkar, *Takeover in Iran: The Inside Story of the 1979 U. S. Embassy Capture* (London: Talonbooks, Limited, 2001).

[42]Sick, *All Fall Down: America's Tragic Encounter with Iran*, pp. 35–55.

[43]Paul B. Ryan, *The Iranian Rescue Mission: Why It Failed* (Annapolis, MD: Naval Institute, 1985), pp. 31–39.

[44]McFadden et al., *No Hiding Place*, pp. 115–25.

[45]Glen Craig, Sheriff, Sacramento County Sheriff's Office, *Training Video on Good Guys Incident* (Sacramento: Sacramento County Sheriff's Office, April 1991).

[46]Mitchell R. Hammer, "Negotiating Across the Cultural Divide: Intercultural Dynamics in Crisis Incidents," in *Dynamic Processes of Crisis Negotiation: Theory, Research, and Practice*, eds. Randall G. Rogan, Mitchell R. Hammer, and Clinton R. Van Zandt (Westport, CT: Praeger, 1997), pp. 105–15.

[47]Simon, *The Terrorist Trap: America's Experience with Terrorism*, pp. 3391–393; see also Iddo Netanyahu, *The Jonathan Netanyahu Story: The First Battle in the War on Terrorism* (Green Forest, AR: New Leaf Press, 2003).

[48]*San Francisco Chronicle*, December 27, 1994, p. 1.

[49]Chris Hansen, "The Lesson of Air France Flight 8969," February 6, 2003, *http://www.msnbc.com*.

[50]*Sacramento Bee*, December 18, 1996, p. Al.

[51]For example, see Suzie Baer, *Peru's MRTA: Tupac Amaru Revolutionary Movement* (New York: Rosen Publishing Group, 2003); Gordon McCormick, *Sharp Dressed*

Men: Peru's Tupac Amaru Revolutionary Movement (New York: National Book Network, 1993).

[52]The Rescue, *Pride Is First for the President*, April 24, 1997, *http://www.geocities.com/CapitolHill/6502/pride.htm.*

[53]Christian Caryl and Eve Conant, "Show of Nerve," *Newsweek*, November 4, 2002, pp. 44–46.

[54]For example, see Frank Bolz, *How to Be a Hostage and Live* (New York: Carol Publishing Group, 1987); Terry Anderson, *Den of Lions: Memoirs of Seven Years* (New York: Crown, 1993).

[55]For example, see Robert K. Spear and Michael Moak, *Surviving Hostage Situations* (Leavenworth, KS: Universal Force Dynamics, 1989); Ben Weir and Carol Weir, *Hostage Bound, Hostage Free* (Philadelphia: Westminster Press, 1987).

[56]For example, see Frank Bolz et al., *Counterterrorism Handbook: Tactics, Procedures and Techniques* (Boca Raton, FL: CRC Press, 2002).

[57]*Sacramento Bee*, January 19, 1986, sec. A, p. 1.

[58]Frank Ochberg, "Hostage Victims," in *Terrorism: Interdisciplinary Perspectives*, eds. Burt Eichelman, David Soskis, and William Reid (Washington, DC: American Psychiatric Association, 1983), p. 86.

[59]Richard Clutterbuck, *Kidnap and Ransom: The Response* (London: Farber and Farber, 1978), pp. 158–64.

Contemporary Terrorism and Bombing

Chapter Objectives

The study of this chapter will enable you to:

- Identify the effects of an explosion
- Explore the historical antecedents of explosive materials
- Distinguish between low- and high-velocity explosives
- Describe the phases of blast/pressure
- Examine several vehicle bomb attack methods
- Outline a law enforcement strategy to cope with vehicle bombs
- Explore incidence of aircraft bombings
- Develop a security program to prevent injuries due to mail bombs

Introduction

In spite of the spectacular nature of hostage-taking incidents, nothing personifies contemporary terrorism more than indiscriminate bombing. Certainly everyone is familiar with the popular caricature of the nineteenth-century anarchist/terrorist, dressed in a long, black coat and broad-brimmed hat with eyes bulging, about to throw a round, black bomb with a fuse extending from the top into a crowd of unsuspecting victims. Unfortunately, the terrorist using the bomb is still the most important strategic attack method of modern terrorism. Slightly more than one-half of all recorded international terrorist incidents in 2001 were bombings.[1] Between 1977 and 2001, the U.S. State Department affirms that 63.5 percent of all recorded terrorist incidents were bombings.[2] According to Rand Terrorism Chronology, 3,684 terrorist bombings occurred worldwide between 1968 and 1997, recording 4,492 deaths and 19,725 injuries.[3] Regardless of whose statistics we use, little doubt remains that bombing is the terrorist weapon of choice. Several factors have contributed to the escalation of bombing as a preferred tactic by today's terrorist groups.

First, bombings are the most effective method of launching a terrorist attack. **Carlos Marighella** writes, "Terrorism is accomplished by placing a bomb . . . so that its destructive power causes an irreparable loss of life to the *enemy*; committed with extreme cold-bloodedness, while acting with bold decisiveness" (my emphasis).[4] Indeed, terrorist bombings are lethal, indiscriminate, and cold-blooded. Several examples illustrate the point. In September 1986, fourteen terrorist bombs indiscriminately exploded in several French cities, killing 15 people; the U.S. embassies in Kenya, and Tanzania were bombed in August 1998, killing over 200 people and injuring 5,000 others. In October 2002, a powerful car bomb killed 192 people in Bali Indonesia, and a midair terrorist explosion aboard Pan Am 103 killed 258 Americans. In June 1996, Tamil terrorists in Sri Lanka randomly bombed trains, busses, and busy market plazas, killing more than 85 innocent victims. But the most devastating bombings over the last four years have occurred in Israel with the introduction of the deadly suicide bomber. Suicide bombers have killed hundreds of Israeli civilians. Nothing so symbolizes the Palestinian resistance to Israeli occupation of the West Bank and Gaza as the ubiquitous suicide bomber. (Suicide bombings are discussed in chapter 7.)

Second, explosives and bomb technology are easily accessible to terrorist groups at a relatively low financial cost. In fact, several "mayhem" manuals are available, which graphically illustrate the simplicity of bomb making.[5] Third, although the making of clandestine explosive devices requires some degree of technical expertise, one person can easily handle the entire process. Fourth, bombings involve far less risk to the terrorist bomber since improved timing devices allow sufficient opportunity for the terrorist to escape detection or injury. Fifth, Internet sources provide detailed instructions on bomb making. Finally, the larger the terrorist explosion the more vigorous the media coverage. Media interest is in "good" pictures. Indeed, bombings provide graphic scenes of mayhem, mutilation, and death. Witness the media coverage on 9/11.

The focus of this chapter is on types of explosives, effects of explosions, and terrorist bomb attack methodologies. Its purpose is to provide criminal justice students with a general understanding of the nature of explosions and explosives. But first, a brief review of the historical development of explosive devices is relevant.

HISTORICAL PERSPECTIVE

The oldest known explosive and propellant is black powder. As with most discoveries that are centuries old, the name of the inventor and even the country of its origin remain in dispute. The principal claimants for the discovery of black powder are the Chinese, the Romans, the Hindus, the Greeks, the Arabs, the English, and the Germans. For example, the Chinese and the Romans of the fourth century were familiar with black powder pyrotechnic displays, while the ancient Greeks manufactured an incendiary composition, similar to that of black powder, referred to as "Greek Fire."

In England, Roger Bacon is generally credited with the invention of black powder in the thirteenth century. However, Bacon apparently was not aware of the projecting qualities of black powder although he was aware that black powder was unstable, made a thunderous noise when exploded, and terrified people. By the fourteenth century, Berthold Schwarz, a German friar, used black powder as a propelling agent; he is generally acknowledged as the inventor of firearms. Eventually, in Europe, black powder became known as Schwarzpulver. Until the seventeenth century, black powder was used as a propellant charge. Cannonballs, for example, were made of solid pieces of stone or iron. But the development of hollow cast iron balls introduced the use of black powder as an explosive filler, thus introducing crude bombs that could be thrown or used as mines. These bombs could easily be ignited by a time fuse.

Laqueur records several incidents where black powder bombs were used with great effect, especially in the terrorist Fenian bombing of Clerkenwell Prison in 1867 in which twelve persons were killed and 120 injured.[6] The unpredictable nature of black powder, however, made it extremely dangerous to handle, and many people blew themselves up while making bombs. Terrorist bombing was made much easier with the invention of nitroglycerine and **dynamite**.

Nitroglycerine, the basis of high explosives, was discovered in 1847 by an Italian chemistry professor at the University of Turin.[7] But the discovery of nitroglycerine remained more or less a scientific curiosity until 1867, when the eminent scientist Alfred Nobel mixed nitroglycerine with an absorbent material, thus making it safer to handle. Nobel also invented the blasting cap to provide a safe and dependable way to detonate dynamite. Nobel's epoch-making discovery of dynamite ushered in a new era of high explosives.[8] Dynamite was widely believed to be the ultimate weapon, and anarchist/revolutionary groups of the period based their whole strategy on its use. However, terrorists, anarchists, and revolutionaries quickly discovered that they could not bomb their way into the hearts and minds of the people. The exaggerated hope of dynamite as the ultimate weapon was not fulfilled. Clearly, the dynamite bomb was not the all-destroying weapon of the future, but it had become a symbol of fear and intimidation. Dynamite continues to be one of the most popular high explosives used by modern terrorist groups.[9]

With the introduction of military explosives shortly before the outbreak of World War I, the technological development of high explosives accelerated. Military explosives differ from commercial explosives such as black powder and dynamite in several respects. Military explosives have a much greater shattering effect, have high rates of detonation, and are relatively insensitive to impact, heat, shock, and friction. Military explosives also must be usable underwater and be of convenient size, shape, and weight for combat use. The most widely used military explosive is TNT (trinitrotoluene). TNT is widely used as a main charge in aerial bombs, artillery shells, and mortar rounds. TNT cannot be detonated by heat, shock, or friction, as black powder or dynamite can.[10]

Another popular military explosive, discovered during World War II and in wide use today, is the mysterious Composition 4 (C-4). **C-4** is the notorious "plastic" explosive, a yellow, puttylike substance that closely resembles children's modeling clay. C-4 is easy and safe to handle and can be molded into a variety of shapes. It has no odor, has a greater shattering effect than TNT, and detonates at a much higher rate.[11] Yet another well-known military explosive is pentaerythritol-tetranitrate, commonly known as PETN.[12] **PETN** is a high explosive in linear form that has a variety of military as well as some commercial uses. It closely resembles ordinary clothesline and is also referred to as datachord, primex, or primacord. Like C-4, PETN is resistant to heat, shock, and friction.

After the first bombing of the World Trade Center in 1993, yet another high explosive came into prominent use. Ammonium nitrate **fertilizer** bombs have been used by a variety of terrorist groups, including the **PIRA**, Tamil Tigers in Sri Lanka, and Middle East groups. Most recently the **Jemaah Islamiya** Organization (JI) used a fertilizer bomb in Bali, Indonesia, on October 20, 2002, that killed over 192 people. Ammonium nitrate is a strong oxidizer and mixed with other materials can cause a massive explosion.

In the bombing of the Murrah Building in Oklahoma City, **Timothy McVeigh** described how he mixed three 55-gallon drums of liquid nitromethane with 108 50-pound bags of ammonium nitrate fertilizer. McVeigh then placed a high explosive known as Tovex sausage around the AN-FO to act as a booster. In the end he had mixed 7,000 pounds of explosives. The explosion would release more energy than the **blast** from a ton of dynamite. McVeigh would use datachord to set off a

FIGURE 6.1 Timothy McVeigh confers with his attorneys at the federal prison in El Reno, Oklahoma. McVeigh was convicted for the terrorist bombing of the Murrah Building and sentenced to death. (AP/Wide World Photos)

nonelectric blasting cap that would instantaneously transfer a spark to the Tovex setting off the explosive mixture of ammonium nitrate and nitromethane. The result was the death of 168 people and the worst terrorist bombing in U.S. history until the 2001 attack on the World Trade Center.[13] (See Figure 6.2).

The ample range of explosive materials now available to contemporary terrorist groups has produced a shock wave of worldwide bombings. The commercial explosives, **black powder** and dynamite, can be easily purchased or stolen from construction or mining sites while military explosives are provided to terrorist groups by such "terrorist" nations as Iraq, Sudan, Iran, Libya, or Syria.[14] New types of delayed fuses are also available to terrorist groups. These include electrically fired devices and bombs fired by pressure, by chemical methods, and by X-ray–sensitive fuses. Even the most powerful bombs can be easily concealed in letters, parcels, shopping bags, suitcases, or vehicles. The technological advances in the manufacture of explosives have produced limitless opportunities for today's terrorist bombers. But the greatest threat of terrorist bombing comes from the very real possibility of nuclear terrorism. Jenkins warns the international community that nuclear blackmail by terrorists is the future threat to democratic nations.[15]

Several future nuclear terrorist scenarios have been identified. First, terrorists now have the technology to construct a fission-type nuclear device. Second, terrorists could contaminate a city with nuclear waste material by detonating a **dirty bomb** in midair and allowing the wind to let the radiation drift over the target.

A dirty bomb is a conventional explosive salted with radioactive isotopes in order to spread nuclear material over a wide area. It is much easier to construct a "dirty nuke" than to build a conventional nuclear bomb. Even though a "dirty nuke" can kill a large number of people, the resulting panic would be devastating. A "dirty nuke" is a pure terror weapon. On May 2, 2002, Jose Padilla was arrested in Chicago after allegedly planning a "dirty bomb" attack in the United States. Padilla is believed to be a follower of Osama bin Laden and trained in terrorist camps in Afghanistan.

Third, a terrorist group could seize a nuclear facility and cause a meltdown. Finally, long-range missiles or mortars, causing widespread nuclear fallout, could attack a nuclear facility. Theoretically possible, these nuclear scenarios pose a serious threat to the entire world.[16]

As the technology of bombing has become more complicated, terrorist groups have greatly increased their technical expertise and the competency required to handle sophisticated explosive material. When manufactured explosives are not available, the ingredients necessary to produce an improvised explosive device are easily obtained. The ingredients required to construct homemade bombs are virtually unlimited and can easily be obtained in hardware or drug stores without arousing much suspicion. Such seemingly innocuous items as starch, flour, sugar, and ammonia-nitrate fertilizers can be treated to become effective explosives. But still, the most widely used main charge explosive is black powder. The black powder pipe bomb is the most popular type of clandestine explosive device used in the United States. This next section reviews the three primary effects of an explosion.

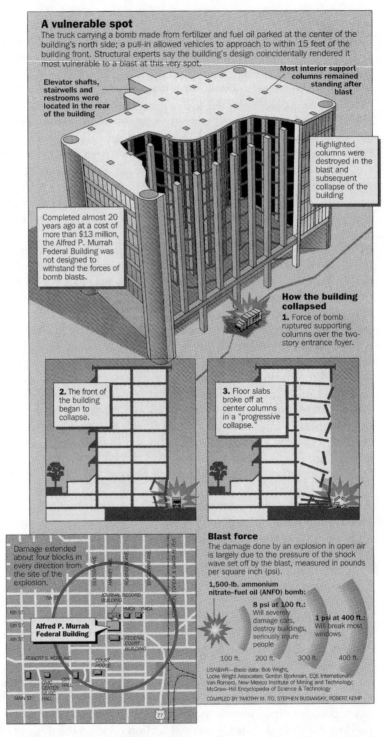

A vulnerable spot
The truck carrying a bomb made from fertilizer and fuel oil parked at the center of the building's north side; a pull-in allowed vehicles to approach to within 15 feet of the building front. Structural experts say the building's design coincidentally rendered it most vulnerable to a blast at this very spot.

Elevator shafts, stairwells and restrooms were located in the rear of the building

Most interior support columns remained standing after blast

Highlighted columns were destroyed in the blast and subsequent collapse of the building

Completed almost 20 years ago at a cost of more than $13 million, the Alfred P. Murrah Federal Building was not designed to withstand the forces of bomb blasts.

How the building collapsed
1. Force of bomb ruptured supporting columns over the two-story entrance foyer.

2. The front of the building began to collapse.

3. Floor slabs broke off at center columns in a "progressive collapse."

Damage extended about four blocks in every direction from the site of the explosion.

Alfred P. Murrah Federal Building

Blast force
The damage done by an explosion in open air is largely due to the pressure of the shock wave set off by the blast, measured in pounds per square inch (psi).

1,500-lb. ammonium nitrate–fuel oil (ANFO) bomb:

8 psi at 100 ft.: Will severely damage cars, destroy buildings, seriously injure people

1 psi at 400 ft.: Will break most windows

100 ft.   200 ft.   300 ft.   400 ft.

USN&WR—Basic data: Bob Wright, Locke Wright Associates; Gordon Bjorkman, EQE International; Van Romero, New Mexico Institute of Mining and Technology; McGraw-Hill Encyclopedia of Science & Technology

COMPILED BY TIMOTHY M. ITO, STEPHEN BUDIANSKY, ROBERT KEMP

FIGURE 6.2 Bombing of Murrah building—Oklahoma City, 1995. (Copyright 1995 U.S. News & World Report, L.P. Reprinted with permission.)

EFFECTS OF AN EXPLOSION

When an explosive is detonated, the black powder, stick of dynamite, block of TNT, or chunk of C-4 is instantaneously converted from a solid into a rapidly expanding mass of gases. The detonation will produce several secondary effects, but three primary effects produce the greatest amount of damage: **fragmentation**, blast pressure, and secondary fires, as illustrated in Figure 6.3.

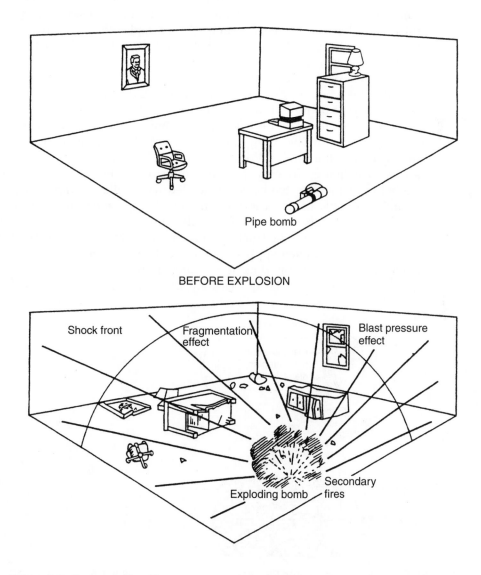

FIGURE 6.3 Fragmentation, blast pressure, and secondary forces produced by an explosion.

Fragmentation

A simple fragmentation bomb is a quantity of explosive filler placed inside a length of pipe capped at each end with a piece of time fuse used for detonation. Once detonated, the explosion will produce a number of shattered fragments of the pipe propelled outward from the point of detonation at extremely high velocity. These small, high-velocity fragments reach a speed of approximately 2,700 feet per second.[17] The bomb fragments travel in a straight line until they lose velocity and fall to the earth or become embedded in an object. In order to increase the number of small, high-velocity fragments flying through the air, the inside of the pipe is often filled with glass, nails, bullets, razor blades, or staples, thereby increasing the number of people killed and injured. Another fiendish explosive device used by terrorist groups to increase the amount of fragmentation, or *shrapnel,* is one in which a couple of sticks of dynamite has a two-inch layer of nails or staples taped on the outside. This type of device is referred to as an IRA nail bomb. Figure 6.4 illustrates the typical pipe bomb and IRA nail bomb.

However, the most destructive fragmentation terrorist explosive device is the vehicle bomb. The configuration of a vehicle bomb is limited only by the imagination of the bomber. Whether a car, van, or truck is used, the consequences are overwhelming. Not only does the explosion create fragments from the vehicle but in many cases the vehicle is loaded with bullets, scrap metal, or a large quantity of nails to increase the amount of fragmentation. Typically, vehicle bombs contain high explosives such as dynamite, TNT, or "plastic." For example, the FBI estimates that the truck driven into the **Marine compound** in Beirut in October 1983 contained approximately 12,000 pounds of TNT.[18] The explosion collapsed a four-story building, left a crater approximately 30 feet deep by 40 feet wide, and killed 241 Marines as they lay sleeping in their bunks.[19] Despite

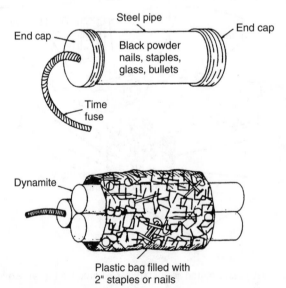

FIGURE 6.4 Black powder pipe bomb and dynamite nail bomb.

FIGURE 6.5   Bombing of the U.S. Marine Compound in Beirut on October 23, 1983. Rescue workers search the debris for survivors. Two hundred forty-one Marines were killed in the bombing. Hizballah/Islamic Jihad claimed credit for the bombing. (Zouki/AP/Wide World Photos)

injuries created by the fragmentation effect, the blast pressure effect can also contribute to increased casualties.

Blast Pressure

The detonation of an explosive charge produces very hot expanding gases. These gases exert pressures of approximately 700 tons per square inch and rush away from the point of detonation at velocities up to 7,000 miles per hour. This mass of expanding gases travels outward in a concentric pattern from the point of origin of the explosion like an immense wave, destroying any object in its path. Similar to a giant ocean wave rushing to meet the beach, the further the pressure wave travels from the point of origin of the explosion, the less power it has until it disappears completely. This wave of pressure is called the blast pressure effect of an explosion. There are two distinct phases to the blast pressure effect: (1) positive pressure phase, and (2) negative pressure phase.[20]

The positive pressure wave is formed at the moment of detonation when the surrounding atmosphere is compressed into a rapidly expanding circle. The leading edge of the positive pressure wave is called the shock front. As the shock front begins to move outward from the point of detonation, closely followed by the positive pressure wave, it introduces a sudden, crushing one-two punch to any object in its path. Therefore, when the positive pressure wave struck, for example, the walls of the Marine compound, the shock front delivered a massive blow to the building followed instantly by the positive pressure phase. The shock front shattered the walls of the compound while the positive pressure waves violently pushed the walls outward in a radiating pattern away from the point of detonation. The entire process of shock front and positive pressure waves lasts only a fraction of a second. The positive pressure waves will continue to dissipate until all the wave's power is expended.[21]

The negative pressure phase occurs as the outward compression of air by the positive pressure phase causes a partial vacuum at the point of detonation. The partial vacuum causes the displaced air to reverse its movement and rush inward to fill the void left by the positive pressure phase. The displaced air has mass and power as it returns toward the point of origin of the explosion. Even though the negative pressure phase is not as powerful as the positive pressure phase, it still has great velocity. In comparative terms, the positive pressure wave is comparable to a hurricane while the negative pressure phase can be compared with a high wind.

As the displaced air rushes toward the point of origin or detonation, it will strike and move objects in its path of destruction. For example, when negative pressure waves struck the already damaged Marine compound, it caused additional portions of the battered building to topple. However, in the negative pressure phase, objects are pulled toward the center of detonation. The negative pressure phase lasts about three times longer than the positive pressure phase and is less powerful in its destruction.

Secondary Fires

The final effect produced by an explosion is the secondary fires, or thermal effect. The secondary fires created by the detonation of low- or high-velocity explosives vary greatly. At the instant of detonation, there is a bright flash, or fireball, that often causes a fire. Only when highly combustible materials are near the point of detonation will secondary fires erupt. For example, if a pipe bomb containing five pounds of black powder is detonated inside a building, the fires generally result from ruptured fuel lines or shorted electrical circuits. Generally, secondary fires cause the least amount of damage of the three primary detonation effects. The next section briefly clarifies the distinction between low- and high-velocity explosives.

VELOCITY AND EXPLOSIVES

The most widely acclaimed system for the classification of explosives is according to the rate of velocity or detonation of explosion. Two major groups of explosives have been identified: (1) low-velocity explosives, and (2) high-velocity explosives.

Low-velocity explosives have rates of detonation below 3,000 feet per second. For example, the most popular low-velocity explosive in use today is black powder, which has a velocity rating of approximately 1,312 feet per second.[22] By comparison, straight dynamite, which is at the low end of high-velocity explosives, has a velocity rating of between 7,000 and 18,000 feet per second. The primary use of low-velocity explosives is as a propellant. The expanding gases of a low-velocity explosive such as black powder have a pushing effect rather than the shattering effect of high-velocity explosives. Low-velocity explosives, that is, black powder, gunpowder, or smokeless powder, are used in a variety of legitimate ways such as the manufacture of fireworks, flares, sporting propellants, blasting and mining operations, and the construction of safety fuses.

Black powder is a mechanical mixture of three common ingredients: (1) potassium nitrate or saltpeter, (2) charcoal or carbon, and (3) sulphur. The explosive characteristics of black powder occur only when the three ingredients are thoroughly mixed together. There are several recipes for the making of black powder; however, the most widely accepted formula is 75 percent saltpeter, 15 percent charcoal, and 10 percent sulfur. The composition of black powder has changed little since it was introduced in the thirteenth century in Europe. It can also be found in a range of colors, from black to gray to brown. In addition, the form of black powder may differ: the grains range from very fine to very coarse. The size of the grains controls the burning speed of black powder; large grains burn more slowly than smaller grains, fine grains burn more rapidly and explode more quickly. Thus, terrorists prefer the fine grain black powders for making homemade pipe bombs.

Black powder is also one of the most hazardous low-velocity explosives. It is easily ignited and can explode, when not confined, for no apparent reason. It is susceptible to friction, heat, and static electricity. Static electrical sparks can easily initiate black powder fires and explosions. Therefore, police officers and other criminal justice personnel working with black powder should wear self-grounding shoes and static-free clothing and work with wooden tools. Additionally, unlike other explosives, black powder does not deteriorate with age.

The black powder pipe bomb is the most widely used clandestine explosive device in the United States, and a number of people have blown themselves up while attempting to make the device. For instance, in one representative year, 1982, 35 percent of all recorded injuries in the United States due to bombings involved the persons who made the bombs.[23] Bombs show no allegiance to their makers. In sum, black powder is an extremely unpredictable low-velocity explosive that should be handled with extreme care.

The most widely used high-velocity explosive is dynamite, which is a combination of liquid nitroglycerine, oxidizers, and an absorbent material. Dynamite is relatively easy to obtain in the United States either by theft or through legal purchase. Consequently, terrorists and criminal bombers prefer dynamite. Commercial dynamites differ widely in their strength and sensitivity. Straight dynamite, for example, is a mixture of liquid nitroglycerine; sodium nitrate, which supplies the oxygen for complete combustion; and wood pulp or ground meal to absorb the shock of the nitroglycerine. The strength of commercial straight dynamite is determined by the percentage of nitroglycerine by weight in the dynamite formula. For example, 60 percent dynamite means the dynamite contains 60 percent nitroglycerine and is quite powerful. When detonated, dynamite gives off a gray-white smoke. Dynamite is usually found in stick form, wrapped in colored wax paper, but is available in a variety of sizes, shapes, strengths, and packages. In addition to straight dynamites, ammonia dynamites, gelatin dynamites, and ammonia-gelatin dynamites are in wide use today in commercial operations.[24]

TABLE 6.1 Types of Explosives

Low Velocity		High Velocity
Black powders		Dynamite
Smokeless powders	Military	TNT
Gun powders: detonate	Explosives	C-4
at 40 feet per second		PETN: detonates at 21,000 feet per second
		Ammonium nitrate
		Fertilizer bombs

Other high-velocity explosives are manufactured for military use. These include TNT, C-4, and PETN. The TNT recovered by law enforcement personnel generally comes in the form of 1/4, 1/2, or 1–pound blocks. After TNT is exposed to sunlight, its light-yellow to light-brown color gradually turns to dark brown. TNT gives off a dirty gray smoke when detonated.

Composition 4 (C-4) is an improved version of Composition 3 (C-3). C-3 was developed for the Korean War but had a tendency to be brittle and break up. C-3 was difficult to handle in hot or cold environments. Subsequently, C-4 was developed for the Vietnam War. C-4 contains 90 percent of the explosive compound RDX, has no odor, and is white to light tan in color. Table 6.1 summarizes the types of explosives most commonly used by modern terrorist groups and criminal bombers.

Now that we have identified the effects of an explosion and the types of explosive materials, our attention turns to the diverse and innovative attack methodologies of modern terrorist groups and criminal bombers.

VEHICLE BOMBS

The use of a vehicle as a bomb delivery system is not new, but it has become the tactic most preferred by such terrorist groups as the IRA and various Mideast factions. Typically, the types of vehicles used to "deliver" explosive materials have been cars and vans. However, with the escalation of terrorism, explosive devices have also been planted on railway cars, busses, large trucks, and airplanes to create increased casualties and to attract greater media attention.

The attack methodologies used to date by terrorists and criminal bombers include the following: (1) placing explosive materials on or in a car to kill the occupants; (2) the use of a vehicle as a launching system for rocket-propelled munitions; (3) the use of a vehicle as a booby trap or antipersonnel device to ambush law enforcement personnel, members of the military, or bomb disposal experts; (4) the use of a hostage for the transportation and delivery of explosives; (5) the use of a vehicle as a fragmentation device when a large amount of explosives is used; (6) the use of multiple vehicle bombs in a coordinated terrorist strike; and (7) the use of a vehicle in a suicide, or "kamikaze," attack. Terrorist groups use all these methods today, but the trend seems to be toward the indiscriminate car bomb, loaded with explosives, parked on a busy commercial street with the purpose of killing a large number of innocent bystanders. A review of car bomb attack methods follows.

Historically, **car bombs** have been used for the purpose of killing the occupants. The car served merely as another location for the act of murder. The motives for such killings were no different than other types of murders that were committed with guns, knives, or poisons. These motives included retaliation, revenge, anger, suicide, financial gain, or hate-love triangles. The procedure for many of these car bombings was to place 2 to 5 pounds of dynamite under the hood on the left side of the engine, under the front seat, on the gas tank, under the dashboards, or any place on the car that would have the greatest killing effect on the intended target.[25]

Organized crime figures of the 1920s, 1930s, and even the 1980s and 1990s are notorious for using car bombs to intimidate rival gangs and to eliminate competition. The practice is still used today. In one incident in 1985, a car bomb was used to murder a government witness who agreed to testify against organized crime figures in a Chicago gambling case.

Likewise, hundreds of accounts exist in which car bombs were used in domestic arguments. In one case, known as the "baby food bombing," the bomber placed two explosive devices contained in baby food jars under the front seat of his spouse's car. The jars were wired to the car's ignition system. Brodie maintains that the most effective place to hide a bomb is under the driver's seat, which is also the most common area for bombs to be placed in domestic quarrels.[26]

Car bombs have also been used in the selective assassination of political figures throughout the world. For example, a remote-controlled bomb killed Orlando Letelier, the former Chilean ambassador to the United States, as he drove through a quiet residential street in Washington, DC. The bomb, a 1.5-pound mixture of TNT and plastic explosive, was fastened to the undercarriage of Letelier's car. The explosion killed Letelier and two passengers as they unsuspectingly drove to work.[27]

Another fairly common terrorist bomb attack method is to place an explosive charge inside a vehicle and park the vehicle along the route of the intended victim. On April 14, 1993, while in Kuwait, there was an attempt to assassinate former President George Bush by using a car bomb. Bush was the target of an assassination plot directed by Iraqi intelligence. Kuwaiti police discovered a 175-pound car bomb, including the remote control detonators, the plastic explosives, and the electronic circuitry. The car bomb had been parked near the motorcade route taken by former President Bush. The bomb was to be set off using a remote control device that would have been lethal for nearly a quarter of a mile. The bomb was disarmed after an Iraqi informant told Kuwaiti police where it was located. Using a remote control switch, the terrorist bomber needs only await the arrival of the intended victim. When the victim is within range, a signal is transmitted to the explosive charge, causing detonation. The remote-controlled car bomb is a popular Provisional IRA tactic.

On August 27, 1979, eighteen British paratroopers were killed by a cleverly planned double car bombing on the border between Northern Ireland and the

Republic of Ireland. A vehicle containing 1,100 pounds of explosives was parked inconspicuously on a country road. As a British troop convoy passed the vehicle, the PIRA bombers detonated the bomb by remote control. Ten British soldiers were killed, and the force of the blast hurled their vehicle 50 feet into the air. British reinforcements quickly arrived at the scene, and a second 800-pound bomb was detonated remotely, killing another eight British paratroopers. The use of two explosive devices in conjunction is a frequently used PIRA tactic. This PIRA attack inflicted the heaviest loss of life on British soldiers since 1921, when thirty-five British troopers were killed in an ambush by Irish Republican rebels.[28]

A second variation of the vehicle bomb attack method is to use the vehicle as a munitions launching system. This terrorist strategy is used to fire rockets and mortars at the intended target—again, a favorite strategy of the Provos.

A stolen flatbed truck that concealed a makeshift mortar-launching system welded to the truck's frame was used by the PIRA to attack a heavily fortified police barracks in Newry, Northern Ireland.[29] Nine shells were launched from a distance of 250 yards away, scoring a direct hit on the Royal Ulster Constabulary police barracks, killing nine police officers and seriously wounding thirty-seven others. Police in Northern Ireland suspected the mortars were fired by remote control. The stolen flatbed truck had been parked on a hill overlooking the rear entrance of the police barracks, making an easy target for the PIRA bombers. Mortar attacks by the PIRA are quite frequent in Northern Ireland but in the past have been notoriously inaccurate. For example, the PIRA fired eighteen mortar rounds from a flatbed truck at a police station and training center in Belfast.[30] The mortar rounds fell harmlessly, and no one was seriously injured. On February 7, 1991, in a daring, well-planned attack, the PIRA attempted to assassinate British Prime Minister John Major at 10 Downing Street with a salvo of mortar rounds fired from a van. A section of the van's roof had been cut away to allow the firing of the homemade "rockets." Three mortar rounds fell within 40 feet of 10 Downing Street, the residence of the British prime minister. The "rockets" shattered the upper windows of 10 Downing Street where Prime Minister Major was in a meeting with British cabinet members. No one was killed or injured. Such attacks, whether successful or not, receive significant media attention, again publicizing the cause of the Republican movement and the "courageousness" of the Irish Republican Army.

The third variation of the vehicle bomb attack method involves the use of the bomb-laden vehicle to ambush law enforcement and military personnel. The ambush attack method usually involves a stolen car or rental vehicle expertly wired with a remote-control firing device. The vehicle bomb is then parked near a police station house or along routes frequented by police or military personnel. As security vehicles approach, the vehicle bomb is detonated without warning, usually killing the unsuspecting security officers.

In July 1986 the PIRA detonated a booby-trapped truck in Belfast, Northern Ireland, while four British security officers were inspecting it, killing two and seriously wounding the others. Hundreds of British soldiers and police officers of the Royal Ulster Constabulary have been killed by such devices. The tactic has also been used recently in Spain, Greece, Australia, and the United States. For example, on July 27, 1986, Basque separatists or terrorists in Spain killed two police officers with a remote-control vehicle bomb as they were about to investigate a complaint of a suspicious vehicle.[31] In Athens, Greece, a car bomb was detonated by remote control as a police bus was passing, killing two and wounding fourteen. In Melbourne, Australia, two rental cars packed with explosives were parked at the front entrance to police headquarters. The first car bomb was detonated, causing little damage and few injuries; however, the second car bomb was detonated fifteen minutes later after a large crowd had gathered at the scene of the first bomb. This second car bomb, or double bomb, caused many casualties, including the serious wounding of fifteen police officers. In the United States the booby-trapped car bomb has also been used by the FALN. In one such incident a number of police officers and firefighters were injured by an exploding van while responding to a fire alarm. Eyewitness accounts indicate that the van was parked and then set on fire. As firefighters attempted to put out the flames, the van was detonated by a remote-controlled firing device. The FALN later claimed credit for the blast in a telephone call to *The New York Times*.

The fourth type of vehicle attack bomb uses the vehicle to deliver or gain access to the intended target. The PIRA was the first terrorist group to popularize this method, which uses the following strategy. In order to penetrate security checkpoints and gain a closer position to the intended target, the PIRA would kidnap a close family member of a legitimate employee (such as a government employee or prison guard) of the bombing target. The legitimate employee would then be instructed to deliver the bomb vehicle to his place of employment. If the employee refused, then the family member being held hostage would be threatened with injury or death. With few choices, the employee would deliver the explosive device using his legitimate identification to penetrate security checkpoints. The tactic has also been used repeatedly in the Middle East with a slight difference.

In the October 1983 bombing of the French embassy in Beirut, explosives were surreptitiously planted in the vehicle of an embassy employee. Unaware that the vehicle contained a large quantity of explosives, the unsuspecting employee was allowed to pass a security checkpoint and park the vehicle on the embassy grounds where sometime later the explosives were detonated.

In the fifth variation of the vehicle terrorist attack method, large quantities of explosives are used; and glass, bullets, or small pieces of metal are contained inside the bomb vehicle. Bomb vehicles containing explosive substances in excess of 100 to 500 pounds and randomly parked in a heavily residential area to maximize the killing of innocent civilians are not unusual.

During the civil war in Lebanon, Hizballah and affiliated groups carried out hundreds of such bomb attacks. During one 17-day period in July and August 1990, Hizballah detonated nine vehicle bombs, killing 103 people and injuring 596. These vehicle bombs were parked on busy commercial and residential streets, thereby increasing the number of civilian casualties.

On June 25, 1996, Muslim terrorists from the Saudi Hizballah detonated a petroleum tanker truck containing approximately 4,000 pounds of ammonium nitrate fertilizer and RDX explosives on the perimeter of the U.S. apartment complex known as **Khobar Towers** in Dhahran, Saudi Arabia. The apartment complex housed U.S. Air Force personnel and their families. The bomb-laden truck initially was denied entry into the Khobar facility but eventually was parked outside the concrete barriers surrounding the facility. The driver got out of the truck and sped away in a small white car driven by another man. The resulting explosion left an 85- by 35-foot crater that killed nineteen U. S. Air Force personnel and inured 500 others.[32] Thirteen Saudis and a Lebanese were indicted on June 22, 2001, on charges of murder and conspiracy for the Khobar towers bombing. The 48-count indictment alleges that the fourteen men were members of the Islamic terrorist group Hizballah, who received financial and spiritual support from Iran. The indictment states that the conspiracy was driven by a desire to drive Americans from Saudi Arabia.[33]

The sixth vehicle attack method uses multiple bombs hidden on vehicles of public transportation. This terrorist attack method involves placing explosive devices, timed to explode during rush hours, on busses or trains, thereby creating mass casualties of innocent civilian bystanders. The method has been used by various Palestinian factions, the PIRA, and more recently by Tamil separatists in Sri Lanka and Kashmiris in India. The intent of such indiscriminate bombings is to gain media attention and create intense fear in the general community. There is no doubt that the selective terrorist bombing of public transportation will continue to escalate. The establishment of effective security controls for all public transportation is difficult to institute.

The seventh bomb attack method involves vehicle bombs containing large quantities of explosives driven by suicide bombers. The most sensational suicide bombings have occurred in the Middle East and have been directed against U.S. targets. On October 23, 1983, a truck loaded with the equivalent of 12,000 pounds of TNT was driven into the Marine compound in Beirut.[34] According to the FBI, this vehicle bomb created the largest conventional blast ever seen by explosive experts. In a simultaneous attack on the French multinational peacekeeping force, a suicide truck bomber killed fifty-eight French paratroopers. Then, on November 5, 1983, a suicide truck bomber penetrated the Israeli military compound in Tyre, Lebanon, killing sixty people.[35] In less than two weeks, suicide truck bombers had killed 359 members of the military forces of the United States, France, and Israel.

The suicide bomb attack method has fully emerged as a strategic weapon that enables nations with inferior military forces to gain a degree of strategic equality with more powerful military forces. Defenses against the suicide car or truck bomb are difficult to maintain. They consist of physical barriers, vehicle mazes, use of increased buffer distances, and well-armed security guards instructed to fire on suspicious vehicles. The fear of the vehicle bomb exists not only in the Middle East. Washington, DC, has been given the look of a government under siege with highway barriers and armed security guards protecting entrances to the White House, U.S. Capitol, and other important government structures. The psychological impact of the suicide bomber has created a situation of overwhelming fear in the United States as well as the Middle East. One must remember that the focus and direction of terrorism is to create fear. Certainly the suicide vehicle bomb accomplishes this major objective of terrorist violence.

In sum, the evolution of the vehicle bomb attack method has produced some definitive trends. The bigger the explosion the greater the casualties, and the more intense the media coverage the greater the publicity for the terrorist group. Since we concluded in earlier chapters that terrorist groups are imitative rather then innovative, they have certainly monitored the successes of vehicle bomb tactics. Most likely we can anticipate the increased use of vehicle bombs by terrorist groups around the world.

As the use of vehicle bombs escalates, law enforcement personnel must devise alternative tactics to identify practical ways to stop the bombing—obviously an extremely difficult responsibility. In some cases, such as with the suicide bomber, it becomes a formidable task to prevent or deter infiltration into an area without seriously disrupting daily routines. However, security forces (law enforcement, military, or sentries) must be on the alert and have sufficient training to handle the vehicle bomb on an individual basis. From the terrorist perspective, the true genius of the vehicle attack method is that the objective and the means of attack are often beyond the imagination of those responsible for providing security and establishing bomb-training curriculums. Security personnel must understand that the vehicle bomb is a fully established mode of indiscriminate political violence. But the use of deadly parcel bombs is probably the most heinous bomb attack method.

LETTER BOMBS

According to Laqueur, Russian terrorists of the 1880s first introduced the terrorist tactic of preparing letter bombs. Russian terrorists made plans to conceal small quantities of explosives in little parcels, then mail the parcels to the tsar and other government officials. However, because of the insurmountable technical difficulties in handling explosives, this plan apparently was not carried out. Additionally, anarchist writers of the 1880s, such as Most, Bakunin, and Nechaev, recommended sending letters and small parcels containing incendiary explosives as a tactic to spread fear among government leaders and bureaucrats. Nonetheless, the first recorded use of a letter bomb or parcel bomb occurred in 1895 when a young German anarchist sent a 25-pound black powder bomb to a Berlin police officer. The bomb was intercepted at the Berlin post office and rendered harmless. By the beginning of World War I, some of the technical difficulties of making letter bombs were overcome, and several prominent European political leaders were killed or seriously injured by exploding parcels. Through the years various terrorist groups, including the Irgun, the Palestine resistance groups, and the IRA, have used letter bombs to spread fear and to introduce "new" terror tactics since the police and potential targets were alert to most of the old terror bomb attack methods.[36]

Theodore Kaczynski, better known as the **Unabomber**, is serving four consecutive life sentences in connection with sixteen parcel bombings and attempted bombings he committed in seven states between 1978 and 1995. Kaczynski's parcel bombs injured ten people and killed three. Two of the fatalities occurred in Sacramento. Kaczynski was motivated by his hatred for advancements in high technology. His bombings had targeted carefully selected individuals, victims he

FIGURE 6.6   Theodore John Kaczynski, a.k.a. the Unabomber, is led into court in Sacramento, CA, where he pled guilty to a series of bombings that killed three people, two in Sacramento. Kaczynski was sentenced to life in prison without the possibility of parole. He is serving his time at Supermax Prison in Florence, Colorado. (Michael Gallacher/Getty Images, Inc—Liaison)

blamed for technological achievements in the United States. Kaczynski acted alone and was not part of any terrorist organization.[37]

Through trial and error the technological problems associated with the construction of letter bombs have been greatly reduced. Explosive devices now can easily be concealed within letters and small packages. The letter bomb creates a far greater security risk than the car bomb or planted bomb. Letter bombs are antipersonnel devices and serve two offensive terrorist functions. First, they may be designed to kill or maim a specific target. Since letter bombs contain only a small amount of explosive material, their intended effect is to injure and maim. Injury from an exploding letter bomb is caused by the explosive shock and the blast pressure, not from fragmentation. Second, letter bombs may be used to harass and intimidate the general public.

Even though the use of letter bombs is an ideal terrorist attack method, they are used infrequently compared with other bomb attack methods, such as the vehicle bomb. Letter bombs tend to be the preferred terrorist tactic during periods of a brief, intensive terrorist bombing campaign directed against specific targets. Such a terrorist letter bomb campaign was waged by Palestinian terrorists against Israeli and American targets in 1972. As with other bomb attack methods, the high-risk targets of letter bombs are embassies, corporations, defense-related industries, police, and government offices. Historically, letter bombs have been sent to a variety of targets.

For example, between 1977 and 1983, 84 recorded letter-bomb incidents occurred in 23 different countries. The United States was the favorite target, with

19 incidents reported, while 47 letter bombs were mailed to Western European targets. By far the favored addresses for letter bombs have been diplomats, to whom 40 of the 84 letter bombs were sent. Seven people were killed and 51 others injured in the 84 reported letter bomb attacks. Terrorist groups representing 18 different ethnic identities claimed credit for 43 (51.1 percent) of the 84 letter bombs, with the senders of the remaining 41 undetermined. Various Irish extremist groups and individuals sent 11 of the deadly letter bombs to British targets, accounting for the largest number of letter bombs sent among known ethnic terrorists.[38]

In another more recent letter-bomb campaign that occurred between December 1996 and January 1997, sixteen letter bombs disguised as holiday greeting cards were delivered through the mails to targets in the United States and United Kingdom. Thirteen of the letter bombs were mailed to the offices of the Al Hayat newspaper in New York City, Washington, DC, and London. One bomb detonated in the London Office of Al Hayat seriously injuring two people. Al Hayat is an independent Arabic-language daily newspaper published in London with worldwide distribution and circulation.

All sixteen letter bombs bore a December 21, 1996, Alexandria, Egypt, postmark without a return address. The bombs were in plain white envelopes, with computer-generated addresses. Three of the letter bombs were discovered at the federal penitentiary in Leavenworth, Kansas. This is still an open case and the FBI currently offers a $5 million reward for information about the perpetrators.[39]

Letter bombs or parcel bombs may be constructed to fit within almost any familiar container. This list includes all types of mail deliveries. Mail bombs are designed to detonate as the letter or package is opened. The explosive charge is activated by the release of a spring-loaded striker system or an electrical circuit. The most common type of mail devices encountered by postal security officers has been sent in large envelopes or small packages. The typical terrorist letter bomb weighs between 2 and 3 ounces and fits neatly into an envelope approximately 5 3/4 inches by 4 inches by 1/4 inches.[40]

In order to function, letter bombs must contain an explosive charge, a detonator, and a fuse to set off the detonator. The type of explosive preferred by letter bombers is C-4, but if C-4 is unavailable, other fast-burning explosives, including various black powder mixtures, can also be used. The most common type of fuse used in letter bomb construction is the percussion fuse. The percussion fuse operates on the same principle as a firing pin in a gun. The spring is released carrying a striker that impacts upon the detonator, igniting the explosive charge. The detonator most commonly discovered in letter bombs is the type used in commercial mining operations. This type of detonator is cylindrical in shape, has a very thin copper casing, and is about 3/16 inch (5 millimeters) in diameter. It is hoped that the identification and understanding of these principles of letter bomb construction will help security and police officers to detect and recognize suspected mail explosive devices.

Some specific things to look for in a suspected letter bomb are the following: (1) letters bombs cannot be constructed of extremely small size or placed in very thin, ordinary envelopes; (2) letter bombs are generally unbalanced, and are heavier on one side or the other; (3) an explosive mail device may have wires or spring holes in its outer wrapping; (4) certain categories of explosives may leave a greasy film on the envelope or paper wrapping, which may indicate also that the explosive is extremely unstable; (5) an unusual odor such as an almond smell may be present; (6) if the envelope is taped down on all sides, it may contain a spring-loaded booby trap; and (7) inspection of the stiffness of the contents of the envelope may reveal the presence of folded paper, cardboard, or an explosive device. The key indicator that an explosive device may be present in an envelope is *feel*. If the suspected letter bomb does not bend or flex and has a feeling of springiness at the top, bottom, or sides of the envelope, this is a clear sign that an explosive device is present. (See Figure 6.7).

As in other bomb attack methods, the target of the bombers should not assume that only one explosive device exists. Letter bombers have been known to send several explosive devices to the same address. Therefore, all mail deliveries for several weeks should be carefully examined. There are several excellent books, monographs, and pamphlets that outline the correct procedure for handling suspected letter bombs and parcel bombs.[41]

Letter bombs are a continued hazard to the high-risk population of diplomats, corporate executives, government officials, and police officers. Therefore, the risks of receiving letter bombs must be continually reevaluated and updated.

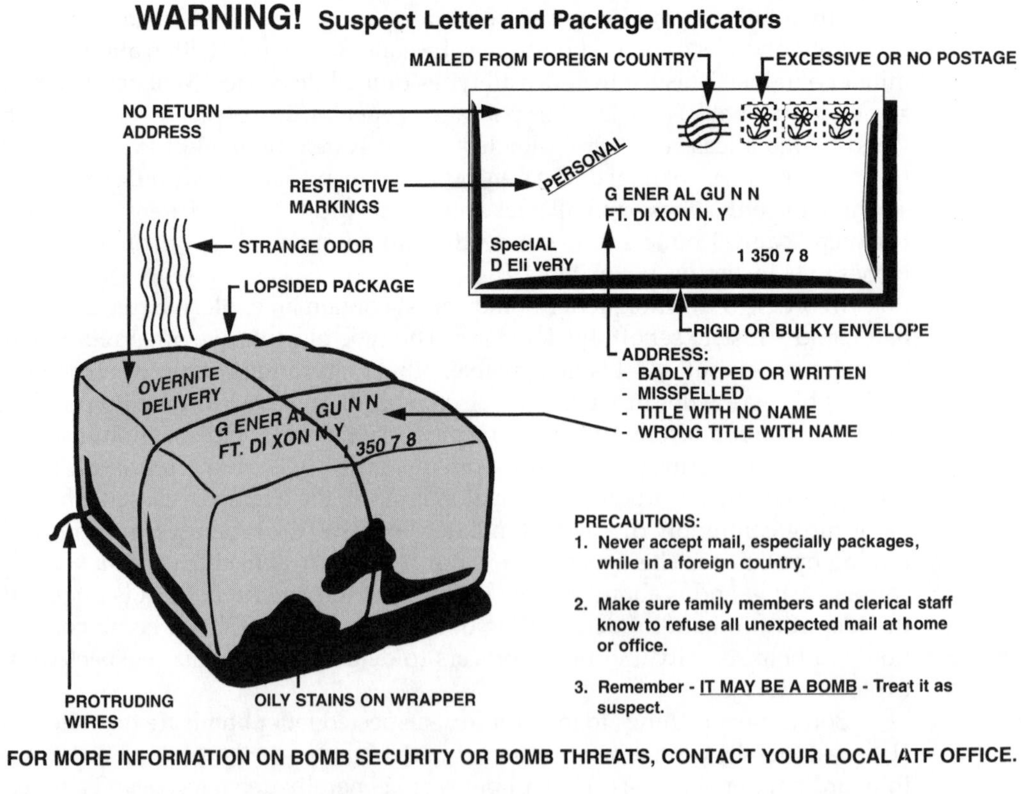

WARNING! Suspect Letter and Package Indicators

FOR MORE INFORMATION ON BOMB SECURITY OR BOMB THREATS, CONTACT YOUR LOCAL ATF OFFICE.

FIGURE 6.7 Package and letter bomb recognition.

Criminal justice management and rank-and-file employees alike must be trained in letter bomb recognition and the proper emergency procedures for handling explosive mail devices.

BOMBINGS ABOARD AIRCRAFT

The bombing of in-flight aircraft is yet another extranormal terrorist attack method. Modern high-performance civil aircraft are extremely vulnerable to in-flight bombing attacks. There are numerous ways of planting bombs on aircraft, even with the heightening of security measures. The motivations behind such terrorist attacks are many, but regardless of the motive, it is apparent that bombers of aircraft hope to destroy all tangible evidence by creating midair explosions. The design of the explosive device and methods of concealment are limited only by the ingenuity of the bomber. Therefore, security arrangements and technical methods of detecting hidden explosive devices on board aircraft must be superior to that of the skillful bomber. If, however, bombers of aircraft are able to penetrate security measures and the aircraft is destroyed, then every effort must be made to quickly recover victims and debris from the explosion. At times the problems of recovery may seem insurmountable, especially if the explosion occurred over deep ocean waters or the aircraft is widely scattered over desert or jungle landscapes. Such was the case after a midair bomb explosion occurred off the coast of Ireland on September 21, 1985.

An Air India Boeing 747 Flight 182 en route to London from Vancouver, British Columbia, Canada, disintegrated in midair about 110 miles off southwestern Ireland, killing all 329 people on board.[42] The midair explosion occurred less than an hour after another explosive device detonated at the Air India baggage check station in Tokyo, killing two baggage handlers and seriously wounding several workers. Both bombings were claimed by Sikh extremists seeking political autonomy from India. After a lengthy investigation, Air India officials concluded that a plastic explosive device, concealed in the forward cargo hold, escaped metal detectors and was the cause of the midair explosion. Indian forensic scientists reconstructed the debris and examined the remains of victims recovered at the scene of the explosion and further determined that two bombs were used by the Sikh terrorists.

On February 11, 2003, Inderjit Singh Reyat pled guilty to manslaughter for his part in the bombing of Air India Flight 182. Reyat had earlier been sentenced to ten years for the Tokyo bombing. Reyat, as the bomb maker, was sentenced to five years for the bombing of Flight 182. Two accomplices are awaiting trial in Vancouver, B.C., for their part in the bombing of Flight 182. The motivation for the two attacks was related to Sikh extremists' ambitions to create an independent Sikh nation in India called Khalistan. Air India is considered a legitimate target since it is a highly visible symbol of the Indian government.[43]

In yet another midair explosion, this one inside a TWA jetliner bound for Athens, four people were hurled to their deaths.[44] The explosion blew a 9- by

3-foot hole in the side of the aircraft; the four innocent victims were sucked out of the hole at approximately 15,000 feet and fell to their deaths. Palestinians claimed credit for the TWA bombing, saying it was in retaliation for a U.S. military strike against Libya. Fortunately, this type of terrorist bombing attack is rare compared with car bombs and letter bombs.

On December 21, 1988, **Pan Am Flight 103**, a Boeing 747, was destroyed by a bomb hidden in the cargo hold of the aircraft. The bombing occurred at 31,000 feet over the Scottish village of Lockerbie, killing all 259 passengers on board as well as eleven people on the ground. Investigators were able to identify the luggage that contained the bomb, which led them to two Libyan suspects. The investigation continued for three years when U.S. and British officials concluded that two Libyans, one a member of the Libya intelligence service, had organized the bombing. In March 1993, the United States was able to convince the United Nations to impose economic sanctions on Libya. Eventually Libyan leader Muammar Qaddafi turned over the two accused Libyans in hopes of having the economic sanctions lifted. The trial began in May 2000, conducted by a Scottish Court sitting in the Netherlands. On January 20, 2001, the Court returned a verdict of guilty for the Libyan intelligence officer Abdel Bassit Ali–al Megrahi and sentenced him to twenty years in prison. His alleged accomplice, Laman Khalifa Fhimah, was acquitted.[45]

Statistics on explosions aboard aircraft between 1949 and 2001 indicate that 80 aircraft were damaged or destroyed by the detonation of an explosive device while in flight. Of the 80 aircraft damaged or destroyed, 17 aircraft were totally destroyed. In all, 1,148 passengers and crew lost their lives. The bombings occurred in various parts of the world covering 38 countries and affecting 43 airlines. During that same period, the United States recorded the damage or destruction of 15 aircraft with a total loss of 126 lives.[46]

To some extent the increase in fatalities can be attributed to the larger size of aircraft used by civil air carriers rather than the increased effectiveness of terrorist bombers. An analysis of the statistics also reveals that the three most popular areas to secrete explosive devices aboard aircraft are cargo baggage holds, the passenger cabin, and the lavatory.

In view of the little information available to students of criminal justice, a brief review of several in-flight aircraft bomb attacks is presented.[47]

1. United Airlines DC–68 (November 1, 1955)
   This aircraft was on a scheduled flight to Portland, Oregon. Approximately 11 minutes after takeoff from San Francisco an explosion disintegrated the aircraft. A dynamite bomb located in the number 4 *baggage compartment* detonated, killing 39 passengers and 5 crew.
2. Canadian Pacific Airlines DC–68 (July 8, 1965)
   An explosive device planted in the *passenger cabin* area detonated, separating the tail section from the aircraft. All 52 aboard were killed. The explosion occurred over British Columbia.

3. British Airways Comet 48 (October 12, 1967)
   On a scheduled flight to Nicosia, Cyprus, at about 28,000 feet an explosion ripped through the tourist *passenger cabin*. All 66 aboard were killed. The recovery of victims and debris revealed evidence of an explosion.

4. Cathway Pacific Airways CV 880 (June 15, 1972)
   En route from Thailand to Hong Kong a bomb in a suitcase under the *passenger seat* exploded killing 81 passengers and crew.

5. Air Vietnam B-727 (September 15, 1974)
   A skyjacker boarded the aircraft in Saigon and ordered the flight to go to Hanoi. The pilot convinced the skyjacker that the plane was low on fuel and therefore a forced landing was necessary. While in the landing pattern, the skyjacker for some reason detonated two hand grenades in the *cockpit*. The pilot lost control of the aircraft and 70 passengers and crew were killed.

6. Gulf Air Bahrain B–737 (September 23, 1983)
   About 30 miles from the airport in Kuwait, a bomb exploded in the *baggage compartment*. While attempting a forced landing in the desert, the aircraft crashed, killing 112 people.

7. Air India B–747 (June 21, 1985)
   Approaching the coast of Ireland at approximately 30,000 feet, the aircraft disintegrated, killing 329 people. Subsequent investigation revealed plastic explosives had been planted in the *baggage compartment* and the *lavatory*.

8. Brazilian TAM Fokker 100 (July 9, 1997)
   An unknown explosive device detonated in flight, killing one passenger and injuring seven others, including the bomber. The device blew a hole in the *fuselage* of the aircraft. The plane landed safely. A passenger, intent on suicide, brought the explosive device on board in his carry-on baggage.

9. Russian Airways (May 30, 2000)
   A homemade improvised explosive device was discovered on board. The device consisted of 400 grams of TNT, a clock mechanism, detonator, battery, and connecting wires. The device was hidden in a tea box in the rear *lavatory* of the plane. The device was discovered just before takeoff.

10. American Airlines Boeing 767 (December 23, 2001)
    Richard Reid, an alleged member of al Qaeda, attempted to ignite an explosive device concealed in his shoes. The device contained several ounces of C-4. Passengers and crew overpowered Reid before he could detonate the explosive device. The flight, which originated in Paris on the way to Miami, contained 185 passengers and 12 crew members. The plane landed safely. Richard Reid pleaded guilty and admitted he was a member of al Qaeda. In January 2003, Reid was sentenced to life in prison plus 30 years.

In sum, the effectiveness of civil-aviation security measures will continue to test the determination of terrorist bombers. Acts of aircraft bombings and attempted bombings are on the increase. This increase in the number of explosions and the number of explosive devices detected by airport security indicates that perhaps aircraft bombings may become the primary threat to civil air carriers as opposed to hijackings. Despite the preventive measures taken of strengthening security systems, it is believed that civil aviation will remain a tempting and vulnerable target to the mentally disturbed, criminal, and terrorist bomber.

CONCLUSIONS

We have reviewed the effects of explosions, types of explosive devices, and bomb attack methodologies, including the use of car bombs, letter bombs, and the bombing of aircraft. This review suggests that terrorist bombers have demonstrated clearly and convincingly that they are willing to escalate the threshold of violence beyond what was previously believed attainable because of stricter police and military security measures. However, stricter security measures have not prevented suicide terrorist bombers from turning Jerusalem into a city of fear. During the month of December 2002, Palestinian terrorists, in an attempt to coerce the Israeli government to end the occupation of the West Bank, detonated six bombs in Jerusalem in one 10-day period. Twenty people were killed and scores were injured. Although the Jerusalem suicide bombings were serious, they were not catastrophic. Nevertheless, the suicide terrorist bombings in Jerusalem may be a harbinger of a more lethal future for democratic countries. Intensive terrorist bombing campaigns could easily be carried out by dedicated terrorist groups.

Therefore, police officers and government security personnel need technical training in bomb recognition, identification of explosive materials, and bomb construction. Too often law enforcement agencies wait until an incident occurs before a decision is made to take precautionary measures for the future. There is no substitute for the well-informed and well-trained police officer.

The next chapter explores a special kind of terrorist bombing—the suicide bomber.

KEY TERMS

Black Powder	Dynamite	Marine Compound
Blast	Fertilizer	Pan Am Flight 103
C-4	Fragmentation	PETN
Car Bombs	Jemaah Islamiyya	PIRA
Carlos Marighella	Khobar Towers	Timothy McVeigh
Dirty Bomb	Letter Bombs	Unabomber

REVIEW QUESTIONS

1. List at least five factors that have contributed to the escalation of terrorist bombing.
2. Describe the difference between commercial and military explosives.

3. Explain the effects of an explosion.
4. Distinguish between the positive and negative pressure phase of an explosion.
5. Discuss the difference between low- and high-velocity explosives.
6. Identify and explain at least five terrorist vehicle bomb attack methods. What strategies would you suggest to prevent the recurring problem of vehicle bombs?
7. Compare and contrast the car bomb and letter bomb methodologies.
8. Describe several techniques for identifying suspected letter bombs.
9. Why are aircraft so vulnerable to terrorist attack?
10. Outline a bomb-training program for police and security personnel.

WEB SITES

Sourcebook of Criminal Justice Statistics 2001
   http://www.albany.edu/sourcebook/
Nobel e–Museum
   http://www.nobel.se.
Bureau of Alcohol, Tobacco, and Firearms
   http://www.atf.gov
International Association of Bomb Technicians and Investigators
   http://www.iabti.org
International Association of Arson Investigators
   http://www.fire-investigators.org
National Center for Forensic Science
   http://www.ncfs.ucf.edu

ENDNOTES

[1]U.S. Department of State, *Patterns of Global Terrorism: 2001* (Washington, DC: U.S. Government Printing Office, 2002), p. 8.

[2]U.S. Department of State, *Terrorist Bombings* (Washington, DC: U.S. Government Printing Office, 2002), p. 1.

[3]Rand Terrorism Chronology, 1968–1997, MIPT—Oklahoma City National Memorial Institute for the Prevention of Terrorism. *http://db.mipt.org.*

[4]Carlos Marighella, *The Terrorist Classic: Manual of the Urban Guerrilla*, trans. Gene Hanrahan (Chapel Hill, NC: Documentary Pub., 1985), p. 84.

[5]For example, see William Powell, *Anarchist Cookbook* (New York: L. Stuart, 1971); Andrew MacDonald, *The Turner Diaries* (Arlington, VA: National Vanguard Books, 1985); Alberto Bayo, *150 Questions for a Guerrilla* (Boulder, CO: Paladin

Press, 1975); Joseph P. Stoffel, *Explosives and Homemade Bombs* (Springfield, IL: Charles C. Thomas, 1972).

[6]Walter Laqueur, *Terrorism* (Boston, MA: Little, Brown, 1977), p. 92.

[7]Arthur P. Van Gelder and Hugo Schlatter, *History of the Explosives Industry in American* (New York: Arno Press, 1972), p. 315.

[8]For example, see Ragnar Sohlman, *The Legacy of Alfred Nobel* (London: Bodley Head, 1983).

[9]For example, see Chris Gray, *Dynamite: A Century of Class Violence in America 1830–1930* (New York: Rebel Press, 1990); William J. Borbidge, *Bombs: Defusing the Threat* (Jacksonville, FL: Institute of Police Management and Technology, 1999).

[10]Department of the Army, *Field Manual 5-250 Explosives and Demolitions* (Washington, DC: U. S. Government Printing Office, 1992).

[11]Robert R. Lenz, *Explosives and Bomb Disposal Guide* (Springfield, IL: Charles C. Thomas, 1971), p. 56.

[12]H. J. Yallop, *Explosion Investigation* (Edinburgh, Scotland: Scottish Academic Press, 1980), p. 90.

[13]Lou Michel and Dan Herbeck, *American Terrorist: Timothy McVeigh and the Oklahoma City Bombing* (New York: Regan Books, 2001), pp. 215–18.

[14]U.S. Department of State, *Terrorist Bombings, p. 4.*

[15]Brian Jenkins, "Terrorism and Nuclear Safeguards Issue," *Rand Paper Series P-5611* (Santa Monica, CA: Rand Corp., 1984), p. 1.

[16]Neil C. Livingstone and Terrell E. Arnold, eds., *Fighting Back: Winning the War against Terrorism* (Lexington, MA.: D. C. Heath, 1986), pp. 32–33.

[17]Yallop, *Explosion Investigation*, pp. 75–77.

[18]*New York Times*, October 23, 1983, sec. 1, p. 1.

[19]For example, see Eric Hammel, *The Root* (New York: Harcourt Brace Jovanovich Publishers, 1985); Jacqueline Akhavan, *The Chemistry of Explosives* (Cambridge, England: Royal Society of Chemistry Information Services, 1998).

[20]Charles L. Roblee and Allen McKechnic, *The Investigation of Fires* (Englewood Cliffs, NJ: Prentice Hall, 1981), p. 98.

[21]For example, see P. W. Cooper and S. R. Kurowski, *Introduction to the Technology of Explosives* (New York: Wiley-VCH, 1997); M. A. Cook, *The Science of High Explosives* (Malabar, FL: Robert E. Krieger Publishing, 1985); Jehuda Yinon, *Forensic and Environmental Detection of Explosives* (New York: John Wiley, 1999).

[22]Van Gelden and Schlatter, *History of Explosives Industry*, p. 281.

[23]U.S. Bureau of Alcohol, Tobacco, and Firearms, *Explosives Incidents 1982* (Washington, DC: U.S. Government Printing Office, 1983), p. 6.

[24]Van Gelden and Schlatter, *History of Explosives Industry*, pp. 403–16.

[25]Thomas G. Brodie, *Bombs and Bombings* (Springfield, IL: Charles C. Thomas, 1972), p. 92.

[26]Ibid., p. 98.

[27]John Dinges and Saul Landau, *Assassination on Embassy Row* (New York: Pantheon, 1980), pp. 2–15.

[28]*London Times*, August 28, 1979, p. 1.

[29]*San Francisco Chronicle*, March 2, 1985, sec. A, p. 8.

[30]*Sacramento Bee*, September 5, 1985, sec. A, p. 12.

[31]*New York Times*, July 27, 1986, sec. 1, p. 2.

[32]John W. Ellis, *Police Analysis and Planning for Vehicular Bombings: Prevention, Defense, and Response* (Springfield, IL: Charles C. Thomas, 1994), pp. 156–64.

[33]Rewards for Justice, *Bombing of Khober Towers*, *http://www.rewardsforjustice.net*.

[34]*Report of the DOD Commission on Beirut International Airport Terrorist Act*, October 23, 1983 (Washington, DC: U.S. Government Printing Office, 1983), pp. 84–86.

[35]*The New York Times*, November 5, 1983, sec. 1, p. 14.

[36]Laqueur, *Terrorism*, pp. 94–95.

[37]For example, see John E. Douglas and Mark Olshaker, *Unabomber: On the Trail of America's Most Wanted Serial Killer* (New York: Pocket Books, 1996); Robert Graysmith, *Unabomber: A Desire to Kill* (Washington, DC: Regency Publishing, 1997); Nancy Gibbs et al. *Mad Genius: The Odyssey, Pursuit, and Capture of the Unabomber Suspect* (New York: Warner Books, 1996).

[38]U.S. Department of State, *Terrorist Bombings*, pp. 4–6.

[39]FBI Homepage, *http://www.rewardsforjustice.net*.

[40]Graham Knowles, *Bomb Security Guide* (Los Angeles, CA: Security World, 1976), p. 93.

[41]For example, see Knowles, *Bomb Security Guide*, pp. 96–102; Frank Moyer, *Police Guide to Bomb Search Techniques* (Boulder, CO: Paladin Press, 1981), pp. 137–46; Richard Clutterbuck, *Living with Terrorism* (London: Faber & Faber, 1976). pp. 83–91.

[42]*New York Times*, September 21, 1985, sec. 1, p. 1.

[43]CBC News: InDepth: The Bombing of Air India Flight 182. *http://www.cbc.ca/news/indepth/airIndia/index.html*.

[44]*New York Times*, June 24, 1985, sec. 1, p. 1.

[45]The Pan Am 103 Crash Web Site. *http://www.geocities.com/CapitalHill/5260/headpage.html*.

[46]U.S. Department of Transportation, Federal Aviation Administration, Office of Civil Aviation Security, *Explosions Aboard Aircraft* (Washington, DC: U.S. Government Printing Office, 2002), pp. 1–13.

[47]Ibid.

SUICIDE BOMBERS:
A GLOBAL PROBLEM

CHAPTER OBJECTIVES

The study of this chapter will enable you to:

- Explore the nature of suicide bombing
- Describe the motivation of suicide bombers
- Identify terrorist groups involved in suicide bombing
- Understand the complexity of suicide
- Develop strategies to interdict suicide bombings
- Speculate as to the future of suicide bombing attacks

INTRODUCTION

In recent years, the terrorist strategy of suicidal bombings has created increasing fear and widespread media attention. Suicide bombings are an incredibly cost-effective method of terrorism. While some suicide bombings are directed toward military targets, most are directed toward civilians. Such events as the suicide bombing of the United States Marine barracks in Beirut in 1983, the assassination of Rajiv Gandhi in 1991, the numerous suicide bombings against innocent civilians in Israel since March 1996, the suicide bombing of the U.S.S. *Cole* in 2000, and the devastating suicide bombings of the World Trade Center and the Pentagon on September 11, 2001, have caused widespread alarm.

It is hardly surprising that the suicide bombers themselves have become one of the most feared terrorist weapons. Suicide is a particularly awful way to die. Suicidologists agree that the mental suffering leading up to suicide is usually prolonged, intense, and well thought through.[1]

The suicide bombers discussed in this chapter are those who carry explosive charges on their bodies or by various vehicles such as a car, truck, boat, bicycle, or an airplane. Unlike previously noted acts of suicidal terrorism, the suicide bomber's intent is to cause a maximum number of innocent casualties. However, the ultimate goal of suicide bombers goes well beyond causing a high number of casualties. Suicide bombers produce fear, intimidation, and anxiety in the larger population. A suicide bombing attack ensures full media coverage and ranks with other outrageous acts of terrorism, such as midair explosions or the threatened use of weapons of mass destruction such as nuclear bombs, anthrax, or smallpox. For our purposes, a suicide bombing is defined as "a politically motivated violent attack carried out by an individual who is fully aware and purposely causes his or her own death by blowing himself or herself up along with the intended target usually to influence an audience." The offender's death is a precondition for the success of the suicide bombing attack.

Suicide bombings, as well as the fear suicide bombers promote in the general population, is not a new phenomenon.

In fact, the suicide bombings of the U.S.S. *Cole,* the World Trade Center, and the Pentagon are reminiscent of earlier suicidal attacks against the United States that may be a template for contemporary suicide bombing attacks. Indeed, if we examine the historical record, it will become clear that strong parallels exist between the Japanese **kamikaze** pilots of World War II and the perpetrators of the recent suicide bombings aimed especially at Israeli and American military and citizen targets.

The most infamous example of suicide bombers occurred during World War II when Japanese kamikaze[2] pilots slammed their bomb-laden planes onto the decks of U.S. naval vessels in the Pacific. In effect, the kamikaze, or Divine Wind, was a flying bomb. Indeed, the term *kamikaze* is now synonymous with suicide attack. The Japanese High Command believed the only way to stop the advancing U.S. naval forces was to organize suicide bombing attack units. The organized suicide attacks were seen by the Japanese military as an effective battle tactic against the overwhelming superiority of U.S. forces.

Popular images of psychopathic fanatical kamikaze pilots, however, appear to be exaggerated. Sasaki writes that kamikaze pilots were volunteers between seventeen and twenty-five years of age, well educated, and well trained with many attending various military pilot-training programs.[3] Even so, why would a Japanese pilot volunteer for certain death? There seem to be several reasons. Extreme patriotism was one certain factor. Complete reverence for the emperor—who was considered a god in Japanese society—was another factor. Some Japanese pilots believed that if one died for the emperor and was praised in the Yasukuni Shrine,[4] he would be in paradise forever. Thus, the kamikazes considered it an honorable mission to take revenge against the advancing U.S. military forces and felt it was a great honor to be selected from the group of volunteers for

FIGURE 7.1 A Japanese kamikaze pilot ties on a ceremonial headband with the rising sun design before crashing his bomb-laden plane onto American naval vessels. (Getty Images, Inc.—Hulton Archive Photos)

a suicide bombing attack. Inoguchi and Nakajima report that most of the volunteer kamikaze pilots were extremely depressed at the thought of a U.S. invasion of the Japanese home islands and the eventual loss of the war.[5] Robins, in his landmark study, reminds us that nowhere is the danger of suicide more acute than in the mood disorders of depression and manic depression.[6] Suicidologists have long agreed that depression is at the heart of all suicidal behaviors. In sum, Pineau reports that the depressed kamikaze pilots believed that everlasting happiness would follow the suicide attacks on U.S. military forces; thus, there was nothing to fear.[7]

In spite of the heroism and self-sacrifice of the kamikaze pilots, they were relatively ineffective and contributed little to the Japanese war effort. Craig describes the kamikaze suicide bombing attacks as the "tactics of despair."[8] Nearly a thousand Japanese kamikaze pilots were lost and over one hundred U.S. naval vessels were damaged or destroyed. The dream of halting the advancing U.S. Navy by suicide bombing attacks remained unrealized.

Suicide bombers again attracted attention during the last two decades of the twentieth century. During that time, eighteen different terrorist organizations

TABLE 7.1   Suicide Bombing Events

Group	Country of Origin	Motive	Target
Kamikaze	Japan	Tactical	U.S. naval vessels in Pacific
Hizballah	Lebanon/Iran	Tactical/revenge/image	Multi-National Force Lebanon/Israel
HAMAS	Palestine/Israel	Revenge	Israeli "soft" (non-military) targets
Islamic Jihad	Lebanon/Iran	Expulsion of foreigners/ revenge	United States/Israel
LTTE	Sri Lanka	Tactical/inspire recruits	Sri Lankan and Indian government and military
Sikhs	India	Independence/separatists	Indian hard and soft targets
Kashmiris	India	Union with Pakistan	Indian government and military officials
PKK	Turkey	Revolution/separatists	Turkish military and soft targets
Gama (Egypt)	Egypt	Retaliation	Foreign tourists in Egypt
Islamic Jihad	Egypt	Retaliation/revenge	Foreign tourists in Egypt
Abu Sayyaf	Southern Philippines	Separatists/independence	Philippine government/ Roman Catholics
MNLF	Southern Philippines	Separatists/independence	Philippine government/ Roman Catholics
al Qaida	Afghanistan/Yemen	Islamic revolution/revenge	United States/Israel
Chechens	Chechnya/Russia	Chechen independence	Russian military
Iranians	Iran	Tactical	Iraqi military
al Aqsa	Israel/Palestine	Revenge/retaliation	Israeli civilians
PFLP	Israel/Palestine	Revenge/retaliation	Israeli civilians
Jemaah Islamiya	Indonesia	Expulsion of foreigners/ revenge	Australian civilians
Iraqi "nationalists"	Iraq	Expulsion of U.S. military	United States military and foreign diplomats

and their sponsors in sixteen different countries have used suicide-bombing attacks in an attempt to realize their political objectives. (See Table 7.1.)

In addition, the *threat* of a suicidal terrorist bombing attack increasingly has become a useful terrorist tactic in attempts to intimidate "unfriendly" governments. For example, after 9/11, government buildings in Washington, DC, as well as U.S. embassies around the world, have been barricaded, and the United States is on heightened security alert to prevent vehicles or airplanes containing bombs being driven into them in kamikaze-style suicide attacks. The media have reinforced these threats by describing the recruitment and training of suicidal terrorists, especially in Islamic countries. Hundreds of so-called fanatical Palestinian suicide bombers offering to sacrifice their lives for the destruction of Israel have been portrayed on the evening news.

DEFINING THE PROBLEM

There are no simple theories for suicide bombings nor are there strategies with which to predict suicide bombing attacks. Nevertheless, Kushner points out that much knowledge exists about who commits suicide bombings.[9] For example, the research on suicide bombers reveals vulnerable age groups, social backgrounds, gender, methods used, locations, times chosen, and types of bombing devices. However, researchers are less certain as to why people carry out suicide bombing attacks. The complexity and privacy of the suicidal mind is a difficult barrier to overcome. The motives of a suicidal person are quite complex. Inevitably, the research literature on **suicidology** reflects the complexities and inconsistencies in our understanding of suicide bombing attacks.

However, suicide to attain a collective political goal is not confined to just suicide-bombing attacks. Suicide is quite prevalent among terrorist groups. Suicide by self-inflicted starvation or a **hunger strike** has a long history. In Ireland, for example, the hunger strike has been a characteristic form of political protest used by the Republican movement for many years. In March 1981 the nationalists groups Provisional Irish Republican Army (PIRA) and **Irish National Liberation Army (INLA)** began a hunger strike that continued until October 1981. When it finally ended, ten hunger strikers were dead. The hunger strikers believed that self-induced starvation was the only logical means of bringing public attention to their cause and was the price to be paid for winning national liberation from British domination of Northern Ireland. According to Poland, PIRA and INLA planned to end the hunger strike only after the British government granted their political demands.[10] Potential hunger strikers were lined up and ready to take the place of a "striker" once he died. It was only pressure from family members on the leadership of PIRA and INLA that finally ended the hunger strike, which probably saved the lives of dozens of young PIRA and INLA nationalists.

Another form of suicide used to support political objectives was carried out in the late 1960s by the notorious Baader-Meinhoff[11] terrorist gang in then West Germany. After a prolonged series of bombings, hostage takings, and attempted assassinations, the Baader-Meinhoff gang was finally apprehended, convicted, and sentenced to life in prison. While there the gang planned an elaborate scheme to "discredit" the West German government and continue the "revolution." Handguns were smuggled into the maximum-security prison housing the Baader-Meinhoff gang by their attorneys. Three members of the gang then committed suicide by self-inflicted gunshots. The scheme of the suicide was intended to suggest that they had, in fact, been murdered by prison authorities. An independent investigation revealed that the three members of the Baader-Meinhoff gang had indeed committed suicide by self-inflicted gunshots, and one gang member had hanged herself.

Another example of suicide for a political cause is **self-immolation**. Suicide by fire or self-immolation is a rare form of suicide, and is almost always associated with political protests. Self-immolation is without exception the most fanatical form of political protest. In the late 1960s an epidemic of suicides and attempted suicides by burning occurred in Southeast Asia after a Buddhist monk set fire to himself on a busy thoroughfare in Saigon to protest the war in Vietnam. Suicide by

Figure 7.2 Buddhist monk commits ritual suicide by self-immolation in Saigon, South Vietnam, to protest religious persecution by the South Vietnamese government in June 1963. (AP/Wide World Photos)

fire seems to be best understood as an extreme form of political protest designed to bring attention to a specific political problem. In one sense the self-immolations of the late 1960s had a profound effect on the peace movement in the United States. After several public self-immolations, public opinion against the Vietnam War began to shift from the battlefield to the negotiating table. The tremendous media coverage of the self-burnings ensured that the political nature of the Vietnam War would not go away. Furthermore, Jamison states that suicide by burning is a rational act where the victims are well aware of what they are doing.[12] More recently Carlson reports that several members of the Falun Gong spiritual group committed suicide by self-immolation in Beijing, China.[13] According to Dallman and Yamamoto, the Falun Gong has been protesting against the oppressive Chinese government for interfering in their religious activities.[14]

In sum, suicide to protest political conditions has a contagious aspect, as well as an indisputable appeal as the solution of last resort. Suicide—by self-starvation, self-inflicted gunshots, self-immolation, or suicide bombings—is described by Lifton as "symbolic immortality."[15] In other words, Lifton claims that human beings require a sense of immortality in the face of inevitable death. Hazani takes Lifton's paradigm further and refers to a variety of suicidal acts of terrorism as "sacrificial immortality."[16] Accordingly, extreme political movements such as the PIRA, **HAMAS**, al Aqsa, or the Tamils require members to sacrifice their lives, by suicide if necessary, for the furtherance of political and nationalistic objectives. If this is the case, then:

1. What common background characteristics are related to suicide bombers?
2. What terrorist groups sponsor and support the tactic of suicide bombings?

3. How are suicide bombers selected or why do they volunteer?
4. Why have suicide bombings occurred at this historical period?
5. Is it possible to predict the next target of a potential suicide bombing attack?

SUICIDE BOMBERS IN THE MIDEAST

The most well-known contemporary suicide bombers originated in the Mideast. Suicide bombing attacks began in Lebanon on April 18, 1983, when a suicide bomber driving a van carrying approximately 400 pounds of high explosives drove into the U.S. Embassy in **Beirut**, killing sixty-three and injuring hundreds more. Among the dead were sixteen Americans, including the CIA station chief in Lebanon. The newly formed Shiite terrorist group, **Hizballah** (Party of God), claimed credit for the attack. Then on October 23, 1983, a suicide bomber, also from Hizballah, drove a three-quarter ton truck loaded with 12,000 pounds of TNT into the U.S. Marine barracks in Beirut, killing 241 Marines. A simultaneous suicide bombing attack was carried out against the French multinational force in Beirut, killing sixty French paratroopers and maiming dozens more.

Martin and Walcott report that between the spring of 1983 and the summer of 1985 there was an unprecedented number of suicidal bombings carried out by Hizballah, Islamic Jihad (Islamic Holy War), and other competing Lebanese Shiite factions in Lebanon. In the thirteen months prior to the suicidal bombing of the Marine barracks, Hizballah and Islamic Jihad had participated in 118 car bomb attacks. During that time Hizballah suicide bombers attacked a variety of targets, including the U.S. military, rival Shiite groups, the Israeli military forces in southern Lebanon, and the Syrian military. Of the 118 car bombs, at least forty were in fact suicide car bombings.[17] Schweitzer estimates that Hizballah was responsible for fifty suicide-bombing attacks between 1983 and 1999.[18]

There is no denying that the Beirut suicide bombings made a marked impression on world public opinion and launched the career of Hizballah as a dangerous terrorist group that continues to this day. Even though there is a strong Islamic prohibition against suicide, Hizballah clerics grant religious dispensation to suicide bombers on the eve of their suicidal mission. Hizballah clerics rationalize that death from a suicide bombing attack is no different from deaths of soldiers who enter battle knowing that some of them will be killed. Based on this perverted moral logic, Hizballah could then recruit, train, and deploy young Shiite men and women in suicidal bombing missions.

By late 1999 Hizballah discontinued its suicide bombing attacks in favor of other "tactical" considerations. Hizballah suicide bombing attacks have also inspired a number of terrorist groups in other countries as well as the Mideast. The most prolific suicide bombers currently in the Mideast have been the Palestinian HAMAS, Palestinian Islamic Jihad (PIJ), the Palestinian al Aqsa Martyrs Brigade, and the Popular Front for the Liberation of Palestine.

Although the PFLP, al Aqsa, Islamic Jihad, and HAMAS targets are not as spectacular as the U.S. Marine headquarters in Beirut, the series of suicide bombing attacks in Jerusalem and elsewhere in Israel are just as vicious. For example,

HAMAS initially focused its suicide attacks against Israeli military targets but found that security surrounding military targets made suicide bombing an unacceptable tactic. As a result, HAMAS shifted its suicide bombing attacks to innocent civilians in crowded Israeli cities. The Israeli home page (*www.israel.org*) lists more than eighty-five suicide bombing attacks since 1993 carried out by Islamic Jihad, HAMAS, Popular Front for the Liberation of Palestine (PFLP), and al Aqsa, causing over 300 fatalities and the wounding of over 2,000 innocent victims.[19]

Beyer describes a typical suicide bombing attack that occurred on a crowded bus carrying Israeli students to classes in the city of Jerusalem. A lone Arab passenger sitting in the back of the bus suddenly reached into the book bag he was carrying and detonated a high explosive bomb filled with nails. Police later estimated the improvised explosive device contained about ten pounds of plastic explosive. The blast instantly incinerated the suicide bomber and four Israelis seated nearby. In addition to the five killed, 107 others were injured, some very seriously. In similar attacks that occurred in March and April 2002, hundreds of Israeli civilians were killed and wounded. The bombs were packed with nails, razor blades, staples, ball bearings, and nuts and bolts to deliberately increase the number of Israeli casualties.[20]

The fear generated by such suicidal attacks has a profound impact on the personal security of Israeli citizens. The horror is compounded by the fact that the bombers purposefully killed themselves. Who would carry out such atrocities and why? Obviously, to question suicide bombers directly involved in suicide attacks is not possible. However, HAMAS, PIJ, al Aqsa, and PFLP suicide bombers often make videotapes the night before the suicide attacks. Oliver and Steinberg,[21] in their definitive research on HAMAS suicide bombers, had access to several of the videotapes. The videotapes were used to memorialize the young suicide bombers and to illustrate to other potential suicide recruits the honor of a heroic "suicide" death for Palestine. The videotapes show young HAMAS recruits strapping high-velocity explosives to their waists and stating that the choice of martyrdom was an opportunity to meet God. At this point there is no turning back for the suicide bomber. The suicide bombers appear to be attracted by a straightforward message of religion and nationalism.

Israeli filmmaker Dan Setton produced a documentary film about HAMAS suicide bombers. The film, *Suicide Bombers: Secrets of the Shaheed,* is a series of interviews of HAMAS members who tried to carry out suicide attacks against Israeli targets but failed. The film portrays the recruitment of suicide bombers in Gaza mosques through the time when, strapped with explosives, they try to blow themselves up. These surviving suicide bombers are alive only because bombs failed to detonate or police intervened before bombs could be set off. From the surviving suicide bombers, Setton puts together a profile of a "typical" suicide bomber: unobtrusive, uneducated, raised within poor families who have no criminal record, and capable of blending easily into a crowd. Even their closest family members are unaware of plans to carry out a suicide bombing attack. Setton is bewildered by how calm the suicide bombers were before their planned attack.[22] But Jamison insists that suicidal people are calmer after deciding to kill themselves because they are relieved of the anxiety and pain related to life.[23]

Setton continues that some suicide bombers are lured by visions of beautiful virgins waiting for them in paradise. In order to prepare for death, suicide bombers perform a bizarre ritual by visiting cemeteries at night and sleeping among the graves of **martyrs**. In one film sequence, a jailed bomb maker casually diagrams how a suicide bomb works. Setton portrays the leaders of HAMAS, who have no plans to sacrifice their own lives, as manipulative, cynical, and charismatic.

Even though Setton's film presents a so-called "inside look" at the motivation for suicide bombings, Merari has other ideas. Merari maintains that HAMAS clerics use three strategies to convince young Muslims to die for Palestine. One technique is to force or trick people to carry out suicidal bombing missions against their will. Merari illustrates one such incident involving a 16-year-old who was apprehended by Israeli police before he could detonate the suicide bomb. The boy claimed he had been forced to go on a suicide bombing mission after HAMAS threatened to kill his family. A second tactic is to seek out mentally disturbed persons who may harbor suicidal tendencies or suffer from other aberrant psychological conditions. A third strategy is to brainwash or indoctrinate potential young recruits to believe that to die for God and Palestine is a great honor—as many kamikaze pilots believed that it was a great honor to die for the defense of Japan and the emperor. In sum, suicide bombing has become a vital part of the struggle to destroy Israel and establish an independent Palestine.[24]

Another explanation for the motivation of Palestinian suicide bombers is what Muir refers to as the paradox of dispossession or "the less one has the less one has to lose."[25] Nasr reports that the majority of Palestinian suicide bombers had no money, no job, no opportunities, no property, little respectability, no skills, little education, and believed their lives were meaningless without taking revenge against the "Zionists."[26]

Beck et al., in an extensive study, stated that one of the most consistent warning signs of suicidal behavior is a sense of hopelessness, despair, and negative feelings about the future.[27] **Emile Durkheim** argued that the egotistical suicidal person becomes detached from society, family, and religion and becomes so deluded in his personal beliefs and feelings that suicide appears to confirm the righteousness of a suicidal attack.[28] Being surrounded by unprecedented violence every day, potential Palestinian suicide bombers were living very depressed and desperate lives. Thus, it became easy to make the transition from a "nobody" to instant recognition as a martyr for Palestine. Katz believes that the simplicity of the suicide bombing attack had great appeal to the leaders of HAMAS, since the "hopelessness and helplessness" described the inner feelings of Palestinian people living under Israeli occupation for thirty-five years.[29]

In theory, the Islamic suicide bomber is required to submit to the will of Allah, but it is his own personal decision to go on a suicide bombing attack. In practice, the candidates for suicide bombing attacks are thoroughly indoctrinated, chosen by Islamic leaders and assured that after martyrdom they will be in heaven with the Prophets. Their families will be financially taken care of, and their afterlife will be filled with perfection. Laqueur refers to the Mideast suicide bomber as a sort of deluxe martyrdom.[30] The Islamic martyr will live on in paradise, eating exquisite food, living in golden palaces, and surrounded by beautiful young virgins, and their families will be provided with monthly stipends. In contrast, suicide martyrs outside of the Islamic faith carry out suicide bombings without the promise of an elaborate reward structure.

Kramer has argued that Islamic suicide bombing attacks are intended to be expressions of both religious faith and nationalistic fervor.[31] There is little doubt that religious fervor, nationalism, and perhaps mental illness is a dangerous mix. Undertaking a suicide bombing attack provides a way of adding meaning to a life that has little prospect of future success. As a young Palestinian stated to Hassan, "the youth of the Islamic resistance who blow themselves up in order to cause casualties are considered the greatest of those who die, because they die as martyrs."[32] Clearly a qualitative difference exists between those *willing* to die and those *wanting* to die. There are dozens of articles on the Internet that justify the suicide bombing attacks by Palestinian youth for Palestinian nationalism and Islamic beliefs. In fact, Jerozolimiski writes that the selection of suicide bombing is an integral aspect of Palestinian terrorism taught to Palestinian children at a very early age.[33]

In conclusion, Hizballah, HAMAS, Palestinian Islamic Jihad, al Aqsa, and the PFLP suicide bombing attacks are the most well known due to the instant media coverage of such events. But the most effective and brutal terrorist group to utilize suicide bombing attacks to date has been the **LTTE (Liberation Tigers of Tamil Eelam)**, the Tamil separatist group of Sri Lanka.

THE LIBERATION TIGERS OF TAMIL EELAM (LTTE)

Since the early 1970s the Tamils, provoked by government discrimination in education, culture, language, and restricted opportunities in the professions, have demanded the creation of a separate Tamil state in the northern and eastern regions of Sri Lanka (to be called Eelam—homeland). By the late 1970s, an all-out archetypical separatist/terrorist war was being waged by the most violent and hard-line Tamil organization, the LTTE. Terrorism had reached epidemic proportions, and Sri Lanka was descending into an outright civil war. According to Grosscup, inspired by the suicide tactics of Hizballah, which had forced the multinational force out of Lebanon, the LTTE shifted its terrorist attacks from ambush and assassination of Indian troops to suicide bombing attacks.[34]

Gunaratna tells us that between July 1987 and December 2000, LTTE carried out over 170 suicide attacks in Sri Lanka and southern India and is responsible for 62 percent of suicide bombing attacks worldwide.[35] Thousands of innocent bystanders have been killed and maimed in LTTE suicide attacks. Joshi contends that LTTE actually has suicide units called the "**Black Tigers**" comprised of both men and women who are more than willing to participate in suicide bombing attacks.[36] In fact, the LTTE has a unique feature not found in other international or national terrorist groups. Every member of the LTTE carries a cyanide capsule around his/her neck. Upon capture he/she may swallow the cyanide capsule to avoid disclosing the group's secrets during coercive interrogation. The media report many instances of LTTE terrorists who take the cyanide capsule rather than risk capture and interrogation that most likely would force them to betray their organization. Joshi reports that many young Black Tigers live under the delusional belief that they will not be harmed and will survive the suicide bombing attack.[37]

The primary focus of LTTE suicide bombing attacks has been the ruling political party in Sri Lanka. The LTTE is the only terrorist group to assassinate two heads of state by a suicide bombing attack. Rajiv Gandhi, former prime minister of India, was assassinated on May 21, 1991, when a female suicide bomber approached him with a bouquet of flowers as a welcoming gesture to his arrival in Sri Lanka. Concealed in the bouquet and around the body of the assassin was a high-explosive bomb packed with small ball bearings to increase the shrapnel effect. The powerful bomb killed Gandhi plus twenty-eight innocent bystanders and wounded hundreds more. In 1993 the president of Sri Lanka was assassinated when a male suicide bomber from LTTE detonated an explosive charge wrapped around his body. Juergensmeyer reminds us that hostilities in Sri Lanka are exacerbated by the religious struggles between the Hindu Tamil minority and the Buddhist Sinhalese majority.[38] Elsewhere in India, **Sikh** and **Kashmiri** extremists have occasionally resorted to suicide bombing as a terrorist tactic in their efforts to gain independence from India.

SIKH TERRORISM

The most serious violence and terrorism between Sikh separatists and the Indian government began after Indian troops invaded the Golden Temple on June 5, 1984, the most holy shrine to Sikh believers.[39] In a two-day military operation to drive Sikh militants from the Golden Temple, over 2,000 Sikhs were killed. What outraged the Sikh community most was the desecration of their most sacred shrine, the Golden Temple, by Indian troops. On October 31, 1984, Sikh extremists seeking revenge for the Golden Temple massacre assassinated Indira Gandhi, prime minister of India. On the following day, angry Hindu mobs slaughtered thousands of innocent Sikhs in Delhi and elsewhere in India. After the rioting, Sikh militants became even more fervent for their need to establish a separate Sikh nation. Marwah and Mahmood contend that the heavy-handed response and torture by the Indian government of Sikh militants helped to increase the ranks of the Sikh nationalist movement and create Sikh suicide martyrs.[40] Similar to the LTTE, HAMAS, and Hizballah, young Sikh extremists from a variety of competing factions from 1981–1994 viewed martyrdom as an honorable and holy way to die, even in a suicide bombing attack.

Vinayak's investigation into the first Sikh suicide bombing attack provides some insight into the suicide bombing strategy. The young Sikh suicide bomber practiced for the suicide bombing event for several weeks. As the suicide bomber prepared to leave on his mission, he gave a note to one of his companions stating that his act of suicide was to honor the memory of the martyrs of the Golden Temple. Apparently inspired by his dedication, other young Sikhs became suicide bombers, giving new life to the Sikh separatist movement. By the mid-1990s Sikh terrorist groups were penetrated by the Indian police and ceased to be a major threat to the Indian government, although the Sikh community still demands the creation of an independent Sikh nation.[41]

KASHMIRI SUICIDE BOMBERS

In Kashmir, where Muslims are the majority, another separatist movement began in 1986. The decades-old dispute between India and Pakistan over the hegemony of Kashmir erupted when the Muslim United Front called for secession from India. By May 1989 the separatists began referring to themselves as "holy warriors" and calling for a Jihad (holy war) against the Hindu government of India. The violence and terrorism between India and Kashmiri separatists continued to escalate, and thousands of people from both sides were killed and maimed by indiscriminate bombings. By the late 1990s the bombing campaign by various competing Kashmiri Muslim factions gave way to the use of suicide bombers. Accordingly, ten suicide bombings occurred in the year 2001.[42] For instance, on December 13, 2001, in an unprecedented attack, five suicide bombers attacked the Indian parliament in Delhi, killing twelve, including the suicide attackers, and injuring twenty-two. The suicide attack on the Indian parliament once more brought India and Pakistan (which allegedly supports Kashmiri terrorism) to the brink of war.

Juergensmeyer reports that Islamic clerics have little interference in recruiting young Kashmiri Muslim men to fight in a holy war.[43] Similar to the kamikaze, Kashmiri suicide bombers are young, well-educated, middle-class recruits who appear to be *willing* to die for God and country. Khurshid states that groups such as the Kashmiri Liberation Front and the Muslim United Front have little trouble attracting young Kashmiri males to carry out suicide bombing attacks against the Indian military forces in Kashmir.[44]

KURDISH SUICIDE BOMBERS: THE PKK

Another group that has resorted to suicide bombing attacks is the **PKK (Kurdistan Workers Party)**. The PKK is composed of Turkish Kurds and represents the same ruthless brand of terrorism as other notorious Mideast terrorist groups. They have murdered more than 10,000 people, mostly innocent Turks and Kurds. The PKK began as an orthodox revolutionary group in 1974, but has evolved into a nationalist/separatist religious group seeking to establish an independent Islamic Kurdistan in Turkey. Criss reports that the PKK received "terrorist" training sponsored by Hizballah in the Bekaa Valley in Lebanon.[45] While training there the PKK discovered the "terrorist strategy" of the suicide bombing attack and emerged as a deadly terrorist group ready to wage war against the Turks.

The PKK resorted to suicide bombing attacks beginning on June 30, 1996, when a female suicide bomber dressed as a pregnant woman in order to conceal the explosives she had hidden beneath her dress. She detonated the bomb, killing herself and ten innocent Turkish victims. Ergil contends that between 1994 and 1996 the PKK carried out twenty-one suicide or attempted suicide bombing attacks.[46] The PKK resorted to suicide bombing terrorism at a time when the Turkish military was gradually destroying the infrastructure of the PKK. In order to boost the morale of its membership and continue to struggle for a separatist Kurdish nation, suicide bombing attacks were chosen. The PKK, under Abdullah Ocalan's leadership, believed that the willingness to sacrifice one's life for Kurdish national goals would consolidate their membership, inspire young Kurds, and cause intense fear among the Turkish population. Apparently the tactic of suicide bombing did not work. After the capture of Abdullah Ocalan in June 1999, the Kurdish suicide bombing campaign was called off.

AL QAEDA

Osama Bin Laden and his terrorist group al Qaeda (the Base or the Base of Allah's support) recently have successfully carried out suicide bombings against the United States. Al Qaeda is responsible for two of the most spectacular and lethal suicide bombing attacks in recent years. The coordinated suicide bombing attacks against the World Trade Center and the Pentagon, which killed over 3,000 innocent people, and the attack on the American embassies in Nairobi and Dar-es-Salaam in August 1998, which killed 300 and left at least 5,000 wounded, demonstrate the lethality of well-planned acts of suicide bombings. Osama Bin Laden and al Qaeda demonstrated that with careful planning and dedicated followers, even the United States was vulnerable to a suicide bombing attack.

Gunaratna states that in a suicide attack reminiscent of the kamikaze, in October 2000 two al Qaeda suicide bombers approached the destroyer, the U.S.S. *Cole,* in the port of Aden, Yemen, in a small boat and detonated an enormous amount of explosives. The explosion ripped a 40- by 450-foot hole in the *Cole,* killed seventeen American sailors, and injured 33 others. The attack was intended to show the powerlessness of the United States in the face of Islam's embrace of martyrdom. The zeal of the two suicide bombers was meant to intimidate and demoralize the United States while simultaneously acting as an inspiration to Muslims around the world. A billion-dollar U.S. warship, armed with sophisticated twenty-first-century high-tech equipment, was all but destroyed by a small boat operated by "martyrs." This act conveys the message that world superpowers are easily vulnerable to suicide attack. Emboldened by the attack on the *Cole,* al Qaeda has demonstrated that a combination of religious zeal and technical know-how can produce horrific results. Gunaratna maintains that suicide attacks are likely to remain al Qaeda's preferred terrorist strategy for the foreseeable future. Al Qaeda will continue to plan spectacular suicide attacks against high-profile or symbolic targets (embassies, naval vessels, government buildings, and famous landmarks) in the United States.[47]

Al Qaeda–affiliated groups also claimed responsibility for two recent suicide bombings. On May 8, 2002, a suicide car bomber of the Jaish-e-Mohammed, a Pakistani terrorist group supported by al Qaeda, pulled up alongside a busload of French guest workers in Pakistan and detonated a powerful bomb, killing fourteen people. In Tunisia on April 11, 2002, the Islamic Army for the Liberation of the Holy Sites claimed credit for the suicide truck bombing of an historic synagogue in Tunis, killing nineteen people. The Islamic Army for the Liberation of the Holy

Sites announced that the synagogue bombing was in retaliation for Israeli crimes against the Palestinians. Unlike the kamikaze, al Qaeda has adopted suicide bombing as a strategic "first" choice.

CHECHEN SUICIDE BOMBERS

Chechen separatists carried out a wave of suicide truck bombings against Russian military forces in Chechnya in 1999 and 2000. After the Russian military declared that Chechen rebel resistance had been crushed, the suicide bombers struck. Five nearly simultaneous suicide truck bombing attacks occurred in four Chechen towns on July 4, 2000. In each of the bombings, large trucks were loaded with explosives. Suicide bombers drove them into buildings housing Russian military troops. Over eighty Russian soldiers and police officers were killed and hundreds were wounded. Commander Kattab, leader of the Chechen rebels, proudly claimed credit for the bombings, stating that "the Kremlin military adventure had no prospects for success against the dedication of the Chechen martyrs." Once again the twin motivators of religion and nationalism have inspired the use of the terrorist strategy of suicide bombing attacks.[48]

On December 6, 2003, two female Chechen suicide bombers attempted to enter the Russian parliment, but the explosives detonated prematurely. Five people were killed and fourteen were injured.

OTHER SUICIDAL TERRORIST GROUPS

Several additional terrorist groups have also claimed suicide bombing as part of their terrorist strategy. Egypt's two leading terrorist groups—Gama'a el-Islamiya and the Egyptian Islamic Jihad—have taken credit for at least two suicide bombing attacks. In a retaliatory attack, a Gama'a suicide bomber drove a vehicle loaded with high explosives into a police barracks in Croatia in October 1995. A Gama'a member had been held in the police barracks awaiting extradition to Egypt. Several police officers were injured by the attack.

In November 1995 the Egyptian Islamic Jihad sent two suicide bombers to attack the Egyptian Embassy in Pakistan in retaliation for Egyptian and Pakistani cooperation in extraditing fugitives of the Egyptian Jihad group to Egypt to stand trial for a variety of terrorist-related offenses. The attack resulted in fifteen fatalities and dozens of seriously injured victims. Like the suicide attacks on the United States by al Qaeda, the suicide bombings of the Egyptian Gama'a and Jihad illustrate that terrorist groups are not hesitant to export suicide attacks to other countries.

The Philippines has witnessed occasions of suicide bombing attempts in the southern Philippine islands of Mindanao. Two Islamic separatist groups, **Abu Sayyaf** and the Moro National Liberation Front, have attacked Philippine military bases with suicide bombers. After police interrogation, several members of Abu Sayyaf claimed that Osama Bin Ladin is providing training for Abu Sayyaf in terrorist techniques and suicide bombing attacks.[49]

SUMMARY

There is little doubt that suicide bombings generate a great deal of fascination and panic among the general population. If, according to the creed of terrorist groups, bombing attacks are considered "propaganda by deed," then the suicide bombing attack is the ultimate propaganda. The impression created by martyrs willing to sacrifice themselves is that the cause is worthy and God is "on our side." In the case of Muslim suicide bombers, however, the Koran does not permit suicide in principle. At the same time, it is the religious duty of every Muslim to fight and die in defense of Allah and Islam—certainly a confusing religious doctrine.

Islamic fundamentalists may live without hope, be poverty stricken, deeply religious, and nationalistic, but only a fraction of them have considered going on suicide bombing attacks. Is there a fraction of suicide bombing candidates who are more idealistic, more easily manipulated by terrorist group leaders, and more willing to sacrifice their lives? Is there perhaps an inclination to overlook the so-called real motives for suicidal behavior? What is the justification for the current appeal of suicide bombing attacks?

For the moment, suicidologists know that some groups of individuals are much more likely to kill themselves: those who suffer from depression, manic depression, drug and alcohol addiction, schizophrenia, personality and mental health disorders, patients recently released from mental hospitals, and adolescents.[50] The World Health Organization estimates that worldwide over one million people commit suicide every year.[51] Jamison estimates that the figure may be twice as high.[52] Worldwide, suicide is the second leading cause of death for females between the ages of 15 and 40. Among males of the same age group, suicide is the fourth leading cause of death. By any standard, suicide in general is a crucial public health problem. Hence, it may be relatively easy for such groups as Hizballah, HAMAS, Islamic Jihad, al Aqsa, or al Qaeda to convince prospective suicide bombers to die for Allah and the motherland.

Merari argues that religion is unimportant to a suicide bomber and that the choice is made by an individual who wishes to die for personal reasons.[53] In fact, he contends the terrorist group simply provides the framework and legitimacy for committing the suicide bombing. Merari continues that there is no evidence to suggest that religious or political leaders could convince a nonsuicidal person to carry out a suicidal bombing attack. Alvarez tends to support the notion that no one mental illness or event causes suicide and no one knows the motivation behind the killing of self.[54]

In addition, the tendency for suicide bombing attacks to incite imitation is persistent, especially if the suicide is highly publicized and romanticized. In 1975 the sociologist David Phillips introduced the phrase "Werther Effect" to describe the phenomenon of suicide contagion.[55] Many researchers believe that highly publicized media accounts of suicide bombing events lead to an increase in suicidal behavior.[56] Motto agrees that suicide has the strongest impact on young people and that the images and context of the suicide are far more important than the act of suicide itself.[57]

Berkan and the American Association of Suicidology offer the following general media guidelines for reporting suicide incidents that may contribute to a reduction or lessening of suicide bombing attacks.[58]

1. Providing sensational coverage of suicide bombing attacks.

    By its nature, news coverage of a suicidal bombing heightens public awareness and fear. Researchers believe this practice is associated with contagion and suicide **clusters**.[59] Police and news reporters can reduce the sensationalism by limiting the morbid details and avoiding the use of dramatic photographs.

2. Presenting suicide bombing as a tactic for reaching political goals.

    Suicide bombing is usually a rare act of a disturbed person. If suicide bombing is presented as an effective means of destroying Israel or the United States, for example, suicide may be perceived by a potentially suicidal person as a viable "military" strategy. In almost twenty years of terrorist suicide bombings, terrorist campaigns have not been won in Palestine, Sri Lanka, Chechnya, or any other nation.

3. Glorifying suicide bombers.

    Such actions may contribute to suicide contagion by suggesting to a susceptible young person that a great deal of honor and glory is associated with the suicide bombing attack. The innocent victims of a suicide bombing are often only given cursory coverage, while extensive coverage is devoted to the suicide bomber, his motives, and his tactics.

4. Presenting simplistic explanations for suicide bombings.

    Any type of suicide is a very complex interacting of many factors. There is more to a suicide bomber's motives than "Allah Akbar." Research on suicidology supports the thesis that people who commit suicide have a history of personal, social, and mental health problems. The overwhelming number of suicides are linked to psychiatric illnesses. At the heart of many suicides are mood, anxiety, and personality disorders. Acknowledgment of these problems will surely demonstrate the complexities involved in suicide bombing attacks.[60]

5. Illustrating and reporting "how to" descriptions of suicide bombing techniques.

    Describing technical details about the method of bombing may be undesirable. Providing details of the mechanism and procedures used to complete the suicide bombing may inspire other suicidal persons. For example, in the documentary *The Shaheed,* a bomb maker casually sketched the simplicity of making a bomb carried by a suicide bomber. Suicide incites imitation and repetition. Livingstone has argued that emphasis on violent acts committed by terrorist bombers may stimulate like-minded terrorists to repeat the same behavior. In Livingstone's view, the evidence suggests that detailed media coverage of suicide bombing attacks is apt to lead to a rash of similar imitative suicide bombings.[61]

In sum, with the exception of Palestinian groups and al Qaeda, most of the terrorist groups involved in suicide bombing attacks actually have either stopped using it or significantly reduced it. According to Jacqard the difference between suicide attacks by al Qaeda and other terrorist groups is the capacity and the global reach of al Qaeda to inflict mass casualties through the use of chemical or biological weapons.[62] Today the greatest potential risk of suicide bombing attacks is the use of weapons of mass destruction. Stern warns us that the use of a chemical, biological, or nuclear weapon by a suicide bomber is now a reality.[63]

Despite all the information available on suicide and suicide bombers, law enforcement still has not been able to protect communities from the lethality of a suicide bombing attack. What can society do to prevent suicide bombings from occurring in the future?

A practical problem that confronts the planning of suicide bombings is the extent of physical security surrounding potential targets. Some targets, such as government officials or embassies, may have elaborate and sophisticated security systems to prevent a suicide bombing attack. Other targets are largely unprotected, such as unguarded buildings and unarmed civilians. Therefore, terrorist suicide bombers will always have opportunities to carry out attacks, since it is impossible to provide protection for all possible targets. The result of such uneven security means that some targets will always be vulnerable to a suicide bombing attack. So what can be done to protect vulnerable citizens from a determined suicide bomber?

While the very size of a large urban area makes it difficult to protect all possible targets, the possibilities of carrying out a suicide bombing attack can be reduced by following a few practical security recommendations.

- First, the deployment of a large number of uniformed soldiers and police may afford some security as they increase the likelihood that suicide bombers will be intercepted on the way to an attack.
- Second, the introduction of intense surveillance of potential targets will make it difficult for suicide bombers to move about undetected. For example, the installation of high-density TV cameras can provide coverage of a vulnerable area.
- Third, the use of covert observation posts on the roofs of houses combined with surveillance equipment can supply information on suspicious persons.
- Fourth, the use of helicopters hovering over areas that are most vulnerable will help, especially to supplement the observation posts.
- Fifth, the setting up of checkpoints will make it difficult for the suicide bomber to move about undetected and should act as a deterrent as the suicide bomber runs the risk of being identified before he can carry out his mission.
- Sixth, the use of dogs can detect explosives concealed in vehicles and on individuals.

In sum, some protection may be possible against suicide bombing attacks, but it is impossible to protect everything and everyone all the time. A determined suicidal terrorist bomber may not be deterred by security measures. The limitations on the amount of physical protection create vulnerabilities that are exploited by terrorist groups planning suicide bombing attacks. As potential targets are hardened, suicide bombers seek out softer targets. In January 2000, an individual bent on committing suicide drove his eighteen-wheeler into the south porch of the State Capitol in Sacramento, California. Surveillance cameras showed the eighteen-wheeler barreling up the steps of the California capitol building into the portico and bursting into flames. Fortunately, the driver of the semitruck was not a suicide bomber. Instead, he was a suicidal person who had spent much of his life in prison and mental institutions and apparently suffered from a variety of mental health and mood disorders. There is little doubt, however, that potential suicide bombers studied how easy it was to attack a hard target such as the California capitol building.

Security measures alone are not sufficient to prevent suicide bombings. The collection of intelligence information is the key to a successful **interdiction** of a suicide bombing attack. Potential suicide bombers need support in order to plan and execute a successful suicide attack. Dershowitz observes that the vast majority of suicide bombers do not act alone and are part of complex organizational structures.[64] Suicide bombers are recruited, trained, and promised rewards by the organization that sends them on suicide attacks. Therefore, by taking preventive measures it may be possible to interdict future suicide bombing attacks. The decision to send a suicide bomber is almost always made by others. A few proactive measures follow.

- First, family members may notice a change in the behavior of a son or daughter planning a suicide attack and notify authorities and perhaps prevent the suicide attack from occurring.
- Second, a successful counterstrategy requires comprehensive intelligence of the recruitment, selection, and training of the suicide bombers. The potential suicide bomber must be identified either when he or she joins the terrorist organization or during the period of "basic training."
- Third, the person who recruits the potential suicide bomber usually follows him or her throughout his "military" preparation and "spiritual" awakening before the planned suicide attack.
- Fourth, the operational groundwork for the suicide attack includes preparation of the explosive device at a clandestine bomb factory, location of a safe house for the suicide bomber, and finally the transport of the suicide bomber and the explosives to the target area without being detected by the police, military, or watchful citizens.
- Fifth, the leaders of terrorist organizations who support and create an atmosphere for the use of suicide attacks should be identified. There is little

doubt that the tactic of suicide bombing is devised and approved by terrorist organizational leaders.

In short, the intelligence apparatus of nations under attack by suicide bombers should concentrate on interrupting the preparations and planning of a suicide attack in order to neutralize the suicide attack in its preparatory stage. When contending with the phenomenon of suicide bombings, nations under attack must keep in mind that suicide operations are not the act of a desperate terrorist or a lone "madman." Rather, suicide attacks are well-planned, well-organized strategic operations that include extensive preparation and the involvement of a large support staff. Therefore, countering suicide bombings requires a combination of target hardening and intelligence gathering to interdict the terrorist organizations responsible for suicide attacks.

Another, perhaps surer, strategy for preventing suicide bombings, especially in Israel, may be for the Israeli government to end the occupation of Palestinian territory and to cease the construction of Israeli settlements in the "occupied territories." Bahour concludes that only Israel can stop the suicide bombing attacks by returning the "occupied territories" to the Palestinians.[65] For many of these groups, the Palestinians included, the political objective for suicide bombers is, most often, the achievement of an independent state. Thus, it may be posited that in most cases of suicide bombing, the best prevention strategy is a political settlement in which some kind of independence is granted. In the wake of September 11, how we respond to suicide bombings and terrorism is becoming the defining issue of our time.

CONCLUSIONS

There are no simple theories for suicide bombing, nor are there strategies to predict it. As yet no one has found a way to stop it. Suicide bombing has a contagious aspect associated with it, and it has an indisputable appeal as the solution of last resort.

The leadership of terrorist organizations also has discovered a number of positive benefits of the suicide attack method. First, many casualties can be expected. Second, widespread media coverage is assured. Third, the suicide bomber can choose the time and place of the attack. Fourth, there is no need to plan an escape and risk being captured and interrogated. Fifth, the suicide attack method is least costly in terms of "battlefield losses." Finally, success is almost guaranteed.

Suicide bombing has become the new benchmark of religious devotion and nationalistic pride. In fact, the suicide bomber also believes he or she benefits from participating in a suicide attack. For example, fulfillment of a religious obligation and eternal life in paradise are certainly benefits. The suicide bomber improves his social status in the community and may receive economic rewards for his family as more benefits.

For these reasons, suicide bombing will continue to be part of the terrorist strategy of many terrorist organizations. Suicide bombing, which has quadrupled over the last twenty years, is without argument the most serious problem facing the war on terrorism. The world is now facing the very real threat of a suicide attack using weapons of mass destruction (WMD). The next chapter concentrates on counterterrorist measures—the best response to the growing threat of terrorism.

KEY TERMS

Abu Sayyaf

Beirut

Black Tigers

Cluster

Emile Durkheim

HAMAS

Hizballah

Hunger Strike

Interdiction

Irish National
  Liberation Army
  (INLA)

Kamikaze

Kashmiri

Kurdistan Workers
  Party (PKK)

Liberation Tigers of
  Tamil Eelam (LTTE)

Martyrs

Self-immolation

Sikh

Suicidology

REVIEW QUESTIONS

1. Who were the kamikaze?
2. What is the Yasukuni Shrine?
3. Identify the country of origin of the following groups:
    a. PKK
    b. Hizballah
    c. Sikhs
    d. Abu Sayyaf
    e. Black Tigers
    f. MNLF
4. Explain the concept of "suicide clusters."
5. What motivates suicide bombers?
6. Why do you think suicide bombing is a "tactical" choice of terrorist groups?
7. Describe the analysis of suicidologists and the motivation for individual acts of suicide.
8. What terrorist group participates in the largest number of recorded suicide attacks? Why?
9. Develop a strategy to interdict and prevent suicide bombings.

WEB SITES

The International Policy Institute for Counter-Terrorism
  http://www.ict.org.il/
Israeli Ministry of Foreign Affairs
  http://www.israel.org/mfa/home.asp
The Jerusalem Post
  http://www.jpost.com
Washington Report on Middle East Affairs
  http://www.wrmea.com/
American Association of Suicidology
  http://www.suicidology.org/

ENDNOTES

[1]For example, see Bruce Hoffman, *Inside Terrorism* (New York: Columbia University Press, 1998); B. Crosby et al., "Suicide by Fire: A Contemporary Method of Political Protest," *International Journal of Social Psychology* 23 (1997), pp. 60–69; Martin Milton and Judy Crompton, "Recent Research on Suicide," *Counseling Psychology Review* 16 (2001), pp. 28–33; James Rogers, "Theoretical Grounding: The 'Missing Link' in Suicide Research," *Journal of Counseling and Development* 79 (Winter 2001), pp. 16–25; Edwin Shneidman, ed., *Comprehending Suicide: Landmarks in 20th Century Suicidology* (Washington, DC: American Psychological Association, 2001); John Westefeld and others, "Suicide: An Overview," *Counseling Psychologist* 28 (July 2000), pp. 445–510.

[2]Kamikaze or Divine Wind is a term originally applied by grateful Japanese to a typhoon that destroyed a Mongol invasion fleet in 1281. Revived in 1945, kamikaze applied to pilots who flew planes loaded with explosives into U.S. naval vessels.

[3]Mako Sasaki, "Who Became Kamikaze Pilots and How Did They Feel toward Their Suicide Mission," *Concord Review,* 2000. Web site: *http://www.tcr.org.*

[4]Yasukuni (Peaceful Country) is a shrine dedicated to Japanese war dead. If a war hero is buried in the Yasukuni Shrine, he becomes godlike and deserves reverence from all visitors. The shrine is dedicated to the Shinto code of Bushido. It is the most important shrine in the Shinto hierarchy of shrines. In one respect the Yasukuni is equivalent to Arlington Cemetery. The shrine contains a special room for kamikaze pilots.

[5]Rikihei Inoguchi and Tadashi Nakajima, *The Divine Wind* (Annapolis, MD: United States Naval Institute, 1958), pp. 36–52.

[6]For example, see Eli Robins, *The Final Months: A Study of the Lives of 134 Persons Who Committed Suicide* (New York: Oxford University Press, 1981).

[7]Roger Pineau, "Spirit of the Divine Wind," *U.S. Naval Institute Proceedings* 84 (January 1958), pp. 23–29.

[8]William Craig, *The Fall of Japan* (New York: Dell Books, 1967), pp. 1–14.

[9]Harvey Kushner, "Suicide Bombers: Business as Usual," *Studies in Conflict and Terrorism* 19 (October–December 1996), pp. 329–37.

[10]James M. Poland, *Understanding Terrorism: Groups, Strategies, and Responses* (Englewood Cliffs, NJ: Prentice Hall, 1988), pp. 53–54.

[11]The Baader-Meinhoff gang, so named after its founders, was active in the Federal Republic of Germany in the 1970s. The original name of the Baader-Meinhoff Gang was the Red Army Faction (RAF). The gang strongly believe that an armed campaign of terrorist violence against the state was the highest form of class struggle.

[12]Kate Jamison, *Night Falls Fast: Understanding Suicide* (New York: Vintage Books, 1999), pp. 142–45.

[13]Peter Carlson, "For Whom the Gong Tolls," *Washington Post*, February 27, 2000, p. 1.

[14]Christine Dallman and Isamu Yamamoto, "China's Falun Gong, the World Is Watching . . . and Joining," *Christian Research Journal* 22 (February 2000), pp. 22–45.

[15]For example, see Robert Lifton, *Destroying the World to Save It: Aum Shinrikyo, Apocalyptic Violence and the New Global Terrorism* (New York: Metropolitan Books, 1999), pp. 292–95; Lifton, *The Broken Connection: On Death and the Continuity of Life* (New York: Simon and Schuster, 1979).

[16]Moshe Hazani, "Sacrificial Immortality: Toward a Theory of Suicide Terrorism and Related Phenomena," in *The Psychoanalytic Study of Society*, eds. C. Boyer et al. (Hillsdale, NJ: Analytic Press, 1993), pp. 415–42.

[17]David Martin and John Wolcott, *Best Laid Plans: The Inside Story of America's War against Terrorism* (New York: Simon and Schuster, Inc., 1988), pp. 125–45.

[18]Yoram Schweitzer, "Suicide Terrorism: Development and Characteristics," (Herzlija, Israel: *The International Policy Institute for Counterterrorism*, 2000). Web site: *http://www.ict.org.il/*.

[19]Israeli Ministry of Foreign Affairs, 2002. Web site: *http://www.israel.org/ mfa/home.asp*.

[20]Lisa Beyer, "Jerusalem Bombing," *New York Times*, August 21, 1995, p. 1.

[21]For example, see Anne Marie Oliver and Paul Steinberg, *Rehearsal for a Happy Death: HAMAS Suicide Bombers in Gaza* (New York: Oxford University Press, 2001); Oliver and Steinberg, "The Politics of Apocalypse in the Underground Media of the Islamic Resistance Movement (HAMAS)," *Center for Millennial Studies* (Boston, MA: Boston University Press, 1997).

[22]*Suicide Bombers: Secrets of the Shaheed*, written and directed by Dan Setton (Set Productions, 1998). Presentation of CineMax: Reel Life.

[23]Jamison, *Night Falls Fast: Understanding Suicide*, pp. 125–27.

[24]Ariel Merari, "The Readiness to Kill and Die: Suicide Terrorism in the Middle East," in *Origins of Terrorism: Psychologies, Ideologies, Theologies, States of Mind*, ed. Walter Reich (Washington, DC: Woodrow Wilson Center Press, 1998), pp. 192–207.

[25]William K. Muir, *Police: Streetcorner Politicians* (Chicago: University of Chicago Press, 1977), p. 61.

[26]For example, see Kameel B. Nasr, *Arab and Israeli Terrorism: The Causes and Effects of Political Violence* (Jefferson, NC: McFarland, 1997); Raphael Israeli, *Islamikaze: Manifestations of Islamic Martyrology* (London: Frank Cass Publishers, 2003).

[27]Aaron T. Beck et al. "Relationship between Hopelessness and Ultimate Suicide: A Replication with Psychiatric Outpatients," *American Journal of Psychiatry* 147 (1990), pp. 190–95.

[28]For example, see Emile Durkheim, *Suicide: A Study in Sociology* (New York: Simon and Schuster, 1997).

[29]For example, see Samuel Katz, *The Hunt for the Engineer: How Israeli Agents Tracked the HAMAS Master Bomber* (New York: Fromme International Publishing, 1999).

[30]Walter Laqueur, *The New Terrorism: Fanaticism and the Arms of Mass Destruction* (Oxford: Oxford University Press, 1999), pp. 140–47.

[31]Martin Kramer, "The Moral Logic of Hizballah," in *Origins of Terrorism: Psychologies, Ideologies, Theologies, States of Mind*, ed. Walter Reich, (Washington, DC: Woodrow Wilson Center Press, 1998), pp. 131–57. See also Barbara Victor, *Armies of Roses: Inside the World of Palestinian Women Suicide Bombers* (Emmaus, PA: Rodale Press, 2003).

[32]Nasra Hassan, "Letter from Gaza: An Arsenal of Believers: Talking to the 'Human Bombs,'" *New Yorker,* November 11, 2001, pp 36–42.

[33]Adam Jerozolimiski, "Islamic Jihad Is Running Four Camps in the Gaza Strip at Which Eight to Twelve-Year-Olds Learn the Importance of Becoming a Suicide Bomber," *Jerusalem Post,* July 20, 2001, p. l.

[34]Beau Grosscup, *The Newest Explosion of Terrorism* (Far Hills, NJ: New Horizon Press, 1998), pp. 234–67.

[35]For example, see Rohen Gunaratna, *International and Regional Security Implications of the Sri Lankan Tamil Insurgency* (St. Albans, United Kingdom: International Foundation of Sri Lankans, 2000).

[36]Charu Joshi, "Ultimate Sacrifice," *Far Eastern Economic Review,* June 1, 2000, pp. 64–67.

[37]Ibid.

[38]Mark Juergensmeyer, *Terror in the Mind of God: The Global Rise of Religious Violence* (Berkeley: University of California Press, 2000), pp. 112–113.

[39]The Golden Temple in Amristar in Punjab Province of India is the symbol of strength of Sikh people worldwide. The Golden Temple is the heart of Sikhism and is equivalent to St. Peters in Rome and Temple Mount in Jerusalem.

[40]For example, see Cynthia Mahmood, *Fighting for Faith and Nation: Dialogues with Sikh Militants* (Philadelphia: University of Pennsylvania Press, 1997); Ved Marwah, *Uncivil Wars: Pathology of Terrorism in India* (New Delhi, India: HarperCollins India, 1995).

[41]Ramsen Vinayak, "Striking Terror," *India Today,* September 30, 1995, p. 27.

[42]*BBC News*, 2001, Web site: *http://news.bbc.co.uk/.*

[43]Juergensmeyer, *Terror in the Mind of God*, p. 210.

[44]For example, see Salmon Khurshid, *Beyond Terrorism: New Hope for Kashmir* (New Delhi, India: UBS Publications, 1994).

[45]Nur Criss, "The Nature of PKK Terrorism in Turkey," *Studies in Conflict and Terrorism*, 18 (January–February 1995), pp. 17–38.

[46]Dogu Egil, "Suicide Terrorism in Turkey," *Civil Wars* 3 (2000), pp. 37–54.

[47]For example, see Rohen Gunaratna, *Inside al Qaeda: A Global Network of Terror* (New York: Columbia University Press, 2002); Roland Jacqard, *In the Name of Osama Bin Laden: Global Terror and the Bin Laden Brotherhood* (London and Durham, NC: Duke University Press, 2002).

[48]*The Russia Journal*, July 8, 2000, Web site: *http://www.russiajournal.com/.*

[49]"The War Comes Home," *Asiaweek*, October 26, 2001, pp. 24–27.

[50]For example, see Edwin Shneidman, *Definition of Suicide* (New York: Aronson, Jason Publishers, 1995); Shneidman, *Voices of Death* (New York: Harper and Row, 1980).

[51]For example, see World Health Organization, *Figures and Facts about Suicide: World Health Organization Mental and Behavioral Disorders Team* (Geneva: World Health Organization, 2001).

[52]Jamison, *Night Falls Fast: Understanding Suicide*, p. 48.

[53]Ariel Merari, "The Readiness to Kill and Die: Suicide Terrorism in the Middle East," in *Origins of Terrorism: Psychologies, Ideologies, Theologies, States of Mind*, ed. Walter Reich, (Washington, DC: Woodrow Wilson Center Press, 1998), pp. 192–207.

[54]For example, see Alfred Alvarez, *The Savage God: A Study of Suicide* (London: Weidenfeld and Nicolson, 1971).

[55]David Phillips, "The Influence of Suggestion on Suicide: Substantive and Theoretical Implications of the Werther Effect," *American Sociological Review* 39 (June 1974), pp. 340–54.

[56]Drew Velting and Madelyn Gould, "Suicide Contagion," in *Review of Suicidology*, ed. W. Maris, et al. (New York: Guilford, 1997), pp. 3–22; Ira Wasserman, "Imitation and Suicide: A Reexamination of the Werther Effect," *American Sociological Review* 49 (June 1984), pp. 427–36.

[57]J. A. Motto, "Suicide and Suggestibility—The Role of the Press," *American Journal of Psychiatry* 124 (August 1967), pp. 252–56.

[58]For example, see William Berkan, *A Guide to Curriculum Planning in Suicide Prevention* (Madison: Wisconsin Department of Public Instruction, 1990).

[59]For example, see Loren Coleman, *Suicide Clusters* (Boston, MA: Faber and Faber, 1986).

[60]For example, see Shneidman, *Definition of Suicide*; Shneidman, *Voices of Death*.

[61]For example, see Neil Livingstone and Terrell Arnold, *Fighting Back: Winning the War against Terrorism* (Lexington, MA: Lexington Books, 1986); Neil Livingstone, *The War against Terrorism* (Lexington, MA: Lexington Books, 1982).

[62]Jacqard, *In the Name of Osama Bin Laden*, p. 48.

[63]Jessica Stern, *The Ultimate Terrorists* (Cambridge, MA: Harvard University Press, 1999), pp. 84–85.

[64]Alan Dershowitz, *Why Terrorism Works: Understanding the Threat, Responding to the Challenge* (New Haven, CT: Yale University Press, 2002), pp. 29–30.

[65]Sam Bahour and Leila Bahour, "Are Palestinians Human," 2002. Web site: *http://www.awitness.org/*.

8

The New Terrorist Threat: Weapons of Mass Destruction

Key Concepts

fanatics	biotoxins	nerve gases
biological weapons	botulinum toxin	ricin
chemical weapons	tularemia	small plutonium device
plague	smallpox	dirty bombs
unit 731	anthrax	agroterrorism
bacteria	viral hemorrhagic fever	Operation Silent Prairie
viruses	choking agents	suicide carrier
rickettsiae	blistering agents	
fungi	blood agents	

Science and technology have made enormous progress, but human, alas, has not changed. There is as much fanaticism and madness as there ever was, and there are now very powerful weapons of mass destruction available to the terrorist.

Walter Laqueur

CONTEXT OF THE THREAT

As noted earlier, terrorism is not a new phenomenon; instead, it is a pattern of behavior with deep roots in the history of most modern nation-states and peoples. Nor are all weapons of mass destruction new; biological and even chemical agents have been used in conflicts for centuries. But most analysts of contemporary terrorism assumed, until recently, that the costs—financial and political—were too high for modern terrorists to seriously attempt the use of such weapons today.

This reasoning contained several errors. The first is that the financial costs of all forms of weapons of mass destruction (WMDs) are too high today to be paid by individuals or groups willing to commit acts of terrorism. Although the cost of building a nuclear bomb is still quite high, access to nuclear material and the technological skills to develop such weapons have become much less restricted since the fall of the Soviet Union. So-called backpack nukes and other small-scale tactical nuclear weapons have made it to the black market in arms sales fueled by the Soviet collapse. Nuclear waste material, too, continues to be generated at an alarming rate, although secure storage of a permanent nature for such material remains a serious problem, making the possibility of a nuclear dirty bomb as a terrorist weapon quite feasible.

The second flaw in the logic lies in the insistence that terrorists would not use nonconventional weapons today, because the use of such weapons would carry too high a political or support network cost. Groups supported by states would, it was reasoned, be unlikely to use WMDs, because to do so would bring down attacks using similar weapons on the sponsor state. To deliberately jeopardize the patron state, thus perhaps causing the cutting off of all lines of support, would be an irrational move. Nor, it was reasoned, would patron states be willing to put such weapons in the hands of groups carrying out terrorist acts, because such retribution would surely fall on the state if the group used the weapon.

This reasoning is based on the assumptions that terrorists are rational actors and that all terrorists' groups are supported by states and would thus be unwilling to damage that relationship by the use of such weapons. As the September 11 attacks demonstrated, terrorist groups today are not necessarily funded by or networked with any particular state, and so cannot be assumed unwilling to use such weapons for this reason. As noted in the chapter discussing the motivations of terrorists, it is also probably erroneous to assume that terrorists are rational actors in the commonly accepted sense. Because they define their world in ways that often make little sense to those who do not see the struggle or the enemy as they do (as discussed in Chapter 4), then to assume their rationale for the use or nonuse of WMDs would meet the world's criteria for logic is itself irrational.

Furthermore, as Walter Laqueur discusses in his book, *The New Terrorists: Fanaticism and the Arms of Mass Destruction,* there are now many terrorists who are **fanatics,** *individuals who are overenthusiastic, zealous beyond the bounds of reason.* Because reason is clearly not, by definition, going to be a factor in the decision-making process of a fanatic terrorist, then to assume he or she would not use WMDs is a forlorn hope, indeed, an irrational act on our part. To know that such weapons exist, to be aware they are much more accessible now to potentially fanatical users, and *not* to attempt to assess the potential for such destructive attacks and their probable consequences, would be irrational—as illogical as the fanatic who may well seek to use such weapons today.

The greater the understanding of the reality of the threat, the potential for destruction of these weapons, and the capability of groups to utilize such weapons, the better will be our ability to deal with the current world situation without either paranoia or desperate security measures. This chapter, then, will deal with these three aspects of terrorism and WMDs: an historical analysis of the reality of the use of WMDs, the types of such weapons that currently exist and their lethality, and the ability of current groups engaged in terrorism to use such weapons.

HISTORICAL USE OF WEAPONS OF MASS DESTRUCTION

Modern WMDs have one new component—nuclear weapons—but the other two major types of WMDs, biological and chemical, have been part of the arsenal of warriors for much longer. The oldest of these, **biological weapons,** *warfare agents that include living microorganisms and toxins produced by microorganisms, plants, or* *animals*, have the longest history to explore. **Chemical weapons,** *often comprised of binary compounds of chemicals that would not, separately, be lethal,* are not necessarily a completely different category of weapon, since agents like strychnine and ricin (which will be discussed later) are called biotoxins. We will begin with the oldest of these weapons—the biological ones—and progress through chemical to nuclear, taking a quick look at each type.

Brief History of Biological Weapons

During the 1990s, there was a widespread belief that biological and chemical weapons were the greatest danger facing humanity. Biological weapons treaties, including the one signed by the United States and the Soviet Union in 1972, gravely declared that nations would no longer produce such weapons and would destroy their current stocks of these weapons. But the use of such weapons had already been part of the history of conflict throughout the world.

The **plague** of the fourteenth century, *reported to have killed about a third of the population of Europe, was supposedly spread by the Tartars, in their siege of the fortress of Caffa in the Crimea.* According to legendary accounts, the Tartars used catapults to hurl plague-infected corpses into the city, becoming one of the first armies in history to engage in germ warfare. Other plagues were also alleged to be either the result of or to be enhanced by the deliberate use of infected skins and/or corpses by military groups. This includes the account mentioned in the chapter discussing terrorism in the United States of the use of blankets infected with smallpox as "peace offerings" to the Native Americans in Pennsylvania in the 1760s.

During World War I, Germany was accused of trying to spread cholera bacilli in Italy, the plague in St. Petersburg, and anthrax in Mesopotamia and Romania. In 1915, German agents in the United States were believed to have injected horses, mules, and cattle with anthrax on their way to Europe during World War I. The germs were produced in Silver Springs, Maryland, a Washington, DC, suburb, at a small German laboratory headed by Dr. Anton Dilger, who produced a liter of anthrax and glanders. The original seed cultures had reportedly been supplied by Berlin.[1]

In the mid-1930s, *Japan created a special biological warfare force* called **unit 731,** led by General Ishi in Manchuria, and many biological agents were produced in the laboratories of this unit. During the Japanese invasion of China in 1937, fleas were infested with many of these agents, including plague, smallpox, typhus, and gas gangrene. Evidence has emerged that these fleas were put in wheat dropped from Japanese planes over Chinese towns toward the end of the war, resulting in hundreds of deaths.

The United Kingdom and the United States also developed germ warfare capabilities during World War II. The United Kingdom's experiments with anthrax at Gruinard Island off the coast of Scotland resulted in contamination of the island, which was only removed at the end of the 1990s. The U.S. biological warfare program, initiated in 1942, continued after the end of the war, headquartered in Fort Detrick, Maryland, during the 1950s and 1960s.

Germ warfare installations also suffered from problems due to accidents. One of the most famous of these occurred in Sverdlovsk, in the Ural Mountains of the Soviet Union in April 1979. Intelligence assessments, later confirmed by Russian files after the collapse of the USSR, indicated that a large airborne release of anthrax spores used for bacteriological warfare resulted in fatalities. Similar, if smaller, accidents have reportedly occurred at facilities around the world, making the production of such weapons more visibly hazardous.

Brief History of Chemical Weapons

There are today a wide range of potential chemical weapons. Unfortunately, many chemicals used regularly for nonlethal purposes can be easily obtained and used—in combination with other chemicals—as chemical weapons. Chemical agents can be divided into many categories, but at least a cursory look at some of the major types of chemical agents will make a discussion of this type of weapon more easily understood.

Biotoxins, mentioned earlier, are one type of chemical agent. This category includes agents such as ricin, abrin, and strychnine. Another type of agent used by the military in many contexts in the twentieth century are the blister agents, including sulfur mustard, known as mustard gas.

Chemical weapons are a much more recent addition to the arsenal of nations and warriors than are biological agents. For the most part, this type of weapon was not used in conflict until the twentieth century, existing only in the form of plans never carried out in the decades at the end of the nineteenth century. The idea of using poison gas against an enemy has been reported in connection with several groups, including the Finians in the 1870s, who allegedly planned to spray it in the House of Commons in London. Similar plans were apparently made, but not carried out, during the Boer War, and even the Japanese War with the Russians in 1905.

It was not until World War I, by the Germans in 1915 at the battle of Ypres, that a chemical weapon—chlorine gas—was used on a large scale, with shocking success. The gas killed 5,000 Allied troops and injured many more. Five months later, in Loos, Belgium, the Allies used poison gas against German troops, again with dreadful success. The military on both sides continued to use gases as weapons, with varying levels of success. Although chlorine gas continued to be used in gas artillery shelling in a number of battles, including but not limited to the battles of Fey-en-Haye, Verdun, and the Somme, an equally effective mixture of chlorine and phosgene (mustard gas) was also used.

About 25 poison gases were used in World War I. The exact casualty count from this type of weapon is unclear; estimates vary between 500,000 and 1,200,000 total of troops and civilians from both sides. History indicates that the Russians may have suffered the worst losses from this weapon when it was used against them in conflict east of Warsaw in 1915. They reportedly lost about 25,000 soldiers in the first such attack, with countless casualties among civilians in towns near the front line.

Gas attacks, though clearly technologically possible, do not appear to have occurred in World War II. Even the Germans, who had clear technical superiority in the range of chemical weaponry developed, decided for a variety of reasons not to use these weapons. Believing, apparently, that Allied forces had also developed tabun and sarin, toxic gases produced in Germany by 1944, Hitler decided not to use these newest lethal weapons (although it turned out that the Allies had *not* developed these toxins during the war).

The next reported use of chemical weapons occurred when Iraq used them during its war with Iran, against both Iranians and later against members of Iraq's own citizenry. Here are a few of the accounts of the use of these agents in this eight-year conflict:

1983. Mustard gas was used at Haj Umrah.

1984. Nerve gases again used, at Al Basra, when Iraqi troops were on the defensive, in retreat.

1985 and 1986. Thousands of Iranian soldiers reportedly killed by gas attacks at Um Rashrash, Hawizeh Marsh, and other locations.

1986 and 1987. Poison gases used against the Kurds at Panjwin and Halabah. Reports indicate that Saddam Hussein used tabun in these attacks. News reports depicted men, women, and children lying in agonized death sprawls on the streets, after planes passed over the villages spraying the toxins.

Brief History of Nuclear Weapons

History of the actual use of nuclear weapons is quite brief. This relatively recently developed WMD has only been used on the occasion of the bombing attacks, by the United States, on the Japanese cities of Hiroshima and Nagasaki in 1945, bringing about an end to the war in the Pacific during World War II. Although atomic, and later nuclear, weapons were only in the hands of a few nations for several decades, this situation has rapidly changed in recent years.

To date there are at least eight states with openly declared national nuclear weapons capabilities: the United States, the United Kingdom, France, Russia, the People's Republic of China, India, Pakistan, and North Korea. However, many more states have secretly developed, and have arguably tested, nuclear weapons, including such states as Israel, Iran, South Africa, Iraq, and a few others. Moreover, several states that emerged from the former Soviet Union, in addition to Russia, have nuclear weapons still within their arsenals, although most have agreed to turn these over to Russia for the purpose of bilateral United States–Russian disarmament, as initiated in the SALT documents and discussions of the 1980s and 1990s.

Proliferation of nuclear weapons has occurred and is no doubt still occurring. This trend makes it less likely that the history of the use of nuclear weapons has terminated with the two attacks in 1945.

TYPES OF WEAPONS OF MASS DESTRUCTION AVAILABLE TODAY

Clearly, WMDs have been used by groups of warriors and nation-states for many years. The possibility that terrorists today would use such weapons cannot be assessed, because there is no history of previous use by others involved in intense struggles.

Moreover, such weapons have not been used exclusively, or even primarily, by non-democratic states or individuals with a careless disregard for the rules of warfare. Instead, a variety of states, many of them democratic and most of whom would today deplore the use of such weapons as barbaric, have been the major forces employing these weapons. Remember that the *only* use of atomic and/or nuclear weapons was by the United States, against predominantly civilian targets (of military significance but civilian populations).

The next step is to examine the types of WMDs available to terrorists today and the relative capacity of each to create mass destruction. Although many of these weapons have been untested on human populations, estimates can be made as to their relative lethality based on laboratory tests. Such tests cannot be definitive, but information provided about these weapons in such tests offer at least some indication of the toxicity of the substances.

Biological Agents

There are four categories of living microorganisms: bacteria, viruses, rickettsiae, and fungi. **Bacteria** are *small free-living organisms;* they can be grown on solid or liquid media and produce diseases that often respond to specific treatment with antibiotics. A familiar example of a bacteria used recently in a terrorist attack is anthrax, an acute infectious disease caused by the spore-forming bacterium *Bacillus anthracis*. Although anthrax most often occurs in hoofed mammals, it can also infect humans, as the anthrax attack in the mail system of the United States in the fall of 2001 clearly proved.

Viruses are *organisms that require living cells in which to replicate*. This type of organism does not respond to antibiotics, but is sometimes responsive to viral compounds, few of which are available. Again, the most familiar example of viruses as a weapon of terror is smallpox, an infection caused by the *Variola* virus, whose use was mentioned earlier.

The latter two groups are less familiar to the general public. **Rickettsiae** are *microorganisms that have characteristics of both bacteria and viruses*. Like bacteria, rickettsiae have metabolic enzymes and cell membranes, utilize oxygen, and are susceptible to a broad spectrum of antibiotics. Like viruses, they grow only within living cells. Q-Fever, a zoonotic disease caused by the rickettsiae *Coxiella burnetii*, is a form of rickettsiae. **Fungi,** *primitive plants that do not utilize photosynthesis, are capable of anaerobic growth, and draw nutrition from decaying vegetable matter,* are a little more familiar, but not in terms of a biological weapon. A diverse group of more than 40 compounds produced by fungi *Trichothecene mycotoxins* have been generated in recent years because they can inhibit protein synthesis, impair DNA synthesis, alter cell and membrane structure and function, and inhibit mitochondrial respiration. T-2, as these are called, used as a biological warfare agent aimed at causing acute exposure via inhalation, could result in the onset of illness within hours of exposure, and death within 12 hours.

Biotoxins, *poisonous substances produced naturally by microorganisms, plants, or animals that may be produced or altered by chemical means,* will be discussed later, in the context of chemical weapons. This category would include agents like ricin, abrin, and strychnine.

As one news analyst noted,

> While the list of the most likely weapons in a bioterror attack is short, it includes agents that, if acquired and effectively disseminated, could cause a significant public health risk. The challenge would be to recognize the danger early to limit the number of casualties.[2]

A quick look at five biological agents currently available today illustrates the breadth of the threat of attack from such weapons. A more in-depth case study of one of these—anthrax—will offer further clues as to the danger that such agents pose.

Botulinum toxin *(Clostridium botulinum) is the single most poisonous substance known.* While it is usually food borne, it could be developed as an aerosol weapon. After infection with this biological agent, symptoms generally include blurred vision as well as difficulty swallowing and speaking within 24 to 36 hours. This agent, a nerve toxin, paralyzes muscles, leading to respiratory failure and death. The Aum Shinrikyo cult in Japan was accused of trying to use botulinum toxin sprayed from airplanes over Tokyo, fortunately without success, at least three times in the 1990s.

Plague *(Yersinia pestis) is an incredibly virulent, but not always lethal, biological agent.* If 110 pounds of this agent were released over a city of 5,000,000 people, about 150,000 would contract the disease, but most would survive if treated early in the infection period. Within one to six days after exposure to the plague bacteria, victims would begin to show symptoms of severe respiratory and gastrointestinal distress. Treatment with antibiotics, however, would be effective as long as it was administered within the early stages of infection.

Tularemia *is a potentially lethal infectious organism developed by the United States as a possible weapon in the 1950s and 1960s.* As a weapon, it could be sprayed in an aerosol cloud. Within three to five days of infection, the victims would suffer fever, chills, headaches, and weakness. Subsequent inflammation and hemorrhaging of the airways can be fatal, and no vaccine is currently available.

Smallpox *is an infectious agent that several nations have tried for decades to effectively weaponize,* but which was eradicated in 1980. Some strains of this disease are maintained, however, in only two nations, officially: the United States and Russia. The former Soviet Union reportedly stockpiled large amounts of this virus for use as weapons, and several other nations, such as Iraq and North Korea, may have covert stashes of smallpox today. The smallpox virus is highly contagious and would quickly spread, because even in the United States, vaccinations for this disease stopped more than 25 years ago. An aerosol release of smallpox, infecting only 50 people, could easily unleash an epidemic, killing about 30 percent of those infected with the painful, disfiguring disease.

Anthrax *is an acute infectious disease caused by the spore-forming bacterium* Bacillus anthracis. It most commonly occurs in mammals such as cattle, sheep, goats, camels, and antelopes, but can also occur in humans exposed to infected animals or tissue from infected animals. Anthrax is unusual in that its spores are hardy: they are resistant to sunlight, heat, and disinfectant, and can remain active in soil and water for years. Anthrax spores tend to clump together in humid conditions, making it somewhat difficult to spray as an aerosol. Anthrax, unlike smallpox, is not contagious—that is, it is highly unlikely that it could be transmitted from direct person-to-person contact.

Since this particular bacteria was used in 2001 as a biological agent, a closer look at anthrax as a biological weapon would be useful at this point. This case study of anthrax is not an account of the attack, but an evaluation of anthrax as a biological weapon.

CASE STUDY   Anthrax

Anthrax is linked to several devastating plagues that killed both humans and livestock. In 1500 B.C., the fifth Egyptian plague, which affected livestock, and the sixth, known as the plague of boils, were linked to anthrax. The Black Bane of the 1600s A.D. was also thought to be anthrax and killed 60,000 cattle in Europe.

Robert Koch confirmed the bacterial origin of anthrax in 1876. Not long after this discovery, anthrax began to emerge as a biological weapon. The biological weapons programs involving anthrax continued after World War II throughout the 1950s and 1960s at various military bases. In the United States, Fort Detrick in Maryland became the focal point for this program until 1969, when President Richard Nixon formally ended the United States' biological weapons program. In 1972, Nixon signed an international convention outlawing the development or stockpiling of biological weapons.

The ratification of this convention did not end the production, testing, and use of biological agents, including anthrax. From 1978–1980, Zimbabwe experienced an outbreak of human anthrax that infected more than 6,000 people and killed as many as 100. Evidence of continued development of anthrax as a biological weapon emerged in 1979 when aerosolized (weaponized) anthrax spores were accidentally released at Compound 19, a military part of Sverdlovsk in the Soviet Union. An explosion at this secret military base near an industrial complex in the Ural Mountains sent a cloud of deadly microbes over a nearby village. Reputed death tolls from this accident vary, with as few as 68 deaths attributed, and as many as 1,000 dying eventually from this contact with a weaponized form of anthrax.

The group Aum Shinrikyo released anthrax in Tokyo several times between 1990 and 1993, but without any reported deaths or infections. Anthrax, even in weaponized form, is difficult to disseminate over a city, because warm air generated by the traffic and compression of population generally forces the air up, not down, making it difficult to spray above the city with any success. In theory a cloud of anthrax spores inhaled by a city's population would create widespread severe, flu-like symptoms, killing 80 percent of those infected within one or two days after their symptoms appeared. As yet, no successful dissemination of this sort has been recorded. Nevertheless, states continue to seek to produce anthrax as a weapon. In 1995, Iraq admitted to UN inspectors that it produced 8,500 liters of concentrated anthrax as part of its biological weapons program.

In 2001, a letter containing anthrax spores was mailed to NBC offices in New York City, one week after the September 11 attacks on the United States. This was the first of a number of incidents at locations in the eastern part of the country, including letters in Florida and Washington, DC. Five deaths to date have been attributed to anthrax attacks.

Anthrax infection can occur in three forms: cutaneous (skin), inhalation, and gastrointestinal.

Cutaneous. About 95 percent of cutaneous anthrax infections occur from a cut or abrasion on the skin, such as when someone is handling wool, hides, or hair products of infected animals. It begins as a raised itchy bump that resembles an insect bite, but soon turns into a painless ulcer, about one to three centimeters in diameter, with a black center in the middle. About 20 percent of untreated cases of cutaneous anthrax result in death. One employee who contracted anthrax in the U.S. incident had the cutaneous form of anthrax.

Inhalation. Inhalation anthrax occurs when anthrax spores enter the lungs, requiring from 2 to 43 days to incubate. Initial symptoms for this form of anthrax may resemble a common cold but will lead to severe breathing problems and to shock after several days. Inhalation anthrax was thought to be fatal in about 90 percent of the cases, because its symptoms initially appear in a form that does not require a visit to a doctor. This assumption was based on incomplete data, however, from the Russian accident mentioned earlier. The data did not include information on those treated for infection who survived or were not infected. It only identified the deaths from the infection. The employee of the Florida tabloid and four of those handling the mail going through a New Jersey postal service died of inhalation anthrax in the 2001 attack.

Intestinal. Intestinal anthrax generally follows consumption of contaminated meat. It is characterized by an acute inflammation of the intestinal tract, and includes symptoms of nausea, loss of appetite, vomiting, and fever, followed by abdominal pain, vomiting blood, and severe diarrhea. Usually, between 25 and 60 percent of cases of this form of anthrax are fatal. This is the type of anthrax that the Soviet Union initially blamed for the deaths in Sverdlovsk.

Anthrax is not contagious and can be treated with antibiotics. To be effective, the treatments must be initiated early, because if not treated in a timely fashion, the disease can be fatal. A cell-free filtrate vaccine for anthrax exists, which contains no dead or live bacteria in the preparation.

Anthrax is a particularly attractive candidate for a successful bioweapon, because its spores are hardy, as noted earlier. However, manufacturing sufficient quantities of any bacteria in stable form is a technical and scientific challenge, and dissemination of anthrax remains a challenge. The use of crop duster planes, for instance, as a tool for dissemination is difficult, because the planes are designed to spray pesticides in a heavy, concentrated stream. In contrast, anthrax as a bioweapon would perform better if scattered in a fine mist over as large an area as possible. The nozzles of crop dusters are best suited to discharge relatively large particles—100 microns in diameter—not tiny one-micron specks of bacteria.

In its natural state, anthrax has a low rate of infection among people. Experts state that it takes a sophisticated lab and advanced skills to turn the natural anthrax spore into an aerosol that can cause death from lung infection. The organism *Bacillus anthracis* can be grown in a lab to produce a weapons-grade form of the bacteria. Removed from a nutrient-rich environment, the bacteria turn into spores, which naturally clump together. These spores are then purified, separated, and concentrated, then combined with fine dust particles to maintain separation and increase the time that the spores can be suspended in the air.

Used as a weapon in the 2001 attacks, the powdery mixture was apparently put into an envelope. When released into the air, such as during processing of mail at mail centers, a high concentration of spores can be drawn deep into the lungs. The spores return to their bacterial state in the lungs and a rapidly developing anthrax infection releases deadly toxins into the person's system.

In addition to the apparent use of anthrax as a weapon through the mail system in the United States after the September 11 attacks, several other countries reported mail that initially tested positive to anthrax contamination. In Pakistan, at least one of four suspected letters received at three locations in Islamabad contained anthrax; in Lithuania, one mailbag at the U.S. Embassy at the capital tested positive, revealing trace elements of anthrax. Although similarly suspicious letters received in Kenya, Brazil, Argentina, and Germany initially tested positive to anthrax, none resulted in confirmed contamination of workers, and most tested negative in subsequent tests for exposure. Nevertheless, the potency of anthrax as a weapon for disruption and expensive response was clearly demonstrated by the limited attacks occurring in the autumn of 2001. ❑

CASE STUDY   Viral Hemorrhagic Fevers

Although biological agents such as anthrax and smallpox have been used as biological weapons in the past, neither are as potentially lethal as some of the viral hemorrhagic fevers studied at the Centers for Disease Control and Prevention in the United States today. Anthrax is, as noted earlier, a bacterial infection and therefore responsive to antibiotics, reducing its lethality if treated promptly. Although smallpox is a virus, it was eliminated from the natural world in 1977, and exists, officially, only in two laboratory repositories: one in the United States and one in Russia. Moreover, while smallpox is very easy to spread through a population, most patients in modern times infected with smallpox recover, although death would probably occur in up to 30 percent of the cases.

Viral hemorrhagic fever (VHF) is a term used to describe *a syndrome that severely affects multiple organs in the body, caused by several distinct families of viruses.*

Although some of the VHF viruses can cause relatively mild illnesses, many of them cause severe, potentially fatal disease. With a few noteworthy exceptions, there is no cure or established drug treatment for VHFs.

The survival of VHFs is dependent on the animal or insect host, called the natural reservoir, and humans are not the natural reservoir for *any* of the VHFs. But humans may become infected when they come into contact with infected hosts, and in the case of some of the more lethal VHFs such as Ebola and Marburg, may transmit the disease from one human host to another. This type of secondary transmission, from infected human to infected human, can occur directly (through close contact with infected people or their body fluids) or indirectly (through contact with objects contaminated with their body fluids).

VHFs like Ebola and Marburg have terrifying symptoms. Initial signs among persons infected would include marked fever, fatigue, dizziness, muscle aches, loss of strength, and exhaustion. As the diseases progressed, however, the person would exhibit signs of bleeding under the skin, in internal organs, and/or from the mouth, eyes, or ears. Although the loss of this blood externally would appear shocking, the patient would not, in most cases, die from loss of blood. Instead, the patient's body would be assaulted with the collapse of many organs within the system, nervous system malfunction, coma, delirium, seizures—and finally death, which would in many respects be a release.

There is no known cure for Ebola or Marburg VHF. Outbreaks of Marburg and Ebola have occurred through human-to-human transmission. The potential for a crusader willing to be a "suicide patient" rather than a suicide bomber, deliberately infecting himself or herself with one of these lethal VHFs to infect people within an "enemy" nation is still remote, given the fortunate scarcity of the virus. But the possibility exists, and if the virus was obtained and replicated in a lab with deliberate intent to use it as a weapon, the results for humankind might be unthinkable.   ❏

Chemical Weapons

Although there are potentially thousands of biological agents that terrorists could use, there are, in all probability, even more poisonous chemical agents available. The agents come in a variety of forms, most often as a liquid rather than a gas, usually dispersed as droplets. Biotoxins, mentioned earlier, are one type of chemical agent, which includes agents such as ricin, abrin, and strychnine. *Chlorine and phosgene* are **choking agents,** used during World War I, and *causes pulmonary edema. Mustard gas, lewsites, and others that cause chemical burns and destroy lung tissue* are called **blistering agents. Blood agents** include other types of chemicals, such as *hydrogen cyanide* and *cyanogen chloride, that attack the respiratory system and usually result in very rapid coma followed by death. The neuromuscular system is attacked* by the **nerve gases,** like *sarin* (used in the Tokyo subway incident), *tabun* (found in Iraq after the Gulf War), *soman,* and *VX.* These agents *block the enzyme cholinesterase, which causes paralysis of the neuromuscular system, resulting in death.*

Most of the substances used to create chemical weapons have a legitimate use. Some, like eserin (a nerve gas), have been used for medicinal purposes. Others are used as cleaning agents, insecticides, herbicides, and rodenticides. This makes many of them available commercially, in some form. As the United States learned in the bombing at Oklahoma City, truckloads of fertilizer can be easily obtained and can be a very lethal weapon in the hands of a terrorist. Evidence of similar efforts by individuals and groups within the United States to secure and even to use chemical agents is a small but growing threat.

Chemical weapons are prolific in number, relatively easy to acquire and stockpile, and not too expensive. They are difficult, however, to manufacture in sufficient quantities for a large-scale attack. More likely, they would be used successfully in isolated attacks of a relatively small nature. Chemical weapons are also difficult to disperse effectively. The attack by the Aum Shinrikyo on the Tokyo subway system in Japan illustrates both the strength, in terms of the psychologically disruptive effects, and the weaknesses, in light of the relative nonlethality of the attack and the problems in dissemination, inherent in the use of chemical weapons by terrorists today.

CASE STUDY   Ricin

Ricin is a *biotoxin found in the bean of the castor plant,* Ricinis communis, and it is one of the most toxic and easily produced plant toxins. Originally cultivated in ancient Egypt as a lubricant and a laxative, castor beans are today used to produce castor oil, which is a brake and hydraulic fuel component found throughout the world. Ironically, ricin can be made from the waste left over from processing castor beans.

Because it is both highly toxic and easily produced, ricin was studied and developed by the United States during both world wars in the twentieth century. Unfortunately, these same characteristics have made ricin an attractive weapon of interest to radical individuals, groups, and governments in recent years as well.

Like anthrax, ricin may cause toxic reactions in people from three possible routes of exposure: inhalation, injection, and oral ingestion (the least toxic method). Inhaling ricin, according to one group of experts, would produce symptoms within 8 hours, and depending on the dose, death within 36 to 72 hours. There is, unfortunately, no known vaccine for ricin and no antidote to the poison to counter it.[3]

Although ricin poisoning is not contagious (it cannot be spread from person to person from casual contact), it has already been used as a weapon in recent history. In 1978, Georgi Markov, a Bulgarian writer and journalist who was living in London, died after he was attacked by a man with an umbrella—an umbrella that had been fixed to inject a poison ricin pellet under Markov's skin. Reports indicate, too, that ricin was used in the Iran-Iraq conflict in the 1980s. Quantities of ricin were reportedly found in caves in Afghanistan used by al-Qaeda prior to the 2001 attacks, and information about ricin appears in the so-called *Jihad Encyclopedia* discovered after September 11. Ricin is intensely more lethal than sarin, which was used in the Tokyo subway attack. ❑

Nuclear Weapons

Options for nuclear weapons today exceed the prohibitive cost and technological limits inherent in the creation of plutonium-based nuclear missiles. Several types of nuclear weapons may be feasible for use by terrorists in the twenty-first century, although none have yet been used in an attack.

A **small plutonium device,** *requiring at least 2.5 kilograms of plutonium, is constructed with a core made of a sphere of compacted plutonium oxide crystals in the center of a large cube of Semtex (or one of the other new, powerful explosives).* The bomb, when complete, would weigh about a ton and would require at least a van or a truck to get it to the target.

A home-produced or stolen nuclear device of moderate size, about 10–15 kilotons, detonated in a major city would destroy several square miles of territory and could cause up to 100,000 casualties. The bomb would have to be transported and strategically placed for maximum effect. The technical skills required, the facility necessary, and access to a large quantity of plutonium are impediments to the use of such a weapon by a group engaged in terrorism.

Dirty bombs do not require the theft of large amounts of the carefully guarded plutonium, nor does their construction require great technical skills or a well-equipped laboratory. These weapons can be made with *nonfissionable radioactive materials, such as cesium 137, cobalt 60, and strontium, exploded by conventional means.* Even though such a bomb would not cause the vast number of fatalities generated by a nuclear blast, they spread nuclear contaminant over water supplies, crops, and other essential parts of a system. These bombs could be used in shopping malls or train stations to disrupt as well as to destroy.

Attacks on nuclear power facilities would also be a form of nuclear terrorism possible today. This has happened many times, in many countries, but without evidence that such attacks have yet generated a major accident with catastrophic loss of lives. Nevertheless, in the wake of the attacks on September 11, nuclear facilities were recognized as vulnerable to the same type of attack—one using a large, well-fueled plane as a "bomb" flown into the facility.

The black market for weapons has had, since the demise of the Soviet Union, incidents in which small, backpack nuclear devices, and even devices as small as landmines were for sale. Although no records obviously exist of such sales, the leaders of the international community have expressed their concern about the possibility of a group engaged in terrorism, or a "rogue state" willing to operate outside of traditional legal norms, acquiring such fully manufactured devices. This possibility has been the subject of discussion at numerous UN meetings and resulted in resolutions condemning such sales and pledging not to facilitate them, but little documented success in the control of such weapons exists to date.

Terrorists and groups appear more willing to experiment with the use of biological or chemical weapons than nuclear weapons today. If terrorists want biological weapons, they can make potent agents from such substances as isopropyl alcohol (easily available at drug stores and supermarkets), from pesticides and herbicides (available at most home and farm supply stores), and from a host of other equally accessible products.

Most experts also agree that it does not take great skills in chemistry to manufacture many different chemical agents. Some are more difficult than others, of course; but a wide range is possible for someone with perhaps a few graduate courses in chemistry.

Chemical weapons are less attractive to terrorists primarily because of the difficulty in their delivery. As evidenced in the sarin gas attack in Tokyo, if the agent is not administered properly, it may afflict many but kill few. If the desire is for dramatic effect, this may not be a critical factor. But if the desire is to disable as well as frighten an enemy, to punish severely rather than merely inconvenience a target, then this problem in dissemination can be a major stumbling block. Factors such as wind direction, temperature, enclosure of space, and moisture can affect the dissemination process. Nerve gas, for example, rapidly hydrolyzes in water and therefore cannot be put, as many biological agents can, into the water system of a city.

ACCESS TO AND USE OF WEAPONS OF MASS DESTRUCTION

Chemical Agents

As weapons of terrorists chemical agents are relatively easily accessible, potentially very lethal, but are limited in usefulness to date by the difficulty in dissemination, unless the desired effect is primarily psychological rather than physical in nature. Most chemical weapons have been available since World War I, and the processes for manufacturing most usual war gases have been published in open literature. Several nations possess chemical weapons, making it possible for them to supply a group with this type of weapon. Yet only the Aum Shinrikyo cult in Japan has attempted to procure and use a chemical weapon in a large-scale terrorist attack.

The reason for this lack of use may lie simply in practical, rather than political, moral, or monetary terms. Most toxic gases are very difficult to handle, control, and deploy effectively. Even toxic industrial gases, like chlorine and hydrogen cyanide, which are easy to procure, are very volatile. These types of agents could only be used in an attack on a target population in an enclosed area, with limited exits (so that those targeted could not escape, and/or to keep the gases from escaping into the atmosphere outside). As one researcher noted, if a terrorist wanted to use a nerve agent by introducing it into the air-handling system in a building (whose inhabitants are the target population), the device must

1. be of a size and shape that is easily carried by one person;
2. be leakproof; and
3. must have an activation process that will result in the agent being dispersed in a way that will not endanger the terrorist operating the device (unless the terrorist is a crusader,

willing to die in the attack), yet strong enough to reach the population in a sufficiently high concentration to cause a high casualty rate.[4]

Nevertheless, trainees at terrorist camps in Afghanistan learned how to use chemical weapons, according to testimony in U.S. courts in July 2001. Ahmed Ressam told the court that his training for chemical attacks included testing the effect of cyanide and sulfuric acid on a dog. "We wanted to know what is the effect of the gas," Ressam told the court.[5]

Biological Agents

In the early 1990s, perception of the possibility of biological attacks was radically altered due to two dramatic events. The first was the discovery of enormous quantities of such weapons in Iraq after the Gulf War, particularly as there was reason to believe that only a portion of them had been found. Moreover, there was also a growing realization that Iraq and other countries, including but not limited to Iran, were continuing preparations for BC (biological/chemical) warfare. While suspicions had existed before the Gulf War, particularly because Iraq had used chemical weapons against both the Iranians and the Kurds resulting in many thousands of deaths, the realization of the buildup of BC had clearly been enormously underestimated.

At the Al Muthanna laboratories in Iraq, 2,850 tons of mustard gas was found to have been produced, along with 790 tons of sarin and 290 tons of tabun. Iraq was found to have 50 warheads with chemical agents in place at the beginning of the Gulf War. In terms of biological weapons, Iraq had also produced anthrax, botulinum toxin, and other biological agents since 1988, with the result that when inspectors began investigating in 1991, they found that 6,500 liters of anthrax and 10,000 liters of botulinum had been weaponized.

Libya has also engaged in intense production of biological agent capabilities. With help from biological firms from Germany, Switzerland, and several other countries, Libya constructed large underground laboratories at Tarhuna and Rabta. Specialists suggest that such facilities could be transformed in less than one day from weapons factories to peaceful pharmaceutical labs. This makes tracking the production of biological agents difficult, and given Libya's long-term relationships with many groups engaging in terrorist acts, makes the access of terrorists to such weapons potentially feasible, until the recent movement of Libya to distance itself from the creation of WMDs.

The second source of world shock on the issue of biological agents came with the breakup of the Soviet Union. Although Russia promised to destroy its BC weapons, it soon became obvious that it was failing to adhere to its promise and was instead preventing access by foreign inspectors after 1993. Records of the amounts of such weapons in existence, and even of the location of facilities manufacturing or storing them, were lost, destroyed, or hidden, with the result that few are certain of precisely how many BC weapons were produced and who currently possess them.

This type of weapon has been linked to several earlier terrorist groups and activities. It was reported in the late 1970s that the RAF in Germany was training Palestinians in the use of bacteriological warfare. A raid by police in Paris uncovered a laboratory with a culture of botulism. The RAF threatened to poison the water supplies of about 20 German cities unless their demand for special legal defense for three of their imprisoned comrades was met. Microbiologists were believed to have been enlisted in efforts by groups in Italy and Lebanon to generate biological weapons for terrorist use. In the United States, 751 persons in the small town of The Dalles, Oregon, were poisoned by salmonella planted in two restaurants by followers of Bhadwan Shree Rajneesh.

A special issue of the *Journal of the American Medical Association* published the first systematic survey of biological agents in 1997. This survey included brucellosis, the plague, tularemia, Q-fever, smallpox, viral encephalitis, viral hemorrhagic fevers, anthracis, and botulinum. The latter three were described as the greatest potential danger, given their toxicity, contagion rate, and because both were found in large quantities in Iraq, where they had already been weaponized.

Although vaccines could be used to neutralize many of the existing agents, and antibiotics could be used to both treat and prevent most, the weaponizing of these agents presents a problem. Through this process, the agent is changed in ways that could make the majority of the safeguards and remedies ineffective.

It is believed that 30 to 40 countries have the capacity to manufacture biological weapons, because many have a pharmaceutical industry to aid in this production. The greatest concentration of existing weapons is believed to be in the Middle East, including not only Iraq and Iran, but Syria, Libya, and the Sudan. The U.S. bombing of the pharmaceutical factory in the Sudan in 1998 when this laboratory was linked by intelligence information with Osama bin Laden illustrates the rising concern over the possible use of this type of agent by terrorists.

Biological agents have been called "the poor man's nuclear bomb." They are difficult to trace, cheap to manufacture, and potentially incredibly lethal. Botulinum, the most deadly toxin available—100,000 times more poisonous than the sarin gas used in the Tokyo subway attack—is theoretically capable, in a quantity as small as one gram, of killing all the inhabitants of a city the size of Stockholm, Sweden. An aerosol distribution is the ideal method of delivery for such an agent. It has been estimated that botulinum, in optimal weather conditions, could kill all living beings in a 100-square kilometer area. Fortunately, ideal weather conditions seldom last, but many would certainly die from such an attack.

Nuclear Devices

Hundreds of pages of photocopied, handwritten, and printed documents, written in a mixture of Arabic, Urdu, Persian, Mandarin, Russian, and English, were recovered from a number of al-Qaeda houses in the Afghan capital a day after its fall to the Northern Alliance forces in November 2001. These pages confirmed, among other things, that al-Qaeda cells were examining materials to make a low-grade, dirty nuclear device. The pages also indicated that their understanding of bomb-related electronic circuitry at least matched that of the Provisional IRA's experts.

According to John Large, a British nuclear consultant, while the organization would not have been able to make a large-scale missile or nuclear device from the documents found, "it was obviously prepared to consider the use of such weapons, so that if it could not manufacture such for itself then, given the opportunity, it would acquire such for use."[6] Included in the documents acquired by *The Times* relating to nuclear physics was a chart depicting a portion of the periodic table of elements, dealing solely with radioactive materials. This portion, according to Large, contained all of the elements needed if one were constructing a dirty bomb.

Access to nuclear materials is problematic, depending on which type of material is sought. The most carefully guarded, weapons-grade uranium and plutonium is perhaps the least accessible. However, numerous attempts have been made to smuggle nuclear materials out of the former Soviet Union, and there are unconfirmed rumors that nations, and perhaps even a group like al-Qaeda, may have obtained a nuclear warhead. Thus far, police and customs officials in Europe have seized only low-quality nuclear waste that, although it could not be made into a real atomic bomb, it could, in sufficient quantity, be used to build a dirty bomb that would spread nuclear contamination.

The easiest access by which a terrorist group might make a nuclear bomb would be to find a government willing to allow access to its laboratories or its arsenals, but few if any such governments are willing to take such a risk today. UN inspectors after the Gulf War found that Iraq had come within months of building an atomic bomb, but the effort apparently took about a decade and cost nearly $10 billion dollars. There is no evidence that any government today has helped terrorist groups acquire nuclear weapons at such prohibitive costs. The potential cost of being linked to the bomb if the terrorists deploy it successfully has also apparently deterred access to this type of weapons through state conduits.

But the number of potential suppliers of nuclear weapons technology continues to expand. Countries such as North Korea, once dependent on external help from other nations in crafting a nuclear weapons program, now enjoy a vigorous missile- and technology-export business with a number of Middle Eastern countries including Iran, Pakistan, and Syria. Moreover, all technologies become less expensive with the passage of time and proliferate as more begin to utilize them. Although there is no immediate threat of nuclear bombs in the hands of terrorists, the next plane flown into a symbolic target like the World Trade Center may have something more lethal aboard than aviation fuel.

Case Study   Agroterrorism

As concern mounts about the potential for terrorist attacks utilizing WMDs, one of the possibilities receiving special attention is that of agricultural biowarfare, or

agroterrorism, which involves *the deliberate introduction of a disease agent either against livestock or in the food chain for purposes of undermining stability or generating fear.* At least 13 nation-states developed, or are suspected to have developed, biological agents with antilivestock or anticrop properties. Specific, verifiable information on such programs is difficult to access, since most biowarfare programs are (or were) clandestine. The list of diseases developed in these programs by just two countries, the United States and the former USSR, is staggering, including (but definitely not limited to) anthrax, brucellosis, equine encephalitis, foot-and-mouth disease, fowl plague, glanders, African swine fever, avian influenza, contagious bovine pleuropneumonia, Newcastle disease virus, wheat blast fungus, rye blast, and tobacco mosaic.

Concern about the potential for agroterrorism led the United States in February 2003 to conduct a terrorism scenario focused on a domestic agroterror attack, **Operation Silent Prairie,** a *simulation of an attack generating an epidemic of foot-and-mouth disease (FMD).* The national livestock population has had no natural immunity to this disease since 1929, when FMD was eradicated in the United States. Given this lack of immunity, by the conclusion of the exercise, FMD hypothetically had ravaged the livestock herds from North Carolina to the San Joaquin Valley, with what would have been devastating economic consequences.

Organized by the National Strategic Gaming Center and held at the National Defense University, the simulation was designed to give senior government officials (18 members of Congress, the Surgeon General, the deputy secretary of agriculture, the deputy secretary of defense, and representatives from the FBI, FEMA, the North Carolina Department of Agriculture, the National Guard Bureau, the Joint Chiefs of Staff, and others participated), insights into the complexities of the emerging global biosecurity challenges. It certainly served to highlight the devastating potential of the bioterror threat.   ❏

CONCLUSIONS

There is growing concern among many who study terrorism that the use of WMDs may become more common in the near future. The legal, political, and financial restraints that have discouraged states from the use of these types of weapons appear less likely to be sufficient to limit the willingness of a group, if it can acquire such a weapon, from its use. Because access to such weapons is clearly growing and groups are already training in the use of the more easily accessed materials, then the likelihood of a threat by terrorists of a WMD seems credible.

Documents obtained from some of the al-Qaeda houses in Afghanistan not only described the organization's efforts to obtain nuclear capabilities, but also outlined this group's plans for chemical weapons. These plans were drawn with large-scale production in mind, with each recipe containing a step-by-step guide explaining how to produce batches that would kill thousands of people. Some of the pages contained photocopies explaining how a device or chemical agent could best be put to devastating effect.

The use of weapons by terrorists, not just al-Qaeda, is clearly not a remote possibility, but an actively sought goal today. Smallpox, which is estimated to have killed 120 million people in the twentieth century alone, offers an incredibly lethal weapon, in weaponized form or in the hands of a **suicide carrier,** *a terrorist willing to be infected with the disease in order to carry it into the target audience to spread it among this group.* If smallpox had not been eradicated, according to the World Health Organization, "the past 20 years would have witnessed some 350 million new victims—roughly the combined populations of the United States and Mexico—and an estimated 40 million deaths—a figure equal to the entire population of Spain or South Africa."[7]

The biological threat is small, in at least two respects: most biological agents are hard to produce and hard to make into weapons. The preparedness of governments to deal with even this small threat, however, was demonstrated in the fall of 2001 by the anthrax attacks in the United States and elsewhere.

In spite of the fact that ordinary airplanes were used as WMDs in the September 11 attacks, the difficulty in generating and appropriately dispersing biological, chemical, and nuclear weapons remains high. But that attack has changed, to some extent, the world's perception of modern terrorists. The suicidal zealotry, the malevolence, and the determination of the individuals who flew the airliners into buildings; their willingness to prepare for the attacks for years; and their clear desire to cause mass casualties have confirmed the possibility that such terrorists would willingly use chemical, biological, or nuclear weapons.

EVALUATION

The attack by the Aum Shinrikyo cult in Japan makes an excellent case study of the use by a modern terrorist organization of a weapon of mass destruction. Carefully study the following account, assessing

> indications that such an attack was eminent,
>
> the skill (or lack of it) in the dissemination of the toxin,
>
> the legal response to the attack, and
>
> the impact on the public (that is, the extent to which a terrorist goal of creating a mood of fear was achieved).

CASE STUDY   Aum Attack on the Tokyo Subway

On March 20, 1995, Aum Shinrikyo (Supreme Truth), a Japanese cult, placed containers of sarin gas on five trains of the Tokyo underground subway network, which came together in the Kasumigaseki station, near many government offices. This attack killed 12 people, injured 5,500, and caused serious chaos in the subway system for days afterwards.

The timing of the attack, as well as its focus on trains full of government workers, was significant. Japanese police were actually planning to raid cult leader Shoko Asahara's Tokyo compound on March 22, expecting to find the chemical agents the

group possessed. Aum had been able to infiltrate the police department with two supporters who warned Asahara of the coming raid. Aum chose to launch the subway attack
on March 20 during the police shift change to divert attention from the planned raid.

The subway attack plan had many flaws and consequently left fewer victims
than might have been expected. The sarin used was not pure, and the means of
distribution—polyethylene bags that had been punctured—was primitive and ineffective. The attack was carefully planned, but rushed into place earlier than anticipated, thus relying on improvisation rather than tested techniques.

The Tokyo attack in 1995 was not the cult's first attempt to use a chemical
weapon. Aum spent more than $30 million developing poisonous gases, even con-
structing a special facility called Satyan 7 to produce sarin gas.[8] In 1994 seven people
were killed and another 264 injured at Matsumoto, a resort west of Tokyo. The event
was thought to be an accident, although members of this cult later admitted to spraying sarin from a van. There had been other minor incidents involving toxic vapors
linked to Aum, and anonymous threats referring to coming attacks had been received
by the police. Some of these letters even named the Tokyo subway as the probable target, but the authorities took only limited action, until after the March attack.

Because the cult owned a billion-dollar computer empire in Japan, it invested
much of its profits in the building of fully equipped laboratories, where it attempted
to create or modify deadly chemical and biological toxins. Aum sent scientists in research teams worldwide in search of deadly biological agents, even exploring the
possibility of securing a culture of the Ebola virus during its outbreak in Zaire.

Evidence gathered after authorities searched the warehouses and labs indicated
that Aum had tried to develop weaponized forms of botulinum and anthrax, as well
as other toxic agents. In 1993, the cult tried twice to spray what they believed to be a
weaponized form of anthrax, in aerosol form, from the top of their compound in
Tokyo. After the 1995 attack, they also admitted to spraying botulinum on the walls
outside the American Embassy in Tokyo. No injuries or deaths were reported from
either of these attempts to use biological agents. The willingness of the group to
spend millions to acquire these lethal agents, and its eagerness to use them was balanced, apparently, by its inability to produce effective strains or to disseminate them
efficiently.

Asahara and the other key leaders in the subway attack were captured by the
Japanese government less than two months after the incident.   ❑

SUGGESTED READINGS

Butler, Richard. *The Greatest Threat: Iraq, Weapons of Mass Destruction, and the Crisis of
    Global Security*. New York: Public Affairs, 2000.
Cole, Leonard A. *The Eleventh Plague: The Politics of Biological and Chemical Warfare*. New
    York: Freeman, 1997.
Falkenrath, Richard A., Robert D. Newman, and Bradley A. Thayer. *America's Achilles' Heel:
    Nuclear, Biological, and Chemical Terrorism and Covert Attack*. Cambridge, MA: MIT
    Press, 1998.

Laqueur, Walter. *The New Terrorism: Fanaticism and the Arms of Mass Destruction.* Oxford: Oxford University Press, 1999.

Miller, Judith, Stephen Engelberg, and William Broad. *Germs: Biological Weapons and America's Secret War.* New York: Simon & Schuster, 2001.

Stern, Jessica. *The Ultimate Terrorists.* Cambridge, MA: Harvard University Press, 1999.

NOTES

1. Walter Laqueur, *The New Terrorism: Fanaticism and the Arms of Mass Destruction* (Oxford: Oxford University Press, 1999), 61.
2. "Guide to Toxic Terror," *The Charlotte Observer,* September 30, 2001, 11A.
3. "A Focus on Ricin Toxin," *Counter-Terrorism Training and Resources for Law Enforcement,* http://www.counterterrorismtraining.gov/focus/focus.html.
4. Raymond A. Zilinskas, "Aum Shinrikyo's Chemical/Biological Terrorism as a Paradigm?" *Politics and the Life Sciences* (September 1996): 238.
5. Sharon Theimer, "Special Report: Attack on America," *The Washington Post,* September 21, 2001, A27.
6. "Scientists Confirm bin Laden Weapons Tests," *The Sunday Times,* December 30, 2001, 2A.
7. David Ensor, "Biological Attack Threat Real, but Small," *CNN Washington Bureau,* September 24, 2001.
8. Mike Dasher, "AUM Shinri Kyo (Supreme Truth)," in *The Encyclopedia of Terrorism*, ed. Cindy Combs and Martin Slann (New York: Facts-on-File, 2002), 22.

PART III

Countering the Threat

9

Counterterrorism: The Use of Special Forces

Key Concepts

Munich massacre	secrecy and surprise	Delta Force
strike forces	killer course	Ranger
Sayaret Mat'kal	GSG-9	Air Force Special
Special Night Squads	Mogadishu	Operations Command
Irgun	U.S. Special Operations	SEALs
King David Hotel	Command	Operation Eagle's Claw
Entebbe raid	U.S. Army Special Forces	Operation Chavin de
Operation Nimrod	Command	Huantar

As soon as men decide that all means are permitted to fight an evil, then their good becomes indistinguishable from the evil that they set out to destroy.

Christopher Dawson

Although international laws of war and peace make it clear that terrorist acts have begun to be regarded as illegal, there does not yet exist a cohesive framework capable of guiding the actions of nations confronted with, or perpetrating, terrorism. In the absence of such a framework, the burden of regulating the acts has fallen upon individual nation-states. The review of U.S. efforts in this direction revealed some of the flaws that exist in national responses to terrorism.

Recent history abounds with examples of individual state efforts to combat the problem of international terrorism, highlighting both the dangers and the degree of success they have achieved. The success and failure of the efforts, and an assessment of the price paid for both success and failure, provide interesting insights into the strengths and limitations of nations engaged in waging single-handed war on terrorism.

Moreover, if international law truly grows or evolves from international norms, then it may be that strategy for dealing with international terrorism internationally will strongly resemble those strategies found successful among nations individually. Thus a review of the responses of nations to terrorism today may provide some clues as to the shape of international responses in the future.

NATIONS WITHOUT DEFENSES

It has been said that the **Munich massacre** *of Israeli athletes by Black September terrorists at the Olympic games in 1972* marked the turning point in the Western world's indifference toward terrorism.[1] Until that event, few of the nations most frequently the victims of terrorist attacks had made any coherent policy for combating terrorism. Although CIA analysts concluded that "terrorists continue to prefer operations in the industrialized democracies of Western Europe and North America,"[2] the very characteristics that cause nations to be included in this category also make it difficult for them to organize defenses against terrorist attacks.

In liberal democracies, dissent is part of the very fabric of the social and political milieu. This adherence to an almost absolute right to disagree sometimes creates conditions that allow radical dissent to become violent opposition before governments are able to prepare for this transformation. In West Germany, for example, before the publicized exploits of the Baader-Meinhof gang, any hint of the formation of an elite army or police unit to combat terrorism would have provoked a storm of protest inside (and outside) of the country.

Similarly, the United States, where both the army and the public bore scars from the traumas of Vietnam and Watergate, was in no condition to prepare for terrorist threats. This was partly due to the demoralizing effect of the Vietnam conflict on the army's special units and partly to the perceived need to curtail (rather than expand) domestic surveillance operations.

Nor were these nations alone in their lack of preparedness. France (in the wake of their protracted Algerian war) shared Germany's abhorrence of secret or special armies, while the British, with their problems in Northern Ireland, were perhaps too confident in their assumption that their anti-IRA network would also deal effectively with any international terrorist. Italy, at this time, was oblivious to the growing potential for terrorism within its borders, misled by a belief that most contemporary terrorism was confined to participants in the Arab-Israeli conflict. In fact, virtually every Western nation, except Israel, lacked the equipment and staff to combat the growing terrorist threat; they also lacked a realization of the impending danger.

At Munich, this complacency and inattention was effectively shattered. When a group of Black September terrorists, with logistical support from German and French sympathizers, captured the Israeli athlete's dormitory in the Olympic village in Munich in 1972, West Germany's response was firm, but it failed to prevent disaster. As the world watched transfixed in helpless terror, the Germans set up an ambush at Furstenfeldbruck Airport. Five sharpshooters succeeded in killing five of the terrorists, but not before the terrorists had killed all nine hostages.[3]

STRIKE FORCES: A FIRST LINE OF DEFENSE?

This spectacular attack and the equally spectacular failure of the government troops to secure the hostages' safety prompted several Western governments to reevaluate the quality of their counterterrorism strike forces. Since 1972, the creation of effective **strike forces,** *military or police units specially trained, equipped, and organized to combat terrorism*, has become a fairly common practice—with varying degrees of success and divergent degrees of legality. A review of the strike forces created by a few nations, their methods of operation, and their patterns of success and failure may help us understand the problems and pitfalls of the use of such forces.

Israel's Sayaret Mat'kal

Israel has been engaged in antiterrorism warfare for perhaps longer than any other nation. It has, as a result, a more extensive history in the use of strike teams. As such, it serves as an interesting case to study to determine the strengths and weaknesses of this tactic for combating terrorism.

In Israel, the Talmudic injunction, "If someone comes to kill you, rise and kill him first," has become the slogan of the **Sayaret Mat'kal.** This *specialized Israeli antiterrorist strike force* is so secretive that the Israelis rarely even mention it by name. It is this unit that was responsible for raids into Beirut to murder Palestinian leaders and for the Entebbe rescue operation in 1976.

Founded nearly a decade after Israel's establishment in 1948, the Sayaret Mat'kal was one of the country's early elite antiterrorist military formations. The application process is severe and only a tiny percentage of applicants are admitted to the training program. The Sayaret Mat'kal specializes in hostage rescue operations in Israel. However, the unit also engages in foreign activities and is understood to have been involved in the 1976 Entebbe operation. Sayaret Mat'kal frequently cooperates with other Israeli counterterrorist organizations such as Sayaret Tzanhanim, the elite paratroop unit.

This unit has both successfully thwarted terrorist attacks, and in its zeal to "strike before being struck" and to punish terrorists, has also been guilty of the murder of innocent persons. When Prime Minister Golda Meir unleashed "hit teams" the day after the Munich massacre, with orders to roam the world seeking out and summarily executing those responsible for the attack, the results were neither entirely legal nor wholly desirable.

One of these "hit teams" assassinated the wrong man. At Lillehammer, Norway, in 1973, an innocent Morrocan waiter was gunned down by a hit team in front of his pregnant Norwegian wife. The team had mistaken the waiter for the architect of the Munich massacre, Ali Hassan Salameh. International indignation forced Israel to temporarily restrain the hit squads.

This was, however, only a brief setback in Israel's use of strike forces in its war on terrorism. In January 1979, one of Israel's hit teams succeeded in killing Salameh with a radio-controlled car bomb in Beirut. This bomb also killed his four bodyguards and five innocent people who happened to be passing by at the time. The Israeli hit team may also have been responsible for the assassination in Tunis on April 16, 1988, of Khalil al-Wazir, the PLO's mastermind of terrorist strategy against Israel.

One of the ironies of Israel's response to this incident is that, as an excusatory footnote to their (unofficial) admission of regret at the loss of innocent lives, the

Israelis suggested that these people were just "in the wrong place at the wrong time."[4] This has unfortunate echoes of the "justification" offered by terrorists of harm to innocent people caused by their bombs.

The innocent persons killed, like Susan Wareham, a British woman working as a secretary for a construction company in Beirut, committed only the mistake (crime?) of being too near Salameh's car when it exploded. Although counterterrorist attacks like this may not deliberately take innocent life, they are undoubtedly culpable of a wanton disregard for the safety of innocent persons. Callous uncaring or deliberate disregard for the safety of innocent persons—the difference may be in the degree of disregard for the sanctity of human life. The net result for the innocent bystander is unhappily the same.

Not all of Israel's counterattacks on terrorism have been so counterproductive. Indeed, the Sayaret Mat'kal is one of the best-trained and equipped special forces units in operation today, with an impressive record of successful missions as well.

This unit is not part of the regular army and reports only to the chief of intelligence. Its members, however, do wear uniforms. This unit does not rely on trained volunteers but instead draws on raw recruits from the Kelet (the recruit depot). Usually an officer of the Sayaret Mat'kal will go to the Kelet to select about 15–20 recruits to form a team.

This team does much of its training in enemy territory, where the bullets are as real as the enemy. Recruits who survive this basic training become permanent members of a squad. Such squads are trained in the use of the .22 Beretta pistol as well as the Uzi, the Israeli-invented machine pistol, and the Kalashnikov, the Russian assault rifle.

The willingness of such teams to commit acts of terrorism in order to counter terrorism may perhaps lie in the very roots of Israel's history. The joint British-Jewish **Special Night Squads,** of which Moshe Dayan was a member, operated during the 1930s. These squads *were trained by their leader,* Orde Wingate, *to kill rather than wait to be killed.*

The **Irgun,** *a successor to these squads in the increasing spiral of violence in the region of Palestine*, boasted Menachem Begin as a member. This organization was responsible for the *bombing at the* **King David Hotel** *on July 22, 1946, which took 91 lives—British, Jewish, and Arab.* The terrorists of the Irgun who perpetrated this violence still meet annually to observe the anniversary of this bombing—at the King David Hotel. Thurston Clarke's account, *By Blood and Fire: The Attack on the King David Hotel*, is detailed and well-documented in a publication by G. P. Putnam's Sons (1981), for those interested in a further review of this incident.

Given this concept that it is better to kill than to wait to be killed, which seems to have pervaded Israel's brief and bloody history, it is perhaps easier to understand both the brilliant successes that reflect the intense training and dedication and the disasters that have occasionally resulted because of the ruthless determination of these special strike force teams.

The Sayaret Mat'kal conducted a raid inside Lebanon in December 1968 that was described as an attempt to force the Lebanese to prevent Palestinian terrorists from mounting their attacks from Lebanon. Earlier that year, the Palestinians had carried out a successful hijacking, taking over an El Al airliner en route from Rome to

Tel Aviv. They had also attacked another El Al plane at Athens airport in Greece, damaging it with automatic fire and grenades. Israeli intelligence reports showed that both terrorist incidents originated in Beirut.

So a commando raid, carried out by the Sayaret Mat'kal, was launched against Beirut International Airport. Thirteen Arab aircraft, including nine jetliners, were destroyed. There were no casualties, because all of the airplanes were cleared of passengers and crew first.

Although the raid was a tactical success, its long-term effects were less rewarding. President De Gaulle condemned the raid as a violation of the sovereignty of a nation-state and used it as a reason for cutting off all arms shipments to Israel. This cutoff came at a time when the Israeli Defense Forces were relying heavily on French equipment. Moreover, the other major supplier of Israeli arms, the United States, expressed its displeasure over the raid but stopped short of cutting off arms shipments.

Furthermore, the Palestinians acquired both publicity and a certain amount of public sympathy for their cause, two of the primary goals of terrorists, with respect to the media. Finally, the airline company that owned and operated the planes, Middle East Airlines, was able to purchase a whole new fleet of jetliners—with the insurance money from the destroyed planes!

Other assault operations were equally "successful" but had perhaps less negative impacts. It was the Sayaret Mat'kal that in 1972 successfully ended the hijacking of a Sabena Boeing 707 jetliner, Flight 517 from Brussels to Tel Aviv. When four members of the Black September Palestinian group hijacked the plane and forced it to land at Lod airport, they announced that they intended to blow up the plane, with its 90 passengers and 10 crew members, unless the Israeli government met their demands for the release of over 300 Arab prisoners.

The Sayaret Mat'kal assault force succeeded in storming the plane and freeing the passengers and crew members. Although one passenger and two of the hijackers were killed, this minimal loss of life became the standard for similar feats, such as that carried out by Germany's GSG-9 at Mogadishu.

When the Palestinians struck again, it was at the Olympic Games in Munich, only months after the Lod Airport rescue. Israeli athletes were the target, and the Sayaret Mat'kal was excluded from the attempts to free those hostages.

This unit also was responsible for the successful **Entebbe raid** in *June 1976 when an Air France Airbus, Flight 139 en route from Tel Aviv to Paris was hijacked after a stop at Athens airport and Israel responded by organizing a brilliant and successful military rescue operation.* The plane, which landed at Entebbe airport in Uganda, carried 248 passengers and crew members. All but 106 of these hostages were released by the terrorists before the Israeli raid. Only the Israeli citizens and Jews of other nationalities were kept hostage, to increase pressure on Israel to agree to the release of 53 "freedom fighters" imprisoned in Israeli prisons.

The military incursion mounted by Israel succeeded in freeing all of the hostages held at the airport, with the exception of three who either misunderstood or did not hear orders by the commandos to lie down as they opened fire on the terrorists. All seven of the terrorists (two of whom were German and five of whom were Palestinian members of the PFLP) were killed, along with a number of Ugandan soldiers, who tried to prevent the Israeli commandos from escaping with the hostages.[5]

International opinion, for the most part, supported Israel, in spite of the fact that Israel militarily invaded Uganda. Part of this approbation derives, no doubt, from a common love for a "winner." But part is due to the perceived legal right of a nation to intervene for "humanitarian" purposes in another country. Although this right of humanitarian intervention is limited, it seemed to most of the community of nations to be acceptable in this case.

Thus, Israel had the first and arguably the most highly trained of the strike forces. Their greatest liability may lie in the fervor with which they pursue their enemies. This zeal has caused them to cross not only national boundaries in their quest for vengeance, but also international law.

The British Special Air Services

On May 5, 1980, a clear crisp Monday morning, Britain's 22nd SAS, the Special Air Service Regiment, supported by special police units, carried out **Operation Nimrod,** *an assault on the Iranian Embassy in the heart of downtown London.* As thousands of people on the streets of London watched, black-clad SAS members swung down from ropes and burst into the building through windows. Wearing gas masks, the assault force moved from room to room throwing stun grenades mixed with CS gas. As they moved through the building, they identified the terrorists, shot them with their Heckler & Koch MP5s or Browning automatic pistols, and bundled the hostages out of the burning building.

This was not the only successful counterterrorist attack carried out by Britain's SAS, but it was unique in at least one sense. Most citizens do not have the opportunity to see their special strike forces in operation on their home soil. Most operations of such forces take place on foreign soil, far from home and the attention of citizens.

Even in Operation Nimrod, however, Britain worked very hard to preserve the speed and secrecy that have become the hallmark of SAS operations. The assault team wore hoods, which served to hide their identities as well as to frighten the terrorists. When the incident was over, the unit handed authority back to the police and quietly made its way to the St. John's Wood barracks for a small celebration before returning to their permanent station at Bradbury Lines in Hereford.

Secrecy and surprise have been *the watchwords of this regiment* ever since it was formed over 40 years ago. Lieutenant David Stirling, of the Scots Guard, is credited with creating this special unit. Under his plan, the SAS was designed to operate in units of five (later reduced to four) men, which continues to be the standard SAS stick.

The units have tended to be made up of a high percentage of Scottish Roman Catholics, perhaps because its founder Stirling was himself a Scots Catholic, and perhaps because the Catholics of Scotland have had a history for generations of guerrilla warfare and traditions of secrecy. All of its members are volunteers, mostly from the Parachute Regiment. It is not a "young" regiment; the average age is about 27.

Each recruit is required to give up his rank and pay (most have already reached the rank of corporal or sergeant before attempting to join) and go back to the rank of trooper. Training in the Welsh countryside is rigorous, literally a killer. Three men died on Brecon Beacons during solo treks in 1979 and 1980, in terrible weather through the Welsh mountains.

Recruits are trained in combat survival, survival in Arctic conditions, and swimming fully clothed. They also receive special parachute training, including night jumps from extraordinary heights. Emphasis is placed on weapons training, using the SAS weapons, the aforementioned Heckler & Koch submachine gun, the Browning .45 automatic pistol, the pump action shotgun, and the Sterling submachine gun fitted with a silencer. In addition, they are given training in foreign weapons, so that they can both use captured weapons and be familiar with weapons that their enemies may use on them.

Out of every 100 men who apply, only about 19 will meet the physical and mental requirements. The initial tests include a series of treks across the Welsh hills, carrying weighted packs. *The final trek covers 37 miles while carrying a 55-pound pack, over some of the toughest country in the Brecon Beacons. It must be covered in 20 hours, and it is literally a* **killer course.** As noted earlier, men have died trying to complete it.

Once they have passed these initial courses, they continue to receive specialized training in such subjects as explosives, battlefield medicine, and the operation of communication equipment. They train in the use of various personal weapons, knives and crossbows for "silent" killing, and submachine guns fitted with silencers. They learn about desert and jungle warfare, and wilderness survival.

After this, they continue to specialize. Their specialties may be in such fields as medicine, languages, skiing, mountaineering, or underwater warfare. Individual skill development is encouraged at all times.

The SAS finds itself operating more often than most other national strike forces, with the possible exception of the Sayaret Mat'kal. This is due to the decades of violence in Northern Ireland. Although the SAS rarely figures in press reports on antiterrorist activities in that region, many operations have been carried out by this unit in cooperation with the British occupying forces. The SAS has also seen overseas service in Aden, Oman, and Borneo. Indeed, much of its training for the guerrilla warfare that it has faced in Northern Ireland finds its origins in the SAS experience in Aden in the mid-1960s.

In Northern Ireland, the SAS served as a backup for the regular army units and the Royal Ulster Constabulary. It was a largely thankless and often a very dangerous job. As members have somewhat cynically noted, if the "Sassmen" (as the Irish have called them) were killed or injured in an ambush, little public mention was made of the incident. But if the SAS was responsible, even indirectly, for the injury or death of any civilians, then public indignation was quite vocal.

Britain, unlike Israel, has indeed been willing to criticize its own strike forces when their actions have resulted in needless injury or loss of life. One judge, in whose court two Sassmen were on trial for responsibility in the death of a civilian in a stakeout of an arms cache, stated that although terrorists might consider themselves outside the rule of law, the army could not.

Forty years of experience as a special forces regiment has made the SAS into one of the best counterterrorist strike forces in the world today. Many nations' own strike forces benefit from training and assistance offered by this unit. Relations between the SAS and Germany's GSG–9 are quite cordial and have resulted in considerable mutual training and assistance efforts.

Relations between the SAS and Israel's Sayaret Mat'kal, however, are far less amiable. Both units can remember a time when the British, under the Palestine Mandate, formed Q Squads to hunt down Jewish terrorists, particularly those of the infamous Stern Gang. In one particularly nasty incident, Roy Farran, responsible for the formation of the Q Squads on SAS principles, was acquitted in a court martial of the murder of a suspected member of the Stern Gang. Israeli terrorists, not satisfied with the verdict, sent a book bomb to Farran's home in England. Roy's brother, Rex, opened the package and was killed as the bomb exploded in his face. The memory of such tragedies and the vindictiveness that caused them, has historically made the relations between these two special forces units strained, although relations improved in the late 1990s.

Moreover, the Sassmen are frequently called upon by their government to protect the leaders of various Arab states. Because many of these states and their leaders were regarded by some in Israel as natural enemies, the SAS and the Sayaret Mat'kal often found themselves on opposite sides of these security situations.

Germany's GSG-9

Grenzschutzgruppe 9 (called **GSG-9**) makes no claim to being a "killer troop" or "hit squad." This group, *formed when the Bavarian State police were unable to deal adequately with the Munich situation in September 1972,* has made a point of being less dependent upon weapons than upon the talents, discipline, and training of its men.

The Federal Border Guard became the parent unit for this special unit, which works out well since it is the only force in Germany directly under the control of the central government. GSG-9 became the ninth unit of the Border Guard, making its headquarters at St. Augustin just outside of Bonn. It was formed very much along the same lines as the SAS, operating with five-man sticks.

Within GSG-9 there is a headquarters unit, a communications and documentation unit, and three fighting units. Its three technical units deal with weapons, research, equipment, backup supply, and maintenance services. Each of its three strike forces has 30 men, comprising a Command Section and five Special Tactical Sections (composed of four men and an officer)—the five-man stick.[6]

This group differs from the Sayaret Mat'kal and the SAS in that it is a civilian police force. Although much of the training given to its members is similar to that of the SAS, it is unique in the training its members receive in knowledge of the law, particularly the law applying to counterterrorism operations. Members of this special force are more conscious of the law, and of their need to stay as far as possible within its bounds, than are other similar strike forces.

This does not mean that GSG-9 does not train its personnel in active counter-terrorism techniques. In fact, Germany's elite force has one of the most sophisticated arsenals in the world. Because the deplorable shooting at Furstenfeldbruck Airport demonstrated the need for marksmanship training, every man of GSG-9 is taught to be an expert marksman, using weapons such as the Mausser 66 sniper's rifle, equipped with infrared sights and light intensifiers for night shooting. Like the SAS, they favor the Heckler & Koch MP5s for their routine work, but they are also armed with .357 Magnum revolvers.

Because they are required to reach any part of Germany within two hours ready for action, units are supplied with Mercedes-Benz autos of special design, and BO 105 type helicopters. They are trained to descend via special ropes from hovering copters.

But these units are trained in more than just combat. They spend a great deal of time studying the origins and tactics of known terrorists, to determine how best to defeat them. Every member of a team learns such useful tricks as how to pick locks and how to handle airport equipment, to facilitate efforts to mount successful attacks against terrorists who have hijacked an airplane.

GSG-9 practices assaults on hijacked airliners, training on mock-ups of aircraft and sometimes on aircraft on loan from Lufthansa. Such training placed them in good stead in **Mogadishu** in 1977. In October of that year, *Zohair Akache's terrorist team hijacked a Lufthansa Boeing 737 with 82 passengers, in support of the Baader-Meinhof gang.* After touring the Middle East in search of an airport willing to let them land, they finally landed at Mogadishu in Somalia.

Unlike the situation in Uganda faced by the Israelis, the Germans found Somalia more than willing to cooperate with them in their efforts to end the hostage situation. Twenty-eight handpicked men stormed the airliner, rescuing all hostages without harm. It was, if not a perfect raid of its kind (the original assault ladders were too short), a very good example of careful planning and execution. No laws were broken, no unnecessary injuries to innocent persons occurred, and both hostages and plane were recovered.

TOO MANY U.S. OPTIONS?

American counterterrorist forces are based in the United States, far from the Middle East where the current war on terrorism is focused. The Joint Special Operations Agency, headed by a two-star general, is charged with preparing guidelines and plans to guide counterterrorist forces during their formation, training, and operations. But this agency has no command authority over the forces.

The **U.S. Special Operations Command** (USSOCOM) *was established by the Department of Defense, under congressional orders, on June 1, 1987, as a single command for all of the special operations units.* This command is located at MacDill Air Force Base, Florida, and commands the following units: the Special Operations

Command (SOCOM) unit based at Fort Bragg, North Carolina; the Naval Warfare Special Operations Command, and the Joint Special Operations Command. The Air Force Special Operations Command is located at Hurlbert Field, Florida. At present, the U.S. Army maintains the highest number of special operations units, with three distinct parts. The U.S. Air Force and the Navy each have one unit, and the U.S. Marines also have one unit, arguably the largest special operations unit, dedicated to amphibious beachfront assaults. The U.S. Navy's SEAL teams are under the command of the Naval Special Warfare Group, headquartered in San Diego, California.

A brief look at some of these units will help make understanding the whole collection a little easier. It may also make clear the problems faced in successful use of such forces.

Special Forces, U.S. Army

The Joint Special Operations Command (JSOC) and the U.S. Army Special Operations Command (USASOC) are both headquartered at Fort Bragg, North Carolina, under SOCOM. JSOC is a multiservice and interdepartmental command, with antiterrorism its primary job. It includes a command staff that overseas the training and operations of Army's Delta Force, the Navy's SEAL Team Six, and in times of national emergency, the FBI's Hostage Rescue Team.

USASOC has more that 25,000 personnel and includes the **U.S. Army Special Forces Command** (SFC), the 75th Ranger Regiment, the 180th Special Operations Aviation Regiment (SOAR), the JFK Special Warfare Center and School, the U.S. Army Civil Affairs and Psychological Operations Command, the U.S. Army Special Operations Support Command, and various chemical reconnaissance units. Each of these "communities" has special roles and missions. For example, SOAR, often referred to as the "Nightstalkers," is the most secret and technologically advanced unit in USASOC, while the SFC is home of the more widely known Green Berets and is regarded as the "brains" portion of the USASOC; the Rangers are referred to as the "muscle" of the SOCOM.

SFC has the highest operations tempo of any community within SOCOM, because the average SF soldier generally spends more than half of every year in the field. These are the *"trained professionals," who with high levels of technical, cultural, and combat skills, trained to work together to solve problems.* In this sense, they are more like a Peace Corps team with guns than a counterterror unit. Yet they continue to be used in areas where terrorism is a serious threat, as in Iraq and Afghanistan during the early part of the war on terrorism. Thus, this community deserves a quick look.

Although a special forces unit has three types of teams, (A, B, and C), the latter two teams are generally not deployable, since they consist of staff and support personnel. Usually, an A-Team consists of 12 men, including a captain, a warrant officer, and ten men who all are at least sergeants. All candidates for such a team must pass a very rigorous training course, much like the SAS. This training includes a "selection" session, with intense physical and mental training, and a Qualification Class (or Q-School). The 25-week process creates candidates who are experts in a variety of tasks, including but not limited to land navigation, basic weapons and demolition, water navigation, intelligence, and reconnaissance. Upon completing Q-School successfully, the candidate must then continue training in his chosen area of specialty, which can take from 6 to 56 weeks to complete.

1st Special Forces Operational Detachment—Delta (Delta Force), U.S. Army

Delta Force *was commissioned under the command of Colonel Charles Beckwith on November 19, 1977, to be primarily a hostage-rescue and counterterrorism force.* Most of its people are drawn from the Ranger units or the Special Forces units by a desire to serve in this very secret unit. Like the SAS, Delta Force is built on the premise of a critical need for secrecy and its training is in many ways similar to that of the SAS.

Very little public information is available about this unit, except in very general terms. It is designed to rapidly resolve hostage or hijacking incidents involving U.S. citizens abroad or on planes traveling beyond U.S. territory. Consequently, its members have a wide range of skills, from rappelling (as the SAS did in London) to parachuting (into hostile territory) to rapid repair of a wide range of vehicles. Most of the training is altered regularly to be certain the men are able to respond to current world situations.

Ranger, U.S. Army

Drawn usually from the Airborne Infantry units, candidates for **Ranger** units must be extremely physically fit initially, since training involves intense physical challenges. The first stage involves successful completion of the Ranger Indoctrination Program (RIP), a three-week course of physical and mental training, including building strengths in swimming, land navigation, and endurance as well as classroom instruction.

The next nine weeks, if one successfully completes RIP, has four phases, each of which presents a different type of challenge. The first phase is another week of RIP, designed to weed out those not completely motivated or physically able to continue. The second phase training takes place in the swamps and forests near Eglin Air Force base in Florida, where the candidates stay "continuously wet, continuously moving, continuously hungry."[7]

During the third phase of Ranger training, candidates operate in a mountainous terrain near Dahlonega, Georgia, again with little sleep or food, learning to rappel down cliffs and to navigate through difficult valleys. Finally, the training groups are sent to the desert near Dugway, Utah, to learn how to navigate without many discernable landmarks and to conduct patrols and ambushes without cover or concealment. The objective for such a multifaceted form of training is to create *a highly mobile infantry unit able to deploy quickly anywhere in the world and to lead through any terrain ground forces that will be deployed to follow.*

Air Force Special Operations Command

The Air Force Special Operations Command (AFSOC) is based at Eglin Air Force Base in Florida. Although the **Air Force Special Operations Command** units cover four different types of mission areas, only one, the Special Operations Forces Mobility, is usually associated with counterterrorism. *This unit consists of numerous fixed- and rotary-winged aircraft, with the pilots and support crews used to insert and recover soldiers of other special ops units of every service branch.* The AFSOC currently has units located strategically throughout the world which are ready to deploy with little advance warning to facilitate counterterrorism efforts by the other branches.

Naval Special Warfare Command

Although it has units stationed around the world, the NAVSPECWARCOM has its home base in Coronado, California. A part of the Naval Special Warfare Groups, the **SEALs** (Sea, Air and Land) *are made up of highly trained and intensely motivated seamen, who have successfully completed 25 weeks of difficult training.* If the volunteer candidates make it through the first five weeks of Basic Underwater Demolition training (the "toughening up" phase), they must then spend a week pushed to the limits of their physical endurance (called "hell week" by the men). Those who successfully complete this will then spend the next 19 weeks learning to navigate great distances underwater, become proficient at underwater demolition, reconnaissance and navigation, and a variety of other skills essential for combat diving, including how to enter and exit a wide range of vehicles to carry out operations at sea.

These seamen also receive jungle, desert, and arctic training, as well as training at Fort Benning and the U.S. Army Parachute School. The final five weeks of their training is in simulations in which they are required to use their new skills to resolve real-world situations they might encounter.

Clearly, the United States has a wide range of military units that could be utilized in counterterrorism efforts. The problems with U.S. counterterrorism forces are equally obvious, particularly those brought on by the lack of cohesive command illustrated by *the abortive attempt to send a strike team into Iran to free Americans held hostage in the U.S. Embassy in Tehran.* **Operation Eagle's Claw,** as this mission was called, was characterized by a confusion of command, insufficient training, and critical equipment failure.

Cloaked in so much secrecy that even some of the military officers involved were not told the aim of the mission for which they were preparing, this operation became a model for what can go wrong in a strike force maneuver. In addition to too much secrecy, there were too many "chiefs" and not enough cooperation between military units. An army officer, Major General James Vaught, was in command overall; Colonel James Kyle of the Air Force had responsibility for fixed-wing aircraft, while Colonel Charles Pitman of the Marines also had command responsibility and Colonel Beckwith controlled the Delta Force unit.

The Delta Force squad lacked sufficient training and experience for such an operation. It had been created by Colonel Beckwith only two years earlier in 1987, and its training program was incomplete and not designed for the type of situation that evolved. Delta Force was underfunded and ill-equipped to handle the hostage raid, having trained primarily in guerrilla warfare and low-intensity conflict.

Today, the United States has taken steps, outlined above, to create a command unit in which to vest coordination for this specialized training and command. However, within the armed services there remain strong rivalries, making it difficult for one branch to create and receive support needed for each of these separate specialized units. In the wake of Operation Eagle's Claw's disaster a call was made for a new special counterterrorism unit, with personnel drawn from all of the armed services, but there has been little success in creating such a unit. Interservice rivalries make its creation very unlikely in the near future.

According to government reports, the Delta Force unit has been deployed several times, other than the highly publicized Operation Eagle's Claw fiasco and the *Achille Lauro* incident. It was, for instance, sent to Venezuela to advise the armed forces there on the ways to retake a hijacked aircraft. It was sent on a similar mission to Oman, to prepare to retake a hijacked plane in nearby Kuwait. At the time of the TWA hijacking, Delta Force was deployed to the Mediterranean. But in each of these cases, its activities stopped short of assault; it simply made preparations for, or advised in preparations for, the assault.

Some have argued this has had a detrimental effect on the morale of the individuals in Delta Force. To always be preparing for but never performing counterterrorist activities is infinitely frustrating, as the men in GSG-9 and SAS could attest. But the United States has been reluctant to field a strike force against the terrorists, until a war on terrorism was declared in 2001. The role that Delta Force plays in this war will remain secret for the foreseeable future, and hence its effectiveness today is impossible to gauge.

Delta Force remains one of the best that the United States has to offer in terms of a strike force. Since the Iranian fiasco, it has proved itself capable of successful missions. The "skyjacking" of the *Achille Lauro* hijackers was an outstandingly successful operation, whose questionable legality has been overshadowed by its brilliant execution, giving a much-needed boost to Delta Force's morale.

Because the United States did not have many indigenous groups engaging in domestic terrorism until the 1990s, unlike Germany and Great Britain who were challenged by events in the 1970s to create units to deal with terrorism domestically, it was able to focus its attentions on training its special forces to operate overseas. Emphasis was placed less on secrecy of identity than on rapid-response capabilities and combat training. If coordination of command problems can be surmounted, these forces may develop into units as efficient and respected as the SAS and GSG-9.

New Units—and New Technologies

In the wake of the Operation Eagle's Claw debacle, the Pentagon began to establish the closest thing this nation has ever had to a secret army. Small, specially trained units were developed that were designed to operate much more covertly than some of the older military units, such as the Navy SEALs. In addition to being given rather exotic code names, such as Yellow Fruit and Seaspray, these units were armed with newer, more sophisticated types of equipment. These included such items as the small, high-tech helicopters with which Task Force 160, operating out of Fort Campbell, train.

These new units were also given more sophisticated communications gear. This gear includes, for example, the one-man satellite-communications radios and dishes.

More important than these technological "toys," however, was the creation of the Intelligence Support Activity (ISA), a far-ranging intelligence organization that gave the Army, for the first time, the ability to engage in full-fledged espionage, fielding its own agents. Through this organization the strike forces were able to gather the information they needed to plan their counterterrorist activities. They were no longer dependent upon the CIA or other intelligence services for vital data, which was too often not available or kept classified at a critical juncture in the planning process. Indeed, their intelligence and reconnaissance efforts in the early stages of the war on terrorism in 2001 facilitated U.S. military response options at this critical juncture.

Even with these innovations, however, these units have had difficulty in rising above the bureaucratic infighting and bungling that has for so long plagued U.S. strike forces. Although the units still exist, their morale, and even their preparedness, is too often in disarray. Seaspray, Yellow Fruit, and the ISA became involved in clandestine operations in Central America, which seriously impaired their credibility with Congress and within the military and intelligence units of the United States. The use (or misuse) of counterterrorism forces in this area has jeopardized America's efforts to develop a credible and respected strike force, respected by and capable of working with units such as the SAS and GSG-9. The struggle in Afghanistan has offered U.S. special forces units and the SAS opportunities for joint operations that, when they are more clearly evaluated after the war, may improve the international perspective of these forces.

A quick look at three different efforts by governments to use special forces to resolve situations involving terrorism may help to illustrate both the strengths and the weaknesses discussed thus far in using special forces to resolve terrorism.

CASE STUDY   Operation Chavin de Huantar

On December 17, 1996, rebels from the Tupac Amaru seized the Japanese Embassy residence in Lima, Peru, during a festive cocktail reception. Demanding the release of 400 of their comrades who were in Peru's prison at the time, the 14 Tupac Amaru guerrillas gradually released hundreds of the hostages, retaining only 72 for the entire seige. Alberto Fujimori, Peru's president, saw little chance for resolving the situation peacefully, because he was determined not to release the prisoners. But he gave the negotiators an opportunity to try. Attempting to alleviate the tension, he arranged the safe passage to Cuba for the rebels if they wished (which they did not choose to accept, as most wanted to remain in Peru). He also appointed Archbishop Luis Cipriani to be the special negotiator.

The 72 hostages who were held for the whole 126-day siege included senior Peruvian officials, Fujimori's brother Pedro, foreign diplomats, and the Japanese ambassador. Britain, Germany, Israel, and the United States all offered to help in the rescue attempt, but were all officially turned down. Fujimori, however, was under intense pressure to resolve the situation as quickly and peacefully as possible.

But he resisted all calls for a quick solution, choosing instead to allow time for his military and intelligence units to create and implement **Operation Chavin de Huantar** (named in honor of a pre-Incan archaeological site that was honeycombed with underground passages), *the rescue mission, using 140 Peruvian special forces troops and professional miners.* During the seemingly endless weeks of the standoff, while negotiations continued, the professional miners were brought into the area near the residence to build large, ventilated and lighted tunnels through which the troops could reach the inside of the compound.

The outstanding success of the operation (with only one of the 72 hostages being killed) can be attributed to split-second timing, well-planned diversions, and superb intelligence. During the months of the incident, listening devices were smuggled into the residence. Some were hidden in a guitar and thermos bottle that the Red Cross workers were given to deliver; others were placed in buttons on clothing brought to the hostages as changes of clothes were needed. During the final four days, intelligence agents posed as doctors and were allowed to enter the compound to check on the health of the hostages, implanting while they were there matchstick-sized two-way microphones that helped intelligence officers on the outside to communicate with the military and police commanders being held among the hostages within.

With this intelligence access, those planning the operation were able to monitor the movements of the guerrillas and hostages each day, noting patterns of behavior. This information made a carefully timed assault possible, because the intelligence officers were able to learn that the Tupac Amaru guards played a game of soccer at about 3 p.m. in the ground-floor living room each day. Prior to this game, the 14 guards stacked their rifles in a corner of the room.

Because the building plans were readily available to government forces, the special forces team had plenty of time to train on mock-ups of the building. Construction of the tunnels, if detected by the hostage takers, could have triggered a violent battle and possibly a massacre of the hostages. To prevent this, Peru's leaders played blaring martial music day and night outside the embassy compound to mask the noise. This diversion also served to deny rest to the hostage takers, demoralizing or at least weakening their resistance and stamina. Moreover, the tunnels were built to offer as many as six different accesses to the compound, which would increase the rebels' confusion when the assault began, thus providing another strategic advantage to the rescue teams.

At 3:10 p.m., the listening devices indicated that the afternoon soccer game had begun, with at least half of the guards participating. By 3:17 p.m., the hostages, who were being held upstairs during the game as usual, were alerted by a hidden receiver held by a military officer who was among the hostages. They moved a desk to block the second-floor entrance and took cover. Three minutes later, nine pounds of explosives were detonated in the tunnel directly under the reception room, where the soccer game was in progress. This explosion killed four of the eight guards and opened a hole through which troops began to pour.

The patience exercised by the Peruvian government in talking with the terrorists through extensive negotiations, using the time to gather intelligence, to build tunnels, and practice the assault, was amply rewarded when the hostages were successfully rescued with the loss of only one hostage's life. Peru presented to the international community an example of the value of careful intelligence and planning in such hostage-rescue situations. The rescue efforts broke no laws, it wasted no civilian or innocent lives (except for the one, who was shot by a guard as the attack began), and the rescue team was given plenty of time to plan a successful final act. Patience and careful planning, based on timely intelligence information, were keys to the success of Operation Chavin de Huantar.[8]   ❑

CASE STUDY   **Mogadishu**

Germany's newly created GSG-9, with only about 180 total personnel who had undergone a few years of counterterrorism-specific training, was nevertheless one of the best units of its kind in the world in 1977. GSG-9 was confronted early in its career with a challenging hostage-rescue operation involving an airline hijacking, which tested the group's ability to operate successfully within the law, without loss of life.

In September and October 1997, shortly after the unit was formed, the RAF took German businessman Hans-Martin Schleyer hostage. The RAF immediately demanded the release of 11 of their comrades-in-arms who were being held in prison in [West] Germany. In spite of attempts by the German government to find a nation willing to take the terrorists, a whole month passed without resolution of the situation. At last, on October 13, French authorities reported that a Lufthansa had been hijacked en route from the Balearic Islands to Germany. The Boeing 737 jet, with 85 passengers and 5 crew members, had been hijacked by an individual calling himself "Captain Mahmoud" (later identified as known terrorist Zohair Youssef Akache) and forced to change course toward Rome.

Landing in Rome, the plane refueled after the hijackers threatened to blow up the plane with all aboard. It flew to Cyprus, where Mahmoud demanded another refueling—then a new problem arose. Word about the hijacking had spread, and many governments publicly resolved not to allow Flight LH 181 to land on their territory. Indeed, in Beirut, the runways were physically blocked with equipment to prevent an unauthorized landing. The pilot eventually landed in Dubai, despite government denial of landing privileges.

At Dubai, the crew was able to communicate with ground officials, telling them there were in fact four terrorists aboard. The long ordeal began to have an effect on terrorists as well as hostages, to the extent that later that same day Mahmoud killed the pilot. He also postponed his original deadline (for the release of the 11 held in prison in Germany) from 4 p.m. to 2:45 a.m. the next day, as he accepted a promise from the [West] German minister of state (who was acting as chief negotiator).

Having changed the deadline, Mahmoud ordered the plane to be flown to Mogadishu, Somalia, where it landed on October 17.

One of GSG-9's 30-man groups had been following the aircraft since its landing in Cyprus, in a modified Lufthansa 707. This group was airborne soon after the German government learned of the plane's Mogadishu destination, having flown from Bonn to Cyprus, to Ankara, and back to Germany before learning of its final destination. A second 30-man unit, including commander Ulrich Wegener, had flown in the mean time from Germany to Dubai, and was thus in a better position to attempt hostage rescue operations.

The Somali government was cooperative and permitted Wegener's group to land. The government also set up a security perimeter of Somali commandos around the airport before their arrival. This enabled the GSG-9 unit to receive vital intelligence about the plane from the security forces. GSG-9 deployed sniper and reconnaissance teams and prepared to carry out an immediate assault on the plane, if the need for such an event arose. An assault was not required, and with the arrival of the second GSG-9 unit, intense planning for hostage rescue began.

As the night progressed, officials concluded that, because Mahmoud was growing increasingly unstable and had already demonstrated a willingness to execute hostages (e.g., the pilot), a rescue operation would be necessary. At 11:15 p.m., sections of the assault team began a covert approach to the plane, accompanied by two SAS men who were skilled in the use of "flash-bang" grenades. In an attempt to draw at least some of the terrorists to the cockpit (to establish their location), Somali commandos at 2:05 a.m. lit a bright signal fire a few hundred feet from the front of the plane. GSG-9 reconnaissance reported that Mahmoud and another terrorist had gone to the cockpit and appeared confused by the fire.

Simultaneously, GSG-9 commandos made entry through the airplane's doors, using special rubber-coated ladders to muffle the sound of their approach. The emergency doors were blown open at 2:07 a.m., with explosive charges. The two SAS men, who had managed to slip undetected onto the plane's wings, tossed their grenades inside, and the GSG-9 teams entered the plane, ordering the hostages to get down. In just a few seconds, three of the terrorists were killed, the fourth severely wounded, with all of the hostages unharmed and one GSG-9 man slightly wounded. The operation was officially over by 2:12 a.m., October 18.

Three days later, the body of Schleyer, the German businessman, kidnapped about a month earlier, was recovered.[9]   ❑

CONCLUSIONS

The use of special forces to combat terrorism has both assets and liabilities. Too little commitment can result in an insufficiently trained and equipped force, as happened to the U.S. forces in the Operation Eagle's Claw disaster. Too zealous a desire to use such forces can result in the loss of innocent lives, as Israel has discovered.

Determination, unsupported by sufficient training or equipment, is also a recipe for disaster, as became evident in November 1985. An Egyptian airliner en route to Cairo from Athens was hijacked and diverted to Malta. Egyptian troops stormed the plane the next day, after the hijackers began to kill some of the hostages on board. As the troops rushed onto the plane, the hijackers tossed grenades at passengers. The death toll was put at 60, 57 of whom died in the rescue attempt.

It is not enough just to have such a force. Nations must train and equip them with adequate information and weaponry to meet an increasingly sophisticated terrorist threat. Nations need also to instill in its strike forces, as Germany has sought to do, a respect for the law and its restraints on strike force activities. So equipped and so trained, such forces can operate to significantly reduce not necessarily the number but the success of terrorist attacks worldwide.

EVALUATION

There are many conflicting views on whether strike forces are legitimate and useful tools in combating terrorism. Some view such strike teams as potential threats to democracy, creating elite troops that could be used to quell demonstrations as well as to stop terrorist attacks. Others view them as essential to a nation's security, operating in ways not open to a large military unit to safeguard a nation's citizens, both at home and abroad.

Below are two quotations that reflect, in part, this divergence of view. Each viewpoint expressed is a bit extreme, tending toward opposite ends of the spectrum of opinion. Read each, and decide which more accurately reflects the appropriate assessment of the need and use for such forces in today's world.

1. "The Israeli argue the case for pre-emptive strikes: it is better to kill their enemies in their own bases and so prevent them mounting their operations, rather than conduct elegant sieges inside Israel. While appreciating the excellence of other forces' pieces of electronic wizardry and the skill of the talk-out experts, their aim is to prevent the need for such expertise arising. Such a policy has its attractions, especially for a beleaguered, small nation like Israel under continual attack from enemies based round its borders. When national survival is at stake all manner of actions become permissable that would not be countenanced in more secure societies."[10]

2. "The danger inherent in the war against terrorism is, of course, the prospect of desperate societies willing to substitute state terror for (non-state) terrorism, to trade individual rights and freedoms for relief from chaos and violence, reconstituting what were once relatively benign governments into coldly efficient, centralized tyrannies, whose populations are held in close check by armies of secret police and informers, widespread electronic eavesdropping, and a constant deluge of propaganda."[11]

SUGGESTED READINGS

Clancy, Tom. *Special Forces: A Guided Tour of U.S. Army Special Forces*. New York: Berkley Books, 2001.

Dobson, Christopher, and Ronald Payne. *Counterattack: The West's Battle Against the Terrorists*. New York: Facts On File, 1982.

"Patterns of Global Terrorism." U.S. Department of State Publications (annual publication—available on the World Wide Web).

Rivers, Gayle. *The Specialists: Revelations of a Counter-terrorist.* New York: Stein and Day, 1985.

Strategic Assessment 1999: Priorities for a Turbulent World. Washington, DC: National Defense University's Institute for National Strategic Studies, 1999, http://specialforces.com

NOTES

1. Christopher Dobson and Ronald Payne, *Counterattack: The West's Battle Against the Terrorists,* New York: Facts On File, 1982, xvi.

2. *Patterns of International Terrorism in 1980: A Research Paper* (Washington, DC: National Foreign Assessment Center, 1980), 1–6.

3. "International Terrorism: Issue Brief No. 1874042" (Washington, DC: Congressional Research Service, 1978), 41–42.

4. Dobson and Payne, *Counterattack,* 84.

5. Seventy-four year old Dora Bloch was not being held with the hostages at the airport. She had been transferred to a Ugandan hospital. After the raid, she disappeared, amid reports that she was dragged screaming from her hospital bed and murdered, on Ugandan President Idi Amin's orders. She has never been seen or heard from since that time.

6. Dobson and Payne, *Counterattack,* 96.

7. Gary Mitchell, "Special Operations Units of the United States Government," in *The Encyclopedia of Terrorism,* ed. Cindy Combs and Martin Slann (New York: Facts On File, 2002).

8. Cindy Combs and Martin Slann, "Operation Chavin de Huantar," in *The Encyclopedia of Terrorism* (New York: Facts On File, 2002), 135–137.

9. Ibid., 121–122.

10. N. C. Livingstone, "Taming Terrorism: In Search of a New U.S. Policy," *International Security Review: Terrorism Report,* 7, no. 1 (Spring 1982): 20.

11. Dobson and Payne, *Counterattack,* 83.

CHAPTER 10

Security Measures: A Frail Defense

Key Concepts

physical security	training programs
penetration teams	taggants
operational security	trace detectors
personnel security	general threat indicators
Operation Eligible Receiver	local threat indicators
infowar	specific threat indicators
hardening the target	shoot-ats

Power, in its most primitive sense, can be defined as the capacity to disrupt or destroy. Terrorists through the use of selective, yet often indiscriminate, violence have been able to force governments to negotiate and often grant concessions to their demands. They have been able to attract worldwide attention to themselves and their goals. Terrorism has forced governments to expend vast amounts of time and resources on security.

M. K. Pilgrim

Confronted with a growing tide of terrorist destruction, governments have indeed been forced to spend increasing amounts of time and money on the problems related to security. Modern society is both fragile and complex, with much interdependence within the systems. As such, the possibilities for interference by terrorism are almost infinite.

Some aspects of security have received more attention than others, due to their spectacular selection as targets of terrorism. It is more than possible that this focus will shift, as new technologies make current security measures obsolete and as successful security systems harden certain targets against attack.

Technological developments during the past few decades have increased dramatically the potential targets and weapons available to persons committing terrorist acts. While the technology accessible to governments has also grown, governments are to some extent more hampered than helped by the technology boom. Governments are simultaneously confronted with a rapidly growing number of targets that must be secured and constrained by democratic principles from utilizing many technological devices to secure those targets. Creating an effective security system that protects against a wide range of terrorist attacks while it continues to afford a maximum exercise of democratic freedoms and privileges is a formidable task indeed.

THREE FACETS OF SECURITY

Security is not a one-dimensional issue. Instead, those confronting security problems are faced with at least three aspects of the situation that must be considered: physical security, operational security, and personnel security. Each of these facets of security is closely related to the others and cannot be easily differentiated in an analysis of counterterrorism security efforts.

But certain features of each aspect can, if explained, offer a better understanding of the security measures that nations and businesses are, even now, taking against terrorist incidents and threats. Let us examine each of these aspects of security briefly.

Physical security has, as its objective, *the hardening of the target against which an attack may be made.* Although no blueprint for successful physical security measures against terrorist attack has been in any sense adopted, there are certain considerations and countermeasures that have begun to achieve acceptance in both the government and the business community.

Both these communities are slowly recognizing that security measures against terrorism must go beyond the level of normal crime prevention. These are not "normal" criminals: their goals, their willingness to sacrifice innocent lives, and their willingness to die in their attacks make them extraordinary criminals, against whom extraordinary measures must be taken if security is to be achieved and maintained.

In order to determine what, if any, extraordinary security measures are needed to protect against a terrorist attack, government and business have employed a number of relatively ordinary tactics. A physical security survey by professionals who are aware of the dangers in a particular area or to a particular business or region is standard procedure. This has, in recent years, begun to include the use of **penetration teams,** *whose job it is to discover holes in security systems through which other teams, such as terrorist attack teams, could presumably penetrate and sabotage or destroy the target.*

The penetration team, or the organization conducting the physical security survey, may suggest in its report that the business utilize certain devices that have proven useful in guarding against attack or sabotage. For example, a variety of intrusion detection devices are available on the market today.

Or such an evaluation may emphasize the importance of such factors as lighting, access control, or physical security and access control codes. Organizations may be advised to inhibit surreptitious approaches by increasing lighting of entryways, fences, hallways, and other points of access. Greater access control is often recommended, usually in the form of limitations on the numbers of individuals cleared to work in the facility as a whole, or in specific, sensitive parts of the operation. One of the more common recommendations for improved physical security is that security and access codes be changed fairly frequently, to make penetration of the operation more difficult.

Some operations, where security has been a relatively minor problem until recently, are being urged to consider the use of personnel, such as guards, whose specific duty it is to ensure physical security. Others, who have already taken this step, have discovered from security surveys that they have need of additional guards or specially trained counterterrorist guards.

Physical security is clearly dependent upon other types of security—operational security and personnel security. Fortress walls, barbed fences, and barred gates are not, in modern times, either reasonable or sufficient protection against determined terrorist fanatics. The operation of the facility itself must be secure, and its personnel well trained in security procedures, to circumvent modern terrorist attacks.

Operational security *has as its objective the denial of opportunity for terrorists to collect such information on either the facility or its activities as might enable it to predict those activities.* To be able to predict those activities would help the terrorist to successfully penetrate the facility or activity and disrupt or destroy it. By denying that information to terrorists, the risk to terrorists carrying out an attack against the activity or facility significantly increases.

Prediction of operational activities usually relies on discerning patterns of behavior, so operational security analysis focuses on identifying those patterns and how they are communicated to personnel. Emphasis is placed on making such patterns less predictable, randomizing activities as far as possible without creating chaos within the organization. Too often, repeated activities create in the minds of the individuals responsible for security a lack of alertness to small differences that may be crucial. The arrival of a particular car at the same time every morning, the use of a van of a specific color and model delivering goods at the same place and time—these routines can deaden the alertness of personnel to such factors as the identity of the driver or the presence of an authorized person in the vehicle. Such a failure to notice, to carry out a thorough security check, can prove fatal to the organization or to some of its personnel.

The training of personnel in operational security measures is also important. Organizations are advised to train personnel in the recognition of intelligence-gathering activities, so that they can more readily spot individuals engaged in such activities. Screening of both employees and casual but regular contacts—such as vendors—is also a major focus of operational security efforts, as all such individuals can constitute a threat to the operation.

Moreover, the organization as a whole is often encouraged to improve its own operational security by a variety of fairly obvious, but essential, measures. These include, but are not limited to

1. maintaining a low profile, so that the organization does not become an attractive, publicity-provoking target;
2. improving communications security, so that it is less possible to penetrate the flow of commands or patterns of communications; and
3. developing counterintelligence capabilities, within both management and security-related personnel, so that the organization need not always be on the defensive in this struggle against terrorism.

Neither operational nor physical security can function effectively without the third crucial type of security: personnel security. **Personnel security** focuses on *the training of personnel to take responsibility on their own for security,* by teaching them to know how to recognize and respond to a potential terrorist threat. For many years, this type of security was directed toward high-threat individuals, those whom the organization regarded as being at a greater risk of attack than most of the rank-and-file personnel.

Many organizations have developed individual crisis management files, which help management to decide which individuals need special security training and protection. Using those files, these at-risk individuals are often advised on how to randomize travel routes and maintain a low profile. Training is also given to certain individuals in special antiterrorism devices, such as bulletproof clothing.

But today, personnel security has taken on added dimensions. Organizations routinely schedule periodic training for all personnel in counterterrorism procedures. Such training is usually designed to heighten awareness among employees of the potential for terrorist attacks, and the preincident phases—particularly intelligence gathering—which may alert personnel to a terrorist attack in progress. The proper use of security measures at all times is stressed, so that employees are less likely to be lulled by a sense of routine into a possibly fatal breach of security procedures.

Most of all, the need to tell someone about suspicious or threatening behavior, to alert the proper authorities to potential threats, has become a major focus in the training of personnel in many organizations. The alertness of personnel to security breaches may well mean the difference between a successful terrorist attack and the failure of such an attempt.

CASE STUDY   NSA's Operation Eligible Receiver

Using a "penetration team" comprised of a group from within the National Security Agency (NSA) in 1998 and software easily obtained from hacker sites on the Internet, **Operation Eligible Receiver** *demonstrated how easy it would be for computer-efficient cyberterrorists to cripple U.S. military and civilian computer networks.* The simulated attack was run during a two-week period, and the results were "frightening," according to a defense official involved in the simulation. This official noted that this attack "run by a set of people using standard Internet techniques, would have basically shut down the command-and-control capability in the Pacific theater for some considerable period of time."[1]

The "game" played by the penetration team was simple: they conducted *information warfare attacks*, or **infowar,** on the Pacific Command (and ultimately on the United States) to soften its policies toward the communist regime in North Korea, with the hackers posing as paid agents for North Korea. The "Red Team" of NSA surrogate hackers, using computers, modems, and software technology easily accessible on what is often called the "dark side of the Internet" (network-scanning software, intrusion tools, and password-breaking "log-in scripts"), were able to inflict crippling damage. According to news reports, they were able to break into computer networks and gain access to the systems that control the electrical power grid for the United States, giving them the power, if they had so desired, to disable the power grid and leave the country in darkness.

This power knock-out option was only a sideshow: the primary target of the attack was the U.S. Pacific Command, which is in charge of the troops (about 100,000) who would be called on to respond to wars in Korea or China. According to one defense official involved in the exercise,

> The most telling thing for the Department of Defense, when all was said and done is that basically for a two-week period the command-and-control capability in the Pacific theater would have been denied by the "infowar" attacks, and that was the period of the exercise.[2]

The attacks were not, of course, run against the infrastructure components, since there was no desire to actually shut down a power grid or disable Pacific Command. But the referees monitoring the simulation were shown the attacks and the structures under attack, and they concluded that the attacks would be successful. Moreover, the pseudo-attackers foiled essentially all efforts to trace them, even though the FBI joined the Pentagon in trying to locate them. Only one of the numerous units of NSA groups (one based in the United States) was uncovered. The others operated without being located or identified.

These attacks, run by "friendly" agents working as teams of hackers to penetrate "secure" computer networks, offered useful insights to government officials in Defense and Justice responsible for the security of such systems. This operation also makes clear the response of the U.S. government in 2003 to a massive power failure in the northeast section of the country, including New York City. Federal agencies were able to announce fairly quickly that this power failure was *not* a terrorist attack, because the parameters for such an attack had already been studied in this operation and did not fit the pattern of the 2003 grid failure. Being able to eliminate the possibility of a security breach as the root of the failure no doubt enabled a more rapid assessment of the real cause and the initiation of appropriate measures to resolve the problem. Thus, security tests cannot only indicate weaknesses in a system; they may also make evaluation of disaster situations at least one step easier.   ❑

AIRPORT SECURITY IN THE UNITED STATES

Nations such as the United States have tried to institute some security measures at one of terrorism's favorite targets: airports. Travelers of commercial airlines in this country were, even before the September 11 attacks, routinely subjected to electronic or manual luggage inspection and to electronic or physical body searches—a practice virtually unknown only a few years ago. In airports in the United States, too, individuals without purchased airline tickets can no longer meet incoming plane guests at the arrival gates, nor can they take their friends or relatives to the departure gates after the security rules were changed in the wake of the attacks.

These are potentially controversial measures, involving some invasion of privacy and some searches without a warrant of persons not accused of any crime. Yet

tizens today have serious objections to these measures. Even the presence of air
als on randomly selected flights and the use of National Guard troops for air-
ecurity were accepted with complacence by most citizens, perhaps in recognition of the fact that threat to their lives and property created by a terrorist is greater
than that incurred in airline security measures.

Such security measures, of course, only offer a measure of protection, in one
country, against only one type of terrorism. If such measures are not universally applied by all nations, then the potential for skyjacking or bombing remains substantial,
even for citizens of countries having such security systems.[3] Moreover, even U.S.
measures until late in 2001 focused primarily on the hijacking of airlines with the use
of conventional weapons, most of which was clearly inappropriate in terms of security preparations for the events of September 11.

Most of the security measures against hijacking with conventional weapons
were enforced by measures that were incomplete and poorly enforced. Consider the
results of investigations of airport security in several major U.S. airports. Federal auditors, testing X-ray procedures for carry-on luggage, reported recently that major
airports missed, on the average, about 20 percent of the auditors' dummy weapons.
One airport missed 66 percent of these weapons! This is clearly a breakdown in both
physical and operational security.

Other surveys suggest that the problem does not lie exclusively with laxity in
X-ray procedures. One audit, for instance, found that Los Angeles International Airport could not account for 6,000 employee identification badges. Two thousand were
missing at Dulles International Airport near Washington, DC. Obviously, personnel
security is also somewhat lax in this industry, contributing to a breach in operational
security.

Consider the results of the informal "penetration team" of *U.S. News & World
Report* reporters who checked several U.S. airports:

1. At Washington National, a reporter with a suitcase walked right past a security checkpoint on the side where arriving passengers walk out of the arrival gate. The reporter
   pretended to make a call at a row of pay phones near the checkpoint, then slipped by
   when the guards' backs were turned. What if his suitcase had contained a bomb?

2. At Chicago's O'Hare International Airport, a visitor found a baggage-room security
   door open. He walked through with his briefcase into the baggage-truck passageway,
   onto the tarmac where planes fuel and load, and up a jetway staircase. He then entered
   the terminal as if deplaning and caught another flight—without ever going through
   security. He could have sabotaged either luggage or a plane, without any contact with
   security.

3. A reporter watched in amazement as janitors at Midway airport in Chicago pushed large
   trash cans up to the passenger checkpoint. The janitors went through metal detectors,
   but they pulled the cans through on the unscreened side. Guards neither inspected the
   trash cans—a serious security breach—nor did they check parcels brought into the same
   area by food vendors.

4. A reporter at Atlanta's Hartsfield Airport watched as an employee punched a code into a
   security door's lock. She then tried the same code on several other doors in the concourse.
   It opened them all! These doors led, among other things, to the planes on the tarmac.[4]

Such lapses in airport security must frighten and worry both those responsible for such security and the passengers and crew whom such security is designed to protect. The lapses are clearly both in personnel and operational security. The argument is made that security personnel operate under the disadvantage of a mandate by their employers to make air travel as pleasant as possible. In other words, we want airport employees to be both unfailingly courteous and unrelentingly suspicious—of everyone. They are trained to put the comfort and convenience of the passengers first—but also to regard all individuals, including those same passengers, as potential threats to the airline's peace and security. It would appear, on the surface, to be an almost impossible task.

Weaknesses in the Security System

It has been suggested by several experts that commercial aviation was used as the "weapon" in the September 11 attacks precisely because of convenient flaws that existed within the security system of this industry. A quick look at a few of these weaknesses will illuminate the logic of this claim.

Ease of Access to the Cockpit

Because none of the September 11 pilots had the pilots or copilots informing air traffic controllers that they were being hijacked, and because the planes were turned into "missiles" flown deliberately into facilities on the ground, it seems reasonable to assume the terrorists were able to take over the cockpits. This was probably done in one of three patterns: by stealth, by the use of sudden overwhelming force, or by creating a disturbance drawing one of the crew to exit the cockpit and thereby create access to the flight deck for the hijackers.

Taking the cockpit by stealth would require access to a key to the cockpit of the plane. Unfortunately, prior to September 11, every flight attendant was required by the standards of the Federal Aviation Authority (FAA) to carry such a key at all times. On American Flight 11 (the first plane to fly into the World Trade Center), one of the flight attendants reported that two flight attendants had been stabbed. The second plane to fly into the WTC, United Flight 175, also reported that one flight attendant had been stabbed and two had been killed. Since each of these attendants had a key to the cockpit, it is reasonable to assume that the terrorists were able to take the cockpit by stealth.[5]

As one expert notes, prior to the events of September 11, "a normal-sized man with a karate kick or a shoulder shove could have broken down a cockpit door without too much exertion."[6] Numerous examples of this weakness were reported by news agencies, including attacks by a passenger on a Boeing 747-400 British Airways flight from London to Nairobi in December 2000 and by a young couple on a flight in February 2001 from Miami to New York. In these as in so many other cases, the passengers were able to breech the cockpit by force—and neither incident involved a large or well-trained attacker.

Finally, it was possible to take the cockpit by creating a distracting disturbance in the passenger area. This security weakness was possible because pilots were instructed, in the event of a disruptive incident in the passenger cabin, to intervene personally by leaving the cockpit and confronting the disruptive passenger. This instruction may have led to access for the terrorists on September 11. After the United flight crashed into the WTC, the operations center in Chicago sent an electronic text message to the airliners (including United Flight 93) that read: "Beware, cockpit intrusion." This message could have been interpreted by the flight crew as an air rage incident, requiring that the pilot exit the cabin to confront the problem. The pilots responded to confirm receipt of the message, and a few minutes later the plane was taken over by four terrorists. The policy of having the pilot exit the cockpit to confront may have facilitated the seizure of the aircraft.

Inadequate Screening Processes

As noted in the account of earlier penetration teams at airports, the screening process for passengers and luggage prior to the events of September 11 were seriously flawed. Perhaps the most obvious evidence of the flaws in this process lies in the handling of at least half of the 19 hijackers. Consider this:

> Nine of the hijackers were selected for special security screenings on the morning of September 11.
>
> Of these, six were chosen for extra security by a computerized screening system.
>
> Two others were singled out because of irregularities in their documents.
>
> One was listed on ticket documents as the travel companion to one who had questionable identification.

Yet they were all, in the end, allowed to board their flights, since on September 11, FAA security regulations required that passengers selected for further screening were only required to have their *checked* baggage further evaluated for possible weapons. Because only one or two of the terrorists actually checked any luggage, there would be no reason for the security process in place at that time to detect the weapons in the carry-on luggage of the terrorists.[7] Clearly, the process needed refining.

IMPACT OF SEPTEMBER 11 ATTACKS ON AIRPORT SECURITY

Although airport security clearly had flaws prior to these attacks, this demonstration of the dreadful consequences of airline hijacking dramatized the issue and forced the government and the industry to rapidly reassess and reorganize to reassure the public. The attacks, as noted earlier, caused airports across the country to be shut down in an effort to prevent further hijackings to occur. It took several days before the airports could be fully reopened, leaving thousands of passengers stranded at airports to which their flights had been diverted when the closings were ordered.

Moreover, we learned that the September 11 hijackers cased airports in the weeks prior to the attacks, taking test runs on flights to identify weaknesses within the system.

Confronted with the task of both reassuring the public that it was safe to fly and immediately taking effective measures to ensure (as far as possible) that such hijackings did not occur again, government and industry took several rapid steps:

1. Banning curbside check-in of luggage.
2. Severely limiting the use of e-tickets.
3. Restricting access to areas beyond the security scanning checkpoints to ticketed passengers only.
4. Assigning members of the National Guard to offer visible security at the check points.

Not all of these initial steps remained permanent or even universally applied at all airports, but they represented a significant effort to improve airport security and the public's perception of that security. At some airports, scrutiny of handbags and carry-on luggage was intense and resulted in the confiscation of fingernail files, pocket knives, letter openers, and a variety of other potential "weapons." Because those who carried out the hijackings in September apparently did not use guns or other conventional weapons for which baggage handlers had been trained to scan, this represented a serious change in the perception of dangerous personal items on the part of airport personnel.

Moreover, new potential threats continued to emerge, challenging previous patterns of security operations at airports. The potential of explosives in shoes became evident with the attempt of an individual to "light" what appeared to be a fuse attached to his shoes on a flight from Paris. Subsequently, airports at several major points around the country began to require passengers to submit to a scanning of their shoes for explosives.

That the people who seized control of the airplanes were not initiating a conventional hijacking situation also demonstrated a need to change security patterns. Pilots had been trained to cooperate, if possible, with hijackers, in efforts to get them to allow the plane to land, to offer opportunities for negotiation or hostage-rescue operations. The cockpits of the planes were seldom equipped with locking systems that would prevent such a takeover of the plane by skilled pilots. Thus, the pilots' training had to be revised, and mechanisms have now been added to most passenger planes that enable the cockpit to be secured from the inside against passengers, if necessary.

The United States struggled with the question as to who should have the task of maintaining internal airport security: private industry (in the form of security personnel businesses) or the federal government. Because the attacks on September 11 were made when airports contracted for their own security personnel with private agencies, the assumption was made that this process was flawed. But both the cost and the practical problems of making airport security a government enterprise are staggering, although it is the route currently being mandated. The hiring and training—including the setting of qualification standards for employment, training regimens, and quality enforcement—have become the responsibility of the federal government, which must also try not to create unemployment problems with its new rules.

In addition, physical security is still not completely effective. Weapons experts have testified before Congress about the possibility of smuggling guns through metal detectors by carrying them on certain spots on the body. Nor are these metal detectors, on which much airline physical security relies, effective at all heights. Although some airports now have technology to detect explosive materials, it is expensive and therefore will not be used in all airports. Training in the search for explosive materials, too, is not yet effective. A gentleman whose shoes showed evidence of explosive materials was stopped in January 2002 at the San Francisco airport and then allowed to walk away before security personnel could check it out, resulting in a shutdown of flights for several hours as airport security tried to locate the individual, without success.

Until after the events in September, no system was in place to X-ray check baggage on domestic flights, according to the FAA. The argument was made that the volume of such baggage was too high and that many weapons forbidden in carry-on baggage (for which the current detectors are designed) were still permitted on checked baggage. After those events, a program to match luggage with passenger flight manifests has been instituted, but only for the first check-in point. Unless all checked baggage is tested for weapons and explosives, a person could still get a bomb into a plane in checked luggage if his or her flight had at least one stop where the passenger could disembark, leaving the luggage (and the bomb) on the next leg of the flight. The argument against the more comprehensive scanning and baggage matching scheme continues to be that it is too expensive in terms of time and money, but the Transportation Safety Administration is beginning to draft and implement rules to make more comprehensive scanning and matching mandatory.

So what are airports to do to harden themselves as targets against terrorism? They could insist on training for security personnel to make them more security conscious, but it might well be at the cost of a loss of the "friendly" image with which airlines have sought to market their services. They could install more detection devices, for weapons as well as explosives, but again unless the laws regarding the type of weapons that may be carried in checked luggage change and the public becomes more reconciled to delays in flights due to essential security checks, then the cost of such measures to the airline industry may seem prohibitive.

THE COSTS OF SECURITY

The costs of such antiterrorism measures are high, materially as well as politically. Unfortunately, a great deal more money is required to erect defenses against terrorist attacks than to commit such acts.

If the cost of defending just one type of industry against attack is so high, then the cost of erecting coordinated international defenses against a multitude of types of terrorist attacks may well be prohibitive. The protection of specific targets against terrorists, including air transport facilities, would be a mammoth task. It is also a task which would not in itself be sufficient to secure entire nations and persons against terrorist attacks of all kinds.

The difficulty, as Robert Kupperman noted, is that potential targets for terrorist attacks are not limited to airports. As he has pointed out, there are numerous vulnerable targets in our sophisticated society. Electrical power systems, for example, are very tempting as accessible targets. A well-placed bomb or shots from a high-powered rifle could conceivably cause a blackout in an entire city. The same is true about the potential for destructive attacks on telephone systems, gas pipelines, dams, water systems, and nuclear power plants.

Kupperman also noted that, with the extensive reliance on computer information systems—for banking, credit cards, real estate, and so forth—that now characterizes industrial societies, the potential for economic disruption by terrorist attacks on those systems may also be substantial, as noted in a preceding chapter. As any computer hacker knows, no matter how carefully a computer system's security may be designed, a blend of time, patience, knowledge, and a little bit of luck will usually suffice to break into it. The potential of cyberterror, discussed in an earlier chapter, in which computers are used to destroy banking systems, public records, even water purification systems, presents a serious threat to many industries in the twenty-first century.

Concern has surfaced, too, over the protection of oil rigs in international waters. There are by now hundreds of oil rigs in the Gulf of Mexico and a rapidly growing number in the North Sea, all of which are vulnerable to terrorist attacks. Recent movies and novels depicting attacks on such rigs serve to highlight the plausibility of this potential disaster.

This industry, so vital to modern economies, is particularly open to attack, according to some experts, not only at its drilling operations, but also at a variety of other points. Although established petroleum and natural gas operations, their pipeline interties, and associated tankage and storage facilities have been the most attractive targets to date, there are many other points at which this industry is vulnerable, as events in the recent war in Iraq and subsequent attacks in Saudi Arabia have demonstrated.

The point is that the list of potential targets that could require security measures is extensive and growing rapidly with the development of modern technological interdependence. It might be possible, although incredibly expensive, for a nation to undertake to protect its own citizens and structures, but destructive attacks in another nation can have a substantial impact on the economy and lifestyle of the "protected" nation.

An attack on a North Sea oil rig, for example, would not only affect the cost of oil in Britain (and any nations that Britain supplies), but it could damage the North Sea countries' fishing industries as well. A successful attack on the computerized international banking system could have serious consequences for many national economies. The poisoning of a water supply in one nation could affect all of the other nations who share the use of that poisoned river or lake.

Just as no nation can entirely protect itself from terrorism by securing all potential terrorist targets, it is probably impossible for any nation, acting alone, to prevent or control the flow of weapons to terrorists. If targets cannot be fully protected, the next security step logically would appear to be an effort to curb the number and types of instruments of destruction available to terrorists. But again, the vast array of security measures required are staggering.

Some of the security measures in place or under consideration involve what is called **hardening the target,** which *involves efforts to make targets less accessible.* As noted earlier, these include the installation of metal detectors and X-ray machines at points of entry, the use of sensor or closed-circuit television to monitor accessways, and other similar technical devices. Such measures also can include the erection of fences, vision barriers, and heavy barriers around the perimeters of the installation. Related security measures can involve increased use of such items as armored cars, security guard forces, and bulletproof vests. An increasing number of executives are enrolling employees in expensive **training programs** designed *to teach skills in such things as high-speed car chases, surviving a kidnapping, and how not to look like a businessman traveling abroad.*

Indeed, companies offering to help make a business or a businessman more secure from terrorism have proliferated. One enterprising woman launched a business in 1987 that offered fake passports from nonexistent countries. Most of her clients were military men and businessmen traveling in the Middle East, South America, and Europe. Donna Walker, president of International Documents Service, pointed out, "When you're up against a bunch of gun-waving crazies, you should have an option"—such as a passport that does not label you as an American.[8]

Whether such exercises in protecting the target are useful or not, they continue to generate both interest and money for the companies providing them. What is not clear is the extent to which they offer real protection against a terrorist attack that is commensurate with the money expended on them.

Nor is it clear whether such measures are either legal or acceptable in a democratic society. Fake passports could well be used by criminals to baffle legitimate customs officials. The erection of heavy barriers and guards around public buildings, although perhaps necessary to protect them from attack, are still unpopular with a democratic public, accustomed to easy access to, for example, their nation's capitol buildings. It is, as the United States found in the wake of the Oklahoma City bombing, neither popular nor practical to harden all buildings that have federal offices against the public that they serve. Similarly, even though the general public supports, as a whole, the *idea* of strengthening airport security in the wake of September 11, individuals still do not want to wait longer or pay more for tickets in order to achieve that enhanced security.

PROTECTING PUBLIC TRANSPORTATION

Public transportation networks in large cities are enticing targets for terrorists because

1. they typically carry large numbers of people;
2. they move in concentrated, predictable geographic areas under routine time frames;
3. they are highly accessible, since they are "public service" operations, and cannot be hardened easily against their primary users—the general public.

Thus, in terms of physical, personnel, and operational security, they are attractive targets for those seeking to reach a large audience and disrupt a system with little effort. The U.S. State Department, in its record of international terrorist attacks in 1996, noted that 92 of these—almost a third—were against transportation and transportation infrastructures. While European, Middle Eastern, and Asian countries rely on their public transit systems much more heavily than the United States and have consequently developed more expertise in protecting these systems, officials were unable to prevent the sarin gas attack on the Tokyo subway in 1995 or the bombings of trains in Madrid in 2004.

Attempts to share learning experiences and technologies have evolved among some of the nations with a shared interest in this security threat. The advanced industrial nations (Canada, France, Germany, Great Britain, Italy, Japan, and the United States—the G-7) plus Russia have met several times in recent years to discuss the need for cooperation. On July 30, 1996, these nations met at the Lyons Summit in France, adopting a 25-point plan for international cooperation to combat terrorist acts. This plan included several significant points:

1. Tightened control on firearms and explosives
2. Improved bomb detection methods
3. Prevention of terrorist communications on the Internet
4. Faster exchange of information on terrorist activities, including those involving chemical, biological, and nuclear materials

Based on the progress made at this summit, two further meetings focusing on land transportation security were held in Washington, DC, in 1996 and 1997. In April 1998, domestic and international presenters (primarily from the G-7 plus Russia) met in Atlanta, Georgia, to discuss current and emerging terrorist threats, results from case studies, lessons learned and techniques developed due to terrorist actions, and new technologies useful in protecting land transportation systems. Some of the developing technologies discussed at this meeting, which may be of particular service in this target area, include weapons detection systems that can identify a weapon containing little or no metal at a distance of 30 feet, less-than-lethal incapacitation technologies that are both legal and socially acceptable (such as laser dazzlers, pyrotechnic devices, enhanced pepper spray delivery systems, and net devices), and sniper fire identification systems, capable of detecting and locating a sniper within a 10- by 10-foot area of an urban environment.[9]

Cooperation with other states is indispensable in the effort to provide security for land transportation systems. The techniques and equipment developed by other nations, if shared, may make future attacks on these vulnerable targets more difficult. But, as the officials at these meetings noted more than once, security for such accessible targets is not possible without a loss of freedom unacceptable to democracies. Furthermore, the events of September 11 demonstrated that the cooperation came *after* the terrorist event, not before, and thus did not prevent the attack but made capture of others involved possible.

EVENTIVE SECURITY

Security has not been exclusively concerned with the hardening of targets that terrorists may—or may not—select today. Some efforts are also being directed at what has been termed "preventive security," meaning the making of terrorist attacks themselves less likely.

One such security technique in use today involves efforts to tag and trace various weapon components. There exist **taggants**—*chemically identifiable trace agents*—for many types of explosives today. It is also possible, although not as easy, to use **trace detectors** *for chemical agents*, which would enable security agents *to detect the presence of dangerous or hazardous chemicals in innocuous-looking containers.*

The use of tagging devices and trace elements for portable rocket security, in addition to more complete inventory control measures, is also under advisement. The advantage in the use of taggants, in addition to an ability to detect certain substances, is an ability to determine the country, and sometimes even the company, of origin. Although this would not necessarily be of immediate use in preventing terrorist attacks, it would be of considerable use in determining responsibility, perhaps thereby making future such attacks less likely.

However, companies and countries manufacturing such materials, from explosives to handguns, from nuclear to chemical and biological weapons, have resisted many attempts to institute a comprehensive tagging effort. Most have argued that laws requiring such security measures violate the rights of businesses engaged in lawful enterprises.

Political reality has made it clear that nations cherish their right to sell arms to whomever they please, under whatever conditions they deem advisable. Even nations that have made no secret of the fact that they sponsor, with arms and war matériel, terrorist groups have little difficulty securing those arms on the world arms market.

Regardless of the motivation, arms are increasingly available to anyone with the money (or a moneyed sponsor) to pay for them. This makes the efforts to limit terrorist access to weapons, as a form of preventive terrorism, largely futile. What terrorists cannot purchase legally on the open arms market they can surely procure illegally on the black market. Fake end-user certificates are readily available from several countries, such as Nigeria.

Moreover, it is difficult, in the shadow world of illegal arms sales, to use most preventive measures effectively. Shell companies, Swiss bank accounts, and the routing of weapons from country to country three or four times to hide the country of origin make the labyrinth of arms deals difficult to penetrate with regulation or preventive action.

The use of taggants might make tracing the country of origin feasible (even through this maze of sale and resale), but it is also highly probable that nations winking at such sales by their industries are going to be unwilling to force those industries to institute measures that might make it easier for a finger to be pointed accurately at violators of arms agreements. For monetary reasons they may have tacitly agreed to the sales; for political reasons they do not want such arms sales easily traced home.

Preventing terrorism becomes, in such cases, less crucial than being held accountable for violation of arms control laws and agreements.

The issue of arms sales becomes particularly critical when the arms being sold are nonconventional weapons. The growing threat of chemical, biological, and nuclear weapons in the hands of terrorists willing and able to use them will be discussed in the next chapter.

THREAT ASSESSMENT: HOW DO YOU KNOW WHEN YOU ARE AT RISK?

How do nations or businesses decide which of their operations or activities are likely to be victims of terrorist attacks? Nations and individuals use three types of indicators to assess the potential threat of terrorism. These can be described as general threat indicators, local threat indicators, and specific threat indicators. Let us look briefly at each of these types of indicators.

General threat indicators are used to *determine whether, within the nation or state, there exist conditions that might stimulate or provoke terrorism*. Such indicators are extremely general and are consequently of little use in predicting the likelihood of a specific terrorist attack. Instead, they are used to assess the climate— political, ideological, religious, and so on—that might influence the willingness of a portion of the population to resort to terrorism. Politically, for example, the presence of an unpopular, repressive, or corrupt government is considered a positive indicator of the probability of terrorism. Similarly, an economic climate that includes extreme poverty and/or high unemployment is regarded as conducive to terrorism.

This does not mean that any nation or region possessing these political or economic conditions will necessarily have a large degree of terrorism. It simply means that the presence of such conditions makes the likelihood of terrorism greater in such places than it might be in areas that do not have similar political or economic climates. These are indicators only, not predictors of terrorism. For instance, one geopolitical indicator has been the concentration of large foreign populations within a nation. In the United States, many such concentrations exist in major cities without outbreaks of terrorism, but they may provide terrorism support networks for future terrorist attacks. In occupied territories or in nations involved in border disputes, such populations have been useful indicators of the probability of terrorism.

Local threat indicators are used *to assess more specific and localized possibilities for terrorism*. Usually, such indicators focus on the forms that dissent tends to take on the local level and the degree of violence involved in the expression of such dissent. The formation of radical groups; reports of stolen firearms, ammunition, and explosives; violence against local property, including looting and arson; violence against individuals, including murders, beatings, threats, and abductions; and the discovery of weapon, ammunition, and explosives caches are all considered local threat indicators. Again, this does not mean that any radical group that forms must necessarily be a terrorist threat, nor that any demonstration against a government or a company must be the prelude to a terrorist attack. These are just some indicators of the possibility of terrorism in a particular location.

Specific threat indicators are used *to evaluate the vulnerability of a particular target to terrorism,* not the likelihood of terrorism in a nation or neighborhood. These indicators include such things as the history of attacks on similar targets, the publicity value of the target, the target's access to infiltration, its counterterror capability and its communications capability, the tactical attractiveness of the target, and the availability of the police or other security personnel.

Some of these indicators are essentially judgment calls, such as the determination as to whether the industry involves a "sensitive" installation, which is generally used to refer to a nuclear, chemical, or other similar facility. Others are very easily quantified, such as the population density in the immediate area.

None of the three types of indicators can be said to predict the probability of a terrorist attack. Nevertheless, government and industry are beginning to rely increasingly on such indicators to help them decide what, if any, terrorist threat exists and what direction such attacks may take. With the cost of installing, staffing, and maintaining security systems spiraling, no one is anxious to spend more than is warranted on protection against a threat that may never materialize. But few are willing, either, to risk remaining unsecured where strong indications exist that terrorist attacks may cripple or destroy costly facilities and irreplaceable lives.

CONCLUSIONS

The question is how much a company, a government, or a people are willing to sacrifice in order to achieve greater security from terrorist attacks. For some, as long as the attack happens to "somebody else," the sacrifice of rights to prevent terrorism will always seem too high a price. To others, the prevention of terrorism will justify the loss of precious rights and freedoms. Governments, trying to strike a delicate balance between the need for its citizens to be secure and the need to protect its citizens' rights, have an increasingly difficult task.

Terrorism is fundamentally an attack on the state. Just as offshore maritime terrorism is a crime waiting to happen, terrorism with nuclear, biological, or chemical weapons is an international disaster waiting to occur. Neither national nor international security measures have proved adequate in terms of either protecting targets or preventing the dissemination of such agents of mass destruction.

As governments and industries come to grips with the rocketing costs of securing themselves against terrorism, serious questions continue to be raised concerning the priority that security should have in the allocation of resources. However real the terrorist threat may be, few are willing as yet to meet the exorbitant costs, both political and economic, of providing adequate security against that threat. The costs that the United States is incurring in the wake of September 11 are enormous; to date it is not clear how long the general public will support the continued use of finite government resources, in a time of recession, to meet the threat of terrorism.

Unlike the issues raised with intelligence-gathering and investigative counter-terrorism measures, in the United States security measures costs were reckoned less in terms of political ideals such as civil liberties than in terms of convenience, and more importantly, money. Until terrorism was perceived to be enough of a threat to the economic well-being of the nation, its citizens, and its industries to justify the expenditure of countless millions of dollars, security remained a weak weapon in the arsenal against terrorism. Until terrorism seriously pinches the pocketbook of nations and businesses, that pocketbook will be slow to open to defeat or prevent that "pinch." Once that pinch is felt, however, the willingness to pay may allow significant steps in security at airports, water systems, nuclear power plants, and many other vulnerable points to evolve.

EVALUATION

Making a decision to take on the cost—in economic, political, and public relations terms—of installing and enforcing security systems is seldom easy. Rarely is there a clear indicator that makes such a decision effortless or obvious. Governments and industries continue to wrestle with the problems, and while their solutions seldom satisfy everyone, it is often difficult to state, unequivocally, what they should do in a given situation.

Consider the following cases, and try to formulate an appropriate response. Remember to take into account both the monetary and political costs of any decision. Could you justify your decision to a corporate board or an irate citizen in terms of cost-effectiveness? That is, does the security measure that you may recommend pay for itself in terms of the security gained, in a way that would recommend itself to a stockholder or taxpayer?

1. In spite of the events of September 11, many airports are reluctant to maintain the initial limits imposed on passengers in terms of curbside baggage check-in, e-ticketing, and allowing friends and relatives to accompany passengers to the boarding areas. Should the FAA require these increased measures, as well as the installation of more and better screening devices for all check-in baggage on all domestic as well as international flights? Could you justify spending large sums for increased security? As a citizen, passenger, and potential target of aircraft terrorism, do you want better security systems in place? Are you willing to pay for them, in higher-priced airline tickets, longer lines, and more flight delays?

2. The 2004 bombings of the trains in Madrid, Spain, were clearly timed to impact the upcoming national elections, which they clearly did. As other nations approach similarly critical transition points in their national government, should additional security be taken to prevent such incidents, or should the events be postponed or cancelled? What types of targets should be protected? Will any type of security really be effective, if individuals or groups engaged in a crusade are determined to carry out such attacks? Should public events, like the Olympics or other types of international sports competitions, be restricted, postponed, or cancelled out of security concerns?

3. Technology now exists, and is used in some airports, that can detect plastic explosives. The equipment is based on the detection of plastic and is similar to a metal detector but much more expensive (about $1 million per unit). Because it was a plastic explosive that caused the destruction of the flight over Lockerbie, Scotland in 1989, this seems an important technological breakthrough. But in order to detect the amount of plastic material used in the Lockerbie bombing, the machine's calibrations would have to be set so low (since it was a small amount) that the machine would detect every credit card that passengers had in their wallets. Setting it high enough not to set off an alarm for every credit card and driver's license (with the ensuing passenger frustration and endless delays) would mean that the Lockerbie bomb would not have been detected by the machine. Should airports be required to have such devices, even though they are very expensive, to prevent the bombing of an airplane? How low should the calibrations on the machines be set—low enough to detect the Lockerbie-type bomb, even though to set it that low would mean long lines and much passenger frustration at having to surrender, even for a moment, credit cards? What if the airport cannot afford the machines? Should the government provide them, as well as training for the security personnel to use them? How real does the threat of a bomb on a plane have to be before the security devices and the ensuing hassles are worth the trouble and the cost?

4. **Shoot-ats** are *incidents in which in-flight aircraft (commercial and general or charter planes) are fired at from the ground (generally by SAMs, antiaircraft artillery, or small arms fire), or from the air.* In November 2002, an Israeli charter jet was shot at by two SA-7s (SAMs) as it was traversing over Mombasa, Kenya. In May 2002, a U.S. military aircraft experienced a shoot-at by an al-Qaeda member also using a SA-7. Can commercial passenger aircraft be secured against this type of attack? What would it cost? Should such protection be mandatory for all civilian aircraft? Who would pay for it?

Suggested Readings

Aberlin, Mary Beth. "Trace Elements: Taggants Can Help Finger Terrorists and Counterfeiters." *The Sciences* 36, no. 6 (November/December 1996): 8–10.

"Corporate Security: Risk Returns." *The Economist* (U.S.), 353, November 20, 1999, 78.

Gleick, Elizabeth. "No Barrier to Mayhem." *Time* 148, July 29, 1996, 42ff.

Hahn, Robert W. "The Cost of Airport Security Measures." *Consumer's Research Magazine,* 80, July 1997, 15ff.

Jain, Vinod K. "Thwarting Terrorism With Technology." *The World & I,* 11, no. 11 (November 1996): 149–155.

Laqueur, Walter. "Postmodern Terrorism." *Foreign Affairs* 75, no. 5 (September/October 1996): 24–36.

Thomas, Andrew R. *Aviation Insecurity: The New Challenges of Air Travel.* Amherst, NY: Prometheus Books, 2003.

Wallis, Rodney. *Combatting Air Terrorism.* Dulles, VA: Potomac Books, 1998.

Notes

1. Bill Gertz, "NSA's Operation Eligible Receiver," *The Washington Times,* April 17, 1998. http://www.landfield.com/isn/mail-archive/1998/Apr/0089.html.

2. Ibid., 2.

3. One CIA official (who requested anonymity) noted that in many less developed nations, the lack of any real security at airports constitutes "a terrorist attack waiting to happen."

4. "The Next Bomb," *Life,* (March 1989): 130–138.

5. Andrew R. Thomas, *Aviation Insecurity: The New Challenges of Air Travel* (Amherst, New York: Prometheus Books, 2003), 33.

6. Ibid., 37.

7. Ibid., 38–39.

8. Walter Laqueur, "Postmodern Terrorism," *Foreign Affairs* 75, no. 5 (September/October 1996), 24.

9. "Protecting Public Transportation From Terrorists," *National Institute of Justice Journal* (March 1998): 17–24.

CHAPTER 11

Police Strategy for Homeland Security

Strategy without tactics is the slowest route to victory. Tactics without strategy is the noise before defeat.

Sun Tzu (circa 500 BC)

INTRODUCTION

As reviewed in Chapter 1, America has moved into a new era, one often cited as the post–9/11 era. The events of that day have significantly changed not only America and its policies, they have also changed the world. Moreover, they have created new demands on federal, state, and local government and have transformed the responsibilities of the police. Although Homeland Security has become the overall umbrella under which policing and security in the post–9/11 world work, as reviewed in Chapter 2, the various organizational roles are still being worked out at the federal level, leaving less time for consideration of the role of state and local police. Although it is repeatedly stated that the police will play a role in homeland security and a very important role, defining that role has been limited. Recognizing that policing in the post–9/11 world has moved into an era of homeland security and that there is a stated role for state and local police, determining exactly what that role is becomes the concern of the rest of this book.

To understand the role of police in homeland security, as the opening quote denotes, it is important to have an understanding of the strategic objectives of homeland security to guide the tactics being used. Strategy provides the goals and objectives for achieving an end and the policies that will allow us to achieve these goals and objectives. In the case of homeland security, strategy determines the goals and objectives for securing the homeland and provides the framework for the formulation and implementation of policies aimed at achieving homeland security. These policies, then, become the basis for all operations and the use of actual tactics on the street. As Harold G. Campbell has explained, "The best defense against terrorism is offensive action, but knowing how and where to act is also of extreme importance."[1] Strategy

307

provides us the framework to know how and where to act. Therefore, determining the proper strategy for state and local police in the pursuit of homeland security is the purpose of this chapter.

STRATEGIES FOR HOMELAND SECURITY

Strategy is the overall framework by which resources are used to achieve certain goals and objectives. A strategy must take into consideration a number of factors that not only shape and influence the development of the strategy, but also will be influenced by the adoption of the strategy itself. As Campbell has also stated, "Homeland security strategy development is, in fact, a comprehensive endeavor that must take into consideration a significant number of seemingly disassociated variables in order to maximize strategic options and foster the creation of an indomitable public policy."[2] He explained that the strategist must be able to understand and recognize critical level variables, to see the relationships between these variables, and to be able to plan for all eventualities. As he succinctly explained, "Strategic level security planners must see the entire battlefield and understand the complexities and interrelations of all the factors, if they are to anticipate the enemy's next move," and "like a Grandmaster in chess, the strategic security planner must be able to think twenty moves ahead in the game and have contingencies in place that serve to counter any moves made by their adversary or strike before the enemy is ready to act."[3] Many of these complexities and variables can be seen in the events that unfolded after 9/11 and can contribute to our understanding of the need for a policing strategy for homeland security.

The primary purpose of a strategy is usually derived from a particular threat. The threat may be one that has already attacked American interests, or it may be one that poses a future threat to national interests; thus strategy is created to prevent these situations from developing. In the case of homeland security, 9/11 was the attack that necessitated the development of a strategy for homeland security, but multiple threats continue to exist in today's post–9/11 world. These include potential future terrorist attacks by Al-Qaeda and other groups, the illegal drug trade, illicit arms and weapons of mass destruction (WMD) trafficking, international organized crime, and illegal immigration for criminal purposes. As various countries and groups continue to modernize and employ modern-day information technology, combined with the infrastructure for the movement of people and resources, America has become more vulnerable to attacks on its own soil. This was made clear to America on 9/11, thus creating the need for a strategy to secure the homeland.

Other considerations derived from 9/11 necessitated the development of a homeland security strategy in the United States. These include the political dimension, the use and need for greater technology, the need for better information coordination, as well as a more unified action among the various agencies responsible for security in the United States. The attacks on America created a need for the United States to meet the challenge of securing the homeland and to recognize the political environment in which this would have to operate. The various levels of government, from the federal government down to the local counties, cities, and tribal governments, create a complex political environment in which to work; thus a strategy to secure the homeland cannot exclude the various levels of government in the development of a strategy, as all levels of government are clearly going to be affected by an overall strategy.

The use of technology by Al-Qaeda and its operatives on 9/11 highlighted the fact that technology can be used against America and its interests. However, technology also serves to enhance our ability to organize, lead, and employ police officers with greater efficiency and effectiveness by providing the ability to inject quality information into the decision-making process. It also provides a number of tools that police officers can use to better perform their job. Because the United States does not have the monopoly on technology, using superior technology and giving officers the skills necessary to adapt this technology to their advantage is critical.

Closely related today to the use of technology is the use of information. As was highlighted from the 9/11 Commission's report, information was often available, but information was not readily shared. Because today's technology gives us the edge of having real-time information, any strategy today must take this into consideration to develop ways in which data can be shared. And, not only must agencies be willing to share information, but they must also be willing to act in a unified manner regarding this information. Therefore, any strategy must take into consideration the politically fragmented system and find ways to share information and unify these various agencies to work together.

BOX 11-1

HOMELAND SECURITY AND NATIONAL SECURITY

The Preamble to the Constitution defines our federal government's basic purpose as "... to form a more perfect Union, establish justice, insure domestic Tranquility, provide for the common defense, promote the general Welfare, and secure the Blessings of Liberty to ourselves and our Posterity." The requirements to provide for the common defense remains as fundamental today as it was when these words were written, more than two hundred years ago.

The *National Security Strategy of the United States* aims to guarantee the sovereignty and independence of the United States, with our fundamental values and institutions intact. It provides a framework for creating and seizing opportunities to strengthen our security and prosperity. The *National Strategy for Homeland Security* complements the *National Security Strategy of the United States* by addressing a very specific and uniquely challenging threat—terrorism in the United States—and by providing a comprehensive framework for organizing the efforts of federal, state, local, and private organizations whose primary functions are often unrelated to national security.

The link between national security and homeland security is a subtle but important one. For more than six decades, America has sought to protect its own sovereignty and independence through a strategy of global presence and engagement. In so doing, America has helped many other countries and peoples advance along the path of democracy, open markets, individual liberty, and peace with their neighbors. Yet there are those who oppose America's role in the world, and who are willing to use violence against us and our friends. Our great power leaves these enemies with few conventional options for doing us harm. One such option is to take advantage of our freedom and openness by secretly inserting terrorists into our country to attack

(continued)

our homeland. Homeland security seeks to deny this avenue of attack to our enemies and thus to provide a secure foundation for America's ongoing global engagement. Thus the *National Security Strategy of the United States* and The *National Strategy for Homeland Security* work as mutually supporting documents, providing guidance to the executive branch departments and agencies.

There are also a number of other, more specific strategies maintained by the United States that are subsumed within the twin concepts of national security and homeland security. The *National Strategy for Combating Terrorism* will define the U.S. war plan against international terrorism. The *National Strategy to Combat Weapons of Mass Destruction* coordinates America's many efforts to deny terrorists and states the materials, technology, and expertise to make and deliver weapons of mass destruction. The *National Strategy to Secure Cyberspace* will describe our initiatives to secure our information systems against deliberate, malicious destruction. The *National Money Laundering Strategy* aims to undercut the illegal flows of money that support terrorism and international criminal activity. The *National Defense Strategy* sets priorities for our most powerful national security instrument. The *National Drug Control Strategy* lays out a comprehensive U.S. effort to combat drug smuggling and consumption. All these documents fit into the framework established by the *National Security Strategy of the United States* and *National Strategy for Homeland Security,* which together take precedence over all other national strategies, programs, and plans.

Source: Office of Homeland Security. (2002). *National Strategy for Homeland Security.* Washington, D.C.: Office of Homeland Security, White House.

DEVELOPING A NATIONAL HOMELAND SECURITY STRATEGY FOR POLICE

Philip McVey decisively pointed out that the primary dilemma facing law enforcement professionals is in regard to the development of a homeland security strategy for their police.[4] He stated that police executives could either do nothing and wait for direction from outside their agencies or they could do something that might possibly be wrong. Neither of these are attractive options for the development of a homeland security strategy or for the police to begin actively playing a role in homeland security. McVey articulated a third alternative and that is to start "with the basic realization that any proposal forthcoming from federal agencies will likely be only strategically general" and that ultimately, "each jurisdiction will have to interpret such a proposal according to the area's unique risk factors and operational capabilities."[5] He then argued that "given this, each agency must lay the necessary groundwork in preparation for those proposals by generating and incorporating into its individual administrative paradigm a basic understanding of the terrorist risks it faces and its own incident management capability."[6] In other words, he argued that each agency will ultimately have to establish its own strategic plan that will have to be continually updated and incorporate other strategies from other sources, whether the federal strategy, a state strategy, or a regional strategy, as well as other strategic plans where the police play an integral role.

As any strategy will generally draw from more than one source, this is also the case for a homeland security strategy. The most defined strategy to date comes from what was created by the Office of Homeland Security under then-director Tom Ridge, the *National Strategy for Homeland Security.*[7] The document was the product of eight months of consultation with a cross section of interested people who contributed to the formation of this national policy.

The opening preface by President Bush makes the argument that "this is a national strategy, not a federal strategy."[8] The document sets out the overall strategy for the entire nation as it relates to homeland security. It attempts to answer four basic questions: (1) What is homeland security and what missions does it entail? (2) What do we seek to accomplish, and what are the most important goals of homeland security? (3) What is the federal executive branch doing now to accomplish these goals and what should do in the future? and (4) What should nonfederal governments, the private sector, and citizens do to help secure the homeland?[9]

The document does address the role of state and local police in homeland security, but it is a much broader document attempting to focus on the broad array of homeland security issues facing America. Thus, the majority of the *National Strategy* is oriented toward the federal government and the various agencies responsible for homeland security. It is, however, the best place to start for developing an overall strategy for state and local law enforcement.

The second source for developing a strategy for Homeland Security comes from the joint efforts of the International City/County Management Association (ICMA) and the International Association of Chiefs of Police (IACP). Both of these associations have pulled together a number of articles that have looked at "best practices" for homeland security, especially as it relates to local police.[10] In addition, the IACP issued their own white paper, resulting from a project that brought together law enforcement leaders from across the country, titled *From Hometown Security to Homeland Security.*[11] The project was launched in November of 2004, and on May 17th of the next year, the IACP issued their white paper with a press release. The white paper was very critical of the *National Strategy for Homeland Security,* charging that the "national strategy" released in 2002 was developed by federal departments and agencies and that despite the assertions of Bush in the preface of the document, it was in fact a federal strategy, not a national strategy. The IACP argued that all levels of government, including local, tribal, state, and federal, should have participated in the development of the strategy to truly make it a *national* strategy.[12] A federally developed homeland security strategy, according to the IACP, that does not reflect the advice, expertise, or consent of public safety organizations at levels of government other than federal could be viewed as overly instructive and cumbersome and possibly impractical. The IACP advocated solving the problem by adopting a national, rather than a federal, approach to future homeland security planning and strategy development.[13]

The third document that is focused directly on policing's needs for a homeland security strategy comes from the Police Executive Research Forum and the Office of Community Oriented Policing Services document *Protecting Your Community From Terrorism: Strategies for Local Law Enforcement.*[14] This document was based on the findings of an executive session that was held in November of 2002, which included federal, state, and local law enforcement leaders. Through several days of discussion, these police executives provided their insight into possible strategies for fighting terrorism on the home front. Specifically they discussed the local–federal partnership, federal and local law enforcement needs, information sharing among agencies, and models of successful partnerships, and they developed a strategy for improving partnerships for the purpose of homeland security. A white paper was then published in 2003 detailing the strategic priorities for local law enforcement.

Finally, longtime policing scholar William V. Pelfrey has offered a "cycle of preparedness" for Homeland Security to establish a framework for preparing for terrorist attacks.[15] His article has adopted a broader framework that represents a solid strategy for local law enforcement to implement Homeland Security at the operational and tactical level.

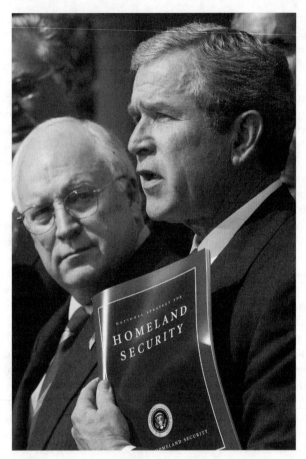

President Bush and Vice President Cheney at the
University of the National Strategy for Homeland Security.
(*Source: AP Wide World Photos*)

National Strategy for Homeland Security

The *National Strategy for Homeland Security* defines "homeland security" as "a concerted national effort to prevent terrorist attacks within the United States, reduce America's vulnerability to terrorism, and minimize the damage and recover from attacks that do occur."[16] The *Strategy* makes the statement that the federal government does play a critical role in homeland security, but the nature of American society and its governance demands a partnership among all levels of governments, as well as with the private sector and American citizens. Therefore, the *Strategy*, it is again argued, is a national strategy, not a federal one.

As the focus of the *Strategy* is aimed at terrorism in the United States, it addresses one of the more difficult problems in developing any strategy or policy aimed at terrorism, which is defining what terrorism means in the first place. The *Strategy* itself talks about "characterizing" terrorism as "any premeditated, unlawful act dangerous to human life or public welfare that is intended to intimidate or coerce civilian populations or governments."[17] Although this characterization may be helpful, what is more useful is deriving a definition that can be used by police, but to do this, one must first arrive at a fuller understanding of what is meant by the use of the term *terrorism.*

According to a leading scholar in the area of terrorism, White has explained that the term *terrorism,* although often defined, has no unified consensus regarding what constitutes terrorism.[18] White explained that the term itself is a very political term and is used to label certain groups as politically and socially unacceptable, thus allowing for governments to increase their legitimacy when using this label against certain groups, which becomes even more complicated when a legitimately recognized government uses terror as a means of ruling.[19] This can become even more problematic when we attempt to reach a consensus to determine what is meant by the threat of terrorism, how to legislate against terrorism, and more importantly, for the police, how to enforce the laws against terrorism. This ambiguity creates a problem for law enforcement in that it becomes difficult to separate common crimes from political crimes, it does not allow for comparison of the terrorist acts, and it makes it difficult to plan against such terrorist acts.[20] But, as McVey has explained, "It is crucial that a common definition of terrorism be developed within and between [law enforcement] agencies" and the definition "must be universally valid and must reliably serve the interests of local law enforcement jurisdictions by being both flexible and relevant."[21]

Despite the fact that there is little consensus regarding a unified definition of terrorism, that has not stopped many individuals from proposing a variety of definitions. One scholar, Jenkins, has explained terrorism as the use or threatened use of force designed to bring about political change.[22] Another scholar, Laqueur, has explained terrorism to be the use of illegitimate force to achieve a political objective by the targeting of innocent people.[23] Still another scholar has defined it as political violence in or against true democracies.[24] Although these and other scholarly definitions are beneficial, their focus is too often on the political and social aspects and not on the criminal aspects, which are of most concern to local law enforcement.

To derive a more acceptable definition for law enforcement, one can look to the writings of those in the law enforcement field. One such person, Friendlander, has defined terrorism as the use of force, violence, or threats thereof to attain political goals through fear, intimidation, or coercion.[25] Another source, the National Advisory Commission on Criminal Justice Standards and Goals, explains terrorism as violent, criminal behavior designed primarily to generate fear in the community, or a substantial segment of it, for political purposes.[26] Although both of these definitions draw on specific concerns for the police, their drawback is that they do not have the legal standing to serve as definitive definitions for the purposes of law enforcement.

The best place to turn for a useful definition of terrorism, as it relates to law enforcement, is the one currently used by the Federal Bureau of Investigation (FBI). The FBI's definition of terrorism is "the unlawful use of force and violence against persons or property to intimidate or coerce a government, the civilian population or any segment thereof, in furtherance of political or social objectives."[27] The benefit to this definition is the fact that it is already defined in the *Code of Federal Regulations* and is used by the FBI as the operational definition of terrorism. Further, the definition addresses the law enforcement aspect of terrorism largely because the FBI considers terrorists to be criminals and thus sees terrorism as a crime. As Dyson has explained, by referencing the "unlawful" use of force, it allows terrorism to be directly associated with criminal activity allowing for this type of illegal behavior to fall under the purview of the FBI.[28] And because the FBI is going to serve as the primary source of intergovernmental relations between local and federal law enforcement regarding issues of terrorism, if local law enforcement adopts the same definition, it resolves a number of definitional and operational problems.

The FBI also further elaborates on the definition of terrorism by dividing terrorism into two categories: domestic and international. The FBI, by way of the U.S. Code, defines domestic terrorism as "activities that involve acts dangerous to human life that are a violation of the criminal laws of the United States or of any state; appear to be intended to intimidate or coerce a civilian population; to influence the policy of a government by mass destruction, assassination, or kidnapping; and occur primarily within the territorial jurisdiction of the United States.[29] And international terrorism is defined by the FBI as "violent acts or acts dangerous to human life that are a violation of the criminal laws of the United States or any state, or that would be a criminal violation if committed within the jurisdiction of the United States or any state. These acts appear to be intended to intimidate or coerce a civilian population; influence the policy of a government by intimidation or coercion; or affect the conduct of a government by mass destruction, assassination or kidnapping and occur primarily outside the territorial jurisdiction of the United States or transcend national boundaries in terms of the means by which they are accomplished, the persons they appear intended to intimidate or coerce, or the locale in which their perpetrators operate or seek asylum."[30]

The FBI's definition of terrorism and the two categories of domestic and international terrorism provide a readily available and working definition of terrorism. Adopting them for local law enforcement purposes will assist not only in the law enforcement intergovernmental relations, but will also assist in law enforcement's understanding of the threat of terrorism. It will also assist in the development of a more unified national strategy for policing in an era of homeland security.

The *National Strategy* then proceeds to describe prevention as the first priority for homeland security. The first strategic goal of homeland security is to deter all potential attacks by detecting them before they strike, deny them from entering the United States and obtaining the instruments of terror, and take "decisive action" to eliminate the threat they pose. The second strategic goal is to reduce America's vulnerability to terrorism. This goal acknowledges the open and free society that we have in America makes this task difficult, and when we shore up one particular area against terrorism, such as airport security, terrorists can adapt and exploit another area of weakness, such as trains and subway transportation. Therefore, as the *National Strategy* articulates, "we must constantly balance the benefits of mitigating this risk against both the economic costs and infringements on individual liberty that this mitigation entails."[31] Finally, the third strategic objective for homeland security is to minimize the damage and recover from attacks that do occur. This strategic objective faces the reality that it is not a matter of *if* but *when* future attacks will occur in the United States and establishes the objective of preparedness for such attacks as one of the primary strategic goals.

Along with these three overarching objectives, the *National Strategy* establishes a number of principles necessary to achieve these objectives. First, it requires responsibility and accountability of the various agencies responsible for protecting the homeland. Although the emphasis is largely on the Department of Homeland Security (DHS), there is the recognition that all the bureaucratic agencies taking part in the security of the nation will have to act responsibly and be held accountable for their actions. Second, it is intent on mobilizing our entire society, not just federal agencies, but federal, state, and local governments, as well as the private sector. Third, it demands that we manage risk and allocate resources judiciously.

BOX 11-2

THE FEDERAL BUREAU OF INVESTIGATION'S DEFINITION OF TERRORISM

...the unlawful use of force and violence against persons or property to intimidate or coerce a government, the civilian population or any segment thereof, in furtherance of political or social objectives.

Source: Federal Bureau of Investigation (2002). *Terrorism in the United States: 2000/2001.* Washington, D.C.: U.S. Government Printing Office. The definition is derived from [18 U.S.C. § 2331(1).

This principle is focused on the use of risk assessment to prioritize America's vulnerabilities and thus allocate more funding to those areas that face the greatest risk. The fourth principle is to seek opportunity from adversity. This principle is focused on dual usage of terrorism preparedness by finding multiple uses for the methods and resources employed to fight terrorism. The fifth principle is that preparedness should be measured to ensure that agencies are achieving the proper level of performance and that these efforts, the sixth principle, should be sustained over the long term. Finally, the seventh and last principle is that efforts should be made to constrain government spending. These seven principles are intended to guide the implementation of the *National Strategy's* three primary objectives to ensure that it is done in a proper fashion.

Threat and Vulnerability

The *National Strategy* then turns to the need to understand the threat America faces and its vulnerabilities. They succinctly state that one fact dominates all homeland security threat assessments, and that is "terrorists are strategic actors."[32] Terrorists choose their targets based on weaknesses and vulnerabilities they observe, and they then move to exploit those weaknesses. Unlike criminals who tend to maintain a particular modus operandi where past behavior predicts future behavior, terrorists tend to learn and adapt to the strategic environment, making them far more difficult to protect against. In the 9/11 attack, terrorists exploited America's vulnerability of airline security. In the wake of the attacks, America has bolstered airport security by federalizing the baggage screeners, enhancing rules and regulations, and controlling access points throughout the airport process. Although this has been very important to protecting against future and similar airline attacks, terrorists recognize that this sector has been target-hardened and thus will select more vulnerable targets for future attacks. Because America is such a free and open society with a very large, diverse, and mobile citizenry, other vulnerabilities exhibit themselves. These include schools, sporting arenas, concerts, office buildings, high-rise residences, and various places of worship. Protecting America's homeland becomes very difficult when one recognizes that the very thing that makes America great also exposes it to potential attacks.

The *National Strategy* highlights this very thought when it reviews five key elements of American life: democracy, liberties, security, economy, and culture. American democracy promotes a very open society that is based on the rule of law. Terrorists tend to operate outside the rules of law and can exploit America's form of democracy. American liberties are the safeguards of individuals against an oppressive government, but terrorists can use these rights to help achieve their own ends. It also raises the possibility that to prevent terrorism in the United States, we may have to trade some of our liberties for more security, thus sacrificing some of what makes America great. The *National Strategy* does recognize this dilemma, for it addresses the issue of security, a primary reason for government to exist in the first place, and it acknowledges that although the federal government has tried to promote security in a global setting, "we have relied primarily on law enforcement and the justice system to provide for domestic peace and order." In addition, two other things that have made America so great are its free market economy and its diverse culture, but terrorism threatens both of these by its intent on damaging our economy and dividing our diverse nation. In a larger sense, these are the threats that terrorism poses to America.

In a more direct sense, terrorism poses a number of threats to America based on the means of attack available. Perhaps the most common threat cited by the news media and government is the threat of weapons of mass destruction, for which the acronym WMD has become part of America's vocabulary. It is true that nuclear, radiological, chemical, and biological weapons do pose a theat. The breakup of the Soviet Union and the proliferation of nuclear capabilities in such countries as Iran and North Korea have increased the availability of radiological materials that could be used in a "dirty bomb" (the use of radiological material in a conventional bomb). In addition, chemical attacks are real threats, for the attack in 1995 in the Tokyo subway has proven how threatening such an attack can be. Moreover, biological attacks can be just as threatening, whether to humans directly or by way of attacking our food sources such as farm produce or livestock. The anthrax attacks immediately following 9/11 demonstrate not only the dangers of such an attack, but they also highlight the fear that these weapons can generate.

Although WMD do pose a serious threat, so do attacks by conventional means. Attacks through car and truck bombs, kidnapping and hostage-taking, and suicide bombings all remain a threat in the United States. The 2005 bombings in the England subway stations highlight the amount of damage and fear such conventional means could have in America. In addition, terrorists have also found ways to exploit technology, in particular the Internet and cell phone communications, to further their attacks. Attacks on the computer systems themselves, whether through worms, viruses, or other means, can have a crippling effect on America's reliance on technology. And finally, it is recognized that terrorists tend to be innovators and may devise new methods of attack that haven't been fully recognized as viable options or truly possible methods of attack. Although some intelligence reports suggested planes could be hijacked and turned into missiles and Tom Clancy integrated this concept into one of his novels, the reality is that few people truly recognized this as a viable threat to America until it happened.

The *National Strategy* also states that the primary threat to America regarding terrorism was Al-Qaeda. The fact that Osama bin Laden and many of his immediate followers are still alive and operating, as well as the threat of Al-Qaeda cells operating on their own in various countries, still poses the greatest threat to America. There are, however, other terrorist groups sympathetic to Al-Qaeda, other international terrorist groups, and even individuals within the United States (as evidenced by the 1995 bombing of the Murrah Federal Building in Oklahoma City) that also pose a threat to America and should be considered in any homeland security strategy.

Organizing for a Secure Homeland

The *National Strategy* recognizes that America has over 87,000 different jurisdictions, consists of over 280 million people, and has a very large private sector ranging from international corporations down to family-run stores. In addition, it is acknowledged that "state, county, municipal, and local governments fund and operate the emergency services that would respond in the event of a terrorist attack,"[33] just as they did on September 11th. How best then to organize for homeland security has been a key concern in developing a strategy for homeland security. Although the *National Strategy* recognizes the various governments, it primarily deals with the federal executive branch and its organization for homeland security. As detailed in the previous chapter, the White House created the Office of Homeland Security and ultimately, through Congressional legislation, the DHS. The *Strategy* also looks to the role that the Department of Defense has taken in regard to homeland security and the creation of Northern Command to oversee military operations in the United States. And it looks to other federal departments and agencies outside the DHS that play a key role, such as the Justice Department, the Federal Bureau of Investigation, and the Central Intelligence Agency. It then discusses intergovernmental coordination and the request by the president that every state create a single Homeland Security Task Force (HSTF) to coordinate homeland security practices between the federal and local governments. It is very clear that under this strategic plan, the national government sees its role as leading on homeland security and encouraging state and local governments to cooperate.

Intelligence and Warning

The *National Strategy* states that intelligence and information analysis is critical to the mission of securing the homeland and that it is not a separate function, but an integral part of the overall strategy. It establishes a framework of four interrelated categories of intelligence and information and then sets out three categories of actions that can follow from intelligence analysis, thus creating "actionable intelligence." The first category of analysis is tactical threat analysis. According to the *National Strategy,* actionable intelligence is essential for preventing acts of terrorism. The timely and thorough analysis and dissemination of information about terrorists and their current and potential activities allow the government to take immediate and near-term action to disrupt and prevent terrorist acts. It also provides a useful warning to specific targets, security and public safety professionals, or the general population.

The second category is strategic analysis of the enemy. Intelligence agencies, it is argued, must have a deep understanding of the organizations that may conduct terrorist attacks against the United States. Knowing the identities, financial and political sources of support, motivation, goals, current and future capabilities, and vulnerabilities of these organizations assist in preventing and preempting future attacks. Intelligence agencies can support the long-term strategies to defeat terrorism by understanding the roots of terrorism overseas and the intentions and capabilities of foreign governments to disrupt terrorist groups in their territories and to assist the United States.

The third category is vulnerability assessment. These assessments are an integral part of the intelligence cycle for homeland security. They allow planners to project the consequences of possible terrorist attacks against specific facilities or different sectors of the economy or government. These projections allow authorities to strengthen defenses against different threats. Such assessments are informed by the use of tools such as computer modeling and analysis.

The fourth category is threat-vulnerability integration. Mapping terrorist threats and capabilities—both current and future—against specific facility and sectoral vulnerabilities will allow authorities to determine which organization poses the greatest threats and which facilities and sectors are most at risk. It will also allow planners to develop thresholds for preemptive or protective action.

The three types of action that can result from the four categories of intelligence analysis listed are tactical prevention, warning and protection, and strategic response. Tactical prevention attempts to use intelligence analysis when it uncovers evidence of terrorist planning by moving to preempt potential attacks. Warning and protective action draws on general knowledge of a possible attack, without the specifics to be able to employ tactical prevention. This allows for security to be upgraded in any affected sector and encourages citizens to be on a higher state of awareness. Finally, strategic response is aimed at refining the strategies used based on a continual update of intelligence information and analysis. This is to prepare for both immediate and long-term strategic planning.

To achieve these strategic goals, the *National Strategy* is highly focused on the national government's assets. It looks to enhancing the analytic capabilities of the FBI, building new capabilities within the DHS, implementing the Homeland Security advisory system, using dual-use analysis to prevent attacks, and using "red team" techniques, which utilizes intelligent knowledge of the potential threats to war game possible actions by the terrorists and to determine how the government would respond.

Border and Transportation Security

The *National Strategy* next focuses on several broad strategic areas that support the primary goals of homeland security, the first being border and transportation security. The *Strategy* recognizes that "virtually every community in America is connected to the global transportation network by the seaports, airports, highways, pipelines, railroads, and waterways that move people and goods into, within, and out of the Nation,"[34] hence border and transportation security are key concerns for any homeland security strategy. The initiatives necessary to ensure the protection of this network consist of the call for ensuring accountability in border and transportation security, which the *National Strategy* places in the hands of the newly formed DHS. The document also argues for the creation of "smart borders," a border management system that uses modern technology to track people and goods coming into the country and where those people and goods go after entry. Once again, the primary responsibility for the deployment of smart borders in the document lies with the DHS. There is some mention that this department would enter into law enforcement databases the names of high-risk aliens who remain in the United States longer than authorized and, when warranted, deport illegal aliens, but this is inherently a top-down approach.

The discussion of border and transportation security also focuses on increasing security of international shipping containers, implementing the Aviation and Transportation Security Act of 2001, recapitalizing the U.S. Coast Guard to enhance its mission of border security, and to reform immigration services. Again, all these are primarily federal government initiatives that, although having direct bearing on local law enforcement, do not necessarily present a particular role for the police.

Domestic Counterterrorism

If there is a section of the *National Strategy for Homeland Security* that speaks best to the role of local law enforcement, it is assuredly the police role in domestic counter-terrorism. The section opens by explaining that "the attacks of September 11 and the catastrophic loss of life and property that resulted have redefined the mission of fed-eral, state and local law enforcement authorities" and that "while law enforcement agencies will continue to investigate and prosecute criminal activity, they should now assign priority to preventing and interdicting terrorist activity within the United States."[35] The *Strategy* further explains that effectively reorienting law enforcement organizations to focus on counterterrorism objectives requires decisive action in a number of areas and that "much work remains to be done before law enforcement agencies can collectively pursue the counterterrorism mission with maximum effect."[36] The document discusses such things as information sharing and coordination of oper-ational activities at all levels and recognizes that "the federal government needs to do a better job of utilizing the distinct capabilities of state and local law enforcement to prevent terrorism by giving them access, where appropriate, to the information in [the] federal databases, and by utilizing state and local information at the federal level."[37] The document acknowledges the success of some FBI-led Joint Terrorism Task Forces before discussing the major initiatives it sees as implementing the strategy of domestic counterterrorism.

The first major initiative is the call for an expansion and improvement of FBI-led Task Forces. It then discusses the facilitation of apprehending potential terrorists by expanding the FBI's National Crime Information Center (NCIC) databases to address terrorism, by having the FBI create a consolidated terrorism watch list, and for the FBI to obtain biographical data on suspected terrorists from foreign law enforcement agen-cies and to enter any fingerprint data into the FBI's Integrated Automated Fingerprint Identification System.

The second major initiative is to continue ongoing investigations and prosecutions of terrorists. Here the document acknowledges the important role that state and local law enforcement play in investigating such crimes as selling false driver's licenses, certificates for transporting hazardous material, and both passports and visas that may be used to further terrorist goals. It also states that local law enforcement plays an important role in reporting unusual behavior and any security anomalies. Although it recognizes the im-portance of state and local law enforcement in this section, it does not necessarily state a specific role for it to play in domestic counterterrorism beyond what policing already does as a matter of course.

The section on domestic counterterrorism also mandates the complete restructuring of the FBI to emphasize preventing terrorist attacks, for the federal agencies to target and attack terrorist financing, and for the Department of Justice to track foreign terror-ists and help bring them to justice. All these, again, are federal government–related en-deavors without any specification of a role for state and local governments.

BOX 11-3

POLICING FOR HOMELAND SECURITY: THE MIAMI-DADE POLICE DEPARTMENT

Phillip Davis, Sam Houston State University

Miami-Dade County, anchored by its seaport and airport, remains the North American gateway to Latin America and the Caribbean. The county is represented by over 2 million residents and continues to stand as the meeting ground for numerous multinational businesses and banks.

Because of these unique qualities, Miami remains a high-risk threat area of terrorism. In addition to producing mass casualties, an attack on the county can damage critical infrastructure, disrupt essential services, and cause severe nationwide economic loss. Miami-Dade County's Comprehensive Emergency Management Plan encompasses an all hazards approach to preparedness and protection of our community. As part of the approach, the county has developed a Domestic Preparedness Strategy (DPS) built on the National Strategy for Homeland Security and the State of Florida's Domestic Security Strategy. The DPS assesses the county's local ability to meet state and federal identified homeland security objectives. Miami-Dade County's funding of homeland security is allocated strategically to achieve the following goals:

> **Goal 1: Preparedness**—achieve a readiness posture that reduces the impact of terrorism
>
> **Goal 2: Response**—meet the community's terrorism response needs
>
> **Goal 3: Recovery**—utilize resources to facilitate the community's recovery from terrorism disasters
>
> **Goal 4: Mitigation**—reduce the community's vulnerabilities to terrorism hazards; prevent the occurrence of avoidable incidents

The county, with cooperation from its municipalities, has produced an extensive list of projects that are based on the assessment of threats and vulnerabilities. To date, Miami-Dade County has approximately $280 million in homeland security needs, while its municipalities have approximately $9 million in homeland security needs. Less than 12 percent, or $80 million, of all county funding applied for from state and federal governments over the past three years has been received.

The county's progress in utilizing funds over the past year includes training first responders, educating the community on terrorism, and obtaining much needed disaster response equipment. Homeland security priorities for the 2004–2005 fiscal year include funding projects such as: securing the Port (Seaport Department, $7 million) and guarding against the threat of terrorism for the county's drinking water (Water & Sewer Department, $85 million).

Source: Miami-Dade County Homeland Security Briefing Book (2004–2005). Retrieved from *http://www.miamidade.gov/Homeland/library/Homeland%20Security%20Briefing%20Book. pdf*

Protecting Critical Infrastructure and Key Assets

The *National Strategy* next emphasizes the need to protect critical infrastructure in America and to safeguard key assets. It details the numerous sectors that are vulnerable to attacks, including agriculture, food, water, public health, emergency services, government, defense industrial base, information and telecommunications, energy, transportation, banking and finance, the chemical industry, and postal and shipping. It then recognizes that government has only a limited amount of resources, and it faces the quandary of determining what must be protected. Once again, the *National Strategy* acknowledges the importance of state and local governments, as well as the private sector, to achieve this strategic goal.

The major initiatives for protecting the critical infrastructure in America are to unify these efforts under the DHS with the creation of a directorate aimed at this particular goal (see Chapter 2). It recommends that the department build a complete and accurate assessment of America's critical infrastructure and to develop a national infrastructure protection plan. It is recognized that to achieve these extremely complex goals, it will have to enable effective partnerships with state and local governments and the private sector. The emphasis here is actually with all levels of government cooperating with the private sector, as the *Strategy* states that the private sector controls 85 percent of America's infrastructure, making this task even more difficult. The primary responsibility for security and addressing public safety risks is placed on the private sector's shoulders, but it is recognized that often government at all levels may have the technical expertise that the private sector lacks. The key, the *Strategy* argues, is to enable, not inhibit, the private sector's ability to carry out its protection responsibilities. The *Strategy*, however, looks to the DHS as offering a single contact and coordinating point for coordinating infrastructure protection and developing a centralized plan.

This section also encourages that cyberspace be secured, that the best analytic and modeling tools be used to develop protective solutions, all of which will cost enormous amounts of money that only the federal government may be able to incur. And it encourages agencies to protect against "inside threats," attacks from its own personnel, and to partner with the international community to protect against "outside threats."

Defending Against Catastrophic Threats

The section of the *National Strategy* that deals with defending against catastrophic threats is primarily focused on the threat of WMD. Overall this section emphasizes the role of the federal government by focusing on the DHS's role in securing against such threats, as well as the role of the Departments of State, Energy, and Defense. The major initiatives under this section include preventing terrorist use of nuclear weapons through better sensors and procedures; detecting chemical and biological materials and attacks; improving chemical sensors and decontamination techniques; developing broad spectrum vaccines, antimicrobials, and antidotes; to harness the scientific knowledge and tools to counter terrorism; and to implement the Select Agent Program, which is the registration of laboratories that deal with hazardous materials.

There is little regarding state and local government in this section of the *National Strategy*, but the one place where state and local governments are invoked raises a very complicated issue for policing. The section falls under the detecting chemical and biological materials and attacks discussion and explains, "The ability to quickly recognize and report biological and chemical attacks will minimize casualties and enable first responders to treat the injured effectively." It succinctly states that "local emergency personnel and health providers must first be able to diagnose symptoms."[38] As police officers are always going to be first responders to any type of terrorist attack, their ability to recognize the type of attack and report it will be critical to launching a quick response. Perhaps more importantly, the faster a police officer can recognize an attack and identify it as such, the faster they will be able to protect themselves and other first responders, thus launching a more successful response.

Emergency Preparedness and Response

The second area that has clear implications for state and local law enforcement falls in the *National Strategy's* objective of emergency preparedness and response. Like the section on domestic counterterrorism, there is a distinct acknowledgment to the role that local police will play in a terrorist attack. It states that "America's first line of defense in the aftermath of any terrorist attack is its first responder community—police officers, firefighters, emergency medical providers, public works personnel, and emergency management officials."[39] It recognizes the three million first responders in the United States that serve at the state and local level, including those serving in specially trained positions, such as hazardous materials teams, search-and-rescue units, bomb squads, and special weapons and tactics units. Despite this acknowledgment, it points to the importance of the DHS and the Federal Emergency Management Administration (FEMA) and the role they play in responding to major emergencies.

The major initiatives outlined in this section include the goal of integrating separate federal response plans into a single all-discipline incident management plan and creating a national incident management system. Both of these would be centralized under the DHS. The *Strategy* does recognize that the Incident Management System is already widely spread throughout state and local governments, hence the federal government through the DHS sees its role as one of ensuring federal grants are in place to continue the promotion of this system to state and local governments. It also encourages all state and local governments to "regularly update their own homeland security plans, based on their existing emergency operation plans, to provide guidance for the integration of their response assets in the event of an attack."[40] Moreover, it urges agencies to work with their neighbors to establish and sign mutual aid agreements to facilitate cooperation among agencies during an actual emergency.

Another major initiative that falls under the purview of local law enforcement is the call to improve tactical counterterrorist capabilities. According to the *National Strategy:*

> With advance warning, we have various federal, state, and local response assets that can intercede and prevent terrorists from carrying out attacks. These include law enforcement, emergency response, and military teams. In the most dangerous of incidents, particularly when terrorists have chemical, biological, radiological, or nuclear weapons in their possession, it is crucial that the individuals who preempt the terrorists do so flawlessly, no matter if they are part of the local SWAT team or the FBI's Hostage Rescue

Team. It is crucial that these individuals be prepared and able to work effectively with each other and with other specialized response personnel. Finally, these teams and other emergency response assets must plan and train for the consequences of failed tactical operations.[41]

The section on emergency preparedness and response also encourages seamless communications among all responders to ensure that the response does not break down due to disparate communication systems. Again, it encourages the DHS to work with state and local governments to achieve this particular goal. In addition, it also sets the goals of preparing health-care providers for catastrophic terrorism, augmenting America's pharmaceutical and vaccine stockpiles, and preparing for chemical, biological, radiological, and nuclear decontamination as goals under preparedness. Moreover, it addresses plans for military support to civil authorities, building the citizen corps to assist in terrorism-related responses, and building a national training and evaluation system. However, all these goals are DHS led, working with other federal agencies and state and local constituents.

Law

The *National Strategy* cites the USA PATRIOT Act as being an important step in ensuring that the nation is prepared to prosecute terrorism under the law, but encourages a detailed review of the legal aspects of terrorism to ensure the proper laws are in place to allow for terrorist-related investigations and prosecutions. This is the one section in the *National Strategy* that identifies different major initiatives for federal and state governments. The major initiatives listed under the federal government consist of, again, ensuring the critical infrastructure for information sharing among federal agencies exists and that this information and intelligence can be properly shared with law enforcement agencies at the state and local level. It also sets the goals of expanding existing extradition authorities, reviewing authority for military assistance in domestic security, and giving the president the ability to reorganize the administration to better organize for homeland security (this authority lapsed in 1984 and has not been renewed).

The major initiatives for the states include coordinating suggested minimum standards for state driver's licenses, enhancing market capacity for terrorism insurance, training for prevention of cyberattacks, suppressing money laundering, ensuring continuity of the judiciary, and reviewing quarantine authority. In nearly all of these "state" initiatives, there is somewhat of a suggestion that federal standards be created. In terms of driver's license "minimum standards," there is a discussion that the "federal government, in consultation with state government agencies and non-governmental organizations, should support state-led efforts to develop suggested minimum standards," leading one to the conclusion that this is more a federal initiative. The ability to enhance market capacity for terrorism insurance, much like flood insurance, is going to need federal support; training for cyberattacks lists the FBI as taking the lead; and suppressing money laundering focuses on the USA PATRIOT Act, a federal law. Finally, most recently, the Bush administration has called for a military role in the event of an outbreak of the pandemic influenza in the United States.[42] Despite the categorization of "state" initiatives, it would appear these are more federal initiatives that require some coordination with current state law.

Science and Technology

The *National Strategy* also emphasizes the importance of science and technology for securing the homeland and is very realistic in its understanding that much of the development in these two areas lies in the private sector. Although the federal government can be involved in terms of funding and developing federal guidelines and standards, most of the development will occur in the private sector. Because the ability of the federal government to marshal resources is far greater than state and local governments, there is little in the way of a direct role for state and local governments under this part of the *National Strategy*.

The major initiatives for the development of science and technology for homeland security included the development of chemical, biological, radiological, and nuclear countermeasures; developing systems for detecting hostile intent; and applying biometric technology to identification devices. It also encourages improving the technical capabilities of first responders, coordinating research and development of the homeland security apparatus, and establishing a national laboratory for homeland security. There is also a call for soliciting independent and private analysis for science and technology research, essentially grants for private-sector development. The *Strategy* also cites the establishment of some mechanism for producing prototype technologies, conducting demonstrations and pilot deployments of these prototypes, and ensuring the system allows for the creation of high-risk, high-payoff homeland security research. These latter goals are focused on the promotion of innovation within the homeland security concept. Finally, the document calls for the DHS to establish the standards for all homeland security technology, once again calling for the DHS to take the lead role.

Information Sharing and Systems

It became readily clear in the aftermath of the terrorists attacks on September 11th that not only did agencies within the federal government not share information horizontally, but there was also a large weakness in sharing information vertically, among federal, state, and local governments. In fact, even before September 11th, there was evidence of a lack of interoperability between agencies in other terrorist attacks such as the 1993 World Trade Center bombing, the 1995 Oklahoma City bombing, and the 1999 Columbine school shootings. The latter truly highlighted the problem when the response to the Columbine shootings consisted of 23 local and county law enforcement agencies, 2 state and 3 federal law enforcement agencies, 6 local fire departments, and 7 local emergency medical services, most of which had incompatible communication procedures and equipment. Clearly any strategic plan for homeland security must address these issues, and it is imperative that any strategy for policing for homeland security must work toward enhancing communication.

The *National Strategy* recognizes that any expansion of information systems engages in a delicate balance of providing information that is both proper and legal with that of providing not only illegal and improper information, but wrong information as well. Therefore, the *National Strategy* invokes five principles to guide any strategic expansion of information systems for homeland security purposes. The first is to balance homeland security concerns with citizens' right to privacy. The second is to view the homeland security community, consisting of federal, state, and local governments, as one entity. Third, they state that information should be captured at the source, then used many times to support multiple requirements, rather than compartmentalizing information at the source and not sharing it with others. The fourth principle is to create databases of record that can serve as trusted sources of information. And the final principle is that homeland security information should provide a dynamic tool for those attempting to prevent or counter terrorism in the homeland.

The major initiatives for information sharing and systems consist of improving the sharing of information across the federal government and then moving to share information across state and local governments, as well as with private industry and citizens when warranted. In regard to sharing information with state and local governments, specifically the police, the document states that the FBI and other federal agencies are augmenting the information available in their crime and terrorism databases such as the National Crime Information Center and the National Law Enforcement Telecommunication systems. They also request that state and local governments use a secure intranet to increase the flow of classified federal information to state and local agencies. And it states that the federal government should make an effort to remove classified information from some documents so that the information can be distributed to state and local authorities. They explain that the "effort will help state and local law enforcement officials learn when individuals suspected of criminal activity are also under federal investigation and will enable federal officials to link their efforts to investigations being undertaken by the states."[43] Interestingly enough, the *Strategy* makes no mention of enhancing the number of state and local law enforcement officers that have security clearances so as to have access to classified material.

Other initiatives under the information sharing section included the call to adopt common "meta-data" standards for electronic information relevant to homeland security, to ensure reliable public health information, and to improve public safety emergency communication. Although the majority of public safety emergency communication is in the hands of the first responders, found at the local level, this section speaks more to the DHS and its initiatives. It does mention the creation of a tactical wireless infrastructure to support first responders at federal, state, and local law enforcement levels, but this is largely a technology pursuit that is being led by the DHS.

International Cooperation

As we are fighting a global war on terrorism, to protect the homeland there is the need for international cooperation not only in the investigation process, but in the political and economic realms as well. Here it is clear the federal government, not only through the DHS, but also in other federal agencies, must take the lead to support the mission of homeland security. To this end, some of the major initiatives are to combat fraudulent travel documents, increase the security of international shipping containers, help foreign nations fight terrorism, and improve cooperation in response to attacks.

The one initiative that has the most direct bearing on state and local law enforcement is the goal of intensifying international law enforcement cooperation. Although this is clearly a Department of Justice and FBI–led initiative, cooperation at this level can have a decisive impact on the state and local level, for information obtained from other countries could provide a key element to state and local law enforcement in preventing and/or preparing for a terrorist attack. Once again, the important element in regard to this type of information sharing between nations is that once received, it is shared with state and local police.

Costs of Homeland Security

Perhaps the most difficult aspect of adding the responsibility of homeland security to state and local police are the costs of this added role. This section does list some principles to guide the allocation of homeland security costs, such as balancing benefits and costs, federal regulations on state and local governments, and the issue of federalism and cost sharing. There are no major initiatives under this section. Rather, it speaks to the costs of securing the homeland and the costs of recovering from attacks. There is simply a recognition that the federal government will have to pay more, but so too will state and local governments and the private sector. For economic recovery it speaks to various federal plans that support state and local government in the event of a terrorist attack, but generally focuses on broader themes such as restoring the financial markets and national economic recovery.

IACP's Principles for a Nationally Coordinated Homeland Security Strategy

In May of 2005, the International Association of Chiefs of Police (IACP) issued a white paper titled *From Hometown Security to Homeland Security: IACP's Principles for a Locally Designed and Nationally Coordinated Homeland Security Strategy.*[44] In that document they explained that as the terrorist attacks of the 1990s occurred, the United States did not significantly alter its security strategy, but then again, neither did law enforcement agencies. They argued that although law enforcement most certainly learned from those incidents, they "did not dramatically adjust their policing philosophies."[45] In the wake of the September 11th attacks, they argued that all agencies, at the federal, state, and local levels, rapidly shifted their attention toward the issue of homeland security. Everyone realized that homeland security would be a national issue, one that had to be addressed not just by the federal government, but by all levels of government. President Bush's own opening statements in the *National Strategy for Homeland Security,* released in 2002, when he stated, "This is a national strategy, not a federal strategy,"[46] emphasized this fact.

The IACP, however, argued that despite the passage of the USA PATRIOT Act, the creation of the DHS, programs supporting state and local governments, as well as the talk of creating a "national" plan, the reality is the national plan is a top-down driven federal plan. The majority of the *National Strategy,* according to the IACP, has focused on the federal government's role in homeland security, particularly the DHS, and when it does invoke state and local agencies, it has the tendency of focusing on what the federal government wants state and local agencies to do. The IACP explained that despite statements to the contrary, the *National Strategy* was primarily created by the federal government with a federal government perspective. They thus argued that the *National Strategy* "was developed without sufficiently seeking or incorporating the advice, expertise, or consent of public safety organizations at the state, tribal, or local level."[47]

Recognizing the deficiencies within the *National Strategy*, the IACP called for the development of a new homeland security strategy, one that would incorporate the perspective of state, tribal, and local public safety agencies, as they will remain the first line in prevention and the first responders to any homeland security plan. Although the IACP is currently working on the development of the strategic goals and objectives critical to state, tribal, and local law enforcement, they did identify five key principles that should continue to guide the development and implementation of a truly national homeland security strategy.

The IACP identified the first principle as a play on the former Speaker of the House Tip O'Neil's statement that "all politics is local," by stating that "all terrorism is local." The IACP clearly states that regardless of the global and international connections, any actual terrorism attack is going to occur at the local level, and it will be local first responders that will deal with the attack. The IACP thus succinctly stated "that it is imperative that as homeland security proposals are designed, they must be developed in an environment that fully acknowledges and accepts the reality that local authorities, not federal, have the primary responsibility for preventing, responding to and recovering from terrorist attacks."[48]

The second principle that the IACP articulates is "that the prevention of terrorist attacks must be viewed as the paramount priority in any national, state, tribal, or local homeland security strategy."[49] The IACP argued that the majority of state and local initiatives by the federal government have centered on the police responding to and participating in the recovery of a terrorist attack. The strategic goal of prevention is largely left to the federal government and its assets, mostly through the Department of Homeland Security and Justice domestically and the Department of State and Defense globally, to thwart any future attacks. The IACP believes that law enforcement can and do play a critical role in preventing terrorism, just as they do in preventing crimes or traffic accidents. A truly national strategy would recognize this fact and integrate it into the goals and objectives focused on the prevention of future terrorist attacks.

The third principle, and reflective of the title of the document, is "hometown security is homeland security." The IACP explained that by way of law enforcement's duties to protect their communities against crime, it is a natural extension that they should also protect their communities against terrorism. If law enforcement agencies each protect their hometown, this will cover the majority of communities, leaving the federal government responsible for issues related to overseas, on federal property, and along our borders. The IACP argued, however, that the federal government has not enhanced resources for local law enforcement, but rather has cut them by way of reductions in the Local Law Enforcement Block Grant Program, the Edward Byrne Memorial Grants, and the Office of Community Oriented Policing Services. The IACP believes this is a move in the wrong direction, and "if our homeland security efforts are to have any chance of succeeding, it is absolutely vital for Congress and the administration to make the necessary resources available that will allow law enforcement agencies to mount effective anticrime programs, which will also serve as effective antiterrorism programs."[50]

The fourth principle the IACP puts forth is largely a reiteration of their largest complaint regarding the *National Strategy for Homeland Security,* in that it is more of a federally coordinated strategy for homeland security than a nationally coordinated strategy. The IACP argues that since September 11th, the emphasis has remained on what the Departments of Homeland Security, Justice, and Defense, are doing to address homeland security. Although there is often discussion about local law enforcement, they are seen more as an effect than a cause. If the federal government creates a regulation for homeland security (the cause) then the local police will have to implement it (the effect). Or if the DHS establishes information-sharing procedures with local law enforcement, the DHS is the cause and the police are the effect. Local police are rarely seen as being the cause of homeland security, only the effect, the ones who execute the policies and procedures. According to the IACP, "a truly national effort will ensure that all levels of government, local, tribal, state, and federal, are participating in the policy design and development process as <u>full and equal partners</u>"[51] (emphasis in the original).

The fifth and final principle articulated by the IACP is the importance of bottom-up engineering; the diversity of the state, tribal, and local public safety community; and noncompetitive collaboration. Although these sound like numerous principles, the element that underlies each of them is the concept that any homeland security strategy should draw from a broad base of resources. In other words, like the concept of community policing, one size does not fit all. America's communities and law enforcement agencies are too diverse to adopt a cookie-cutter approach to homeland security. Rather, any homeland security strategy should first draw on the diversity by collaborating to determine the best strategies for prevention, response, and recovery, and then develop a homeland strategy that all agencies can draw on. To do this, they encourage bottom-up engineering or, more simply put, tapping into the knowledge of those on the front lines of the war on terror, those that are in fact securing the homeland, and those that have been and will be first responders in the future. Police officers bring a unique perspective and insight into the issues of security and prevention and should not be ignored. This is the same for police agencies, regardless of size or jurisdiction, as this diversity can bring further insights into the process of developing a national strategy. And finally, the IACP argues that resources for homeland security should not be competitive in nature emphasizing only large urban areas, but rather should be noncompetitive and that grants should not be given to large urban areas at the expense of protecting smaller jurisdictions throughout the United States.

These five principles are intended to guide the development of a national strategy, which the IACP is now working to develop, one that will "address critical areas of need, such as the development of prevention and response plans, hiring and training needs, and resource and funding strategies."[52] Their goal is to incorporate the views of federal, state, tribal, and local law enforcement to develop a strategic blueprint and to "identify, collect, and disseminate best practices and innovations in areas such as intelligence gathering and information sharing, threat assessment, deployment strategies, equipment needs and standards, and public-private partnerships."[53] In doing so, the IACP intends to reach out beyond just members of the law enforcement community and attempt to solicit input from all public safety agencies, including fire and emergency services.

Santa Ana Police Department morning briefing. (*Source: PhotoEdit Inc.*)

Homeland Security Best Practices—ICMA

As alluded to in their white paper, the IACP has in fact already advanced the concept of identifying, collecting, and disseminating best practices and innovations when the ICMA published its collection of articles entitled *Homeland Security: Best Practices for Local Government*.[54] Numerous articles written by police chiefs and others from the IACP were featured in this publication that attempted to identify successful practices of local government, particularly local law enforcement, for homeland security. The book was organized in the same manner as FEMA organizes its strategic goals, namely mitigation, preparedness, response, and recovery. The document serves not entirely as a strategic plan, but it is organized in such a manner as to, in the words of the IACP, create a blueprint for a strategic model.

The editor recognizes, like others, that on September 11th, the people that responded to the terrorist attacks were primarily from local governments, not federal agencies or the military. To discuss emergency management, they use the federal framework of mitigation, preparedness, response, and recovery. Mitigation is defined as those efforts to prevent man-made or natural disasters or to lessen their effects. Preparedness looks at how well government is readied to respond to disasters of all types, including terrorist attacks. Response deals with the government's actual reaction to such disasters, and recovery focuses on the ability of government to clean up debris, restore the environment, rebuild infrastructure, and reinstate public services to its citizens. Using this framework, the collection of articles then details various concepts necessary to achieve these overarching goals, similar to strategic planning.[55]

Mitigation

Under the mitigation section, several of the authors deal with the issue of information gathering, developing intelligence, and then sharing both information and intelligence. Police officers on a routine basis collect information, whether through field interviews and "routine" traffic stops or by more formal investigations into reported crimes. This information is collected and maintained by agencies in a variety of manners, but not necessarily in a way that coverts information (raw data) into intelligence (analyzed data). Although police departments prior to the 1970s typically maintained intelligence units, most were disbanded in the 1960s and 1970s due to the civil rights movement and a series of laws, rules, and regulations regarding the maintenance of police intelligence. In addition, many of these laws prevented or limited the sharing of such information, so unless agencies had bona fide crime information, raw data and even analyzed data, unless it pertained directly to known criminal activity, could not be shared.

There was a distinct realization that in the post–September 11th environment, this was detrimental to agencies attempting to prevent future terrorist attacks, and there has been a call for change. To effectively mitigate future attacks, police officers need to be able to collect information, analyze that information, and distribute it through various information systems. In addition, this type of information and intelligence contributes to an agency's ability to engage in threat assessments, the analysis of potential threats to a particular community and that government's ability to counter such a threat. Threat assessments assist agencies in determining the allocation of resources, but lacking information and analyzed information (intelligence), governments cannot make the necessary analysis for threat assessments. Therefore, to mitigate or prevent future terrorist attacks, it is argued that police must find legal means by which they can collect, analyze, and disseminate information and intelligence. Many have come to call this strategic goal "intelligence-driven" policing.

One particular article in this section by Douglas Bodrero[56] makes the argument that intelligence gathering and analysis and threat assessments are a critical goal to preventing future terrorist attacks. But, he also stated there are three other critical steps to prevention, and they include training to understand the threat and prepare for it, to develop or continue working with terrorism task forces and working groups, and that state and local agencies should develop counterterrorism plans, and that these should continually be updated to address changes in the intelligence environment and the recognition of new threats.

Preparedness

Under the preparedness section there is a common theme among the articles, that in order to be adequately prepared for a terrorist attack, it is imperative that agencies make the determination of who is to be in charge before any incident occurs. This can be done through the task force or working group process, or by way of mutual aid agreements between neighboring agencies. In addition, there is the consistent call for all such emergencies to be handled through the Emergency Operations Centers (EOC) concept. The EOC should be located in an easily accessible location, should have predetermined staffing, and should be exercised on a regular basis, so that when called on, the EOC can begin managing an incident in the immediate aftermath of an attack and carry it through both the response and recovery stages.

Another theme that runs through this section is the focus on the broader picture, specifically the different sectors of the community that will be affected. This includes such sectors as fire and emergency medical services, the medical community itself, public works, the private sector, and others. Each of these will play a critical role during the response and recovery phases, and therefore their participation in the preparedness stage is critical. In addition, one of the key tasks during this stage is the development of plans. One particular plan emphasized in this section was that for the evacuation of high-rise buildings, but other plans are needed as well. One only has to look to the mass evacuation of Houston, Texas, as Hurricane Rita swept toward its coast in September of 2005, to understand that plans were not fully in place to make the major highways and interstates one-way leaving Houston. This emphasizes the need for continual planning to address any eventuality that may occur. And plans, once put in place, must be continually updated as environment, threat, and intelligence change over time.

Response

The section related to response has one primary theme running through the various articles and that is the ability in a terrorist attack to communicate and share information during the actual incident. It is noted that although there is the common issue of police, fire, and emergency medical services responding to an attack and needing to communicate, other entities such as public works will be a crucial element with which to communicate. In addition, although much of the focus is on internal and cross-agency communication, there is also a strong need to communicate with the public. This is often not factored into the plan or if it is, during a response it is only with some delay that public notifications are made. Despite the history of the public emergency broadcast system, it was not invoked after the attacks on September 11th, and public notifications are usually only made through press conferences. Real-time or close to real-time information should be given to citizens to allow them to react in a proper and informed manner, rather than relying on rumor and innuendo that often surface in the event of a major incident.

In addition, in the immediate aftermath of a major incident the one source of information for citizens to notify government is through the dispatch centers, which often become overloaded during a crisis. A key part of the communications process is citizens calling dispatchers and dispatchers notifying public safety personnel of critical information. If this system breaks down or becomes overloaded, coordination in the response phase becomes quickly ineffective. Strategic goals and planning in this regard are critical to the response phase.

One innovative means for assisting in the response phase is the use of geographic information systems. The article by Russ Johnson details how the New York Office of Emergency Management (OEM) had a storehouse of geographic information on transportation systems, subway services, power grids, operational and staging areas available, and areas of personnel services, particularly food and water stations. In addition, geographic mapping also allows for visual blueprints of various key buildings, such as malls, schools, and courthouses that can provide key information to not only the emergency operation center personnel for planning purposes, but also to those officers that are the first responders. The use of this technology should most assuredly be part of any strategic homeland security plan.

Recovery

The recovery section deals primarily with planning for the worst-case scenarios such as stress management, particularly critical incident stress, and how to deal with line-of-duty deaths. Although many agencies have developed these types of plans over time, those agencies that do not have these in place should make it an integral part of their planning. The successful cleanup of disaster sites, the restoration of public services, and the rebuilding of infrastructures all deal with more physical elements of the recovery process, what this particular section reminds the strategic planners of is the mental elements of the recovery process.

Strategies for Local Law Enforcement—COPS and PERF

As previously described, in November of 2002, the Police Executive Research Forum, a widely known and respected police think tank, drew on a grant from the Office of Community Oriented Policing Services to conduct an executive session aimed at developing some broad strategic goals related to policing for homeland security. The executive session included a cross section of federal, state, and local law enforcement, collaborating together to identify key law enforcement strategies that were seen as the immediate priorities of police for engaging in homeland security. They identified seven priorities, which consisted of promoting effective local–federal partnerships, security clearances and information sharing, joint terrorism task forces, FBI strategies, intelligence, multijurisdictional information sharing, and training and awareness. Although many of these are highly related, the premise behind each will be discussed.

The first priority listed was the promotion of effective local–federal partnerships through information exchange and access. Many of the local agencies felt that communication with federal agencies tended to be a one-way street, local to federal, but not the other way around. The call was to build this relationship through processes and protocols, much in the way that the various joint task forces have operated. The priority also incorporated partnerships not only between federal and local agencies, but also with the media and the community. However, put simply, greater cooperation across all levels of officials and across sectors is critical to a successful homeland security strategy.

The second priority listed included security clearances and information sharing. The purpose of enhancing local–federal partnerships is to increase information exchanges, but in many cases the information that the federal government has is classified and therefore cannot be shared with local law enforcement unless they have clearances. In addition, even if one individual in the agency has a clearance, he or she may not be able to share that information within the police department due to the information being classified. The executive committee recognized this as an obstacle that must be overcome. Simply making police agencies aware of the security clearance dilemma and the process for applying for a security clearance can alleviate suspicions, but further administrative cooperation and streamlining of the process may be necessary to ensure that information and intelligence can be shared so that it may be acted on.

The third priority was the enhancement of joint terrorism task forces. Although these have been in existence since the first one in New York in 1980, they are few and far between and do not necessarily create a perfect solution. The executives all agreed that the joint task forces on terrorism generally lacked "the structure, appropriate number of analysts and administrative personnel to support investigations and other critical resources." Therefore, although they are held up as solid models for local and federal partnerships, they are not perfect. In addition, they cited the fact that in many cases the task forces are redundant, as there are often overlapping task forces, and that too many task forces would become unwieldy and would drain resources.

The fourth priority was related to FBI strategies, which attempted to recognize the goals and responsibilities of the FBI and how they differ from local law enforcement. Ultimately, this section was dedicated to enhancing local police and FBI cooperation by having each recognize the legal, political, and economic restraints that the other faces.

The fifth priority was the collection, analysis, and dissemination of intelligence. Here there was the recognition that information sharing must be maintained, but that the FBI ultimately was the primary source for channeling information and intelligence. A key recommendation was that law enforcement agencies at all levels be given the assistance and training to develop intelligence units, a function most have not performed since the 1960s. And, once again, there was the call for the FBI to feed information back down to local agencies so that they may incorporate the available intelligence into their threat assessments and homeland security planning, recognizing again the constraints of classified material.

The sixth priority was multijurisdictional information sharing that focused on information sharing between not only the federal and local agencies, but also between federal, state, and local agencies that all share a similar geographical area. Finally, the seventh priority was to ensure that state and local agencies receive the proper training, not only for their line officers, but for their executives and midlevel managers as well.

A Framework to Prepare for Terrorist Threats

More recently, in 2005, Dr. William V. Pelfrey, longtime scholar of policing, wrote an article titled, "The Cycle of Preparedness: Establishing a Framework to Prepare for Terrorist Threats."[57] In this article, Pelfrey identified the fact that our numerous governmental agencies at all levels must not only prepare for terrorist threats, but also simultaneously plan for natural disasters. Although this may seem like an impossible task, he argued that by breaking down the concept of preparedness into its various components, it will be easier to prepare for the homeland security role. He explained that it is an accepted proposition that we must prepare for these eventualities. He stated what is most critical is identifying "a strategic framework that provides governmental and non-governmental entities the ability to prepare in stages."[58] He, therefore, proposed a strategic framework, which he labeled the "cycle of preparedness" to guide agencies toward this end.

Pelfrey explained that he sees the overall concept of homeland security as one of preparedness. He used the concept of preparedness as an umbrella term for many of the concepts previously stated under the other strategic plans reviewed. He then labeled these particular concepts as phases and titled them prevention, awareness of attack, response, recovery. He sees these four phases as a cyclical process, primarily emphasizing the first phase, prevention, until an attack or natural disaster occurs. At that point, the concept preparedness moves through the next three phases until returning to prevention.

In terms of the first phase, prevention, Pelfrey draws heavily on the Office for Domestic Preparedness' *Guidelines for Homeland Security 2003*[59] to articulate what elements make up the strategic goal of prevention. He quoted the *National Strategy for Homeland Security* stating the prevention consists of such objectives as "deterring all potential terrorists from attacking America through our uncompromising commitment to defeating terrorism wherever it appears," "detect terrorists before they strike," "prevent them and their instruments of terror from entering our country," and "take decisive action to eliminate the threat they pose."[60] Prevention, then, according to Pelfrey "is the process of identifying the risks associated with terrorism most likely to affect the security, safety, and well-being of the community and eliminating or mitigating those risks through all legal means."[61] To strategically apply the concepts of prevention, Pelfrey asserted that we must focus on the specific objectives of protection, deterrence, preemption, and mitigation. The key is to protect citizens, deter terrorism, take action against known terrorists' activity, and to work toward reducing the harm an attack will cause by being prepared to respond promptly.

To more fully operationalize these concepts (the subject of the next chapter), Pelfrey focused on two distinct elements necessary under the prevention phase. He drew these elements from the *Office of Domestic Preparedness Guidelines,* and they include collaboration and information sharing.[62] Collaboration focuses on the numerous governmental and police agencies working together both laterally and vertically, between neighboring and overlapping jurisdictions, including the private sector, as well as between federal, state, and local agencies. Information sharing is focused on the "process of gathering, storing, analyzing, and disseminating data, information, and intelligence between and among different agencies, organizations, and individuals, on a need-to-know basis, for the common purpose of foreseeing or recognizing terrorist threats, actions, and behaviors."[63] The combination of these two concepts, collaboration and information sharing, are thus the key elements to preventing future terrorist attacks.

The second phase of the preparedness cycle is awareness of an attack. Although intuitively one might think this phase is rather simplistic and ultimately recognizable, this is not always the case. In general, most people treated the first plane into the World Trade Center as a very serious accident. However, when the second plane flew into the World Trade Center it became very clear to all that it was, in fact, a terrorist attack. Some type of biological agent introduced into the food supply such as mad cow disease, could potentially be treated as a natural occurrence and never fully recognized as a terrorist attack. The key to this phase is recognizing an attack for what it truly is, for until we recognize an attack has occurred, we cannot launch the appropriate response. As Pelfrey stated, "The speed of the recognition is the key to the mediation of the harm."[64] And once an attack is recognized for what it is, we can begin to quickly transition to the next phase: response.

The third phase of Pelfrey's cycle of preparedness is the response phase. Citing the *National Strategy for Homeland Security,*[65] Pelfrey stated that the following passage, which describes emergency preparedness is really about response:

> We need a comprehensive national system to bring together and command all necessary response assets quickly and effectively. We must equip, train, and exercise many different response units to mobilize for any emergency without warning . . . to create

and employ a system that will improve our response to all disasters, both manmade and natural."[66]

Pelfrey then breaks down the necessary elements of the response, consisting of the strategies of "containment of the scene, control of the scene, management of the incident, and identification of the perpetrators, keeping in mind that preservation of life is the first priority of response."[67] Once the initial response is achieved, the routine that follows will be the transition to the next phase, that of recovery.

The fourth phase is the recovery phase. Regardless of whether man-made or natural, recovery can be seen as the "process of rehabilitating, restoring, and repairing the harm done."[68] Pelfrey makes the argument that like the other phases, planning and training must go into the recovery phase, which will determine how recovery will be handled by the agencies involved. And like the other phases, this phase must be managed properly for it to succeed. In addition, one other strategic consideration during this phase is the protection of those working during the recovery phase. One only has to look at the thousands of workers at ground zero at the World Trade Center working amidst the unstable rumble, often in no more protection than street clothes, to recognize the importance of this strategic concern.

After working through the four phases of the cycle of preparedness, Pelfrey then articulated the need for true preparation in advance for each of the four phases. He created a matrix that factors in each of the four phases and its goals and objectives and then crosses those with the need for planning, training, equipping, exercising, evaluating, and revisions based on the evaluations. By breaking each of the phases down into elements and ensuring that each of the preparedness considerations are met, it allows managers to implement this strategic plan in a rational and doable manner. Working through each of these considerations for each of the goals and objectives of preparedness will help ensure that the strategic plan is truly operationalized.

BOX 11-4

STRATEGY CHECKLIST

1. Align the strategic objectives that support state and urban area goals to the seven national priorities. This does not require an update to existing objectives if those objectives already reflect the National Priorities. However, the alignment of those objectives to the national priorities should be clearly articulated.

   Does the strategy address Regional Collaboration?
   Does the strategy address the National Incident Management System?
   Does the strategy address information sharing and collaboration?
   Does the strategy address interoperable communications?
   Does the strategy address police as first responder safety?

2. Describe the strategies, goals, and objectives within the framework of the mission areas: prevent, prepare, protect, respond, recover, assess.

(continued)

Does the strategy address prevention?
Does the strategy address preparedness?
Does the strategy address protection?
Does the strategy address response?
Does the strategy address recovery?
Does the strategy address assessment?

3. Local jurisdictions participation in the strategic planning process.

Does the strategic process include participation from local jurisdictions?

4. Address citizen preparedness and volunteer efforts.

Does the strategy appropriately address citizen preparedness and volunteer efforts?

5. Regionalization and mutual aid.

Does the strategy address multiple agencies?
Does the strategy address regionalization?
Does the strategy address mutual aid agreements?

Source: Adapted from Department of Homeland Security. (2005). *State and Urban Area Homeland Security Strategy: Guidance on Aligning Strategies with the National Preparedness Goal.* Available online at *http://www.ojp.usdoj.gov/odp/docs/StrategyGuidance_22JUL2005.pdf*

Downloaded on August 15, 2005.

A COHESIVE STRATEGY FOR HOMELAND SECURITY

The move to a new era of policing, the era of homeland security, necessitates a strategic plan for the implementation of such a broad and sweeping change in law enforcement. The development of a strategy provides police agencies with the policy or framework with which to operationalize the myriad concepts associated with homeland security. The dilemma, however, as McVey has pointed out, is whether or not to wait for a strategy to be handed down or develop one's own without any sense of whether one is planning strategically in the right direction.[69] Responding to the first option, McVey sums it up nicely when he states that "fortunately, there is a third alternative for local law enforcement" and "it begins with the basic realization that any proposal forthcoming from federal agencies will likely be only strategically general."[70] In fact, not only was the *National Strategy for Homeland Security* strategically general, as the IACP pointed out, it was largely a federal strategy aimed at what the federal government can do to implement homeland security. In fact, there is nothing inherently wrong with this, as the federal government's strategic plan should emphasize federal activity. The only complaint is that it was sold as an all-encompassing national strategy, rather than a federal strategy. And so, McVey explained that "each jurisdiction will have to interpret such a proposal according to the area's unique risk factors and operations capabilities" and thus "each agency must lay the necessary groundwork in preparation for those proposals by generating and incorporating into its individual administrative paradigm a basic understanding of the terrorist risks it faces and its own incident management capability."[71] Simply put, each agency or a grouping of agencies (such as those in a metroplex environment), should develop their own strategic plan for homeland security.

To develop a strategic plan, it is important to draw on as many sources as possible for its creation. Despite the federal leanings toward the *National Strategy for Homeland Security,* it should not be ignored as being useless to a local police department, but rather a police department's strategic plan should incorporate elements of the *National Strategy.* In fact, a local strategic plan should be nested into the larger *National Strategy,* thus finding ways of being linked to one another to ensure the implementation of similar goals and fostering both collaboration and information sharing. Yet, as McVey pointed out, it must fit the needs, risks, and threats particular to the jurisdiction and police department of concern. Thus the next question is, Where to start?

Drawing on all of the previous documents that have focused on strategic goals and objectives, an underlying consistency exists that provides a framework for the development of a strategic plan. Beginning with these particular elements and incorporating those factors that are particular to a police department's jurisdiction will allow for the generation of a strategic plan to oversee any police department's move to homeland security.

The strategic goals of homeland security would appear to consist of five overarching goals, and they are Prevention, Preparedness, Response, Recovery, and Assessment/ Adaptation. Every document reviewed has focused heavily on the concept of prevention. In fact, drawing on the IACP white paper, they stated that it was the IACP's belief "that the prevention of terrorist attacks must be viewed as the paramount priority in any national, state, tribal, or local homeland security strategy."[72] The *National Strategy* was also in accordance with the IACP in that it stated, "The first priority of homeland security is to prevent terrorist attacks."[73] Therefore, any strategic plan must begin with this goal and order its strategic applications around it. As Pelfrey has stated, some of the key strategic applications for prevention include protection, deterrence, and preemption.[74] Agencies should look to ways of altering the environment to protect people from terrorism (e.g., target hardening and Crime Prevention Through Environmental Design (CPTED) principles), they should implement means for deterring potential terrorists, and they should rapidly and forcefully preempt any terrorist attacks once detected. And, as *The Office for Domestic Preparedness Guidelines* explained, prevention and deterrence should focus on collaboration, information sharing, threat recognition, risk management, and intervention. Each of these strategic applications work toward the goal of prevention.

The second strategic goal should be that of preparedness. Unlike prevention, preparedness is the realization that a future attack or natural disaster is inevitable and that the agency should be prepared to respond to such an event. The strategic applications under preparedness include "proper planning, resource allocation, training and simulated disaster response exercises . . . to ensure that skills, equipment and other resources can be effectively coordinated when an emergency occurs."[75] Much of the strategic application is working through mutual aid agreements, determining which agency in a multiagency metroplex would be officially in charge, the emergency operation center command structure, governmental resources that can be drawn on, personnel readiness, and ensuring that plans and standard operating procedures are put into place. Each of these strategic applications works toward the goal of preparedness.

The third strategic goal is response. Incorporated within response is Pelfrey's third phase, and that is the importance of threat recognition. Once a threat is recognized, initiating the initial response to a terrorist attack is the next strategic goal. Strategic applications of the goal of response, beyond threat recognition, include the mechanism for issuing appropriate warnings and information to the public, accessing the proper personnel to initiate the response, ensuring the proper incident management and coordination with other police and government agencies. In addition, "other important aspects of the response phase include search-and-rescue operations, evacuations according to established procedures, damage assessments, and the proper handling of fatalities."[76] Response is focused on the various elements of the agency having the capabilities necessary to perform their function in a terrorist attack or natural disaster and being able to adequately deploy in such an environment. Each of these strategic applications works toward the goal of response.

The fourth strategic goal is that of recovery. Once the initial response is made and the event moves from the crisis mode to that of managing the scene, the agency will move into the recovery phase. This phase will include such things as "the cleanup of debris, the restoration of the environment, the reinstitution of public services, and the rebuilding of the public infrastructure."[77] The strategic application for recovery has to do with that ability to manage in this environment, especially under the strain of limited resources and personnel. Providing security and traffic control for the area that was impacted becomes a key concern during the response phase. In addition, part of the goal is providing protection to those officers engaging in the recovery effort, both physically and mentally. In the former case, the proper equipment must be on hand to work through the recovery phase and in the latter, the necessary counseling must be provided to effectively deal with the critical incident stress officers will face. Each of these strategic applications works toward the goal of recovery.

Finally, the last strategic goal is that of assessment. Although often subordinated to a final strategic application within the recovery phase, assessment here is detailed as its own strategic goal. Each agency should have the mechanisms in place to adequately assess how effective an agency was during the response to a true attack or natural disaster, regardless of scale, as well as the ability to assess effectiveness through simulated exercises, whether computer simulated or hands-on field exercises. Incorporating feedback obtained from action reviews and lessons learned must find their way into the strategic application under prevention, awareness, response, and recovery.

In addition to the strategic goals, a number of strategic objectives also underlie and support each of the strategic goals. Each of these in their own right must be addressed by police agencies and become an integral part of the strategic plan to move an agency into the era of homeland security. These objectives include organization, collaboration, intelligence, information/intelligence sharing, law, and science and technology. Agencies must determine how best to organize for homeland security. This will be largely determined by the level of personnel and resources available, the size of the jurisdiction and agency, resources available, threat and risk assessments, and a host of other factors influencing the agency. Whether this means restructuring the organization, centralizing the command or certain elements of command, or adding a new division to the agency must be determined by the capabilities and constraints of each agency. Central to the organizational considerations, however, should be the ability to achieve the strategic goals for homeland security. One element of organization that will more than likely fit into any plan is the reliance on the Incident Management System and the use of an incident command center.

Collaboration again cannot be ignored for its importance in working not only with other governmental agencies within one's own jurisdiction, but also with neighboring jurisdictions as well. In addition, collaborations with other regional agencies are important as is developing working relations under the concepts of homeland security with state and federal agencies. Although clearly collaboration is important in regard to the goal of prevention, it is also critical in all of the strategic goals.

Intelligence gathering and analysis is also a critical objective for law enforcement and one that has not been used by many departments over the previous 30 years. However, if policing for homeland security is to concentrate primarily on prevention, it will largely be driven by intelligence. Information must be collected and analyzed before it becomes intelligence. Having a means of data collection and the ability to analyze the data is critical to developing intelligence. Once this intelligence becomes available, the ability to disseminate to the agencies or units that are tasked with responding to threats and preempting strikes is critical to the success of the prevention goal. Therefore, drawing on both the collaboration and intelligence objectives necessitates the emphasis of yet another key objective, and that is information and intelligence sharing. Once information is attained or data has been analyzed into usable intelligence, some mechanism must exist to move the intelligence both laterally and vertically.

Also undergirding the strategic goals are the objectives of the law and both science and technology. In many cases the strategic goals of homeland security may run into problems with the law. For instance the creation of intelligence units within police departments may potentially be blocked by laws passed in the 1960s and 1970s. These types of impediments must be dealt with prior to the strategic goals being accomplished. In addition, laws may need to be created to support investigations into terrorism or to apply the law to the situation of terrorism. In addition, the application of both science and technology may be a necessary element for achieving the strategic goals, as it is technology that may provide the proper solution to achieving these goals.

CONCLUSION

As policing moves into this new era of homeland security and faces challenges hitherto unfaced in America, there is a clear and present need for a strategic plan to guide police agencies' implementation of homeland security. The federal government has issued its *National Strategy for Homeland Security,* but there has been criticism that it is much too focused on the federal government and not the nation as a whole. In addition, other writings exist that have focused on the strategic goals of homeland security, but they have presented little in the way of a complete framework from which to work. Drawing on Pelfrey's "Cycle of Preparedness" can provide a good starting point for developing a strategy, but it is important that local agencies, when developing their own strategic plan, look to multiple sources for the development of its own plan. Although a locally developed strategic plan is critical for the implementation of homeland security policy, it must be compatible with strategic plans at the federal, state, and local levels, so as to avoid conflicts in its implementation. Basing a strategic plan on the common themes presented in the strategic documents provides five goals: Prevention, Preparedness, Response, Recovery, and Assessment; as well as six strategic objectives: organization, collaboration, intelligence, information/intelligence sharing, law, and science and technology. Taken together, these five strategic goals and the various strategic objectives provide the necessary framework for which police departments can begin developing a useful strategy for homeland security. Drawing on these strategies, police can then begin to look at police operations for homeland security, the subject of the next chapter.

ENDNOTES

1. Campbell, H. G. (2005). "Logic Models in Support of Homeland Security Strategy Development." *Journal of Homeland Security and Emergency Management* 2, no. 2: 1–7, p. 1.
2. *ibid.*
3. *ibid.*
4. McVey, P. M. (2003). "The Local Role in Fighting Terrorism." In *Homeland Security: Best Practices for Local Government,* edited by R. L. Kemp, 125–130. Washington, D.C.: International City/County Management Association.
5. McVey, P. M. (2003). "The Local Role in Fighting Terrorism." In *Homeland Security: Best Practices for Local Government,* edited by R. L. Kemp, 125–130, at page 125. Washington, D.C.: International City/County Management Association.
6. *ibid.*
7. Office of Homeland Security. (2002). *National Strategy for Homeland Security.* Washington, D.C.: U.S. G.P.O. Available online at http://www.whitehouse.gov/ homeland/ book/nat_strat_hls.pdf; downloaded January 4, 2005.
8. See Preface Office of Homeland Security. (2002). *National Strategy for Homeland Security.* Washington, D.C.: U.S. G.P.O. Available online at http://www.whitehouse.gov/ homeland/book/nat_strat_hls.pdf; downloaded January 4, 2005.
9. See Preface Office of Homeland Security. (2002). *National Strategy for Homeland Security.* Washington, D.C.: U.S. G.P.O. Available online at http:// www.whitehouse.gov/ homeland/book/nat_strat_hls.pdf; downloaded January 4, 2005.
10. Kemp, R. L. (2003). *Homeland Security: Best Practices for Local Government.* Washington, D.C.: International City/County Management Association.
11. International Association of Chiefs of Police. (2005). *From Hometown Security to Homeland Security.* Washington, D.C.: International Association of Chiefs of Police. Available online at http://www.theiacp.org/leg_policy/HomelandSecurityWP.PDF; downloaded on September 20, 2005.
12. Reese, S. (2005). "State and Local Homeland Security: Unresolved Issues for the 109th Congress." *CRS Report for Congress.* Washington, D.C.: Congressional Research Service. Available online at http://www.fas.org/sgp/crs/homesec/RL32941.pdf; downloaded September 20, 2005.
13. *ibid.*

14. Murphy, G. R. and Plotkin, M. R. (2003). *Protecting Your Community From Terrorism: The Strategies for Local Law Enforcement Series. Volume 1: Improving Local-Federal Partnerships.* Washington, D.C.: Police Executive Research Forum and the Office of Community Oriented Policing Services. Available online at http://www.cops.usdoj.gov/mime/open.pdf?Item=1362; downloaded April 17, 2005.
15. Pelfrey, W. V. (2005). "The Cycle of Preparedness: Establishing a Framework to Prepare for Terrorist Threats." *Journal of Homeland Security and Emergency Management* 2, no. 1: 1–21.
16. Office of Homeland Security. (2002). *National Strategy for Homeland Security.* Washington, D.C.: U.S. G.P.O. Available online at http://www.whitehouse.gov/homeland/book/nat_strat_hls.pdf; downloaded January 4, 2005, p. 2.
17. *ibid.*
18. White, J. R. (1998). *Terrorism: An Introduction.* 2nd ed. Belmont, CA: West/Wadsworth Publishing Company, chapter 1.
19. *ibid.*
20. Poland, J. M. (2005). *Understanding Terrorism: Groups, Strategies, and Responses.* Upper Saddle River, NJ: Prentice Hall, p. 9.
21. McVey, P. M. (2002). "An Effective Homeland Defense Partnership." *The Police Chief* 69 (4): 174–180, p. 174.
22. Jenkins, B. M. (1983). *New Modes of Conflict.* Santa Monica, CA: Rand Corporation.
23. Laqueur, W. (1999). *The New Terrorism: Fanaticism and the Arms of Mass Destruction.* New York: Oxford University Press.
24. Heymann, P. B. (1998). *Terrorism and America: A Commonsense Strategy for a Democratic Society.* Cambridge, MA: The MIT Press, p. 6.
25. Friendlander, R. A. (1981). *Terrorism and the Law: What Price Safety?* Gaithersburg, MD: International Association of Chiefs of Police, p. 3.
26. National Advisory Committee on Criminal Justice Standards and Goals, Law Enforcement Assistance Administration. (1976). *Disorders and Terrorism.* Washington, D.C.: U.S. Government Printing Office, p. 3.
27. Federal Bureau of Investigation (2005). *FBI Homepage.* Available online at http://www.fbi.gov; See also Federal Bureau of Investigation (2002). *Terrorism in the United States: 2000/2001.* Washington, D.C.: U.S. Government Printing Office.
28. Dyson, W. (2005). *Terrorism: An Investigator's Handbook.* 2nd ed. Newark, NJ: Matthew Bender.
29. Federal Bureau of Investigation (2002). *Terrorism in the United States: 2000/2001.* Washington, D.C.: U.S. Government Printing Office. The definition is derived from 18 U.S.C. § 2331(5).
30. Federal Bureau of Investigation (2002). *Terrorism in the United States: 2000/2001.* Washington, D.C.: U.S. Government Printing Office. The definition is derived from 18 U.S.C. § 2331(1).
31. Office of Homeland Security. (2002). *National Strategy for Homeland Security.* Washington, D.C.: U.S. G.P.O. Available online at http://www.whitehouse.gov/homeland/book/nat_strat_hls.pdf; downloaded January 4, 2005, p. 2.
32. Office of Homeland Security. (2002). *National Strategy for Homeland Security.* Washington, D.C.: U.S. G.P.O. Available online at http://www.whitehouse.gov/homeland/book/nat_strat_hls.pdf; downloaded January 4, 2005, p. 7.

33. Office of Homeland Security. (2002). *National Strategy for Homeland Security.* Washington, D.C.: U.S. G.P.O. Available online at http://www.whitehouse.gov/homeland/book/nat_strat_hls.pdf; downloaded January 4, 2005, p. 12.
34. Office of Homeland Security. (2002). *National Strategy for Homeland Security.* Washington, D.C.: U.S. G.P.O. Available online at http://www.whitehouse.gov/homeland/book/nat_strat_hls.pdf; downloaded January 4, 2005, p. 21.
35. Office of Homeland Security. (2002). *National Strategy for Homeland Security.* Washington, D.C.: U.S. G.P.O. Available online at http://www.whitehouse.gov/homeland/book/nat_strat_hls.pdf; downloaded January 4, 2005, p. 25.
36. *ibid.*
37. Office of Homeland Security. (2002). *National Strategy for Homeland Security.* Washington, D.C.: U.S. G.P.O. Available online at http://www.whitehouse.gov/homeland/book/nat_strat_hls.pdf; downloaded January 4, 2005, p. 25–26.
38. Office of Homeland Security. (2002). *National Strategy for Homeland Security.* Washington, D.C.: U.S. G.P.O. Available online at http://www.whitehouse.gov/homeland/book/nat_strat_hls.pdf; downloaded January 4, 2005, p. 38.
39. Office of Homeland Security. (2002). *National Strategy for Homeland Security.* Washington, D.C.: U.S. G.P.O. Available online at http://www.whitehouse.gov/homeland/book/nat_strat_hls.pdf; downloaded January 4, 2005, p. 41.
40. Office of Homeland Security. (2002). *National Strategy for Homeland Security.* Washington, D.C.: U.S. G.P.O. Available online at http://www.whitehouse.gov/homeland/book/nat_strat_hls.pdf; downloaded January 4, 2005, p. 43.
41. *ibid.*
42. Brown, D. (2005). "Military's Role in a Flu Pandemic." *Washington Post.* Available online at http://www.washingtonpost.com; downloaded October 5, 2005.
43. Office of Homeland Security. (2002). *National Strategy for Homeland Security.* Washington, D.C.: U.S. G.P.O. Available online at http://www.whitehouse.gov/homeland/book/nat_strat_hls.pdf; downloaded January 4, 2005, p. 57.
44. International Association of Chiefs of Police. (2005). *From Hometown Security to Homeland Security.* Washington, D.C.: International Association of Chiefs of Police. Available online at http://www.theiacp.org/leg_policy/HomelandSecurityWP.PDF; downloaded on September 20, 2005.
45. International Association of Chiefs of Police. (2005). *From Hometown Security to Homeland Security.* Washington, D.C.: International Association of Chiefs of Police. Available online at http://www.theiacp.org/leg_policy/HomelandSecurityWP.PDF; downloaded on September 20, 2005, p. 1.
46. Office of Homeland Security. (2002). *National Strategy for Homeland Security.* Washington, D.C.: U.S. G.P.O. Available online at http://www.whitehouse.gov/homeland/book/nat_strat_hls.pdf; downloaded January 4, 2005, p. iii.
47. International Association of Chiefs of Police. (2005). *From Hometown Security to Homeland Security.* Washington, D.C.: International Association of Chiefs of Police. Available online at http://www.theiacp.org/leg_policy/HomelandSecurityWP.PDF; downloaded on September 20, 2005, p. 2.
48. International Association of Chiefs of Police. (2005). *From Hometown Security to Homeland Security.* Washington, D.C.: International Association of Chiefs of Police. Available online at http://www.theiacp.org/leg_policy/HomelandSecurityWP.PDF; downloaded on September 20, 2005, p. 3.

49. *ibid.*

50. International Association of Chiefs of Police. (2005). *From Hometown Security to Homeland Security.* Washington, D.C.: International Association of Chiefs of Police. Available online at http://www.theiacp.org/leg_policy/HomelandSecurityWP.PDF; downloaded on September 20, 2005, p. 5.

51. International Association of Chiefs of Police. (2005). *From Hometown Security to Homeland Security.* Washington, D.C.: International Association of Chiefs of Police. Available online at http://www.theiacp.org/leg_policy/HomelandSecurityWP.PDF; downloaded on September 20, 2005, p. 6.

52. International Association of Chiefs of Police. (2005). *From Hometown Security to Homeland Security.* Washington, D.C.: International Association of Chiefs of Police. Available online at http://www.theiacp.org/leg_policy/HomelandSecurityWP.PDF; downloaded on September 20, 2005, p. 7.

53. International Association of Chiefs of Police. (2005). *From Hometown Security to Homeland Security.* Washington, D.C.: International Association of Chiefs of Police. Available online at http://www.theiacp.org/leg_policy/HomelandSecurityWP.PDF; downloaded on September 20, 2005, p. 3.

54. Kemp, R. L. (2003). *Homeland Security: Best Practices for Local Government.* Washington, D.C.: International City/County Management Association.

55. Kemp, R. L. (2003). *Homeland Security: Best Practices for Local Government.* Washington, D.C.: International City/County Management Association.

56. Bodrero, D. D. (2003). "Preventing Terrorist Acts: A New Challenge for Law Enforcement." In *Homeland Security: Best Practices for Local Government,* Edited by R. L. Kemp, 39–44. Washington, D.C.: International City/County Management Association.

57. Pelfrey, W. V. (2005). "The Cycle of Preparedness: Establishing a Framework to Prepare for Terrorist Threats." *Journal of Homeland Security and Emergency Management* 2, no. 1: 1–21; available online at http://www.bepress.com/jhsem/vol12/iss1/5

58. Pelfrey, W. V. (2005). "The Cycle of Preparedness: Establishing a Framework to Prepare for Terrorist Threats." *Journal of Homeland Security and Emergency Management* 2, no. 1: 1–21; available online at http://www.bepress.com/jhsem/vol12/iss1/5, p. 1.

59. Office of Domestic Preparedness. (2003). *The Office for Domestic Preparedness Guidelines for Homeland Security, June 2003: Prevention and Deterrence.* Washington, D.C.: U.S. Department of Homeland Security.

60. Office of Homeland Security. (2002). *National Strategy for Homeland Security.* Washington, D.C.: U.S. G.P.O. Available online at http://www.whitehouse.gov/homeland/book/nat_strat_hls.pdf; downloaded January 4, 2005.

61. Pelfrey, W. V. (2005). "The Cycle of Preparedness: Establishing a Framework to Prepare for Terrorist Threats." *Journal of Homeland Security and Emergency Management* 2, no. 1: 1–21; available online at http://www.bepress.com/jhsem/vol12/iss1/5, p. 7.

62. Office of Domestic Preparedness. (2003). *The Office of Domestic Preparedness Guidelines for Homeland Security June 2003: Prevention and Deterrence.* Washington, D.C.: U.S. Department of Homeland Security.

63. Office of Domestic Preparedness. (2003). *The Office of Domestic Preparedness Guidelines for Homeland Security June 2003: Prevention and Deterrence.* Washington, D.C.: U.S. Department of Homeland Security; Pelfrey, W. V. (2005). "The Cycle of Preparedness: Establishing a Framework to Prepare for Terrorist Threats." *Journal of*

Homeland Security and Emergency Management 2, no. 1: 1–21; available online at http:// www.bepress.com/jhsem/vol12/iss1/5, p. 9.

64. Pelfrey, W. V. (2005). "The Cycle of Preparedness: Establishing a Framework to Prepare for Terrorist Threats." *Journal of Homeland Security and Emergency Management* 2, no. 1: 1–21; available online at http://www.bepress.com/jhsem/vol12/iss1/5, p. 10.

65. Office of Homeland Security. (2002). *National Strategy for Homeland Security.* Washington, D.C.: U.S. G.P.O. Available online at http://www.whitehouse.gov/homeland/book/nat_strat_hls.pdf; downloaded January 4, 2005.

66. Office of Homeland Security. (2002). *National Strategy for Homeland Security.* Washington, D.C.: U.S. G.P.O. Available online at http://www.whitehouse.gov/homeland/book/nat_strat_hls.pdf; downloaded January 4, 2005; Pelfrey, W. V. (2005). "The Cycle of Preparedness: Establishing a Framework to Prepare for Terrorist Threats." *Journal of Homeland Security and Emergency Management* 2, no. 1: 1–21; available online at http://www.bepress.com/jhsem/vol12/iss1/5, p. 10.

67. Pelfrey, W. V. (2005). "The Cycle of Preparedness: Establishing a Framework to Prepare for Terrorist Threats." *Journal of Homeland Security and Emergency Management* 2, no. 1: 1–21; available online at http://www.bepress.com/jhsem/vol12/iss1/5, p. 11.

68. *ibid.*

69. McVey, P. M. (2003). "The Local Role in Fighting Terrorism." In *Homeland Security: Best Practices for Local Government,* edited by R. L. Kemp, 125–130, at page 125. Washington, D.C.: International City/County Management Association.

70. *ibid.*

71. *ibid.*

72. International Association of Chiefs of Police. (2005). *From Hometown Security to Homeland Security.* Washington, D.C.: International Association of Chiefs of Police. Available online at http://www.theiacp.org/leg_policy/HomelandSecurityWP.PDF; downloaded on September 20, 2005, p. 3.

73. Office of Homeland Security. (2002). *National Strategy for Homeland Security.* Washington, D.C.: U.S. G.P.O. Available online at http://www.whitehouse.gov/homeland/book/nat_strat_hls.pdf; downloaded January 4, 2005, p. 2.

74. Pelfrey, W. V. (2005). "The Cycle of Preparedness: Establishing a Framework to Prepare for Terrorist Threats." *Journal of Homeland Security and Emergency Management* 2, no. 1: 1–21; available online at http://www.bepress.com/jhsem/vol12/iss1/5

75. Kemp, R. L., ed. (2003). *Homeland Security: Best Practices for Local Government.* Washington, D.C.: International City/County Management Association, p. 4.

76. *ibid.*

77. *ibid.*

CHAPTER 12

Police Operations for Homeland Security

It is essential to relate what is strategically desirable to what is tactically possible with the forces at your disposal. To this end it is necessary to decide the development of operations before the initial blow is delivered.

Field Marshal Bernard Montgomery

INTRODUCTION

The operational level of policing is a transitional realm between good police strategy and tactics. It is where police management translates strategic goals and objectives writ large into a plan of action. It is moving from a general theory of how best to deal with securing the homeland, to a practical method that is aimed at achieving these goals. It is in essence the process by which the homeland security strategy is translated into operational plans for tactical action. Although it retains some aspects of being a science, because we do not deal with definitives in the police operational environment, it is in large part an art. It is the operational art of employing police officers to obtain the strategic goals and objectives by properly planning and directing officers on the street. It also includes the necessary planning to ensure that officers are prepared for all eventualities so that the police agency may achieve their strategic goals.

Police operations in the past have not entirely adhered to the strategic-operational-tactical process for the deployment of its police. Operational planning has generally been very limited and is usually found through simple policies in the standard operating procedures. In fact, police operations have largely been handled by the dispatchers with management intervention only in the event of a significant incident such as a hostage situation, bank robbery, or murder scene. Police operations under homeland security present a far more dynamic method of police planning, command, and conduct of police operations. It looks to reconceptualize how police departments organize and manage their assets, it looks to risk assessment and threat assessments to determine how assets should be deployed, and it draws on police intelligence for the actual deployment of these police assets. Drawing on these three concepts, it presents a far more advanced method of police operations, one that bridges the gap between homeland security strategy and street-level tactics.

The purpose of this chapter, then, is to understand police operations for homeland security by defining operations and analyzing it under the homeland security concept. It will then discuss police organization and management for homeland security, specifically looking at police planning, incident command, and partnering with other agencies through mutual aid agreements and joint task forces. It will further discuss the concept of operational planning through risk and threat assessments to develop plans and determine the allocation of police resources. And, finally, it will review the process of turning police information into usable and actionable intelligence for intelligence-led policing.

POLICE OPERATIONS FOR HOMELAND SECURITY

Historically, police operations have been grounded in traditions that date back to the late 19th and early 20th centuries. As police operations developed with the teaching and writing of August Vollmer, O. W. Wilson, and others, it began to take on more defined, albeit simplistic, methods. Traditionally, patrol officers responded to crimes and calls for service. Traffic units would handle any traffic offenses and would issue tickets. And detectives would investigate crimes. It was not until the 1960s that, according to Cordner, Gaines, and Kappeler, a slow revolution occurred in the way that police services were delivered.[1] The police community relations era, brought on by a number of social events such as the civil rights movement and protests over the Vietnam War, became the subject of focus for the police as the traditional methods of the past conflicted heavily with the environment of the 1960s. Police departments across the United States began implementing changes to its methods of police operations to deliver its services under these new concepts.

The primary methods of police operations, however, continued largely unchanged. The only true changes were appendages added to the organizational structure focused on specialized police services, ranging from team-policing units to special weapons and tactics (SWAT) units. It was not until the 1980s and 1990s that police operations began to see significant changes as a result of the community-oriented policing movement.[2] Police officers were now being assigned to permanent beats in neighborhoods and being required to partner with citizens to identify and solve problems. In addition, elements of crime prevention began to become a primary emphasis of police operations under this new model of policing. These concepts were seen as not only an operational change, but also as the adoption of a new philosophy of policing.

Despite several incidents that may have served as warning signs of what was to come, such as the first World Trade Center Bombing and the Oklahoma City Bombing, it was not until September 11th that police operations began to take on the consideration of adding homeland security to its operational functions. Dealing with terrorists was not often considered a standard police operation. Yet, it is not just terrorist bombings that have necessitated the move toward homeland security. The increasingly global society within which we live has generated numerous problems of global and transnational crimes. Ranging from organized crime and drug cartels to the abduction of women and children from other countries for the purposes of prostitution, the crimes have highlighted the impact that global crimes can have on local communities. In addition, the rapid spread of technology, specifically the Internet, has generated a whole new means of criminal activity and offenses that must be dealt with by local police, despite the fact that many of these crimes are occurring at the national or international level. Today's global society and the criminal elements inherent in it have necessitated changes in police operations.

Understanding what is meant by police operations under the concepts of homeland security is the first step in understanding the changes demanded in today's environment. As police operations have no definitive concept of linking strategy with tactics, it is perhaps necessary to turn to a bureaucratic agency that has a long history of dealing with the operational art and that is the military. Drawing on the military's conceptual understanding of operations without the language of war, it defines it as

> the level . . . at which . . . major operations are planned, conducted, and sustained to accomplish strategic objectives within . . . operational areas. Activities at this level link tactics and strategy by establishing operational objectives needed to accomplish the strategic objectives, sequencing events to achieve the operational objectives, initiating actions, and applying resources to bring about and sustain these events. These activities imply a broader dimension of time and space than do tactics; they ensure the logistics and administrative support of tactical [police] forces, and provide the means by which tactical successes are exploited to achieve strategic objectives.[3]

The intent here is not to apply a military model to policing, but to draw on aspects of operational activities that would be complimentary to policing for homeland security. In this case, police operations would be the level at which police responses and activities are planned, conducted, and sustained to achieve the strategic goals of homeland security reviewed in Chapter 11. Police operations would then determine, based on the strategic goals and objectives, what the operational objectives would be, how these can be accomplished, and it would determine how police assets, both personnel and equipment, could be deployed to achieve these objectives. This deployment of personnel and equipment also dictates what tactics police need to learn and be ready to use in the event the operational plans are put into motion.

The definition of operations also speaks to the "broader dimension of time and space," which focuses on the necessity for operational planning to think in terms of how long these plans will realistically take and what type of space is needed to accomplish these objectives. Time and space also denote constraints that must be factored into any plan. For instance, if New York City in a terrorist threat is to secure all bridges leading into and out of the island, it must consider the time necessary to move assets into place, but it must also think it terms of space, which may be the size of the bridge, the number of bridges, as well as the waterways under the bridges. Hence police operational planning in this case must ensure that the logistical and administrative support exists for the tactical forces (the police) to be able to achieve this strategic objective.

Another way of considering this is the concept of operational challenges, first denoted by the former Chairman of the Joint Chiefs of Staff, General Colin Powell. Powell explained that any operation must consider certain challenges, and these include (1) What political and social conditions (objectives) must be produced in the operational area to achieve the strategic goals? (Ends); (2) What sequence of actions is most likely to produce that condition? (Ways); How should the resources of the [police] be applied to accomplish that sequence of actions?; and (3) What is the likely cost or risk to the [police] in performing that sequence of actions?[4] Using these operational challenges the planning process should always exhibit a clear strategic aim. It must determine what is to be achieved by this strategic aim, it should identify the operational objectives, determine the steps necessary to achieve the objectives, and it must organize and apply the resources to accomplish each of these steps. These operational challenges hold true not only in operational planning, but also in the case of a significant event.

To apply these operational concepts to policing for homeland security, it is not necessary to scrap the traditions that have long built up through policing's history. Rather, we must continue to build on the framework that exists, but policing must apply new methods of doing business to prepare itself for this new role. Namely, it must begin to either adopt some of the changes that have circulated throughout policing or, where adopted, it must continue to adapt these concepts to the homeland security role. First and foremost it must look at the organizational structure and management of police. A number of concepts that already existed can be readily adopted or adapted, including decision-making processes, incident command structures, CompStat, mutual aid agreements, and Joint Task Forces. Second, it must utilize the methods of risk and threat assessment to more adequately develop its plans for homeland security. And, third, because risk and threat assessments are intelligence driven and these assessments factor into the planning process, information gathering, intelligence analysis, and sharing of both information and intelligence are critical to today's intelligence-led policing. It is to these three concepts that we now turn.

ORGANIZATION AND MANAGEMENT FOR HOMELAND SECURITY

Police organization in America has generally reflected the traditional aspects of police operations. As police operations have focused on patrol, traffic, and investigations, police organization has generally reflected this operational style by creating patrol, traffic, and investigation divisions, as well as an administrative division for managing the functions of the department. The patrol division has traditionally consisted of three to four shifts, centered on three eight-hour shifts for 24-hour coverage, and sometimes a fourth shift that serves as a power shift to overlay the busiest times for police calls-for-service, the late evening to early morning time frame. The traffic division has generally been a weekday coverage system for those time periods when traffic is at its peak, and investigations, like patrol, have generally adhered to a 24-hour coverage cycle with skeletal crews in the early morning hours.

Police management in America has generally consisted of shift commanders and midlevel management, sergeants that manage the police work in the field. The shift command has typically been a highly administrative entity, whereas field supervisors have served as the basic method of police officer oversight. For the most part, however, police management does not necessarily manage but rather administers. What typically drives the police department are calls-for-service, received by the "police operations center" dispatchers, who then allocate departmental resources by sending one or two police officers to the scene. Command of the scene then reverts to the police officers in the field and remains as such until a field supervisor supercedes the authority of the officer. This latter case is rare and usually only involves serious incidents that need to be coordinated, such as a hostage situation or bank robbery. It is an even rarer case when the actual shift commander supersedes the field supervisor's authority to take command of a situation. Therefore, police management cannot necessarily be defined as managing police assets, but rather serves as the administrator of police rules and regulations.

Mark H. Moore, a well-respected scholar of policing, has made a similar argument in a book entitled, *Impossible Jobs in Public Management.*[5] As he explained, "Police leadership is . . . handicapped by a startling lack of operational control over officers" and that departments function "under a carefully constructed illusion of control created to satisfy citizen demands for accountability."[6] Moore cites the focus on policies and procedures, a strict chain-of-command, and an emphasis on training as the mechanisms for police leadership appearing to have strict control over its officers. However, as Moore outrightly explains,

> The reality is quite different, however. For the most part, the police operate on their own. Although they must be responsive to dispatchers, they tell the dispatchers when they are available for service and where they are located. Their supervisors are often absorbed with other duties and cannot always find them. Supervisors respond to calls with the officers only on the most important occasions. As a practical matter, although the written procedures and hierarchical structure create deterrents for misconduct, the officer controls most of the information about his or her whereabouts and activities, and that fact defeats the effectiveness of these control arrangements.[7]

The drawback to this method of police management is largely found within the police decision-making process. Dispatchers generally make isolated decisions to allocate police resources. Police officers in the field make isolated decisions of how to properly handle a situation. These officers then direct departmental assets for solving the call-for-service. Throughout this process, the officer reports back to dispatch, which is "monitored" by police supervisors in the field and those at the police station. At no time, on a typical call, are there decisions being made by anyone other than individual actors based on the individual's environment as presented.

In the event of a crisis, officers continue to make decisions and communicate with dispatch, who in turn makes decisions for the allocation of resources. At this point, field supervisors intervene to collect as much information to make decisions and determine how to allocate resources. This is often slowed by the fact that they are in a situation where they have to be "brought up to speed" to understand the nature of the incident. They are essentially attempting to gather facts from both the officer on the scene and the dispatcher to once again make what is largely an isolated decision. It is not until the event becomes a major incident that any type of staffing system is summoned to move the organization into incident management.

Once an agency moves into the incident command system form of management, there is often a significant lag time between the commencement of the incident and the incident command system's ability to effectively manage the crisis. These time lags consist of personnel being off-duty, not always in communication with the department when off-duty, and because the incident command center tends to be at a specific location, which requires activation. Although several personnel from the incident command system may be available to take control of the situation, once again the decision-making process follows largely the same format, an isolated individual making decisions based on information being fed to him or her from the field and dispatch. It is not until the full incident command system is up and running that decisions are made with the greatest amount of input from the staff or management team operating the incident command center. In the case of another terrorist attack or a significant natural disaster, this is far too long a lag time for effective decision making to be obtained.

The National Commission on Terrorist Attacks Upon the United States in their *9/11 Commission Report,* stated that

> The attacks on 9/11 demonstrated that even the most robust emergency response capabilities can be overwhelmed if an attack is large enough. Teamwork, collaboration, and cooperation at an incident site are critical to a successful response. Key decisionmakers who are represented at the incident command level help to ensure an effective response, the efficient use of resources, and responder safety.[8]

The 9/11 Commission concluded that "emergency response agencies nationwide should adopt the Incident Command System (ICS)."[9] It is their belief that by using the ICS in critical incidents that what will ultimately be improved is the decision-making process. The problem, however, is that even if practiced on a regular basis, the lag time of having a fully operational ICS is too great a time when it comes to a critical incident. Therefore, what is needed is a full-time, fully staffed ICS that manages police resources on a routine basis. The ICS would become the method for routine police operations, which would conduct centralized planning, and all decision making would be preformed by the ICS staff. Despite the ICS implementing centralized planning, agencies would continue utilizing decentralized execution, thus continuing to rely on the professionalism and discretion of the officers on scene. What is needed, then, is an entirely new way of thinking about police decision making.

Problem-Oriented Policing

Herman Goldstein, in his seminal book *Problem-Oriented Policing,*[10] has documented that research into policing prior to the 1970s was greatly lacking. There were images of what the police did and then there were the realities, but the gulf between these was not well understood. Research coming out of the 1970s demonstrated that not only were the problems of policing a result of poor management, they were also a result of the complexities of the police role in society. It was found that police operational methods (e.g., preventative patrol, investigations, and rapid response) were not as successful at deterring or solving crime as conventional wisdom held. There was the realization that the police do far more than enforce the law and deal with criminal matters, despite an overreliance on the criminal law. Perhaps most important was the recognition of policing's broad use of discretion when dealing with problems on the street.

What Herman Goldstein noticed was that police decision making was driven by calls-for-service and was isolated within the frame of the incident itself. In other words, when the police responded to a call, they treated the incident as if it had neither a past nor a future, and that it was an isolated incident. Even when officers acknowledged that they would often go back to the same address and deal with the same problems, they still did not treat the incident as the symptoms of a problem, but rather the problem itself. The goal was to deal with it as quickly and professionally as possible and move on to the next problem. Goldstein thus argued that a more rational method of dealing with problems—substantive problems—should be the goal of policing.

Goldstein's solution was the adoption of what he called "problem-solving" or "problem-oriented policing."[11] The goal is to begin analyzing calls-for-service and attempting to label the underlying problem, not the symptoms of the problem. Linking problems with other incidents may reveal the substantive problem that underlies the calls-for-service. These can then be more effectively dealt with through the development of alternatives and the implementation of a possible solution, tailor-made to the problem under consideration. The goal of problem-oriented policing was thus focused on the ability to strengthen the police decision-making process and to increase the accountability of the police to the public it serves. As Goldstein explained,

> This process, of course, is clear when alternatives require the approval of a mayor, city manager, city council, or legislature. It is less clear when the police administrator is the sole decision maker. But numerous opportunities exist for clarifying these processes so that a higher degree of accountability is achieved. This improved accountability, in [Goldstein's] opinion, can best be achieved by having police administrators assume a greater responsibility for decisions that, either by design or default, are already theirs to make. They are in the best position to weigh alternative responses to citywide problems. They are most likely to have the staff and resources required to conduct analyses, to implement policies, and to achieve conformity with them. Administrators are also in the best position to determine the latitude of decision making that can be delegated to officers on the street and the methods by which this decision making can be reviewed.[12]

Despite the call for administrators to take more responsibility in the decision-making process, the concepts of problem-oriented policing have largely developed into a method of police service delivery. This has especially been true with the application of the SARA model of policing, which is a hands-on adaptation of Goldstein's concept that stands for scanning, analysis, response, and assessment.[13] Officers are taught to use the SARA model to look for incidents that might be related in the beats they police (scanning), to begin analyzing the problem by the collection of as much data as possible, to then develop potential means of effectively dealing with the problem (analysis) and implementing the response (response), and finally, to evaluate the response for its effectiveness (assessment).

Combined with the concepts of community-oriented policing, officers have been encouraged to problem solve with citizens in the neighborhoods they police. However, most problem solving tends to be officer initiated and officer conducted.[14] Police administration is often brought into play when officers develop solutions that require the use of additional police assets, such as personnel or equipment. On a daily basis, however, police administration generally only functions to manage the process by ensuring that officers are engaged in problem-solving cases, that they report on the status of their problem-oriented policing cases, and that they turn in final reports on completion. Rather than managing the problem-solving cases themselves, police administrators tend to only manage the paperwork that tracks the problems. As one author has concluded, "problem solving policing, no matter how well conceived or designed, cannot succeed unless the individual designated to take the lead in solving problems has the requisite knowledge, skills, authority and discretion to intelligently identify problems and construct viable tactical responses, as well as the organizational power

Chief Daryl Gates of the Los Angeles P.D., one of the creator's of COMPSTAT. *(Source: AP Wide World Photos)*

to marshal and apply resources to address them."[15] In other words, line officers are
not the proper level for solving substantive problems; the proper level lies, as Goldstein stated, with police administration. So, despite the calls for a more engaged police administration in the decision-making process, Goldstein's problem-oriented policing
developed simply into a method of policing, a tactic without good operational control,
support, or guidance.

The one concept in policing history that did develop into a system by which police administrators were forced to take on a more dynamic role in police decision making was the
implementation of CompStat by Police Commissioner William Bratton of the New York City
Police Department. CompStat recognized that the police commanders with a field perspective are "in a better position than beat officers to understand and harmonize the agency's
overall policies with the particular social dynamics operating within their geographic com-
pass."[16] In other words, the NYPD's application of CompStat was the first attempt in policing history where an agency attempted to place the responsibility of decision making where
it should be, with police management.[17]

CompStat

CompStat was created by the New York City Police Department under Police Commissioner William Bratton in the early 1990s.[18] Bratton's Deputy Commissioner, Jack Maple, is often the person credited as being the brainchild behind the concept.[19] The term *CompStat* has generally been said to have been derived from the concept of "compare statistics" or "compare stats," which was then shortened to CompStat. It was developed because police precinct reporting to the police headquarters in the New York City Police Department (NYPD) was dreadfully slow and was often three to six months old by the time it was fully collected and received. Bratton and Maple argued that the inability to have up-to-date and timely crime statistics was an impediment to good decision making for solving crime problems across the city.[20] Precinct commanders were then ordered to obtain current crime statistics on the seven major crime categories, and they were to report to a meeting of precinct commanders with the police commissioner. These meetings would evolve into the process of implementing CompStat.[21]

The precinct commanders would meet with Bratton and his staff to discuss the major crime concerns in their precincts and what they were doing to address the problems. At first the precinct commanders did not know what to expect, but once the process began with monthly meetings, the requirement became that they must be prepared to discuss the crimes that were occurring in their precincts and the methods they were using to address the problems. Failure to do so could possibly mean removal as a precinct commander. Those that were successful with their presentations were then held accountable for reducing the higher crime problems in their respective jurisdictions. Ultimately what was developed was a system of command profiles that tracked the capabilities of precinct commanders and special unit commanders (such as detective squad supervisors and narcotics supervisors) to determine their success in reducing crime. Again, those that demonstrated poor performance were removed and those that demonstrated high success were promoted.

The CompStat meetings eventually developed from low-tech paper handouts to a more high-tech conference room, emphasizing computer technology, video monitors, with projection screens. Data was presented via presentation software, and crime mapping data was presented, showing crimes over the previous month. Eventually, this command and control center became dubbed the "war room," and the department was essentially run through this method of command and decision making. In addition to the precinct commanders, other staff members were mandated to attend, despite the fact that they may not have to actually present. Their presence at these meetings allowed "for the immediate development of integrated plans and strategies" and gave precinct commanders the ability to "get on-the-spot commitments for the resources and assistance he or she need[ed] from ancillary and operational units."[22] Bringing together the high-level administrators, staff, and precinct commanders who were thus being held accountable for the actions of their subordinates brought police management and leadership to a vastly different level and attempted to overcome many of the criticisms of police management.

One realization after CompStat had been running was its lack of operational implementation. Although crime statistics were reviewed, trends and relationships discussed, and possible solutions generated, there was no mechanism for actually assigning responsibility or

BOX 12-1

COMPSTAT AS A MANAGEMENT APPROACH

Larry Hoover, Sam Houston State University

The notion that CompStat is a management approach instead of a strategy or even a set of strategies should not be quickly dismissed. Indeed, it should be noted that CompStat is strikingly similar to the generic principles of organizational success articulated by Peters and Waterman in their classic work, *In Search of Excellence.*

* **A bias for action** (immediate and definitive response to crime trends);
* **Close to the customer** (responsive to citizen complaints of crime problems);
* **Autonomy and entrepreneurship** (delegation to precinct commanders with innovation expected);
* **Productivity through people** (tough minded accountability);
* **Hands-on, value-driven** (the police can control crime, and we are here to do so);
* **Stick to the knitting** (crime control, not quality of life);
* **Simple form, lean staff** (back in uniform, back to patrol); and
* **Simultaneous loose-tight properties** (monitored at headquarters, but implemented at the precinct level with precinct-to-precinct variation).

Source: Reprinted with permission from Hoover, L.T. (2004). "CompStat as a Strategy: A Texas Perspective Part I—Conceptual Framework." *TELEMASP Bulletin* 11(4): 1–7.

implementing the solutions. The solution was the creation of a post-CompStat meeting that the high-ranking officers would attend to work out these types of operational issues. However, this was not a full-time operational unit, but rather an additional staff meeting to ensure proper coordination.[23]

The goals and objectives of CompStat reached far beyond anything policing had seen throughout its history.[24] It was a unique method for attempting to manage the issue of crime, holding management accountable, and coordinating the numerous police elements into a communicative decision-making process. Vincent Henry, in his book on CompStat, perhaps explains the overall strategy behind CompStat best. He explains that

> CompStat meetings permit executives and managers to monitor practically every aspect of the agency's activities—from fulfilling the primary mission of reducing crime and making the city's streets safer to closely observing and controlling virtually every systemic change instituted in the agency's systems, practices, structures and culture. CompStat meetings are, in a sense, a window through which the department's executives and managers can glimpse every aspect of its operations as well as the process and directions of every change taking place. They are also a mechanism by which the agency's operations and practices can be continually assessed and fine-tuned to ensure their continued success, and through which important messages can be subtly or overtly transmitted and reinforced.[25]

For all intents and purposes, what CompStat in New York City was able to do was to apply an administrative process by which police decision making was being conducted at the executive level, rather than at the street level. Police leadership was actually beginning to both lead and manage the department.

The greatest deficiency to the CompStat process for department decision making, however, was actually the same factor that created CompStat in the first place, the lack of good current data. Although CompStat took what was often spotty records three to six months old and brought them up-to-date with monthly presentations, the one-month lag time was a deficiency in allowing the police department to operate in real time. Although many of the crime problems an agency faces are long term, many are not. The once-a-month format continued to demonstrate a significant lag time. The NYPD, after moving through a period of unscheduled surprise meetings, eventually went to weekly and then twice weekly meetings to address this problem. The process, however, was still largely reactive.

CompStat would further evolve in both the NYPD, as well as the Los Angeles Police Department, where William Bratton would assume the role of Police Chief. Ultimately, what Compstat has come to focus on are four key principles.[26] The first principle is the call for timely and accurate intelligence to determine how best to use police resources. The second principle was the use of effective tactics to ensure that the methods being deployed by the department are the most effective for the problem at hand. The third principle is the use of rapid deployment to move resources where they are needed most through a strong operational plan. And finally, the fourth principle is to relentlessly follow up and assess whether or not the tactics used were the most appropriate to use that information for future deployments of police personnel and resources. Operational planning, however, was still largely relegated to the weekly CompStat meetings.

In August of 2002, in the wake of the 9-11 terrorist attacks, Chief Charles H. Ramsey of the Washington, D.C., Metropolitan Police instituted the CompStat process in his department and made it a daily occurrence. For 90 minutes each weekday morning, the Washington, D.C., police force's top commanders and detectives would meet in a similar "war room" to review the latest crimes and disorder in Washington, D.C. The purpose was to bring management up-to-date on the latest intelligence, develop solutions to any serious problems, and begin the process of communication and interaction to solve those problems.[27] By moving to a daily briefing, it allowed the department to operate in near real time insofar as police decision making at the executive level can be conducted. What is lacking, however, is an executable staff system that can implement the plans and operations coming from the daily meetings, as well as being prepared to react to major incidents. This is still left largely to the purview of the dispatchers and police officers in the field.

To fully implement a real-time police decision-making process at the administrative level it is necessary to continue the daily CompStat briefings, but it must be the responsibility of the CompStat players to continue the planning process outside these briefings. In other words, the staff must continue to work these operational issues together to produce the final operational plan that will deploy officers tactically. More importantly, when a major incident does occur, if this staff is already operating 24/7, there is no need to initiate the emergency operations center, as it is already in place and operational. Although

BOX 12-2

CRITICAL COMPONENTS OF COMPSTAT

Larry Hoover, Sam Houston State University

* Most Critical Component = Some kind of Discretionary Quick Deployment Resource.
* Specificity, or Targeted Enforcement, is an essential component.
* Multiple units are typically employed for Tactical Response.
* In large agencies, CompStat should be conducted both at headquarters and substation level.
* Geographic Information System Display is very useful, but is only an enhancement.
* An experienced GIS operator who can instantly modify the display (e.g., zoom or overlay multiple family dwellings) is essential if GIS is to be useful.
* CompStat is as much about values and motivations as it is strategy.

Source: Reprinted with permission from Hoover, L. T. (2004). "CompStat as a Strategy: A Texas Perspective Part II—Texas Practices." *TELEMASP Bulletin* 11(5): 1–15.

it may be staffed only with the primary players on each shift, the time it takes to respond to an incident is far less than if the emergency operations center is vacant or staffed by only one or two officers. In addition, it places full control of police operations in the hands of the police staff, it allows for the maximum amount of information to provide for the best information and intelligence to make informative decisions, and it forces police management to actually lead the department, rather than feigning leadership, as was previously discussed.

Incident Command/Emergency Operations Center as Police Operations

Prior to the events of September 11th and the actions of the Bush administration, exactly how the emergency operation center should work would most likely have been best left up to each individual department. A number of factors go into the determination of how best to organize such an entity. The so-called war room methods are generally a given, but space constraints, location, the proper personnel that need to be present, technology, and budget constraints, among other factors, all contribute to the determination of how best to organize. Questions revolve around whether or not the emergency operation center should be colocated with the police dispatch, at the police headquarters, or should the department purchase a mobile headquarters that can move closer to the scene? Other questions revolve around the proper staffing, who should be in command, what key players and staff members should have authorization to the emergency operations center, and how these entities communicate to one another. Still other questions center around the mechanisms for communication and information, such as television screens, computers, handwritten messages, e-mails, whiteboards, phone lines, or just plain old-fashioned shouting. All these issues generally had to be resolved, and many of these resulted in failures. In some cases state-of-the-art command centers were poorly located, such as was seen on September 11th, where the emergency operation center was located in one of the World Trade Center towers and proved inaccessible. In other cases, large and expensive recreational vehicles were purchased and equipped to be "close to the scene," making them more of a liability than an asset. And often these centers were seldom trained on or seldom used, and when used created an impediment due to unfamiliarity with the technology and equipment. All that hopefully will have ceased on February 28, 2003.

President Bush, on February 28, 2003, issued Homeland Security Presidential Directive Number 5, calling for the standardization of the National Incident Management System (NIMS) and the use of the ICS for all emergency operations.[28] NIMS provides a consistent framework for entities at all jurisdictional levels to work together to manage domestic incidents, regardless of cause, size, or complexity. The goal is to promote interoperability and compatibility among the federal, state, and local agencies and to provide a core set of guidelines, standards, and protocols for command and management, preparedness, resource management, communications and information management, supporting technologies, and both the management and maintenance of NIMS.[29] By creating a standardized system for managing incidents, it allows for greater ease of cross-boundary communication and helps to foster the multijurisdictional efforts that are often necessitated by major incidents. A good example of the need for this system was Hurricane Katrina, which devastated the New Orleans area, but was not merely relegated to the city of New Orleans. Or the following Hurricane Rita, that struck the Texas shores, which necessitated multiple jurisdictions to handle the evacuation of Galveston and Houston. In sum, it avoids the problem cited by one law enforcement official that "we co-locate on a regular basis, but we don't have the ability to communicate."[30]

The primary aspect of the NIMS for police command is the use of the ICS.[31] The ICS was developed in the aftermath of a devastating wildfire in California. During 13 days in 1970, 16 lives were lost, 700 structures were destroyed, and over one-half million acres burned. The overall cost and loss associated with these fires totaled $18 million per day. Although all the responding agencies cooperated to the best of their ability, numerous problems with communication and coordination hampered their effectiveness. As a result, the Congress mandated that the U.S. Forest Service design a system that would make a quantum jump in the capabilities of Southern California wildland fire protection agencies to effectively coordinate interagency action and to allocate suppression resources in dynamic, multiple-fire situations.

The California Department of Forestry and Fire Protection (CDF), the Governor's Office of Emergency Services (OES); the Los Angeles, Ventura, and Santa Barbara County Fire Departments; and the Los Angeles City Fire Department joined with the U.S. Forest Service to develop the system. This system became known as FIRESCOPE (FIrefighting RESources of California Organized for Potential Emergencies).

In 1973, the first "FIRESCOPE Technical Team" was established to guide the research and development design. Two major components came from this work, the ICS and the Multi-Agency Coordination System (MACS). The FIRESCOPE ICS is primarily a command and control system delineating job responsibilities and organizational structure for the purpose of managing day-to-day operations for all types of emergency incidents.

By the midseventies, the FIRESCOPE agencies had formally agreed on ICS common terminology and procedures, then conducted limited field testing of ICS. By 1980, parts of ICS had been used successfully on several major wildland and urban fire incidents. It was formally adopted by the Los Angeles Fire Department, the CDF, and the OES and endorsed by the State Board of Fire Services.

Also during the 1970s, the National Wildfire Coordinating Group (NWCG) was chartered to coordinate fire management programs of the various participating federal and state agencies. By 1980, FIRESCOPE ICS training was under development. Recognizing that in addition to the local users for which it was designed, the FIRESCOPE training could satisfy the needs of other state and federal agencies, the NWCG conducted an analysis of FIRESCOPE ICS for possible national application.

By 1981, ICS was widely used throughout Southern California by the major fire agencies. In addition, the use of ICS in response to nonfire incidents was increasing. Although FIRESCOPE ICS was originally developed to assist in the response to wildland fires, it was quickly recognized as a system that could help public safety responders provide effective and coordinated incident management for a wide range of situations, including floods, hazardous materials accidents, earthquakes, and aircraft crashes. It was flexible enough to manage catastrophic incidents involving thousands of emergency response and management personnel. By introducing relatively minor terminology, organizational and procedural modifications to FIRESCOPE ICS, the National Interagency Incident Management System (NIIMS ICS) became adaptable to an all-hazards environment.

Although tactically each type of incident may be handled somewhat differently, the overall incident management approach still utilizes the major functions of the ICS. The FIRESCOPE board of directors and the NWCG recommended national application of ICS. In 1982, all FIRESCOPE ICS documentation was revised and adopted as the NIIMS. In the years since FIRESCOPE and the NIIMS were blended, the FIRESCOPE agencies and the NWCG have worked together to update and maintain the Incident Command System Operational System Description. This document would later serve as the basis for the NIIMS ICS.

The NIIMS ICS is readily adaptable to policing and in fact has already been implemented in numerous departments across the country. One of the benefits of the Arlington County Police Department's efficient response on September 11th, stemmed from a number of the command staff having received ICS training.[32] In addition, as a result of the HSPD-5, the Department of Homeland Security (DHS) has begun training police departments in the use of the ICS. Because HSPD-5 provides a framework for emergency incident command, it takes little additional effort to incorporate the concepts of ICS as a permanent fixture of police-level command. In other words, ICS should be the method of dealing with the daily routine of policing. Combined with the management capabilities of CompStat, its ability to operate in real time and manage the police department's personnel and resources, as well as being operational prior to a major incident, the ICS system is the most appropriate method for police management and leadership in a post–9-11 world.

The actual operational methods of the ICS consist of the command staff and the general staff.[33] The command staff has four positions, with the primary position being the Incident Commander. The Incident Commander then has three special staff personnel that report directly to him or her and assist in the command of the ICS. These positions include the Public Information Officer (PIO), the Safety Officer (SO), and the Liaison Officer (LO). The PIO is responsible for interfacing with the public, media, and/or other agencies with incident-related information requirements.

The SO monitors incident operations and advises the Incident Commander on all matters related to operational safety, including the health and safety of emergency response personnel. The SO is ultimately responsible to the Incident Commander, but he or she does have the emergency authority to stop and/or prevent unsafe acts during incident operations.

The LO is the point of contact for representatives of other government agencies, nongovernmental agencies (such as the Red Cross), and/or private companies.

Other possible command staff personnel may include a police chaplain, the Internal Affairs Inspector, and possibly the lead legal counsel for the department. These additional staff are generally left to the discretion of the Incident Commander. Finally, other members that are related to the command staff that may be present in the ICS are the assistants for the various staff members.

The General Staff includes incident management personnel who represent the major functional elements of the ICS, and these include the Operations Section Chief, Planning Section Chief, Logistics Section Chief, the Finance/Administration Section Chief, and the Information and Intelligence Officer. The Operations Section is responsible for all activities focused on reduction of the immediate hazard, saving lives and property, establishing situational control, and restoration of normal operations. The Operational Section Chief will establish an operational plan and will specify the tactical objectives necessary to carry out the operational plan. The Operational Section Chief will obviously have a staff of his or her own to assist in the development of incident plans and orders, but the actions of the Operation Section lie with the Chief and ultimately the Incident Commander.

The Planning Section of the General Staff collects, evaluates, and disseminates incident situation informational and intelligence to the Incident Commander and incident management personnel. The Planning Section also prepares status reports, displays situation information, maintains status of resources assigned to the incident, and develops and documents the Incident Action Plan based on guidance from the Incident Commander.

The Logistics Section is responsible for all support requirements needed to facilitate effective and efficient incident management. These support requirements include ensuring that the proper supplies, food, technology, and medical services are available to the responders.

The Finance/Administration Section of the General Staff is established when the agency involved in incident management requires finance and other administrative support. These needs may include cost/benefit analysis, procurement requirements, and compensation/claims issues.

The Information and Intelligence Section provides analysis and sharing of both information and intelligence during an incident. Intelligence can include national security or classified information but also can include operational information from open sources such as risk assessments, medical intelligence, weather information, structural designs of buildings, blueprints of various facilities, and hazardous chemical information.

In a major incident these staffs must come together to determine the operational plan and specifically the tactical objectives that will accomplish the operational plan in support of the overall strategy. The Incident Commander drawing on the input of the two staff elements is then in a position to make informative decisions by gaining input from the various sections as the operations proceed. This method has been proven to be highly effective in a number of settings, ranging from the U.S. military to political campaigns. More recently it has become a mainstay of decision making for special-interest groups to respond faster to any actions or language that may go against their particular issue, and even Wal-Mart has created a similar mechanism to deal with negative publicity. But again, the concept of only activating this in the event of major incidents slows down the effectiveness of such an operation. To move to a "full-time" ICS it would necessitate some administrative changes.

Moving to a full-time ICS would mean that each of the sections, except the Operations and Finance/Administration Sections, would require at least one staff member to be on duty at all times. The PIO, SO, and LO of the command staff would need to have someone subordinate, an assistant, to staff these positions around the clock, having the capability of calling back the primary officer in a major incident. The Planning, Logistics, and Information/Intelligence Sections would also have to maintain at least a skeleton crew on duty at all times. The Finance/Administration would be able to serve on call as the ICS would not necessarily need this individual or staff until a major incident. Finally, the shift commander could serve as the "Incident Commander" during that particular shift with his or her management personnel serving as the Operations Section Chief and Staff controlling the tactical deployment of officers.

The actual facility may be colocated with police dispatch, but with technological capabilities, that is not mandatory. However, consideration should be given to security when selecting a location, and a secondary site should be identified in case of the disabling of the primary ICS. It is from this facility that the ICS should be used to develop and disseminate operational orders, manage information, maintain staff estimates regarding personnel and equipment, and both control and assess operations. Information must be channeled to the ICS, and all orders should be processed through the ICS. Dispatch will retain its function, but it will be overseen by the Operations Section. Information must also be available to all those involved in the ICS; therefore, computer imaging, plasma screens on the walls, and a databank of television monitors would provide for as much information as possible for the staff to make decisions.

The use of other technologies should be considered as well, especially those technologies that the ICS can access and those that give the ICS more enhanced real-time information to contribute to the decision-making process. Three examples include closed-circuit cameras, geographic information systems with global positional satellites, and crime prevention through environmental design (CPTED). In the case of closed-circuit television cameras, the research is still somewhat mixed as to whether or not they reduce crime.[34] In some cases they have been found to reduce crime, in some cases they have displaced crimes, and in others they have proven useful in investigations. A recent survey conducted by the International Association of Chiefs of Police found that 80 percent of police departments reported used some form of closed-circuit televisions, many of which

BOX 12-3

HOMELAND SECURITY OPERATIONS CENTER (HSOC)

Phillip Davis, Sam Houston State University

The Homeland Security Operations Center (HSOC) serves as the nation's nerve center for information sharing and domestic incident management—dramatically increasing the vertical coordination between federal, state, territorial, tribal, local, and private-sector partners. The HSOC collects and fuses information from a variety of sources every day to help deter, detect, and prevent terrorist acts. Operating 24 hours a day, seven days a week, 365 days a year, the HSOC provides real-time situational awareness and monitoring of the homeland, coordinates incidents and response activities, and, in conjunction with the DHS Office of Information Analysis, issues advisories and bulletins concerning threats to homeland security, as well as specific protective measures. Information on domestic incident management is shared with Emergency Operations Centers at all levels through the Homeland Security Information Network (HSIN).

HSOC Structure

The HSOC represents over 35 agencies ranging from state and local law enforcement to federal intelligence agencies. Information is shared and fused on a daily basis by the two halves of the HSOC that are referred to as the "intelligence side" and the "law enforcement side." Each half is identical and functions in tandem with the other but requires a different level of clearance to access information. The "intelligence side" focuses on pieces of highly classified intelligence and how the information contributes to the current threat picture for any given area. The "law enforcement side" is dedicated to tracking the different enforcement activities across the country that may have a terrorist nexus. The two pieces fused together create a real-time snapshot of the nation's threat environment at any moment.

Source: U.S. Department of Homeland Security, Homeland Security Operations Center Fact Sheet.
Source: http://www.dhs.gov/dhspublic/display?theme=30&content=3813

were located in police cars, interrogation rooms, and access to courts and other government buildings.[35] While 63 percent of the respondents found these cameras useful in investigations and 54 percent said they were helpful in gathering evidence, only 20 percent reported they helped to reduce crime. Incorporated into the ICS operation center, however, they may also provide additional information for informative decisions, something not fully appreciated to date. Therefore, despite the controversy often surrounding them, the use of these cameras will most likely continue and could prove invaluable to the ICS system.[36]

The second example is the use of geographic information systems (GIS) and global positioning satellites (GPS).[37] In the case of GIS, with the various layers of geographic information available to police, ICS command centers can draw on this type of information through a computer tabletop screen in both daily routine patrol and major incidents. The impact of weather on certain areas prone to flood can give law enforcement an

BOX 12-4

DEPARTMENT OF HOMELAND SECURITY INCIDENT MANAGEMENT ROLE

Interagency Incident Management Group (IIMG)

Phillip Davis, Sam Houston State University

The IIMG is a headquarters-level group comprised of senior representatives from DHS components, other federal departments and agencies, and nongovernmental organizations. The IIMG provides strategic situational awareness, synthesizes key intelligence and operational information, frames operational courses of action and policy recommendations, anticipates evolving requirements, and provides decision support to the secretary of Homeland Security and other national authorities during periods of elevated alert and national domestic incidents.

Quick Response. During incidents such as Hurricane Isabel, the December 2003 Orange Alert, and the blackout in New York City, the IIMG was "stood-up" in less than 90 minutes and hosted assistant secretary-level members of the represented agencies to provide strategic leadership.

Source: U.S. Department of Homeland Security, Homeland Security Operations Center Fact Sheet.
Source: http://www.dhs.gov/dhspublic/display?theme=30&content=3813

idea of where to move citizens to safe locations. In the event of a major incident, it can help the ICS staff determine where best to stage operations, alternate locations for managing a situation, and methods of ingress and egress from the incident. Coupled with the capability of global positioning satellites, if all police vehicles incorporated a GPS receiving device, it would allow the command center, and specifically the Operations Section, to know the location of police assets at all times.[38] This can help the ICS command and general staff make decisions of how best deploy officers tactically in the event of a major incident, based on their real-time location. The U.S. military has been using a very similar system in both Iraq and Afghanistan known as "blue-force tracker," giving the command tactical operations center the capability of controlling actions on the battlefield. A similar system would support the operational goals of a full-time ICS.

The third example, CPTED has moved from a concept to a technological approach to preventing crime. CPTED concepts also lend themselves to preventing terrorism or reducing the harm caused by terrorist incidents, based on architectural design of buildings and streets, as well as the placement of such things as streetlights, landscaping, traffic control devices, sidewalks, parks, and other recreational areas. Using CPTED can assist in risk assessments and can have both a strategic and operational application to Homeland Security policing.[39]

Police Decision-Making Process

The confluence of a full-time ICS police center, alongside the organizational staff structure to compliment it, combined with the CompStat format of daily briefings, lends itself to a

NYPD Officers from the Bronx, NY undergoing In-Tac (In-Service Tactical) training in a classroom. *(Source: NYPD Photographic Unit)*

police decision-making process that can operate in real time. What is, in essence, being advocated is the implementation of CompStat full-time. Ultimately the goal of conducting operations in this manner is to utilize the staff to create good operational plans, make informative decisions during crises, and to deploy the police tactically in a manner that will best accomplish the operational objectives. By achieving these objectives, it allows the department to achieve its strategic goals of policing in an era of homeland security. And, overall, it places the management of the police department in the hands of the police department's leadership, advocating for centralized decision making and decentralized execution.

To achieve this level of operations, the police must use a mechanism to adequately deal with not only the daily routine operations, but also with major incidents as they arise. The staff format is the structure, but what is also needed is a process of decision making for the full-time ICS staff to receive information on situations, work through a process of developing good operational plans, then directing the tactical deployment from the police command center or "war room." Once again, the development of the problem-solving methods articulated by Goldstein and CompStat as developed by Bratton lend themselves readily.

The ICS should monitor the dispatch calls for services as a means of early warning that an incident is developing. The Operations Section would obviously be responsible for monitoring both radio and computer traffic to this regard. In addition, officers on the street can communicate their observations, thus providing for further input they more readily identify a situation developing. Once information begins to enter the ICS command center, the staff must identify the possible threats and begin to mobilize police officers on patrol, discretionary quick response units, special police units, detectives, or other personnel deemed appropriate. This does not simply mean that all available officers are dispatched to the scene as is common; it simply means that officers are made aware of a situation developing.

Once officers are mobilized, then the staff must begin the process of analyzing the situation with the information currently available. Specific information that is lacking must be identified and attempts to obtain that information made. It is during this time period that a tentative plan is made. Ideally, the ICS staff can draw on plans that previously existed within the Planning Section and modify these to fit the situation at hand. These standard operating procedures allow for a baseline for planning operations and can be updated in the after-action analysis that should be conducted. Regardless, the situation must be analyzed, and the Incident Commander and his or her staff should identify the threat and develop the basic who, what, when, where, and how the situation will be handled. The staff must also consider the key tactical tasks that must be conducted, what the goal or end-state of the operation is to be (Operations Officer), and they must constantly consider the constraints under which they operate (Liaison and Logistics Officers) and the risks posed by the operation (Safety Officer).

In addition to the key tasks cited earlier, the Incident Commander and his or her staff must develop various courses of action for dealing with the problem or incident. These courses of action must be distinguishable from one another, and they must be feasible to the operational capabilities of the department as well as from a legal standpoint. The various courses of action must also conform to the overall strategic goals of the department, and they must be acceptable in terms of a cost and benefit analysis, where the costs of resources and risks do not outweigh the benefits of the course of action. If each course of action satisfies these requirements, then the agency must analyze each of the courses of action for their positive and negative ramifications independently, and then they must compare them against one another. Although staff input into selecting the best course of action is highly desirable and should be the norm, ultimately the decision lies with the Incident Commander. Once the particular course of action is selected, the ICS staff must then began to put the final plan together based on the option selected.

Once a tentative plan is put into place, the ICS staff must began issuing the operational orders to the various units on standby, and they must be directed. The order must consider all the input from the various sections, including the identification of the threat and personnel responding to the threat, the operational plan, and the logistics and communication coordination necessary to achieve the tactical objectives. It must also assign responsibility to subordinate leaders, those in the field, to ensure that the tactical aspects of the plan will be implemented. And, as new information or intelligence becomes available and officers on the scene communicate updated information, the ICS staff must remain flexible enough to adapt its plans to the situation.

Although this form of decision making can be sped up to handle major crises that occur without warning, such as 9-11, it can also be used in terms of crime trend analysis and problem solving in the same format as CompStat. Although the process does become highly abbreviated, it is still suggested that each of the steps, identification of the situation, analysis, course of action development/analysis/comparison, and operational orders developed, would all remain a part of the process.

Finally, drawing on the cycle of preparedness identified by William V. Pelfrey, it is imperative that the ICS staff, after any incident, exercise, or implementation of a response to crime trends, evaluate its success.[40] At a minimum, an after-action review should be conducted, one that allows all the members of the staff to assess what went well and what went poorly. The key is to identify ways of improving the police response in the future to similar incidents. All this should be captured by the Planning Section to then be incorporated into standing plans. As Pelfrey articulated, the process should be one of constant planning, training, equipping, exercising, evaluating, and revising.[41] And, in the case of a major incident, a formal after-action report should be made available in a published format that not only all of those working within the agency may benefit, but those from other police agencies may benefit as well. A good example of this is the Arlington County Police Department's After-Action Report from their response on September 11th.[42]

Although there are numerous operational considerations when it comes to police operations under homeland security, three major factors will clearly influence operations and operational planning. These considerations include multijurisdictional partnerships, both risk and threat assessments, and law enforcement intelligence. Each of these will be expounded on in detail.

BOX 12-5

HAYWARD POLICE DEPARTMENT AND HOMELAND SECURITY

Hayward is a municipality near San Francisco with a population of about 144,600. Its police department has almost 200 sworn officers. After receiving a Department of Homeland Security grant, the Hayward Police Department created a full-time detective position focused specifically on homeland security issues. By contacting the Financial Investigations Program (FIP) of the California Department of Justice's Bureau of Narcotics Enforcement, the Hayward Police Department was able to access FinCEN data regarding suspicious financial transactions. The department requests reports on suspicious activity by ZIP Code and received 450 suspicious activity reports. An analysis of the reports revealed links to an outlaw motorcycle gang, possible organized crime groups, and terrorist financing.

As a result, the Hayward Police Department is conducting a joint investigation with the U.S. Bureau of Immigration and Customs into a subject with ties to terrorist financing and who has laundered more than $100 million during a three-year period.

The Hayward Police Department also has been able to access investigative and analytic support from the U.S. Department of Justice's FIP, including access to a wide range of commercial databases. One outcome of this work is the improved relationship between the police department and its local financial institutions. The institutions now contact the police proactively about suspicious financial activity reports, cutting the lag time between when a suspicious activity occurs and when police learn about it.

As a result of this success in the financial investigative area, the Hayward Police Department new requests a FinCEN check on every subject who is investigated for possible terrorist connections.

Source: Peterson, M. (2005). *Intelligence-Led Policing: The New Intelligence Architecture.* Washington, D.C.: Bureau of Justice Assistance, p. 23.

PARTNERSHIPS

The call for partnerships under homeland security has been very strong in post–9-11. It has differed from the community policing era in that the demands for partnerships are now primarily focused on partnering with other police departments, as well as state and federal law enforcement agencies, whereas under community policing, it was primarily about the police partnering with the community. Although this should not be diminished under the era of homeland security, as partnerships are assuredly still needed with citizens, the media, nongovernmental agencies, and other governmental agencies, the focus is on the coordination of police services across jurisdictional boundaries. Whether this is through enhanced mutual aid agreements, networking, data sharing, communication, or the implementation of the ICS unified command, partnerships are an important operational aspect of homeland security, and they begin with the mutual aid agreements.

Historically, law enforcement mutual aid agreements have been used most often on a limited basis for the sharing of personnel and resources to establish multiagency investigative teams and task forces.[43] Typically, the enabling agreement between jurisdictions takes the form of memorandums of understanding. Such agreements are limited in scope and purpose to address specific crime problems that cut across jurisdictional boundaries. Most familiar to law enforcement agencies are automatic mutual aid agreements in which units from neighboring jurisdictions are automatically dispatched to incident scenes. These are interlocal agreements that are usually basic contracts or even informal agreements. Mutual agreements for homeland security, however, should be more formalized than these types of agreements and should be designed to provide a wide range of services and resources to afflicted jurisdictions over longer periods.

Law enforcement has long recognized that such multijurisdictional, multiagency operations reap major benefits in combating broad-based criminal activities that cut across jurisdictional boundaries. For example, contiguous jurisdictions have successfully used major case squads in a variety of contexts for decades. In the early 1980s, the Federal Bureau of Investigation (FBI) set up a Joint Terrorism Task Force (JTTF) in New York City to serve as a link for regional operations among federal, state, and local agencies. The JTTF, as well as the Joint Drug Task Forces, soon spread to other major cities nationwide and have been widely hailed as effective partnerships.

In light of these successful interjurisdictional enterprises, it is not surprising that the same collaborative approach has been taken in local, state, and national attempts to address the threats of international and domestic terrorism. The utility of these agreements was demonstrated dramatically during and immediately following the events surrounding September 11, 2001, when well-orchestrated mutual aid agreements among regional agencies in New York and interstate agreements among other adjoining states were activated to deal with the cataclysmic events and aftermath of that day. Fire companies, law enforcement officers, other first responders, and a wide variety of other assistance were brought from throughout New York State as well as from far-flung regions of the country. In New York State, such personnel were activated under regional mutual aid agreements to assist at the scene. They also were used to backfill positions of first responders in jurisdictions surrounding New York City that were temporarily vacated by those who were directly engaged in rescue efforts at the World Trade Center so that fire and law enforcement services could continue unabated in these surrounding jurisdictions.

For these and other reasons, President George W. Bush launched the National Mutual Aid and Resource Management Initiative to assist first responders outside major metropolitan agencies in establishing mutual aid agreements or in renewing and refining existing agreements. The key concepts of this initiative are to establish preincident agreements, develop protocols for response, identify resources available for response, and to ideally create an automated resource management system that can track these resources. As part of the effort to ensure that America is prepared for future attacks and can mitigate the damage caused by such an attack, police agencies, in support of the strategies for homeland security, are encouraged to give operational consideration to mutual aid agreements to develop their partnerships with other agencies.

Mutual aid agreements should be regarded as another form of law enforcement partnership. Mutual aid may have been conceived primarily to respond to disasters and emergencies, but it also is well suited for preventing such occurrences. The organizational and collaborative approaches developed through mutual aid agreements bring together key decision makers who can share information that serves their individual and collective interests on many levels. This may be derived through shared intelligence. Local law enforcement officials can obtain a great deal about terrorist and other criminal activity in general and assist in identifying threats that are common local or regional concerns. It may come from the training received by one agency in the region that can be shared with officers in partnership with other agencies in the region through the train-the-trainer approach or similar means. There is also the case that these partnerships may assist in potential target identification and developing law enforcement agency threat assessments. Local law enforcement agencies that work closely together to identify regional threats, share intelligence, and work constructively to develop mutual aid agreements are more likely to prevent an emergency or disaster and to mitigate the damage caused by one.

Mutual aid agreements codify an understanding between two or more entities to provide support in a given context. Parties to agreements can include two, three, or more response agencies, private organizations, hospitals, public utilities, governments, and virtually any type of organization that can bring resources to bear during an emergency. Such agreements may be as expansive or as limited as the parties desire. Because of the varying levels of jurisdictions there are several types of mutual aid agreements, and they include (1) automatic mutual aid, where units from neighboring jurisdictions are automatically dispatched to the scene; (2) mutual aid, where neighboring jurisdictions agree to assist in incidents when requested to do so by another agency; (3) regional mutual aid, where agencies from a particular region, when called on, can assist local units for extended period of times; (4) statewide mutual aid, where agencies across the entire state and state-level resources can be called on to assist in a catastrophic event; and (5) interstate agreements, where out-of-state assistance can be utilized to assist in the recovery phase of a significant event. Depending on the geographical nature of the jurisdictions, both risk and threat assessments, and the level at which the mutual aid agreements are being negotiated, will determine the type of mutual aid agreement under consideration.

It is recommended that a committee be established to create or update mutual aid agreements. A wide variety of stakeholders should be involved in drafting a mutual aid agreement. The committee members should negotiate the agreement and approve it or recommend its approval on behalf of their respective organizations. Jurisdictions must determine who needs to be at the negotiating table so that the agreement will be as inclusive and responsive as possible. The respective heads of the law enforcement agencies involved should be included, as well as potentially the heads of other emergency response agencies, emergency management agencies, elected officials, and legal representatives. The committee should determine the boundaries of the agreement, the needs of each agency, what resources (personnel, equipment, etc.) they can bring to the table, and what stipulations they have on the agreement. Once this is ironed out, the parties should work with their agencies' stakeholders and legal advisors to craft the mutual aid agreement. These agreements can then be brought to future meetings to merge the various drafts into one document. The preference is to present the documents on-screen and edit "live" while everyone can read and review the language. Once the committee approves, the heads of agencies should be briefed for their input, and ultimately the agreement should be signed by all interested parties.

As the mutual aid agreement is signed, it is essential that the agreement turn into an operation plan. Therefore, it is critical that the agreement address as many factors as possible so that the operational plan can be drawn up. Considerations should include (1) department officials who are authorized to request assistance from other participating law enforcement agencies should be clearly identified; (2) the agreement must set forth the circumstances under which assistance may be granted; (3) it should specify the acceptable methods by which requests for assistance may be transmitted between agencies; (4) it should specify the forms of assistance that are to be rendered; (5) it should specify the extent and duration of any assistance rendered between jurisdictions; (6) it should detail under what circumstance assistance can be withdrawn; (7) command and control issues must be addressed in the agreements; (8) financial responsibility for the provision of services must be clearly defined; (9) claims for reimbursement must be established in the agreement, addressing the costs of personnel, equipment, supplies, and the record keeping process; (10) it should include conditions and procedures for the withdrawal of a participating agency from the agreement itself; (11) it should identify whether the agreement will be binding on subsequent agency chief executives; (12) it should deal with an agency's inability to respond to a request as not forming the basis of a breach of contract; (13) it should not contain provisions for summoning state or federal aid; (14) it should define the responsibilities of chief executive officers; and (15) it should provide for the inclusion of other public and private entities in prevention, preparation, and response to regional emergencies.[44] All these factors should be addressed in the mutual aid agreement, so that the operational plan can be properly developed.

The operational plan should consider the process by which mutual aid is obtained. Normally, a request for assistance begins at the line level when a supervisor becomes aware of a situation that may require assistance from a participating law enforcement agency. All such communications must receive approval of the chief law enforcement officer of the agency or a designated officer who has been delegated authority to make such decisions in the absence or on behalf of the chief executive officer. All initial requests should be sent through the law enforcement agency's communications center and routed to the authorized in a timely manner.

After a request is filed, a decision to provide assistance must be made by the law enforcement agency contacted for assistance. Agencies that participate in the plan are not legally obligated to provide assistance if doing so would unreasonably diminish the safety and welfare of their community. Once a decision has been make on deployment, personnel or units should be dispatched through the emergency communications center. Dispatchers should prohibit on- or off-duty units who are listening in from self-dispatching to the incident scene. This can be a common practice in emergency situations, but it is unacceptable. Self-dispatch can create chaos at an incident scene.

The incident commander is responsible for making initial and ongoing assessments of the personnel and resource requirements necessary to adequately address and control the emergency. Personnel and resources should report to a preestablished staging area or one identified by the incident commander. In the event that multiple jurisdictions are affected by the incident, under the NIMS, the use of a unified command is implemented.[45] This unified command can be one aspect of the mutual aid agreement and operational plan, which should address the possibility that an event may cover multiple jurisdictions, a single jurisdiction with multiagency involvement, or multiple jurisdictions with multiagency involvement. The unified command allows agencies to work together effectively without affecting individual agency authority, responsibility, or accountability. It does this by providing guidelines to enable agencies with different legal, geographic, and functional responsibilities to coordinate, plan, and interact effectively. This allows for both joint planning and joint execution, while attempting to avoid duplication of effort and general inefficiencies.

RISK ASSESSMENT AND RISK MANAGEMENT

In the aftermath of 9-11, the Heritage Foundation put together a Homeland Security Task Force to begin looking at the priorities of federal, state, and local governments in regard to the entire scope of Homeland Security issues.[46] One of the working groups of this task force focused on intelligence and law enforcement. Its number one stated priority was to "require the Office of Homeland Security to direct the assessment of threats to critical assets nationwide."[47] It argued that the key steps to accomplishing this priority consisted of assessing the threats, identifying critical targets, determining their vulnerabilities, and assessing risk. What should naturally follow, they urged, is the establishment of a national strategy to protect the homeland based on the national assessments. Although this is highly encouraged, local agencies cannot and should not wait for a national identification of risks and how to manage these risks. Each law enforcement agency should begin the process of conducting risk assessments to help develop their own risk management plan. Any risk assessment or management plan conducted at the regional, state, or federal level can simply be factored into the assessments already conducted by the local agency. The only drawback to this is that many law enforcement agencies have either not conducted these types of assessments in decades or they never have conducted these assessments at all. Therefore, it is necessary for law enforcement agencies under homeland security to learn what each of these assessments, threat, criticality, vulnerability, and ultimately risk, entails, and how they are conducted.

To understand the concept of threat assessments, it is important first to understand the concept of threat. Roper defines a threat as "any indication, circumstance or event with the potential to cause loss or damage to an asset" in the case of "the intention and capability of an adversary to undertake actions that would be detrimental to U.S. interests."[48] To be helpful in assessing vulnerability and risk, threats need to be characterized in some detail.[49] Important characteristics include type (e.g., insider, terrorist, military, hurricane, tornado), intent or motivation, triggers (i.e., events that might initiate an attack), capability (e.g., skills, specific knowledge, access to materials or equipment), methods (e.g., use of individual suicide bombers, truck bombs, assault, cyber), and trends (i.e., what techniques have groups used in the past or experimented with). Information useful to characterize the threat can come from the intelligence community, law enforcement intelligence units, specialists, news reports, analysis and investigations of past incidents, received threats, or "red teams" whose purpose is to "think" like a terrorist. Threat assessment typically also involves assumptions and speculation because information on specific threats may be scant, incomplete, or vague.

Once potential threats have been identified (both generically, e.g., terrorists, and specifically, e.g., Al-Qaeda) and characterized, a threat assessment estimates the "likelihood of adversary activity against a given asset or group of assets."[50] The DHS defines a threat assessment as

> a systematic effort to identify and evaluate existing or potential terrorist threats to a jurisdiction and its target assets. Due to the difficulty in accurately assessing terrorist capabilities, intentions, and tactics, threat assessments may yield only general information about potential risks.[51]

However, it should be noted that these assessments for law enforcement purposes must consider the full spectrum of threats, such as natural disasters, criminal activity, and major incidents, as well as any terrorist activity.

Focusing more specifically on the possibility of a terrorist attack, the likelihood of an attack is generally considered a function of at least two parameters.[52] The first is whether or not the asset represents a tempting target based on the goals and motivations of the adversary (i.e., Would a successful attack on that asset further the goals and objectives of the attacker?). The second is whether the adversary has the capability to attack the asset by various methods. Other parameters to consider include past history of such attacks against such targets by the same adversary or by others, the availability of the asset as a target (e.g., Is the location of the target fixed or does it change and how would the adversary know of the target's existence or movement?). The asset's vulnerability to various methods of attack (risk assessments) may also affect the attractiveness of the asset as a target.

To conduct a threat assessment, law enforcement must draw on these characterizations of the threat, consider the parameters, and draw on as many sources as possible. Threat assessments must be compiled from comprehensive and rigorous research and analysis.[53] Law enforcement cannot function unilaterally. Threat assessments that do not incorporate the knowledge, assessments, and understanding of state, local, and private organizations and agencies with the potential threats being assessed are inherently incomplete. For example, a threat assessment of water district facilities should include the most comprehensive data available from local police, sheriff, and fire departments; health services; emergency management organizations; and other applicable local, state, and federal agencies that may be affected by an attack on the water district's infrastructure. The threat assessments should also assimilate germane, open-source, or nonproprietary threat assessments, as well as intelligence information. Lastly, the assessment must provide a high level of awareness and understanding regarding the changing threat and threat environment faced by a government entity.

Essential data to collect for analysis prior to conducting a threat assessment include (1) the type of adversary, whether or not it is a terrorist, employee, or other; (2) category of adversary, such as foreign or domestic, terrorist or criminal; (3) objective of each type of adversary, examples include theft, sabotage, or mass destruction; (4) the number of adversaries expected for each category, for instance single suicide bomber or multiples, one or more terrorist cells, gang or gangs; (5) target selected by adversaries, such as critical infrastructure, government buildings, symbolic structures such as monuments; (6) the type of planning activities required to accomplish the objective, for example long-term casing, photography, monitoring of police patrols; (7) most likely or "worst-case" time an adversary could attack, when facility is fully staffed, rush hour, holidays; (8) range of adversary tactics, such as force, deceit; and (9) the capabilities of the adversary, their knowledge, motivations, skills, weapons, and equipment.[54]

It should also be clear that a threat assessment need not be static in time.[55] Threats (i.e., the likelihood that an adversary may attack) may rise and fall over time, depending on events, anniversary dates, an increase in capabilities, or the need for the adversary to reassert itself. Intelligence may detect activity that indicates preattack activity or a lull in such activity, or an explicit threat may be made. This is why continual updates of threat assessments must be made to keep them relevant to police operations. To this end, law enforcement executives must ensure that an officer or unit is trained and assigned to identify potential targets and can recommend enhancements for security at those targets.[56] The proper individual, under the staff process previously described, to assign this responsibility to is the Information and Intelligence Officer and his or her staff. However, action must be taken by all departments, including those with limited resources. Ideally, the entire patrol force should be trained to conduct intelligence gathering and reporting for the Intelligence staff to adequately conduct updates on their threat assessments.

In addition to assessing threats, it is also important that agencies conduct what are known as criticality and vulnerability assessments. The former attempts to identify key targets in a jurisdiction, whereas the latter attempts to determine how weak these targets are in relation to an attack. The DHS defines criticality assessments as

> a systematic effort to identify and evaluate important or critical assets within a jurisdiction. Criticality assessments help planners determine the relative importance of assets, helping to prioritize the allocation of resources to the most critical assets.[57]

The Department defines vulnerability assessments as

> the identification of weaknesses in physical structures, personnel protection systems, processes, or other areas that may be exploited by terrorists. The vulnerability assessments also may suggest options to eliminate or mitigate those weaknesses.[58]

These two assessments combined will give us an idea as to which assets present the greatest targets to the terrorists and which are most vulnerable to their attacks.

The measure of criticality, or asset value, determines the ultimate importance of the asset. Loss of life and/or damage to essential assets are of paramount concern to law enforcement executives. Loss of symbolic targets, which can result in the press coverage that terrorists seek, is also important, as it can destroy people's faith in the ability of law enforcement and government to protect the public.

Assessing criticality can at times involve some degree of subjectivity. Assessment may rely on the intimate knowledge of law enforcement agency professionals and their colleagues in other government agencies to gauge the importance of each potential target. However, clear objective thought must prevail when loss of human life is possible. Certain facilities are inherently vulnerable and should be addressed as critical infrastructure or key assets of law enforcement. These include transportation facilities, public utilities, public and government facilities, financial and banking institutions, defense-related centers, and health-care facilities, as well as cyber/information technology.[59] However, not every asset is as important as another. To focus assessment resources, all the methodologies reviewed suggest that the assessment should focus on those assets judged to be most critical. Criticality is typically defined as a measure of the consequences associated with the loss or degradation of a particular asset. The more the loss of an asset threatens the survival or viability of its owners, of those located nearby, or of others who depend on it (including the nation as a whole), the more critical it becomes.[60]

The consequences can be categorized in a number of ways, including economic, environmental, health, and technological. The immediate impact can have tremendous implications for not only the local jurisdiction, but again, across the country. However, although the immediate impact is important, so too is the amount of time and resources required to replace the lost capability. And another issue is that the loss of particular assets may create secondary effects, which can begin affecting other areas of infrastructure. For example, the loss of electric power can lead to problems in the supply of safe drinking water. Therefore, integral to the criticality assessment is a determination of all these factors when ranking those assets that present attractive targets to terrorists and ranking them by their criticality, the impact, that their loss or damage would have on the local community.

Once the facilities and assets have been identified as being potential targets and their criticality determined, the next assessment is to determine their vulnerability. Roper defines vulnerability as a "weakness that can be exploited to gain access to a given asset."[61] Weaknesses, like criticality, can be categorized in a number of ways: physical (e.g., accessibility, relative locations, visibility, toughness, strength), technical (e.g., susceptible to cyberattack, energy surges, contamination), operational (e.g., policies, procedures, personal habits), or organizational (e.g., would taking out police headquarters severely disrupt operations). Existing countermeasures may already exist to address these weaknesses. A vulnerability assessment must evaluate the reliability and effectiveness of those existing countermeasures in detail. For example, security guards may provide a certain degree of deterrence against unauthorized access to a certain asset. However, to assess their effectiveness, a number of additional questions may need to be asked. For example, how many security guards are on duty? Do they patrol or monitor surveillance equipment? How equipped or well trained are they to delay or repulse an attempt to gain access? Have they successfully repulsed any attempt to gain unauthorized access before?[62]

Vulnerabilities are assessed by the analyst against specific attacks. There are three steps to assessing vulnerabilities.[63] The first is to determine how an adversary could carry out a specific kind of attack against a specific asset (or group of assets). The second is to evaluate existing countermeasures for their reliability and their effectiveness to deter, detect, or delay the specific attack. And third, estimate current state of vulnerability and assign it a value. To measure the vulnerability, it is important to look at four areas: (1) Is the target available (i.e., is it present and/or predictable as it relates to the adversary's ability to plan and

BOX 12-6

CRITICAL INFRASTRUCTURE AND KEY RESOURCE SECTORS

Agriculture and food

Public health and health care

Drinking water

Wastewater treatment system

Energy

Banking and finance

National monuments and icons

Defense industrial base

Information technology

Chemical

Transportation systems

Emergency services

Postal and shipping

Dams

Government facilities

Commercial facilities

Nuclear reactors, materials, and waste

Source: U.S. Department of Homeland Security. (2005). *State and Urban Area Homeland Security Strategy: Guidance on Aligning Strategies with the National Preparedness Goal.* Available online at http://www.ojp.usdoj.gov/odp/docs/StrategyGuidance_22JUL2005.pdf; downloaded on August 15, 2005.

operate)? (2) Is it accessible (i.e., how easily can the adversary get to or near the target? (3) What are the "organic" countermeasures in place (i.e., what is the existing security plan, communication capabilities, intrusion detection systems, guard force)? and (4) Is the target hard (i.e., based on the target's design complexity and material construction characteristics, how effectively can it withstand the attack)?

Once the Information and Intelligence officer and his or her staff has conducted threat assessments and both criticality and vulnerability assessments, it is important that they combine this information into a risk assessment. Risk implies uncertain consequences to which Roper defines risk as the ". . . probability of loss or damage, and its impact."[64] The DHS defines risk assessment as "essentially an estimate of the expected losses should a specific target/attack scenario occurs."[65] Therefore, risk assessments factor in the threat by asking how likely it is that an adversary will attack those identified assets, it factors in criticality by asking what is the likely impact if the asset is lost or harmed by the threat, and it factors in vulnerability by asking what are the most likely vulnerabilities that the adversary or adversaries will use to target the identified asset.[66]

Risk assessments can be either qualitative or quantitative in nature. Threat assessments can be categorized as consisting of five categories: negligible, low, medium, high, and critical.[67] The presence of a terrorist group, its capabilities, intent, and history, all combine to determine the threat assessment levels. These levels can then be converted into numerical numbers ranging from 1 to 5, with the higher value being the more serious threat. Both criticality and vulnerability can also be measured in a very similar way, using the qualitative terms and turning them into numeric values. The comprehensive results of each of these assessments can be summarized into a risk statement with an adjectival or numeric rating. The risk equation used in most systems is expressed in this basic formula:

$$Risk = Threat \times Vulnerability \times Criticality$$

In this equation, risk is defined as the extent to which an asset is exposed to a hazard or danger. Threat times vulnerability represents the probability of an unwanted event occurring, and criticality equals the consequence of loss or damage to the critical infrastructure or key asset. Using this methodology allows the Information and Intelligence officer the ability to determine what assets face the greatest risk, thus allowing for an agency to engage more realistically in risk management.

Risk management is essentially the process of using risk assessments to identify and prioritize risk reduction activities. It is the decision-making process inherent in determining which assets to secure, the methods and resources used to address the security, and the cost-benefit calculus associated with those decisions.[68] Risk assessments help determine which assets to secure by weighting them toward those facing the higher risk. However, despite having an adjectival or numeric weighting it is still imperative that which key assets are going to be secured go through the decision-making process, as there are other factors involved. In addition, the decision-making process is also used to identify ways to reduce risk. Risks can be reduced in a number of ways: by reducing threats (e.g., through eliminating or intercepting the adversary before they strike), by reducing vulnerabilities (e.g., target hardening), or by reducing the impact or consequences (e.g., building backup systems or isolate facilities from major populations).[69] Countermeasures include physical security (fencing, camera surveillance, seismic monitoring devices, barricades), cybersecurity (firewalls, antivirus software, secure computer networks), personnel security, and other proactive methods that industry uses to secure critical infrastructure and key assets.[70] Countermeasures, such as expansion of agency staffing, installation of equipment and new technology, or target hardening, must be evaluated or tested periodically to ensure that improvements are actually working as intended.

For each potential countermeasure the cost-benefit for risk reduction should be determined.[71] More than one countermeasure may exist for a particular asset, or one countermeasure may reduce the risk for a number of assets. Multiple countermeasures should be assessed together to determine their net effects. The analysts should also assess the feasibility, acceptability, and suitability of each countermeasure. Although cost effectiveness is usually the recommended measure for setting priorities, it is imperative that these decisions go through the CompStat-like decision-making process, as decision makers may use other measures. Finally, it is imperative that the process be thought of as a continual process and one that should constantly be updated as new information and intelligence is obtained. As police intelligence may very

BOX 12-7

COMPARISON OF COMPSTAT AND INTELLIGENCE-LED POLICING

CompStat	Commonalities	Intelligence-Led Policing
* Single jurisdiction	* Each has a goal of prevention	* Multijurisdiction
* Incident driven	* Each requires organizational flexibility	* Threat driven
* Street crime and burglary	* Each requires consistent information input	* Criminal enterprises and terrorism
* Crime mapping	* Each requires a significant analytic component	* Commodity flow; trafficking and transiting logistics
* Time sensitive (24-hour feedback and response)	* "Bottom-up" driven with respect to operational needs	* Strategic
* Disrupt crime series (e.g., burglary ring)		* Disrupt enterprises
* Drives operations: patrol, tactical unit, & investigators		* Drives operations: JTTF, organized crime investigations, task forces
* Analysis of offender MOs		* Analysis of enterprise MOs

Correlated goals and methodologies make both concepts complement each other.

Source: Carter, D. (2002). *Law Enforcement Intelligence: A Guide for State, Local, and Tribal Law Enforcement Agencies.* Washington, D.C.: U.S. Department of Justice, p. 43.

well alter the equations of risk assessment, thus altering the risk management plan, it is imperative that the police intelligence process be as well defined as the risk management process.

POLICE INTELLIGENCE

Perhaps the greatest clarion call of policing for Homeland Security has been the call for increased focus on intelligence-driven policing and police intelligence units.[72] According to Professor Doug Moore, who specializes in the area of security, at the time of 9-11 there were probably only 50 to 100 police departments that had the ability to collect information for international terrorism, but that most of those collecting information did not have the capability for analysis.[73] He bluntly stated that at the time, police needed to update their criminal analysis capabilities. Adding on the intelligence analysis component would stress most agencies who did not have the training or resources to be able to conduct this type of police intelligence. And even if they did, he highlighted the fact that at the time, most local polices faced the problem of sharing information. Although these issues have not been fully resolved, work is being done at the federal, state, and local levels to address these specific problems to improve local policing's ability to collect information, analyze that information, and then share it with the appropriate agencies.

According to Peterson, introducing intelligence-led policing into law enforcement is problematic for a number of reasons.[74] First, many agencies do not understand what intelligence is or how to manage it. Second, agencies must work to prevent and respond to day-to-day crime at the same time they are working to prevent terrorism. Third, the realities of funding and personnel resources are often obstacles to intelligence-led policing. She concludes that although the current intelligence operations of most law enforcement agencies prevent them from becoming active participants in the intelligence infrastructure, this problem is not insurmountable.

A number of the homeland security grants have focused on this specific issue (see Chapter 2). In addition, the DHS and numerous police associations have made this a key strategic priority (see Chapter 11). Moreover, several recent publications by the U.S. Department of Justice have detailed the importance of intelligence-led policing, and they have laid the groundwork for perhaps one of the most important elements of policing for homeland security.[75] Intelligence then, is a key part of police operations for homeland security and must become an integral part of the process.

There are essentially two broad purposes for an intelligence function within a law enforcement agency: prevention and planning/resource allocation.[76] The first purpose, prevention, includes gaining or developing information related to threats of terrorism or crime and using this information to apprehend offenders, harden targets, and use strategies that will eliminate or mitigate the threat. The second purpose is planning and resource allocation. The intelligence function provides information to decision makers about the changing nature of threats, the characteristics and methodologies of threats, and emerging threat idiosyncrasies for the purpose of developing response strategies and reallocating resources, as necessary, to accomplish effective prevention.

Despite the many definitions of the word *intelligence* that have been promulgated over the years, the simplest and clearest is "information plus analysis equals intelligence."[77] This formula clarifies the distinction between collected information and produced intelligence. It notes that without analysis, there is no intelligence. Intelligence is not what is collected, it is what is produced after collected data is evaluated and analyzed. Therefore, information may be defined as "pieces of raw, unanalyzed data that identifies persons, evidence, events or illustrates processes that indicate the incidence of a criminal event or witnesses or evidence of a criminal event,"[78] whereas law enforcement intelligence may be defined as "the product of an analytic process that provides an integrated perspective to disparate information about crime, crime trends, crime and security threats, and conditions associated with criminality."[79] Law enforcement intelligence analysis, therefore, should be done by a trained intelligence professional, and under the decision-making staff structure described earlier it will fall to the Information and Intelligence officer and his or her staff. This intelligence will then tell the staff everything they need to know to make informed decisions and develop courses of action.

Intelligence is often denoted as falling into one of three categories; strategic, operational, and tactical intelligence.[80] Strategic intelligence deals with the "big-picture" issues such as planning and manpower allocation. Operational intelligence is sometimes used to refer to intelligence that supports long-term investigations into multiple, similar targets. Operational intelligence is concerned primarily with identifying, targeting, detecting, and intervening in criminal activity. Tactical intelligence contributes directly to the success of specific investigations. It directs immediate action. Once again, strategic intelligence, like police strategy, guides the operational plan by allowing police executives to think about how best to structure the department and organize for homeland security. Operational intelligence provides police operations, the concern of this chapter, with how to effectively use this intelligence to act on it. Tactical intelligence is the type of intelligence that the police department can use to deploy its resources and will help drive police tactics in the field.

Historically, policing actually began moving toward the use of intelligence units in the 1970s. The original blueprint for intelligence work was published by the Law Enforcement Assistance Administration of the U.S. Department of Justice in 1971.[81] In 1973, the National Advisory Commission on Criminal Justice Standards and Goals made a strong statement about intelligence. It called on every law enforcement agency and every state to immediately establish and maintain the capability to gather and evaluate information and to disseminate intelligence in a manner that protects every individual's right to privacy while it curtails organized crime and public disorder.

When first instituted, intelligence units within law enforcement departments were not governed by policies that protected civil liberties and prevented intelligence excesses.[82] During the 1970s, a number of intelligence units ran afoul of good practices, and as a result, some agencies shut down their intelligence functions voluntarily, by court order, or from political pressure. In 1976, in response to the problem of intelligence abuses, standards were developed that required a criminal predicate for subjects to be entered in criminal intelligence files. Guidelines were then developed, but most agencies either avoided starting up intelligence units again or they relied on other initiatives such as the Regional Information Sharing System (RISS) that shared "information" and avoided the term *intelligence*. Although there was some development in enhancing the area of law enforcement intelligence analysis, it was not until 9-11 that the necessity of these units was recognized.

Intelligence is critical for the decision-making process, planning, targeting, and crime prevention. Gathering information and deciding what to do with it are common occurrences in law enforcement operations. Law enforcement officers and managers are beset by large quantities of information, yet decisions are often based on information that may be incomplete, inaccurate, or misdirected. The move from information gathering to informed decision making depends on the intelligence/analytic process and results in a best estimate of what has happened or what will happen.

Intelligence is also critical to effective planning and subsequent action. In many law enforcement agencies, planning and subsequent action is performed without an understanding of the crime problems facing the jurisdiction and without sufficient operation input. In these instances, planning bears no resemblance to analysis or intelligence. Instead it relates only to funding issues and operational constraints.

Targeting and prioritization are other critical roles of intelligence, as seen earlier with risk management. Law enforcement agencies with tight budgets and personnel reductions or shortages must use their available resources carefully, targeting individuals, locations, and operations that promise the greatest results and the best chances for success.

The final area in which intelligence is critical is crime prevention. Using intelligence from previous crimes in local and other jurisdictions, indicators can be created and shared among law enforcement agencies. Comparing the indicators from local neighborhoods, analysts can anticipate crime trends and agencies can take preventive measures to intervene or mitigate the impact of those crimes.

The actual intelligence process consists of six steps: planning and direction, collection, processing/collation, analysis, dissemination, and reevaluation.[83] The first step, planning and direction, is key to the intelligence process. Effective planning assesses existing data and ensures that additional data collected will fill any gaps in the information already on file. As one federal manager put it, "Don't tell me what I know, tell me what

---

BOX 12-8

NATIONAL ADVISORY COMMISSION ON CRIMINAL JUSTICE STANDARDS AND GOALS (NAC) AND POLICE INTELLIGENCE

In 1971, the National Advisory Commission on Criminal Justice Standards and Goals (NAC) was created to make recommendations for increased efficacy of the entire criminal justice system. "For the first time national criminal justice standards and goals for crime reduction and prevention at the state and local levels" were to be prepared. Included in the commission's report were recommendations directed at establishing and operating intelligence functions for state and local law enforcement agencies. These recommendations included the following:

Establishing Intelligence Functions

* Each state should develop a centralized law enforcement intelligence function with the participation of each police agency within the state.
* States should consider establishing regional intelligence networks across contiguous states to enhance criminal information-sharing processes.
* Every local law enforcement agency should establish its own intelligence function in accordance with its respective state's intelligence function.

Intelligence Function Operations

* Each state and local intelligence function should provide support to federal agencies.
* Operational policies and procedures should be developed for each local, state, and regional intelligence function to ensure efficiency and effectiveness.
* Each agency should have a designated official who reports directly to the chief and oversees all intelligence operations.
* Each agency should develop procedures to ensure the proper screening, securing, and disseminating of intelligence-related information.

Source: Carter, D. (2002). *Law Enforcement Intelligence: A Guide for State, Local, and Tribal Law Enforcement Agencies.* Washington, D.C.: U.S. Department of Justice, pp. 30–31; National Advisory Commission on Criminal Justice Standards. (1971). *Report of the Task Force on Organized Crime.* Washington, D.C.: U.S. Department of Justice.

I don't know."[84] To be effective, then, intelligence collection must be planned and focused, its methods must be coordinated, and its guidelines must prohibit illegal methods of obtaining information. Inaccurate collection efforts can result in a flawed result, regardless of the analytical skills used. Planning also requires an agency to identify the outcomes it wants to achieve from its collection efforts. This identification directs the scope of the officers' and detectives' investigations—for example, a straightforward inquiry to identify crime groups operating in a jurisdiction or a more complex inquiry to determine the likelihood that criminal extremists will attack a visiting dignitary.

The second step of the intelligence process is collection. Intelligence analysis requires collecting and processing large amounts of information. Data collection is the most labor-intensive aspect of the intelligence process. Traditionally, it has been the most emphasized segment of the process, with law enforcement agencies and prosecutors dedicating significant resources to gathering data. New technology and new or updated laws have supported this emphasis. Historically, the following have been the most common forms of data collection used in intelligence units: physical surveillance, electronic surveillance, confidential informants, undercover operators, newspaper records, and public records. To a large degree, most of these forms of data collection are very familiar to law enforcement.

The third step is processing and collation. This step involves sifting through available data to eliminate useless, irrelevant, or incorrect information and to put the data into a logical order. This organization makes it easier to identify relationships among entities and uncover relevant information. Today, collation is performed using sophisticated databases for retrieving and comparing data and many have text-mining capabilities. This step also involves evaluating the data being entered. Information placed into an intelligence file is evaluated for the validity of the information and the reliability of its source. And, information placed into an intelligence system must meet a standard of relevance in that it must be relevant to criminal activity.

The fourth step of the intelligence process is analysis. Analysis converts information into intelligence. Analysis, then, is quite simply a process of deriving meaning from data. The analytical process tells what information is present or missing from the facts or evidence. In law enforcement intelligence operations, data are analyzed to provide further leads in investigation, to present hypotheses about who committed a crime or how it was committed, to predict future crime patterns, and to assess threats facing a jurisdiction. Thus, analysis includes synthesizing data, developing inferences or conclusions, and making recommendations for action based on the data and inferences. These inferences constitute the finished intelligence product. This final product should identify the targeted consumer of the information (patrol officers, administrators, task force members, etc.), convey the critical information clearly, identify time parameters wherein the intelligence is actionable, and provide recommendations for specific courses of action.[85] It is important to remember that the analyst *recommends* but does not direct or decide on policy alternatives to minimize crime problems.

The fifth step of the process is dissemination. This requires getting intelligence to those who have the need and the right to use it in whatever form is deemed most appropriate. Intelligence reports kept within the intelligence unit fail to fulfill their mission. Those who need the information are most often outside the intelligence unit; therefore, the current dissemination protocol is to share by rule and to withhold by exception. It is here that the sharing of intelligence within, between, and across law enforcement agencies becomes critical for operational planning and tactical execution to have any meaning. One impediment that must be overcome in regard to the dissemination of intelligence is the lack of proper security clearances among the law enforcement community. It is time that all qualifying law enforcement officers in the United States obtain at a minimum a secret clearance to overcome these impediments. Those in the command staff should be considered for top secret clearances. Officers now designated to secure our homeland should not be left out of this step for the excuse that they don't have the proper security clearance.

The sixth and final step is reevaluation. This is the task of examining intelligence products to determine their effectiveness. Part of this assessment comes from the consumers of intelligence, that is, the managers, investigators, and officers to whom the intelligence is directed. One way to reevaluate intelligence is to include a feedback form with each product that is disseminated. Another way is to have the staff assess the "useability" of the intelligence reports in terms of their decision making, operational planning, and tactical execution. Did the reports present actionable intelligence, and how good was it?

The responsibility for the intelligence process once again falls to the Information and Intelligence Officer and his or her staff. As David Carter has explained, "State, local and tribal law enforcement will be its most effective when a single source in every agency is the conduit of critical information, whether it is the Terrorist Intelligence Unit of the Los Angeles Police Department, the sole intelligence analyst of the Lansing, Michigan Police Department, or the patrol sergeant who understands the language of intelligence and is the information sharing contact point in the Mercedes, Texas Police Department."[86] By having the Intelligence Officer handle all the intelligence information for the agency, he or she can control what is coming in and what is going out from the unit. More importantly, that individual than brings an enormous amount of knowledge, experience, and intelligence to the decision-making process so that well-informed decisions are made by

BOX 12-9

HOMELAND SECURITY OPERATIONS BY EXAMPLE: THE HOUSTON POLICE DEPARTMENT

Phillip Davis, Sam Houston State University

The Houston, Texas, Police Department has established a plan for any potential acts of terrorism. The plan is divided into two stages: crisis management and consequence management. During the crisis management phase of operations, the Houston Police Department will be in command of all responses to the terrorist incident. This includes all command and control of the investigation and whatever tasks are necessary to prevent the event from escalating. The consequence management phase of operations, however, is commanded by the Houston Office of Emergency Management. This phase of operations is primarily concerned with managing whatever negative effects have been created by the terrorist incident.

Source: The City of Houston. Houston Office of Emergency Management. *Annex V Terrorism Incident Response & Management Plan.* Retrieved from *http://www.houstontx.gov/oem/ANNEX%20V%202002.pdf*

the staff. Although it is important that this individual have a strong voice on the police decision-making process, by having them as only a member of the staff, it prevents final decisions being made simply on the recommendation of one individual.

CONCLUSION

Strategy drives operations. A police strategy for homeland security should then drive police operations for homeland security. This would necessitate that police leadership have a strong operational control over its police force. Yet, as Mark Moore has explained, "Police leadership is . . . handicapped by a startling lack of operational control over officers," and departments function "under a carefully constructed illusion of control created to satisfy citizen demands for accountability."[87] Due to this lack of operational control and capability for centralized decision making, police operations and police management under homeland security must change.

What is promising is the development of both CompStat and the ICS. By merging these two systems together into a full-time, staff-driven, operational control system, police departments will be better organized to deal with issues of homeland security, consisting of both natural disasters and terrorist threats and attacks. Centralized decision making through an informed staff, driven by a homeland security strategy, will establish a strong system of police operations. A system that can establish strong centralized plans, coupled with decentralized execution, will adapt well to the modern environment of policing for homeland security. Combined with an emphasis on partnerships, the ability to manage risk, and the capability of intelligence-led policing, today's modern police departments will operationally be prepared to deal with all threats, natural, criminal, and terroristic.

ENDNOTES

1. Cordner, G. W., Gaines, L. W., and Kappeler, V. E. (1996). *Police Operations: Analysis and Evaluations.* Cincinnati, OH: Anderson Publishing Company.
2. Oliver, W. M. (2003). *Community-Oriented Policing: A Systemic Approach to Policing.* 3rd ed. Upper Saddle River, NJ: Prentice Hall.
3. U.S. Department of Defense. (2001). *Joint Pub 1-02: Department of Defense Dictionary of Military Terms and Associated Terms.* Washington, D.C.: U.S. G.P.O., p. 275.
4. U.S. Department of Defense. (2002). *Joint Pub 5-001: Joint Doctrine for Campaign Planning.* Washington, D.C.: U.S. G.P.O.
5. Moore, M. H. (1990). In *Impossible Jobs in Public Management,* edited by E.C. Hargrove and J. C. Glidewell, 72–102. Lawrence, KS: University Press of Kansas.
6. Moore, M. H. (1990). In *Impossible Jobs in Public Management,* edited by E. C. Hargrove and J. C. Glidewell, 72–102. Lawrence, KS: University Press of Kansas, p. 82.
7. *ibid.*
8. National Commission on Terrorist Attacks Upon the United States. (2003). *The 9/11 Commission Report.* New York: W.W. Norton & Company, p. 396.
9. National Commission on Terrorist Attacks Upon the United States. (2003). *The 9/11 Commission Report.* New York: W.W. Norton & Company, p. 397.

10. Goldstein, H. (1990). *Problem-Oriented Policing.* New York: McGraw-Hill Publishing Company.

11. *ibid.*

12. *ibid.*

13. Eck, J. E. and Spelman, W. (1987). *Problem-Solving: Problem-Oriented Policing in New-port News.* Washington, D.C.: Police Executive Research Forum/U.S. Department of Justice and the National Institute of Justice.

14. Oliver, W. M. (2003). *Community-Oriented Policing: A Systemic Approach to Policing.* 3rd ed. Upper Saddle River, NJ: Prentice Hall.

15. Henry, V. E. (2002). *The COMPSTAT Paradigm: Management Accountability in Policing, Business and the Public Sector.* Flushing, NY: Looseleaf Law Publications, Inc., p. 147.

16. Henry, V. E. (2002). *The COMPSTAT Paradigm: Management Accountability in Policing, Business and the Public Sector.* Flushing, NY: Looseleaf Law Publications, Inc., pp. 147–148.

17. McDonald, P. P. (2004). "Implementing CompStat: Critical Points to Consider." *The Police Chief* 71(1): 1–6; available online at http://www.policechiefmagazine.org; downloaded July 14, 2004.

18. Henry, V. E. (2002). *The Compstat Paradigm: Management and Accountability in Policing Business and the Public Sector.* Flushing, NY: Looseleaf Law Publications, Inc.; Silverman, E. B. (1999). *NYPD Battles Crime: Innovative Strategies in Policing.* Boston, MA: Northeastern University Press.

19. Maple, J. & Mitchell, C. (2000). *The Crime Fighter: Putting the Bad Guys Out of Business.* New York: Broadway Publications.

20. Bratton, W., with Knobler, P. (1998). *The Turnaround: How America's Top Cop Reversed the Crime Epidemic.* New York: Random House Publishers.

21. Henry, V. E. (2002). *The Compstat Paradigm: Management and Accountability in Policing Business and the Public Sector.* Flushing, NY: Looseleaf Law Publications, Inc.; Silverman, E. B. (1999). *NYPD Battles Crime: Innovative Strategies in Policing.* Boston, MA: Northeastern University Press.

22. Henry, V. E. (2002). *The Compstat Paradigm: Management and Accountability in Policing Business and the Public Sector.* Flushing, NY: Looseleaf Law Publications, Inc., p. 20.

23. Silverman, E. B. (1999). *NYPD Battles Crime: Innovative Strategies in Policing.* Boston, MA: Northeastern University Press.

24. McDonald, P. P. (2004). "Implementing CompStat: Critical Points to Consider." *The Police Chief* 71(1): 1–6; available online at http://www.policechiefmagazine.org; downloaded July 14, 2004.

25. Henry, V. E. (2002). *The Compstat Paradigm: Management and Accountability in Policing Business and the Public Sector.* Flushing, NY: Looseleaf Law Publications, Inc., p. 21.

26. McDonald, P. P. (2004). "Implementing CompStat: Critical Points to Consider." *The Police Chief* 71(1): 1–6, available online at http://www.policechiefmagazine.org; downloaded July 14, 2004; Schick, W. (2004). "CompStat in the Los Angeles Police Department." *The Police Chief* 71(1): 1–7, available online at http://www.policechiefmagazine.org; downloaded July 14, 2004

27. Wilber, D. Q. (2004). "90 Minutes a Day that Shape Fight to Cut Crime." *Washington Post.* Available online at http://www.washingtonpost.com; downloaded June 1, 2004, p. B01.

28. Bush, G. W. (2003). *Homeland Security Presidential Directive/HSPD 5.* Available online at http://www.whitehouse.gov/news/releases/2003/02/20030228 9.html; downloaded on July 17, 2004.
29. Department of Homeland Security. (2005). *State and Urban Area Homeland Security Strategy: Guidance on Aligning Strategies with the National Preparedness Goal.* Available online at http://www.ojp.usdoj.gov/odp/ docs/StrategyGuidance_22JUL2005.pdf; downloaded on August 15, 2005.
30. LaTorrette, T., Peterson, D. J., Bartis, J. T., Jackson, B. A., and Houser, A. (2003). *Protecting Emergency Responders: Community Views of Safety and Health Risks and Personal Protection Needs. Volume 2.* Santa Monica, CA: RAND Corporation, p. 70.
31. FEMA. (2004). *NIMS and the Incident Command System.* Available online at www.fema.gov/nims; downloaded on July 13, 2005.
32. Arlington County. (2002). *Arlington County After-Action Report.* Arlington County, VA: Arlington County.
33. FEMA. (2005). *National Incident Management System: National Standard Curriculum Training Development Guidance.* Available online at http://www.fema.gov/pdf/nims/nsctd.pdf Downloaded August 15, 2005.
34. National Institute of Justice. (2003). "CCTV: Constant Cameras Track Violators." *NIJ Journal,* No. 249: 16–23.
35. International Association of Chiefs of Police. (2001). "The Use of CCTV/Video Cameras in Law Enforcement." *IACP Executive Brief.* Available online at http:// www.theiacp.org/documents/pdfs/Publications/UseofCCTV%2Epdf; downloaded November 1, 2004.
36. Maghan, J., O'Reilly, G. W., and Ho Shon, P. C. (2002). "Technology, Policing, and Implications of In-Car Videos." *Police Quarterly* 5(1): 25–42.
37. See Alpert, D. (2003). *GIS/GPS Law Enforcement Master Bibliography.* 2nd ed.Washington, D.C.: Police Executive Research Forum; Regional Community Policing Institute. (2004). *Global Positioning Satellite System (GPS).* Available online at http://www.wsurcpi.org/tech/COPS%20Act%20GPS.pdf; downloaded on August 2, 2005.
38. LaTorrette, T., Peterson, D. J., Bartis, J. T., Jackson, B. A., and Houser, A. (2003). *Protecting Emergency Responders: Community Views of Safety and Health Risks and Personal Protection Needs. Volume 2.* Santa Monica, CA: RAND Corporation, pp. 79–80.
39. Stephens, D. W. and Hartmann, F. X. (2002). "The Policing Challenge." In *Beyond the Beltway: Focusing on Hometown Security,* edited by J. N. Kayyem, 15–22. Boston, MA: John F. Kennedy School of Government, Harvard University.
40. Pelfrey, W. V. (2005). "The Cycle of Preparedness: Establishing a Framework to Prepare for Terrorist Threats." *Journal of Homeland Security and Emergency Management* 2, no. 1: 1–21; available online at http://www.bepress.com/jhsem/vol12/iss1/5
41. *ibid.*
42. Arlington County. (2002). *Arlington County After-Action Report.* Arlington County, VA: Arlington County.
43. This section is derived from Lynn, Pl. (2005). *Mutual Aid: Multijurisdictional Partnerships for Meeting Regional Threats.* Washington, D.C.: Bureau of Justice Assistance.
44. Lynn, Phil. (2005). *Mutual Aid: Multijurisdictional Partnerships for Meeting Regional Threats.* Washington, D.C.: Bureau of Justice Assistance, pp. 13–20.
45. FEMA. (2004). *NIMS and the Incident Command System.* Available online at www.fema.gov/nims; downloaded on July 13, 2005.

46. Holmes, K. R. (2004). *The Heritage Foundation Homeland Security Task Force Executive Summary.* Washington, D.C.: The Heritage Foundation.

47. Holmes, K. R. (2004). *The Heritage Foundation Homeland Security Task Force Executive Summary.* Washington, D.C.: The Heritage Foundation, p. 54.

48. Roper, C. (1999). *Risk Management for Security Professionals.* Boston, MA: Butterworth-Heinemann, p. 43.

49. This section is derived from Moteff, J. (2004). "Risk Management and Critical Infrastructure Protection: Assessing, Integrating, and Managing Threats, Vulnerabilities and Consequences." *CRS Report for Congress.* Washington, D.C.: Congressional Research Service.

50. Moteff, J. (2004). "Risk Management and Critical Infrastructure Protection: Assessing, Integrating, and Managing Threats, Vulnerabilities and Consequences." *CRS Report for Congress.* Washington, D.C.: Congressional Research Service, p. 7.

51. Leson, J. (2005). *Assessing and Managing the Terrorism Threat.* Washington, D.C.: Bureau of Justice Assistance, p. 5.

52. Moteff, J. (2004). "Risk Management and Critical Infrastructure Protection: Assessing, Integrating, and Managing Threats, Vulnerabilities and Consequences." *CRS Report for Congress.* Washington, D.C.: Congressional Research Service.

53. Leson, J. (2005). *Assessing and Managing the Terrorism Threat.* Washington, D.C.: Bureau of Justice Assistance.

54. Leson, J. (2005). *Assessing and Managing the Terrorism Threat.* Washington, D.C.: Bureau of Justice Assistance, p. 6.

55. Moteff, J. (2004). "Risk Management and Critical Infrastructure Protection: Assessing, Integrating, and Managing Threats, Vulnerabilities and Consequences." *CRS Report for Congress.* Washington, D.C.: Congressional Research Service.

56. Leson, J. (2005). *Assessing and Managing the Terrorism Threat.* Washington, D.C.: Bureau of Justice Assistance.

57. Leson, J. (2005). *Assessing and Managing the Terrorism Threat.* Washington, D.C.: Bureau of Justice Assistance, p. 5.

58. Leson, J. (2005). *Assessing and Managing the Terrorism Threat.* Washington, D.C.: Bureau of Justice Assistance, p. 7.

59. Leson, J. (2005). *Assessing and Managing the Terrorism Threat.* Washington, D.C.: Bureau of Justice Assistance.

60. Moteff, J. (2004). "Risk Management and Critical Infrastructure Protection: Assessing, Integrating, and Managing Threats, Vulnerabilities and Consequences." *CRS Report for Congress.* Washington, D.C.: Congressional Research Service.

61. Roper, C. (1999). *Risk Management for Security Professionals.* Boston, MA: Butterworth-Heinemann, p. 63.

62. Moteff, J. (2004). "Risk Management and Critical Infrastructure Protection: Assessing, Integrating, and Managing Threats, Vulnerabilities and Consequences." *CRS Report for Congress.* Washington, D.C.: Congressional Research Service.

63. *ibid.*

64. Moteff, J. (2004). "Risk Management and Critical Infrastructure Protection: Assessing, Integrating, and Managing Threats, Vulnerabilities and Consequences." *CRS Report for Congress.* Washington, D.C.: Congressional Research Service, p. 9.

65. *ibid.*

CHAPTER 12   POLICE OPERATIONS FOR HOMELAND SECURITY   **385**

66. Leson, J. (2005). *Assessing and Managing the Terrorism Threat.* Washington, D.C.: Bureau of Justice Assistance.

67. *ibid.*

68. Office for Domestic Preparedness. (2003). *The Office for Domestic Preparedness Guidelines for Homeland Security June 2003: Prevention and Deterrence.* Washington, D.C.: U.S. Department of Homeland Security.

69. Moteff, J. (2004). "Risk Management and Critical Infrastructure Protection: Assessing, Integrating, and Managing Threats, Vulnerabilities and Consequences." *CRS Report for Congress.* Washington, D.C.: Congressional Research Service.

70. Leson, J. (2005). *Assessing and Managing the Terrorism Threat.* Washington, D.C.: Bureau of Justice Assistance.

71. Moteff, J. (2004). "Risk Management and Critical Infrastructure Protection: Assessing, Integrating, and Managing Threats, Vulnerabilities and Consequences." *CRS Report for Congress.* Washington, D.C.: Congressional Research Service.

72. Carafano, J. J., Rosenzweig, P., and Kochems, A. (2005). "An Agenda for Increasing State and Local Government Efforts to Combat Terrorism." *Backgrounder,* No. 1826. Washington, D.C.: The Heritage Foundation; Marrin, S. (2003). "Homeland Security Intelligence: Just the Beginning." *Journal of Homeland Security,* November. Available online at http://www.homelandsecurity.org/journal/Articles/marrin.html; downloaded May 2, 2005; Moore, D. (2002). "Homeland Intelligence." Radio Interview with Professor Doug Moore, aired September 1, 2002. Available online at http://www.cjcenter.org/media/radio/; accessed January 15, 2004.

73. Moore, D. (2002). "Homeland Intelligence." Radio Interview with Professor Doug Moore, aired September 1, 2002. Available online at http://www.cjcenter.org/media/ radio/; accessed January 15, 2004.

74. Peterson, M. (2005). *Intelligence-Led Policing: The New Intelligence Architecture.* Washington, D.C.: Bureau of Justice Assistance.

75. Carter, D. (2004). *Law Enforcement Intelligence: A Guide for State, Local, and Tribal Law Enforcement Agencies.* Washington, D.C.: U.S. Department of Justice; Peterson, M. (2005). *Intelligence-Led Policing: The New Intelligence Architecture.* Washington, D.C.: Bureau of Justice Assistance.

76. Carter, D. (2002). *Law Enforcement Intelligence: A Guide for State, Local, and Tribal Law Enforcement Agencies.* Washington, D.C.: U.S. Department of Justice.

77. Peterson, M. (2005). *Intelligence-Led Policing: The New Intelligence Architecture.* Washington, D.C.: Bureau of Justice Assistance, p. 3.

78. Global Intelligence Working Group. (2004). *Criminal Intelligence for the Chief Executive.* As quoted in Carter, D. (2002). *Law Enforcement Intelligence: A Guide for State, Local, and Tribal Law Enforcement Agencies.* Washington, D.C.: U.S. Department of Justice, p. 9.

79. Carter, D. L. (2002). *Law Enforcement Intelligence Operations.* 8th ed. Tallahassee, FL: SMC Sciences, Inc., as cited in Carter, D. (2002). *Law Enforcement Intelligence: A Guide for State, Local, and Tribal Law Enforcement Agencies.* Washington, D.C.: U.S. Department of Justice, p. 10.

80. Peterson, M. (2005). *Intelligence-Led Policing: The New Intelligence Architecture.* Washington, D.C.: Bureau of Justice Assistance.

81. *ibid.*

82. Peterson, M. (2005). *Intelligence-Led Policing: The New Intelligence Architecture.* Washington, D.C.: Bureau of Justice Assistance; see also Carter, D. (2002). *Law Enforcement Intelligence: A Guide for State, Local, and Tribal Law Enforcement Agencies.* Washington, D.C.: U.S. Department of Justice, Chapter 3.

83. Peterson, M. (2005). *Intelligence-Led Policing: The New Intelligence Architecture.* Washington, D.C.: Bureau of Justice Assistance; see also Carter, D. (2002). *Law Enforcement Intelligence: A Guide for State, Local, and Tribal Law Enforcement Agencies.* Washington, D.C.: U.S. Department of Justice, Chapter 5.

84. Peterson, M. (2005). *Intelligence-Led Policing: The New Intelligence Architecture.* Washington, D.C.: Bureau of Justice Assistance; see also Carter, D. (2002). *Law Enforcement Intelligence: A Guide for State, Local, and Tribal Law Enforcement Agencies.* Washington, D.C.: U.S. Department of Justice.

85. Carter, D. (2002). *Law Enforcement Intelligence: A Guide for State, Local, and Tribal Law Enforcement Agencies.* Washington, D.C.: U.S. Department of Justice.

86. Carter, D. (2002). *Law Enforcement Intelligence: A Guide for State, Local, and Tribal Law Enforcement Agencies.* Washington, D.C.: U.S. Department of Justice, p. 2.

87. Moore, M. H. (1990). In *Impossible Jobs in Public Management*, edited by E. C. Hargrove and J. C. Glidewell, 72–102. Lawrence, KS: University Press of Kansas, p. 82.

Moving Forward

13

Defending Liberty

Today and Tomorrow

Enhancing national security to prevent a terrorist attack often requires the solving of other problems, such as cyber-security and immigration control. Terrorists can use the Internet to cause more destruction than a bomb. If illegal immigrants can easily enter the United States by the thousands daily, then terrorists can just as easily enter the country.

America's immigration system is also outdated, unsuited to the needs of our economy and to the values of our country. We should not be content with laws that punish hardworking people who want only to provide for their families, and deny businesses willing workers, and invite chaos at our border. It is time for an immigration policy that permits temporary guest workers to fill jobs Americans will not take, that rejects amnesty, that tells us who is entering and leaving our country, and that closes the border to drug dealers and terrorists.

—President George Bush, State of the Union Address, February 2, 2005

Chapter Outline _____

Learning Objectives _____

- The reader will understand why additional efforts are necessary to defend the homeland against terror attacks.
- The reader will understand how cyber-terrorism could be a greater threat than bombs.
- The reader will understand how terrorists use the Internet and will know the advantages of the Internet to the terrorists.
- The reader will realize why terror-proofing the Internet is a very difficult task.
- The reader will know of the government's response to cyber-security threats.
- The reader will appreciate the difficulty of the task of border security and immigration control.
- The reader will know the various programs initiated to enhance border security and immigration control.
- The reader will understand the role of deportation in immigration control.
- The reader will appreciate the impact of border security and immigration control initiatives on the U.S. relationship with Canada and Mexico.

Introduction: A Threat with No End in Sight

Following the September 11, 2001 attacks, the United States took immediate actions to address what were considered the most threatening vulnerabilities to attacks by terrorists: airline security and prevention of nuclear, biological, and chemical terrorist attacks. However, the prevention of terrorism is not limited to these threats. As the United States strives to prevent terrorists from striking homeland targets, it has become evident that in addition to the first steps that were taken to defend the homeland, additional actions are necessary. For example, in his 2005 State of the Union Address, President Bush pointed out the problem with securing the U.S. borders against terrorism while at the same time permitting the flow of legitimate persons and commerce. Defending the homeland against terrorism requires a two-prong strategy: (1) defending against immediate threats and (2) defending the homeland by identifying problems and future threats that must be addressed.

One of the most significant problems in fighting terrorism is maintaining the high level of vigilance necessary for identifying and responding to possible future threats for an indefinite period of time.[1] For example, as election day approached for the 2004 presidential elections, federal and local government agencies maintained a high level of alert in anticipation of a possible terrorist attack. Police officers in major cities were required to work 12-hour shifts with few or no days off. New York City and Washington, D.C., spent millions of dollars in overtime pay. Many cities spent money they did not have to respond to the heightened security alert preceding the presidential elections.[2] After the election, the Department of Homeland Security (DHS) lowered the terror alert for the financial sector in New York, Washington, and northern New Jersey and many were relieved to "have gotten by without any major terrorist attacks." However, after the elections in November it was necessary to again gear up for possible terrorist attacks for the presidential inauguration ceremonies. It is a never-ending cycle of continuous preparation against possible terrorist attacks.

The process of staying prepared for a terrorist attack is an ongoing challenge and a challenge that can change from day to day. Staying prepared requires accurate information, equipment, training, funding, and, most important, the ability to anticipate what the threats of terrorism could be tomorrow. The federal government and the DHS have focused their major efforts on responding to the threat of terrorist attacks on aviation and using nuclear, chemical, and biological weapons of mass destruction. This chapter discusses two other concerns that may require more serious counterterrorism attention in the immediate future: (1) cyber-terrorism and (2) immigration control and border security.

Continuous Vigilance

The Department of Homeland Security warned that the relaxing of vigilance against terrorism is a "very dangerous train of thought"[3] and that there is every indication that attacks on the homeland by foreign-sponsored terrorists continues to be a significant concern.[4] The DHS has also warned that there are signs that terrorist groups have long-term plans for attacking the United States. In support of this assertion, DHS points out that the Osama bin Laden video released just before the 2004 presidential elections came with English subtitles. Also, a 75-minute video in English from "Azzam the American" released to ABC news on

October 22, 2004, was obviously intended for an American audience. Al-Qaida is targeting Americans with their warnings of violent jihad. There is evidence that al-Qaida's anti-American diatribe is having an affect on some in the United States, as there are more and more reports of persons arrested for rendering support to foreign terrorist groups.

In fact, intelligence officials are beginning to examine why the United States has not experienced another terrorist attack.[5] Did the vigilance of the DHS and other federal and local agencies detour planned attacks? Has the operational capacities of such terrorist groups such as al-Qaida been reduced by overseas military actions and stepped up anti-terrorism actions by foreign nations? Whatever the explanation, counterterrorism experts warn that continuous vigilance is "a relatively new phenomenon" in the United States and that local and federal governments need to develop permanent, long-term plans for vigilance against terrorism. Shortsighted plans that assume vigilance will be maintained by working overtime and deficit spending will result in burnout and decreased response capacity. Already some large-city police departments are experiencing this burnout among their officers, evidenced by high absenteeism rates as officers are calling in sick from working 12-hour shifts for an extended period of time.[6]

Experts are warning that local governments are going to have to be more innovative in building a response capacity and may have to effect change in policies and permanent increases in staffing levels to maintain the vigilance necessary to meet the threat. The Police Executive Research Forum, a Washington-based think tank that helps large police departments, has warned that defense of the homeland against terrorist attacks "is a threat with no end in sight."[7] Counterterrorism experts remind the public and government agencies that Israel has endured over three decades of terrorist attacks with no end in sight.

There are two major vulnerabilities the United States has identified as needing immediate attention: cyber-terrorism and immigration control and border security. To enhance anti-terrorism security and to defend the homeland against terror attacks it will be necessary to make major changes to improve anti-terrorism security.

Cyber-Terrorism

The *National Strategy to Secure Cyberspace* report said that in the 1950s and 1960s the federal government created a national system to protect against the new threat of attack from aircraft and missiles.[8] In the twenty-first century the *National Strategy to Secure Cyberspace* calls for similar actions by the federal government to protect against a new and different kind of national threat—attacks through cyber-space. Defending cyber-space is a new challenge that emerged with the invention of the Internet. Defending cyber-space from attack by terrorists is a new threat that has become a prominent concern since the 9/11 attacks.

The Federal Bureau of Investigation has defined *cyber-terrorism* as "the premeditated, politically motivated attack against information, computer systems, computer programs, and data which result in violence against noncombatant targets by subnational groups or clandestine agents."[9] This definition includes actions by both domestic terrorists and international terrorists operating either in the United States or in a foreign country. There have been no documented cases of a "pure cyber-attack" by international terrorists but the National Research Council has warned that "tomorrow's terrorist may be able to do more damage with a keyboard than with a bomb." Former cyber-security czar Richard Clarke warned Congress in 2003 that there is a "dangerous tendency to dismiss the consequences of an attack on the nation's computer networks because no one has died in a cyber-attack and there has never been a smoking ruin for cameras to see."[10]

Even before the 9/11 attacks experts have warned that cyber-terrorism presents a great potential threat to the United States. Since the 9/11 attacks experts have warned of the specter of a "digital Pearl Harbor."[11] Former Central Intelligence Agency Director Robert Gates warned, "Cyberterrorism could be the most devastating weapon of mass destruction yet and could cripple the U.S. economy."[12]

Terrorists could use the strategy of cyber-terrorism in the following four ways: (1) use of the Internet to promote terrorism; (2) use of the Internet to gather information for attacks (cyber-attacks) and as a tool to attack businesses and websites to disrupt the economy and cause financial loss (cyber-intelligence); (3) attacks on critical infrastructures using the Internet to effect physical damage, and (4) cyber-warfare.

Use of the Internet to Promote Terrorism

Military action by the United States has disrupted the terrorist training camps in Afghanistan and Iraq. Also, the United States has increasingly pressured other Middle Eastern nations to take actions against terrorist training camps within their borders. The result is that terrorist groups are turning to the Internet as their new sanctuary.[13] The Internet has become a key tool for both domestic and international terrorist organizations. For international terrorist groups such as al-Qaida the Internet is their new "base." Anonymous Arabic-language Internet websites provide cyber-sanctuaries for terrorists that are often more difficult to detect and eliminate than physical training camps. Deputy Defense Secretary Paul D. Wolfowitz, in testimony before the House Armed Services Committee, said that terrorists use the Internet as a tool "to conceal their identities, to move money, to encrypt messages, even to plan and conduct operations remotely."[14] It is known that al-Qaida and its affiliates have always used email and the Internet as communication tools. The Internet allows al-Qaida to use a legitimate technology to assist in planning terrorism, recruiting new members, and gathering information that will assist them in their attacks. The Internet has become one of the prime tools of the terrorists.[15]

In addition to using the Internet to communicate with each other, terrorist groups use the Internet to distribute their violent messages and call for jihad worldwide. Al-Qaida can use the Internet to develop a global supply chain of angry people to fill their ranks.[16] There are several hundreds of jihadist sites on the Internet.[17] Often the Internet company hosting the Arabic-language jihadist websites is not aware of the nature and purpose of the website.[18] Al-Qaida even has a "virtual university" on the Internet that teaches "electronic jihad."[19] Besides urging attacks against American and Israeli targets, these websites provide information resources for terrorists. Website visitors can read instructions on using a cell phone to remotely detonate a bomb, instructions for manufacturing small missiles, advice on the art of kidnapping, and instructions on military tactics.[20]

Federal agencies, including the National Security Agency, the FBI, and the Department of Homeland Security, monitor suspected terror sites on the Internet and sometimes track users. However, the sheer number and anonymity of these jihadist websites makes it virtually impossible to stem the flow of radical Islamic propaganda.[21] Another problem in stopping violent jihadist groups from using the Internet is that censoring Internet websites often raises the constitutional challenge of First Amendment rights. For example, many of the jihadist websites distribute videos of kidnapped hostages pleading for their lives or graphic uncensored videos of beheadings. Terrorists have been quick to understand the power of graphic images and the powerful tool that atrocity footage can be. For example, websites showing beheadings usually get 200,000 visitors a day.[22] However, censoring these violent images "opens the floodgates to really marginalizing a lot of the free speech that has been a hallmark of the American legal and political system."[23] Thus, these websites are able to distribute videos of retributive humiliation and vengeful, purifying executions that encourage terrorism and spread its propaganda of fear and humiliation. The videos proclaim that there are no innocent foreigners and that the United States, with all its power and might, is unable to ensure the protections of civilian immunity. Also, terrorists hope the images on these websites will be a crucial first step toward cracking the will to continue the fight.[24] This strategy has been particularly evident in Iraq. There, some of the citizens of coalition forces have been so influenced by the emotional videos showing kidnapped civilians pleading for their lives and their subsequent execution that they have pressured their government to withdraw their troops or support from the war in Iraq.

Cyber-Intelligence and Cyber-Attacks

Cyber-Intelligence.   In addition to being an effective method for the distribution of propaganda, the Internet is a strategic tool for terrorists to gather intelligence to assist in planning attacks and a tool to attack businesses and websites to disrupt the economy and cause financial loss.

The Internet has proven to be one of the most valuable sources of intelligence for planning attacks for terrorists. Prior to the 9/11 attacks the amount of information that could be of strategic importance to terrorists that could be accessed by the Internet was overwhelming. Routinely, data about electrical power, gas and oil storage, transportation, banking and finance, water supply, emergency services, and the continuity of government operations were available from the Internet. Even information that would clearly be of value in the planning of an attack—such as the operational status information of nuclear plants, toxic-release inventory, a listing of all factories and other sources that emit poisonous pollution, information about dangerous pesticides and detailed maps of power lines, gas lines, and locations of critical emergency supplies used by state Emergency Management Offices—was easily accessible as public documents on the Internet. Even after the 9/11 attacks many sites did not remove information that could equip potential terrorists to carry out an attack, such as the location of fuel storage tanks, maps of electrical grids, information on dams and reservoirs, and building floor plans of state and federal buildings.

Removal of information from the Internet has prompted some cries of censorship and infringement of freedom of speech and information. For example, environmental protection groups used to use information that was available on the Internet to monitor nuclear power plants, hazardous waste sites, and other toxic waste information. States have removed most of this information from the Internet and now the environmental groups must use the Freedom of Information Law to obtain such information. However, some states are even refusing to release information under the Freedom of Information Law, claiming that the information "serves no other purpose than to equip potential terrorists."[25]

The search to find the correct balance between the right of the public to know and the duty of local, state, and federal governments to secure information that could be used by terrorists to inflict damage is ongoing. Activist groups accuse the government of making information secret to protect administrative mismanagement, to cover up failure to comply with clean air and toxic guidelines, and to make it more difficult to monitor compliance. These groups often charge that the removal of the information from the Internet does not protect against terrorist attacks but does protect government and businesses from lawsuits and fines. Government officials deny such charges and claim their actions do not deny the public access to legitimate information. For example, following the 9/11 attacks, New York State Energy Department erased a detailed map of power lines and substations from its site. Requests for the information under the Freedom of Information Act can be censored if it is determined that release of the information would endanger people's lives or compromise criminal investigations. Citing these exemptions, officials are refusing to release information such as the diameter and location of a suspension bridge's cables and fasteners, fencing and gates around nuclear plants, and access roads leading to water reservoirs.[26]

Cyber-Attacks.   Security experts have warned for several years that cyber-terrorism presents a great potential threat to the United States.[27] Even before the 9/11 attacks, the information technology revolution was quietly and quickly changing the way business and government operate. The Internet has become the world's communications network linking banking, businesses, manufacturing, and utilities. In the past, waterways, surface transportation, and air transportation were the vital communication and transportation systems considered to be the engine of commerce. Today, networked computers and the Internet is the lifeline of businesses and government. Unfortunately, however, the Internet was developed without a great deal of thought about security.[28] This great dependence on information transferred by the Internet and networked computers has created a new vulnerability for society with the potential to bring commerce to a halt and to impact the lives of millions of people worldwide. Intelligence gathered from confiscated computers from al-Qaida members, interrogations of captured terrorists, and past actions clearly indicate that terrorist groups are planning attacks to disrupt or disable the Internet and other global communications networks.[29]

Cyber-attacks did not originate with terrorists. In fact, terrorists account for only a small fraction of such attacks. It is estimated that about 90 percent of the cyber-attacks are perpetrated by amateurs. Of the remaining 10 percent, 9.9 percent are perpetrated by professional hackers or corporate spies. That leaves only 0.1 percent of cyber-attacks that can be attributed to terrorists and enemy nations. Some experts dismiss the threat of cyber-terrorism. According to one panel of security experts, "The nation's computer networks face greater threats from non-terrorist hackers, viruses and poorly designed software than from a major cyberterrorism attack."[30] Although the threat of cyber-terrorism is minimum according to some, many fear that the *fear* of cyber-terrorism is greater than the actual threat that can be documented. In addition, although there have been no catastrophic cyber-attacks by terrorists, the same could be said of attacks using airplanes as flying missiles prior to September 11, 2001. Thus, cyber-terrorism is a great concern by both governments and businesses.

Computer systems and networks are vulnerable for two major reasons: (1) inadequate security to prevent unauthorized users from obtaining access and (2) software and network flaws that allow unauthorized users to exploit a flaw in the software or network to gain unauthorized access to the computer system or network. Such flaws are called *bugs*. The term originated in 1945 when Rear Admiral Grace Murray Hopper discovered that the cause of a computer malfunction was a moth trapped between relays in a Navy computer. She called it a "bug" and the term has been used since to refer to problems with computers and networks. *Debugging* is the term used to describe efforts to fix computer and network problems.

One of the most common causes of bugs is a flaw in the software. Companies such as Microsoft are constantly issuing "patches" to fix flaws or bugs in their software. However, sometimes hackers and terrorists learn of this flaw before a patch is distributed or use this flaw to gain access to computers that have not installed the software update. Unfortunately, rather than experiencing a decrease in vulnerabilities due to software and hardware flaws, there has been a significant increase in such vulnerabilities. From 2000 to 2002 the number of known vulnerabilities in software and hardware that could permit unauthorized access or allow an attack to cause damage increased from 1,090 to 4,129—a four-fold increase. Microsoft, the leading software company, reported 128 publicly disclosed security flaws in Windows during the 12-month period from June 1, 2002, to May 31, 2003. From the time a security flaw is disclosed to the time a patch is issued and applied, companies are at risk of a cyber-attack. Microsoft reported an average of 25 days between disclosure and release of a fix, and this performance is one of the best in the software business, as other operating system software companies report up to 82 days between the disclosure and release of a patch.

Companies and governments use software and network security programs and devices to defend against unauthorized entry whether due to a software vulnerability or to the efforts of a hacker. These software programs are called *anti-virus programs*. Another defense against unauthorized entry into a computer system or network is a *firewall*, which is an intrusion-detection system designed to detect unauthorized users and not allow them entry into the system. Surveys of computer networks report that about 90 percent of network systems use anti-virus programs, firewalls, and intrusion-detection systems. Nevertheless, 90 percent reported that security breaches had taken place, with 85 percent reporting their systems had been damaged by computer viruses.

Reports by the General Accounting Office have repeatedly warned that federal systems are not being adequately protected from computer-based threats, even though these systems process, store, and transmit enormous amounts of sensitive data and are indispensable to many federal agency operations.[31] Tests of government computer systems in 2001, 2002, and 2003 indicated that nearly all of the 24 agencies tested have "significant information security weaknesses that place a broad array of federal operations and assets at risk of fraud, misuse, and disruption." Among these agencies were the Department of Defense, the Department of State, the Department of Energy, and the Federal Emergency Management Agency. All four of these agencies have primary roles in the war on terrorism.[32]

Viruses and Worms. Computers and networks can be attacked using Trojan horses, worms, and viruses. All three of these are called *malicious code* and all three are similar in that they are software programs or instructions that when executed cause the computer to perform a task. However, they have unique characteristics. A *Trojan horse* is a software program that claims to be one thing while in fact it has a "hidden" software program that performs another task—often unknown to the user. A Trojan horse software program usually promises the user to perform some useful function to cause the user to install the program. Once installed, another program is launched that operates in the background, unknown to the user. A common Trojan horse program is a program that promises to place local weather information on the user's computer. The program performs this function but it also sends information about the user's visits to websites to a predetermined Internet address so that this information can be used to target the user to receive advertisements related to the sites he or she visits. This type of Trojan horse is commonly called *spyware*. Terrorists could use a Trojan horse program to have government or private company computers send confidential information to them.

Worms usually exploit software vulnerabilities and propagate without user intervention. Engineers at Xerox Palo Alto Research Center first discovered the computer worm. The worm was a short program that scours a network of idle processors in order to provide more efficient computer use. Modern worms are a form of a computer virus that does destructive damage to data on computers. Some well-known cyber-attacks using worms—none of them initiated by terrorists—are the Code Red worm in 2001, the Klex worm in 2002, the Slammer worm in 2003, and the MyDoom worm in 2004.

Viruses are a type of malicious code that requires the user to execute the program. Opening an email attachment or going to a particular webpage could trigger this action. One of the first PC viruses ever created was "The Brain" released in 1986 by programmers in Pakistan. Some well-known viruses—none of them initiated by terrorists—are the Melissa and the Chernobyl viruses released in 1999, the I Love You virus released in 2000, the Anna Kournikova virus released in 2001, and the SoBig.F virus released in 2003. It is estimated that nearly 63,000 viruses have rolled through the Internet, causing an estimated $65 billion in damages.[33] Despite the fact that none of these viruses has been linked to terrorism, half of those surveyed by the Pew Internet and American Life Project said they worried about terrorists damaging the Internet.[34]

Types of Cyber-Attacks.   There are five main types of cyber-attacks: (1) incursion, (2) destruction, (3) disinformation, (4) denial of service, and (5) defacement of websites. *Incursion attacks* are carried out with the purpose of gaining unauthorized access to a computer system or network. Such attacks are most commonly carried out to obtain data or to manipulate information. The motive for incursion attacks among nonterrorists is for financial gain, such as embezzlement, or for sabotage. For example, disgruntled employees or former employees may want to cause economic damage to the database. Young males, sometimes preteen boys, seeking thrills and notoriety, commit a good number of incursion attacks. Successful incursion attacks are usually carried out by taking advantage of loopholes in computer systems and networks, insider information (e.g., knowledge of passwords), or flaws in the software that allow unauthorized "backdoor" entries.

Destruction involves entry into a computer system or network for the purpose of inflicting severe damage or destroying them. Such destruction usually causes significant financial loss to the target. The damage can be erasing databases, corrupting data, releasing sensitive data to the public or competitors, and causing the system to crash. This type of attack is usually carried out by disgruntled employees or former employees seeking revenge or criminal hackers as a kind of vandalism. For terrorists, the motivation would be to cause economic damage to private business or to disrupt government operations.

Disinformation attacks are used to spread rumors or information that can have severe impact to a particular target. Such cyber-attacks can be carried out using legitimate bulletin boards or by creating websites, some claiming to be "news" websites, to disseminate the disinformation. A common criminal use of this type of cyber-attack is to influence the price of a company's stock. This type of cyber-attack is commonly used by radical jihadist websites. Many of the websites purport to be "news" sites but they disseminate false information about U.S. actions and policies. During war this is commonly referred to as *propaganda*.

Denial of service (DOS) is one of the most common forms of cyber-attack. The main objective in a DOS attack is to disable or disrupt the online operations of a website by flooding the targeted servers with a huge number of packets or requests for service. A DOS attack usually involves a worm that takes control of remote computers without the knowledge of the computer user. The worm is programmed to initiate requests for service on a predetermined time or event. A successful DOS attack will cause the target server to shut down due to its inability to handle the incoming messages. A denial of service attack in 2002 generated such a volume of messages that it nearly overwhelmed the entire Internet.[35]

The final type of cyber-attack is *defacement of websites*. This type of attack is a form of digital vandalism. The targeted website can be changed totally to include messages and images from the cyber-attacker. The attack can cause the website to be taken down to avoid embarrassment caused by the defacement and can cause financial losses and loss of services as legitimate users are denied access to the website while the vulnerability is detected and patched and the website restored. The motivation for this type of attack is primarily propaganda or publicity. Defacement of website attacks have been successfully executed against the White House website, the Department of Defense website, and George Bush's reelection campaign website.

Attacks on Critical Infrastructures Using the Internet

Cyber-terrorist attacks can be grouped into three main categories: (1) simple–unstructured, (2) advanced–structured, and (3) complex–coordinated.[36] *Simple–unstructured* attacks are directed against individual systems using software created by other people. This is the most common form of hacking by amateurs. *Advanced–structured* attacks are directed toward multiple systems or networks and the hacker may use hacking software he or she created. *Complex–coordinated* attacks are capable of causing mass disruptions against integrated and heterogeneous defenses. Using complex–coordinated attacks, terrorists have the ability to use the Internet as a direct instrument of bloodshed. These complex–coordinated cyber-attacks do more than cause damage to computer databases and networks. They have the ability to give terrorists control of the physical structures controlled by computers.[37]

What gives terrorists the ability to use computers to cause damage in the real world are the use of digital control systems (DCS) and supervisory control and data acquisition systems (SCADA). These specialized digital devices are used by the millions as the brains of critical infrastructure in the United States.[38] The report of *The National Strategy to Secure*

Cyberspace states that over the last 20 years DCS and SCADA control systems have transformed the way many industries in the United States control and monitor equipment. These two systems do tasks such as collect measurements, throw railway switches, close circuit breakers, and adjust values in the pipes that carry water, oil, and gas. They can also be designed to control a single device or to monitor and control multiple devices. They can be programmed to make decisions as to what to do and when to do it. The use of DCS and SCADA systems has allowed industry to replace many tasks that were previously performed manually with digital controls. They are used in almost every sector of the economy, including water, transportation, chemicals, energy, and manufacturing.[39] Using the Internet to take control of DCS and SCADA systems, terrorists could use virtual tools to destroy real-world lives and property. Terrorists could combine physical attacks, using explosives with cyber-attacks to escalate the damage caused by a physical attack. For example, terrorists could detonate a truck bomb and simultaneously disable the 911 communications systems to prevent officials from responding to the situation.

When DCS and SCADA systems were designed it was not anticipated that there would be public access to these digital control systems, as they were controlled by local computers without access to the Internet. During the last 20 years many of these systems have been connected to the Internet because this allows companies to reduce personnel and costs. However, connecting these digital control systems to the Internet has created new vulnerabilities. A statement by the Commerce Department's Critical Infrastructure Assurance Office warns that the prevalence of these digital control systems connected by the Internet to run physical assets places the nation at risk. "Digital controls are so pervasive that terrorists might use them to cause damage on a scale that otherwise would not be available except through a very systematic and comprehensive physical attack."[40]

There have been no documented cases of al-Qaida conducting such cyber-attacks. However, there have been cases where cyber-attacks on DCS and SCADA systems by persons who are not international terrorists have been successful in causing physical damage or could have caused damage. In 1998, a 12-year-old hacker broke into the computer system that runs Arizona's Roosevelt Dam. He had complete command of the SCADA system controlling the dam's floodgates. Had he been more malicious or a terrorist, he could have opened the floodgates and caused extensive damage.[41] In 2000, computer hacker Vitek Boden, age 48, was able to gain access to the digital control system of the Maroocky Shire wastewater system in Queensland, Australia. He was able to take control of the digital control system and dump hundreds of thousands of gallons of putrid sludge into parks, rivers, and the manicured grounds of a Hyatt Regency hotel. The release of wastewater killed marine life, polluted creek water, and made it impossible for people to use the beaches. What is astonishing is that he was able to make 46 successful incursions without being detected. The utility's managers could not determine why the wastewater system's controls were malfunctioning until Boden was captured.[42]

In the United States there have been a number of successful cyber-attacks on the 911 system and the telephone system. Successful cyber-attacks on the Internet have brought down police and fire departments' emergency communication systems and disrupted telephone services to thousands of customers.[43] In January 2003, a cyber-attack shut down the monitoring system of a nuclear power plant. Fortunately the plant was off-line or the cyber-attack would have resulted in a major disaster.[44]

A major concern of government officials is the vulnerability of the North American power grid. Equipment failures not due to cyber-attacks by terrorists have demonstrated that it is possible for the grid to go down and that disruption of the power grid causes enormous financial damage, causes fear and disruption of everyday life, and exposes cities to vulnerabilities due to disruption of communications and emergency services such as fire and police. The Commerce Department has conducted mock cyber SCADA attacks against the power grid. These mock attacks have always succeeded in bringing down the power grid.[45]

Cyber-Warfare

Cyber-attacks by terrorists are a concern, but some government officials, including Richard A. Clarke, former head of the Office of Cyberspace Security under President Bush, consider cyber-attacks by nation-states "the most dangerous threat to this country's computer security."[46] Clarke has indicated that he suspects that about five or six nation-states have attempted cyber-attacks on national security computers.[47] The report of *The National Strategy to Secure Cyberspace* stated that in 1998, attackers carried out a sophisticated, tightly orchestrated series of cyber-intrusions into the computers of the Department of Defense, the National Aeronautical and Space Administration (NASA), and government research labs. The intrusions were targeted against those organizations that conduct advanced technical research on national security, including atmospheric and oceanographic topics as well as aircraft and cockpit design.[48] In 1999 and 2000, unidentified hackers downloaded scores of "sensitive but unclassified" internal documents from the Los Alamos and Livermore national laboratories. Defense Department investigators traced the electronic trail back to an unnamed foreign country.[49] Officials in the United States believe it is possible that a foreign government helped create the Code Red virus that took control of 314,000 servers in 2001 and directed them to attack White House computers.[50]

Tests of the security of national military and security computers have indicated that the government's computers and security networks are vulnerable.[51] Continued testing of the Department of Defense computer and network security by the Government Accounting Office continues to reveal security flaws that make unauthorized intrusion possible. The concern with lax cyber-security is two-fold: (1) agents of nation-states may take information that would prove harmful to United States security and (2) agents of nation-states may place malicious software such as a virus, worm, or Trojan horse program on network computers with the goal that the malicious software would be transferred to more sensitive networks.[52]

It is easy for the perpetrators of a cyber-attack to conceal their identity; thus, cyber-attacks have proven attractive strategies for attacking the United States, especially by poorer nations. Nations that would never consider a military assault against the United States may be tempted to launch a cyber-attack. Cyber-warfare could be carried out at a fraction of the cost of a conventional war, expose the attacker to much less risk of retaliation, and be initiated anywhere in the world. It is not necessary to physically enter the United States to launch a cyber-attack. Mock attacks by the Central Intelligence Agency and the National Security Agency have concluded that cyber-terrorism could be the most devastating weapon of mass destruction and could cripple the U.S. economy.[53]

The Internet is a prime target of terrorists because the high-tech economy of the United States is dependent on it. Furthermore, the economy of countries from which most terrorists originate is usually not as dependent on the Internet. Therefore, a disruption of the Internet would have a far greater impact on the United States.[54] Former Central Intelligence Director Robert Gates has warned that as terrorists become more motivated by radical religion, the less the terrorists are concerned about the scale of their violence and the number of innocent lives they are prepared to take.[55] Thus, concerns about both cyber-attacks from terrorists and cyber-attacks from nations have caused the federal government and military to take actions to develop robust defense capacities against cyber-attacks.

Whereas the United States worries about cyber-attacks by foreign nations, the nation has also given consideration to the use of cyber-weapons against nations. For example, in the 1999 U.S. military action in Kosovo, the U.S. military jammed Serbian computer networks.[56] However, the United States has never conducted a large-scale, strategic cyber-attack.[57] The extent of the U.S. arsenal of cyber-weapons, offensive capacity, and defense capacity is "among the most tightly held national security secrets, even more guarded than nuclear capabilities."[58] It is known that National Security Presidential Directive 16, a classified document issued in July 2002, directed government and military officials to develop a national-level policy for determining when and how the United States would launch cyber-attacks against enemy computer networks.[59]

In considering the rules of engagement for cyber-weapons, the United States needs to consider such factors as expected outcomes and military advantages of cyber-attacks and collateral damage. For example, a computer attack on an enemy nation's electric power grid intended to disable military facilities may also cut off power to civilian users, such as hospitals.[60] Also, the United States has to consider that U.S. businesses and governmental entities depend on technology to a far greater degree than do relatively underdeveloped countries, rogue nations, and terrorist groups. If the United States initiates offensive cyber-attacks against such countries, it could trigger counter–cyber-attacks that would be much more harmful to the United States than to the nation the United States attacked.[61]

Defending Cyber-Space

Defense against cyber-attacks is somewhat different from defense against physical attacks by terrorists. In defending against physical attacks, the primary goal is to prevent such attacks through intelligence, preparation, and target hardening. The primary goal in cyber-attacks "is not to prevent cyber-attacks but to withstand them."[62] Cyber-networks are constantly exposed to anonymous cyber-attacks in the United States. There is no way to prevent such attacks, so the primary defense is to develop firewalls, hardware, and software that can detect a cyber-attack and prevent the malicious program from gaining access to the network or damaging data. In developing a defense strategy against cyber-terrorism, the federal government has had to contend with three unique obstacles that make cyber-terrorism different from traditional terrorism: (1) hackers versus terrorists, (2) private initiatives, and (3) the role of the federal government.

Hackers versus Terrorists.
First, most cyber-based attacks are crimes, not attacks, by cyber-terrorists.[63] Furthermore, most of the cases of major cyber-attacks have been initiated by amateurs or hackers, not terrorists. Some of the cyber-attacks have been initiated by teenagers as young as 14 years old. It is difficult for the federal government to develop a

national policy and national agency to respond to a problem that should be the responsibility of law enforcement officials. The problem is that law enforcement and the courts are not effective agents in preventing cyber-terrorism. Laws against cyber-terrorism do not keep pace with the technology of the crime. For example, it was not possible to prosecute the person who was responsible for the "I Love You" virus that did 7 billion dollars worth of damage, because his native country did not have laws against releasing the malicious code and there was no U.S. law that allowed him to be extradited for prosecution in the United States.

Even when there are laws against cyber-attacks, such laws are very difficult to enforce and often carry only minimum punishments. David Smith, the person responsible for the Melissa virus, which was responsible for millions of dollars of damage, received only a 20-month sentence for sending the virus. Also, many of those responsible for cyber-attacks are teenagers who are often protected from harsh punishment by the juvenile courts. The federal government has taken some steps to remedy this problem, however. In November 2003, legislation was passed making certain computer crimes federal crimes punishable by harsher sentences. For example, under the new legislation a person who is responsible for a cyber-attack that intends to cause deaths, such as tying up 911 emergency telephone lines or shutting down the power grid, could face a life sentence. However, for the most part, local and state law enforcement authorities are not well equipped to detect and prosecute those responsible for cyber-crime.

Private Initiatives Necessary.   The second problem in defending against cyber-attacks is that most critical infrastructures, and the cyber-space on which they rely, are privately owned and operated.[64] Not only is there no single government oversight agency responsible for cyber-security but also the federal government often has no authority or responsibility at all. Thus, cyber-security to a great deal depends on private initiatives. Often the most the federal government can do is to encourage individuals and private businesses to take steps to increase cyber-security.[65] The report of the *National Strategy to Secure Cyberspace* indicated that the majority of security vulnerabilities could be mitigated through good security practices.[66] However, many individuals and businesses may not be willing to pay the additional costs necessary to promote cyber-security.[67] For example, one of the most deadly cyber-attacks by terrorists would be an attack where terrorists took control of digital control systems and supervisory control and data acquisition systems with the purpose of overriding critical controls of nuclear power plants, dams, wastewater treatment, traffic signal controls, or other devices that could cause real damage and death. One of the simple ways to prevent such a disaster is to provide human control in all vital systems so as to prevent misuse by such terrorists. However, the very reason that such digital control systems were initiated was to save the cost of human supervision.

Efforts by both the government and consumers to encourage private software developers to eliminate vulnerabilities in their software has not eliminated one of the most common causes of cyber-insecurity—software with vulnerabilities that allow intrusions and malicious code attacks by exploiting vulnerabilities in the software. Some have argued for software companies to be held legally responsible for damages due to software vulnerabilities. They suggest that software developers should be held accountable for what they produce, sell, and distribute to the public.[68] Critics have argued that leaving it to software companies to improve their software security has not worked and that regulation and legislation is necessary. If adopted, such regulations and legislation would mandate the use of firewalls, anti-virus software, and increased security practices.

A 2003 survey by the Pew Internet and American Life Project indicated that nearly 60 percent of Internet users say they favor the government requiring U.S. corporations to disclose more information about their vulnerabilities. Most do not believe that voluntary efforts to secure the Internet are sufficient.[69] Many businesses, however, fear that regulation would place financial burdens on them that would destroy their ability to be competitive in the marketplace. For example, broadband Internet providers argue that if they modify their services, as suggested in several legislative proposals to make it easier for police to perform wiretaps, such costs would be prohibitive.[70] Colleges say that to modify their campus-based networks to make it easier for law enforcement to monitor Internet-based voice conversations could cause colleges to incur significant costs without compensation.[71] Other advocates argue that if the government is allowed to require security enhancements to the Internet, such regulations would "dumb down the genius of the Net to match the limited visions of the regulator."[72]

The Federal Government's Role. The report of the *National Strategy to Secure Cyberspace* concluded that "public-private engagement is a key component of our strategy to secure cyberspace."[73] However, although the report concluded that the federal government alone cannot sufficiently defend America's cyber-space, the report also concluded that the federal government plays a key role in securing cyber-space.[74] Worms and viruses can infect millions of computers in a very brief time and can cause millions or billions of dollars in damage. The speed and anonymity of cyber-attacks makes the distinction among the actions of terrorists, criminals, and nation-states difficult. Often this distinction is only possible after the attack occurs.[75] Thus, the task is to define the role of the federal government in cyber-security.

In October 2001, President Bush issued Executive Order 13231, authorizing a federal cyber-protection program that consists of continuous efforts to secure information systems for critical infrastructure, including emergency preparedness communications and the physical assets that support such systems.[76] Unlike the federal role in aviation security, the federal government has chosen to take a limited role in cyber-protection that depends to a great extent on partnerships with private businesses and individuals. The report of the *National Strategy to Secure Cyberspace* concluded that private-sector organizations and all individuals must make their own decisions as to what security measures they will adopt based on cost effectiveness analysis and risk-management and mitigation strategies.[77] The federal government has taken the role of encouraging rather than legislating that the public and private institutions and cyber-centers perform analysis, conduct watch and warning activities, enable information exchange, and facilitate restoration efforts.[78] Basically, the federal government's position is that "each American who depends on cyberspace, the network of information networks, must secure the part that they own or for which they are responsible."[79]

The federal government under President Bush's Executive Order 13231 and President Clinton's Presidential Directive Decision 63 (May 22, 1998) has outlined its responsibility for cyber-security and the partnerships it envisions with the public and private sector. Operating under these directives, the federal government established lead agencies responsible for various infrastructure sections. The overall critical infrastructure protection responsibilities of the federal government are summarized in Table 13.1. Each lead agency is responsible for developing its own plan (1) to protect those computers and networks for which it is responsible and (2) to partner with the various public and private infrastructure sectors for which it is the lead agency to encourage policies and actions that will enhance cyber security.

With the creation of the Department of Homeland Security, the DHS assumed a key role in cyber-security. One of the directorates of the DHS is the National Cyber Security Division (NCSD). This division is the federal government's cornerstone for cyber-security coordination and preparedness, including implementation of the *National Strategy to Secure Cyberspace*. The operational arm of the NCSD is the United States Computer Emergency Readiness Team (US-CERT), established in September 2003. The DHS defines the *US-CERT* as "a public-private partnership charged with improving computer security preparedness and response to cyber attacks in the United States." The specific mission of US-CERT is to (1) analyze and reduce cyber-threats and vulnerabilities, (2) disseminate cyber-threat warning information, and (3) coordinate incident response activities.

In January 2004, the National Cyber Security division of DHS initiated the National Cyber Alert System. This system is similar to the DHS color-coded threat alert advisories in that it delivers "timely and actionable information" to pubic and private sectors concerning computer security vulnerabilities and cyber-attacks. Unlike the National Threat Advisory

TABLE 13.1   *Critical Infrastructure Lead Agencies*

Lead Agency	Sectors
Department of Homeland Security	• Information and telecommunications • Transportation (aviation, rail, mass transit, waterborne commerce, pipelines, and highways, including trucking and intelligent transportation systems • Postal and shipping • Emergency services • Continuity of government
Department of the Treasury	• Banking and finance
Department of Health and Human Services	• Public health (including prevention, surveillance, laboratory services, and personal health services) • Food (all except for meat and poultry)
Department of Energy	• Energy (electric power, oil and gas production, and storage)
Environmental Protection Agency	• Water • Chemical industry and hazardous materials
Department of Agriculture	• Agriculture • Food (meat and poultry)
Department of Defense	• Defense industrial base

Source: The National Strategy to Secure Cyberspace, Washington, DC: GPO, February 2003, p. 16.

System, those concerned with computer security have to sign up with the National Cyber Alert System (www.US-CERT.gov/cas) to receive information by email concerning vulnerabilities and threats. There is no charge for this service; even individuals can sign up for cyber-security tips, bulletins, and alerts. Private businesses have offered a similar service for a fee. For example, both Symantec, an independent security services and software publisher, and IBM offer a similar cyber-threat warning network. Similar to the US-CERT National Cyber Alert System, the services of Symantec and IBM provide "a first-line defense" against cyber-attack

Immigration Control and Border Security

The 9/11 Commission criticized the former office of Immigration and Naturalization Services (INS), claiming that INS failed to prevent terrorists involved in the 9/11 attacks from entering the United States even though some of them were listed on the State Department's watch list. The commission also claimed that INS failed to monitor and take steps to remove potential terrorists who entered the United States illegally or who remained in the United States after their visas had expired. The public and the Bush Administration apparently shared this concern, as a crackdown on immigration control and border security was quickly initiated.

Concern over ineffective immigration control and porous border security led to the dismantling of INS and the transfer of responsibility for immigration control and border security to the newly created Department of Homeland Security. The Immigration and Naturalization Service (INS) was abolished March 1, 2003, and its functions and units incorporated into the new DHS.[80] Immigration enforcement functions were placed within the directorate of Border and Transportation Security (BTS), either directly, or under Customs and Border Protection (CBP), which includes the Border Patrol and INS Inspectors or Immigration and Customs Enforcement (ICE). ICE assumed responsibility for the enforcement and investigation components previously performed by INS, such as investigations, intelligence, detention and removals.[81]

The challenge of securing the borders against terrorists is staggering in its scope. There are more than 300 legal ports of entry but the 8,000 miles of Canadian and Mexican borders, plus the Atlantic and Pacific coastlines, provide virtually an unlimited number of possible illegal points of entry. Congress limits the number of legal immigrations into the United States but even with the number of immigrants capped, a tremendous number of people must be screened and processed. In 2002, there were 1,063,732 legal immigrations into the United States, and in 2003, there were 705,827 legal immigrations.[82] On top of this number of legal immigrations, DHS must also detect and remove illegal immigrants. The number of illegal immigrants who enter the United States is as many or more than the number of legal immigrants. For example, there were 1 million deportable aliens located by DHS during 2003, 186,000 deportations, and more than 79,000 criminal alien deportations.[83]

To enhance border security and protect against terrorists entering the United States, the Department of Homeland Security and the newly created departments of Bureau of Customs and Border Protection and the Bureau of Immigration and Customs Enforcement undertook a number of aggressive programs to change existing policies and to enact new policies to defend the homeland against terrorism. The purpose of these programs was to

BOX 13.1 • *Up Close and Personal: May I See Your ID?*

Official identification documents are a major concern in the war on terrorism. The DHS wants to stop terrorists from being able to obtain government identification cards. This concern was sparked by the fact that two of the 9/11 hijackers illegally obtained Virginia identification cards. Following the 9/11 attacks many states tightened rules on issuing identification cards and driver's licenses. Many states refuse to issue driver's license to illegal immigrants; whereas other states argue that it is better to have illegal immigrants licensed rather than driving without testing that a license would require. Without a license or state identification card, immigrants find that they are unable to open bank accounts and to utilize services that require the user to provide official identification. The problem extends not only to illegal immigrants but also to legal immigrants who find that their paperwork is not in order or does not meet the new more stringent DHS standards. Often these immigrants find that although they were able to obtain identification cards and driver's licenses prior to 9/11, they are now unable to renew their ID cards and driver's licenses.[84]

To enhance national security, the government has focused on the merits of a national identification card and a standardized driver's license. Each state issues a driver's license of its own design with whatever information on the license deemed appropriate by the state. The Department of Homeland Security has argued for a single standard "look" with certain information being required on all state driver's licenses. The agency maintains that this would help law enforcement officials, airline security officials, and immigration and customs officials to be able to spot fraudulent identification documents.

Since each state can issue a driver's license of its own design, disputes can arise as to what can be required to obtain a driver's license. Lultaana Freeman, formerly Sandra Keller, was denied a Florida driver's license because she refused to have her photograph taken without her veil. She previously had been issued a driver's license from the state of Illinois and the state of Florida in which she was photographed in her veil. However, following the 9/11 attacks, Florida changed its policy and issued her a letter advising that she would have to have a new photograph taken without her veil or her driver's license would be canceled. Citing objections based on religious practices of the Muslim faith, she refused to be photographed without her veil.

The American Civil Liberties Union filed suit to force the state of Florida to issue a driver's license with a photograph of her veiled. The ACLU claimed that the requirement to be photographed without a veil was arbitrary, as a driver's license can be obtained without a photograph in 14 states. The court ruled against Lultaana Freeman, accepting the lawyers' for state argument that a driver's license showing only a covered face would hinder law enforcement officials. Florida Circuit Judge Janet C. Thorpe said the state of Florida was justified in requiring persons to be photographed without a veil. Judge Thorpe stated in her ruling, "Although the court acknowledges the plaintiff herself most likely poses no threat to national security, there likely are people who would be willing to use a ruling permitting the wearing of full-face cloaks in driver's license photos by pretending to ascribe to religious beliefs in order to carry out activities that would threaten lives."

Questions

1. Freeman was photographed without a veil after she was arrested in 1998 on a domestic battery charge. Also, Muslim women in the Middle East are required to be photographed without their veil for passports. Do you agree with the State Court's ruling that people should not be able to obtain a driver's license without a photograph in which the person can be identified? Why or why not?

2. The ACLU argued the state of Florida does not have compelling state interest in having a face photograph of Freeman on her driver's license without her veil and if required to do so the state would be forcing Freeman to violate her religious beliefs. When there is a conflict between religious beliefs and concern for national security, what should be the criteria in balancing the two conflicting rights?

stop terrorists from entering the United States and to ensure that aliens who entered the United States illegally and those who entered legally but lost their legal status were detected and deported. These new border security strategies and programs have focused on (1) controlling and identifying who enters and exits the United States, (2) more scrutiny of foreign students entering the United States for the alleged purpose of attending school, and (3) enhancing security by the adoption of "smart" passports.

Immigration Control

The Department of Homeland Security initiated several programs with the goal of enhancing border security by identifying and deporting people with criminal backgrounds or indirect ties to terrorism. Among these new programs, the most controversial was one that sought to identify "special-interest" immigrants who allegedly had direct or indirect connections to terrorist groups. This program resulted in the arrest of more than 700 people, most from Middle Eastern countries, who were charged with violating immigration laws.[85] Additional security screening for visa applications was required for applicants from 26 predominately Muslim countries. Also, DHS initiated the Absconder Apprehension Initiative. The purpose of the program was to identify and expedite the expulsion of immigrants who were facing deportation from countries with an al-Qaida presence.

US-VISIT. The DHS has initiated new requirements for travelers to the United States. Two of the most sweeping policies are the fingerprinting and photographing of foreign visitors and passenger screening. The new policy, known as United States Visitor and Immigrant Status Indicator Technology, or US-VISIT, requires foreign visitors to be fingerprinted and photographed when they enter the United States at first applied only to those visitors from countries for which entry visas were required. However, fearing that terrorists may take advantage of the exemption of foreign visitors from European countries and other nations—such as Brunei, Singapore, Japan, Australia, and New Zealand—the policy was changed in April 2004 to require fingerprints and photographs of *all* visitors. The program started with air travelers but will eventually extend to most if not all airports, seaports, and land border crossings. Foreign visitors' reactions to the new fingerprint and photo requirement have been mixed, with some visitors praising the efficiency of the system and others saying the new requirement "makes them feel like a criminal."[86]

The policy requires that foreign visitors be photographed and provide a digital fingerprint of their left and right index fingers. The procedure usually takes less than a minute. One of the shortcomings of the policy is that fingerprints are not checked against the Federal Bureau of Investigation databank of fingerprints. The FBI fingerprint database, one of the most comprehensive in the world, contains more than 47 million prints. The digital fingerprints of travelers are checked only against the limited database of the DHS. The reason for this practice is that the FBI fingerprint database uses fingerprints from all 10 fingers, whereas the DHS database uses only fingerprints from the index fingers. The DHS and the FBI have not developed a common database that will share the fingerprint data collected from foreign travelers. A small percentage of the fingerprints from foreign travelers is cross-checked with the FBI database, but 99 percent of foreign visitors to the United States do not have their fingerprints checked against the FBI database.[87] The Department of Homeland Security has defended the incompatibility of the two fingerprint databases, saying that to take all 10 prints of the millions of visitors would be "expensive, time-consuming and unnecessary" and that the DHS fingerprint database was "not designed for booking criminals."[88]

Airline Passenger Screening.   The second strategy initiated by DHS to enhance border security is passenger screening. In 2004, DHS formalized plans to screen airline passengers against a list of potential terror suspects. This screening was previously performed by the airlines. Passenger name screening requires that the names of passengers provided by the airlines are checked against government watch lists to ensure that suspected terrorists do not board airplanes and that law enforcement officials are promptly notified of potential security risks.[89]

The DHS administration of passenger screening was suppose to result in greater efficiency and was to be less intrusive. However, bugs in the passenger screening system have resulted in passenger lists being screened after the airplane has departed for the United States. Some of these flights have been turned back and the offending passenger made to deplane. Some flights have actually landed in the United States only to discover a passenger on the no-fly list.

One of the more prominent errors of this sort was when Yusuf Islam, better known to Americans as Cat Stevens, the musician popular in the 1960s and 1970s, was flagged in a flight from London to New York in September 2004. The musician's name was not discovered until it was too late to turn the plane back. The airplane was diverted to Bangor, Maine, where Yusuf Islam, or Cat Stevens, was removed, taken into custody, and deported back to London. The deportation of Cat Stevens resulted in a questioning of the effectiveness of the passenger screening program and furthermore a questioning of the criteria used to place names on the list. Many argued that Cat Stevens is known for his peace activities, including opposition to the U.S. war effort, and that he is a moderate Muslim and has taken a public stance against terrorism.[90] Such critics argue that the watch lists "demonstrate the failure of American domestic and security policy, both tactically and strategically, to discern who the bad guys really are."[91] This potential flaw in the passenger screening system was again emphasized when Senator Edward M. Kennedy (D-MA) found he was on the no-fly list from March 1 to April 6, 2004, as a suspected terrorist.[92] While on the no-fly list, Senator Kennedy found that he could not purchase an airline ticket and that the airlines would not explain to him why they refused to allow him to board. Even after the mistake was allegedly corrected by DHS, Senator Kennedy reported that he continued to be stopped from boarding flights.[93]

The Challenges Facing DHS.   The Department of Homeland Security's efforts to secure the borders were evaluated by the 9/11 Commission. The commission concluded that immigration policies initiated by DHS have been "ineffective, producing little, if any, information leading to the identification or apprehension of terrorists."[94] These programs have neither prevented potential terrorists from entering the country nor clearly distinguished potential terrorists who should be removed from the country. For example, after assuming control over visas, the new DHS supervised departments issued visas to 105 foreign men who should have been prevented from entering the United States because their names appeared on government lists of suspected terrorists.[95]

Furthermore, DHS has struggled to keep foreign tourists informed of the new requirements. A significant number of foreign travelers who were not previously required to have visas have found themselves afoul of the new immigration policies. The treatment of these travelers has generated international criticism of U.S. policies. In late 2004, a significant number of British travelers found themselves arrested, handcuffed, and confined without access to a lawyer or the ability to inform others of their situation.[96] The treatment of foreign travelers from countries previously exempt from visa requirements received significant media attention in 2004 when approximately 15 journalists and actress Olivia Newton-John were handcuffed, arrested, fingerprinted, held in detention, and finally deported because they had failed to obtain the newly required special visa, known as an *I-visa,* when visiting the United States for professional reasons.

The I-visa requirement has its roots in the 1952 McCarthy era as a strategy to screen subversives from entering the United States. Foreign journalists and professional news media organizations have criticized the policy of greater scrutiny for journalists as discriminatory practices.[97] When applying for I-visas, journalists are required to declare who they are going to interview, the nature of the article they plan to write, and the fee they will be paid. Foreign journalists can be rejected for visas. If rejected, they have no right to appeal. Foreign journalists object to having to reveal this information, especially since U.S. journalists entering Britain and other European countries covered by this requirement are not required to disclose similar information about their visits.[98] Following the negative press over the

BOX 13.2 • *Case Study: Security or Discrimination?*

People who look like they are of Middle Eastern descent are claiming they are being discriminated against because others assume they are terrorists. In December 2001, an Arab American member of President Bush's Secret Service security detail was denied passage on an American Airlines flight after the flight's pilot questioned the validity of the agent's credentials.[99]

In 2002, an Indian doctor who was a naturalized citizen and former U.S. Army major was detained by air marshals but later released without charge allegedly because they "didn't like the way [he] looked."[100] On September 13, 2003, two Canadian Islamic leaders were denied entry into the United States and detained for 16 hours and jailed because security officials found a business card that contained the name of an organization allegedly tied to terrorism. The Canadian Islamic leaders alleged, "One of the agents told them, 'You guys have picked the wrong time to fly.'"[101] In July 2003, the Federal Bureau of Investigation's highest-ranking Arab American agent filed a racial discrimination lawsuit against the bureau, charging that he was kept out of the investigation of the

September 11, 2001, hijackings because of his ancestry.[102] On December 29, 2004, U.S. border agents detained, searched, fingerprinted, and photographed approximately 30 persons returning from a religious conference in Toronto. A spokesperson for the Department of Homeland Security's Customs and Border Protection Bureau said that agents had orders to detain anyone who said they attended the three-day convention, entitled "Reviving the Islam Spirit," on the belief that such gatherings could promote terrorism.[103] The order to stop all persons attending the conference was justified by the statement that "the threat of terrorism provided no room for error."[104]

Questions

1. Do you believe that heightened security to detect terrorists who may attempt to enter the United States has resulted in unintended discrimination against innocent persons of Middle East ancestry?

2. What would you suggest as guidelines for airlines and customs and immigration for screening for possible terrorists?

policy, the DHS issued new guidelines allowing for more flexibility in admitting first-time offenders.

International Students: Separating Friend from Foe

Several of the hijackers in the 9/11 attacks entered the United States claiming they were entering to study. The screening used by INS prior to 9/11 was a manual system that made it very difficult to determine the legitimacy of immigrants' claims that they were students. To enter as a student, the government issues what are known as *I-20 visa permits*. However, under the system in place prior to the 9/11 attacks, it was very difficult for custom officials to know if a student enrolled and attended the college or program indicated on his or her application.

To close this vulnerability a new tracking system for international students was implemented. The new system converted what was a manual procedure into an automated process and provided stricter monitoring of the activities of international students. The new system, called the Student and Exchange Visitor Information System (SEVIS), is a web-based system for maintaining information on international students and exchange visitors in the United States. It is administered by U.S. Immigration and Customs Enforcement (ICE) and U.S. Customs and Border Protection (CBP). Immigration and Customs Enforcement asserts that "SEVIS is designed to keep our nation safe while facilitating the entry and exit process for foreign students in the United States and for students seeking to study in the United States."[105] The cost of the SEVIS program is paid for by fees collected from those applying for the student, exchange visitor, or scholar visa.

In 2004, more than 770,000 students and exchange visitors and more than 100,000 dependents of students registered with SEVIS. Unlike the previous I-20 visa system, SEVIS provides tracking of students from entry to exit. If an international student enters the United States but does not register and attend classes at the university or school on record, ICE is alerted to this fact. In 2004, 36,600 potential student violators were reported to ICE Compliance Enforcement Unit (CEU). More than 2,900 of these reported violators were "no shows," or students who entered the country but failed to register and attend classes. As a result of investigations triggered by reported violations, CEU made 155 arrests in 2004.

In addition to registering and tracking all student and scholar visitors, SEVIS has the added advantage of being an effective tool to detect corrupt school officials who sell fraudulent Forms I-20 and transcripts. U.S. Immigration and Customs Enforcement has proclaimed, "SEVIS is one of the pillars of ICE's mission of restoring integrity to the immigration system."[106]

Although ICE has praised SEVIS, many U.S. universities have expressed the opinion that the new immigration policies concerning students and scholars has made it difficult for legitimate international students to come to the United States. These universities have also complained that international students have been subjected to misunderstandings and misinterpretations of the regulations, often resulting in their deportation for minor violations or differences of opinions as to the requirements of the law.[107] The number of international students entering the United States has dropped significantly and many credit the drop to the difficulties students are having in getting approval of their visas due to the new screening requirements.[108]

In addition to entry screening, the DHS and the FBI have engaged in active programs to investigate students, especially those from predominately Muslim countries.[109] These investigations often involve on-campus interviews with university administrators and students. Under these new regulations, university officials are "data monitors for the government" and fulfill a "law enforcement" role in tracking the compliance of students.[110] In addition to casting a new relationship between the student and the university, there are charges that although providing new scrutiny against terrorists entering as students, these new policies have adversely impacted important research being performed by international scholars and scientists in the United States.[111] For example, one review of the impact of these policies reported that due to delays and barriers in obtaining visas or permission to reenter the United States, research projects have been delayed, including research programs to create new HIV drugs, work on a vaccine for West Nile virus, research on leukemia, and work on sensors that could detect bio-warfare agents.[112]

High-Tech Passports: The Promise for More Secure Borders?

The passport is one of the primary means of establishing the identity of international visitors to the United States. The fraudulent use of passports has been a concern, as one estimate is that there are as many as 400,000 stolen blank passports.[113] To enhance passport security, the Department of State has initiated a program to move toward "smart" passports. Smart passports would contain microchips with approximately 64 kilobytes of data. The electronic passports would contain data about the traveler, such as name, birth date, and issuing office, as well as biometric identifier data, such as a photograph of the holder's face, digital fingerprints, and iris scans. The technology would permit computers to query the chip on selected data, including the use of facial recognition technology that would match the image on the passport with the traveler. Furthermore, the electronic passports are designed to be able to be read by wireless technology. This would allow travelers to pass through a checkpoint with their passports and have their data confirmed electronically. This feature would greatly speed up the processing of international travelers through customs. The biometric system would cut down the subjectivity in photo identification. The current technology of biometric systems can discriminate the difference between identical twins.[114]

The use of smart passports was initiated in 2004. Initially, the United States had proposed that citizens from most of the countries in Western Europe would be required to have smart passports with machine-readable biometric data by the end of 2004. However, this deadline proved unworkable, as many countries failed to convert their old passports over to the new smart passports. The State Department has endorsed proposals calling for the implementation of smart passports within one to three years of the original deadline.[115]

The adoption of biometric technologies has been held back for years by concerns about privacy, reliability, and the lack of international uniform standards.[116] The 9/11 attacks were the tipping point, resulting in the decision to go with enhanced security rather than worry about privacy concerns. Using the new smart passports, a traveler entering the United States puts his or her index fingers on scanners and stands in front of facial recognition cameras. The traveler's fingerprints and photograph are compared to that on his or her passport. This system provides fast, positive identification of the traveler.

However, the system also provides the potential for abuse. Concern is expressed that electronic passports may be vulnerable to electronic snooping. The wireless technology of the machine-readable passport could enable someone to capture identification data by merely being in close proximity to the traveler's passport with appropriate equipment to read the data illegally. This practice, called *skimming,* is a common technology used by identity thieves.[117] One of the reasons electronic passports would be so vulnerable to snooping is the lack of encryption of the data in the current design. The reason cited for the lack of data encryption is that all countries will need to be able to read the passports and encryption could be a barrier. Thus, the data are not encrypted and anyone skimming the data would have no problem capturing enough information about the traveler to engage in identity theft. One low-tech solution to this problem may be simply to incorporate a layer of metal foil into the cover of the passport so that it can be read only when opened.[118]

The American Civil Liberties Union has raised the concern that the new smart passports could contribute to the continuing loss of privacy.[119] Such passports would make it possible to monitor the movement of individuals globally. Smart passports could be used to track not only the entry and exit of international travelers but also track their movement within the United States. It should be noted that U.S. citizens will also be required to have smart passports. This change is spurred by both DHS initiates and initiates by foreign governments. As the United States requires international travelers to have smart passports, foreign countries in turn are requiring U.S. citizens to have similar passports.

Deportation: A Simple Solution or Misguided Bureaucracy?

As stricter immigration controls have been adopted, the need for enforcement action and sanctions has become more important. Strict immigration controls without enforcement would be useless. The Department of State and the Department of Homeland Security have aggressively pursued deportation as one of the primary strategies to respond to violations of immigration polices. This new aggressive use of deportation has been championed as an effective strategy to defend the United States against terrorists.

Prior to September 11, 2001, the Immigration and Naturalization Service was responsible for enforcing immigration law and INS was criticized for its lax enforcement of immigration laws and removal of aliens who no longer were entitled to remain in the United States. Following the 9/11 attacks this function was transferred to the Department of Homeland Security (DHS) and immigration laws were enforced with a new vigor. Old laws that had not been enforced by INS were strictly enforced by DHS. The Department of Homeland Security placed a never before seen emphasis on strict enforcement of immigration status and deportation of those found to be in violation of their immigration status. For example, in the months following the 9/11 attacks 762 people were arrested for immigration violations.[120] In 2003, DHS removals of illegal aliens increased to more than 186,000. The investigative actions of DHS resulted in the identification of 1 million deportable aliens in 2003. New policies, most of them evoked with the purported purpose of fighting terrorism, have subjected many more aliens to deportation.

Removal from the United States.   Aliens can be removed from the United States primarily by three means: voluntary departure, withdrawal of application for admission, and

BOX 13.3 • *Consider This: Getting under Your Skin*

The Department of Homeland Security has recommended a national identification card and a standardized format for a driver's license. The federal government is moving toward the adoption of a single governmentwide ID card for federal employees and contractors, known as Personal Identity Verification Project, to prevent terrorists, criminals, and other unauthorized people from getting into government buildings and computer systems. New identification cards are containing more and more information, as new high-tech identification cards can be encoded with a fairly large amount of digital information.

However, these forms of identification fall far short of the under-the-skin identity badge developed by Applied Digital Solutions based in Delray Beach, Florida. Applied Digital Solutions has developed an under-the-skin identification badge, known as VeriChip, that has been approved for implantation by the Food and Drug Administration. Implanted ID tags have been commonly used with livestock and pets for years. Applied Digital Solutions has developed a radio frequency identification tag that is 12mm by 2.1mm, or about the size of a large grain of rice, that can be inserted under the skin with nothing more than a syringe—the same technology used to insert identification tags in animals. The radio frequency identification tag uses passive technology and cannot be used to track a person by satellite or other surveillance technology. The information on the chip can be read only by a scanner that cannot be more than a few feet away. The chips used by Applied Digital Solutions are not encoded with personal data. The chips are encoded with a unique 16-digit identification number. The technology is relatively low cost, with each chip costing about $200.

Applied Digital Solutions is emphasizing the uses of the chips primarily for medical purposes whereby a patient's medical records would be tied to the chip's identification number. However, there is nothing to prevent the chip's technology from being used in other ways. In fact, Applied Digital Solutions is marketing its use for other purposes, including homeland security. Applied Digi-tal Solutions reports that government officials in Mexico are using the implanted identification chips to identify people to control access to secure rooms and documents, and some businesses offer the chip as an alternative to traditional identification cards for identifying customers.[121] Applied Digital Solutions has promoted the chip as a means to provide positive identification of children in the event they are kidnapped or abducted. The implanted ID chip could also supplement existing identification systems or it could replace traditional identification cards and could be used to control access to nuclear power plants and government buildings. The technology could also replace dog tags as military identification. In addition, the government could adopt such technology to identify and track criminals and parolees. The government could also use such a chip to track visitors to the United States.

It is not unreasonable to assume that the chip's technology will evolve and it is not unrealistic to expect that a chip could be developed that could track a person's movement or at least could be read from a greater distance. With further development of the chip's technology, it is not science fiction to imagine that frequent flyers who had such chips implanted could be quickly and positively screened through expedited check-in lines or passengers could be matched to their baggage by such technology.

Questions

1. Applied Digital Solutions is emphasizing the implanted identification chip's use to identify medical records of a patient. Do you believe the use of such technology could quickly expand to other nonmedical uses such as security control? How widely do you think this technology will be accepted? Is this going to be the new identification card of the future or will this technology be rejected? Why?

2. What are your feelings about such technology? If you worked in a secure facility—such as a nuclear power plant, a government

(continued)

BOX 13.3 • Continued

building, a bio-chemical laboratory, or a weapons research facility—and your employer offered employees the option of an implanted identification chip in lieu of a traditional identification card, which would you choose? Why?

3. What, if any, are the possible abuses or problems that you can see if such identification technology were to become commonly used in the United States?

formal removal of an alien. Of the approximately 1.5 million removals of aliens in 2003, the largest number of removals was by voluntary departure. More than 99 percent of the 887,115 aliens deported through voluntary departure involved aliens who were apprehended by the Border Patrol and removed quickly. *Voluntary departure* is the most common procedure with noncriminal aliens who are apprehended by the Border Patrol during an attempted illegal entry. In voluntary departure, aliens agree that their entry was illegal, waive their rights to a hearing, remain in custody, and are removed under supervision.[122] Most of the aliens removed through voluntary departure were apprehended crossing the United States–Mexican border.

The next largest number of aliens are removed by *withdrawal of application for admission.* In 2003, 431,807 aliens withdrew their application for admission. Somewhat similar to voluntary departure, in withdrawal of application for admission, aliens who customs inspectors determine are inadmissible during the custom processing phase are allowed to withdraw their application for admission.

Of the 1.5 million aliens removed from the United States in 2003, only 186,151 were formally removed. Actions to initiate the *formal removal of an alien* from the United States are commenced when the presence of that alien is deemed inconsistent with public welfare.[123] Under new policies adopted after 9/11 an immigration officer may determine that an arriving alien is inadmissible because the alien engaged in fraud or misrepresentation or lacks proper documents. Under these circumstances the officer can order the alien removed without further hearing or review, unless the alien states a fear of persecution or an intention to apply for asylum.[124] Furthermore, aliens who are formally removed are subject to fines or imprisonment. In 2003, 79,395 of the 186,073 formal removals were for criminal activity by the alien. Nine countries accounted for almost 92 percent of all formal removals. None of these countries were Middle East countries. (See Table 13.2.)

One controversial aspect of formal removal or deportation of aliens has been the secrecy with which formal removals can be executed. After the 9/11 attacks the court has upheld the right of immigration authorities to hold hearings in secret on possible immigration violations. If immigration officials cite possible terrorist ties as the reason for the formal removal, the Court has upheld that national security justifies the withholding of the names of persons arrested on immigration charges. The courts have ruled that disclosing the names of people arrested on immigration charges could help al-Qaida discover how law enforcement officials were conducting the nation's antiterrorist campaign.[125]

TABLE 13.2   *Nine Top Countries Accounting for Formal Removals in 2003*

Country	Number Removed	Number of Criminals
Mexico	137,819	62,518
Honduras	7,700	1,862
Guatemala	6,674	1,483
El Salvador	4,933	1,982
Brazil	3,797	210
Dominican Republic	3,284	2,139
Colombia	2,081	1,319
Jamaica	1,999	1,480
Haiti	1,032	516

Source: Department of Homeland Security, *2003 Yearbook of Immigration Statistics,* Washington, DC: GPO, September 2004, p. 150.

The Department of Homeland Security has aggressively sought to identify and re-move aliens from the United States. After the 9/11 attacks INS and DHS began a policy of strict enforcement of immigration laws, particularly focused against immigrants from pre-dominantly Muslim countries.[126] One of the first programs to focus on enforcing immigra-tion policies was the Alien Absconder Apprehension Initiative. Prior to the 9/11 attacks INS had a poor record for deporting aliens who were no longer legally qualified to remain in the United States.[127]

In the post-9/11 environment, many aliens have been deported for offenses that prior to 9/11 most likely would not have come to the attention of immigration officials. For ex-ample, aliens who have legal permanent status can be and are deported for committing mis-demeanor crimes. Officials at the Department of Homeland Security regularly scrutinize the records of jails and prisons in search of aliens eligible for deportation. In New York City's Rikers Island jail, an average of 226 inmates per month for the later part of 2004 were iden-tified as deportable aliens.[128] Immigration proceedings are civil, thus, unlike those accused of criminal offenses, aliens identified for deportation hearings have no right to a public de-fender if they cannot afford counsel. Some foreign visitors have found themselves deported for suspected terror-related activities when law enforcement authorities have become suspi-cious of what they were photographing. Visitors have been formally deported for photo-graphing bridges, overpasses, nuclear power plants, water-treatment plants, and other similar structures that could be possible terrorist targets.[129]

Children and Citizenship.   Immigration authorities do not differentiate between children and adults in their enforcement. As a result, about 5,000 unaccompanied minors were ap-prehended in 2004 and processed for deportation.[130] In some cases children are processed for deportation but in other cases parents have been deported while minor children have re-mained in the United States. For example, children born in the United States of immigrants who have been found to be no longer qualified to remain in the United States can stay even though their parents are deported. It is estimated that tens of thousands of children every year lose a parent to deportation.[131]

In the post-9/11 environment even citizenship has proven no guarantee against deportation. For example, in January 2005, U.S. Immigration and Customs Enforcement sought to remove a Haitian American who obtained citizenship six months prior to being convicted of a felony.

Our Neighbors: Canada and Mexico

The crackdown on border security and immigration control has had the largest impact not on Middle Eastern countries but on our neighbors to the north and south, Canada and Mexico. Although neither country is associated with terrorist groups, fear that Middle East terrorists could enter the United States through Canada or Mexico has resulted in enhanced border security between the United States and these countries.

Canada.   Historically, the United States–Canadian border has been a "good-neighbor" border with large stretches of the border unguarded and fairly easy for one to cross illegally. For example, prior to the 9/11 attacks only 35 agents guarded more than 450 miles of border between Erie, Pennsylvania, and Watertown, New York. Also, despite the large expanse of the border, much of the border lacked air surveillance.[132] Increased concern that terrorists could descend on the United States from Canada has resulted in increased surveillance, border-crossing checkpoints, and the adoption of high-tech border monitoring equipment.

The Canadian border poses difficult challenges to close to terrorists because it is possible to cross the border by air, water, and land, and much of the border is relatively deserted wilderness. A compounding factor is the fact that new immigration controls can cause strain on the "good-neighbor" policy between the United States and Canada whereby U.S. citizens and Canadian citizens cross the border freely and frequently for business and tourism. For example, when the United States set up border-crossing checkpoints on Interstate 87 north of Albany, several major crashes resulting in traffic fatalities occurred that were attributed to unsafe conditions near or at the checkpoints.[133] Also, as aliens desire to cross the Canadian–United States border illegally, some Canadian citizens may be tempted to provide illegal border-crossing services for the lucrative profit that can be realized from guiding people across the border. Few aliens seeking to cross from Canada into the United States attempt the crossing without a guide. Smuggling people across the border is lucrative business; depending on the nationality of the alien, one can make as much as $40,000 for each adult they help cross the border.[134]

Mexico.   The closing of the United States–Mexican border to terrorists is complicated by a long-standing history of a great number of illegal crossings by Mexicans seeking employment in the United States. Furthermore, the amount of commercial traffic resulting from North American Free Trade Agreement (NAFTA) and tourist traffic crossing the United States–Mexico border is so great that any delay in border inspections would cause a tremendous back-up of traffic at border crossings. For example, Laredo, Texas, each year has 4.6 million pedestrians, 1.4 million trucks, 6.8 million private vehicles, and more than 40,000 buses cross its four international bridges, according to U.S. Customs and Border Protection.[135] Thus, while border inspections are necessary, timely inspections are essential, thereby creating conflict between efficiency and border security.

Unlike the Canadian–United States border, relations between the United States and Mexico over illegal immigration has always been strained. Illegal immigration, inspired primarily by the desire for better economic well-being, has resulted in a porous border with thousands of illegal crossings per week, despite fences, guards, checkpoints, high-tech night surveillance, and aerial surveillance of the border. It is difficult to separate discussion of preventing terrorists from crossing the border from stemming illegal immigration by Mexican citizens seeking jobs in the United States. Plus, border security is compounded by the desire to stop the flow of illegal drugs into the United States, as the United States–Mexico border is a major route for illegal drug traffic. Thus, border security is a triple challenge as DHS strives to keep out illegal immigrants, drug smugglers, and terrorists. Due to the large number of illegal crossings, DHS has declared that the U.S.–Mexican border "is not a secure border."[136]

For example, prior to the 9/11 attacks there were many "unofficial" but illegal border-crossing points where people crossed back and forth without difficulty or oversight of the border patrol. One example of such an unofficial crossing was near the small town of Lajitas, Texas, where prior to 9/11 residents of both countries could freely cross from one to the other by a short boat ride. People had been using this unofficial crossing for decades and its frequent use was reflected by the fact that the illegal boat ride across the border cost only $1 from Mexico to the United States and $2 from the United States to Mexico. After the 9/11 attacks the unofficial, illegal crossing was closed and anyone caught crossing the river now faces a $5,000 fine and possible jail time.[137]

The Department of Homeland Security continues to invest millions of dollars to enhance border security with Mexico. The fear is that if it is so easy for illegal immigrants to cross, terrorists could cross with the same ease. However, U.S. officials have expressed concern that the Mexican government has not viewed border security with the same perspective. One of the examples cited by U.S. officials of the Mexican government's apparently lax attitude toward illegal border crossings was the Mexican government's publication of 1.5 million copies of a 32-page "comic book" format guide for migrants. These pamphlets instructed migrants on how to illegally cross into the United States and how to minimize the possibility of getting caught by American law enforcement officials once in the United States. Mexico's ambassador to the United States denied that the intent of the book was to promote illegal immigration. He claimed the purpose of the book was to promote safety by instructing those engaging in illegal border crossings about the hazards of drowning or dehydration.[138] However, U.S. officials claimed the guide book is "tantamount to the Mexican government printing a 'how-to' guide to illegally entering the United States."[139] U.S. lawmakers point out that although the book discusses the hazards of crossing the border illegally, it also provides advice on how to avoid arrest and detection by U.S. law enforcement officials after crossing into the United States.[140]

Conclusion: Can the United States Be Terror-Proofed?

Is it possible to turn off the Internet? No. Is it possible to stop illegal immigration into the United States? No. The threats of terrorism stemming from possible cyber-attacks and illegal immigration are threats that have no end in sight. The United States will always be at risk from cyber-attacks. The changing nature of the Internet make it impossible to design software and hardware that would provide 100 percent protection against cyber-attacks and still allow the Internet to be used as it was intended.

Also, there is no solution in sight for the problem of illegal immigration, especially at the southern border of the United States. Following the 9/11 attacks one Customs Service official declared, "Short of building a wall from the Pacific Ocean to the Gulf of Mexico, the task of actually securing the border, most agree, is impossible. It would take a million people, I suppose—maybe more."[141] Three years after the 9/11 attacks and all the effort, money, and resources that that have gone into securing the border of the United States, a survey of border agents and immigration inspectors reported that 60 percent of border patrol agents and immigration officers surveyed said the DHS could do more to stop potential terrorists from entering the country.[142] Responding to data reported by the survey, the President of the National Border Patrol Council said, "Prior to September 22, 2001, it was extremely easy to enter the United States illegally. Incredibly, this has not changed in any meaningful way."[143]

The war on terrorism has had tremendous influence on government policies, actions, and strategies to enhance domestic security to prevent another 9/11-type attack by terrorists. In trying to defend the homeland it is important to understand the larger picture. Often the problem is to shift the focus from the terrorist to the root cause of the problem or the primary reason for the vulnerability. For example, terrorists may be able to use the Internet to execute a crippling cyber-attack on the United States not because terrorists are "super computer programmers" but because the Internet and the computer software and hardware used to access the Internet are full of bugs, flaws, defects, and vulnerabilities. It has been demonstrated that small children with only limited computer skills can hack into databases and control systems. To provide an effective deterrent against cyber-attacks by terrorists it will be necessary to focus attention on the practices of computer users and the quality of software and hardware used by private citizens, commercial companies, and the government.

Likewise, additional border patrol agents, immigration officers, high-tech passports, fences, and surveillance cannot solve border security, especially the United States–Mexican border. Given the incredible number of persons entering the United States, it is impossible for DHS to identify terrorists from among the hundreds of millions of persons who enter the United States each year.[144] However, so long as every person entering the United States is scrutinized as a possible terrorist, DHS will have to continue to demand more and more resources. Some critics argue that the DHS and the U.S. government have taken the wrong approach to securing the United States–Mexican border. They maintain that the waves of illegal immigrants who cross into the United States from Mexico is primarily a labor-market regulation issue rather than a border-security issue.[145] Millions of Mexican citizens will continue to enter the United States illegally so long as there is poverty in Mexico and jobs in the United States. If DHS devotes its time and resources to screening the millions of nonterrorists, it will make it more and more difficult for border agents to focus on identifying potential terrorists. Many argue that the solution to terror-proofing the borders is not more border agents and surveillance but better intelligence so that emphasis can be placed on identifying terrorists attempting to enter the United States.[146]

Finally, the race to secure the borders against terrorists must face the reality that in 2004, 34 million U.S. residents were born outside the United States. Nearly one-third of the total U.S. foreign-born population is from Mexico.[147] Census data project that Hispanics will become the largest single group of minority persons in the United States and that in the southwestern states, including California, Hispanics may eventually be the majority rather than a minority population. Given this demographic shift, it will be necessary to give serious consideration to what the immigration policy of the United States should be.

Cyber-terrorism, border security, and immigration control are not the only long-term challenges the United States will face in the war on terrorism. There are many other threats that need to be addressed to defend the homeland against terrorists. The war on terrorism is going to be one of the most protracted conflicts the United States has seen. Just as the Cold War following World War II in which the United States feared attack from communist countries lasted decades, there is every indication that the war on terrorism will last decades. Given this possibility, it will be necessary to take the time and effort necessary to address the root causes of potential threats rather than throw money at temporary fixes to the symptoms of the problem.

Chapter Summary

- In addition to the anti-terrorism efforts immediately following the 9/11 attacks there are other security issues that need to be addressed, and the need for constant vigilance will continue indefinitely.
- Two threats important to homeland security are cyber-terrorism and immigration control and border security.
- Some fear that tomorrow's terrorist may be able to do more damage with a keyboard than with a bomb.
- The primary tool of the cyber-terrorist is the Internet. Terrorists can use the Internet for intelligence gathering, education, communication, and to launch cyber-attacks.
- Terrorists do not initiate most cyber-attacks but the terrorists use the same tools: viruses, Trojan horses, worms, denial of service, and defacement of websites.
- Internet attacks on digital control systems (DCS) and supervisory control and data acquisition systems could enable a terrorist to do damage to physical infrastructure resulting in economic damage or loss of life.
- Nation-states could use cyber-attacks as a form of cyber-warfare.
- Defending against cyber-attacks is difficult because the Internet is under private control.
- Department of Homeland Security has assumed a key role in cyber-security through the National Cyber Security Division and the United States Computer Emergency Reading Team (US-CERT). Similar to the color-coded terror alerts issued to the public by DHS, US-CERT issues national cyber-alerts.
- Following the 9/11 attacks immigration control and border security were considered so lacking that a major overhaul resulted in these responsibilities being transferred to the Department of Homeland Security.
- Those departments under DHS responsible for immigration control and border security have undertaken aggressive programs to stop illegal immigration, apprehend and deport aliens residing illegally in the United States, and identify terrorists attempting to enter the United States.

- Major initiatives by DHS include the Absconder Apprehension Initiative, the registration of certain male aliens from predominantly Muslim countries, SEVIS, smart passports, and US-VISIT.
- Efforts to enhance border security have had a major impact on the U.S. relations with Canada and Mexico.
- The war on terrorism is going to be one of the most protracted conflicts the United States has seen, and it will be necessary to constantly examine vulnerabilities and adopt new strategies to enhance security.

Terrorism and You

Understanding This Chapter

1. Why is it necessary to look beyond the threats of hijacking and nuclear, biological, and chemical attacks at other potential terror attacks?

2. How is it possible for terrorists to use the Internet to launch a terrorist attack on the United States? Could terrorists do physical harm or cause the loss of life by the use of an Internet attack? Explain your answer.

3. What makes the Internet and computer systems vulnerable to terror attacks?

4. Why is there a concern over attacks on DCS and SCADA systems?

5. What has been the response of the United States in answering the threat of cyber-attacks? What are the primary agencies responsible for cyber-security?

6. Why were responsibilities for immigration control and border security transferred to the Department of Homeland Security?

7. What programs did DHS initiate to enhance immigration control and border security? What have been the criticisms of these programs?

8. How has immigration control and border security affected relationships with Mexico and Canada?

Thinking about How Terrorism Touches You

1. Efforts to enhance Internet security have resulted in the removal of certain information from the Internet. Have you been affected by the removal of any information from the Internet? Do you think removal of sensitive information that could be used by terrorists is a prudent decision or an infringement on freedom of speech? Why?

2. Have you suffered an attack by a virus, worm, or Trojan horse? If so, how did this affect you?

3. Should the private software and hardware industry be made liable for damage due to cyber-attacks if the software or hardware contained bugs that make the attack possible? If this would increase the cost of software and hardware, how much more would you be willing to pay?

4. Do you know of any international student who has been adversely impacted by the new DHS immigration policies? If yes, what were the circumstances?

5. If your name was accidentally placed on the "no-fly" list, how do you think this would affect you? What would you do to correct the error? How long do you think it would take to correct the error?

6. Does it concern you that your passport may contain personal data and biometric data that could be scanned by identity thieves? Why or why not?

Important Terms and Concepts

Absconder Apprehension Initiative
Anti-Virus Programs
Bugs
Customs and Border Protection (CBP)
Cyber-Terrorism
Digital Control Systems (DCS)
Directorate of Border and Transportation Security (BTS)
Executive Order 13231
Firewall
Formal Removal
Hacker
Immigration and Customs Enforcement (ICE)
Internet
National Cyber Alert System
National Cyber Security Division (NCSD)

National Security Agency
Patches
Smart Passports
Student and Exchange Visitor Information System (SEVIS)
Supervisory Control and Data Acquisition Systems (SCADA)
Trojan Horses
United States Computer Emergency Readiness Team (US-CERT)
US-VISIT
Viruses
Voluntary Departure
Withdrawal of Application
Worms

Endnotes

1. Sari Horwitz, "Police Show Strain from Endless Alerts," *Washington Post,* October 18, 2004, p. A1.

2. Ibid.

3. Associated Press, "Gov't: Al-Qaida Threat Still Significant," New York Time Online, www.nytimes.com, November 13, 2004.

4. Ibid.

5. Ibid.

6. Sari Horwitz, "Police Show Strain from Endless Alerts," *Washington Post,* October 18, 2004, p. A1.

7. Ibid.

8. *The National Strategy to Secure Cyberspace.* Washington, DC: GPO, February 2003, p. 19.

9. Ronald L. Dick, "Cyber Terrorism and Critical Infrastructure Protection," www.fbi.gov/congress/congress 02/nipc072402.htm, July 24, 2002.

10. Brian Krebs, "Feds Falling Short on Cybersecurity," *Washington Post,* www.washingtonpost.com, April 8, 2003.

11. John Schwartz, "Decoding Computer Intruders," New York Times Online, www.nytimes.com, April 24, 2003.

12. Associated Press, "Ex-CIA Chief Gates Warns on Cyberterror," New York Times Online, www.nytimes.com, December 5, 2004.

13. Tom Regan, "Terrorism and the 'Net," *Christian Science Monitor,* www.csmonitor.com, October 7, 2004.

14. Eric Lipton and Eric Lichtblau, "Even Near Home, a New Front Is Opening in the Terror Battle," New York Times Online, www.nytimes.com, September 23, 2004.

15. Tom Regan, "Terrorism and the 'Net," *Christian Science Monitor,* www.csmonitor.com, October 7, 2004.

16. Thomas L. Friedman, "Origin of Species," New York Times Online, www.nytimes.com, March 14, 2004.

17. Eric Lipton and Eric Lichtblau, "Even Near Home, a New Front Is Opening in the Terror Battle," New York Times Online, www.nytimes.com, September 23, 2004.

18. Ibid.

19. Tom Regan, "Terrorism and the 'Net," *Christian Science Monitor,* www.csmonitor.com, October 7, 2004.

20. Eric Lipton and Eric Lichtblau, "Even Near Home, a New Front Is Opening in the Terror Battle," New York Times Online, www.nytimes.com, September 23, 2004.

21. Ibid.

22. Michael Ignatieff, "The Terrorist as Auteur," New York Times Online, www.nytimes.com, November 14, 2004.

23. Eric Lipton and Eric Lichtblau, "Even Near Home, a New Front Is Opening in the Terror Battle," New York Times Online, www.nytimes.com, September 23, 2004.

24. Michael Ignatieff, "The Terrorist as Auteur," New York Times Online, www.nytimes.com, November 14, 2004.

25. James C. McKinley, Jr, "State Pulls Data from Internet in Attempt to Thwart Terrorists," New York Times Online, www.nytimes.com, February 26, 2002.

26. Ibid.

27. John Schwartz, "Decoding Computer Intruders," New York Times Online, www.nytimes.com, April 24, 2003.

28. *The National Strategy to Secure Cyberspace.* Washington, DC: GPO, February 2003, p. 5.

29. Brian Krebs, "U.S. Government Flunks Computer Security Tests," *Washington Post,* www.washingtonpost .com, November 19, 2002.

30. Patrick Marshall, "Cyberterrorism: A Clear and Present Danger?" *Federal Computer Week,* November 22, 2004.

31. United States General Accounting Office, *Critical Infrastructure Protection: Significant Challenges in Safeguarding Government and Privately Controlled Systems from Computer-Based Attacks.* Washington, DC: GAO, September 2001, p. 5.

32. Brian Krebs, "U.S. Government Flunks Computer Security Tests," *Washington Post,* www.washingtonpost .com, November 19, 2002; Brian Krebs, "Ex-Officials Urge U.S. to Boost Cybersecurity," *Washington Post,* April 9, 2003, p. E5.

33. Martha Mendoza, "Computer Virus Writers Rarely Go to Jail," *Pocono Record,* August 31, 2003, p. 5A.

34. Amy Harmon, "Digital Vandalism Spurs a Call for Oversight," New York Times Online, www.nytimes.com, September 1, 2003.

35. David McGuire and Brian Krebs, "Attack on Internet Called Largest Ever," *Washington Post,* www .washingtonpost.com, October 22, 2002.

36. Shamsuddin Abdul Jalil, "Countering Cyber Terrorism Effectively: Are We Ready to Rumble?" www.giac.org/practical/GSEC/ Shamsuddin_Abdul_Jalil _GSEC.pdf, 2003.

37. Barton Gellman, "Cyber-Attacks by Al Qaeda Feared," *Washington Post,* June 27, 2002, p. 1A.

38. Ibid.

39. *The National Strategy to Secure Cyberspace.* Washington, DC: GPO, February 2003, p. 32.

40. Barton Gellman, "Cyber-Attacks by Al Qaeda Feared," *Washington Post,* June 27, 2002, p. 1A.

41. Ibid.

42. Ibid.

43. Associated Press, " 'Net Attack Did Extensive Damage," *Pocono Record,* January 28, 2003, p. A5.

44. Jim Bencivenga, "Software: Weak Link in Cybersecurity?" *Christian Science Monitor,* www.csmonitor .com, April 2, 2004.

45. Barton Gellman, "Cyber-Attacks by Al Qaeda Feared," *Washington Post,* June 27, 2002, p. 1A.

46. Ariana Eunjung Cha and Jonathan Krim, "White House Officials Debating Rules for Cyberwarfare," *Washington Post,* August 22, 2002, p. A2.

47. Ibid.

48. *The National Strategy to Secure Cyberspace.* Washington, DC: GPO, February 2003, p. 50.

49. Ariana Eunjung Cha and Jonathan Krim, "White House Officials Debating Rules for Cyberwarfare," *Washington Post,* August 22, 2002, p. A2.

50. Ibid.

51. Robert O'Harrow, Jr. "Sleuths Invade Military PCs with Ease," *Washington Post,* August 16, 2002, p. A1.

52. Ibid.

53. Associated Press, "Ex-CIA Chief Gates Warns on Cyberterror," New York Times Online, www.nytimes.com, December 5, 2004.

54. Ibid.

55. Ibid.

56. Ariana Eunjung Cha and Jonathan Krim, "White House Officials Debating Rules for Cyberwarfare," *Washington Post,* August 22, 2002, p. A2.

57. Bradley Graham, "Bush Orders Guidelines for Cyber-Warfare," *Washington Post,* February 2003, p. A1.

58. Ibid.

59. Ibid.

60. Bradley Graham, "Bush Orders Guidelines for Cyber-Warfare," *Washington Post,* February 2003, p. A1.

61. Ariana Eunjung Cha and Jonathan Krim, "White House Officials Debating Rules for Cyberwarfare," *Washington Post,* August 22, 2002, p. A2.

62. Ibid.

63. *The National Strategy to Secure Cyberspace.* Washington, DC: Government Printing Office, 2003, p. 28.

64. Ibid.

65. Jonathan Krim, "Cyber-Security Strategy Depends on Power of Suggestion," *Washington Post,* February 15, 2003, p. E1.

66. *The National Strategy to Secure Cyberspace.* Washington, DC: Government Printing Office, 2003, p. 9.

67. Jim Bencivenga, "Software: Weak Link in Cybersecurity?" *Christian Science Monitor,* www.csmonitor .com, April 2, 2004.

68. Ibid.

69. Amy Harmon, "Digital Vandalism Spurs a Call for Oversight," New York Times Online, www.nytimes.com, September 1, 2003.

70. Jim Bencivenga, "Software: Weak Link in Cybersecurity?" *Christian Science Monitor,* www.csmonitor.com, April 2, 2004.

71. Andrea L. Foster, "Colleges Fear that Agencies' Surveillance Request will Require Expensive Network Changes," *Chronicle of Higher Education,* http://chronicle.com/daily/2004/042004041402n.htm, April 14, 2004.

72. Stephen Labatron, "Easing the Internet Regulations Challenges Surveillance Efforts," New York Times Online, www.nytimes.com, January 22, 2004.

73. *The National Strategy to Secure Cyberspace.* Washington, DC: Government Printing Office, 2003, p. ix.

74. Ibid., p. xiii.

75. Ibid., p. viii.

76. Ibid., p. 14.

77. Ibid., p. 3.

78. Ibid.

79. Ibid., p. 11.

80. U.S. Citizenship and Immigration Services. "INS into DHS," http://uscis.gov/graphics/othergov/roadmap.htm, January 20, 2005.

81. Ibid.

82. Department of Homeland Security, *2003 Yearbook of Immigration Statistics.* Washington, DC: Government Printing Office, September 2004, p. 3.

83. Ibid.

84. Rachel L. Swarns, "Immigrants Feel the Pinch of Post-9/11 Laws," New York Times Online, www.nytimes.com, June 25, 2003.

85. Michael Janoesky, "9/11 Panel Calls Policies on Immigration Ineffective," New York Times Online, www.nytimes.com, April 17, 2004.

86. Rachel L. Swarns, "Foreign Travelers Face Fingerprints and Jet Lag," New York Times Online, www.nytimes.com, October 1, 2004.

87. Elisabeth Bumiller, "Report Finds Infighting Over Prints," New York Times Online, www.nytimes.com, December 30, 2004.

88. Ibid.

89. "Government to Begin Passenger Screening," New York Times Online, www.nytimes.com, August 27, 2004.

90. Mansoor Ijaz, "One Way to Alienate Moderate Muslims: Depart Cat," *Christian Science Monitor,* www.csmonitor.com, September 24, 2004.

91. Ibid.

92. Rachel L. Swarns, "Senator? Terrorist? A Watch List Stops Kennedy at Airport," New York Times Online, www.nytimes.com, August 20, 2004.

93. Ibid.

94. Michael Janoesky, "9/11 Panel Calls Policies on Immigration Ineffective," New York Times Online, www.nytimes.com, April 17, 2004.

95. Associated Press, "U.S. Issued Visas to 105 Men on Anti-Terror List," *Pocono Record,* November 27, 2002, p. A5.

96. Rachel L. Swarns, "Detention of British Travelers Brings New Policy," New York Times Online, www.nytimes.com, August 16, 2004.

97. Tom Regan, "Foreign Reporters Cry Foul," *Christian Science Monitor,* www.csmonitor.com, June 8, 2004.

98. Elena Lappin, "Your Country Is Safe from Me," New York Times Online, www.nytimes.com, July 4, 2004.

99. "Guard for Bush Isn't Allowed Aboard Flight," New York Times Online, www.nytimes.com, December 27, 2001.

100. Associated Press, "Air Passenger Cries Racism," New York Times Online, www.nytimes.com, September 19, 2002.

101. Associated Press, "Canadian Imams Detained, Told They 'Picked Wrong Time to Fly,' " *Pocono Record,* September 13, 2003, p. A5.

102. David Johnston, "F.B.I. Is Accused of Bias by Arab-American Agent," New York Times Online, www.nytimes.com, July 2003. Washington, DC: GPO, February 2003.

103. Associated Press, "Islamic Group Protests Detention at Border," New York Times Online, www.nytimes.com, December 20, 2004.

104. Ibid.

105. U.S. Immigration and Customs Enforcement, "Fact Sheet SEVIS: One Year of Success," www.ice.gov/graphics/news/factsheets/sevis_1year_success.htm, August 3, 2004.

106. Ibid.

107. "Closing the Gates," *Chronicle of Higher Education,* April 11, 2003, pp. A12+.

108. Burton Bollag, "Enrollment of Foreign Students Drops in U.S." *Chronicle of Higher Education,* November 19, 2004, pp. 1+.

109. Michael Arnone, "Watchful Eyes: The FBI Steps Up Its Work on Campuses, Spurring Fear and Anger Among Many Academics," *Chronicle of Higher Education,* April 11, 2003, pp. A14+.

110. "Closing the Gates," *Chronicle of Higher Education,* April 11, 2003, pp. A13.

111. Lila Guterman, "Stalled at the Border," *Chronicle of Higher Education,* April 11, 2003, pp. 20–21.

112. Ibid.

113. Associated Press, "Interpol Says Hundreds of Thousands of Stolen Blank Passports Aid Terrorists," *Pocono Record,* February 28, 2004, p. A5.

114. Jennifer Lee, "Passports and Visas to Add High-Tech Identity Features," New York Times Online, www.nytimes.com, August 24, 2003.

115. Philip Shenon, "New Passport Rules are Put Off by U.S." New York Times Online, www.nytimes.com, September 9, 2003.

116. Jennifer Lee, "Passports and Visas to Add High-Tech Identity Features," New York Times Online, www.nytimes.com, August 24, 2003.

117. Matthew L. Wald, "New High-Tech Passports Raise Snooping Concerns," New York Times Online, www.nytimes.com, November 26, 2004.

118. Ibid.

119. Ibid.

120. Eric Lichtblau, "Treatment of Detained Immigrants Is Under Investigation," New York Times Online, www.nytimes.com, June 26, 2003.

121. Barnaby J. Feder and Tom Zeller, Jr., "Identity Badge Worn Under Skin Approved for Use in Health Care," New York Times Online, www.nytimes.com, October 14, 2004.

122. Department of Homeland Security, *2003 Yearbook of Immigration Statistics.* Washington, DC: Government Printing Office, September 2004, p. 146.

123. Ibid.

124. Ibid.

125. Neil A. Lewis, "Secrecy Is Backed on 9/11 Detainees," New York Times Online, www.nytimes.com, June 18, 2003.

126. Nina Bernstein, "Old Deportation Orders Put Many Out Unjustly, Critics Say," New York Times Online, www.nytimes.com, February 19, 2004.

127. Ibid.

128. Nina Bernstein, "When a MetroCard Led Far Out of Town," New York Times Online, www.nytimes.com, October 11, 2004.

129. Kirk Semple, "Man Arrested Over Photos After 9/11 Is Deported," New York Times Online, www.nytimes.com, August 14, 2004.

130. Nina Bernstein, "Children Alone and Scared, Fighting Deportation," New York Times Online, www.nytimes.com, March 26, 2004.

131. Nina Bernstein, "A Mother Deported, and a Child Left Behind," New York Times Online, www.nytimes.com, November 24, 2004.

132. David Staba, "A Canadian Gate Where Illegal Immigrants Knock," New York Times Online, www.nytimes.com, June 15, 2004.

133. Al Baker, "Checkpoint Near Canada Called Unsafe," New York Times Online, www.nytimes.com, October 23, 2004.

134. David Staba, "A Canadian Gate Where Illegal Immigrants Knock," New York Times Online, www.nytimes.com, June 15, 2004.

135. Associated Press, "New Border Security Technology Faces Test," New York Times Online, www.nytimes.com, November 15, 2004.

136. Eric Lichtblau, "U.S. Takes Steps to Tighten Mexican Border," New York Times Online, www.nytimes.com, March 16, 2004.

137. Jim Yardley, "Because of 9/11, a Uniting River Now Divides," New York Times Online, www.nytimes.com, August 1, 2002.

138. Mary Jordan, "Guide for Mexican Migrants Draws Ire," New York Times Online, www.nytimes.com, January 6, 2005.

139. Ibid.

140. Ibid.

141. Tim Weiner, "Border Customs Agents Are Pushed to the Limit," New York Times Online, www.nytimes.com, July 25, 2002.

142. Rachel L. Swarns, "Study Finds Most Border Officers Feel Security Ought to Be Better," New York Times Online, www.nytimes.com, August 24, 2004.

143. Ibid.

144. Kris Axtman and Peter Grier, "What It Will Take to Terror-Proof Border," *Christian Science Monitor,* www.csmonitor.com, December 10, 2004.

145. Ibid.

146. Ibid.

147. Associated Press, "Summary: Foreign-Born Population Tops 34M," New York Times Online, www.nytimes.com, November 23, 2004.

14

The Cost of Freedom

Terrorism is cheap. Anti-terrorism is very expensive and requires extensive efforts by all levels of government and all citizens. Protecting against a terrorist attack involves more than a one-time response and expense. The United States has become a terror-focused government. Defending the homeland has become its key mission and, to a great extent, the measure of success.

America's prosperity requires restraining the spending appetite of the federal government. I welcome the bipartisan enthusiasm for spending discipline. . . . In the three and a half years since September the 11, 2001, we've taken unprecedented actions to protect Americans. We've created a new department of government to defend our homeland, focused the F.B.I. on preventing terrorism, begun to reform our intelligence agencies, broken up terror cells across the country, expanded research on defenses against biological and chemical attack, improved border security and trained more than a half million first responders. Police and firefighters, air marshals, researchers, and so many others are working every day to make our homeland safer, and we thank them all.

—President George W. Bush, State of the Union Address, February 2, 2005

Chapter Outline

Learning Objectives

- The reader will understand how terrorism is financed.
- The reader will understand what the United States is doing to cut off funding for terrorism.
- The reader will appreciate how much is spent on the war on terrorism and the problems that arise in determining how much and how to spend this money.
- The reader will understand that in addition to economic costs there are noneconomic costs in the war on terrorism that can be just as important or more important than the economic costs.
- The reader will appreciate the worldview of the United States as it becomes a terror-focused country and to appreciate how other countries have addressed their terror problems.

Introduction: Counting the Costs

The United States has entered an era of terror-focused government. There is a price tag—a hefty price tag—for this new focus. In his 2005 State of the Union Address, President Bush promised economic discipline and spending restraints. He also promised international and domestic security against terror. This chapter will examine the cost of the war on terrorism. It will look at both economic and noneconomic costs. Noneconomic costs such as psychological well-being, trust in government, and loss of privacy are difficult or impossible to quantify but they have a great impact on quality of life. Often these are the measures that define the standards of a democratic society. This chapter will also discuss the very important topic of foreign relations. This book has focused on domestic issues in the war on terrorism but there are important lessons to be learned from looking at the worldview.

How Terrorists Get Their Money

The cost of terrorism is relatively inexpensive, and terrorists seem to have the money they need to engage in a protracted conflict. The September 11 attacks cost al-Qaida an estimated $500,000. However, the al-Qaida network spent less than $50,000 on each of its major attacks.[1] For example, the Madrid (Spain) train bomb attack is estimated to have cost about $10,000 to carry out. The attack on the U.S. destroyer *Cole* in October 2000 is estimated to have cost about $5,000 to $10,000. These cost estimates cover materials as well as gifts to family members of the suicide bombers.

The ability to finance worldwide terrorist attacks is one of the most valuable assets of the al-Qaida network. The wellspring of cash that finances terrorism is a network of illegal enterprises, including unscrupulous charities, drug trafficking, robbery, extortion, kidnapping, credit card fraud, cigarette smuggling, blackmailing, and arms smuggling. American government officials recognize that cutting off terrorists' funding is an important means of disrupting their operations and to that end have engaged in significant efforts to do so.[2] These efforts have affected the financial health of al-Qaida, as it is estimated its annual budget has been reduced from $35 million prior to September 11, 2001, to $5 million to $10 million in 2003, and more than $200 million in terrorists' assets has been frozen worldwide since the 9/11 attacks. Despite significant efforts to cut off funding for terrorism, a United Nations report on the effect of U.N. sanctions against al-Qaida and the Taliban has indicated that terrorists' networks have shown great flexibility and adaptability in keeping the pipeline of money flowing to fund their activities.[3]

Fund-Raising for Terrorism

The United States Treasury Department reports that unwitting or unscrupulous charities are among the biggest financiers of global terrorism. One of the factors that enables unscrupulous charities to raise large amounts of money and to divert the cash to fund terrorism is that observant Muslims consider giving to charity a religious obligation. Generally, Muslims are expected to give 2.5 percent of their annual income to charity. Taking advantage of this religious tenet, terrorist groups have established a network of charities to funnel money to fund terrorism. This network is worldwide and operates extensively in the United States. Since 9/11 the Bush Administration has designated more than 390 groups and individuals as "global terrorists" and has frozen the assets of these groups and individuals and banned charitable giving to these groups and individuals.[4] Of this number, 27 have been Islamic charities that have been designated as financiers or supporters of terrorism. Most are international relief agencies that for years canvassed the mosques and raised millions.[5] Persons donating to these banned "charities" can be investigated and may be arrested for supporting terrorism.

Charities are important in funding terrorism in two ways. First, charities serve as a direct source of income. One of the biggest Islamic charity funneling money to support terrorism in the United States was the Holy Land Foundation. In July 2004, five former leaders of the Holy Land Foundation were arrested on charges that they funneled $13 million to Palestinian terrorists to support suicide bombers and their families.[6] Former Attorney General John Ashcroft claimed the Holy Land Foundation was the "North American front for Hamas."[7] Many who contribute to these charities that support terrorism do so unwittingly, as the charities claim that they support needy Islamic families and children and hide their support of terrorism from the public. For example, Global Relief Foundation, an Illinois-based charity, sent 90 percent of its donations abroad in 2003 for the support of the al-Qaida, Osama bin Laden, and other known terrorist groups, but most people who contributed to Global Relief Foundation were probably not aware of this fact.[8]

Second, charities are important because they provide a conduit to move money worldwide that has been raised through various illegal enterprises. For example, money that has been raised by various enterprises, including criminal activities, can be "donated" to these charities that support terrorists. Then the charities, under the cover of transferring the money from the United States to overseas, can legally move the money overseas where it will be siphoned off by various terrorist front organizations.

Funding Terrorism through Criminal Enterprises

Of the various criminal enterprises to fund terrorism, drug trafficking is at the top of the list of illegal money-raising activities. The 1992 United Nations International Narcotics Control board report warned of the link between illegal drugs and terrorism. President George W. Bush declared, "It's important for Americans to know that the traffic in drugs finances the work of terror, sustaining terrorists, that terrorists use drug profits to fund their cells to commit acts of murder." The Drug Enforcement Agency (DEA) warns the public that there is a link between drug trafficking and global terrorism, as terrorists use the drug trade to fund attacks.[9] The Islamic terrorists responsible for the Madrid train bombings financed their plot with sales of hashish and Ecstasy.

In the United States there have been a number of specific incidences that demonstrate the link between the funding of terrorism and the illegal drug trade in the United States. For example, a series of DEA drug raids in January 2002 uncovered a methamphetamine drug operation in the Midwest involving men of Middle Eastern descent who were shipping money made from drug sales back to Middle East terrorist groups such as Hezbollah. In January 2004, two Michigan men were charged in connection with a drug ring that authorities alleged provided financial support for Hezbollah.[10] In March 2004, two men pleaded guilty in federal court in San Diego in a scheme to trade hashish and heroin for anti-aircraft missiles that in turn were to be supplied to the Taliban and al-Qaida.[11]

One of the largest sources of income for terrorism from the drug trade is opium from Afghanistan. Despite the U.S. invasion of Afghanistan and the displacing of the Taliban from power, in 2004, opium from Afghanistan accounted for 87 percent of the world supply, according to data from the United Nations. The opium drug trade accounted for about 60 percent of Afghanistan's 2003 gross domestic product. The opium trade is so ubiquitous in Afghanistan and the link to terror so direct that Antonio Maria Costa, executive director of the Vienna-based United Nations Office on Drugs and Crime, commenting on the illegal drug trade in Afghanistan, said, "The terrorists and traffickers are the same people."[12] The Afghanistan opium drug trade was estimated at about $2.8 billion dollars in 2004. However, little of the profits from the illegal drug trade goes to those who grow the poppies used to produce opium. Most of the profits from the drug trade go to the drug traffickers, warlords, and militia leaders, according to the United Nations.

Cutting Off the Flow of Cash

Overseas the United States is attempting to cut off the cash terrorists realize from drug trafficking by a two-prong strategy. First, the United States has various in-country programs to reduce drug production. For example, the United States and the United Nations have various programs in Afghanistan to discourage farmers from growing poppies and to encourage cultivation of other crops. One of the difficulties in discouraging farmers from growing poppies is the large difference in price between poppies and legal crops. An Afghanistan farmer may realize about $390 (U.S. dollars) per hex acre income from wheat but the same hex acre of poppies will net $4,600 (U.S. dollars). Thus, it is little surprise that a 2004 United Nations survey of opium production in Afghanistan indicated opium production up 64 percent from 2003. The survey indicated that there were about 2.3 million people, or about 10 percent of the total population, cultivating opium, up 35 percent from 2003.

Second, to cut off the flow of cash to terrorism from drug trafficking overseas, the United States Navy and Coast Guard patrol the high seas to detect and apprehend drug traffickers. Using intelligence and photo imaging data of ship movements, the United States Navy and Coast Guard intercept and inspect ships suspected of transporting illegal drugs. For example, in December 2003, the United States Navy seized two tons of hashish in the Persian Gulf, worth about $8 million to $10 million.[13] In September 2004, the Coast Guard seized about 27 tons of cocaine in the Eastern Pacific. For 2004, the Coast Guard seized in excess of $7.3 billion in illegal drugs.[14]

A new tactic being used in the United States to cut off the flow of illegal cash to terrorists has been the scanning of financial records of persons and organizations suspected to have ties with terrorism to detect "high-risk" financial transactions. In December 2004, the Department of Homeland Security began using various computer databases to allow investigators to match financial transactions against a list of some 250,000 people and firms with suspected ties to terrorist financing, drug trafficking, money laundering, and other financial crimes. Using a network of various private databases, the Department of Homeland Security tries to match financial transactions with people and organizations on the department's terrorist watch list.[15]

Numerous federal agencies are involved in the effort to cut off the funds of terrorists. Table 14.1 lists the various key U.S. government entities responsible for deterring terrorist financing. The list includes the Central Intelligence Agency, the Department of Homeland Security, the Department of Justice, the National Security Council, the Department of State, and the Department of Treasury.

The Cost of the War on Terrorism

The cost of terrorism may be cheap but the cost of the war on terrorism is terribly expensive. In 2004, the Department of Homeland Security spent $5 million to buy an entire 640-acre town and 1,200 surrounding acres in New Mexico for the purposes of training first responders in simulated terrorist attacks and other disasters.[16] The cost of airline security continues to rise, which means passengers and airlines have to pay more and more. In 2004, the report of the National Commission on Terrorist Attacks Upon the United States said it would cost at least $1 billion annually for the next five years in order to close the remaining gaps in airline security.[17] The security surcharge enacted to have passengers pay for additional security screening is providing insufficient funds to cover all of the new security procedures, which is resulting in proposals to double the surcharge. Both the airline industry and passengers are becoming concerned about the rising cost of security.[18] In addition to security costs are the costs of research. For example, the Department of Homeland Security awarded the University of Maryland $12 million to develop a new research center on the behavioral and social underpinnings of terrorism. The goal of the research is to help the government predict when and where attacks will occur, to better prepare the public for attacks, and to recover more quickly.[19] The cost of the war on terrorism impacts not only federal agencies but also state and municipal agencies. For example, in 2004, Washington D.C., police spent $10.6 million on overtime and equipment for security checkpoints.[20] During the Orange terror alert of 2004, the Delaware River Joint Toll Bridge Commission spent $2 million for state police in New Jersey and Pennsylvania to patrol five of its most critical bridges.[21]

It is impossible to calculate the total spending of all government and private agencies in the war on terrorism. However, the 2004 budget for only the key federal agencies involved in the war on terrorism was $52.8 million. Figure 14.1 shows that the majority of this ($23.9 million) went to the Department of Homeland Defense and the Department of Defense received the second highest amount ($15.2 million). This amount to fight the war on terrorism does not include the $200 billion for the U.S. military troops and equipment in Afghanistan and Iraq. There is no end sight to the cost of the war on terrorism. The Bush Administration has asked for an increase in the 2005 Department of Homeland Security budget and all indications are that the cost of the war on terrorism to other agencies will continue to rise.

Kinks in the System

Not only is the war on terrorism costly but there is also considerable debate as to how the money is spent. The nation's counterterrorism budget has been described by New York City Mayor Michael Bloomberg as "pork barrel politics at its worst."[22] The reason for Bloomberg's criticism is that the formula for distributing federal grants and subsidies to

TABLE 14.1   *Key U.S. Government Entities Responsible for Deterring Terrorist Financing*

Department	Bureau/Division/Office	Role
Central Intelligence Agency		Leads gathering, analyzing, and disseminating intelligence on foreign terrorist organizations and their financing mechanisms; charged with promoting coordination and information-sharing between all intelligence community agencies.
Homeland Security	Bureau of Customs and Border Protection	Detects movement of bulk cash across U.S. borders and maintains data about movement of commodities into and out of the United States.
	Bureau of Immigration and Customs Enforcement (ICE—formerly part of the Treasury's U.S. Customs Service)	Participates in investigations of terrorist financing cases involving U.S. border activities and the movement of trade, currency, or commodities.
	U.S. Secret Service	Participates in investigations of terrorist financing cases, including those involving counterfeiting.
Justice	Bureau of Alcohol, Tobacco, Firearms, and Explosives (ATF)	Participates in investigations of terrorist financing cases, including alcohol, tobacco, firearms, and explosives.
	Civil Division	Defends challenges to terrorist designations.
	Criminal Division	Develops, coordinates, and prosecutes terrorist financing cases; participates in financial analysis and develops relevant financial tools; promotes international efforts and delivers training to other nations.
	Drug Enforcement Administration (DEA)	Participates in investigations of terrorist financing cases involving narcotics and other illicit drugs.
	Federal Bureau of Investigation (FBI)	Leads all terrorist financing investigations and operations; primary responsibility for collecting foreign intelligence and counterintelligence information within the United States.
National Security Council		Manages the overall interagency framework for combating terrorism.
State	Bureau of Economic and Business Affairs	Chairs coalition subgroup of a National Security Council Policy Coordinating Committee, which leads U.S. government efforts to develop strategies and activities to obtain international cooperation.
	Bureau of International Narcotics and Law Enforcement Affairs	Implements U.S. technical assistance and training to foreign governments on terrorist financing.
	Office of the Coordinator for Counterterrorism	Coordinates U.S. counterterrorism policy and efforts with foreign governments to deter terrorist financing.
Treasury	Executive Office for Terrorist Financing and Financial Crime	Develops U.S. strategies and policies to deter terrorist financing, domestically and internationally; develops and implements the National Money Laundering Strategy as well as other policies and programs to prevent financial crimes.
	Financial Crimes Enforcement Network (FinCEN)	Supports law enforcement investigations to prevent and detect money laundering, terrorist financing, and other financial crime through use of analytical tools and information-sharing mechanisms; administers the Bank Secrecy Act.
	Internal Revenue Service (IRS) Criminal Investigation	Participates in investigations of terrorist financing cases with an emphasis on charitable organizations.

(continued)

TABLE 14.1   Continued

Department	Bureau/Division/Office	Role
Treasury *(continued)*	IRS Tax Exempt and Government Entities	Administers the eligibility requirements and other IRS tax law that apply to charitable and other organizations that claim exemption from federal income tax.
	Office of Foreign Assets Control	Develops and implements U.S. strategies and policies to deter terrorist financing; imposes controls on transactions; and freezes foreign assets under U.S. jurisdiction.
	Office of the General Counsel	Chairs Policy Coordination Committee for Terrorist Financing, which coordinates U.S. government efforts to identify and deter terrorist financing; coordinates U.S. government actions regarding implementation of, and imposition of, economic sanctions under Executive Order 13224 with respect to the freezing of terrorist-related assets.
	Office of International Affairs	Provides advice, training, and technical assistance to nations on issues including terrorist financing deterrence.

Source: Terrorist Financing (Washington, D.C.: GAO, November 2003), pp. 8–9.

states and cities uses a state-by-state allocation system rather than a threat-based formula. Starting with the assumption that any city could be a terrorist target, Congress allocated federal grants and subsidies with the goal to provide something to everyone, rather than focus on high-risk cities. Using this system, states that have had no or little threat of attack by terrorists have received substantial federal counterterrorism funding. This funding formula re-

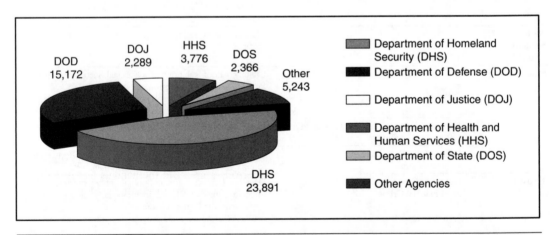

FIGURE 14.1   *Budget Authority for Combating Terrorism by Agency for Fiscal Year 2004 (Total Budget Authority Is $52,732 Million)*

Source: GAO Subcommittee on National Security, Emerging Threats, and International Relations, Committee on Government Reform, House of Representatives, *Combating Terrorism: Evaluation of Selected Characteristics in National Strategies Related to Terrorism.* GAO-04-408T (Washington, D.C.: GAO, February 3, 2004).

Note: "Other Agencies" includes the Departments of Energy ($1,588 million), Agriculture ($368 million), Transportation ($283 million), Commerce ($153 million), Veterans Affairs ($145 million), Interior ($115 million), Treasury ($90 million), Labor ($67 million), Housing and Urban Development ($2 million), and 18 other independent agencies (totaling $2,432 million).

BOX 14.1 • *Consider This: 88009*

The Department of Homeland Defense owns Playas, New Mexico, 88009. The 640-acre township includes a 25-unit apartment complex, community center, grocery store, medical clinic, fitness centers, a bank, a gas station, a post office, a bowling alley, and an airstrip. The DHS also purchased 1,200 acres surrounding the town. The town is located in a remote area of southwestern New Mexico. Playas was built in the early 1970s to house the employees and infrastructure of the Phelps Dodge copper smelter. Once a town of about 1,000, the company shut down in 1999, leaving a virtual ghost town of about 40 families. When the copper-smelting operation shut down in 1999, the Phelps Dodge Corporation put the town up for sale.

The DHS wanted Playas so it could transform the town into a terrorist response training center. When approached by DHS to help facilitate the $5 million purchase of Playas, Senator Pete Domenici responded, "Are you crazy?" The residents living in Playas will be allowed to continue to live in one end of the town.

The DHS partnered with New Mexico Tech and New Mexico State University to open the Play-

as Research and Training Center. The agency will use Playas for national homeland security training and research programs. New Mexico State University will focus on agricultural and food supply security. The Department of Homeland Security will use Playas as a real-world training center for training first responders, including medical personnel, and for emergency operations and training in prevention and response to suicide bombings and other related programs.

New Mexico Tech, a state-supported research university, has signed a five-year contract with DHS to operate the Playas Research and Training Center. It is probably the only university in the United States to own an entire town.

Question

1. The purchase price for Playas was $5 million but annual operating costs and training costs will also cost millions. Do you think it is a worthwhile investment for the DHS to buy an entire town for training purposes? Why or why not?

sults in Alaska, which has 649,000 residents, receiving nearly $92 per resident in security funds in 2003 and 2004, compared with states such as New York, which received $32 per resident, California, which received $22, and Texas and Florida, which received $21 each.[23] As a result, high-risk cities are unable to fund needed security improvements, whereas rural states are trying to find ways to spend the money.

A proposal to provide extra security aid to high-risk cities was vetoed by the House in June 2004. However, in December 2004, the Department of Homeland Security shifted a larger share of its annual $3.5 billion in anti-terrorism grants to the nation's largest cities.[24] Recognizing the importance of getting adequate counterterrorism funding to high-risk cities, the DHS will funnel 42 percent of its aid to New York, Washington, and Los Angeles.[25] Another change is that DHS funding will be shifted to directly funding cities rather than using state programs as conduits for federal counterterrorism funding. State programs tend to diffuse the federal subsidies to both urban and rural areas in response to political pressure. According to DHS officials the new policy reflects the high-risk threat to these cities due to the large number of possible targets such as bridges, signature buildings, government facilities, and symbolic targets.[26]

In addition to criticisms regarding the distribution of federal funds, states and cities are complaining that the funds authorized by Congress are not reaching the local authorities.[27] A Congressional analysis found that in 2004, more than 80 percent ($5 billion) of the counterterrorism money approved by Congress to help cities, counties, and states remains stuck in the administrative pipeline.[28] For various reasons the money is not getting to the agencies that need it to buy equipment, train personnel, pay overtime, and provide for security enhancements. Much of the blame for the delay is due to delays at the state level. State agencies have been unable to develop criteria, guidelines, and administrative procedures to distribute the federal money they receive to counties and cities.[29]

Of greater concern to some is not that money is stuck in the pipeline but the fear that federal counterterrorism grants and subsidies will stop flowing through the pipeline. Many states and cities have exhausted their reserve funds in building up their capacity to respond to terror threats and must rely on federal funding to continue to be able to protect tunnels, ports, airports, building, financial districts, schools, transportation arteries, and other possible terror targets. States and cities are relying more on federal funding, but the federal government is having difficulty providing the funds that states expect and need. The federal government is engaged in deficit spending and the cost of the war in Iraq continues to escalate. As a result, the federal government is finding it necessary to cut back both on its own counterterrorism spending and on its grants and subsidies to states and cities. For example, in October 2004, a budget shortfall of about $500 million at the department of Immigration and Customs Enforcement restricted ICE's ability to conduct terror investigations and forced ICE to release on bond 25,000 illegal immigrants because it lacked space to incarcerate them.[30] Federal cutbacks in the funding given to states in turn have forced states and cities to cut back spending on counterterrorism programs.[31]

Terror-Related Fraud

The nation's financial crisis has caused some to question the $40 million second inauguration of President Bush as they wondered if the money could not be better spent.[32] Although some may consider the inauguration excessive, of greater concern has been terror-related fraud. Millions of dollars have been siphoned off by terror-related fraud, committed by individuals, by businesses, and by the government.

Immediately following the 9/11 attacks many unscrupulous individuals engaged in criminal schemes to claim compensation or to establish fraudulent charities to bilk the public for money. For example, an Arkansas woman tried to defraud a fund for victims of the September 11, 2001, attacks, claiming that her dead brother was a firefighter who was killed in the attacks. The scope of the fraud can be appreciated when you consider that the average settlement paid to families of firefighters averaged more than $4 million.[33] In another case, a Michigan man claimed that his brother died in the collapse of the Twin Towers. The man received more than $268,000 before it was discovered that the claim was fraudulent. Insurance companies allege that numerous businesses have filed fraudulent 9/11-related claims.[34] Even state governments have been accused of using anti-terrorism funds improperly. The governor of Alaska proposed to buy a personal jet with anti-terrorism funds, claiming it was necessary for responding quickly to possible terror attacks. An audit of the state of Texas spending of anti-terror funds indicated that nearly $600 million in federal anti-terrorism funds was spent improperly.[35] Despite the potential seriousness of such misappropriation, some of the alleged abuses appear mind-boggling. For example, it is alleged that one jurisdiction purchased a trailer that was used to haul lawn mowers to "lawn mower drag races," claiming the trailer was "emergency equipment."[36]

The Other Costs of the War on Terrorism: Extremism in the Defense of Liberty

The human rights group Amnesty International released a statement in 2003, saying, "The world has become more dangerous, and governments more repressive, since the effort to fight terrorism began after the September 11, 2001, attacks on the United States. What would have been unacceptable on September 10, 2001, is now becoming almost the norm."[37] One of the difficult costs to calculate in the war on terrorism is the cost of extremism in the defense of liberty. Extremism in the name of protecting the homeland deprives citizens of liberty, creates conflict, diminishes the stature of the United States as perceived by foreign countries, and can be counterproductive in fighting true threats of terrorism.

Extremism in the defense of liberty can manifest itself in numerous ways—often in unexpected situations. For example, consider the debate between community residents of Little Egg Harbor, New Jersey, when a National Guard F-16 fighter jet's accidental release of gunfire resulted in the strafing of Little Egg Harbor Intermediate School with 27 rounds of 20mm cannon fire in November 2004. While some residents expressed concern and fear for their safety and that of their children, others argued that it was "profoundly unpatriotic to question the military during a time of war."[38] In another example where national defense was offered as the defense, three laboratory workers at Boston University were exposed to harmful bacteria at a bio-defense laboratory in January 2005. When some community residents expressed concerns over community safety, the risk was justified with the defense, "The nation needs this lab."[39]

Government agencies have used and continue to use the war on terrorism as the overriding reason in responding to criticisms of community safety and actions that otherwise would not be justified or permitted. At times the government agencies use the claim of national security to circumvent exiting laws. For example, the Defense Department has claimed that to sustain the national defense mission, it needs waivers from environmental laws, such as the Clean Air Act, toxic waste disposal requirements, and the endangered species laws.[40] The Defense Department requested and received exemptions from Congress to these laws and regulations, claiming that compliance would impede the Defense Department's ability to conduct combat exercises and weapons testing necessary for national security.[41] Environmental groups decry the circumvention of environmental controls in the name of national security and have filed lawsuits to force the Department of Defense to comply with Clean Air laws and toxic waste disposal regulations.

Two concerns that constantly emerge in the discussion of excessive actions by the government that are justified by arguments of national security are (1) infringement on privacy rights and government secrecy and (2) the government's alleged use of torture in interrogating terrorists. The war on terrorism has resulted in government actions in these two areas that alarm many critics.

The War on Terrorism and Privacy

As a result of the search for terrorists in the United States and abroad, U.S. citizens are losing more and more of their privacy while government is keeping more and more

BOX 14.2 • *Case Study: Freedom of Speech*

From the time of the Revolutionary War freedom of speech has always been restricted during war. If not by legislation, freedom of speech has been chilled by public opposition against anti-war speech. The war on terrorism is no exception. Professor Ward Churchill of the University of Colorado at Boulder is the lightning rod of the free speech controversy in the war on terrorism. Churchill, who teaches ethic studies, called those who died in the 2001 attacks "little Eichmanns." In an essay he wrote he said that the victims of the 9/11 attack "were not innocent civilians but a technocratic corps at the very heart of America's global financial empire."[42] Churchill has written other essays and books critical of the United States and Israel and their policies toward the Palestinians, including charges of genocide against the Palestinians. He has been denounced by families of victims of the 9/11 attack, the governor of Colorado, Bill O'Reilly of Fox TV, and others. Churchill's public speaking engagements have been canceled and one college has refused to pay him his speaker's fee, which he claims is owed to him.

Professor Churchill issued a defense of his remarks, saying,

> I am not a defender of the September 11 attacks, but simply pointing out that if U.S. foreign policy results in massive death and destruction abroad, we cannot feign innocence when some of that destruction is returned. . . . I have never characterized all the September 11 victims as "Nazis." What I said was that the "technocrats of empire" working in the World Trade Center were the equivalent of "little Eichmanns." It should be emphasized that I applied the "little Eichmanns" characterization only to those described as "technicians." Thus, it was obviously not directed to the children, janitors, food service workers, firemen and random passers-by killed in the 9/11 attack.

Fox TV commentator Bill O'Reilly has called for the firing of Professor Churchill as has the governor of Colorado and numerous other public officials and citizens.[43] The University of Colorado Boulder Faculty Assembly called his remarks "controversial, offensive, and odious" but expressed support for his right to express them.[44] The American Civil Liberties Union renounced the calls for his termination. The ACLU said,

> Freedom of faculty members to express views, however unpopular or distasteful, is an essential condition of an institution of higher learning that is truly free. We deplore threats of violence heaped upon Professor Churchill, and we reject the notion that some viewpoints are so offensive or disturbing that the academic community should not allow them to be heard and debated. Also reprehensible are inflammatory statements by public officials that interfere in the decisions of the academic community.

Questions

1. Professor Churchill has received hundreds of death threats, his public speeches have been disrupted by violent demonstrators, and his vehicle has been vandalized. The Colorado Senate and House have passed resolutions denouncing Churchill's comments as "evil and inflammatory." Does the right to freedom of speech protect Churchill's remarks or is there a line at which point "freedom of speech" becomes treason? If so, do Churchill's remarks cross that line?

2. What are the standards for the acceptable limits on freedom of speech? Who gets veto power over controversial speakers and when should retaliation occur for those who voice unpopular dissent?

3. Some have compared the reaction to Professor Churchill's remarks to McCarthyism and have argued that "well-meaning college administrators who sought to defuse controversy by treating the principle of free speech as one that was expendable in a time of international crisis and domestic anxiety" have done the greatest damage to academic freedom. Does freedom of speech guarantee a professor the right to express any opinion, even if there are strong beliefs that his opinions are not based on fact or truth?

4. Many figures in history have expressed controversial opinions during their lifetimes.

BOX 14.2 • Continued

Some of these persons have been recognized by history as great leaders who expressed what were unpopular opinions at the time, but these opinions would later become guiding principles for society. For example, during his lifetime many of the speeches of Martin Luther King, Jr. were denounced as Communist-inspired and detrimental to the welfare of the nation. Nelson Mandela was imprisoned for his rhetoric against apartheid in South Africa. How can society distinguish between free speech that denounces popular beliefs that are later to be recognized as social evils and treason or other harmful speech that should be banned?

information from the public. One of the most intrusive and influential factors in the loss of privacy is the USA Patriot Act of 2001. The Patriot Act has had far-reaching impact on privacy. Its provisions for secret searches, less restrictions on wiretaps, and a general lowering of the standard of proof for certain law enforcement actions are well known and have been previously discussed. However, there are provisions of the Patriot Act and other laws and regulations that are less well known but just as intrusive. The anti–money-laundering compliance laws, for example, require that persons purchasing real estate submit to a name check to determine if their name is on the government's list of people blocked from participating in "any transaction or dealing . . . in property or interests" within the United States. People on this list have been identified by White House Executive Order 132224 "to have committed, or to pose a significant risk of committing, acts of terrorism."[45] If a person's name matches a name on the list, the transaction must be immediately halted and a report filed with the Treasury Department.[46] The buyer pays the fee for the name search.

Following the 9/11 attacks stricter employment documentation and screening laws were passed based on the rationale that it would make it more difficult for "sleeper" terrorists to remain in the United States or to obtain jobs where they could use their employment to carry out a terror attack. As a result of this legislation, thousands of airline workers lost their jobs. Especially controversial was the provision that required U.S. citizenship for certain airline workers when U.S. citizenship is not even a requirement for military service. Also, new restrictions prohibit persons with felon convictions from obtaining employment on federal contract jobs or military bases. Because there is no time limit on when one was convicted, some workers with long-past felony convictions found themselves unemployed due to the Patriot Act.[47]

News reporters have also experienced the impact of post-9/11 legislation and policies regarding privacy. They have expressed concern over the government's attempts to gather information against suspected terror suspects by issuing subpoenas for reporters' notes and confidential sources.[48] The news media argue that without the protection of the First Amendment to protect confidential sources and interview and investigation records of the reporter, it is not possible to have a free press.[49]

While government agencies have reduced the privacy rights of citizens, they have increased government secrecy. Some members of Congress accuse the Bush Administration of excessive secrecy in the war on terrorism.[50] Senator Charles E. Grassley (R-IA) cited the retroactively classifying of information the Justice Department gave to Congress as an example of government secrecy that appears to do "harm to transparency in government, and it looks like an attempt to cover up the F.B.I.'s problems in translating intelligence."[51] In 2002, Congress heard testimony from a Federal Bureau of Investigation translator who accused the FBI of incompetence and a lack of urgency in translating intelligence documents. In 2004, two years after the testimony, the Justice Department retroactively classified the information and warned congressional members and staffers not to disseminate the information contained in the briefings. Also, the FBI refused to allow the translator to testify in lawsuits filed by families of the September 11 attack victims, claiming her testimony would violate "the state secret privilege."[52] Congressional members expressed surprise at the Justice Department's actions and suggested that the purpose of the action was to "quash Congressional oversight."[53]

Many have become fearful that the government's encroachment on privacy rights has or will become excessive. Not only do critics of government's encroachment on privacy claim violation of constitutional rights by current practices but they also point to possible future violations as the government positions itself to collect even more data on individuals. One example cited of data gathered by the government that could be subject to misuse is the Department of Education's proposal to create a comprehensive database of enrollment records of all college and university students in the United States.[54] The record-keeping proposal is justified by the argument that Congress needs the data to provide accountability in elementary and high schools by having the ability to see which students go on to postsecondary education and to track their progress. The Department of Education issued assurances that the data would not be used for other purposes or given to other federal agencies such as the Department of Homeland Security. Critics counter by arguing, "Since the September 11 attacks, the balance between privacy and the public interest [has] been shifting. We're in a different time now, a very different climate. There's the huge possibility that the database could be misused."[55]

The skepticism of the critics that such a database would not be available to DHS or other government agencies is based on the fact that over the years many databases that initially appeared to have no connection to homeland security have been appropriated by the DHS. In fact, DHS has come to rely on databases gathered by private companies as a primary source of intelligence about individuals. One of the largest private companies that provides personal data about individuals to the DHS, which it in turn uses for actionable intelligence, is ChoicePoint Inc.[56] ChoicePoint gathers comprehensive personal data about individuals, including financial data, data about relatives, DNA identification data, criminal records, testing for illegal drug use, criminal background, personal data, and credit record. ChoicePoint even has access to private databases, such as lists of employees who have admitted to shoplifting whether they were charged and convicted or just admitted the offense to their employer.[57] ChoicePoint claims to have "billions of details" about individuals in their databases and "the ability to access all relevant information with a single query."[58] Thus, it is little surprise that the Department of Homeland Security has contracted with ChoicePoint for intelligence data to assist in investigating terrorist activity and to track down people who pose a threat.

The War on Terrorism and Torture

The pictures of what appears to be the torture of the prisoners of Abu Ghraib prison in Iraq shocked the citizens of the United States and resulted in the investigation and prosecution of those who allegedly were responsible for the torture and mistreatment of Iraqi prisoners. Since the revelation of alleged torture at Abu Ghraib, numerous other allegations of torture of alleged terrorist suspects have emerged. Investigations by the International Committee of the Red Cross have charged that "the American military has intentionally used psychological and sometimes physical coercion tantamount to torture on prisoners at Guantanamo Bay, Cuba."[59] Allegations of torture closer to home come from aliens of Middle East descent who were detained in New York following the 9/11 attacks who claim they were mistreated and physically abused by correctional officials.[60]

The U.S. government has claimed that "a few bad apples" were responsible for the abuse of prisoners at Abu Ghraib, but there is evidence to suggest that the United States has chosen to systematically engage in or permit the torture of terror suspects. Critics of the government's alleged torture of terror suspects accuse the U.S. government of being so shocked by the September 11 attacks that "the United States government was willing to consider doing almost anything—including actions previously thought morally suspect—to prevent another such catastrophe."[61] The emergence of "torture memos" exchanged between the Justice Department and the president seem to suggest that the Bush Administration operated on the premise that in a time of necessity, the president and the military could disregard torture conventions, international treaties, and the law of the land.[62] In legal memorandums by the Justice Department and the Defense Department, President Bush was advised that the Geneva Convention and other anti-torture covenants do not apply to suspected terrorist detainees.[63] President Bush has publicly declared that the United States rejects the use of torture, but allegations by accused terror suspects and various investigations seem to suggest that the United States has used what many would call torture in interrogating suspected terrorists.

Another charge against the Bush Administration is that the Central Intelligence Agency and the government has engaged in a practice called *rendition*. Rendition is when the U.S. government arranges for the transfer of a suspected terrorist from the United States or another country to a country such as Pakistan or Egypt, where the suspect can be interrogated by the use of torture by local authorities. The CIA and the Bush Administration deny any involvement in such alleged clandestine transfer of terror suspects, but various investigations and charges by persons who have allegedly been the victims of such torture appear to provide evidence that such charges are credible.[64]

The Bush Administration has retreated from an August 2002 legal memorandum that defined torture extremely narrowly. The 2002 memorandum asserted that "mistreatment rose to the level of torture only if it produced severe pain equivalent to that associated with organ failure or death."[65] The 2002 memorandum advised the President that "the Geneva Conventions did not bind the United States in its treatment of detainees captured in the fighting in Afghanistan."[66] In December 2004, the Bush Administration redefined its definition of torture while still denying that the administration sanctioned or had sanctioned the use of torture. However, to some it appears that from 2002 to 2004, the 2002 memorandum reflected the policy and practice of the Bush Administration. This charge is reinforced by the assertion of the International Committee of the Red Cross that U.S. personnel have engaged in torture of detainees, both in Iraq and at Guantanamo.[67] The sanctioned use of torture by government officials and the failure to condemn such use when evidence suggests charges are credible is a high price to pay for the war on terrorism. It is a challenge to the Constitution and the rights that citizens believe are held sacred.

Correcting Extremism

Although there are charges that the United States has engaged in extremism in the defense of the homeland, one must also consider the "self-correction" that occurs as extreme practices are made public and criticized, and the government retreats from the abusive practice or policy. There are several examples that can be cited to illustrate this self-correcting process, including (1) the Treasury Department's restrictions on U.S. publications by authors in embargoed countries, (2) DHS's rules against disclosure of nonclassified information by its employees, (3) the Department of Defense's policy on mandatory anthrax shots, (4) the CIA's proposal for domestic spying, and (5) the Transportation Security Administration's policy on search of females.

As discussed in previous chapters, the United States can direct foreign policy by prohibiting individuals and businesses from engaging in economic trade with countries under sanctions. The U.S. Treasury Department Office of Foreign Assets Control (OFAC) applied sanctions against U.S. citizens who were alleged to have engaged in trade with Iraq prior to the U.S. invasion of Iraq. In 2003, OFAC issued advisories that essentially made it impossible for authors from sanctioned nations to have scholarly writings published in the United States. Critics quickly pointed out that the ban in effect discouraged the publication of dissident speech from within these oppressive regimes. Publishers joined in a successful lawsuit to effect a change in the policy. In December 2004, OFAC issued new guidelines that eased the restrictions on authors from sanctioned countries to allow U.S. publishers to work with them as long as they are not government representatives.[68]

In another example of a reversal of a policy criticized as overly repressive was the DHS's policy that "prohibits department employees from giving the public sensitive but unclassified information" and authorized the government to "conduct inspections at any time or place to ensure that the agreement is obeyed."[69] The two unions that represent the DHS employees, the National Treasury Employees Union, and the American Federation of Government Employees, argued that the policy was overly broad in what information it restricted employees from disclosing and that it gave "government unprecedented leeway to search employee homes and personal belongings in violation of the Fourth Amendment."[70] In January 2005, responding to threats of lawsuits, DHS dropped its requirement for new employees to sign the oppressive nondisclosure agreement and instituted a program to provide training on the proper education and training for handling sensitive information.[71] The two unions and civil liberties groups approved of the change in policy but still expressed concern of the "broad and vaguely defined" definition of information that was prohibited from disclosure.[72]

The Department of Defense feared that front-line troops may be exposed to deadly bio-warfare agents and wanted to inoculate troops against such agents if possible. An experimental vaccine against anthrax was developed and the Department of Defense adopted a mandatory vaccination program. Soldiers who refused vaccination were subject to disciplinary action and/or dismissal from the service. Numerous soldiers objected to the mandatory vaccinations and some health experts called into question the safety of the experimental vaccine. Soldiers opposed to the mandatory vaccination filed suit against the Department of Defense. The courts sided with the soldiers and ruled that the mandatory vaccination program was illegal. The court ruled, "Congress has prohibited the administration of investigational drugs to service members without their consent. This court will not permit the government to circumvent this requirement."[73] Lawyers for the soldiers said they would initiate an effort to ensure the government reverses all punishments that were imposed for refusing an order to take the vaccine and will seek compensation for service members who contended they were harmed.[74]

The previous examples illustrate how the court can be a significant force in correcting extremism in the defense of liberty. However, not all self-corrections have required court intervention or the threat of court intervention. Two examples of how public opinion and debate can cause a change in government polices are the discontinuation of the Total Information Awareness (TIA) program by the CIA and the change of policy of the TSA on search of females.

The CIA wanted to develop a program called Total Information Awareness, a secret program that would allow the CIA to develop the ability to spy on American citizens in the United States and to develop a database that could track a person's entire existence.[75] The program would have authorized spy agencies to gather intelligence inside the United States and would have allowed them to recruit citizens as informants on other citizens.[76] The agency would not have to disclose to citizens that intelligence data had been gathered nor would the agency have to have probable cause of terror-related activities or to have approval of the courts to gather intelligence on citizens. When the program concept became known to the public, both public opposition and congressional opposition forced the CIA to abandon the program. Congress refused to fund the program and the firestorm of public criticism discouraged the government from developing the program.[77]

When two women blew up Soviet airliners by smuggled bombs on board the aircraft by secreting them in their bras, the Transportation Security Administration instituted new search procedures for female travelers in the United States. The new search procedures required TSA personnel to search between the breasts of female passengers when performing pat-down security searches. Furthermore, the new policy did not require TSA screeners to have reasonable suspicions to justify the search of females passengers. The policy allowed men to perform the search and the search was conducted at the security checkpoint without any privacy. If the woman was wearing heavy outer clothing, such as a jacket, she was required to remove it. Many women complained that the underclothing they were wearing under their jacket was not appropriate to expose in public. There were numerous complaints from women about the new policy. Women complained that they were being "groped," randomly selected for searches, treated rudely during the search, and sometimes asked personal and inappropriate questions by the TSA personnel. The policy required TSA screeners to use the "back of their hand" to perform the search but many women complained this procedure was not followed. After many complaints and much negative media coverage of the policy, in December 2004, TSA changed the policy and TSA screeners stopped searching between female passengers' breasts during the pat-down search.

These examples indicate that extremism can be tempered. Policies that allegedly violate constitutional rights can be changed. Practices that are intrusive and offensive but do little to enhance security can be stopped. Thus, while there are indeed numerous criticisms of the overzealousness of the government in defending the homeland against terrorism, there is reason to believe that bad policy and practices can be changed.

The Growing Conflict with Foreigners

Hidden costs associated with the war on terrorism can be so enormous that the costs can be unbearable. One of these costs is the changing attitude of Americans toward foreigners—particularly those from Mexico and Middle Eastern countries. Suspicion and distrust of Hispanic immigrants was prevalent prior to the 9/11 attacks but it seems the new focus on national security has highlighted these feelings. Although there is little to connect Hispanic immigrants to terrorism, it appears that many persons conceal their prejudice toward Hispanic immigrants using the guise of national security. In many communities, and not just limited to southwestern-border states, Hispanics find local residents bitter or even violently opposed to the presence of Hispanics in their city.[78]

Hispanic immigrants, and even Hispanic American citizens, often are fearful and mistrusting of law enforcement officials. Some communities report that Latinos are reluctant to contact the police if they are victims of a crime or a witness to a crime.[79] Even when law enforcement attempts to build bridges with the Latino community, residents are suspicious of their motives. For example, when the Fairfax County police held a Spanish-language child safety seat demonstration in Herndon, Virginia, despite a large Latino population, no one showed up. Police officials said they believe the lack of attendance was because the "Hispanic community thought it was a ploy to snare the undocumented."[80] Law enforcement officials report that fear of the police is so widespread that some immigrants hoard food and stay indoors because "they are afraid of venturing outside their homes, believing they will get stopped by police and asked to produce documents that prove their immigration status."[81]

Some argue that Hispanic immigration threatens to "disrupt the political and cultural integrity of the Untied States."[82] Dr. Samuel Huntington, chair of Harvard University's Academy for International and Area Studies, warns that Hispanic immigration threatens the United States with the loss of its "core Anglo-Protestant culture and may soon be divided into two peoples with two cultures (Anglo and Hispanic) and two languages (English and Spanish)."[83]

The greatest conflict, however, is developing between Americans and Muslims. A national poll reported that one in four Americans holds a negative stereotype of Muslims, and almost one-third respond with a negative image when they hear the word *Muslim*.[84] A 2003 poll by the Pew Research Center reported that 46 percent of Americans believe that Islam is more likely than other religions to encourage violence among its believers and 42 percent of Americans believe all Muslims are anti-American.

Muslims are aware of the prejudice of Americans toward them. A poll by the University of Michigan in 2004 of Arab Americans and Muslim Americans in the Detroit area (the largest concentration of Arab Americans in the United States) reported that 60 percent say they are worried about the future of their families. Fifteen percent say they have suffered some form of harassment or intimidation. People who appear to be of Middle Eastern descent, even if they are from India or some other country not identified with the war on terrorism, say they have a feeling of persecution. They feel especially singled out during high terror alerts and at airport security checkpoints. In New York and New Jersey, Muslim residents of communities say they feel there is conflict and tension between the Muslim community and their neighbors.[85] The Federal Bureau of Investigation has issued warnings that tend to confirm this bias toward the Muslim community. The FBI has cautioned that terrorist attacks or the Iraq war could prompt a wave of hate crimes against Arab Americans, Muslims, and other minorities in the United States. Other indicators of bias against people who appear to be from Middle Eastern countries are reports of discrimination by private businesses and reported dismissals from jobs with little or no explanation other than vague reasons citing national security. Many Muslim parents report that they fear that their children may become targets of bigotry.[86]

Racial Profiling

Prior to September 11, 2001, racial profiling was not considered an acceptable practice by law enforcement officers. A 1999 Gallup Poll reported that 81 percent of the public disapproved of racial profiling. Prior to the 9/11 attacks racial profiling referred primarily to selective enforcement against Latinos and blacks. Although the public still disapproves of racial profiling against Latinos and blacks in routine law enforcement investigations, there is support for racial profiling of young Middle Eastern men at airports and national security checkpoints. There is also support for racial profiling in identifying illegal immigrants from Mexico.

The DHS and the Justice Department have been careful to deny that their policies related to immigration enforcement and investigation screening are based on racial profiling. Actions by the DHS and the Justice Department, however, seem to suggest that race often is a primary, perhaps the only, factor in selecting a person for an interview, further screening, or additional security.

Some have argued that "Middle Eastern males should be targeted for search because, 'based on historical experience, [they] seem more likely than others to include suicide bombers or just bombers.'"[87] Thus, although there is still a general disapproval for racial profiling when applied to Latinos and blacks, the public approves of profiling young, Middle Eastern or Islamic men at airports or other high-risk security venues.[88]

Studies have indicated that since the 9/11 attacks in some cities the number of Middle Easterners cited for offenses by law enforcement has been significantly higher than all others charged with offenses.[89] This statistic raises the question: Is there racial profiling of Middle Easterners? Local law enforcement officials deny targeting Middle Eastern males. They claim that any increase in citations to Middle Eastern males is due to changes in patrol or police procedures, not racial profiling. The Justice Department denies that there is racial profiling by federal law enforcement agencies. The department said it conducted a survey of federal operations and concluded that racial profiling by federal law enforcement agents does not appear to be a systemic problem.[90]

In 2003, the Bush Administration issued a policy statement from the Justice Department regarding guidelines on racial profiling. The guidelines govern the conduct of 70 federal law enforcement agencies. The guidelines do not ban racial profiling. They do bar federal agents from using race or ethnicity in their routine investigations but the guidelines allow for clear exemptions for investigations involving terrorism and national security matters.

International Relations

The focus of this book has been on defending the homeland against terrorism, but it is also necessary to examine how U.S. domestic policy aimed at fighting terrorism has influenced foreign relations that in turn has influenced the effectiveness of the United States to fight terrorism. In his 2005 Inaugural Address, President Bush told Americans that spreading liberty around the world was "the calling of our time." In spreading liberty around the world, he said that America "will not impose our own style of government on the unwilling. Our goal instead is to help others find their own voice, attain their own freedom and make their own way." There is a high cost to be paid for this calling.

The Bush Administration has at times has compared the war on terrorism to the Cold War with the Soviet Union. The rhetoric has painted an image of the United States and "freedom-loving" nations in a united fight against terrorism. In this "international" war on terrorism American politicians claim they are leading a popular war against an unpopular enemy. President Bush declared in his 2005 State of the Union Address that in leading the war on terrorism the United States will behave as a benevolent superpower. He said, "The United States has no right, no desire, and no intention to impose our form of government on anyone else. This is one of the main differences between us and our enemies. They seek to impose and expand an empire of oppression, in which a tiny group of brutal, self-appointed rulers control every aspect of every life." Most Americans accept this premise and believe that "while the U.S. necessarily shapes foreign polices to support our national interests, those same interests are not necessarily in opposition to the interests of other nations and cultures. . . . To the contrary, Americans are convinced that the U.S. . . . elevates values emphasizing freedom."[91] The rest of the world does not share this viewpoint.

Terrorism is not a common enemy of the nations of the world. It is a philosophy, a policy, a tactic. The use of terrorism by one group does not unite them and identify them with a worldwide network of terrorists with common goals. The terrorist attacks on the United States are perpetuated by a specific group of enemies, not by a single worldwide group of terrorists. Unlike the Cold War, where sides were divided into those who supported the Soviet Union and communism and those who supported the United States and democracy, the war on terrorism has multifactional fronts, groups, and players. There is no overarching theme that unites the United States and its allies against a common enemy.[92]

There are two key reasons many nations do not attach the same significance to the U.S. war on terrorism as Americans do. First, many nations have endured their own war on terrorism for years or decades. Simply stated, the war on terrorism is old news to them. In 2003, there were 175 worldwide significant terrorism events according to the U.S. State Department Patterns of Global Terrorism report. Only 1.5 percent of terrorism's casualties in 2003 were U.S. citizens. Many countries are fighting and have been fighting their own war on terrorism. Groups around the world have used terror tactics to attack their government. Terrorism is and has been a significant problem in Israel, the Philippines, Russia, Peru, Spain, numerous countries in Africa, and many other nations. Many nations have been engaged in a war on terrorism much longer and with greater ferocity than the United States. For example, since 2000, Israel has had more than 120 suicide bombings. African nations have experienced terrorism on a scale described by some as genocide and Iraq experiences nearly daily suicide bombings or assassinations by terrorists. Russia has been battling the Chechens for decades and Spain has suffered attacks by the Basque terrorists for decades.

Indonesia has had nearly constant conflicts with terrorists, as has Peru in battling the Shinning Path. Terror is a global struggle but each nation battles enemies unique to it, whereas the Bush Administration has described the war on terrorism as a global battle against a common enemy. Thus, many nations find that the U.S. war on terrorism is not the universal pivotal global struggle of the age.[93]

Some nations are critical of the tactics that the United States has adopted in its war on terrorism and the impact of these tactics on their nation. For example, President Luiz Inácio Lula da Silva of Brazil criticized the U.S. strategy, saying, "The exploitation of fear is a highly developed and refined science, but Brazil is not convinced by this culture that triumphed in the American election. What concerns us in Latin America is that, in the name of defending its security, the United States will escalate the wars it has begun."[94]

The second reason that many nations are less concerned than the United States with the war on terrorism is because many of them have more pressing priorities, such as poverty, clean water, economic revival, trade, and other internal economic issues that pose grave dangers to their country. The United States enjoys a level of economic prosperity and wellbeing that far exceeds that of most nations of the world. In many countries the issues of adequate health care, clean water, transportation infrastructure, education, and other services that are taken for granted in the United States are major concerns of the government.

President Bush has said that the lack of support for the war on terrorism from certain Middle Eastern countries is because they "hate our freedom." This analysis as to the cause of the unpopularity of the United States fails to take into account the impact of U.S. policy on those countries. The Report of the Defense Science Board Task Force on Strategic Communication concluded that Middle Eastern countries do not hate America's freedom, but rather they hate America's policies. In particular, they object to "what they see as one-sided support in favor of Israel and against Palestinian rights, and the long-standing, even increasing, support for what Muslims collectively see as tyrannies, most notably Egypt, Saudi Arabia, Jordan, Pakistan and the Gulf states." French terror expert Xavier Raufer asserts that the Bush Administration is "20 years behind the curve" in understanding international terrorism and the opposition to the United States.

Polls of international opinion toward the United States show that approval of the United States has significantly dropped since the 9/11 attacks. Among Arab countries the favorable attitudes toward the United States are extremely low and are dropping. Table 14.2 reports the results of public opinion polls conducted in 2004 on how Arabs view the United States. This poll indicates that even among so-called Arab "allies," such as Egypt, which receives over $2 billion annually in foreign aid from the United States, public disapproval of the United States is at record lows. In June 2004, 98 percent of Egyptians polled stated they had an unfavorable view of the United States. In Saudi Arabia, another "ally" in the war on terrorism, only 4 percent of those polled had a favorable attitude toward the United States. A large majority in Saudi Arabia believe that the United States "seeks to weaken and dominate Islam itself."[95] The highest approval rating among the Arab countries polled was 20 percent (Lebanon).

Even among European "friends," the percent of people polled who report they view the United States favorably is dropping. Table 14.3 indicates that in England, France, and Germany approval rate of the United States has dropped 17 to 26 percent. Only in Britain did more respondents report a favorable attitude (58 percent) toward the United States than an unfavorable attitude. These polls tend to support the assumption that the United States has become more alienated from other nations because of its strategy on the war on terrorism.

TABLE 14.2   *Arab Opinion of the United States*

Country	June 2004		April 2002	
	Favorable	*Unfavorable*	*Favorable*	*Unfavorable*
Morocco	11	88	38	61
Saudi Arabia	4	94	12	87
Jordan	15	78	34	61
Lebanon	20	69	26	70
UAE	14	73	11	87
Egypt	2	98	15	76

Source: "Impressions of America 2004: How Arabs View America, How Arabs Learn about America," A Six Nation Survey Conducted by Zogby International, July 2004.

Lessons from Others

As mentioned, many other countries have had to deal with the problem of terrorism. Like the United States, many of these countries face the problem of how to defend their homeland against terror without "trampling on individual rights or risking charges of discrimination."[96] Many of these countries face the same problems as the United States in striking this balance and, thus, there are lessons to be learned by studying their response to terrorism.

A common struggle among "democratic" countries has been what to do with "suspected" terrorists, especially foreign terror suspects. Often the country does not have sufficient evidence to arrest, try, and convict the suspected terrorist but fears that if left at liberty the person may commit terrorist acts. Like the United States, many allow suspected terrorists to be held without charges or trial. However, some countries, unlike the practices of the Bush Administration, place a limit on how long terrorist suspects can be held without charges. For example, in Spain, terrorism suspects can be held for up to 13 days without charge and as long as four years without trial.[97]

Some countries have laws that provide for punishments very different from those in the United States. For example, in France, it is against the law to associate with terrorists.[98] In the United States, such a law most likely would be considered a violation of the First Amendment. Israel imposes "collective punishment" on all who provide "aid and comfort" to terrorists, even if they had no part in the terror act. The United States has no such similar punishment, and "collective punishment" for those not responsible for a terrorist crime most likely would be unconstitutional in the United States. However, in Israel, to deter suicide

TABLE 14.3   *Percentage of People Who View the U.S. Favorably*

Country	Summer 2002	March 2003	May 2003	March 2004
Britain	75%	48%	70%	58%
France	63%	31%	43%	37%
Germany	61%	25%	45%	38%

Source: Pew Research Center for the People and the Press, 2004.

bombings the military has the authority to destroy the home of the suicide bomber—even if the bomber was not the owner of the home and even if others without knowledge of the actions of the bomber lived in or owned the house. Nearly always this punishment causes "innocent" parties to suffer homelessness. For example, when a relative living in a home with others commits a suicide bombing, the house where they lived is destroyed, even if the other family members can demonstrate they had no knowledge of the bomber's intention. The government says such harsh retaliation is necessary to motivate family members to encourage people living in the same house from deterring other household members from becoming involved in terrorism. Since 2001, Israel has demolished more than 612 homes of Palestinian militants involved in attacks on Israelis, resulting in approximately 4,000 people being left homeless.[99] Without doubt, collective punishment would be unconstitutional in the United States.

Often foreign countries face the same ethical dilemmas as the United States in responding to terrorism. For example, following the 9/11 attacks Germany passed a law, the Air Safety Act, that, like the United States, allows the defense minister to order hijacked aircraft shot down. In January 2005, President Hörst Kohler voiced concern that the law may be unconstitutional. The German debate as to the legal and ethical authority to take innocent lives as a measure to stop a greater harm by terrorists is not that different from the debate in the United States. In the 9/11 attacks the order to shoot down the third hijacked aircraft came too late to execute. However, the debate as to the ethical and legal consequences of "what if" the order had been executed and the military shot down the aircraft is still of great concern to many. Is it ethical to take the lives of hundreds of innocent people for the greater good of protecting the homeland?

Britain has had a similar problem as the United States with foreigners suspected of terrorism. Like the United States, Britain practiced indefinite detention of foreigners suspected of terrorism without charging or trying them. However, in December 2004, the British Court ruled that indefinite detention without trial or charges violated European human rights laws. In ruling on the practice of indefinite detention, Judge Lord Leonard Hoffman said in his criticism of the practice, "It calls into question the very existence of an ancient liberty of which this country has until now been very proud: freedom from arbitrary arrest and detention. The real threat to the life of the nation, in the sense of a people living in accordance with its traditional laws and political values, comes not from terrorism but from laws such as these."[100]

Unable to hold suspected foreign terrorists without charge or trial, Britain had to come up with alternative policies that would protect the public but preserve civil liberties. In January 2005, the British government unveiled its new policies. Instead of imprisoning suspected foreign terrorists, the Home Secretary will have the power to give suspects curfews, tag them with electronic bracelets, limit their access to telephones and the Internet, restrict their communications with "named individuals," and, if necessary, place them under house arrest.[101] As the U.S. courts consider the constitutionality of "enemy combatants" being held without charge or trial, it may be necessary for the government to examine the new British policies in case the courts rule against the government.

The United States is spending millions of dollars to explore the causes of terrorism. Many European countries, especially France and Spain, offer insight into this question, as they are finding that their prisons are becoming breeding grounds for new recruits for radical Islamic terror groups. The problem is most severe in France, where Muslims make up only 10 percent of the country's population but account for approximately 60 percent of the prison population.[102] In Europe, Islam is becoming the religion of the repressed. The United States may want to examine the effect of repression and economic distress as a cause of terrorism. If repression and economic distress are identified as key factors in promoting terrorism, this finding may influence policies and practices governing illegal immigration from Mexico. Many claim that the key motivation for illegal immigrants is economic distress.

Conclusion: A Terror-Focused Government

The U.S. government has become a terror-focused government. Defending the homeland has become its key mission and, to a great extent, the measure of success. Many have joined ranks with the government in defending the homeland against terrorism and are working to root out potential threats. For example, Member of Freedom House, a conservative-learning rights organization based in New York, searched Mosques in the United States to see if they could find evidence of any threat to America. They reported that books and publications containing the hate-filled, vitriolic writings of the minority Muslim Wahhabi sect were found in mosques throughout America.[103] Some examples of the anti-American and anti-Jewish writings include such statements as "It is a religious obligation to hate Christians and Jews" and "It is forbidden for a Muslim to become a citizen of a county (such as the United States) governed by infidels."

Officials throughout the United States have embraced the fight against terrorism, sometimes too enthusiastically. For example, in October 2003, Lt. General William G. Boykin, in a speech before an evangelical Christian audience, likened the war against Islamic militants to a battle against "Satan," resulting in criticism by Muslims that his rhetoric encouraged prejudice against all Muslims.[104] Sometimes government officials have invoked the analogy of the war on terrorism in inappropriate circumstances, as when in February 2004, Education Secretary Rod Paige called the nation's largest teachers' union a "terrorist organization."

Financing the war on terrorism has become a key component of the government's budget at all levels: local, state, and federal. Also, there are many hidden costs in conducting the war on terrorism, including financial costs and intangible costs, such as psychological well-being, trust in government, and erosion of privacy. Who pays for the various counterterrorism actions often is at the heart of the debate in determining how to better defend the homeland. For example, the federal government wants states to adopt a "standard" driver's license and to verify that applicants are U.S. citizens or legal immigrants before issuing an applicant a license. State officials do not dispute the wisdom and intent of the measure but argue that such federal mandates would be a massive unfunded mandate on the states and would require state officials to take on the role of immigration officers.[105]

Counterterrorism actions are not only expensive, they sometimes ensnarl innocent citizens in a maze of red tape causing them to suffer emotional and economic loss or cause some to question the legitimacy of the government's action. For example, citizens who have discovered their names placed on government watch lists find that there is no explanation as to how their names were placed on the list or how to remove the names from the list if they believe the names are listed without cause. In November 2004, 680 people had filed complaints with the DHS that their names have been mistakenly placed on the watch list. Some citizens have had to resort to suing the government, as they have been unable to have their names removed from the watch list.

Floo Floo Bird Syndrome

In examining the response of the United States to the war on terrorism, columnist William Safire said, "The architect Frank Lloyd Wright warned of the floo floo bird, 'the peculiar and especial bird who always flew backward . . . because it didn't give a darn where it was going, but just had to see where it had been.' "[106] Safire accused that in responding to the war on terrorism, the United States was similar to the floo floo bird. He said, "With our eyes fixed on our rearview mirror, we obsessively review catastrophes past when we should be looking thorough our windshield at dangers ahead." The United States has spent millions of dollars examining the 9/11 attacks. Millions more have been spent on aviation security to make sure that there is not a repeat of the 9/11 attacks. At the slightest hint of a possible security weak point, new policies and practices have been adopted to further ensure that there is not a repeat of a 9/11-type attack. Many are critical that such focus on preventing future attacks like the past attacks will lead to the same situation that made the 9/11 attacks possible in the first place: a lack of anticipation of new threats. At the time of the 9/11 attacks airline security focused on threats that were identified in the 1960s and 1970s. Despite warnings from various sources of the danger of terrorists using aircraft in a way that had never before been experienced in the United States, government officials and airline security officials did not anticipate this new strategy.[107]

Another danger of the floo floo bird syndrome is that sometimes blame is assessed against people based on present information but information that was not known to them or others at the time of the incident. One example is the tendency to accuse or suspect those who donated to Muslim "charities" that are now on the government's list of supporters of terrorism as supporting terrorism when they did not know of the charity's support of terrorism at the time of their donation. For example, an investigation of a mosque accused of ties with terrorism revealed that the mosque was established and financed by the former Houston Rockets star Hakeem Olajuwon. Olajuwon issued a statement that said, "he had not known of any links to terrorism when the donations were made, before the government's crackdown on the groups, and would not have given the money if he had known."[108]

The war on terrorism is an expensive war. It will take a great toll on the United States, both economically and noneconomically. It will be a long war. It is a difficult mission to defend the homeland against all possible attacks. The consequences of a nuclear, biological, or chemical attack could be so devastating that all costs in preventing such attacks would pale if such an attack were successful. A successful cyber-attack by terrorists could cause billions of dollars in damage and could result in causalities exceeding that of the 9/11 attacks. If a cyber-attack caused such damage, there would be much regret that more was not spent on cyber-counterterrorism. However, there is not an endless pot of money for counterterrorism. Although terrorism may be cheap, the war on terrorism is expensive. Deciding what is the right amount to spend on counterterrorism will be one of the major decisions by local, state, and federal government for years, perhaps decades, to come in this new age of terror-focused government.

BOX 14.3 • *Up Close and Personal: Should Those Wrongly Accused Be Compensated?*

On a tip, Tarek Albasti, and eight other Evansville, Indiana, Muslim men, were rounded up by Federal Bureau of Investigation agents, shackled, paraded in front of a newspaper photographer, and jailed for a week. Forty agents investigated them for a week and in the end, the tip turned out to be false and the men were released. But four of the men were then listed in the national crime registry as having been accused of terrorism, even though they were never charged. The branding prevented them from flying, renting apartments, and landing jobs.[109] (They were later removed from the watch list.)

The source of tips accusing persons of terrorism can often come from unreliable sources. Vindictive family members provide some tips as a means to get back at the accused due to a family feud. Some tips are provided by people who hope that by providing federal agents with information it will help them with their own immigration problems. Some tips are provided by ex-wives as a way of striking back at their former husbands. If the same tips were received accusing a person of criminal activity, few courts would authorize a search warrant, much less an arrest warrant.

However, the policy of the Department of Homeland Security and the Department of Justice is that in the event of charges of terrorism, suspects are to be immediately imprisoned and held without bail, if possible, until it can be determined if the suspects have terrorist ties. Often suspects are arrested and detained without interviewing or assessing the validity of the information provided by the tipster. As a result, numerous people have been detained on suspicion of terrorism based on false allegations. For example, Mohamed Alajji, a Michigan trucker born in Yemen, was jailed for seven days before agents interviewed his accuser, who turned out to be making false claims against him to press a family feud.[110] Alajji was set free but the ordeal destroyed his business and he was forced to return to Yemen. In another case, Esshassah Fouad was accused by his former wife of plotting terrorism. He was jailed until it was determined the charges against him were false. However, Fouad was charged with violating his immigration status by not attending school, despite his defense that he had missed school because he was in jail.[111]

Questions

1. The Justice Department defends the immediate jailing of those accused of terrorism before the facts of the case can be verified, claiming, "With terrorism you do not have the luxury of sometimes waiting to figure out if the guy is truly a terrorist." Do you believe the risk of failing to apprehend a terrorist outweighs the risk of imprisoning an innocent person? Why or why not?

2. Is jailing those accused of terrorism without first confirming or investigating the evidence a "double-standard" in that in the criminal justice system normally the assumption of innocence requires that the prosecutor provide evidence to justify the jailing of a suspect? Explain your answer.

3. Should people who are falsely imprisoned while the government investigates the tips against them be financially compensated by the government? Why or why not?

4. Should there be a punishment against federal agents for falsely imprisoning suspects? Why or why not?

5. Other than false imprisonment of innocent persons, what are the potential harms that can result from a policy in which accused suspects are imprisoned first and the tip verified after they have been imprisoned?

Chapter Summary

- The United States has entered an era of terror-focused government.
- The cost of terrorism is relatively inexpensive. The average terrorist attack costs about $50,000.
- Terror is financed by criminal enterprises. The major source of funding from criminal enterprises comes from drug trafficking.
- Terror is financed by unwitting or unscrupulous charities.
- Many government agencies are working to cut off the flow of cash to terror groups.
- The cost of counterterrorism is very expensive to local, state, and federal governments.
- Local and state governments have relied on the federal government for funding but the federal government is having difficulty providing them the funds they need.
- Some counterterrorism funding is misspent.
- In addition to economic costs, the war on terrorism has noneconomic costs. Chief among these are extremism in the defense of liberty, loss of privacy, and loss of trust in government.
- Some extreme policies and practices are self-correcting in that the government takes actions to reverse these policies and practices. Sometimes this action is spurred by the courts.
- Prejudice against foreigners, particularly Hispanics and those of Middle Eastern descent, is a concern.
- Many foreign nations do not approve of U.S. actions and policies in the war on terrorism.
- Foreign countries have similar problems with terror as the United States, and there are lessons that the United States could learn from observing how these countries respond.
- The United States must anticipate new strategies that terrorists may use and not become focused on defending the homeland against the same terror tactics that have been used in the past.

Terrorism and You

Understanding This Chapter

1. How is terror financed?

2. What is the federal government doing to cut off the flow of cash to terrorists?

3. Why is the war on terrorism so expensive?

4. What are some of the noneconomic costs of the war on terrorism?

5. What are some examples of extremism in the defense of liberty?

6. What are some examples of self-correcting actions taken by the government in the correction of extremism in the defense of liberty?

7. How has the war on terrorism affected relations with and attitudes toward Hispanics and persons of Middle Eastern descent in the United States?

8. What is the worldview of the U.S. actions in the war on terrorism?

Thinking about How Terrorism Touches You

1. What impact, if any, do you think that the government's crackdown on charities that support terrorism has on "legitimate" charities that help needy people in the Middle East?

2. Do you think that people in the United States who use illegal drugs believe that they are supporting terror? Explain.

3. Have you felt any loss of privacy or personal freedom due to the war on terrorism? Explain.

4. Do you think the use of extreme interrogation tactics to obtain information from terror suspects is justified? Why?

5. Do you think TSA agents at airline checkpoints should pay more attention to Arab-looking people than other passengers? Why?

6. What do you think of the fact that many countries view the United States as an aggressive superpower and disapprove of the nation's in the war on terrorism?

7. In the 2004 presidential election, did the candidates' stand on terrorism influence your vote? Explain.

Important Terms and Concepts

Collective Punishment
Extremism in the Defense of Liberty
Floo Floo Bird Syndrome
Global Relief Foundation
Holy Land Foundation
Playas Research and Training Center
Pork Barrel Politics
Racial Profiling

Rendition
Terror-Focused Government
Torture
Total Information Awareness
U.S. Treasury Department Office of Foreign Assets Control (OFAC)
Ward Churchill

Endnotes

1. Associated Press, "U.N.: Most Terror Attacks Cost Under \$50G," New York Times Online, www.nytimes.com, August 27, 2004.

2. "Terrorist Financing." Washington, DC: GAO-01-163, November 2003, p. 1.

3. Associated Press, "U.N.: Most Terror Attacks Cost Under \$50G," New York Times Online, www.nytimes.com, August 27, 2004.

4. David B. Ottaway, "Islamic Group Banned by Many Is Not on U.S. Terrorist List," *Washington Post,* Washingtonpost.com, December 27, 2004.

5. Laurie Goodstein, "Since 9/11, Muslims Look Closer to Home," New York Times Online, www.nytimes.com, November 15, 2004.

6. Eric Lichtblau, "Arrests Tie Charity Group to Palestinian Terrorists," New York Times Online, www.nytimes.com, July 28, 2004.

7. "Terrorist Financing." Washington, DC: GAO-01-163, November 2003, p. 14.

8. Ibid., p. 15

9. Donna Leinwand, "Exhibit Links Terror, Drug Traffic," *USA Today,* September 13, 2004, p. 6D.

10. Associated Press, "Hezbollah Allegedly Linked to Drug Ring," New York Times Online, www.nytimes.com, January 21, 2004.

11. "National Briefing: West," New York Times Online, www.nytimes.com, March 4, 2004.

12. Associated Press, "Drug Profits in U.S. Linked to Middle East Terrorists," *Pocono Record,* September 2, 2002, p. A5.

13. Thom Shanker, "Navy Seizes Hashish; Sees Ties to Al Qaeda," New York Times Online, www.nytimes.com, December 20, 2003.

14. Department of Homeland Security, "27 Tons of Cocaine Seized from Two Vessels in Pacific," www.DHS.gov/dhspublic/display?content=4046, September 27, 2004.

15. Eric Lichtblau, "Homeland Security Department Experiments with New Tool to Track Financial Crime," New York Times Online, www.nytimes.com, December 12, 2004.

16. Associated Press, "N.M. Town Is Anti-Terror Training Center," New York Times Online, www.nytimes.com, December 2, 2004.

17. Sara Kehaulani Goo, "Deadlines Urged for Terror Fixes," *Washington Post,* August 17, 2004, p. A13.

18. Eric Lichtblau, "Color Crazed: Terror Policy: Between Fear and Freedom," New York Times Online, www.nytimes.com, January 11, 2004.

19. Kelly Field, "U. of Maryland Wins Federal Grant for Research Center on What Makes a Terrorist," *Chronicle of Higher Education,* http://chronicle.com/daily/2005/01/2005011103n.htm, January 11, 2005.

20. Spencer S. Hsu and Sari Horwitz, "Spending on Capital Checkpoints at Issue," *Washington Post,* November 21, 2004, p. C7.

21. Kedvin Amerman, "$2 Million Police Presence for Toll Bridges," *Pocono Record,* February 24, 2004, p. A3.

22. Philip Shenon and Kevin Flynn, "Mayor Tells Panel 'Pork Barrel Politics' Is Increasing Risk of Terrorism for City," New York Times Online, www.nytimes.com, May 20, 2004.

23. Dean E. Murphy, "Security Grants Still Steaming to Rural States," New York Times Online, www.nytimes.com, October 12, 2004.

24. Eric Lipton, "Big Cities Will Get More in Antiterrorism Grants," New York Times Online, www.nytimes.com, December 22, 2004.

25. Ibid.

26. Ibid.

27. Eric Lichtblau and Joel Brinkley, "$5 Billion in Antiterror Aid Is Reported Stuck in Pipeline," New York Times Online, www.nytimes.com, April 28, 2004.

28. Ibid.

29. Ibid.

30. John Mintz, "Cutbacks Threaten Work of Homeland Security Unit," *Washington Post,* October 31, 2004, p. A6.

31. Josh Benson, "Codey Fears Cutbacks in Security," New York Times Online, www.nytimes.com, December 9, 2004.

32. Anne E. Kornblut, "Laura Bush Defends Gala in Time of War and Disaster," New York Times Online, www.nytimes.com, January 15, 2005.

33. Associated Press, "$38.1B Said Paid to Those Affected by 9/11," New York Times Online, www.nytimes.com, November 9, 2004.

34. Michael Slackman, "2 Insurers Say Bank's Suit Tries to Capitalize on 9/11," New York Times Online, www.nytimes.com, August 26, 2003.

35. Associated Press, "Audit Finds Texas Improperly Spent Terror Funds," New York Times Online, www.nytimes.com, January 8, 2005.

36. Ibid.

37. Sarah Lyall, "Amnesty Calls World Less Safe," New York Times Online, www.nytimes.com, May 29, 2003.

38. Associated Press, "Strafing of School Divides N.J. Region," New York Times Online, www.nytimes.com, November 28, 2004.

39. Scott Shane, "Exposure at Germ Lab Reignites a Public Health Debate," New York Times Online, www.nytimes.com, January 24, 2005.

40. Felicity Barringer, "Pentagon Is Pressing to Bypass Environmental Laws for War Games and Arms Testing," New York Times Online, www.nytimes.com, December 28, 2004.

41. Ibid.

42. Brian Braiker, "The Patriot Search," *Newsweek,* June 9, 2004.

43. Ibid.

44. Scott Smallwood, "Colorado Regents Will Investigate Professor Who Compared September 11 Victims to Nazis," *Chronicle of Higher Education,* http://chronicle.com/daily/2005/022005020405n.htm, February 4, 2005.

45. Scott Smallwood, "Anatomy of a Free-Speech Firestorm: How a Professor's 3-Year-Old Essay Sparked a National Controversy," *Chronicle of Higher Education,* http://chronicle.com/daily/2005/0220005021003n.htm, February 10, 2005.

46. Associated Press, "UC Faculty Backs Professor on Free Speech," New York Times Online, www.nytimes.com, February 2, 2005.

47. Associated Press, "Patriot Act Affects Ex-Con from Nebraska," *Seattle Post-Intelligencer,* June 4, 2004.

48. Julia Preston, "Reporters' Subpoenas Are Being Fought in the Case of Lawyer Accused of Aiding Terrorism," New York Times Online, www.nytimes.com, June 15, 2004.

49. Ibid.

50. Eric Lichtblau, "Material Given to Congress in 2002 is Now Classified," New York Times Online, www.nytimes.com, May 20, 2004.

51. Ibid.

52. Ibid.

53. Ibid.

54. Diana Jean Schemo, "Federal Plan to Keep Data on Students Worries Some," New York Times Online, www.nytimes.com, November 29, 2004.

55. Ibid.

56. Robert O'Harrow, Jr., "In Age of Security, Firm Mines Wealth of Personal Data," *Washington Post,* January 20, 2005, p. A1.

57. Ibid.

58. Ibid.

59. Neil A. Lewis, "Red Cross Finds Detainee Abuse in Guantanamo," New York Times Online, www.nytimes.com, November 30, 2004.

60. Nina Bernstein, "Lawyers Sue Over Tapes with Detainees," New York Times Online, www.nytimes.com, July 2, 2004.

61. Peter Grier, "Bush Team and the Limits on Torture," *Christian Science Monitor,* June 10, 2004, p 1.

62. Ibid.

63. Ibid.

64. Dana Priest, "Jet Is an Open Secret in Terror War," *Washington Post,* December 27, 2004, p. A1.

65. Neil A. Lewis, "Justice Dept. Broadens Definition of Torture," New York Times Online, www.nytimes.com, December 31, 2004.

66. Ibid.

67. Neil A. Lewis, "Justice Dept. Toughens Rule on Torture," New York Times Online, www.nytimes.com, January 1, 2005.

68. Lila Guterman, "Treasury Department Removes Restrictions on U.S. Publications by Authors in Embargoed Countries, *Chronicle of Higher Education,* http://chronicle.com/daily/2004/12/2004121602n.htm, December 16, 2004.

69. Brian Wingfield, "Unions for Border Workers Criticize Rules on Disclosure," New York Times Online, www.nytimes.com, November 30, 2004.

70. Ibid.

71. John Files, "Security Dept. Eases Its Nondisclosure Rule," New York Times Online, www.nytimes.com, January 18, 2005.

72. Ibid.

73. Marc Kaufman, "U.S. Barred from Forcing Troops to Get Anthrax Shots," *Washington Post,* October 28, 2004, p. A1.

74. Ibid.

75. Tom Regan, "Terrorism & Security," *Christian Science Monitor,* www.csmonitor.com/2004/0223/dailyUpdate .html, February 23, 2004.

76. Tom Regan, "Pentagon Seeks OK to Spy on Americans," Christian Science Monitor, www.csmonitor.com/2004/0617/dailyUpdate.html, June 17, 2004.

77. Tom Regan, "Terrorism & Security," *Christian Science Monitor,* www.csmonitor.com/2004/0223/dailyUpdate .html, February 23, 2004.

78. Patrick Healy, "L.I. Clash on Immigrants Is Graining Political Force," New York Times Online, www.nytimes.com, November 29, 2004.

79. David Cho and Tom Jackman, "Law Raises Immigrants' Suspicions," *Washington Post,* July 11, 2004, p. C1.

80. Ibid.

81. Ibid.

82. David Glenn, "Critics Assail Scholar's Article Arguing that Hispanic Immigration Threatens U.S.," *Chronicle of Higher Education,* http://chronicle.com/daily/2004/02/200402401.htm, February 24, 2004.

83. Ibid.

84. Caryle Murphy, "Distrust of Muslims Common in U.S., Poll Finds," *Washington Post,* October 5, 2004, p. A2.

85. Associated Press, "N.J. Killings Spark New Anti-Muslim Bias," New York Times Online, www.nytimes .com, January 22, 2005.

86. Anemona Hartocollis and Charlie LeDuff, "Parents Fear Their Children Will Be the Targets of Bigotry," New York Times Online, www.nytimes.com, September 15, 2001.

87. Tracey Maclin, "'Voluntary' Interviews and Airport Searches of Middle Eastern Men: The Fourth Amendment in a Time of Terror," *Mississippi Law Journal,* January 21, 2005, p. 521.

88. Ibid.

89. Associated Press, "Dearborn, Mich., Arabs Cited More Often," New York Times Online, www.nytimes.com, November 20, 2003.

90. Eric Lichtblau, "Bush Issues Federal Ban on Racial Profiling," New York Times Online, www.nytimes.com, June 17, 2003.

91. *Report of the Defense Science Board Task Force on Strategic Communication.* Washington, DC: Defense Science Board, 2004. p. 44.

92. Bruce Nussbaum, John Rossant, and Stan Crock, "Fighting A New Cold War," *Business Week,* www .keepmedia.com/pubs/BusinessWeek/2004/03/29/397908, March 29, 2004.

93. Roger Cohen, "An Obsession the World Doesn't Share," New York Times Online, www.nytimes.com, December 5, 2004.

94. Ibid.

95. *Report of the Defense Science Board Task Force on Strategic Communication.* Washington, DC: Defense Science Board, 2004, p. 46.

96. Craig S. Smith, "Dutch Try to Thwart Terror Without Being Overzealous," New York Times Online, www.nytimes.com, November 25, 2004.

97. Ibid.

98. Ibid.

99. Associated Press, "Israel Destroys Teen Suicide Bomber's Home," *Pocono Record,* November 3, 2004, p. A7.

100. Lizette Alvarez, "Britain's Highest Court Overturns Anti-Terrorism Law," New York Times Online, www.nytimes.com, December 16, 2004.

101. Lizette Alvarez, "Britain Offers Plan to Restrain, Not Jail, Foreign Terror Suspects," New York Times Online, www.nytimes.com, January 27, 2004.

102. Craig S. Smith, "In Europe's Jails, Neglect of Islam Breeds Trouble," New York Times Online, www.nytimes.com, December 8, 2004.

103. John Mintz, "Report Cites 'Hate' Writings in U.S. Mosques," *Washington Post,* February 6, 2005, p. A18.

104. Douglas Jehl, "U.S. General Apologizes for Remarks about Islam," New York Times Online, www.nytimes.com, October 18, 2003.

105. Associated Press, "House Agrees to Citizenship Check for Licenses," New York Times Online, www.nytimes.com, February 10, 2005.

106. William Safire, "The Floo Floo Bird," New York Times Online, www.nytimes.com, April 5, 2004.

107. Eric Lichtblau, "9/11 Report Cites Many Warnings about Hijackings," New York Times Online, www.nytimes.com, February 10, 2005.

108. Associated Press, "Terror Fronts Got Money from Olajuwon's Mosque," New York Times Onine, www.nytimes.com, February 10, 2005.

109. Michael Moss, "False Terrorism Tips to F.B.I. Uproot Lives of Suspects," New York Times Online, www.nytimes.com, June 19, 2003.

110. Ibid.

111. Ibid.

PART V

Appendices

The President's Address to a Joint Session of Congress and the American People September 20, 2001

THE PRESIDENT: Mr. Speaker, Mr. President Pro Tempore, members of Congress, and fellow Americans:

In the normal course of events, Presidents come to this chamber to report on the state of the Union. Tonight, no such report is needed. It has already been delivered by the American people.

We have seen it in the courage of passengers, who rushed terrorists to save others on the ground—passengers like an exceptional man named Todd Beamer. And would you please help me to welcome his wife, Lisa Beamer, here tonight.

We have seen the state of our Union in the endurance of rescuers, working past exhaustion. We have seen the unfurling of flags, the lighting of candles, the giving of blood, the saying of prayers—in English, Hebrew, and Arabic. We have seen the decency of a loving and giving people who have made the grief of strangers their own.

My fellow citizens, for the last nine days, the entire world has seen for itself the state of our Union—and it is strong.

Tonight we are a country awakened to danger and called to defend freedom. Our grief has turned to anger, and anger to resolution. Whether we bring our enemies to justice, or bring justice to our enemies, justice will be done.

I thank the Congress for its leadership at such an important time. All of America was touched on the evening of the tragedy to see Republicans and Democrats joined together on the steps of this Capitol, singing "God Bless America." And you did more than sing;

you acted, by delivering $40 billion to rebuild our communities and meet the needs of our military.

Speaker Hastert, Minority Leader Gephardt, Majority Leader Daschle and Senator Lott, I thank you for your friendship, for your leadership and for your service to our country.

And on behalf of the American people, I thank the world for its outpouring of support. America will never forget the sounds of our National Anthem playing at Buckingham Palace, on the streets of Paris, and at Berlin's Brandenburg Gate.

We will not forget South Korean children gathering to pray outside our embassy in Seoul, or the prayers of sympathy offered at a mosque in Cairo. We will not forget moments of silence and days of mourning in Australia and Africa and Latin America.

Nor will we forget the citizens of 80 other nations who died with our own: dozens of Pakistanis; more than 130 Israelis; more than 250 citizens of India; men and women from El Salvador, Iran, Mexico and Japan; and hundreds of British citizens. America has no truer friend than Great Britain. Once again, we are joined together in a great cause—so honored the British Prime Minister has crossed an ocean to show his unity of purpose with America. Thank you for coming, friend.

On September the 11th, enemies of freedom committed an act of war against our country. Americans have known wars—but for the past 136 years, they have been wars on foreign soil, except for one Sunday in 1941. Americans have known the casualties of war—but not at the center of a great city on a peaceful morning. Americans have known surprise attacks—but never before on thousands of civilians. All of this was brought upon us in a single day—and night fell on a different world, a world where freedom itself is under attack.

Americans have many questions tonight. Americans are asking: Who attacked our country? The evidence we have gathered all points to a collection of loosely affiliated terrorist organizations known as al Qaeda. They are the same murderers indicted for bombing American embassies in Tanzania and Kenya, and responsible for bombing the USS Cole.

Al Qaeda is to terror what the mafia is to crime. But its goal is not making money; its goal is remaking the world—and imposing its radical beliefs on people everywhere.

The terrorists practice a fringe form of Islamic extremism that has been rejected by Muslim scholars and the vast majority of Muslim clerics—a fringe movement that perverts the peaceful teachings of Islam. The terrorists' directive commands them to kill Christians and Jews, to kill all Americans, and make no distinction among military and civilians, including women and children.

This group and its leader—a person named Osama bin Laden—are linked to many other organizations in different countries, including the Egyptian Islamic Jihad and the Islamic Movement of Uzbekistan. There are thousands of these terrorists in more than 60 countries. They are recruited from their own nations and neighborhoods and brought to camps in places like Afghanistan, where they are trained in the tactics of terror. They are sent back to their homes or sent to hide in countries around the world to plot evil and destruction.

The leadership of al Qaeda has great influence in Afghanistan and supports the Taliban regime in controlling most of that country. In Afghanistan, we see al Qaeda's vision for the world.

Afghanistan's people have been brutalized—many are starving and many have fled. Women are not allowed to attend school. You can be jailed for owning a television. Religion can be practiced only as their leaders dictate. A man can be jailed in Afghanistan if his beard is not long enough.

The United States respects the people of Afghanistan—after all, we are currently its largest source of humanitarian aid—but we condemn the Taliban regime. It is not only repressing its own people, it is threatening people everywhere by sponsoring and sheltering and supplying terrorists. By aiding and abetting murder, the Taliban regime is committing murder.

And tonight, the United States of America makes the following demands on the Taliban: Deliver to United States authorities all the leaders of al Qaeda who hide in your land. Release all foreign nationals, including American citizens, you have unjustly imprisoned. Protect foreign journalists, diplomats and aid workers in your country. Close immediately and permanently every terrorist training camp in Afghanistan, and hand over every terrorist, and every person in their support structure, to appropriate authorities. Give the United States full access to terrorist training camps, so we can make sure they are no longer operating.

These demands are not open to negotiation or discussion. The Taliban must act, and act immediately. They will hand over the terrorists, or they will share in their fate.

I also want to speak tonight directly to Muslims throughout the world. We respect your faith. It's practiced freely by many millions of Americans, and by millions more in countries that America counts as friends. Its teachings are good and peaceful, and those who commit evil in the name of Allah blaspheme the name of Allah. The terrorists are traitors to their own faith, trying, in effect, to hijack Islam itself. The enemy of America is not our many Muslim friends; it is not our many Arab friends. Our enemy is a radical network of terrorists, and every government that supports them.

Our war on terror begins with al Qaeda, but it does not end there. It will not end until every terrorist group of global reach has been found, stopped and defeated.

Americans are asking, why do they hate us? They hate what we see right here in this chamber—a democratically elected government. Their leaders are self-appointed. They hate our freedoms—our freedom of religion, our freedom of speech, our freedom to vote and assemble and disagree with each other.

They want to overthrow existing governments in many Muslim countries, such as Egypt, Saudi Arabia, and Jordan. They want to drive Israel out of the Middle East. They want to drive Christians and Jews out of vast regions of Asia and Africa.

These terrorists kill not merely to end lives, but to disrupt and end a way of life. With every atrocity, they hope that America grows fearful, retreating from the world and forsaking our friends. They stand against us, because we stand in their way.

We are not deceived by their pretenses to piety. We have seen their kind before. They are the heirs of all the murderous ideologies of the 20th century. By sacrificing human life to serve their radical visions—by abandoning every value except the will to power—they follow in the path of fascism, and Nazism, and totalitarianism. And they will follow that path all the way, to where it ends: in history's unmarked grave of discarded lies.

Americans are asking: How will we fight and win this war? We will direct every resource at our command—every means of diplomacy, every tool of intelligence, every instrument of law enforcement, every financial influence, and every necessary weapon of war—to the disruption and to the defeat of the global terror network.

This war will not be like the war against Iraq a decade ago, with a decisive liberation of territory and a swift conclusion. It will not look like the air war above Kosovo two years ago, where no ground troops were used and not a single American was lost in combat.

Our response involves far more than instant retaliation and isolated strikes. Americans should not expect one battle, but a lengthy campaign, unlike any other we have ever seen. It may include dramatic strikes, visible on TV, and covert operations, secret even in success. We will starve terrorists of funding, turn them one against another, drive them from place to place, until there is no refuge or no rest. And we will pursue nations that provide aid or safe haven to terrorism. Every nation, in every region, now has a decision to make. Either you are with us, or you are with the terrorists. From this day forward, any nation that continues to harbor or support terrorism will be regarded by the United States as a hostile regime.

Our nation has been put on notice: We are not immune from attack. We will take defensive measures against terrorism to protect Americans. Today, dozens of federal departments and agencies, as well as state and local governments, have responsibilities affecting homeland security. These efforts must be coordinated at the highest level. So tonight I announce the creation of a Cabinet-level position reporting directly to me—the Office of Homeland Security.

And tonight I also announce a distinguished American to lead this effort, to strengthen American security: a military veteran, an effective governor, a true patriot, a trusted friend—Pennsylvania's Tom Ridge. He will lead, oversee and coordinate a comprehensive national strategy to safeguard our country against terrorism, and respond to any attacks that may come.

These measures are essential. But the only way to defeat terrorism as a threat to our way of life is to stop it, eliminate it, and destroy it where it grows.

Many will be involved in this effort, from FBI agents to intelligence operatives to the reservists we have called to active duty. All deserve our thanks, and all have our prayers. And tonight, a few miles from the damaged Pentagon, I have a message for our military: Be ready. I've called the Armed Forces to alert, and there is a reason. The hour is coming when America will act, and you will make us proud.

This is not, however, just America's fight. And what is at stake is not just America's freedom. This is the world's fight. This is civilization's fight. This is the fight of all who believe in progress and pluralism, tolerance and freedom.

We ask every nation to join us. We will ask, and we will need, the help of police forces, intelligence services, and banking systems around the world. The United States is grateful that many nations and many international organizations have already responded—with sympathy and with support. Nations from Latin America, to Asia, to Africa, to Europe, to the Islamic world. Perhaps the NATO Charter reflects best the attitude of the world: An attack on one is an attack on all.

The civilized world is rallying to America's side. They understand that if this terror goes unpunished, their own cities, their own citizens may be next. Terror, unanswered, can not only bring down buildings, it can threaten the stability of legitimate governments. And you know what—we're not going to allow it.

Americans are asking: What is expected of us? I ask you to live your lives, and hug your children. I know many citizens have fears tonight, and I ask you to be calm and resolute, even in the face of a continuing threat.

I ask you to uphold the values of America, and remember why so many have come here. We are in a fight for our principles, and our first responsibility is to live by them. No one should be singled out for unfair treatment or unkind words because of their ethnic background or religious faith.

I ask you to continue to support the victims of this tragedy with your contributions. Those who want to give can go to a central source of information, libertyunites.org, to find the names of groups providing direct help in New York, Pennsylvania, and Virginia.

The thousands of FBI agents who are now at work in this investigation may need your cooperation, and I ask you to give it.

I ask for your patience, with the delays and inconveniences that may accompany tighter security; and for your patience in what will be a long struggle.

I ask your continued participation and confidence in the American economy. Terrorists attacked a symbol of American prosperity. They did not touch its source. America is successful because of the hard work, and creativity, and enterprise of our people. These were the true strengths of our economy before September 11th, and they are our strengths today.

And, finally, please continue praying for the victims of terror and their families, for those in uniform, and for our great country. Prayer has comforted us in sorrow, and will help strengthen us for the journey ahead.

Tonight I thank my fellow Americans for what you have already done and for what you will do. And ladies and gentlemen of the Congress, I thank you, their representatives, for what you have already done and for what we will do together.

Tonight, we face new and sudden national challenges. We will come together to improve air safety, to dramatically expand the number of air marshals on domestic flights, and take new measures to prevent hijacking. We will come together to promote stability and keep our airlines flying, with direct assistance during this emergency.

We will come together to give law enforcement the additional tools it needs to track down terror here at home. We will come together to strengthen our intelligence capabilities to know the plans of terrorists before they act, and find them before they strike.

We will come together to take active steps that strengthen America's economy, and put our people back to work.

Tonight we welcome two leaders who embody the extraordinary spirit of all New Yorkers: Governor George Pataki, and Mayor Rudolph Giuliani. As a symbol of America's resolve, my administration will work with Congress, and these two leaders, to show the world that we will rebuild New York City.

After all that has just passed—all the lives taken, and all the possibilities and hopes that died with them—it is natural to wonder if America's future is one of fear. Some speak of an age of terror. I know there are struggles ahead, and dangers to face. But this country will define our times, not be defined by them. As long as the United States of America is determined and strong, this will not be an age of terror; this will be an age of liberty, here and across the world.

Great harm has been done to us. We have suffered great loss. And in our grief and anger we have found our mission and our moment. Freedom and fear are at war. The advance of human freedom—the great achievement of our time, and the great hope of every time—now depends on us. Our nation—this generation—will lift a dark threat of violence from our people and our future. We will rally the world to this cause by our efforts, by our courage. We will not tire, we will not falter, and we will not fail.

It is my hope that in the months and years ahead, life will return almost to normal. We'll go back to our lives and routines, and that is good. Even grief recedes with time and grace. But our resolve must not pass. Each of us will remember what happened that day, and to whom it happened. We'll remember the moment the news came—where we were and what we were doing. Some will remember an image of a fire, or a story of rescue. Some will carry memories of a face and a voice gone forever.

And I will carry this: It is the police shield of a man named George Howard, who died at the World Trade Center trying to save others. It was given to me by his mom, Arlene, as a proud memorial to her son. This is my reminder of lives that ended, and a task that does not end.

I will not forget this wound to our country or those who inflicted it. I will not yield; I will not rest; I will not relent in waging this struggle for freedom and security for the American people.

The course of this conflict is not known, yet its outcome is certain. Freedom and fear, justice and cruelty, have always been at war, and we know that God is not neutral between them.

Fellow citizens, we'll meet violence with patient justice—assured of the rightness of our cause, and confident of the victories to come. In all that lies before us, may God grant us wisdom, and may He watch over the United States of America.

Thank you.

Executive Order Establishing the Office of Homeland Security and the Homeland Security Council October 8, 2001

By the authority vested in me as President by the Constitution and the laws of the United States of America, it is hereby ordered as follows:

Section 1. Establishment. I hereby establish within the Executive Office of the President an Office of Homeland Security (the "Office") to be headed by the Assistant to the President for Homeland Security.

Sec. 2. Mission. The mission of the Office shall be to develop and coordinate the implementation of a comprehensive national strategy to secure the United States from terrorist threats or attacks. The Office shall perform the functions necessary to carry out this mission, including the functions specified in section 3 of this order.

Sec. 3. Functions. The functions of the Office shall be to coordinate the executive branch's efforts to detect, prepare for, prevent, protect against, respond to, and recover from terrorist attacks within the United States.

(a) National Strategy. The Office shall work with executive departments and agencies, State and local governments, and private entities to ensure the adequacy of the national strategy for detecting, preparing for, preventing, protecting against, responding to, and recovering from terrorist threats or attacks within the United States and shall periodically review and coordinate revisions to that strategy as necessary.

(b) Detection. The Office shall identify priorities and coordinate efforts for collection and analysis of information within the United States regarding threats of terrorism against the United States and activities of terrorists or terrorist groups within the United

States. The Office also shall identify, in coordination with the Assistant to the President for National Security Affairs, priorities for collection of intelligence outside the United States regarding threats of terrorism within the United States.

(i) In performing these functions, the Office shall work with Federal, State, and local agencies, as appropriate, to:

(A) facilitate collection from State and local governments and private entities of information pertaining to terrorist threats or activities within the United States;

(B) coordinate and prioritize the requirements for foreign intelligence relating to terrorism within the United States of executive departments and agencies responsible for homeland security and provide these requirements and priorities to the Director of Central Intelligence and other agencies responsible for collection of foreign intelligence;

(C) coordinate efforts to ensure that all executive departments and agencies that have intelligence collection responsibilities have sufficient technological capabilities and resources to collect intelligence and data relating to terrorist activities or possible terrorist acts within the United States, working with the Assistant to the President for National Security Affairs, as appropriate;

(D) coordinate development of monitoring protocols and equipment for use in detecting the release of biological, chemical, and radiological hazards; and

(E) ensure that, to the extent permitted by law, all appropriate and necessary intelligence and law enforcement information relating to homeland security is disseminated to and exchanged among appropriate executive departments and agencies responsible for homeland security and, where appropriate for reasons of homeland security, promote exchange of such information with and among State and local governments and private entities.

(ii) Executive departments and agencies shall, to the extent permitted by law, make available to the Office all information relating to terrorist threats and activities within the United States.

(c) Preparedness. The Office of Homeland Security shall coordinate national efforts to prepare for and mitigate the consequences of terrorist threats or attacks within the United States. In performing this function, the Office shall work with Federal, State, and local agencies, and private entities, as appropriate, to:

(i) review and assess the adequacy of the portions of all Federal emergency response plans that pertain to terrorist threats or attacks within the United States;

(ii) coordinate domestic exercises and simulations designed to assess and practice systems that would be called upon to respond to a terrorist threat or attack within the United States and coordinate programs and activities for training Federal, State, and local employees who would be called upon to respond to such a threat or attack;

(iii) coordinate national efforts to ensure public health preparedness for a terrorist attack, including reviewing vaccination policies and reviewing the adequacy of and, if necessary, increasing vaccine and pharmaceutical stockpiles and hospital capacity;

(iv) coordinate Federal assistance to State and local authorities and nongovernmental organizations to prepare for and respond to terrorist threats or attacks within the United States;

(v) ensure that national preparedness programs and activities for terrorist threats or attacks are developed and are regularly evaluated under appropriate standards and that resources are allocated to improving and sustaining preparedness based on such evaluations; and

(vi) ensure the readiness and coordinated deployment of Federal response teams to respond to terrorist threats or attacks, working with the Assistant to the President for National Security Affairs, when appropriate.

(d) Prevention. The Office shall coordinate efforts to prevent terrorist attacks within the United States. In performing this function, the Office shall work with Federal, State, and local agencies, and private entities, as appropriate, to:

(i) facilitate the exchange of information among such agencies relating to immigration and visa matters and shipments of cargo; and, working with the Assistant to the President for National Security Affairs, ensure coordination among such agencies to prevent the entry of terrorists and terrorist materials and supplies into the United States and facilitate removal of such terrorists from the United States, when appropriate;

(ii) coordinate efforts to investigate terrorist threats and attacks within the United States; and

(iii) coordinate efforts to improve the security of United States borders, territorial waters, and airspace in order to prevent acts of terrorism within the United States, working with the Assistant to the President for National Security Affairs, when appropriate.

(e) Protection. The Office shall coordinate efforts to protect the United States and its critical infrastructure from the consequences of terrorist attacks. In performing this function, the Office shall work with Federal, State, and local agencies, and private entities, as appropriate, to:

(i) strengthen measures for protecting energy production, transmission, and distribution services and critical facilities; other utilities; telecommunications; facilities that produce, use, store, or dispose of nuclear material; and other critical infrastructure services and critical facilities within the United States from terrorist attack;

(ii) coordinate efforts to protect critical public and privately owned information systems within the United States from terrorist attack;

(iii) develop criteria for reviewing whether appropriate security measures are in place at major public and privately owned facilities within the United States;

(iv) coordinate domestic efforts to ensure that special events determined by appropriate senior officials to have national significance are protected from terrorist attack;

(v) coordinate efforts to protect transportation systems within the United States, including railways, highways, shipping, ports and waterways, and airports and civilian aircraft, from terrorist attack;

(vi) coordinate efforts to protect United States livestock, agriculture, and systems for the provision of water and food for human use and consumption from terrorist attack; and

(vii) coordinate efforts to prevent unauthorized access to, development of, and unlawful importation into the United States of, chemical, biological, radiological, nuclear, explosive, or other related materials that have the potential to be used in terrorist attacks.

(f) Response and Recovery. The Office shall coordinate efforts to respond to and promote recovery from terrorist threats or attacks within the United States. In performing this function, the Office shall work with Federal, State, and local agencies, and private entities, as appropriate, to:

(i) coordinate efforts to ensure rapid restoration of transportation systems, energy production, transmission, and distribution systems; telecommunications; other utilities; and other critical infrastructure facilities after disruption by a terrorist threat or attack;

(ii) coordinate efforts to ensure rapid restoration of public and private critical information systems after disruption by a terrorist threat or attack;

(iii) work with the National Economic Council to coordinate efforts to stabilize United States financial markets after a terrorist threat or attack and manage the immediate economic and financial consequences of the incident;

(iv) coordinate Federal plans and programs to provide medical, financial, and other assistance to victims of terrorist attacks and their families; and

(v) coordinate containment and removal of biological, chemical, radiological, explosive, or other hazardous materials in the event of a terrorist threat or attack involving such hazards and coordinate efforts to mitigate the effects of such an attack.

(g) Incident Management. The Assistant to the President for Homeland Security shall be the individual primarily responsible for coordinating the domestic response efforts of all departments and agencies in the event of an imminent terrorist threat and during and in the immediate aftermath of a terrorist attack within the United States and shall be the principal point of contact for and to the President with respect to coordination of such efforts. The Assistant to the President for Homeland Security shall coordinate with the Assistant to the President for National Security Affairs, as appropriate.

(h) Continuity of Government. The Assistant to the President for Homeland Security, in coordination with the Assistant to the President for National Security Affairs, shall review plans and preparations for ensuring the continuity of the Federal Government in the event of a terrorist attack that threatens the safety and security of the United States Government or its leadership.

(i) Public Affairs. The Office, subject to the direction of the White House Office of Communications, shall coordinate the strategy of the executive branch for communicating with the public in the event of a terrorist threat or attack within the United States. The Office also shall coordinate the development of programs for educating the public about the nature of terrorist threats and appropriate precautions and responses.

(j) Cooperation with State and Local Governments and Private Entities. The Office shall encourage and invite the participation of State and local governments and private entities, as appropriate, in carrying out the Office's functions.

(k) Review of Legal Authorities and Development of Legislative Proposals. The Office shall coordinate a periodic review and assessment of the legal authorities available to executive departments and agencies to permit them to perform the functions described in this order. When the Office determines that such legal authorities are inadequate, the Office shall develop, in consultation with executive departments and agencies, proposals for presidential action and legislative proposals for submission to the Office of Management and Budget to enhance the ability of executive departments and agencies to perform those functions. The Office shall work with State and local governments in assessing the adequacy of their legal authorities to permit them to detect, prepare for, prevent, protect against, and recover from terrorist threats and attacks.

(l) Budget Review. The Assistant to the President for Homeland Security, in consultation with the Director of the Office of Management and Budget (the "Director") and the heads of executive departments and agencies, shall identify programs that contribute to the Administration's strategy for homeland security and, in the development of the President's annual budget submission, shall review and provide advice to the heads of departments and agencies for such programs. The Assistant to the President for Homeland Security shall provide advice to the Director on the level and use of funding in departments and agencies for homeland security-related activities and, prior to the Director's forwarding of the proposed annual budget submission to the President for transmittal to the Congress, shall certify to the Director the funding levels that the Assistant to the President for Homeland Security believes are necessary and appropriate for the homeland security-related activities of the executive branch.

Sec. 4. Administration.

(a) The Office of Homeland Security shall be directed by the Assistant to the President for Homeland Security.

(b) The Office of Administration within the Executive Office of the President shall provide the Office of Homeland Security with such personnel, funding, and administrative support, to the extent permitted by law and subject to the availability of appropriations, as directed by the Chief of Staff to carry out the provisions of this order.

(c) Heads of executive departments and agencies are authorized, to the extent permitted by law, to detail or assign personnel of such departments and agencies to the Office of Homeland Security upon request of the Assistant to the President for Homeland Security, subject to the approval of the Chief of Staff.

Sec. 5. Establishment of Homeland Security Council.

(a) I hereby establish a Homeland Security Council (the "Council"), which shall be responsible for advising and assisting the President with respect to all aspects of homeland security. The Council shall serve as the mechanism for ensuring coordination of homeland security-related activities of executive departments and agencies and effective development and implementation of homeland security policies.

(b) The Council shall have as its members the President, the Vice President, the Secretary of the Treasury, the Secretary of Defense, the Attorney General, the Secretary of Health and Human Services, the Secretary of Transportation, the Director of the Federal Emergency Management Agency, the Director of the Federal Bureau of Investigation, the Director of Central Intelligence, the Assistant to the President for Homeland Security, and such other officers of the executive branch as the President may from time to time designate. The Chief of Staff, the Chief of Staff to the Vice President, the Assistant to the President for National Security Affairs, the Counsel to the President, and the Director of the Office of Management and Budget also are invited to attend any Council meeting. The Secretary of State, the Secretary of Agriculture, the Secretary of the Interior, the Secretary of Energy, the Secretary of Labor, the Secretary of Commerce, the Secretary of Veterans Affairs, the Administrator of the Environmental Protection Agency, the Assistant to the President for Economic Policy, and the Assistant to the President for Domestic Policy shall be invited to attend meetings pertaining to their responsibilities. The heads of other executive departments and agencies and other senior officials shall be invited to attend Council meetings when appropriate.

(c) The Council shall meet at the President's direction. When the President is absent from a meeting of the Council, at the President's direction the Vice President may preside. The Assistant to the President for Homeland Security shall be responsible, at the President's direction, for determining the agenda, ensuring that necessary papers are prepared, and recording Council actions and Presidential decisions.

Sec. 6. Original Classification Authority. I hereby delegate the authority to classify information originally as Top Secret, in accordance with Executive Order 12958 or any successor Executive Order, to the Assistant to the President for Homeland Security.

Sec. 7. Continuing Authorities. This order does not alter the existing authorities of United States Government departments and agencies. All executive departments and agencies are directed to assist the Council and the Assistant to the President for Homeland Security in carrying out the purposes of this order.

Sec. 8. General Provisions.

(a) This order does not create any right or benefit, substantive or procedural, enforceable at law or equity by a party against the United States, its departments, agencies or instrumentalities, its officers or employees, or any other person.

(b) References in this order to State and local governments shall be construed to include tribal governments and United States territories and other possessions.

(c) References to the "United States" shall be construed to include United States territories and possessions.

Sec. 9. Amendments to Executive Order 12656. Executive Order 12656 of November 18, 1988, as amended, is hereby further amended as follows:

(a) Section 101(a) is amended by adding at the end of the fourth sentence: ", except that the Homeland Security Council shall be responsible for administering such policy with respect to terrorist threats and attacks within the United States."

(b) Section 104(a) is amended by adding at the end: ", except that the Homeland Security Council is the principal forum for consideration of policy relating to terrorist threats and attacks within the United States."

(c) Section 104(b) is amended by inserting the words "and the Homeland Security Council" after the words "National Security Council."

(d) The first sentence of section 104(c) is amended by inserting the words "and the Homeland Security Council" after the words "National Security Council."

(e) The second sentence of section 104(c) is replaced with the following two sentences: "Pursuant to such procedures for the organization and management of the National Security Council and Homeland Security Council processes as the President may establish, the Director of the Federal Emergency Management Agency also shall assist in the implementation of and management of those processes as the President may establish. The Director of the Federal Emergency Management Agency also shall assist in the implementation of national security emergency preparedness policy by coordinating with the other Federal departments and agencies and with State and local governments, and by providing periodic reports to the National Security Council and the Homeland Security Council on implementation of national security emergency preparedness policy."

(f) Section 201(7) is amended by inserting the words "and the Homeland Security Council" after the words "National Security Council."

(g) Section 206 is amended by inserting the words "and the Homeland Security Council" after the words "National Security Council."

(h) Section 208 is amended by inserting the words "or the Homeland Security Council" after the words "National Security Council."

GEORGE W. BUSH

APPENDIX C: MAPS

Israel

Israel

- ✪ National Capital
- Haifa • City
- — International Boundary
- — District Boundary
- *Haifa* District Name

50 km

0 ——— 50 Miles

LEBANON

SYRIA

GOLAN HEIGHTS (Israeli occupied)

•Nahariyya
•Akko
•Haifa
Haifa
Tiberias
Nazareth
•Hadera
•Netanya
Herzliyya•
•Nablus
•Tel-Aviv Yafo
Tel Aviv
WEST BANK
Ramla•
•Ashdod
Jerusalem✪
•Bethlehem
•Ashqelon
GAZA STRIP•Gaza
•Hebron
•Rafah
•Beersheba
Dead Sea
•Dimona
Oron•
JORDAN
•Mizpe Ramon

Mediterranean Sea

EGYPT

Yotvata•

Elat
Gulf of Aqaba

* Israel occupied with current status subject to the Israeli-Palestinian Interim Agreement - permanent status to be determined through further negotiations

471

Europe

South America

Sea of Okhotsk

RUSSIA

MONGOLIA

Ulaanbaatar

KAZAKHSTAN

C H I N A

Beijing

Sea of Japan

JAPAN

Tokyo
Osaka

NORTH KOREA
Pyongyang

SOUTH KOREA
Seoul
Pusan

Yellow Sea

East China Sea

Ryukyu Islands (JAPAN)

Tropic of Cancer

Taipei
Taiwan

Shanghai

Nanjing

Wuhan
Changsha

Fuzhou

Guangzhou
Hong Kong (U.K.)
Macau (Port.)

Philippine Sea

Northern Mariana Islands (U.S.)
Guam (U.S.)

Trust Territory of the Pacific Islands (U.S.)

FEDERATED STATES OF MICRONESIA

PAPUA NEW GUINEA
Port Moresby
Wewak

AUSTRALIA

Darwin
Wyndham

Cairns

PHILIPPINES
Manila
Cebu
Davao

Sulu Sea
Celebes Sea

I N D O N E S I A

Jayapura
Sorong

Ambon
Banda Sea

Kupang

Jakarta
Surabaya

Ashmore and Cartier Islands (Aust.)

Dampier

MALAYSIA
Kuala Lumpur
SINGAPORE

VIETNAM
Hanoi
Ho Chi Minh City
Da Nang

THAILAND
Bangkok

BURMA
Rangoon
Mandalay

Bay of Bengal

I N D I A

New Delhi
Bombay
Madras
Bangalore
Hyderabad
Calcutta

NEPAL
Kathmandu

BHUTAN
Thimphu

BANGLADESH
Dhaka

SRI LANKA
Colombo

MALDIVES
Male

Indian Ocean

British Indian Ocean Territory (U.K.)

Equator

Scale 1:50,000,000
Miller Cylindrical Projection

PAKISTAN
Islamabad
Lahore
Karachi

AFGHANISTAN
Kabul

Arabian Sea

IRAN
Tehran

OMAN
Muscat

U.A.E.
Abu Dhabi

SAUDI ARABIA
Riyadh

QATAR
Doha

Kuwait

IRAQ
Baghdad

Mecca
Medina

Red Sea

YEMEN
Sanaa
Aden

Socotra (YEMEN)

SOMALIA
Mogadishu

ETHIOPIA
Addis Ababa

DJIBOUTI

ERITREA
Asmara

SUDAN
Khartoum

EGYPT

KENYA
Nairobi
Mombasa

UGANDA
Kampala

TANZANIA
Dar es Salaam

MOZAMBIQUE
Beira

MADAGASCAR
Antananarivo

SEYCHELLES
Victoria

MAURITIUS
Port Louis

Réunion

COMOROS
Moroni

TURKEY
Ankara

SYRIA
Damascus

Black Sea

Caspian Sea

Moscow

UKRAINE

Aral Sea

India

AFGHANISTAN

Indian Claim

Chinese line
of control

CHINA

Srinagar Leh
Jammu and Kashmir
Himachal
Pradesh
Simla
Chandigarh Chandigarh
Punjab
PAKISTAN
Haryana
New Delhi Delhi
NEPAL
Uttar Pradesh
Rajasthan Jaipur Agra
Lucknow
Ganglok SIKKIM
BHUTAN
Kanpur
Bernares Patna
Siliguri
Shillong
Pradesh Ledo
Nagaland
Assam Kohima
Bihar
BANGLADESH
Imphal
Manipur
Kandla Gandhinagar
Ahmadabad
Bhopal Jabalpur
West Bengal
Asansol Triputa Ajal Mizeram
Gujarat Baroda
Madhya Pradesh
Jamshedpur
Calcutta
Veraval
Diu Daman
Nagpur Raipur
MYANMAR
Dadra and Nagar Haveli
Bhubaneswar Cuttack
Puri
Bombay
Maharashtra
Orissa
Poona
Vishakhapatnam
Hyderabad
Arabian Sea
Andhra
Bay of Bengal
Goa Panaji
Pradesh
Mormugao Guntakal
Karnataka
Bangalore Madras
Mangalore
Andaman and
Nicobar Islands Port Blair
Pondicherry
Cuddalore
Kavaratti Island
Calicut
Tamil Nadu
Madurai
Kerala
Trivandrum
SRI
LANKA

India

⊕ National Capital

Raipur • City

—— International Boundary

—— State/Territory Boundary

Punjab State/Territory Name

300 km

0   300 Miles

China

RUSSIA

Lake Baikal

KAZAKHSTAN

Lake Balkhash

.Karamay

MONGOLIA

.Kulja

.Urumqi

KYRGYZSTAN

.Kashgar   *Xinjiang*

Yumen.

.Hailar

Heilongjiang

.Qiqihar

.Harbin

.Changchun

Nei Mongol

Jilin

Shenyang

.Liaoning NORTH KOREA

Hebei

Beijing .Dalian

Yinchuan

Taiyuan

Tianjin.

.Yantai

SOUTH KOREA

Ningxia

Shanxi

Golmud .

Xining

.Lanzhou

Shandong

Qinghai

Gansu Xi'an .

Jiangsu

Yellow Sea

.Shiqunhe

Shaanxi

Henan *Anhui*

.Shanghai

Xizang

Hubei

Sichuan

Wuhan .

Zhejiang

Lhasa .

Chengdu

. Chongqing

Nanchang

East China Sea

NEPAL

Changsha .

Jiangxi

BHUTAN

Guizhou

Hunan

Fuzhou.

INDIA

BANGLADESH

Guiyang .

Fujian

Xiamen.

Kunming .

Guangxi

Guangdong

TAIWAN

Yunnan

Nanning Guangzhou

Hong Kong (U.K.)

MYANMAR   VIETNAM

LAOS

Haikou

Hainan

South China Sea

PHILIPPINES

THAILAND

CAMBODIA

China

- ⊕ National Capital
- Xi'an • City
- ――― International Boundary
- ――― Provincial Boundary
- *Hunan* Province Name
- - - - - Disputed Boundary

500 km

0   500 Miles

GLOSSARY

17 November a terrorist group formed in 1973 in Athens, Greece, in honor of thirty-four university students who were killed by police during a student demonstration.

Abimael Guzman founder of the Sendero Luminoso or Shining Path terrorist group in Peru.

Abu Abbas leader of the Palestine Liberation Front (PLF).

Abu Sayyaf the "bearer of the sword" is an Islamic insurgency movement on the island of Basilan in the Philippines. Abu Sayyaf has links to al Qaeda.

Abu Zubaydah chief of operations for al Qaeda; currently in U.S. custody.

al Aqsa a Palestinian nationalistic group affiliated with the PLO noted for its use of suicide bombings against Israeli civilian targets.

Allon Plan probably the best-known peace plan for the Mideast, advocating a territorial compromise between Israel and the PLO.

al Qaeda an international terrorist network founded by Osama bin Laden, responsible for the September 11, 2001, attacks against the United States.

Amal Arabic for "hope"; a Lebanese Shi'ite terrorist group active in the 1970s.

Anarchism a political ideology that opposes governmental controls of human activity.

ANO the Abu Nidal Organization is a Palestinian terrorist group.

Anthrax a lethal biological agent used to kill five people in the United States in October and November of 2001.

Antiterrorism Act sets forth a formal list of foreign terrorist organizations; enacted in 1996. This

was the first comprehensive American antiterrorism legislation.

Asahara the founder and leader of the religious cult Aum Shinrikyo.

Assassins a division of the Shi'ite Islami Muslim sect. The name assassin is derived from the Arabic hashashin or "hashish eaters."

Assets seizure the seizure of the financial assets and records of known terrorists and drug dealers.

ATEDP Act the Anti-Terrorism and Effective Death Penalty Act passed by the U.S. Congress in 1996. This was the first comprehensive U.S. antiterrorism legislation.

Atrocity a brutal and barbaric attack on innocent noncombatants.

Balfour Declaration a statement of British policy from Foreign Secretary Arthur J. Balfour on November 2, 1917, that promised to create a Jewish state in Palestine.

Bali bombing the first recorded suicide bombing in Indonesia that occurred on October 12, 2002, killing over 190 people.

Basque nationalist terrorist group formed in 1969 seeking to establish an independent Basque nation in the regions of northern Spain and southwestern France.

Beirut the capital of Lebanon where the first recorded suicide bombing occurred in the Mideast at the American Embassy on April 18, 1983.

Bhopal a Union Carbide plant in India where a chemical storage tank exploded killing 4,000 people.

Black Panthers an African American organization founded in Oakland, California, in 1966.

Black powder   a low-velocity explosive used to make clandestine bombs.

Black September   a Palestinian terrorist group founded in 1970 that carried out the terrorist hostage-taking event at the Munich Olympics in 1972.

Black Tigers   suicide units of the Tamil Tigers (LTTE) comprised of both men and women "willing" to carry out suicide bombing attacks.

Blast   relates to the amount of energy released during an explosion.

Bojinka Plot   or the "Big Bang." Involved plan to blow up eleven commercial jets while in flight, to assassinate Pope John Paul and President Clinton, and to blow up the CIA Headquarters in Langley, Virginia.

C-4   a high-velocity military explosive.

Car bombs   a vehicle bomb introduced by PIRA that has become a favorite bombing technique of terrorists worldwide.

Carlos Marighella   author of *The Mini-Manual of Urban Guerrilla Warfare*.

Censorship   the concept of a free press.

Chlorine gas   a chemical agent that destroys the cells in the respiratory system; cited as the first use of a chemical weapon by a terrorist group.

Cluster   refers to an increase in suicide activity after widespread news reporting of suicide incidents, for example, suicide bombings.

Contagion   the theory that anytime someone does something new or novel and are successful others will attempt to emulate that success. The copycat syndrome.

Conventions   international treaties agreed upon to fight the growing threat of terrorism.

Covert operation   counterterrorist measures that seek to disrupt, resolve, or destroy terrorist operations and planning, for example, Delta Force.

Cyanide gas   a rapidly acting chemical agent that prevents the cells of the body from getting oxygen. Cyanide is most potent in enclosed spaces.

D. B. Cooper   the first to successfully hijack a commercial jet liner.

Delta Force   a specially trained American counterterrorist unit that operates in small covert teams.

Department of Homeland Security   U.S. federal agency created to secure the U.S. homeland from terrorist attacks.

Desert One   the code name used for the rendezvous point used in an attempt to rescue American hostages in Iran in April 1980.

Dev Sol   Revolutionary Way; originally formed in 1978 for the purpose of attacking Turkish national security interests and military targets.

Dirty bomb   a conventional explosive combined with radioactive isotopes in order to spread nuclear material over a wide area.

Disinformation   the deliberate spread of false, misleading, or incomplete information.

Dynamite   a high-velocity explosive invented by Alfred Nobel in 1867.

Emile Durkheim   a noted sociologist who studied suicidal behavior.

Entebbe   an airport in Uganda where Israeli commandos rescued over 100 hostages who had been taken hostage by the PFLP.

Extradition   international agreements to return criminal fugitives to law enforcement agencies of cooperating countries.

FALN   a Puerto Rican nationalist/terrorist group active in the United States in the 1970s and 1980s. Historically the most active terrorist group in the United States.

FARC   Fuerzas Armadas Revolucionarias de Colombia was formed in 1964 as a military wing of the Colombian Communist Party, a marxist-motivated terrorist group determined to overthrown the Colombia government.

Fatah   the largest group within the PLO founded by Yassir Arafat in 1957. The term means victory, conquest, or freedom.

Fatwah   an Islamic religious decree.

Fear   the focus, purpose, and direction of terrorism is the creation of fear and panic.

Fertilizer   ammonium nitrate bombs used by a variety of terrorist groups.

FLQ   the Front for the Liberation of Quebec was active in Canada in the late 1960s and early 1970s and took credit for a series of bombing incidents and hostage takings.

Fragmentation   one of the primary effects produced during an explosion.

George Habash founder of the PFLP (Popular Front for the Liberation of Palestine).

GIA the Armed Islamic Group; the most active terrorist group in Algeria.

Good Guys an electronics store located in Sacramento, CA, where forty-one people were taken hostage, three were killed, and eleven were wounded on April 4, 1991.

Guilt transfer a propaganda technique.

Gush Emunium "The Block of the Faithful"; a Jewish religious group that strongly believes that the Jewish nation and the Jewish land are both sacred since they were both chosen by God.

HAMAS the Islamic Resistance Movement well known for its suicide attacks against Israel civilians. The goal of HAMAS is to destroy Israel, the PLO, and the Peace Talks.

Hanafi a Muslim sect that took over 300 hostages at three different locations in Washington, DC, in 1977.

Hizballah the Party of God, an Islamic Movement that supports an Islamic revolution in the Mideast; responsible for the bombing of the U.S. Marine barracks on September 23, 1983.

Hostage reaction psychological states that a hostage goes through during captivity.

HRT/NEST the Hostage Rescue Team/ Nuclear Emergency Search Team. The HRT is organized under the authority of the FBI, while NEST is controlled by the U.S. Department of Energy.

Hunger strike a classic political tactic to obtain widespread media attention.

INLA the Irish National Liberation Army was formed in 1974 after a split in the ranks of the PIRA and the IRA.

Interdiction to prevent suicide bombings before they are carried out.

Irgun/Stern Gang Zionist terrorists organizations responsible for the terror attack on the Palestinian village of Dir Yassin in 1948.

Jammu/Kashmir an ethno-national and Islamic extremist movement that has waged a terrorist war against Indian occupation of Kashmir.

JDL the Jewish Defense league founded by Rabbi Meir Kahane.

Jemmah Islamiyyah an Indonesian terrorist group responsible for the Bali bombing in October 2002.

Judea and Samaria the land of the ancient Hebrews whereby the religious Jews maintain they have an intrinsic right to settle.

Kamikaze literally, "divine wind" in Japanese. During World War II kamikaze suicide pilots flew bomb-laden planes into U.S. naval vessels in the Pacific.

Kashmiri a native inhabitant of Kashmir.

Khobar Towers on October 25, 1996, Islamic terrorists detonated a truck bomb at Khobar Towers in Dhahran, Saudia Arabia, that killed nineteen U.S. Air Force personnel and injured 500 others.

Ku Klux Klan a white supremacist organization founded in Pulaski, Tennessee, in 1866. The KKK is the oldest continuous terrorist organization in the United States.

Letter bombs a bombing technique first introduced by Russian terrorists in the 1880s.

Libya a Mideast nation that was attacked by the United States after a terrorist incident that killed an American soldier.

London Syndrome refers to a situation in which a hostage continuously argues or threatens the hostage takers and the hostage is killed by the hostage takers.

LTTE the Liberation Tigers of Tamil Elam, a Tamil separatist/terrorist group of Sri Lanka.

Marine compound on October 23, 1983, the Marine Compound in Beirut, Lebanon, was destroyed by a suicide bomber that killed 241 Marines.

Martyrs people who die for their religious faith or for some other greater cause. A term often used to describe suicide bombers.

Meir Kahane founder of the JDL and the Kach party in Israel, who was assassinated by an extremist Muslim in 1990 in New York City.

MEK the national liberation movement of Iran which seeks to overthrown the Iranian government.

Microtagging a process whereby tiny chips of microtaggants are blended into explosive substances and color coded to identify the manufacturer and batch of explosives.

Mir Aimal Kansi a Pakistani gunman who killed two and wounded three CIA employees on January 25, 1993. Kansi was eventually captured and executed by lethal injection on November 14, 2002.

Morality the conformity to ideals of virtuous human conduct.

Mujihaddin Islamic extremists who wage war in defense of Islam. Literally translated as Holy Warriors.

Munich Olympics on September 5, 1972, Israeli athletes were taken hostage by members of the Black September Organization. Eleven Israeli athletes were killed by the hostage takers.

Narodnaya Volya the People's Will, a nineteenth-century Russian terrorist group.

National Alliance a white supremacist group that follows the teachings of William Pierce.

Negotiator professionally trained hostage mediator.

NPA the New People's Army; a Filipino-Marxist guerrilla group formed in 1969 that specializes in urban terrorism.

Ocalan the founder of the Kurdish Workers' Party (PKK).

Occupied Territories a Palestinian reference to the West Bank and Gaza.

Omagh on August 15, 1998, the town center of Omagh was destroyed by a powerful car bomb killing thirty people, the deadliest bombing in the thirty-year history of the "Irish troubles." The RIRA took credit for the bombing.

Oslo Peace Process granted Palestinians control of Gaza and a limited area of the West Bank. The Oslo Peace Process was an attempt to gradually partition Palestine into an Arab and Jewish state.

Palestinian Authority is an autonomous Palestinian government established after the Oslo Peace Accords in 1993.

Pan Am 103 an airliner that exploded over Lockerbie, Scotland, on December 21, 1988. Two hundred seventy people were killed, and Libya took credit for the bombing.

PETN a high-velocity explosive in linear form.

PFLP the Popular Front for the Liberation of Palestine founded by George Habash in 1967. The first terrorist group to introduce sky jacking to attract media attention.

Phalangist a right-wing Lebanese Christian militia responsible for the massacre at Sabra and Shitila.

Phineas Priesthood a white supremacist movement that follows the religious principles of the Christian Identity Movement. The name is taken from a verse in the Bible, Numbers 25:6.

PIRA the Provisional Irish Republican Army known for its use of car bombs. The goal of PIRA is to unite Ireland and drive the British out of Northen Ireland.

PKK the Kurdistan Workers Party. The PKK is a nationalist/separatist group seeking to establish an independent Islamic Kurdistan in Turkey.

Political objective the motivation for acts of indiscriminate terrorism.

Posse Comitatus Act enacted in 1878, the act prohibits the use of U.S. military forces in domestic civil situations, such as riot control.

Preemptive strike counterterrorist actions that proactively search for terrorist organizations prior to any terrorist episode.

Rajneeshee followers of a religious cult leader who poisoned ten salad bars in Oregon with salmonella bacteria.

RATF the Revolutionary Armed Task Force; a left-wing terrorist group active in the United States in the 1980s.

Red Brigades an Italian terrorist group most active in the 1970s and 1980s.

Salafist a branch of Islam that adheres to rigid and utopian principles of life. Salaism is followed by the GSPC of Algeria.

Salmonella a bacteria that is a common cause of food poisoning. The Rajneeshees intentionally contaminated ten salad bars with a strain of salmonella in the Dalles region of Oregon in September 1984.

Sarin gas a potent nerve agent; the Aum Shinrikyo cult released sarin gas into the Tokyo subway system in March 1995, killing twelve people.

SAS the Special Air Service is a secretive counterterrorism military unit attached to the British Army.

Sayeret Matkal an elite Israeli counterterrorist reconnaissance unit.

SBS the Special Boat Service is another British counterterrorist unit attached to the British Royal Navy.

Self-immolation a rare form of suicide by fire and almost always associated with political protests.

Shoah the catastrophe or a term used to describe the Holocaust.

Sicarii Jewish rebels who opposed Roman rule in 66 A.D. Considered by historians to be the first terrorist group.

Sikh an adherent of a monotheistic religion of India founded about 1500 A.D.

Skyjacking the hijacking of commercial jet aircraft.

SLA the Symbionese Liberation Army; active in the United States in the early 1970s. The SLA took Patty Hearst hostage in 1974.

Special Operations elite military units deployed to interdict terrorist operations.

S.S. *Mayaguez* on May 12, 1975, a Cambodian gunboat seized the *Mayaguez* off the coast of Cambodia; thirty-nine Americans were taken hostage.

Stockholm Syndrome a psychological aberration in which hostages begin to identify and sympathize with their captors.

Suicidology the study of the theory, causes, and motives of suicidal behavior.

Tanzim in Arabic meaning organization; associated with Yassir Arafat's Fatah movement.

Terrorism the premeditated, deliberate, systematic murder, mayhem, and threatening of the innocent to create fear and intimidation in order to gain a political or tactical advantage, usually to influence an audience.

Time and trust generally considered the most important factors in a hostage-taking episode.

Timothy McVeigh responsible for the ammonium nitrate and fuel oil (ANFO) bomb that destroyed the Alfred P. Murrah Federal Building in Oklahoma City on April 19, 1995, killing 168 people. McVeigh was executed in June 2001.

TTIC the Terrorist Threat Integration Center is a newly organized U.S. government agency to coordinate the intelligence-gathering capabilities of the FBI, CIA, and the Division of Homeland Security.

Tupac Amaru a marxist–terrorist movement in Peru most active in the 1980s and the early 1990s.

Tupamaros a marxist terrorist movement active in Uruguay in the 1960s and 1970s. One of the first groups to exploit terrorism and media attention.

Turner Diaries a novel written by William Pierce, founder of the National Alliance, under the pseudonym Andrew MacDonald. Considered by white supremacist to be the "bible" of right-wing activity in the United States.

Typology a way of categorizing hostage takers; the classification of terrorist groups based on types.

Uighurs the largest Turkish-speaking ethnic minority in Xinjiang province in China. The Uighurs support a moderate form of Sufi Islam.

Unabomber the name given to Ted Kaczynski, a serial bomber who carried out attacks with mail bombs, killing three people. Kaczynski was sentenced to four life sentences.

USA PATRIOT Act following the September 11, 2001, attacks, the Bush administration proposed legislation titled "Providing Appropriate Tools Required to Intercept and Obstruct Terrorist Act," popularly known as the Patriot Act. The Act gives law enforcement far-reaching police powers to detain immigrants, expand wire tapping, to use the military to patrol U.S. borders, and to conduct warrantless searches.

Uzbekistan part of the former Soviet Union created in 1998.

WCOTC the World Church of the Creator founded by Ben Klassen in 1973. A white supremacist organization that believes in a coming racial holy war.

William Pierce the founder of the National Alliance and author of the *Turner Diaries* and *The Hunter*.

WUO/BLA the Weather Underground Organization and the Black Liberation Army. Left-wing terrorist groups active in the United States between 1968 and 1984.

Xinjiang Islamic-dominated province of northwestern China.

Yom Kippur War on October 6, 1973, the Syrian and Egyptian armies simultaneously attacked Israel. Yom Kippur is the Day of Atonement in the Jewish religion.

Zakarias Moussaoui a suspect in the September 11, 2001 terrorist attacks; considered by the FBI to be the "20th hijacker."

Zionism the revival of Jewish national life, culture, language, and religion in the Holy Land.

Index